The '45

The '45

CHRISTOPHER DUFFY

CASSELL

Cassell
Wellington House, 125 Strand, London WC2R 0BB

First published 2003

British Library Cataloguing-in-Publication Data
A catalogue record for this book is available from the British Library

The Penicuik drawings appearing at the head of each chapter and
on p. 24 are reproduced by kind permission of the late Sir John
Clerk of Penicuik, Bt. These drawings were first reproduced in
Witness to Rebellion, by Dr Ian Gordon Brown and Hugh Cheape
(Tuckwell Press, 1996). See also footnote on p. 24.

The photographs in the picture section between pp. 320 and 321
of Prince Charles Edward Stuart, James, 3rd Duke of Perth, and
William Augustus, Duke of Cumberland are © Hulton Getty
Pictures. All other photographs in this section are © the author.

The maps and battle plans listed on pp. 7–8 and the illustrations on
pp. 152, 428, 457, 462 and 475 are drawn by the author.

ISBN 0-304-35525-9

Distributed in the United States by Sterling Publishing Co. Inc,
387 Park Avenue South New York NY 10016-8810

Contents

List of maps and battle plans

Acknowledgements

EVERY PASSABLY SERIOUS HISTORICAL STUDY is inevitably a joint enterprise. In addition to those later acknowledged in the Introduction, I must also to register my thanks to Christian Aikman, Hugh Allison, Dr Leopold Auer (Haus-Hof- und Staatsarchiv, Vienna), Geoff Bailey (Falkirk Museums), Jim Beck, Rachel Bervie (Curator, Montrose Museum), Paul Craddock (Department of Scientific Research, British Library), Samuel Gibiat (Service Historique de l'Armée de Terre, Vincennes), Dr Paddy Griffith, Richard Hall (Cumbria Record Office, Kendal), Dr Hollenberg (Hessian State Archives, Marburg), Dr Bertil Johanssen (Riksarkivet, Stockholm), Professor Phil Jones (Climate Research Unit, University of East Anglia), William Kenyon (Clifton Hall Hotel), Father Roddy McAuley (Benbecula), Phil Mackie (Seven Years War Association), the staff of the Library of the National Maritime Museum, Major Mike Ranson, Jeremy Smith (Prints and Maps Section, Guildhall Library), Mavis Smith (Ministry of Defence Library), Edwin Stubbs (Tolls Farm, Wincle, Cheshire), Angela Tarnowski (Derby Museum and Art Gallery), David Taylor (Librarian, Local Studies Unit, Manchester City Council), Brian Vizek (Chicago), Helen Young (University of London Library, Senate House) and Sue Young (Map Room, British Library). Judith Fisher of Edinburgh gave assistance throughout by tracking down those short-print-run books and articles that rarely find their way to the libraries. Although I am almost a caricature of a particular kind of Englishman, I must say that I have encountered nothing but kindness in my exploration of Scotland. The continuing hospitality of the MacLeod family helped to determine Loch Linnhe as my principal base.

I owe a particular debt to the people who gave their encouragement at decisive stages of the present enterprise – to Professor Jeremy Black (Exeter University), and to a trio of my fellow members of the 1745 Association, namely Sonia Cameron Jacks, Peter Lole and Ross Mackenzie. I dedicate this book to them.

Preface

East Lothian, 19–21 September 1745

TWO ARMIES WERE MOVING TO CONTACT in the country to the east of Edinburgh: the Jacobite Highlanders under Prince Charles Edward Stuart were filing out of their camp at Duddingston; and Lieutenant General Sir John Cope, commander of the British forces in Scotland, had brought his army by sea directly from Aberdeen to the southern side of the Firth of Forth. Having shrunk from doing battle with the Jacobites in the Highlands, Cope was now determined to strike off the head of rebellion at a single stroke.

On the morning of 19 September 1745 the redcoats' column extended for several miles along the road west from Dunbar, and 'all along on the march, by riding through the ranks and encouraging the men, [Cope] raised their spirits to such a degree that all expressed the strongest desire for action. Even the dragoons breathed nothing but revenge, and threatened the rebels with destruction'.[1] A march of 11 miles brought the thirsty army to Haddington, and Cope chose to encamp just outside the town, rather than push on through a tract of waterless country. That evening Richard Jack, a volunteer who had set out that morning to reconnoitre the Jacobite forces, returned with the first useful information on their numbers and position.[2]

A detailed study of a Highland soldier after Prestonpans

Cope's troops were on the march by 9 a.m. the following morning. For the first 3 miles he followed the post road, then turned off to the right between Trabroun and Elvingston in preference to following the highway as it crossed the tangled terrain at Tranent. He was still making for the crossing of the Esk at Musselburgh, this time along a minor road closer to the coast. On learning that the Jacobites were approaching the same crossing from the opposite side, he called a halt on the open ground north of Tranent. 'The field was entirely clear of the crop, the last sheaves having been carried in the night before, and neither cottage, tree or bush were in its whole extent, except one solitary thorn bush which grew ... between Seton and Preston fields.'[3] Cope wished to give free play to his cavalry and artillery, such as they were, and was unwilling to commit himself any further towards the west, where his route would have been squeezed into a narrow avenue between the substantial stone walls of two estates, those of Preston House to the north, and Colonel James Gardiner's Bankton House to the south.

The day before, on 19 September, Prince Charles had moved his forces from the King's Park to new bivouacs at Duddingston (where they had been seen by Richard Jack), and in the evening he and his advisers resolved to confront Cope well to the east of Edinburgh. They were well informed about his infantry and cavalry (in fact 2,034 rank and file, including 650 dragoons), but not about his artillery. At this stage of the rising 'the cannon and the cavalry were what the Highlanders seemed to dread most, for the foot they

Prestonpans, the approach marches

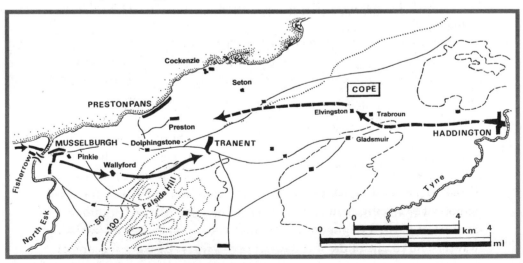

did not mind on account of their having shunned fighting in the Highlands'.[4]

Very early on the 20th the Jacobites were joined by 100 of the Grants of Glen Urquhart and Glen Moriston, and 'that morning the Prince put himself at the head of his army at Duddingston, and presenting his sword, said, "My friends, I have flung away the scabbard!"'.[5] The men answered with a cheer, and at 6 a.m. they ran rather than marched from their bivouacs. A village girl saw them on their way through Easter Duddingston: 'The Highlanders strode on with their squalid clothes and various arms, their rough limbs and uncombed hair, looking around them with an air of fierce resolution. The Prince rode among his officers at a little distance from the flank of the column, preferring to amble over the dry stubble fields beside the road'. She noted his 'graceful carriage and comely looks, his long hair straggling below his neck, and the flap of his tartan cloak thrown back by the wind, so as to make the jewelled St Andrew dangle for a moment clear in the air by its silken ribbon'.[6]

The Jacobites continued through Fisherrow, and made an unopposed crossing of the Esk by the spectacular Roman bridge which gave on to Musselburgh. Lord George Murray, setting the lead with the regiment of Lochiel, directed the march around the south of the town and Pinkie Park. Learning that Cope was at or near Prestonpans, he at once made for what he judged to be the key ground, the long, smooth grassy ridge of Falside Hill, rising to the south of that village. He pressed on through Wallyford and gained the top of the hill.

> The afternoon was gloriously fine, no clouds obscured the sun's bright rays or cast a shadow of gloom over the beautiful landscape which lay in front of the Highlanders' position; far away across the blue Forth rose the distant hills of Fife, dimly seen through the autumn haze; quiet fishing villages, with white-washed red-tiled cottages, were dotted here and there on the margin of the coastline; to the right the Bass Rock swam upon a sea of azure, and the Berwick Law raised its conical summit; to the left Arthur's Seat raised its quaintly outlined form against the western sky, enshrouded in the blue reek of the great city at its base; and almost at their feet, bathed in the warm glow of the golden September sun, great stretches of yellow stubble fields from which the corn had been newly reaped.[7]

Falside Hill offered a splendid overview of the redcoats' position, but it was important to investigate matters more closely, and to that end Major James Stewart of Perth's Regiment and a number of companions made their way forward to one of the shallow coal-pits. (Here it became evident that

Stewart was somewhat encumbered: a friend extracted a pistol from his breeches' pocket, then, to the increasing amusement of his companions, Stewart first drew out two small pistols, then two larger pistols with double barrels, all of this in addition to the blunderbuss he had over his arm.)[8] The more the Jacobites examined Cope's position the more they were 'convinced of the impossibility of attacking it; and we were all thrown into consternation, and quite at a loss what course to take. On even ground, the courage and bravery of the Highlanders might supply the place of numbers, but what could eighteen hundred men do against four thousand [sic], in a position inaccessible at every point?'[9]

Cope had the formidable walls of Preston and Bankton parks to his front or west, while his left or southern flank was covered by the Tranent Meadows, the misleading name for a long belt of marshes that ran almost due east from Preston. They were something of a geological curiosity for they owed their existence to a natural underground wall of impermeable quartz-dolerite which ran to the east of Preston, and prevented the water from Falside Hill from escaping to the sea. As an additional obstacle a ditch, 8 feet wide and 4 feet deep, bordered the southern edge of the quagmire and broadened towards the millponds at Seton.

Early in the same afternoon the Jacobites arrayed themselves in a north-facing line of battle along the ridge as far as the mining village of Tranent. 'This was not a proper situation for Highlanders, for they must have nothing before them that can hinder them to run at the enemy, but there was no other party to be taken until night, for it would not be prudent, so near as we were to them [about half a mile], to march and expose our flank to 'um.'[10] In all the haste, contact had been lost between Lord George Murray on the one hand, and Prince Charles and his adviser Colonel John William O'Sullivan on the other. The Prince saw that by veering as it had done to the south, his army had left the way to Edinburgh open. He accordingly sent back the reserve (two battalions of the Atholl Brigade) to seal off the roads in that direction. When the news came to Lord George Murray, that gentleman threw his musket on the ground and threatened to resign on the spot if the troops were not recalled. Prince Charles humoured him by complying, but events were to show that the redcoats might have been trapped and annihilated if the Athollmen had stayed in their blocking position.

Lord George Murray flared up again when he learned that O'Sullivan had posted fifty-odd of the Lochiel's Camerons in the churchyard of Tranent and the little wood just on the far side of the Heugh. These features lay towards the foot of the ridge below Tranent village, and overlooked the railway and the nearby marsh. O'Sullivan was following the best rules of the military art, for the churchyard was a ready-made strongpoint, but, as events were to show, on this occasion Lord George's instincts proved to be correct.

All might have been well if a civilian official with the Hanoverians, the extraordinarily active Walter Grossett, had not taken it on himself to investigate. Writing of himself in the third person, he describes how 'in order to observe the situation of the rebels, he (the witness) going a second time up a hollow way to the right [the Heugh] that leads through the town of Tranent, was surprised by a party of them, who lay concealed in a churchyard on one side of the said hollow way, and a thicket wood on the other, and from whence they fired on the witness, after they had him fairly betwixt them, in the said hollow way, but ... they all missed him'.[11]

Cope's little collection of ordnance happened to be at hand, and for the first and last time in many months the Hanoverian artillery made good practice. Two of the cannon were run forward to the near side of the marsh and peppered the churchyard and copse with diminutive roundshot, which caused a number of casualties among the Camerons posted there by O'Sullivan. Vindicated, Lord George pulled them out of the enclosure.[12]

Cope was meanwhile adjusting his position in response to the Jacobite motions. Upon the enemy appearing on Falside Hill he changed his original west-facing line to one fronting the marsh to the south, then moved them back when the Atholl Brigade began to retire towards Musselburgh. Alexander Carlyle, one of the Edinburgh Volunteers, was meanwhile keeping watch from the steeple of his father's house at Prestonpans, and sent a servant to report his observations to Cope. 'Coming down the field I asked the messenger if they had not paid him for his danger. Not a farthing had they given him, which being of a piece with the rest of the general's conduct, raised no sanguine hopes for tomorrow.' Carlyle's visit to an old neighbour, Colonel Gardiner, was no more encouraging. He found this Christian soldier 'grave, but serene and resigned; and he concluded by praying God to bless me, and that he could not wish for a better night to lie on the field; and then called for his cloak and other conveniences for lying down, as he said they would be awakened early enough in the morning'.[13]

When night was falling Cope made his fourth adjustment of the day, which was to realign his army once more to face the marsh, though a little further to the east of where they had been before in order to cover the railway (for horse-drawn coal carts) that ran across the Meadows, which he assumed to be the only means by which they could get at him across the bog.

The redcoats rested under arms on this cold and misty night. Cope detached 200 dragoons and 300 of his infantry on outpost duty, and ordered three large fires to be maintained along the front of his army, 'which discovered to the rebels what was doing in his camp, whereas in theirs not a word was heard, not the least sign seen, except a lantern with a candle, which, like a meteor, blazed a little, and then disappeared'.[14] His four coehorn mortars lobbed their bombs towards the assumed position of the enemy, but it transpired that the fuzes had been 'damnified' by long storage in Edinburgh Castle, and Cope ordered the fire to cease.

At dusk there had been an exchange of musketry between an outpost at Bankton House and a number of unidentified Jacobites. Colonel Peregrine Lascelles then noted that at 9 p.m. 'all the dogs in the village of Tranent began to bark with the utmost fury, which, it was believed, was occasioned by the motions of the rebels. Upon which I visited some of the most advanced posts of sentries, and found all very alert, but could see or hear nothing but the barking of the dogs, which ceased about half past ten'.[15] Considerable numbers of the enemy were evidently moving from west to east on the far side of the marsh, though it was impossible to tell whether the whole force was being committed that way. Believing that he could be of no further use, Carlyle returned to his father's manse in Prestonpans, where he found the house crowded with uninvited guests, including a number of the Edinburgh Volunteers. 'They were very noisy and boastful of their achievements, one of them having the dragoon's broadsword who had fallen into the coal-pit, and others the musket he had taken from a Highland soldier between the lines.'[16]

What had been happening? The Jacobite army was indeed moving east to join the Camerons, whom Lord George Murray had positioned on the far side of Tranent. At a first meeting, Prince Charles and his senior officers had fallen in with a proposal of Lord George Murray to take the army on a wide right-flanking move well out to the east of the line of the bogs, and then successively north and west to fall on the unprotected left flank of Cope's army. Robert Anderson, the son of the owner of the Meadows, had listened to the debate without presuming to intervene. He was in the habit of going wildfowling in the marshes, and when a Jacobite officer now happened to ask his opinion, he revealed the existence of a difficult but practicable track that ran by Riggonhead Farm. The council reconvened, and at once decided to follow Anderson's path, which would accomplish the same end as Lord George's move but by a shorter route.

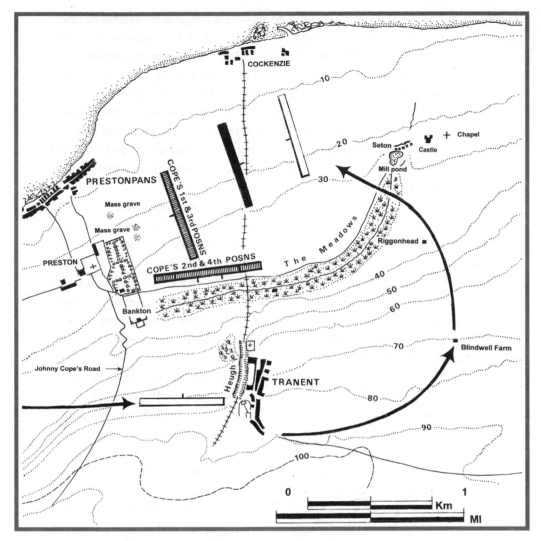

Prestonpans, 21 September 1745

The Jacobite column set off just before 4 a.m. on 21 September.
The Duke of Perth made good progress with the Clan Donald regiments,
which according to ancient custom were designated the right wing. Lord
George had the local command of the left wing, which came up
behind and was led by Prince Charles in person. In leaping one of the
ditches the Prince had fallen on his knees on the far side, and had to
be hauled to his feet. In spite of this bad omen, both wings of the main
force were clear of the marsh at first light, and the three files converted into
ranks by a quarter-turn to the left, and moved in a slanting, discontinuous

line towards the enemy, with Lord George's wing likely to engage first.

Towards 5 a.m. the redcoats saw indistinct forms on the near side of the swamp, and in the half-light the Highlanders in their dark plaids looked like nothing so much as a line of bushes. Once he grasped what was afoot, Cope responded with some speed. He wheeled his main force of infantry to the left by platoons, and marched them north to form a 670-pace line of battle parallel to the advancing Jacobites. He did not have the time to reassign the 300 troops of the outposts to the parent regiments, and so he formed them up in haste on the right flank of the infantry line. A dragoon regiment was posted on either flank. Out to the left (or north), Hamilton's 14th was deployed in the classic formation of two squadrons up in line, and the third in reserve, though when Cope hastened up to inspect them he found that the troopers had not bothered to draw their swords. The three squadrons of Gardiner's 13th on the right were split up in an awkward fashion: only one of the squadron's (Whitney's) was in line with the infantry, on account of the overcrowding caused by the insertion of the outpost troops; Colonel Gardiner had a squadron under his personal command to the right rear of the artillery (below), and the third of his squadrons was posted to the right rear of the main line.

The entire artillery (four coehorn mortars and six 1½-pounder cannon) were kept together in a single battery and stationed on the far right, which was not an ideal arrangement, but the only one which allowed Major Eaglesfield Griffith of the Royal Artillery and Lieutenant Colonel Charles Whitefoord of the Marines to serve the pieces in person. They had nobody to help them except a handful of invalids and sailors, and no assistance was volunteered by the small artillery guard that stood just to the rear. The action was opened when Griffith and Whitefoord ran along their line of pieces and touched them off one by one, like pyrotechnicians at a firework display. One of the six cannon remained silent, for it had fired a signal shot and there was nobody to reload it. After that, the dragoons opened a fire by volleys with their carbines.

As commander of the Jacobite right wing, the Duke of Perth had been much concerned to leave enough space to allow the left wing under Lord George to form up on the northern side of the marsh, with the result that a gap opened in the Jacobite array, and Perth's wing actually outflanked the long line of the redcoats by a useful one hundred paces. This advantage gave added impetus to the three regiments of the Clan Donald when they advanced in good order and closed with the enemy. Men and horses began to fall among Hamilton's Dragoons, and the sight of Lieutenant Colonel Wright being pinned beneath his mount helped to induce a general flight which carried the reserve squadron along with it. In the morning murk 'it can never be known whither the officers were trecherows as there men were cowherds and there horse raw and unmanaged, for it is certain, in the wheeling, the horse on the wings did the first execution and trod down and distressed and confused our foot'.[17]

Cope's centre right wing was already staggering under Lord George's attack. Among the redcoats Captain Drummond later claimed to have a good view of Colonel Lascelles of the 58th, and testified on his behalf that he saw him 'on the front of the line to the left of me, with a pair of pistols hung on [his] belt, and when the rebels came turning up with a confused noise and hallowing, a good many of the soldiers behind [him] took off their hats, crying to give an huzza, when I observed [him] endeavouring to stop their huzzaing, but the humour seemed to prevail among them, [he] took off

Prestonpans, the battle array

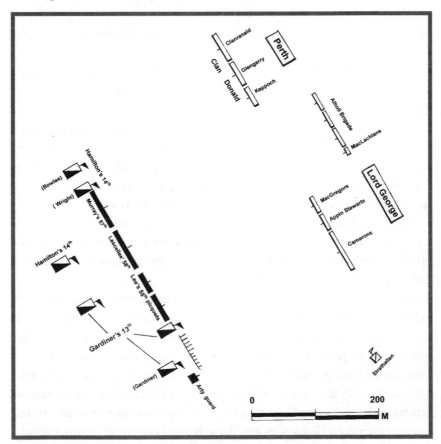

[his] hat and waving it in the air cried: "In the name of God, huzza!"'.[18] The oncoming Highlanders raised a cheer of their own, and did not level their pieces 'until they were very near, being always sure that their one fire should do execution, which they having done, immediately threw down their guns, and drawing their broadswords rushed in upon them like a torrent and carried all before them'.[19] The range of the Highlanders' volley had been so close that the wads of their charges flew among the enemy troops.

The first point of impact was probably the artillery and the terrified guard behind, and Griffith and Whitefoord were overwhelmed before they had any opportunity to reload. At the orders of the Earl of Loudoun, Lieutenant Colonel Shugborough Whitney now wheeled his squadron of Gardiner's to the right to charge into the Highlanders. He relates that he was

> at this time about twenty yards from the flank of this column. I gave the word of command to my squadron to charge into the middle of them, but most unluckily half a moment after that I had my left arm shattered by a musket ball ... I must observe to you that before I left the front of my squadron I ordered my lieutenant to charge in, he came with alacrity to the head of the standard, but having a wild, unruly horse, he fell a-plunging and never ceased till he threw the lieutenant on his back to the ground; by which means a second lucky occasion of doing good service was lost.[20]

The troopers fled.

Colonel Lascelles tried to wheel some of the platoons of his 58th to lend support to the breaking dragoons, but he was 'obliged to stop immediately afterwards, as some files of the platoons upon the right were crouching and creeping gently backwards, with their arms recovered, occasioned by a continued irregular fire over their heads, which I soon set to rights by my example and reproaches'.[21]

The one unit which should have been in a position to stem the Highland breakthrough was the squadron under the immediate command of Colonel Gardiner. It turned tail and ran after some of its horses had been wounded by musket shots. The remaining squadron, which stood in reserve behind the infantry, was carried away in the onrush, and Gardiner himself was deserted by all but a small knot of his men. He snatched up a half-pike and put himself at the head of a leaderless party of infantry, 'at whose head he fought till he was brought down by three wounds, one in his shoulder by a ball, another in the forehead by a broadsword, and the third, which was the mortal stroke, in the hinder part of the head, by a Lochaber axe: this wound was given him by a Highlander who came behind him, while he was reaching

a stroke at an officer with whom he was engaged'.[22] Afterwards the Hanoverians traced the deed to a lad who was being held prisoner by them in Lincoln
Castle. By another account the author was one Samuel Cameron, of
Kilmallie in Lochaber, whose descendants liked to believe he had acted in
self-defence.[23]

The line of redcoat infantry was now completely exposed, and the
platoons disintegrated in succession from their right flank, being utterly
defenceless in close-quarter fighting. 'It seems strange that Cope disarmed the
King's forces of all their most usefull weapons against Highlanders, and when
they marched north ordered all there swords to be laid up in Stirling Castle,
so that at the time of ingaging not one of them had a sword; they had there
bagenets screwed when they were attacked, and non to give the word
of command.'[24]

The experience of Carlyle confirms the general belief that the action was
decided within an extraordinarily short time. He had spent the night in a
neighbour's house, where he was awakened by artillery fire. He ran to a
viewpoint in the garden, and even then, 'which could hardly be more than ten
or fifteen minutes after firing the first cannon, the whole prospect was filled
with runaways, and Highlanders pursuing them. Many had turned their coats
as prisoners, but were still trying to reach the town in hopes of escaping.
The pursuing Highlanders, when they could not overtake, fired at them,
and I saw two of them fall in the glebe'.[25]

The fleeing Hanoverians crowded towards Preston and Bankton parks,
and the panic was augmented when the redcoats lapped around the enclos-
ing walls, which were of stone, and reached up to 12 feet high. All attempts
to make a stand were in vain, with the exception of that of Lieutenant Colonel
Sir Peter Halkett of Lee's Regiment, who was a very brave and (as events
were to show) a very honourable officer. Together with a small party he held
the Highlanders at bay from behind a ditch. Nobody else was willing to
follow his example, and he surrendered at the personal summons of Lord
George Murray.

As a result of their crossing the marsh, and their turn to the west, the
Jacobites were now facing in the opposite direction from their original line
of march from Musselburgh. The victory had been won entirely by the
divisions of Perth and Lord George, and if Lord Nairne and the Athollmen
had remained where they had been reassigned by Prince Charles, behind
Prestonpans, it is likely that not just Lieutenant Colonel Halkett but the
whole of Cope's army would have been forced to surrender.

Some of the fleeing dragoons made off west towards Edinburgh, 'with ther horses all in fro' and foame',[26] and a party actually galloped up the High Street and into the Castle, with young Colquhoun Grant in pursuit. They shut the gates behind them only just in time, and Grant thrust his dirk into the woodwork in frustration.

The rest of the fugitives made south by 'Johnny Cope's Road' past Bankton House and, not far beyond, the leading elements were encountered by two gentlemen who had set out from Dalkeith. They had hoped to join the army, 'but on their way thither met one in livery, who called himself Colonel Hamilton's servant, riding a dragoon horse, and several dragoon horses following, several with and some without saddles, and the bridles among their feet or broken … They were informed that the dragoon horse would not stand fire, and had immediately fallen into disorder … Soon after they saw many dragoons flying, some one way, some another'.[27]

The flight continued almost without intermission all the way over the Lammermuir Hills, and on by way of Lauder to Coldstream and Cornhill, where the runaways rested overnight. They made for Berwick the next day, and Brigadier Thomas Fowke and Colonel Lascelles had the misfortune to encounter Lord Mark Kerr: 'This old general asked them very gravely where the army was. They looked confounded, and said totally routed. He held up his hands, "Good God! I have seen some battles, heard of many, but never of the first news of a defeat being brought by the general officers before." In short, sad it is to say, but we learn no account but that the general officers being run away at the first fire of the Highlanders, the men were almost left to themselves, made a little resistance, and submitted, so that all was over in a quarter of an hour'.[28]

Behind them the abandoned field looked as if a hurricane had spread the contents of a slaughterhouse over the ground. A Whig gentleman learned of a friend who, 'being found among the dead after all was over, remained so butchered and mangled as scarce to be known; for his hands were cut off, and his head cleft to the chin, and his flesh almost stripped from his bones. A poor grenadier, seeing a blow aimed at him, naturally get up his hands over his head, and not only had his hand lopped off, but also his skull cut above an inch deep, so that he expired on the spot'.[29]

Prince Charles forbade any gloating at the defeat of his father's subjects, and ordered all possible care to be taken of the wounded, though nothing could be done for Colonel Gardiner, who died from his wounds (most probably in the minister's house in Tranent). Andrew Henderson caught sight of the Prince at this time, as he was standing by the side of a road. 'He was clad as an ordinary captain, in a coarse plaid and blue bonnet, his boots and knees much dirtied; he seemed to have fallen into a ditch, which I was told by one of the Lifeguards he had.'[30] Charles spent the following night in nearby Musselburgh in the great house of Pinkie, the mansion of the Marquis of Tweeddale, who as Secretary of Scotland had just put the bounty of £30,000 on his head. Notwithstanding this, nothing in Pinkie House was taken or damaged.

The Jacobites brought no artillery with them to the battle, and to all practical purposes they had no cavalry (Lord Strathallan's little troop having been ordered to remain at Tranent), but Prince Charles could be forgiven for believing that his Highlanders were invincible. In their attack they had scorned the popping of the Hanoverian artillery, and 'never after that did regard cannon, which had formerly been so terrible to them'.[31] They had charged cavalry, and they had withstood the fire of the redcoat infantry and returned it at point-blank range.

Cope was ultimately acquitted by a court martial of any major misconduct in the campaign and battle, and criticized only on the minor count of having failed to provide sufficient artillerymen. That did not accord with the opinion of the beaten army. Henderson, 'surveying the field before the dead were stripped, asked some of the wounded what was become of Cope? And they all, but especially the English soldiers, spoke most disrespectfully and bitterly of him'.[32] One of the captured officers testified that 'by scorning our foe, we are become the scorn of our friends'.[33]

The survivors were divided among themselves, and an ugly dispute broke out between Whitney (one of the late Gardiner's squadron commanders), and Lascelles of the 58th. Lascelles spoke disparagingly about the dragoons, claiming to have heard Gardiner pleading with his disintegrating troopers: 'What dragoons, are you going to desert me?'. Whitney, however, asserted that the allegation was a double impossibility, first, because the 58th had been 400 yards from Gardiner's station, and second, because Lascelles had been seen at Haddington so soon after the battle that Whitney doubted he had been in action at all.[34] Lascelles riposted by giving a detailed account of his doings, and by eliciting letters of indignant support from a number of his officers.

In such a way *The '45* begins, if not with a bang, at least with a swish and a grisly thud. And the events at Prestonpans correspond to the stereotype of the Jacobite rising as it has been transmitted to our times, namely that of the Highlander (barbaric, or primitively virtuous, according to one's predilections) bent on carving his adored master's way to a throne with a broadsword.

But let us skip forward from 20 September 1745 at Prestonpans to 23 December at Inverurie, a little place not far from Aberdeen. Here we find plaid-clad Highlanders pitted against a mixed force of regular troops and Lowlanders. The regulars took the lead, making a river crossing under fire, driving the Highlanders up the village street by a regular volleys, and finally chasing them over the fields beyond. A Jacobite defeat? No. Because the regulars and Lowlanders were Jacobites, and the Highlanders were fighting for King George. The conventional imagining of the '45 has no place for such possibilities, but they must be admitted into any reasonably balanced and comprehensive history of that episode.

A battle scene, probably of Prestonpans or Falkirk

The drawing reproduced here, and those that illustrate each chapter opening page, come from a remarkable collection of contemporary sketches recently discovered and identified by Dr Iain Gordon Brown, Principal Curator of the National Library of Scotland, many of which are reproduced in *Witness to Rebellion*, published by the Tuckwell Press in 1996. The caricatures especially give a unique and valuable perspective to the events and personalities of the '45, and the publisher is grateful to all concerned, particularly the late Sir John Clerk, Bt., for allowing these drawings to be reproduced here.

Introduction

A STUDY OF THIS KIND MUST EXTEND beyond the fighting to embrace the origins of the Jacobite cause, the nature of British society as it existed in the middle of the eighteenth century and the very landscapes of the British Isles. I wish I could claim that the present offering was informed from the outset by any such ambition. It wasn't. The first spark was engendered not very long ago, on a visit to northern Britain. Once among the Highlands and the Fells I was struck at once by the congruence between the romantic landscapes and the story of the '45. Back home, curiosity was overtaken by something like awe when I began to learn of the wealth of the relevant documentation, and of the decades of fine scholarship that have been devoted to the examination of the '45, culminating in the rediscovery of Scottish history in the Scottish universities.

What was surprising was that the whole proved to hang together so badly. I had thought it might be within my competence to contribute a specialized study of military topography, drawing on what I knew of warfare at that period, and experiences of counter-insurgency over a heathery and boggy patch of the British Isles. I had assumed that for the rest I could refer readers to a comprehensive corpus of accepted knowledge. Further reading showed that such a consensus was almost totally absent.

Latter-day supporters of the Hanoverian regime and the Jacobite cause are sunk deeply into entrenched positions, and their exchanges take the form of the academic equivalent of hand grenades and mortar bombs. Self-proclaimed hard-edged historians are at odds with the students of culture. The geographical setting is taken for granted, except for works in the tradition of 'The Footsteps of Bonnie Prince Charlie', and to find reasonable maps we have to go back all the way to the well-nigh inaccessible William Drummond Norie (1901). Important tactical realities are ignored once we stray outside the works of Stuart Reid, and the military history is studied without enough regard to the wider context. The coverage of topics is uneven, to the extent that far more has been written about the wanderings of the Prince after Culloden than about the perspectives of the London government and its forces during the whole episode of the '45.

The cumulative effect has been to isolate the '45 from the standards of examination that we would normally apply to other episodes of the past.

Perceptions are even now shaped by the propaganda of King George's supporters in 1745 and 1746. The neo-Hanoverians have always been happy to take its assertions at face value, while the neo-Jacobites have played into their hands by giving the commemoration of the '45 an overwhelmingly Highland character. To test this claim I have made a point of asking professional historians at random about their impression of the Jacobite forces. With slight variations in wording, the answer has invariably been: 'thieving Catholic Highland bastards'. Then, unbidden, and with a tap to the side of the nose, the experts will often add that the Jacobites were beaten because the Duke of Cumberland taught his troops a new bayonet drill. Neither statement can be accepted without a great many qualifications.

By this roundabout route I came to the realization that there is a need to integrate the story of the '45 into the mainstream of historical studies. *The '45* brings together a number of ways in which this ambition might be attained:

Perspectives

We need to look at the events of the '45 in the context of the usages of warfare at that time. Only then is it possible to ask what was interesting and distinctive about the practices of the Jacobites and their opponents. What I found surprised me, and I think it might surprise you. Conversely, there are issues that respond best to a plodding and literal-minded approach, such as asking what forces might have been available to the government to defend London in December 1745, and how the army proposed to deploy them. The latter questions, astonishingly enough, have never been addressed in a serious way before. I thought I might be mistaken on this point, but a re-reading of the literature confirms that this in fact the case.

Evidence

Documentary series like the Newcastle Papers, the State Papers Domestic and the Cumberland Papers are familiar enough, but they prove to contain many out-of-the-way corners which show, for example, that the '45 set communities in altogether unsuspected parts of Britain at lethal odds. Again, a sweep of foreign archives brought to light the dispatches of foreign diplomats, the reports of Lord John Drummond to the French War Ministry, and the records of the Hessian corps (which will form the basis of a separate study). Students with more time at their disposal would probably uncover a great deal more. Jeremy Black and Frank McLynn, for example, have shown what can be gleaned from English county record offices, while the doings of Marshal Wade's Dutch corps remain unexplored territory that might well repay investigation.

New kinds of evidence also have their place. A number of '-ologies' are just beginning to make their impact on military history, and they have found their way into the present work through a number of chance encounters. While traversing the field of Prestonpans I was fortunate enough to meet Tom Hogg (Minister of Tranent), who has made a detailed study of the geology of the field of Prestonpans, and who brought home to me just how decisively the battle was shaped by what lay below the ground. The truly inspirational work on military topography by the Department of Earth Sciences at my local University of Greenwich validated this approach. I also began to assemble a mass of meteorological data from ships' logs and other sources, and it was heartening to find that the effort was worth while when I made contact with Dr Denis Wheeler of the University of Sunderland, and Dr Clive Wilkinson of the National Maritime Museum. The science of military archaeology also has its place, and Tony Pollard and Neil Oliver of Glasgow University have established with new precision the extent of the fighting at Culloden.

When, inevitably, I touch on familiar themes, I refresh the text as far as possible from unfamiliar sources. At the risk of producing 'a *Hamlet* without the Prince', I refer readers who seek details on the career of Charles Edward to the standard biography by Frank McLynn (1988). The picture of the Prince in my own book has been painted layer by layer, always with reference to his words and deeds in the '45, and setting entirely aside the preconceptions to be found in the conventional literature. I have to say that I found him to be an extraordinarily impressive character. The same process has thrown into prominence figures who have hitherto remained hidden in the background, like those of the Duke of Perth or Major General Bland, but somewhat diminished the lustre of Lord George Murray. However, revisionism for its own sake is a contemptible exercise. The enterprise of the '45 remains miraculous in what it so nearly achieved, and miraculous in the grip it has retained on the public imagination.

On my maps I have tried to represent the topography as far as possible as it existed at that period, and for purposes of modern touring I refer readers to the maps of the Ordnance Survey. The wording in the quotations from documents is reproduced faithfully, except where the original punctuation, spelling or use of capitals interferes with the understanding. After some hesitation I have applied the word 'Hanoverian' to the London government and its supporters; 'British' did not quite fit the bill, for it suggested that all of the British supported King George, which was far from being the case.

Dates are given by the Julian (Old Style) calendar, which in 1745–6 ran eleven days behind the continental Gregorian calendar. Thus a date which is presented as 8 July corresponds to 19 July on the continental mainland.

The Highlands, and the Notion of the Highlands

Nothing is better calculated to induce stupefaction in an intelligent reader than a parade of geological terms, yet we will miss some important dimensions of the Jacobite enterprise of 1745–6 if we leave its physical framework out of account – and not just the basic geology, but the effect that the resulting landscapes had on the perceptions of the people of that generation. It would even be possible to talk about the setting of the '45 in brute geological terms. How volcanic upsurges created features like the crags in and about Edinburgh, the massif Ben Nevis and the chaotic Trossachs. How the collision of plates of the earth's crust folded upwards to create the Pennines, and the Downs of south-east England. How, in thinkable time, the glaciers of the Ice Age ploughed the deep troughs of the Scottish lochs.

If we are to understand the effect of the landscape on so many aspects of the '45, we need a brief reminder of what that landscape comprised. As the British Isles became free of permanent ice cover some 10,000 years ago, an outwash of debris from the retreating ice created the Cheshire Plain to the south-west of the Pennines; and on the opposite side of the hills a post-glacial lake dried gradually into the Plain of York. Before long the land was blanketed in woods, of which the most celebrated is the near-mythical Caledonian Forest. Then, as early as 7,500 years ago, they began to retreat in the face of human settlement. In the uplands the assault was second in brutality only to the last Ice Age, for in that testing environment the saplings had no chance at all to reclaim the ground, and acidic and barren moors spread now over the Pennines and the Scottish Highlands.

The environment of the '45 was not limited to the physical, for geology by itself cannot begin to explain how different generations can see the same patch of ground and carry away totally different impressions. This is so-called cognitive geography, in which (with the Jesuit poet Gerard Manley Hopkins) we can talk about 'mountains of the mind'. In the 1740s an army officer would espy impassable 'defiles' and 'ravines' where today we would see respectable paths and shallow valleys. To present-day geographers the uplands begin at 700 feet, and the mountains qualify only from 2,000, but in the middle of the eighteenth century the people living around Holmfirth in the western Pennines counted as 'mountaineers'. In November 1745 one British general described the gentle Bow Hills above Lyme Park in Cheshire as an impassable barrier. In those days civilized people could derive a frisson of excitement by climbing Richmond Hill in Surrey, but their tolerance ended there, and in their eyes the whole effect of the palace of the Douglases at Drumlanrig was spoilt by its setting amid mountains of 'the wildest and most hideous aspect'.[1]

More was at work than just the difficulty of getting about, for the middle of the eighteenth century was the Age of Reason, when thinking people set such store by usefulness and good order. In that respect, at least, the English Pennines and the Lake District did not qualify as fully blown highlands, despite their altitude, for they were populated with hard-working folk who used the force of the gushing streams to power a great range of crafts and industries. It was otherwise in the Scottish Highlands, where 'an eye accustomed to flowery pastures and waving harvests is astonished and repelled by this wide extent of hopeless sterility',[2] and where the mountains, 'always horrid to behold, looked positively diseased when the heather was in bloom'.[3] In 1745, to men who were willing to be affronted by the Jacobite cause, it seemed that the very personifications of Disorder were on the march into England from the North.

PART ONE

THE FABRIC OF BRITAIN

CHAPTER 1

The Historical Setting

WHAT WE KNOW AS 'JACOBITISM' was the ultimate product of three causes of tension:

❖ that between Scotland and England

❖ the division between Catholics and Protestants as a whole, and, most significantly, the split between two kinds of Protestantism: the Episcopal and the Presbyterian

❖ differing notions as to the proper extent of 'kingcraft'.

In 1603, after the death of the great Queen Elizabeth I, King James VI of the Scottish House of Stuart became King James I of England by a planned and peaceful succession. The centuries of intermittent warfare between England and Scotland were at an end, and within a few years the lawless Borders were pacified. The sovereignty of James – and in due course of his two sons – was personal and exercised individually over the two kingdoms, which retained all their internal institutions intact.

By the late 1630s King Charles I, the heir of James, was at religious and constitutional odds with the Presbyterian interest in both of the kingdoms, and

Clergymen were powerful as advocates of the Hanoverian cause

a rough polarization obtained between the differing factions: on the one hand, the Presbyterians (who managed their religious affairs by committee) and the supporters of parliamentary power; and on the other, the defenders of the divinely ordained right of the Stuarts to rule and of the episcopal form of church government, which claimed descent from the Catholic Church independent of Rome.

The first people to resort to arms were the Scottish Presbyterian signatories of the National Covenant of February 1638. In 1643 the majority of the signatories established an alliance with the Parliamentary cause in England, and the result was to widen significantly the scope of the English Civil War, which had broken out in the previous year. In 1644 the Marquis of Montrose (who had broken with the more extreme Covenanters) ravaged through central Scotland on behalf of the king with a small but tough army of Highlanders and professional soldiers who had been brought across from Ireland. This phase in his career ended when he was defeated at Philiphaugh on 13 September 1645, and in the same year the Presbyterian cause triumphed in England. Following lengthy intrigues and negotiations Charles I was executed by the English Parliamentarians in 1649, whereupon his eldest son, another Charles (a man of flexible principle as well as notoriously flexible morals), accepted the Covenant and thereby gained the support of the Presbyterian Scots in his bid to regain his birthright as King Charles II.

Oliver Cromwell, by now the undisputed leader of the army of the English Parliament, defeated the Scots at Dunbar (23 September 1650), just where the Lammermuir Hills receded from the coast of the North Sea. The final effort of the unlikely alliance between Stuart and Presbyterian Scots was a push deep down the western side of England, which was terminated by Cromwell's second victory, at Worcester, exactly a year after his battle at Dunbar. Charles was lucky to escape with his young hide.

Cromwell now extended his rule into Scotland not so much by brute force as by an intelligent use of seaborne mobility, a programme of fort-building at strategic points with battalion outposts to support patrols into the country, and by grasping Highland politics by their complicated innards.[1]

His rule in Britain as a whole, meanwhile, had degenerated into a military dictatorship. He died unmourned in 1658, and in May 1660 Charles II was welcomed back as monarch, albeit one in an uneasy partnership with Parliament. Scottish historians cannot agree whether the policies of the last reigning Stuarts were good or bad for Scotland, but in the event both Scotland and England were overtaken by the crisis which threatened the monarchy after Charles II died in 1685 and his younger brother succeeded as James II. The new king was a Catholic, infused with all the zeal of a convert, and his temperament allied rigidity with susceptibility to panic in a most unhappy combination. A son (James Francis Edward, the future James III, or 'The Old Pretender' to his enemies) was born on 10 June 1688, which opened the prospect of an indefinite succession of Popish monarchs, and persuaded a group of English magnates that they must take drastic action. At their invitation Prince William of Orange, the ruler of Holland, landed in the English West Country with a Dutch army on 5 November 1688. James did not wait to test the strength of his own support in his kingdom and army but fled to France on 23 December. This step enabled the English Parliament to proclaim the fiction that James had abdicated the throne, and the Scottish Estates declared the same on behalf of their own country on 4 April 1689.

Supporters of King James in England were overwhelmed by the pace of events, but in Scotland a rising on his behalf was led by John Graham of Claverhouse, Viscount Dundee. A charismatic leader after the style of Montrose, Viscount Dundee beat a force of Williamite Scots at the Pass of Killiecrankie on 27 July 1689. Dundee was killed at the moment of his triumph and more than three weeks were lost before his orphaned army tried to break into the Lowlands on the far side of the passage by way of Strathtay. On 21 August, in a fight of singular ferocity, they were defeated in the blazing town of Dunkeld by the Cameronian regiment, a body of dedicated Presbyterians newly raised by the Scottish Parliament. By that time the Highlanders had already begun to go home, an indication of the difficulty of keeping the clans together once impetus had been lost. The Williamites overcame the last armed resistance in the Haughs of Cromdale on 1 May 1690, and seven months later the exiled James gave the clans permission to make their peace with the government.

The little branch of the MacDonalds that lived in Glencoe now became the victim of a difference of policy between governmental supporters in Scotland, one of whom, Sir John Dalrymple, Master of Stair, seized the opportunity to set an example in severity to this Jacobite clan. On 13 February 1692 a party of Scottish soldiers from Fort William, given shelter in Glencoe, took up arms and killed some thirty-eight of their MacDonald hosts. Although the scale of the bloodletting was not particularly great by the standards of remoter Scottish history, it violated the traditions of Highland hospitality, and William III stoked up the resentment by obstructing the attempts to establish the blame.

The second half of the 1690s was a period of poor harvests, famine and mass emigration in Scotland, and the dismal associations of the Williamite regime were compounded when the Darien Scheme finally collapsed in 1700. This had been an unsuccessful attempt to establish a Scottish trading settlement in Central America and the Scots naturally blamed the English for the disaster. Many private fortunes been lost and, equally depressingly, Scotland had failed in its bid to establish an independent presence overseas – one of the qualifications for a truly modern state.

By now we have got a little ahead of our story, for we still have to take account of the subjugation of Catholic Ireland. William was a persistent enemy of the France of Louis XIV, which was the most formidable land power of Europe, and by inviting William to England in 1688 the 'Whig' grandees had linked England with the efforts of Holland, Imperial Austria and their associates (including the Pope) to contain French expansionism.

On 12 March 1689 the French opened an outer flank in the war by landing James II on the coast of Ireland with a body of about 4,000 French troops. These forces, even with the addition of considerably greater numbers of Irish, were unable to reduce the northern strongholds of Enniskillen and Londonderry, which were held by Protestant settlers from England and the Lowlands of Scotland. William landed in Ireland in 1690. He beat King James's army on the Boyne on 1 July, and two days later James took ship back to France. However, the resistance of the enemy in central and western Ireland was determined and prolonged, and on 3 October 1691 the Williamite forces granted notably lenient terms of surrender to the garrison of Limerick. Catholic rights in Ireland were guaranteed and no fewer than 12,000 Irish troops and some 4,000 women and other civilians gained a free passage to a new life in France.

The results reached far into the next century. Whatever might have been pledged in 1691, the English authorities eroded the Limerick guarantees so severely that many of the Irish began to look to a French intervention on behalf of the Stuarts as the only way to regain their liberties. Before long the continuing emigration virtually eliminated the natural leaders of the Irish in their homeland, but at the same time it built up an Irish power base in France, which embraced the formidable troops of the Irish Brigade and the wealthy Irish trading houses.

Meanwhile, a significant element in the Protestant Episcopal tradition in both England and Scotland was being excluded from public life. Those who were later to become known as 'Non-Jurors' were numbered among the bishops and clergymen who, during the reign of James II, had hoped to deflect the Catholic king from his more extreme courses. Whilst they had no intention of displacing him or his royal house, which incorporated the notion of sacred hereditary monarchy, once Dutch William was seated on the throne by legal fraud they found it impossible to join the other Episcopalians who were willing to take the requisite oaths of loyalty. In 1690 five bishops and some 400 English clergy were deprived of their offices and livings. Their brethren in Scotland numbered up to 600 and they were in a still worse case, for there the 'Piskies' were ousted as the state church in favour of the Presbyterian 'Church of Scotland by Law Established'.

By the mid 1690s, therefore, 'Jacobitism' had come to exist in both name and substance, its main features being:

❖ An ambition to restore the exiled Stuart line

❖ The potential of armed French intervention to restore the Stuarts

❖ The association of an idealistic section of the Episcopalian church with the Stuart cause

❖ Increasing alienation between London and groups in Scotland.

The last feature, national antagonism, was sharpened by a number of constitutional impostures which the English Parliament now forced through. William III died in 1702 and was succeeded by Queen Anne, the daughter of James II. Although Stuart by name, she was a Protestant by religion and committed to supporting the Act of Settlement (24 April 1701), whereby in the event of her dying without heirs the English throne would pass to the House of Hanover, rulers of a leading Protestant state of north Germany. The English Parliament bludgeoned its Scottish counterpart into recognizing the Hanoverian succession, and in 1707 an unscrupulous campaign of bribery and intimidation persuaded the Scottish Parliament to vote itself out of existence by accepting a Union of the two Crowns. Scotland held to its legal, educational and ecclesiastical systems and its apparatus of local government, but it lost its currency and other essentials of sovereignty. The long-term economic effects of the Union were on the whole favourable to Scotland, but the impact was uneven, and almost everyone suffered in one way or another when English customs and excise dues were extended to Scotland, most notoriously the hated Malt Tax in 1725.[2]

1708

Between 1708 and 1719 the Protestant British state, with minimal effort, brushed off no less than three armed enterprises which the Jacobites launched against it, in addition to various Jacobite conspiracies and foreign negotiations which came to nothing.

The undertaking of 1708 was launched at the height of the War of the Spanish Succession and was a full-blooded French expedition on behalf of the Stuart King James III, who had inherited the claim to the throne after his father James II died in 1701. The initiative had come from Colonel James Hooke, who claimed that Scottish lairds had promised to raise 30,000 men who would march with French support into north-eastern England. 'Nothing', he claimed, 'could hinder them from making themselves masters of the city of Newcastle and of its coal mines, which are so necessary for firing [fuel] in London, that the inhabitants of that place could not be deprived of them for six weeks without being reduced to the greatest extremity'.[3]

The French contingent set out from Dunkirk on board fifteen fast-sailing privateer-transports, with an escort of eight warships, and with the immediate purpose of landing James, together with arms and the 6,000 French troops at Burntisland, on the north side of the Firth of Forth opposite Edinburgh. The French commander, the comte de Forbin, made his first landfall 100 miles too far to the north, and when, finally, he reached the Forth on 12 March, he missed the Jacobite pilots and signals. The next day he regained the open sea to avoid being bottled up by Admiral Byng's British squadron, which had meanwhile arrived in the offing. Thus the expedition disappeared over the horizon without a Jacobite in Scotland having drawn his sword, though the potential for something of consequence had certainly been there.[4]

The '15

The next rising broke out in radically changed circumstances. It counted very much against the Jacobites that France had made its peace with Britain, on 31 March 1713. The French recognized the Protestant succession, and no substantial aid was to be forthcoming from their nation to the Jacobites for more than a generation. At the same time the opportunities for domestic support for an uprising were never to be so great. Elements in the anti-Whig 'Tory' party had been living in hopes of a peaceful Stuart succession, but they had been unable to extract from James III what seemed to them to be the essential precondition, that he should embrace Protestantism. They had still taken no decisive action when on 1 August 1714 Queen Anne died unexpectedly. The Act of Succession now came into force and the Elector of Hanover was at once proclaimed king as 'George I'. All pretence of maintaining a line of sacred monarchy was at an end, for the hereditary claim of the Hanoverians was very remote and in Scotland the feelings of alienation were reinforced by the growing unpopularity of the Union.

The '15 was innocent of the grand strategic purpose that lay behind the expedition of 1708, however unrealistic that might have been. Up to 20,000 Jacobites took up arms in Scotland alone, but this time the rising remained incoherent and well-nigh leaderless, and was characterized by groups of men who hung about doing nothing in particular, or moved indecisively over the landscape doing not much more. The contrast with the '45 is striking.

The largest faction coalesced around John, 6th Earl of Mar, who raised the Jacobite standard at Braemar on 6 September. Eight days later the Jacobites occupied Perth, which became their unofficial capital. They would have enjoyed a great superiority of force if they had moved at once to brush aside their Whiggish Scots opponents from Stirling, for Stirling commanded the passage into the Lowlands between the lower Forth to the east and the swamps of Blairdrummond and Flanders that extended towards the Trossachs in the west. John, 2nd Duke of Argyll, moved swiftly to deny the opportunity to the Jacobites. 'The crux of the crisis lay in a duel between two great Scots magnates, Argyll and Mar, for control of Stirling, the strategic key in the middle of the Lowlands without which a Jacobite army could not open the door to co-operate with its many sympathisers in southern Scotland and northern England.'[5]

The Duke of Argyll was still inferior in numbers, if not in enterprise, when he marched north in November to Dunblane. The marshes were threatening to freeze over, and perhaps Argyll believed that it was no longer possible to bottle up the Jacobites in the Highlands just by sitting tight at Stirling. The rival forces clashed indecisively at Sheriffmuir on 13 November. Both 'armies' then pulled back to their bases, but the outcome was a clear defeat for the Jacobites at the campaign level, for they had thereby renounced the attempt to break across the Stirling gap into the Lowlands.

The one Jacobite leader with any initiative was Brigadier William Mac-Kintosh of Borlum, who had brought a body of 1,500 or so Highlanders across the south side of the Forth on fishing boats, and on 13 October essayed a bold and nearly successful *coup de main* against Edinburgh Castle. Borlum then worked his way south to Kelso, where the retinues of Lowland and Border lairds and Northumberland gentry formed a second grouping.

The lords Kenmure, Nithsdale, Carnforth and Winton were the leading Scots, and James Radcliffe, 3rd Earl of Derwentwater, the most prominent Englishman, but the command was invested in the talkative Thomas Forster, the one English Protestant of any influence, but described by a Whig as 'an idle, drunken, senseless man, not good enough to head a company of militia'.[6] This was harsh, for the Jacobite plans for a rising in Northumberland had been thrown over in favour of a rising in south-west England, which dispersed at the end of September, and after that Forster had been left with no directions at all.

In theory Forster could have swung north to take the weak forces of the Duke of Argyll in the rear, but instead his army turned into north-western England by way of Appleby (3 November), Kendal (4–5 November) and Kirkby Lonsdale. It was a recruiting drive writ large and not an all-out invasion such as Prince Charles would direct in 1745.

Not many recruits came forward in Westmorland, and although between four and five hundred Catholics signed up in Lancashire, the local High Church Anglicans failed to live up to their promises. The march came to an end on the Ribble at Preston, where the Jacobites set about barricading the approaches against the aggressive General Charles Willis. The Scots were all for breaking out while there was still time. They were ignored by the English command, which surrendered the whole force unilaterally on 14 November. Whereas the Lancashire Catholics believed that they had been let down by the Anglicans, the Scots believed that they had been let down by the English as a whole, and the Ribble remained in Scottish thoughts as a psychological as much as a physical barrier.

In such a way the Jacobite military initiatives came to an end on 13 and 14 November, the dates of Sheriffmuir and the surrender at Preston. The '15 was nevertheless perpetuated in an empty and symbolic way when James III landed at Peterhead on 22 December and proceeded to hold court at Perth, where the Jacobites built a line of defences that extended from the old Cromwellian citadel on the Tay below the town, to the marshes of the same river to the north. Without the determination to defend them these works counted for as little as the barricades at Preston, and on 31 January 1716 the Jacobites abandoned them without a fight as soon as the Duke of Argyll embarked on his second and final offensive. Argyll was not moving particularly fast, but in order to delay him still further James was persuaded to burn the towns of Auchterarder, Crieff and Blackford, which was not the best way to endear those places to the Jacobite cause. On 4 February James and the Earl of Mar embarked furtively from Montrose for France, whereupon their men marched north to Badenoch and dispersed to their homes or places of refuge.

Altogether the Hanoverian authorities executed thirty Jacobites, among whom the Earl of Derwentwater was the most prominent. Several hundred lesser persons were transported to the colonies, and the government ordered large-scale confiscations of the estates of the implicated gentry through the agency of the Commissioners for Annexed Estates and the new York Buildings Company. However, a number of Whig gentlemen sheltered their Jacobite neighbours from the worst of the confiscations, or helped them to regain the lands that had been lost, and even the Duke of Argyll was more of a Scotsman than the people in London suspected, for he was no great lover of the Union and harboured no great hatred of Jacobitism as such. Understandably a number of people, most notably the 2nd Earl of Breadalbane, declined to come out in support of Prince Charles in 1745,[7] but the Hanoverian government began to suspect that the Jacobites had escaped lightly, and in 1746 the Duke of Cumberland became convinced that the underhand deals had been responsible for perpetuating militant Jacobitism.

1719

The foray of 1719 was the last in our trio of Jacobite enterprises and counts as the most bizarre. It was a side-show in an aftermath of the War of the Austrian Succession, at a time when Britain was supporting the Austrians against Spain in a contest for power in the Mediterranean. In December 1718 Admiral Byng with an Anglo-Dutch force defeated a Spanish squadron off Cape Passero in Sicily. Spain was enjoying a brief resurgence of power and ambition, and the Spanish minister Cardinal Alberoni believed that he could best hit back by landing 5,000 Spanish troops in the Jacobite cause in the south-west of England. In March 1719 the expedition was scattered by a storm, and the only element which went ahead was a diversion targeted on the Western Highlands. George Keith, the hereditary 10th Earl Marischal of Scotland, duly sailed from Spain with 307 Spanish troops on board two frigates. A further party bearing the Marquis of Tullibardine (the dispossessed Jacobite heir of the Duke of Atholl) took ship from France, and on 4 April the two groups met at Stornoway on the Isle of Lewis.

The enterprise was bedevilled from the start by disputes among the leaders concerning both the command and the objectives. Keith, who commanded the Spanish, was all for reaching the mainland and dashing along the Great Glen to seize Inverness while it was still held weakly by governmental forces. Tullibardine claimed to be in charge of all the Scottish Jacobites and was unwilling to venture any further until he was convinced that the main expedition was on its way.

On 13 April 1719 the bickering force reached the mainland at Loch Alsh and established its principal magazine in the old MacKenzie castle of Eilean Donan. The expedition made contact with the influential local chiefs MacDonald of Clanranald and Donald Cameron of Lochiel, and altogether about 1,600 Highlanders arrived on the scene in dribs and drabs. However, the arguing continued unabated and the initiative passed to the Hanoverians. A flotilla of three frigates first bombarded Eilean Donan, then landed a force which accepted the surrender of the forty Spaniards who held the shattered castle. The principal body of the Jacobites progressed less than 10 miles along Loch Duich and into Glenshiel before they had to do battle with General Wightman, an energetic individual who had gathered reinforcements at Inverness and then marched at speed along Loch Ness and up by way of Glen Moriston.

The action of Glenshiel was fought on 10 June at the narrow north-western exit of the glen just above Shiel Bridge. The Jacobites held a strong position on either side of the pass, which is probably why they did not choose to launch a Highland charge and instead engaged with musketry. Wightman on his side made innovative use of four or six coehorn mortars. These light and stubby pieces were normally reserved for siegework, but Wightman now used them as a substitute for howitzers and he sent explosive shells arching across the glen. The day ended with the Highlanders and the Jacobite leaders scampering to safety over the mountains and the Spanish left to surrender (being finally shipped home at Spanish cost).

The little battle had therefore been decisive, though General Wade noted five years later that the muskets landed by the Spanish were still in the hands of the Highlanders, 'many of which I have seen in my passage through that country, and I judge them to be the same from the peculiar make, and the fashion of their locks'.[8]

The Launch of the '45

One of the most curious aspects of the Jacobite '45 was that it was not the natural projection of a prospering movement. On contrary, by the early months of 1745 the cause had never seemed more deeply buried under a weight of frustrations and disappointments.

In 1714, as we have seen, the Hanoverian elector George had succeeded to the throne of Britain. The English Tories had hesitated to commit themselves either to the 'King George' in waiting, or to the exiled James III, and their triumphant rivals, the Whigs, now excluded them from government altogether. By this time also, Britain and France had made peace at Utrecht (1713) and in November 1716 the two powers made a treaty of friendship, which in the event preserved the peace between them for more than a quarter of a century. There was no further room for French support of the Stuarts. James III and his followers had to leave France, and in 1717 he settled his doubly exiled court in Rome. His first son, Charles Edward, was born there in the Palazzo Muti-Papazzuri on 20 December 1720. A second son, Henry Benedict, the future cardinal, was born in 1725.

The Jacobites were impotent to prevent the accession of Britain's second Hanoverian monarch, George II, in 1727, and so the Stuarts were now removed from the exercise of power by two reigns – or three, if we include the Protestant and hemmed-about Queen Anne. Hanoverian rule consolidated in the course of the 1730s, a period of tranquillity associated with the prime minister, Sir Robert Walpole. Walpole was a master of political manipulation at home and clung to the friendship with France even after an overseas conflict, the 'War of Jenkins' Ear', opened between Britain and Spain in 1739.

For the English Jacobites the early 1740s were years when their hopes were revived, but then shattered in a cruel and seemingly terminal way. In 1742 the long rule of Walpole was at last brought down by an alliance of Parliamentary expediency between the Tories and the 'country' faction among the Whigs. In fact these nominally independent Whigs were merely manoeuvring for a place in the new administration, which was headed by the Duke of Newcastle and his brother Henry Pelham. A number of leading Tories, deserted by all but a few of their Whiggish friends, began to look for help to the Continent. Here the last pillar of the Anglo-French peace collapsed when the French minister Cardinal Fleury died in January 1743.

By the spring of 1743 Britain and France were at war, and a group of Tory peers and gentlemen commissioned Lord Francis Sempill to sound out prospects of help from France. Among the aristocrats in question, the Duke of Beaufort was influential in the south-western counties of England, while Sir Watkin Williams Wynn had important lands and an important following in Wales, and his friend James Barry, 4th Earl of Barrymore, owned estates and influence in the counties of Cheshire, Lancashire, Yorkshire and the strategically important Essex just east of London.

The French army in Germany was beaten at Dettingen on 27 June 1743, and French interests were doing badly in Germany as a whole; to Louis XV and some of his ministers it seemed that the best way to divert the attention of the Hanoverian regime in Britain was a new enterprise in favour of the Stuarts. At that period 'scientific' and other innocent individuals were free to travel between warring countries and so between August and October 1743 the French king's Master of Horse, James Butler, toured England for the nominal purpose of buying bloodstock, but really to sound out the state of the Jacobite cause. He reported to Louis that he had found a high level of latent support, but that the Duke of Beaufort and the other magnates insisted that they were powerless to move until a force of French regulars was landed within close marching distance of London.

The French planning went ahead on that basis. The direction of the expedition was given to the the foremost commander of his time, Marshal de Saxe, and between 12,000 and 15,000 French troops assembled at Dunkirk in readiness to make the short passage to Essex on merchant transports, once a French fleet under Admiral de Roquefort had diverted or beaten the fleet of Sir John Norris. On 24 February 1744 the rival forces were facing up to do battle in the Channel narrows when a great storm swept them both away. Norris lost one of his ships with all hands. Roquefort made it back to Brest with his squadron battered but intact, though there was heavy damage among the transports waiting at Dunkirk. However, the invasion was less at the mercy of the winds than of the French ministers who opposed a landing *per se*, and the scenes in Dunkirk harbour on 28 February gave them all the excuse they needed to cancel the project outright. The essential precondition for the rising of the English Jacobites had been eliminated, or so it seemed, for all time.

All of this had been passing with only the remotest connection with Jacobitism in Scotland. There was no Tory party in that land which could serve as an environment where Jacobites could make social and political contacts. There was only an indirect connection between attachment to the Stuarts and the Scottish resentment against Hanoverian rule – a hostility which provoked the extended Malt Tax Riot in Whiggish Glasgow in 1725, and the Porteous Riots which erupted in Edinburgh in September 1736 after a popular smuggler had been arrested. There were still differences between the Highland social order and that of the Lowlands.

It was left to an individual to make some important connections. The elderly John Gordon of Glenbucket did not begin to rank as a landowner to compare with the members of the Beaufort circle in England, for he had sold his estate and was now living as a tenant farmer. Nor was he impressive as a physical specimen, being bent and crippled (and scarcely able to hold himself in the saddle by the time of the '45). What mattered was his devotion to the Stuart cause and his charisma, which enabled him, although not a chief, to command a personal following among the Highlanders of Strathdon and Glenlivet.

Glenbucket took himself to France in 1737 and found that Cardinal Fleury was not to be moved from his attachment to Walpole's Britain. Undeterred, Glenbucket travelled to Rome in January the next year and persuaded the Stuart court that it was in a position to exploit the unpopularity of the Hanoverian regime in Scotland. He returned to Scotland with the Stuart rank of major general, and more than any other man he kept Scottish Jacobitism alive until a number of magnates began to take an active interest in the cause in 1739, the year hostilities broke out between Spain and Britain.

The Association or Concert was a group of Scottish noblemen and gentry roughly comparable with that of the Duke of Beaufort and his friends in England, though there was no direct connection between the two. The leading figures included the Catholic Duke of Perth, his uncle Lord John Drummond of Fairntower, Lord Lovat, Donald Cameron of Lochiel and Lord Linton (Earl of Traquair from 1741). The Peebles gentleman John Murray of Broughton hurried backwards and forwards to co-ordinate the Highland and Lowland elements and link the Association as a whole with the Stuarts on the Continent. Each Associator was assigned an area in which he was to use his credit to drum up support for the Jacobites, though Murray of Broughton found that little of any use had been done by the time he reviewed progress on behalf of Prince Charles in 1742.

In 1744 Prince Charles travelled incognito from Rome to Paris. Murray of Broughton met him there at the stables of the Tuileries Palace and by his own account told him that he could count on the support of 4,000 Highlanders at the most, and that he must abandon his declared intention of coming to Scotland. Murray of Broughton reported as much when he returned to Scotland in October, though Lord Elcho and other Jacobites suspected that he had in fact encouraged Charles in his scheme. Early in 1745 the Association drew up a paper which set out its objections to any such enterprise unless it was supported by 6,000 French troops. The delivery was entrusted to Lord Traquair, but he returned from London in April to report that he had found no suitable means of getting the message to its destination.

The Prince was having much better luck with his Irish supporters than with his English or Scottish ones. Indeed from one perspective the '45 was essentially an Irish initiative, a point worth making when so much has been written about Charles's 'excessive' regard for his Irish companions. Lord Clare, the commander of the Irish Brigade in the French service, introduced him to a circle of Irish shipowners who were based in French ports and building up fortunes from smuggling, slavery, privateering and open trading – all activities that were considered equally legitimate in the French commercial culture. They were willing to get him to Scotland, along with arms, ammunition, cash and volunteers. French officials also helped, though they thought they were merely sponsoring a cruise in Scottish waters.

Sir Walter Ruttlidge provided a captured 64-gun British warship, renamed *Elisabeth*, which carried 1,500 muskets, 1,800 broadswords and 700 'volunteers' from the regiment of Clare in the Irish Brigade in the service of France. Prince Charles himself was to sail in the nimble 16-gun privateer *Doutelle*, which bore a further cargo of muskets and swords, along with 4,000 *louis d'or*.

The *Doutelle* left Nantes on 22 June 1745. The ship made a successful rendezvous with the *Elisabeth* at Belle-Isle off the southern coast of Brittany on 4 July and they sailed together on the following day. On 9 July the two vessels had the misfortune of encountering the 64-gun *Lion* about 100 miles west of Lizard Point. The two big warships were exactly matched. *Elisabeth* was reduced to a splintery near-wreck. *Lion* had all her rigging shot away, 'so that we lay muzzled, and could do nothing with our sails', and took many shots in the hull 'which killed us 45 men and some of them were between wind and water and wounded 107'. *Doutelle* is usually represented as hanging back from the fray, but for a little ship she did well, twice attempting at the beginning of the action to rake *Lion*, 'but was beat off by our chase guns fore and aft'. The combatants drew apart. *Elisabeth* was too badly damaged to continue on the expedition or even transfer her cargo to the *Doutelle* and she had to put back to France. The officers of *Lion* assumed that they had thwarted a French sailing, 'probably bound for Newfoundland or some other of their garrisons in America', and so no attempt was made to convey an alarm to England.[9] Prince Charles sailed on alone in the *Doutelle* and on 23 July 1745 landed in the Outer Hebrides, on the little island of Eriskay.

Prince Charles might be charged with irresponsibility, for persisting in his scheme when there so was so little evidence of support in Britain and when his expedition was so puny in scale even before the battle with the *Lion*. A little thought shows that his options were narrow. Overt backing from the

French government would have been noted by British agents in Paris, just as preparations for a full-scale invasion would scarcely have escaped the attention of the many British informants in the north French ports. Again, a swelling Jacobite movement in Britain would have alerted the Newcastle administration in London and even its complacent representatives in Scotland.

As it was, the Hanoverian interest in Scotland took only the most desultory notice of the unaccountable state of excitement in the Western Highlands, which were rife with rumours of a Stuart return, and where the coming of the young Prince was hymned by the Gaelic bard Alexander MacDonald.

On 5 June 1745 the Skye chief Norman MacLeod, a supporter of the government, wrote to the Scottish Lord President, Duncan Forbes of Culloden, to tell him to ignore an 'extraordinary tale' that Prince Charles had ambitions in the Highlands.[10] To be absolutely sure, MacLeod set out observers along the string of the Outer Hebrides and also on the mainland, from Glenelg opposite Skye to the isolated headland of Ardnamurchan to the south-west. He wrote to Duncan Forbes again on 15 July, that 'as I've heard nothing further from any of these places, but peace and quiet, I think you may entirely depend on it, that either there never was such a thing intended, or if there was, that the project is entirely defeated and blown into the air'.[11]

CHAPTER 2

The Divided Lands:
England, Wales and Ireland

AS TOURISTS STROLL DOWN THE Royal Mile in Edinburgh today they see shops on either hand which invite them to purchase outfits of male Highland dress, complete with short jacket, kilt and sporran. Men of Whiggish principles have on offer an 'Argyll' rig-out. A would-be Jacobite can fit himself out with the almost identical 'Prince Charles' gear, and imagine perhaps how hordes of devoted clansmen might run down heather-clad hillsides to throw themselves at his feet. Such indeed is the image of the Prince and his followers, scarcely disturbed by the efforts of generations of historians to uncover the realities. It is not true, as often alleged, that there were more Scots fighting against Prince Charles at Culloden than for him. However, Jacobitism was an English, Welsh and Irish phenomenon as well as a Scottish one, and in Scotland there were more Lowlanders in the Jacobite ranks than Highlanders.

So where does the misapprehension come from? It comes from the enduring and unifying image of the heroic Jacobite Highlander, an image cultivated by the Jacobites themselves. It suited the supporters of the House

Possible scenes of the port of Bristo (Edinburgh) under Highland control

of Hanover in equal degree to represent the armed Jacobites as bug-ridden, dangerous brigands who (without any contradiction being perceived) were somehow also pathetic and incompetent. An English Protestant patriotism took on new life, and formed about the unlikely figure of George, Elector of Hanover and King of England.[1]

All Jacobites shared at least the nominal commitment to restore the House of Stuart to the throne or thrones of Britain, whatever the reservations actually harboured by groups or individuals. A genuine Jacobite culture also existed, and it combined, on the one hand, a sentimental attachment to a defeated past, and on the other all the excitement of renewal. It was no coincidence that a walk through the countryside in springtime and early summer revealed on every side the emblems which the Jacobites had appropriated for themselves – butterflies, daffodils, wild white roses, honeysuckle, and acorns embowered in sprigs of oak leaves. Genteel young ladies worked the motifs into their embroidered cushions and samplers, noted printers were eager to run off Jacobite tracts and proclamations, and the list of Jacobite artists is impressive – the classical painters John Alexander and his son Cosmo, Allan Ramsay, and the Robert Strange who designed the Jacobite currency and became an engraver of European renown.

The coming of Prince Charles himself paralleled that of the returning pagan god of spring: 'The spirit of the sun or the god who, according to the ancient creed, guided it in its course, was figured as a lively young man with long, yellow, dishevelled hair … This imaginary conceit of the Hyperborean Apollo made its way to the Highlands, where to this day he is called by the name of Gruagich, "the fair haired"'.[2]

The Underdogs and Personal Advantage

Groups as diverse as Whig grandees, crusading Protestants, and the merchant classes of Liverpool and Glasgow had gained in various ways from developments such as the Glorious Revolution of 1688, the anti-Catholic penal laws, the Union of England and Scotland, the burgeoning trade with the North American colonies, the passing of the throne to the House of Hanover in 1714, the reinforced laws in defence of order and property, or the nearly thirty years of political jobbery that were associated with the name of Walpole.

Other interests had suffered, and for those Jacobitism offered a serious appeal, or at least the potential for change. Prince Charles hoped that the excluded Tories would be drawn by his political programme, embracing as it did short parliaments, the removal of political placemen from public office, a free press, and an enduring peace and the abolition of the standing army. It is significant that in the Derby election of 1742 Tory voters, but not a single Whig, were to be found among the frame-work knitters, wool-combers, butchers, tailors, brick-makers, blacksmiths and tanners.[3] The best gun-founders of the kingdom had been supporters of the Stuarts, and not just Tories,[4] and before Radicalism emerged in the 1760s Jacobitism was seen as the creed of the distressed craftsman and small trader, the highwayman, the smuggler and the adventurer – all folk who had in one way or another been marginalized in Hanoverian Britain, which seemed to be run by rich and influential men for their private advantage.

The purest form of Jacobitism in the ideological sense was probably to be found in Manchester and the east-coast ports of Scotland, where sentiment was swayed by religion, or in committed individuals like Lord George Murray, who took a course which he recognized from the outset as being against his own best interests. He wrote to his Whiggish brother James, the Hanoverian Duke of Atholl: 'I own frankly now that I am to engage, that what I may do may be reckoned and will be reckoned desperate. All appearances seem to be against me. Interest, prudence, and the obligations to you which I lie under, will prevent most people in my situation from taking a resolution that may probably end in my utter ruin. My life, my fortune, my expectations, the happiness of my wife and children are all at stake (and the chances are against me), and yet a principle of (what seems to me) honour, and my duty to King and Country, outweighs everything'.[5]

The clan leaders were divided, and the great majority of the 'Jacobite' chiefs declared for Prince Charles only after weighing the odds. Lord Lovat and MacDonnell of Glengarry played a waiting game as long as they could, while the infamous Ludovick, son of the 'Hanoverian' Grant of Grant, remained an ambiguous figure until the end.

The men of the '45 were heirs of three or four generations of political turmoil, during which time their families had evolved strategies to ensure the continuation of their lines and fortunes, which often seemed more important to them than individual survival. If a Catholic gentleman 'came out' for the Jacobites, he might well sign over his estate to a reliable Protestant for safe-keeping. A father would assign his estate to his eldest son, or stay at home, and see his offspring take the risk on one side or another.

If Prince Charles turned up on your doorstep in person, you could, without compromising yourself, arrange to be away from home, like Sir Robert

Menzies or Lord Nathaniel Curzon of Kedleston, or, like Richard Lowthian of Dumfries, you could make yourself so drunk that you were in no fit state to be presented. (Although this did not necessarily save you from being embarrassed by the more impressionable members of your family.)

William Boyd, the Earl of Kilmarnock, was heavily in debt to a number of the tradesmen of Falkirk, and he represents a classic example of the 'men of desperate fortune' who lacked ideological backbone, but looked to change, almost any change, as an opportunity to resolve their tangled financial or legal affairs. There were also local underdogs, who often came out on one side or the other as a chance to overthrow the 'overdogs' and who only by the working of chance were labelled as being for or against the government.[6]

Religion and the Jacobites

Creeds and codes generally sat lightly on Prince Charles. He was a child of the Age of Reason, and what he saw of the royal courts of Europe convinced him that the modern monarchs were essentially godless.[7] The wonder is that he did not abjure Catholicism in 1745, as he was to do five years later when he visited England incognito, in one of the most curious episodes of his idiosyncratic career.

There was no organic link between the Catholicism of the Jacobites in England and that of the Catholics in Scotland. English Catholicism was largely the survival of the religion of pre-Reformation days, maintained most often through the protection of recusant families and their house priests. Catholicism in Scotland had been for a time totally leaderless, and, as it existed in the 1740s, it was divided into Highland and Lowland branches. (These features will be discussed in a little more detail later on.)

Where religion bound Scottish and English Jacobitism most closely was in the commitment shown by the High Church Non-Jurors, those men and women who looked to the House of Stuart as the embodiment of the Divine Right of Kings, unlawfully (and they hoped temporarily) broken by the usurpations of William of Orange in 1688 and the Hanoverians in 1714.

Non-Jurism was seated most firmly in the eastern Lowlands of Scotland, in Oxford, and in Manchester, where the noted Non-Juror Dr Thomas Deacon declared to a Whiggish friend that he had no alternative but to support the rising, in the full knowledge that he had nothing to gain in the material sense, and that he and his family might suffer, for 'a conscientious man ought not to regard what may happen to him in this world'.[8]

On balance the Non-Jurors were deeper-thinking and more committed

The British Isles

than the general run of Anglicans, and the Hanoverian authorities came to regard any display of religious enthusiasm as suspicious. If they had listened to John Wesley they would have known that he was no kind of rebel, but his Methodist preachers in Cornwall awakened alarm when they went about in lay clothes, gathered crowds about them in the fields, and managed to live with no visible means of support. A Mr Baron reported to the Duke of Newcastle that he concluded that 'they could not belong to the established church, and began to conjecture they must have some further view than the reformation they pretended in religion, which hath been so often a cloak to cover the most wicked designs against the state'. They had deluded the most ignorant people of the lower orders, and distributed bits of paper which bore the words: 'As Moses lifted up the serpent in the wilderness, so must the Son of Man be lifted up'. That indeed was dangerous language.[9]

One of the undoubted Methodist Jacobites was the Sergeant Dunbar who deserted from Sowle's Regiment and fought on the Jacobite side at Falkirk. He appropriated the scarlet and gold uniform of the Hanoverian Major Lockhart, and was still wearing it when he was hanged, along with thirty-five other deserters, in Cumberland's camp after Culloden. 'He was one of Whitfield's disciples, and when he walked to the gallows he was attended by near a dozen Methodists of his own former regiment, with books in their hands all the way singing hymns. He refused to have a Kirk minister with him, but seemingly behaved with decency and courage, and though he talked much of Jesus Christ, yet he died without acknowledging his treason and the justice of his punishment.'[10]

Jacobite England and Wales

Looking back in December 1745, on their retreat homeward from Derby, the disillusioned Scottish Jacobites were angry that the professed English adherents to Prince Charles had apparently withheld their support. Yet there is a world of difference between having an attachment to a cause, and taking specific and life-endangering action when its representative suddenly arrives in your midst. Not for the first time we find agreement between Whig propagandists and neo-Jacobite historians such as William Drummond Norie, for whom 'English Jacobitism was a myth, a mere unsubstantial phantom upon which it would be madness to depend for any practical support', and for whom King George was 'a boorish German debauchee at whose feet the English people, forgetful of their honour, pride and national traditions, grovelled in lazy, indifferent content'.[11] That has a good ring to it, but is it also true?

One answer probably lies in what Prince Charles expected of the English Jacobites, which was limited and specific. The perceptive Maxwell of Kirkconnell points out that the uprising in England had been predicated on a force of at least 7,000 French troops landing and taking the lead.[12] The Jacobite agent Laurence Wolfe agreed, and adds that

> the principal reason for which the well-affected people in England dared not rise in any other form and join the Prince's army, is their want of officers to lead the undisciplined men which the Prince could not spare them, and as it was well known the Prince could never keep his ground in England with

so small an army as 9,000 [sic] men in case the landing could not be effected
from France. It was as well known again that the English could not bear
the same fatigue of long marches at a precipitate retreat as the Scots, and
consequently they must have been sacrificed.[13]

The practicalities also deserve consideration. The route of the Jacobite
invasion of England lay not through Northumberland, where the gentry
were primed on the Prince's behalf, but through notoriously Whiggish Cumberland and Westmorland, and on through Lancashire, where the Jacobites
were divided and out of contact. Little more than 200 Lancashire men
enlisted with Prince Charles on his march through their county, which is few
enough in absolute terms, but we have to compare like with like; the figure
actually compares well with the rate of recruiting in Scotland, where the
Jacobite authorities had much longer to gather their troops and did not
hesitate to use force in the process. Outside the walls of Carlisle no part of
England could count as being under secure Jacobite control for more than a
day or two at a time, and the Jacobite forces moved so quickly that it was as
difficult for would-be recruits to catch up with them, as it was for the
Hanoverian armies. In that respect the very speed of the Scottish Jacobites,
together with their skill at diversion, actually worked against them.

By the nature of things the Jacobites of England and Wales were much
more under the thumb of the authorities than were their counterparts in the
Highlands and the eastern Lowlands of Scotland. The papers of the dukes
of Newcastle and Cumberland are replete with the kind of tale-bearing and
denunciation that were to be found in Gestapo headquarters in German
towns in the 1930s. In England and Wales in 1745 and 1746 the attention of
the authorities was repeatedly drawn by tales of waggons on the move with
mysterious freight, gatherings of gentry on remote estates, and the existence
of hiding places in Catholic country houses.[14]

The contest between the army of Prince Charles and the Hanoverian
forces was fought out by very small forces indeed by the standards of continental European warfare, and a great number – and conceivably a majority
– of the gentry and people of England and Wales were indifferent to the
outcome, or at least willing to come to terms with whatever party came out
on top, as had happened in 1688. The English and Welsh, unlike the Scots
and the Irish, had largely abandoned the practice of serving in foreign armies;
moreover, 'while we had the marches [borders] of Wales and Scotland to
fight upon, our gentry were very martial; but having peace at home, and
few volunteers going abroad; enjoying so great affluence at home, and

delighting so much in effeminate pleasures, whatever the common people may be, *our* gentry are now the least martial of any in *Europe*'.[15]

Maxwell of Kirkconnell indicates that under the Hanoverian regime the people had been overawed by armies of well-disciplined troops. 'There is an artificial and an acquired courage, as well as natural; the former is only got by the use of arms and the practice of war, both [of which] the common people of England are utter strangers to.'[16] In relation to subject peoples in general, the duc de Richelieu pointed out that the advent of disciplined regular armies had reinforced central power, and the peoples 'had been deprived of the means of rebelling against authority, to the extent that, regardless of the secret opinion of the majority, they cannot prevail against those who hold the reins of authority'.[17] The terms of some tenancies still required tenants to render armed service to their landlords upon demand, but in the conditions of the time such provisions were a dead letter.

The English and Welsh were also disarmed in the physical sense, for the tough Game Laws had deprived non-landowners of their firearms and we cannot count the flimsy fowling pieces or the rusty iron weapons that hung in the baronial halls. For this reason the Duke of Cumberland had to send home the thousands of civilians who had been summoned to aid his siege of Carlisle. The British government itself was short of arms for a time, and early in September 1745 it was found that there was little spare capacity in the West Midlands workshops.[18]

The only significant exceptions to the picture of a disarmed Britain were to be found along the coast. The smugglers of Kent and eastern Sussex had guns, and would probably have been willing to use them in the Jacobite interest. On the Hanoverian side, the authorities were able to call on the reserves of cannon and gunpowder to be found in the merchant ships in the north-western ports, where the Whigs prevailed. The Duke of Cumberland exploited this resource to great effect when he borrowed heavy cannon and roundshot from Whitehaven and used them to crack open the walls of Carlisle.

To sign up to the loyal Associations and subscriptions was a relatively painless way of making your mark with the Hanoverian regime, but even so the response in many areas of England and Wales was decidedly patchy. The London government sent Lord Tyrawley to reinforce the efforts of Lord Edgcumbe to raise the far West Country. On the way he had heard encouraging words from magnates like the Earl of Pembroke and Lord Ilchester at Wilton, which suggested that there 'excellent dispositions in the Nation, but I am very much mistaken if they produce anything towards the defence of it, for, when I came to talk with the principal people I have mentioned, I cannot find that at any country meeting these persons have been at for promoting of Associations, that any good has resulted from their meetings but a just sense of danger, and an opinion that something ought to be done, without being able to conclude on any point to be reduced into action'.[19] When, finally, the Duke of Cumberland was following the retreating Jacobites through Lancashire, his secretary complained that the gentlemen had allowed the rebels to traverse their counry without a show of opposition, and now very few of thcm had 'so much as shown themselves to the Duke, which is a matter of respect certainly due to him, and this spirit of indifference reigns at a time when the whole country is in danger of being overrun by a foreign enemy'.[20]

The English Catholics

In the middle of the eighteenth century English popular anti-Catholicism was at one of its peaks, and John Marchant, in his history of the rising, could summon up pictures of 'legions of Popish priests swarming in City and country, poisoning the minds, and debauching the loyalty of the common people'.[21] English Catholics as a whole now came under the most intense scrutiny, and the authorities invoked an accumulation of anti-Catholic penal laws dating back to the time of Elizabeth I. They required Catholics to render oaths of Allegiance and ecclesiastic Supremacy to the monarch, and amongst other things forbade them from keeping a horse worth more than five pounds, venturing more than 5 miles from their own houses, and living anywhere within 10 miles of London. Hardwicke, the Lord Chancellor, observed that 'the true difficulty … lies in this: that the laws against the Papists, as they stand in the statute book, are so severe that they are the cause of their own non-execution'.[22]

On 5 September 1745 the government declared in the name of the king that the legislation must take full effect, and it went on to initiate a series of sweeps of the areas that were inhabited most notoriously by Catholics. On 10 November a deputy lieutenant reported to the Duke of Newcastle from Lancashire that he had carried out the instructions to search for weapons and horses. He had little to show at the moment, but he suspected that there were plenty of illegal objects somewhere, 'as we are surrounded by Papists, some of whom are of good family and large estates'.[23] A *razzia* later in the same month yielded up 300 horses. In effect the English Catholics had been let out on a long lead, and it was now being pulled very tight.

When the Jacobite army entered England in 1745 it was politically important for Prince Charles to disavow any connection between his cause and that of the Catholics. He was persuaded to demote the Catholic Duke of Perth from his rank of lieutenant general, and as a matter of principle his circle had already forsworn any attempt to contact the Catholic clergy of Lancashire (p. 67), which was probably the most Catholic of all the counties and now lay squarely on his way through England. On his side Edward Howard, the Jacobite 9th Duke of Norfolk, did not dare to show his true sympathies. He was the unofficial leader of the Catholic community in England, and had been 'out' in 1715, but he was under the thumb of a disapproving wife, and he now displayed an almost craven loyalty to the Hanoverian regime.[24]

The Duke of Newcastle had been anticipated by Sir William Gage and several other Catholic gentlemen of Suffolk, who on 20 September 1745 waited on the Duke of Grafton at Euston Hall 'to assure His Grace of their peaceable disposition, etc.'.[25] Tendencies like these have encouraged historians to declare outright that there was a divorce between Jacobitism and the English Catholics, which is one of those untrue truisms that have bedevilled the understanding of the '45. Many of the Catholic gentry were plotting for the Prince, as we shall see, and when popular Jacobite disorder broke out in England it more often than not had a Catholic flavour. The English Catholics remained in a state of excitement long after the army of Prince Charles had retired into Scotland, and as late as 20 March 1746 one of their number, Thomas Mayott of Mountnossing, could enter the Rose and Crown public house in Romford in Essex, and on spotting the barber–surgeon James Hewit, 'this same Mayott hugging this deponent said "I'm informed you are one of us, but won't own it, but I've got that at home will remind you [that] you are in the wrong", and insisted on this deponent drinking Prince Charles's health, and said he was then about 20,000 strong, and also said, "Pray God send that he may be 40,000 before tomorrow"'.[26]

The Jacobites and their Enemies

When we wish to ferret out areas of active Jacobite support south of the Border we do not receive much help from the most obvious source, which is the detailed report of King Louis' agent James Butler. Outside London Butler's information was superficial, based principally on the pedigree and landed wealth of the supposed Jacobite gentry and peers, and on their party political stance. He did not understand that the word 'Jacobite' did not apply to all Tories, let alone the representatives of the wider 'country' interest. He set much store by the help of the Duke of Beaufort, who did not act in 1745 (p. 64), and on that of the Duke of Bedford, who in the event raised a regiment (not a very good one) in support of the government. He knew that certain areas had been corrupted – Cambridge by its notorious university, and Norfolk by the machinations of Walpole – but he was unaware of the weight which powerful Whiggish landowners carried in counties like Sussex, Derbyshire, Cheshire and Lancashire, all of which he assumed to be solidly in the Jacobite interest.

London and the South-East

In the case of Britain south of the Border, it seems logical to begin our investigations in London before making a wider *tour d'horizon*. In London James Butler found a welcome among significant elements in the City proper, which was ruled by twenty-six aldermen and the 236 members of the Common Council of the City – at least 186 of whom he counted as zealous Jacobites. He had also high hopes of the citizens of Westminster, whose Free Electors were famously impervious to the influence of the Whig-dominated Parliament that sat in their midst.

All the same, it was typical of Butler's narrow circle of interests that he did not mention in his report the use that might have been made of the itinerant Irishmen who converged towards harvest time on the villages of Hampstead, Highgate and Hackney to the north and east of London. The Bishop of London wrote to the Duke of Newcastle on 28 September 1745 that one of his clergymen had travelled from Cambridge and discovered that large parties of ragged Irishmen were on their way to London, where they might act with the numerous Catholics in support of a French invasion.[27] Suspicions were attached to their drinking dens in Charing Cross, Whitehall and Westminster, and most notoriously to 'the Hole in the Wall in Panton Street'.[28]

The county of Essex, immediately to the east of London, figured prominently in a French and Jacobite invasion scheme in 1743,[29] and in the more specific design of 1744, when two of the local Tory Members of Parliament, Sir Robert Abdy and Thomas Bramptson, were privy to the secret.

When the French returned to the notion of invading England next year their schemes were directed elsewhere. Meanwhile, Essex remained within easy reach of the authorities. They descended on the house of the widowed Lady Petre at Brentwood, and on 22 December two deputy lieutenants led a raid on her other house at Lower Cheam in Surrey, to the south of London, where they discovered nothing more incriminating than a pair of pistols,

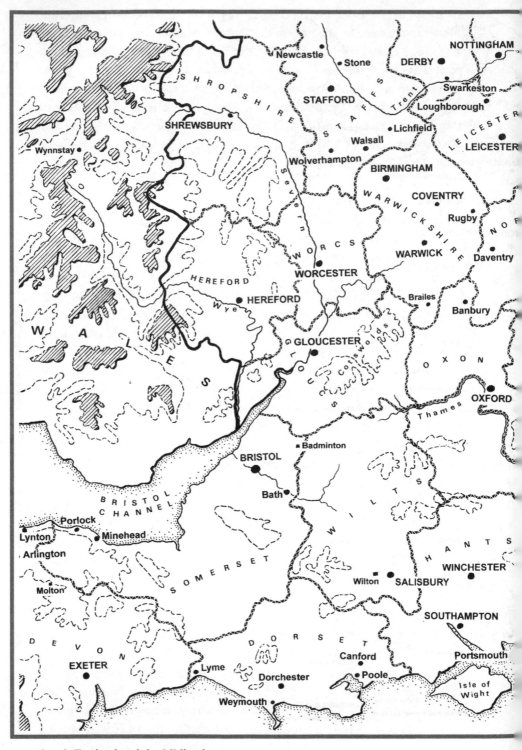

South England and the Midlands

Newark

L I N C S

Gt. North Rd.

Rutland

I R E

RE

Market Harborough

Stamford

Lyveden New Bield

ORTHAMPTON

NORTHAMPTON

H A N T S

H U N T S

King's Lynn

Magdalen Bridge

Stow Bridge

St Germans Bridge

Downham Market Bridge

C A M B S

Ouse

N O R F O L K

NORWICH

Yarmouth

Lowestoft

BEDFORD

Biggleswade

B E D S

Luton

H E R T S

Welwyn

Ware

St ALBANS

CHILTERNS

CAMBRIDGE

Euston

S U F F O L K

IPSWICH

Hollesley Bay

Colchester

E S S E X

Maldon

Chelmsford

Mountnossing

Brentwood

Romford

Barnet

Middlesex

London

C H I L T E R N S

READING

S U R R E Y

Cheam

Guildford

East Grinstead

Midhurst

S U S S E X

Nutley

Goodwood

Slindon

LEWES

Shoreham

Hastings

Newhaven

Chatham

Rochester

MAIDSTONE

K E N T

Canterbury

Ramsgate

ASHFORD

Goudhurst

Hawkhurst

Dover

Folkestone

The Downs

Rye

Calais

Boulogne

0   50

Km

MI

Over 200 m   Over 400 m

and a Romish priest who was hiding in the rafters.[30] That part of the world was dominated by the Speaker of the House of Commons, Lord Onslow, who formed the Surrey Association on 27 September.

The deeper parts of Kent and Sussex were near to London as the crow flies, but almost inaccessible in winter. The coastal smugglers lay on the far side of the Weald (and of the law), and were potentially valuable allies of the Prince and the French on account of their political sympathies and violent ways. At times the writ of the Duke of Richmond, as the leader of the Whigs in West Sussex, scarcely extended beyond his house at Goodwood. Midhurst, just to the north, was the home of the Catholic and Jacobite family of Browne, and it was reported that 'the Papists are so numerous there, that they cannot get men to enlist in the Association for carrying on in defence of His Majesty's Person and Government, the tradesmen being afraid they shall be turned out of their business; and from Slindon in that neighbourhood, that the few Protestants there dare not, openly, so much as wish well to His Majesty's arms against the rebels'.[31]

The Middle and Far South-West

Old loyalties to the Stuarts lived on in the south-western counties of England, which had been one of the strongholds of Royalism in the Civil War. At the time of the '45 the most prominent Jacobite of the region was the 3rd Duke of Beaufort who, from his house at Badminton, ruled extensive estates across the region, and whose influence extended beyond the Bristol Channel and into Wales. However, the history of the '15 showed how little capacity for independent action was enjoyed by the south-western Jacobites, and Beaufort now waited in vain for news of the French landing on which everything was supposed to depend.

This did not prevent a number of the Jacobites from acting on their own accord. A number of the gentry of Hampshire, Dorset and Devon were drawn into schemes to liberate the French and Spanish prisoners in Plymouth in concert with a French landing in the West Country. The Earl of Shaftesbury had to report to the Duke of Newcastle that 'there is a general want of arms amongst the people who I have reason firmly to believe would use them in defence of His Majesty and their country. Our ... coast is defenceless and unguarded, and in particular the three ports of Poole, Weymouth and Lyme. At the first, from its situation, there is little room to apprehend a descent, at either of the two latter should an attempt be made, though there are a few cannon, yet I question whether there are any persons who know how to use them; and as for small arms, I believe there are none at all'.[32]

The hopes of the Jacobites revived at the news of the progress of Prince Charles through England, and on 8 December 1745 the Collector of Customs at Minehead, on the Somerset shore of the Bristol Channel, learned that

> several Roman Catholics did lately assemble themselves in a body at a house called Molton, a country seat not usually inhabited about fourteen or fifteen miles hence, consisting in number of about twenty persons, including servants, exceeding well mounted and horses newly shod. They gave out that they intended to embark for Wales, doubtless in favour of the Pretender. I immediately dispatched messengers to watch Porlock and Lynmouth, and particular care shall be taken they shall not take water this way. They are persons of great distinction. One [is] Mr Chichester of Arlington in Devon; Mr Pastern, I think, lives eastwards; Mr Row of Lyland within six miles hence.[33]

By that time Prince Charles was well on his way back to the North.

The idea of landing in Cornwall had more than once appealed to would-be invaders of Britain as a useful diversion, for they could occupy the Tamar (the border river with Devon) as a ready-made defence line, and compel the London government to detach considerable forces to this remote part of the world. The far west figured in this way in the last of the duc de Richelieu's invasion schemes, in January 1746, but he had no support from his masters, and so the local allegiances were never tested. Most probably the prevailing sentiment was one of particularism. By 19 November 1745 Lord Edgcumbe had given up all hope of enlisting the local men into the militia: 'they all protest great readiness to defend their country, but they mean their county; besides as most of our young fellows prefer the sea service, that is one great reason of scarcity, but the greatest of all ... is that they imagine they may be sent out of the kingdom anywhere, notwithstanding all that is said and shown to them to the contrary, and that at six months' end they will be entitled to their discharge'.[34]

The Upper Thames

On 28 September 1745 the Duke of Newcastle wrote to the Duke of St Albans, as a deputy lieutenant of Berkshire, to tell him 'of an intelligence, which is just come to my hands, relating to the proceedings of the Papists and disaffected people at Reading, which you will see are represented to be very insolent. Your Grace will therefore be pleased to give direction for making the necessary enquiries into the state of the truth of the facts therein mentioned'.[35] The reports were confirmed.

Oxford, further up the Thames, was one of the capitals of sentimental Jacobitism of the High Church kind, and during their advance through England Prince Charles and his generals considered directing their march by way of that place, so that they could take the impressionable undergraduates into safekeeping and use them as more or less willing hostages for the co-operation of their parents. The Oxfordshire Tories indeed refused to sub-scribe to a Loyal Association, but the outright Jacobites in Oxford towns scarcely dared show their noses, and when four troops of Ligonier's Horse drew up in the High Street outside Queen's College on the night of 20 November it was 'impossible to express with what demonstrations of joy they were received, which was visible in every countenance; the innkeepers with great alacrity furnished them and their horses with all necessaries, for which they refused to be paid a farthing; and great numbers of the scholars of this University employed themselves in giving the soldiers liquor, in order to encourage them to fight bravely in defence of His Majesty King George, the Protestant Religion, and the Laws and Liberties of the Kingdom'.[36]

The Midlands

Earlier in November news had come to Oxford from 'one Richardson, a farmer of Brailes in the County of Warwick', to the effect that 'the Protestants there were in the greatest consternation by the threats and menaces of the Papists; for the Papists threatened to turn the Protestants out of the church before Christmas Day next; and further declared that in a great house in the parish, wherein one [George] Bishop lives (who he apprehends is a Romish priest) they constantly go to Mass. Upon enquiring of him (the said Richardson) what number of Papists he believed were in the parish? he replied about an hundred families'.[37]

Brailes, or more properly Upper and Lower Brailes, was a spread-out village about 10 miles to the west of Banbury. The Catholics lived under the protection of the Sheldons of Weston House, and more immediately that of the Bishop family, owners of the 'great house' just mentioned, where in 1726 Edward Sheldon opened a chapel (extant today) in an adjoining malt barn, and within a few stones' throw of the large parish church of St George. The power of the Catholics had already been shown in the 1730s when they turned it against the unpopular Welsh vicar Walter Evans, who described his parish as 'The Mouth of Hell'. He was gone by 1737.

The divide extended across the region. In the West Midlands the iron-masters and country gentlemen were eager to display their loyalty to the regime, and at the same time strong Jacobite traditions and a strong penchant for violence lived on among the coal miners and ironworkers of Birmingham, Wolverhampton, Walsall and Dudley. To the north-west Jacobitism was strong in Staffordshire generally, and particularly in Lichfield, which was not only the birthplace of Dr Samuel Johnson, but also, like the town of Stafford itself, one of the Duke of Cumberland's staging posts on his way north in December 1745. The reception accorded to the duke and his troops in Stafford was openly unfriendly.[38]

Chatsworth in Derbyshire was the seat of the Cavendish dukes of Devonshire, who for decades had counted among the grandest of the Whig grandees. The current duke was deep in the counsels of the government, and recruited an infamously bad regiment of Bluecoats in its cause. However, the army of Prince Charles was made very welcome when it tramped through the western part of that county on its way to Derby town, probably owing to the influence of the Jacobite Squire Meynell of Bradley Hall, and of the Tory Curzons of Kedleston, who were local rivals of the Cavendishes of Chatsworth.

Wales and Cheshire

At that period Wales still counted in ordinary parlance as part of England, and one thar provided possibly its finest troops.[39] These men had been a mainstay of the Royalist cause in the Civil War, and Wales in the mid 1740s was much under the sway of a couple of Jacobite Tory magnates, and of the numerous gentry of the same persuasion. The inclinations of the Duke of Beaufort carried great weight in the southern counties, where the membership of the Jacobite club of the Society of Sea Sergeants extended across Pembroke, Carmarthen, Cardigan and Glamorgan. One of the intended intermediaries between the army of Prince Charles and the Welsh Jacobites was a native of that region, the Monmouth gentleman and barrister David Morgan, who was described in a hostile pamphlet as 'a morose husband, a tyrannical master, a litigious neighbour, and an oppressive landlord, and a false friend; he had pride without the least condescension, avarice without a spark of generosity, ill-nature without a grain of benevolence'.[40]

The leading man in North Wales was Sir Watkin Williams Wynn of Wynnstay, Member of Parliament for Denbigh. Sir Watkin was the leading light in the Cycle of the White Rose, a Jacobite club dating from 1710, which had important followings in Denbigh, Montgomery and Flint, and the neighbouring parts of the English counties of Shropshire and Cheshire. He worked in close association with the Jacobite magnate James Barry, 4th Earl of Barrymore, who had his seat in south Cheshire at Marbury Hall. Prince Charles hoped that North Wales and adjacent England would rise at their bidding, just as South Wales would follow the initiative of the Duke of Beaufort.

Although Lord Herbert, 'who is beloved as a father by his tenants in Shropshire',[41] was reported to have raised 5,000 of his people for the government, the loyalty of the county town of Shrewsbury was decidedly suspect and there were concerns for the northern border region as a whole. By the middle of November 1745 the Duke of Newcastle had information that as soon as Prince Charles's army entered Lancashire, large numbers of the Flintshire Jacobites were going to seize Chester and march across Cheshire to join the Jacobite forces. Newcastle sent orders for the troops already destined for Chester to hasten their progress and for the rector of Hawarden in Flintshire to be placed under arrest.[42]

As things turned out the Duke of Beaufort was completely out of touch, and David Morgan was arrested on his way through Staffordshire before he could reach Wales. In Cheshire the Tory Sir Robert Grosvernor (Eaton Hall) was about to go over to the Whigs and Barrymore was beset by local enemies, including his own son (Lord Buttevant), who intercepted a vital letter which Prince Charles had intended for his father.

Why Sir Watkin Williams Wynn failed to respond is still a mystery. His message from Prince Charles too was intercepted, though it is quite possible that some of the Welsh gentry actually rode out but were unable to make contact with the Jacobite army before it started back north. A report from a Jacobite agent offers a possible explanation, for it claims that Sir Watkins was being detained in London, 'and he does not dare to leave, out of fear of being arrested. He has already been questioned two or three times, but the dukes of Bedford and Richmond have given personal guarantees for his good conduct'.[43] His wife now made herself busy burning papers which, she said, could have led to half of Wales being hanged.

Barrymore's houses at Marbury and Rock Savage lay in southern Cheshire. To the east the county extended into the Pennine foothills. Presbyterianism had been strong in the 'panhandle' into Yorkshire in the far north-east since the time of Elizabeth I, and the most influential gentry supported Parliament in the Civil War. Elsewhere the sub-Pennine region had its nests of Catholics and Jacobites, and one of the Duke of Newcastle's informants wrote to him on 5 October 1745 that

> having some business very lately at the Duke of Norfolk's at Worksop Manor in Nottinghamshire, I afterwards went into Lancashire and Cheshire [and] in my way thither I put up at an inn about four miles from Stockport. As soon

as I told the innkeeper that I came from His Grace the Duke of Norfolk, and that my business was of great secrecy, he presently imagined it was concerning the rebellion. I did not undeceive him. I was soon visited by several persons who appeared like gentlemen, and heard abundance of their treasonable discourse, for they took me for one of themselves. The next morning the innkeeper told me he was sure I was a priest, and that the gentlemen I saw were all ready to join the rebels if they marched that way. I also learned from him that this house was built by subscription of the dis-affected thereabouts, and that he had formerly lived as servant to Legh of Lyme. There are a great many disaffected people in that neighbourhood.[44]

The inn must have been situated near Higher Poynton, and the 'Legh' in question was Sir Peter Legh XII (1669–1744) of Lyme Hall nearby, whose family had held their estate in the Pennine foothills since the Middle Ages. The Leghs had supported Parliament in the Civil War, but they formed a strong attachment to the Stuarts in the reign of Charles II, when the Duke of York (the future James II) had hunted in their park. Sir Peter was the leading light and probably also the founder of the Cheshire Club, an association of Jacobite landowners who met in the Stag Parlour of Lyme from the 1690s. There was much Stuart symbolism in the furnishings of the Parlour, and in 1725 Sir Peter commissioned Giacomo Leoni, a favourite architect of the Tory aristocracy, to re-face the Hall. Unfortunately for the purposes of Prince Charles this Sir Peter died in 1744, and in the following year his nephew and successor Sir Peter Legh XIII reconvened the Cheshire Club and persuaded his friends not to risk their lives and fortunes with the armed Jacobite cause (p. 275).

Manchester and Lancashire

Manchester was located to the north of the upper Mersey in Lancashire. It was one of the fastest rising of the manufacturing and trading towns, but its politics had scarcely evolved since the Civil War, and were still dominated by a feud between the Presbyterians and the supporters of the House of Stuart. The Jacobites looked for their lead to the Collegiate Church (the future Manchester Cathedral), where Dr John Clayton functioned as the high priest of the peculiarly intense Mancunian form of High Anglicanism, and had strong links with Dr Thomas Deacon, the Non-Juring Bishop of Manchester.

The rallying cry of the Jacobites was 'Down with the Rump!' (a reference to a short-lived puppet Parliament under Cromwell). Their opponents repaid the sentiments in kind, and when they heard that most of the Jacobite Manchester Regiment had been captured at Carlisle, they wrote to the Duke of Newcastle to declare that it was 'the earnest request of all the King's friends in this town, that every individual of these abandoned wretches may suffer in or near Manchester, for it was the Manchester rebels who were the most outrageous against the king's friends, coming into their houses and shops with drawn swords and cocked pistols, demanding their money or they would blow out their brains and burn their houses. From some persons they took twenty, from some forty, and from some one hundred pounds'.[45]

The most considerable of the Manchester Jacobites in military rank was Francis Townley of Townley Hall, Colonel of the Manchester Regiment. By his own account he was born in about 1708 to a Catholic family, and served as a child page to the Dowager Queen of Spain. An unsympathetic biographer takes up the story, and claims that as a growing lad Townley, being of 'a gay and volatile disposition', deemed 'it would be labour lost to pester his brains with rules and precepts how to understand old authors that he should not be a farthing better for'.[46] He inherited his father's fortune sooner than was good for him, and left Lancashire in 1728 to enter the French military service, being commissioned into the Regiment of Limousin from which he returned not long before the rising. As an officer of Prince Charles he was 'exceeding active in raising and disciplining the regiment ... in all their marches from town to town he seemed fond of appearing at the head of it; and when the Pretender was proclaimed, he showed himself in all his military accoutrements and giving all the lustre in his power to the mock pageantry'.[47]

In Lancashire 200 Jacobites assembled at Ormskirk on the night of 25 November 1745, and made bold to beat up for recruits and proclaim King James III before they were attacked and dispersed by the Protestant townsmen. Twenty of the rebels were made prisoner. The Earl of Derby, as Lord Lieutenant, had written to the Duke of Newcastle on 22 October 1745 that the Lancashire Protestants were well disposed, and that the loyal subscription would amount to £13,000, but 'as to officers, if we can get as many as seven companies required 'tis as many as I expect; this Your Grace may probably wonder at, but such is the unhappy condition of this country, that many of our best estates are in Popish hands, and at this time we have few young gentlemen in the Protestant families; for my own part I am so unfortunately situated, that I know but one within eight miles of me [at Knowsley], that would take the command of a company'.[48]

However, the potential for Jacobite support among the local Catholics was not realized, and the number of Lancashire Jacobites who were willing to put themselves to any real risk did not exceed 400, including the Manchester Regiment and the Ormskirk rebels. Partly it was the result of the chastening memory of what had happened in 1715, when the Non-Jurors left the 'coming out' to the Catholics; and partly it came from the considered decision of the Jacobite leadership to have nothing to do with the Catholic clergy of Lancashire, as Sir Thomas Sheridan informed John William O'Sullivan, much to the latter's surprise.[49] In the geographical sense the Jacobites of Lancashire were boxed in – by the Pennines to the east, by the militant Protestants of Rossendale just to the north of Manchester, by the Mersey marshes to the south, by the prospering and very Whiggish port of Liverpool to the south-west, and to the north by the counties of Cumberland and Westmorland, which for two generations had been almost entirely under the subjugation of the earls of Lonsdale.

Yorkshire

Yorkshire was the largest county in England, and the Archdiocese of York was larger still, embracing all of Yorkshire (except the area of Richmond), together with Nottinghamshire and part of northern Lancashire. The prelate, Archbishop Thomas Herring, had been timorously conscientious as an ecclesiastical administrator, but he now emerged as a powerhouse of energy on behalf of the government, very much in the mould of those senior lawyers who were to hold the Hanoverian cause together in Scotland. Yorkshire was as polarized in its way as Lancashire. A meeting of the gentry of the county at York on 24 September 1745 gave the lead to all those Loyal Associations that were to spring up elsewhere in England. The city Catholics nevertheless supported a Mass House almost in the shadow of the cathedral, and probably with the connivance of the independently minded Corporation and the assertive local Tories. Herring then put on 'a lay military habit, in order to spirit forward the execution of what His Grace has so bravely and pathetically recommended in his speech to the Association there'.[50]

Outside the city the agents and supporters of the government had a freer hand. They were prompted by the survival of pockets of Catholicism among the isolated communities towards Lancashire (and Craven in particular), in the eastern part of the Vale of York, and in the Cleveland Hills and the North York Moors. These might provide support for the Highlanders, who, it was feared, might cut eastwards across the Pennines during their invasion of England. As late as 25 December 1745 Chancellor

Northern England

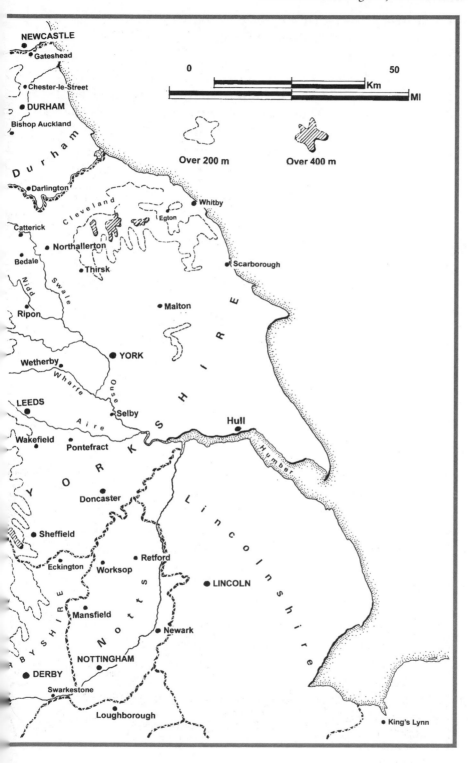

Over 200 m Over 400 m

Hardwicke in London observed that it would be inadvisable for the regular army to draw on recruits from Yorkshire – 'that great county, where there are many Papists, and no militia'.[51]

Among the Catholic communities was that of Egton in the North York Moors, a village of honey-coloured stone that crowned a steep valley to the descent of the Yorkshire Esk. The people lit a bonfire when news reached them of the Jacobite victory at Prestonpans, which provoked the loyal ships' carpenters of nearby Whitby into setting out with the tools of the trade to demolish the village and massacre its inhabitants. The shipwrights were dissuaded from their purpose, though Archbishop Herring connived in the demolition of Catholic chapels in places like Stokesley.

The Jacobites never came through Yorkshire, but the celebrated Dr John Burton contrived to make contact with them on their way south, and Andrew Blood or Blyde, 'of a reputable family in Yorkshire', gained a commission with Prince Charles as a captain. 'During his imprisonment in Newgate he behaved with great decency, kept very much in his room, and never mixed with the noisy mirth and riotous living of his fellow-prisoners.'[52]

The prisoners still being held on suspicion of treason in York Castle on 9 March 1746 included John Martin and several other Catholic priests, and a number of laymen who had uttered treasonable words.[53] The most famous of the Yorkshire suspects, Dr John Burton, was hauled off to the Tower of London for prolonged and not very productive interrogation.

The Far North-East

The militant Protestants were altogether in the ascendant in the County Palatine of Durham. The Durham Association Regiment was possibly the best of those generally poor units, and patrolled the roads to search or detain Catholics, Non-Jurors and other suspects. On 15 October 1746 a number of those people were herded together at Durham, and required, apparently with mixed success, to take the oaths of Allegiance and Supremacy. The business of wrecking Catholic Mass Houses (a speciality of north-eastern England) went ahead unchecked. A Catholic chapel and two suspicious houses were badly damaged in Gateshead, while a couple who were about to be married in the chapel at Sunderland were barely able to escape with their lives when 200 mariners and townspeople arrived on the spot, 'upon which the sailors immediately pulled down the altar and crucifix, together with all the seats, the priest's robes, all their books, the furniture, and every individual thing in the room, and burned them on a fire in the street made for the purpose, and also a large library of books and papers belonging to the priest'.[54]

In such a context it was very unwise of a Durham landowner, George Turnbull of Chamboise in the parish of Bedlington, to say in the hearing of his tale-bearing steward 'that if the Highlanders came to Morpeth, that the said George Turnbull would go and meet them, for that he would see several friends and acquaintances among them'. The steward was promised a big increase in pay, and he suspected that his master's good mood was occasioned by the progress of the rebels.[55]

The attempts of Prince Charles to establish contacts with leading English Jacobites almost certainly extend beyond the couple that have been logged by the historians. Another shortcoming of the historiography is that it writes off the Jacobitism of Northumberland as still reeling under the impact of its failure in 1715, and by 1745 irrelevant almost to the point of non-existence.

By the testimony of James Wilson, a Jacobite clerk, one of the concerns of Prince Charles and his circle at Holyrood was to form links with the Northumberland Jacobites. Andrew Lumisden, personal secretary to the Jacobite Secretary of State, John Murray of Broughton, had already been on missions to Northumberland, the northernmost of the English counties; several times before the rising, and now Murray of Broughton initiated further correspondence with identified supporters. Wilson heard a number of letters being read out in the presence of the Prince, all signed by the veteran Jacobite 'Bowrie' Charlton of Redesmouth on behalf of himself and his friends, who promised all possible aid if Prince Charles came to the border.[56]

The names that came to light in the course of the Hanoverian investigations were those of the conservative Northumbrian gentry – amongst them Thomas Barton, Thomas Errington the Chief of Beaufort, Sir John Swinburne of Capheaton, and Ralph Widdrington of the widespread family of the same name. The elusive Robert Windegate, steward to Mr Errington, acted as liaison inside the group in Northumberland. The other support of the Jacobites was located in the south-east corner of the county and at the opposite end of the social scale, among the Tyne keelmen (lightermen) of Newcastle, 'a mutinous race, for which reason the town is always garrisoned'.[57] They were Scottish Presbyterians, but this did not, as generally supposed, prevent many of their number from being partisans of the Prince.

The Northumberland Jacobites suffered reverses that were altogether beyond their control. One was the decision of Prince Charles, under pressure from Lord George Murray, to invade England along the western side of the Pennines instead of the eastern, a path that would have taken him through Northumberland. Here, according to the interrogation of his captured agent, John Hickson, he would have seized Tynemouth Castle along with its cannon and ammunition. The pieces would have been planted on the hill which commanded Newcastle from the north-east, and probably have forced the town to surrender without a shot.

A further blow occurred when the Royal Navy succeeded in capturing the grandest of the Northumbrian Jacobite nobles, Charles Radcliffe, 5th Earl of Derwentwater, when he was on his way from France to Scotland. He was put on trial and ultimately executed on 11 December 1746.

The Northumberland Jacobites gathered their wits, and in the middle of March 1746 we find them far advanced in a scheme to seize Newcastle, in concert with 1,500-odd keelmen, and make off with money and cannon to take advantage of a supposedly favourable turn of events in Scotland, where it was reported (quite erroneously) that the Hessian contingent had been cut off and that 5,000 Highlanders were in Glasgow.

The design, far-fetched though it might appear, was taken more seriously by the government than any of the plots that had so far been detected in England. The particulars were extracted from the interrogation of a Jacobite messenger, Daniel MacKenzie, and on 17 April (the day after Culloden) the Duke of Newcastle, Mr Henry Pelham and all the other principal officers of government met in a special session in which they determined to seize the suspects.[58]

On the night of 18/19 April a party of leaderless and blundering keelmen made what was probably an attempt to put their part of the scheme into effect when they tried to bluff their way past the guards at the Sandgate. They were repulsed, and they had to go their way, muttering impotently about revenge.[59]

Ireland

Nineteenth-century trends in Scottish and Irish nationalism promoted the destructive work which had begun in 1493, when the suppression of the Lordship of the Isles and the subsequent long-drawn-out decline of the empire of the MacDonalds served to divide British Gaeldom into its two branches. However, the process was still far from complete in the 1740s. West Highland Catholicism was enjoying the new lease of life which it had been given by the Irish missionaries, and old men in the halls of the clan chiefs even now looked to Ireland for the authentic traditions of harping.

The Gaelic bards of Ireland ceded nothing to their Scottish counterparts in their enthusiasm for the coming of Prince Charles, and their sensitivity to the mourning of nature after he failed, when the salmon deserted the waterfall, the birds fell silent, the branches of the oaks contorted, and the mist shrouded the mountains. The Catholics of Connaught had worn plaid after Prestonpans, and the Irish Gaels had looked to Charles as the fair-haired Prince who would end the tyranny of the black-haired fanatics, the 'swarthy Johns' (the English), and who would more specifically restore the ancient rights to land, arms and religious freedom. Folk treasured the rumours that Prince Charles had been seen in Cork, Donegal, and in Galway, where in September 1745 the sighting of the ships of the East India Company fleet was 'saluted with bonfires all along the coast, the people imagining them to be their friends, the French or Spaniards'.[60]

There remained, however, significant differences between Irish and Scottish Jacobitism, and the poetry of the Irish bards carried indications of both the weaknesses and strengths of the Irish variety, showing, as it did, an awareness of the detail and significance of events beyond their homeland. In such a way the remembrance of the Battle of Fontenoy (11 May 1745) was implanted in the Irish national tradition, and the name of the Austrian field marshal Daun was hymned in the Seven Years War (1756–63). Irish Jacobitism, in any form which might have promoted the overthrow of the Hanoverian regime, was represented most formidably in military and commercial institutions abroad, but it was very feeble in its homeland.

The Catholic Irish nobility and gentry had been leaving for the Catholic courts and armies of continental Europe for centuries, but only in the 1740s did the London government take measures to stem the flow of recruits to the Irish Brigade in the French service, the contingents of which provided the main source of disciplined manpower to the Prince in the later stages of the rising. These 'brave hounds' were drawn from the five regiments of Irish infantry (Bulkeley, Clare, Dillon, Roth and Berwick), and from the FitzJames' Regiment of heavy horse. The Irish Brigade was deployed as an instrument of French policy, but even the French war ministry could not be sure of the Brigade's total dedication to French, as distinct from Stuart, interests, and the Brigade's red coats and the Irish and English motifs of its insignia gave it the appearance of King James' army in exile, and presented a potent symbol of the Stuart claim to Britain as a whole.

The refugee Irish military men and their families were accompanied by Irish clergy, doctors, men of learning and merchants, who formed a recognizable society in corners as diverse as Prague in Bohemia, or the western ports of France, where the Franco-Irish entrepreneurs Antoine Walsh, Walter Ruttlidge and Dominique O'Heguerty made it possible for Prince Charles to gather his resources and undertake his voyage to Scotland. Probably they were hoping that a restored Stuart monarchy would put them and Ireland in an advantageous commercial position and promote an Atlantic trading empire in concert, rather than competition, with France and Spain. More fundamentally, 'Jacobitism provided the Irish diaspora with useful practical, cultural and psychological baggage in foreign countries. It was a badge of loyalty, which would have been easily carried and provided a sheet anchor in the uncertainty and dislocation of exile'.[61]

The resources of Irish Jacobitism abroad did not translate into a local threat to Hanoverian rule in Ireland. Protestant Jacobitism, of the kind which was significant in Scotland and England, had shrunk to a handful of Church of Ireland bishops and landed magnates, the most important of the latter being James, 4th Earl of Barrymore, who in 1745 was under virtual house arrest in London, removed alike from his estates in Ireland and Wales.

Generations of confiscations had reduced the land in Catholic Irish ownership to one-seventh of the whole, while the Penal Laws continued to deny literate and ambitious Catholics any possibility of military or professional employment in their homeland. The mass of the Catholic population was deprived of its natural leadership, and weakened still further by the poor harvests from 1739 to 1741 which killed one-fifth of the Catholic population as a whole and even more in Munster, which was the heartland of Irish Jacobitism. Little is known about the attempts of Prince Charles to summon up support in Ireland. The government spy Dudley Bradstreet, whose word is generally reliable, told the Duke of Newcastle in December 1745 that the Jacobites in Scotland intended to send twenty or thirty agents, mostly Catholic, to Connaught, and that the most active person in the scheme was a certain Gordon, a British military military man who had been in garrison in Ireland.[62]

The weakness of Irish Jacobitism was not at once apparent when news came of the progress of the rising in Scotland. The Ulster Protestants were typically belligerent in mood, at least in their strongholds, but there were concerns in the Glens of Antrim nearby, and a distinct sense of vulnerability in the scattered Protestant communities in Cork, south Munster and Connaught. Lord Chesterfield (Lord Lieutenant in Ireland from January 1745 to August 1746) had amongst other things the responsibility for security, and he complained to the Duke of Newcastle that the means at his immediate disposal were limited, for the fortifications were in disrepair, the militia in many of the counties in a state of neglect, and the regular troops amounted to just 9,325 men (six regiments of horse and six of foot).[63]

These precious regulars were depleted when reinforcements were shipped

to England in the emergency after the battle of Prestonpans, but Chesterfield realized that he had a valuable resource in the Ulster Protestants, among
whom he recruited four regiments of volunteers on his own initiative. He
redeployed his remaining regulars in such a way that he could concentrate
them within forty-eight hours in either County Cork or County Galway,
which were overwhelmingly Catholic, and where a French invasion was most
to be feared. Chesterfield placed a wholesale ban on the export of provisions
lest they should go to the Scottish Jacobites, and he was soon able to inform
the Duke of Newcastle that 'the Papists here are not only quiet, but even
their priests preach quiet to 'em. The most considerable of 'em have been
with me to assure me of their firm resolution not to disturb the government,
and to thank me for not having disturbed them as usual at this time. I told 'em
fairly that the lenity of the government should continue as long as their good
behaviour deserved it, but that if they gave the least disturbance, they should
be treated with a rigour they had never yet experienced'.[64]

Chesterfield was in fact striking an effective balance, for he kept potential rebellion in check by the threat of violence, while he refused to be panicked
into untimely action by the Protestants. Upon a Church of Ireland bishop
running into his chamber to tell him that the Jacobites were about to rise,
he consulted his watch, and remarked: 'I fancy they are, my lord, for it is
nine o'clock'.[65]

In late October 1745 Chesterfield's concern shifted to the danger of a
Scots Jacobite invasion from the mainland of Britain. On the 27th he ordered
15,000 militia to Country Down to guard against a rumoured Highland
descent, and there were renewed alarms after the Jacobite army crossed into
England on 8 November, and again early in December when Chesterfield
feared that the Jacobites were heading into Wales and might undertake an
invasion from there.

After Prince Charles retreated from Derby, Lord Chesterfield made bold
to arrest a number of leading Irish Jacobites, and by March 1746 it was
possible to think of the Ulstermen as 'a hardy race of zealous Protestants',
who might be used to extirpate the Camerons and MacDonalds from the
face of the earth.[66] So much for solidarity between the Ulster Protestants
and the Scots.

CHAPTER 3

The Divided Lands:
Scotland

IT IS POSSIBLE TO FIX ON A NUMBER of general characteristics that define the Scottish Jacobites. The Stuarts were a Scottish dynasty, and one which many Scots came to see as incorporating the notion of Scottish national independence, even if Prince Charles never committed himself outright on the subject. If the Non-Juring Anglicans throughout Britain were naturally predisposed towards Jacobitism, the identification in Scotland was nearly absolute, for there the Presbyterian model of church government had ousted the Episcopal as the state church, which was not the case in England. The relevant Act of Parliament had been passed in 1690, and it stated that 'prelacy, and the superiority of any office in the Church above presbyteries, hath been a great and insupportable grievance and trouble to this nation, and contrary to the inclination of the generality of the people ever since the Reformation'.[1] Only a minority of the Episcopal clergy availed themselves of the opportunity held out to them from 1712, which was to renounce the Stuarts and so be admitted as 'qualified' ministers.

The Non-Juring Church in Scotland was at least as vital as the Presby-

A caricature of MacDonnell of Glengarry

terian, and its services were certainly more entertaining. Edmund Burt often admired 'the zeal of a pretty well-dressed Jacobite, when I have seen her go down one of the narrow, steep "wyndes" in Edinburgh, through an accumulation of the worst kind of filth, and whip up a blind staircase almost as foul, yet with an air as dégagé, as if she were going to meet a favourite lover in some poetic bower; and indeed, the difference between the generality of those people and the Presbyterians, especially the women, is visible when they come from their respective instructors, for the former appear with cheerful countenances, and the other look as if they have been convicted and sentenced by their gloomy preachers'.[2]

Presbyterianism smacked of committee or 'democratical' rule, and for the conservative gentry and professional men it was further tainted with the mob excesses of the Scottish Reformation, and thus with a threat to the social order. Outside Edinburgh, the strongholds of the Episcopalians of the Non-Juring variety extended along the coastlands north of the Tay.[3]

Scottish Non-Jurism, therefore, was firmly identified with Jacobitism. It did not necessarily work the other way around, however, that Presbyterian ministers invariably supported the government. Presbyterian clansmen and Lowlanders liked to have Presbyterian preachers with them. One of that kind was Minister James Robe of Kilsyth, who set out to qualify himself to join the Jacobite army by buying sword and pistols, and had his horse trained against gunfire by an old soldier. When at last Robe mounted and fired a pistol, the horse bolted and threw him from the saddle. He complained to the veteran trooper, who had to point out that he had shot the beast through the ear. Most Presbyterians, however, could be counted as solid friends of the government, and in March 1746 the Synod of Aberdeen went so far as to set up a spy network among its ministers.[4]

Hanoverian propaganda scarcely needed to encourage English public opinion to new pitches of hysteria concerning the hordes of Catholic Highlanders who supposedly made up the Jacobite army that broke across the border in November 1745. A sense of perspective is restored when we consider that the Protestant Jacobite Episcopalians north of the Tay numbered at least 200,000, and the Catholics less than one-tenth of that number at probably well under 20,000. The list of areas with Catholic associations is very long, but it consisted either of small and isolated communities in the east or of large but thinly populated tracts of ground in the west. The division corresponds roughly with the two types of Scottish Catholicism, which were totally out of contact until 1738 and then found themselves at odds.

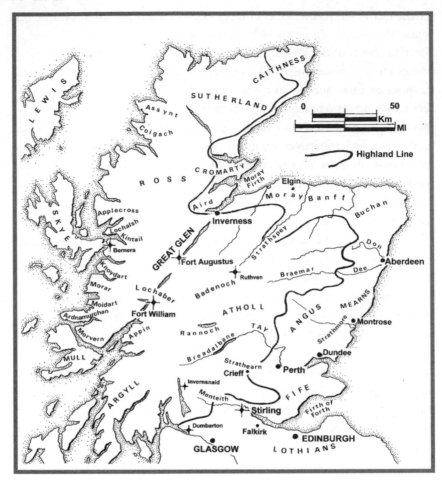

Scotland, principal features

    Along the North Sea coastlands and the eastern Highlands the life of
the Catholics resembled that of their counterparts in England, being
sheltered by Catholic or at least tolerant landowners. Typical Catholic
enclaves were those of Strathfarrar, the Aird, the Enzie of Banff, Braemar,
Glenlivet and Strathdon. The Catholic priests were typically lodged in
noble piles such as Drummond Castle, and sometimes furnished with house
rules as to how they should behave. Relations between the eastern Catholics
and their Episcopalian neighbours were generally good, and one of
Cumberland's officers complained that the only people the army could rely
on were the Presbyterians, for the Episcopalians were all Jacobites. 'Their
ceremonies too, are very near those of the Papists: for in this county in
particular, and in the next county, they have confession; some of them pray

for the dead, and to the Virgin Mary, and mix water with the sacramental wine.'[5]

The priests of the Western Highlands had much more the character of missionaries, who ministered to communities which had survived intact but leaderless, or had sunk into a state of spiritual vacuum. The Presbyterian Kirk was in no state to exploit the opportunity, since the training of its ministers was long and arduous and its representatives were therefore spread thinly. They had, moreover, the task of disciplining entire communities. For the same reasons the Presbyterians were going to lose much ground in the North American colonies to the Baptists and Methodists. The Franciscans from Ireland made their first appearance in the 1620s, and fitted very well indeed with the traditions of the wandering holy men of the West.

MacDonald of Clanranald counted as the foremost of the avowed Catholic chiefs, and the people of his clan, together with those of the Mac-Donnells of Glengarry and the Catholics among the Keppoch MacDonnells, were reckoned to be the leading Catholic Highlanders. The Romish element in the Scots Jacobite forces was a distinct political embarrassment, and, when it was a question of bringing the Jacobite army into England, Lord George Murray and other advisers told Prince Charles that it would be unwise to let the English see Catholics in prominent positions of command. That was why the Duke of Perth had to relinquish his rank as lieutenant general, and Prince Charles had to withdraw the commission he had given to the experienced Irish soldier Sir Francis Geoghegan to raise a regiment in England.

None of this spared the Catholic priests from being the object of particular attention on the part of the Hanoverian general Bland when he advanced through the hinterland of Aberdeen in March 1746. He reported on the 19th that he had arrested three priests in Strathbogie as a matter of routine. He wrote from the same place on the 22nd that he had 'taken up one William Reed, a Popish priest, and who owns himself as such, lurking about the country; though I have nothing to say against him, but that he is one, and consequently a spy upon all our motions'.[6]

It is impossible to leave the subject of Scottish Jacobitism in general without touching on the role of women, which has no counterpart among the English Jacobites. These keepers of the flame showed themselves in many different manifestations, though even the Hanoverian volunteer James Ray had to admit that 'many of the prettiest ladies in Scotland are Jacobites, and members of Non-Juring meeting houses'.[7] Young Whiggish (as well as Jacobite) females were overtaken by fits of excited vapours in the presence of the Prince, but it should be noted that at this stage Charles preferred to keep himself at a distance from social functions, and that almost all of the Jacobite women of the '45 were committed to his cause before he reached Scotland, and put themselves to considerable trouble for his sake.

The dedication of the gentlewomen was shared at the opposite end of the social order by women like the Jacobite 'Florence Nightingale' Anne McKay of Skye, who withstood torture rather than betray her acquaintances, and Mary MacKenzie of Lochaber, who was a follower of Cromartie's Regiment, and is described as a 'lusty, healthy lass, knits and spins'.[8] She was deported.

Female influence, along with Non-Juring Episcopalianism, must therefore be counted as one of the most powerful cohesive forces in Scottish Jacobitism. It was not besotted romanticism, or the work of an excluded group that was clamouring for recognition, but rather an expression of the unofficial standing of women in Scottish society. Some of them never adopted their husbands' names, and they ran many an estate, farm or business when their husbands were absent.

Local Scottish Life and Allegiance

The Lowlands

The representation of the Highlanders in the Jacobite rank and file was disproportionately high, at between 43 and 46 per cent, which was some 15 per cent greater than the Highlander, element in the population of Scotland as a whole. However, the Lowland troops were still in the absolute majority at between 54 and 57 per cent, with the largest single groups coming from the eastern coastlands of Aberdeen, Banff and Moray. The Highland chiefs carried great political weight in the Jacobite counsels, and on the day of battle the Highland gentlemen in the front rank were literally the cutting edge of the Jacobite cause. Yet Prince Charles's only Highland general was Robertson of Struan, and he lived on the doorstep of the Lowlands. The Lowlanders and their leaders therefore made up the bedrock of the 'Highland army', and their circumstances demand some attention.

The variety of the economy and the styles of life in the Lowlands resembled those of England rather than the Highlands, even if manufacturing was poorly developed.[9] Lowland agriculture was predominantly arable, and its chief product was oatmeal, which fed the nearby towns and was sold to the Highlanders in return for cash, for black cattle on the hoof, or for the cattle products of hides, butter, cheese and tallow. Landowners had more freedom than did their counterparts in England to enclose the common land, which gave them an incentive to improve their estates by crop rotation and other agricultural practices. New towns and villages were being established, and there was large-scale planting of commercial forests. On 8 February 1746 the lairds of Kinnoul and Dupplin wrote in some alarm to the secretary of the Duke of Cumberland to assure him that the farmers and tenants of their estate had been unswervingly loyal to the government. They offered Dupplin House for his accommodation, and they asked him in particular 'to take care of the trees and plantations at Dupplin, which are very extensive, young and valuable'.[10]

The majority of at least the better-off Lowland country people lived in half-timbered houses, or ones of 'cruck' construction (formed around infilled pairs of naturally curved timbers which met overhead like Gothic arches). Virtually none survives today, for they have succumbed to decay or the tendency for the population to be resettled in estate villages. Hamilton Palace, Dalkeith and Kirkliston were grand country seats as they would have been recognized in England, but the classic residence of the old-fashioned landowners was still the tall, gabled and turreted tower house of stone on the pattern first set at Threave Castle.

With its 50,000 inhabitants, Edinburgh was still the most considerable town in Britain next to London. The population of its fast-growing and more commercially minded rival Glasgow had already reached 25,000, for no town in Scotland had benefited more from the Union, which brought the opening up of the tobacco trade with the North American colonies. Less dramatic rises were observed in Aberdeen, Dundee, Dumfries, Perth, Stirling and Edinburgh itself. In Scotland generally, manufacturing was being held back by the import of cheap English goods, though the output of linen was increasing fast, and the little places on the droving routes to the South were busier than ever before, because the English had developed a taste for the black Highland cattle.

Something of these movements could be read from the architecture. Glasgow already wore the aspect of a Scottish 'Liverpool', with its regularly laid-out streets of modern houses and public buildings. The construction of Edinburgh's New Town had to wait until later in the century, and meanwhile the original town, with its piled-up tenements and intervening courts and alleys, crowded down the volcanic ridge from the Castle esplanade to Canongate.

The way of living of the gentlemen of the Lowlands and the Highland fringes did not differ radically from that of the style of the 'country' interest in England. The Scottish gentry and professional classes were generally well educated. Most of the burghs had their own grammar schools, and some of the boys went further afield, as witness Lord Elcho, who had attended Winchester in England and found that the pupils were divided into the factions of the 'Jacobites' and the 'Georgites'. Concerning the Scottish universities, Dr Johnson observed that their students went there as boys and left before they became adults. 'Men bred in the universities of Scotland cannot be expected to be often decorated with the splendour of ornamental knowledge, but they obtain a mediocrity of knowledge, between learning and ignorance, not inadequate for the purposes of common life.'[11] That was unfair, for England had only two universities (Oxford and Cambridge), while Scotland could already show five (St Andrews, Glasgow, Edinburgh and the two at Aberdeen). These considerations are important, for they indicate that the officer corps of the Lowland regiments and the higher leadership of the Jacobite army as a whole was at least as literate and well informed as that of the regular European armies of the time.

In terms of political allegiance, Glasgow was heavily committed to the Hanoverians, and the nearby shires of Renfrew, Lanark and Dumfries proved to be singularly barren recruiting ground for the Jacobites. While the country people of East Lothian were on the whole hostile to the government, to judge by the experiences of Cope's army in the campaign of Prestonpans, in Edinburgh they were at the least in a strong minority, and Musselburgh was deemed a nest of Jacobites.

Away from the Central Lowlands, Prince Charles sought to cultivate the gentry of the Southern Uplands. However, he was able to establish effective contact only with individuals like Sir David Murray of Stanhope and his cousin John Murray of Broughton, while little towns like Jedburgh were alarmed at the thought of the Highlanders arriving among them. If we are to believe Lady Jane Nimmo, the Whigs of Berwickshire were deterred from taking up arms on the other side because they distrusted their self-appointed military leader, the Earl of Home. 'Some of his relations speak treason with open mouth, particularly Mr James Purves, who has been all this while spreading treasonable papers about this country, and is now arrived here himself with a white cockade in his hat ... The Chevalier himself or his Jesuits could not have hit on a more successful method to alienate the affection of His Majesty's subjects in this shire than ... to propose Lord Home to them.'[12]

All of this indicates how far the warlike traditions of the lands of the Armstrongs, Douglases, Kerrs and Scotts had abated since James I of England

and VI of Scotland had established the common monarchy, and society in the Borders had become 'luxurious and effeminate'.[13]

Although it figures little in the general perception of the rising, the strongest and most consistent support that Prince Charles enjoyed in Britain came from the north-eastern Scottish shires of Angus, the Mearns and Aberdeen. Although they qualified as lowlanders in the geographic sense, their culture and outlook had little in common with that of the Lowlanders of the Midland Valley, from whom they were isolated by the bridgeless Tay and the snow-streaked mountains. Their celebrated cattle grazed on flat pastures, and the grain prospered on Strathmore, a broad sweep of well-drained arable land formed from the Old Red Sandstone that extended up the eastern side of Scotland. The higher ground to the west was penetrated by the valleys of the Dee, Don, Deveron and Spey, which were being cultivated and settled up to an altitude of 1,000 feet, while new fishing villages were springing up along the northern coast into Banff and Moray. The established trade was orientated as much to northern Europe as to the Lowlands proper or England. New Aberdeen on the Dee supplied the vessels of the Dutch fleet and the VOP (Dutch East India Company) with cured pork, while Montrose shipped out the grain of the hinterland, and imported Swedish iron from Gothenburg. Political allegiances were divided, as in the rest of Britain, but opinions in this region were coloured most strongly by Non-Juring Episcopalianism, Jacobitism and a habituation to smuggling. Moreover, the high tensions with the local Presbyterians had the effect of bringing the classes together, which helped the Jacobite landowners to rally their tenants for the Prince.

Taken from north to south, the principal harbours were those of Fraserburgh, Peterhead, the port town of Aberdeen, Stonehaven, Dunnottar, Johnshaven, Montrose, Arbroath and Carnoustie. Out of these places, Montrose recruited two companies for the Prince's army and was notable as the main channel of reinforcements and military gear from France. Its harbour channel was deep, reaching six fathoms three days before the spring tides, 'the breadth is scarcely a quarter of a mile, but the basin instantly expands into a beautiful circle of considerable diameter; but unfortunately most of it is dry at low water, except where the South Esk forms its channel, in which vessels of sixty tons will float even at the lowest ebb ... The houses are of stone, and like those in Flanders, often with their gable ends towards the street ... Numbers of genteel families, independent of any trade, reside here as a place of agreeable retreat, and numbers keep their carriages; these are principally of the Church of England [Episcopalians]'.[14] Another two

The Central Lowlands

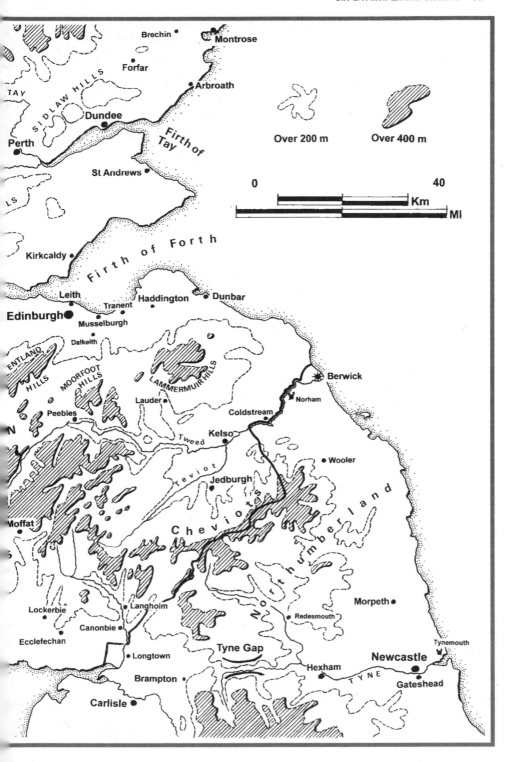

Brechin

Montrose

Forfar

Arbroath

SIDLAW HILLS

TAY

Dundee

Firth of Tay

Perth

St Andrews

LS

Over 200 m

Over 400 m

0   40

Km

MI

Kirkcaldy

Firth of Forth

Leith   Tranent   Haddington   Dunbar

Edinburgh

Musselburgh

Dalkeith

ENTLAND HILLS

MOORFOOT HILLS

LAMMERMUIR HILLS

Berwick

Norham

Lauder

Coldstream

Peebles

Kelso

Tweed

Wooler

Teviot

Jedburgh

Moffat

C h e v i o t s

N o r t h u m b e r l a n d

Lockerbie   Langholm

Morpeth

Canonbie

Redesmouth

Ecclefechan

Tyne Gap

Tynemouth

Longtown

Newcastle

Brampton

Hexham

TYNE

Gateshead

Carlisle

companies came from Arbroath, which must have represented a high proportion of the able-bodied male population, and a small battalion was raised in Aberdeen thanks to the work of James Moir, 4th Laird of Stoneywood, who had an estate just outside the town.

The estates of the Gordons extended from coastal Moray and across the Grampians to meet the lands of the MacDonalds. The situation of the Gordon dukes was typical of the magnates whose influence spanned the two Scottish cultures, in that they were not clan chiefs as such, but could call on a 'following' of Highlanders as well as the gentlemen of their low country. Historically the dukes of Gordon had been among the leading champions of Catholicism in Scotland, but the 3rd Duke Cosmo, the head of the house at the time of the '45, had been brought up as a Protestant and a Whig, and his conduct during the rising was equivocal, if not as blatantly cynical as that of the Grants. In September 1745 he seems to have connived at the way the old family factor, Gordon of Glenbucket, carried away arms and horses for the Jacobites, yet in March the next year he abandoned his duchess (who was in a delicate condition) to the Jacobites in Gordon Castle and made for the Hanoverian camp.[15]

The historic role of the house of Gordon had been taken over by a younger brother, Lord Lewis Gordon, who had abandoned a career in the Royal Navy, and who now proved to be one of the most energetic and ruthless of the Jacobite leaders. He first set himself the task of recruiting a battalion from the Catholic area of Strathdon, and from the mixed Catholic and Protestant populations of Strathbogie and the Enzie. The early enlistment went well, and especially because the Jacobites had freed the people from the hated Malt Tax, but once the genuine volunteers had left Strathbogie, those remaining proved recalcitrant. Lord Lewis therefore turned to force, 'threatening to burn the houses and farmyards of such as stood out. This soon had the desired effect, for the burning of a single house or farm stack terrified the whole'.[16]

Alexander, 4th Lord Forbes of Pitsligo (1678–1762) was a respected Jacobite of the earlier generation. 'He was justly esteemed a polite and learned gentleman, and of great integrity and honour in private life, but entirely enthusiastic on the Jacobite principles.'[17] His moral authority resembled that of Cameron of Lochiel in the Western Highlands, and he was able to win over a number of the gentlemen of Buchan, the area north of Aberdeen where the North Sea coast turned west towards the Moray Firth. Among those who responded to his appeal were Forbes of Brucehill, and the Gordons of Glastirrum, Carnousie and Cupbairdy. 'Carnousie's and Cupbairdy's journey was a great surprise. The latter had no manner of tincture that way, but being a rambling young lad was determined mainly by comradeship, and something too by the high regard he had for Lord Pitsligo. Carnousie was esteemed a wise, solid man and someone not at all wedded to kingcraft. But as many debts of his never heard of formerly are appearing, this somewhat unravels the mystery.'[18]

During the campaign in England this Arthur Gordon Carnousie was again and again seen marching into the towns at the head of Pitsligo's Horse 'dressed in a Highland habit with a broadsword by his side ... a brace of pistols before him ... a tin cockade in his bonnet like a St Andrew's cross, with a motto on it ... *nemo me impune lacessit*'[19] (loosely translated, 'No one insults me and gets away with it'). When he saw that his army was returning to Scotland Carnousie tried to abandon the cause, but his feelers were ignored by the Hanoverian authorities and he was forced to serve on with the Prince.

The Duke of Cumberland and his officers found Angus and Aberdeenshire distinctly unwelcoming in 1746, which 'had a strong effect in disposing him to treat it, after his victory, as a conquered country. Most of the gentlemen, throughout Angus at least, he found absent with the insurgent army; others paid him so little respect as to recruit almost before his eyes. In the town of Forfar, a small party of Charles's forces beat up for new adherents on the day before he entered the town'.[20]

The hostility to the Hanoverian forces was open and active in the country behind Montrose, namely northern Strathmore with Glen Esk and Glen Cova. The most important noble family of the region was the house of Airlie, which was Jacobite by tradition, and although the countess disapproved of the rising (and thus saved her house from being burned), the 20-year-old heir, Lord David Ogilvy, was able to raise one of the best regiments of the Jacobite army. In March 1746 the Duke of Cumberland was alarmed to see a new insurrection break out there in what he had assumed was a pacified area, and he sent an expedition under Major Lafansille to plunder and burn the houses of the people and gentry.

The Highlands

Who were the Highlanders? The term 'Highland Line' signifies a cultural division between a productive agriculture, viable towns, a settled society and a people whose language and clothing were recognizably variants of those worn by the English, and a Gaelic-speaking people whose economy was based primarily on the rearing of cattle (or the thieving thereof), who obeyed custom rather than law, and whose men went about armed and typically wore the plaid.

Unfortunately for the purposes of understanding, the division did not follow a simple north–south divide, with everything north of the Tay counting as the Highlands. That would have excluded the eastern coastlands, which extended all the way up the North Sea coast by way of Aberdeen, and then along the shores of the Moray and Dornoch firths. In other words, Scotland beyond the Tay had its own Lowland and Highland zones, with the Highland style of life predominating in the west, and the flatter ground in the east forming a cultural extension of the Central Lowlands. The Line as it existed in the 1740s described a series of sinuous curves. The Gaelic culture had retreated from the Black Isle, but it stood firm west of Inverness, Dunkeld and Port of Menteith, and its ways and loyalties remained almost unknown to the Scots of the Central Lowlands and the Borders. A Berwickshire gentleman protested that although he had 'no other connection with Highlanders than the common appelation of Scotsmen, I blush this moment at the thoughts that these wretches are acting as allies of France and traitors of Great Britain'.[21]

In that pre-industrial age the population was spread more evenly than was later to be the case, and by the calculations of the Rev. Alexander Webster in 1755 the Highlands contained 51 per cent of Scotland's total population of 1,265,000, and 71 per cent of the total land surface of 29,795 square miles. Webster's understanding of the 'Highland Belt' extended beyond the Highland Line to embrace the eastern coastal lowlands, which would reduce the population of the Highlands to about 30 per cent of the whole; but by any reckoning the Highlands still constituted a significant part of the Scotland of his day.[22]

Although, numerically speaking, the Jacobite forces were predominantly of Lowland origin, it is significant that the army of Prince Charles was commonly called the 'Highland army', and that the rising has ever since been assumed to have borne a Highland character. The rising began and ended in the Highlands, which explains a little. More important was the deliberate choice of the Jacobite leadership to associate their cause with the Highland culture, which carried connotations of patriotism and primitive virtue. Even the officers of the hastily raised Manchester Regiment fitted themselves out with sashes of white silk and tartan, and the only troops totally without allusion to the Highland garb were those of the red-coated Irish Brigade. One of their officers wrote: 'I am rather pleased to be in command of a picquet which will keep its uniform, otherwise I would have to dress myself in the

Highland style, march without breeches, and wear a little bonnet instead of a hat, as do all the dukes, lords, colonels, officers and soldiers of this army except the picquets. It is not that I would be ashamed to appear in Highland dress, but I prefer my own.'[23]

At the heart of the Highland culture lay the clan. It was not tribal, but an admixture of the patriarchal and feudal, and it had arisen in the Middle Ages when geographically isolated communities gathered for self-protection around strong leaders, whose status in time evolved into that of hereditary chiefs. The chief took dues in kind from his clansmen, he had judicial powers of life or death over them, and he could summon them to go forth with him to fight. 'A person is sent out at full speed with a pole burnt at one end, and bloody at the other, and with a cross at the top, which is called the "crosh-tairie", "the cross of shame", or "the fiery cross": the first from the disgrace they would undergo if they declined appearing; the second from the penalty of having fire and sword carried through their country in case of refusal. The first-bearer delivers it to the next person he meets, and he running at full speed to the third, and so on.'[24]

The clan system would not have lasted as long as it did if it had been tyrannical and inflexible. Surnames among the ordinary clansmen were used in a very loose way, and commonly adopted to accord with that of the clan chief (in return for a good meal, in the case of the 'Boll' Frasers), and abandoned again if the men drifted elsewhere. The name which was ultimately committed to paper was usually one that was chosen for no particular reason from the string that was in use by an individual or family.

Some clansmen might hold their lands of one chief but owe personal allegiance to another, and come under the legal 'regality' of a third; and just as a negligent chief could lose credit, so one who was dynamic could build up his 'following' by living up to what was expected of him by tradition. And what was that? It was the duty of safeguarding the clan tradition, the *Duthchas*, or clan heritage, a notion that embraced protection, hospitality, and a sense of shared kinship among the clan, however illusory that relationship might be.

In the 1490s the Scottish king James IV terminated the Lordship of the Isles, and ended the supremacy which the leaders of the MacDonalds had exercised over the Western Highlands and islands since the twelfth century. In 1609, after the union of the Crowns, King James VI of Scotland and I of England promulgated the Statutes of Iona, whereby the clan chiefs were thenceforward obliged to send their sons to the Lowlands for education. With exceptions like these, the Crown preferred to exercise its influence in the Highlands by indirect means, typically by granting royal charters to confirm favoured chiefs in their lands, and by the long-enduring alliances with the Gordons and the powerful clans of the Campbells and MacKays.

At the risk of some simplification, the clan structure may be reduced to the following layers:

❖ First came the clan chief, together with the chiefs of any cadet (junior branches) of the same name. They exercised the principal commands in time of strife

❖ The tacksmen were normally related by blood to the clan chief. They held their lands on lease from him, and repaid him by rents and other obligations, of which the most important was to provide a quota of armed men. The tacksmen were the linchpins of the clan system, for they acted as the ordinary officers of the clan in time of war, and were the immediate instrument of control of the ordinary clansmen

❖ The ordinary clansmen repaid the tacksmen for their little holdings by services, cash rents or agricultural products, and keeping themselves in readiness to take up arms at their behest. At the time of the '45 nearly all clan chiefs assumed that it was in their own interest to maintain the greatest number of followers on their lands. Only later (following the example of the dukes of Argyll) did the chiefs come to see the ordinary clansmen as a nuisance, occupying valley floors that could more profitably be turned over to grazing

❖ Below the clansmen existed a scarcely recorded layer of landless labourers, who were available at short notice to fill up the numbers of fighting men or cattle raiders.

A sept was essentially a sub-clan, affiliated (not necessarily permanently) to one of the more powerful clans (discussed in detail in Appendix I, pp. 552–69).

The lives of the chiefs and the ordinary clansmen invite further attention. By the 1770s, when the destruction of the clan system was already well advanced, Dr Johnson and the Welshman Thomas Pennant allowed themselves the luxury of some regret. Pennant figured to himself a warrior-chief in the old style, 'the dread of neighbouring chieftains; the delight of my people, their protector, their friend, their father ... hetacombs of beeves and deer covered my rude but welcome table. My nearest relations sat next to me, and then succeeded the bravest of my clan; and below them the emulous youth leaned forward, to hear the gallant recital of our past actions'.[25]

The traditional chief went to call on his neighbours accompanied by a clattering retinue comprising his hanchman (secretary and bodyguard), his bard, his spokesman, four gillies and, most importantly, the piper and his party. 'In the morning, when the chief is dressing, he walks backward and forward, close under his window, without doors playing on his bagpipes, with a most upright attitude and majestic stride.' The piper diverted his chief's guests at meals, and inspired his men in battle, 'and the moment he has done with his instrument, he disdainfully throws it on the ground, as being only the passive means of conveying his skill to the ear, and not a proper weight for him to carry at other times. But, for a contrary reason, his gilly snatches it up, which is, that the pipe may not suffer indignity from neglect'.[26]

The best pipers learned their skill from the MacCrimmons, hereditary pipers to the MacLeods of Dunvegan since the sixteenth century. MacLeod of Dunvegan was blackmailed into supporting the government in 1745, and so it was that Donald Ban MacCrimmon was found in the enemy ranks when he was killed at the Rout of Moy on the night of 16/17 February 1746. This was embarrassing to the Jacobites, who put it about that a stray shot from his own side had been responsible for this tragedy.

About forty clans survived at the time of the '45. Few of the chiefs were Jacobite by principle, and those who sooner or later committed themselves to Prince Charles often did so conditionally, and were rarely given to the ideology that moved so many of the Manchester men or the eastern Scottish Jacobites. The successful clan chief was almost by definition a ruthless Highland politician, and it was not for nothing that words like 'henchman', 'blackmail' or 'lifting' (in the sense of stealing) were products of that society.

The clan chiefs were also men of the wider world. They were at least as well educated as the Lowland gentry, and some of them were active businessmen and agricultural improvers in their own right. Thus Donald Cameron of Lochiel exported timber from his estates, he had interests in West Indian plantations, he traded with the North American colonies, he engaged in smuggling enterprises with France, and he tried (not very successfully, it seems) to reclaim Corpach Moss. Already in 1735 a shipload of 100 clansmen from the over-populated Cameron lands set sail for Jamaica under the leadership of his younger brother Ewen. Another of the undertakings in the neighbourhood was that of the Leadmining Company, which worked the veins of lead at Strontian in Sunart, its owner a Lowland gentleman of Jacobite persuasion, Sir Alexander Murray of Stanhope, who lost his immensely lucrative enterprise as a result of the failure of the '45.

In Perthshire the Highlands merged with great estates of the northern Central Lowlands which were run on feudal lines. Here the Jacobites were clearly numbered among the leading 'improvers'. The famous larches of the

The Northern Highlands

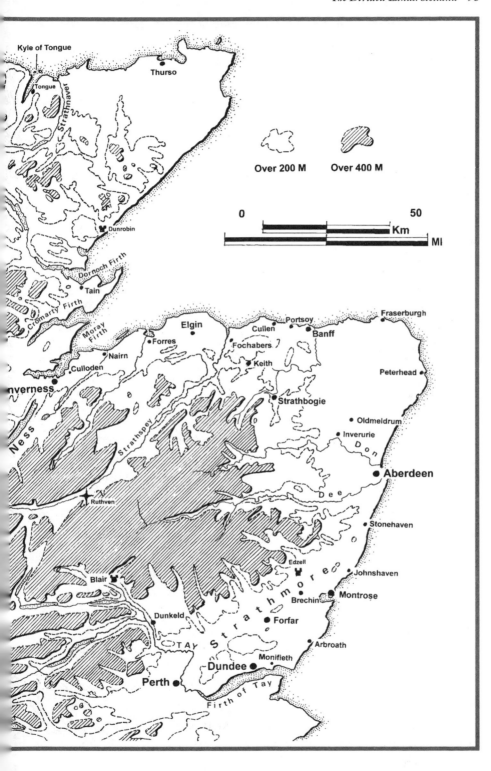

Over 200 M   Over 400 M

0   50
Km
MI

Kyle of Tongue
Tongue
Thurso
Strathnaver
Dunrobin
Dornoch Firth
Tain
Cromarty Firth
Moray Firth
Forres
Nairn
Culloden
Inverness
Ness
Elgin
Cullen   Portsoy
Fochabers   Banff
Keith
Fraserburgh
Peterhead
Strathbogie
Oldmeldrum
Inverurie
Don
Strathspey
Aberdeen
Ruthven
Dee
Stonehaven
Edzell
Johnshaven
Blair
Strathmore
Brechin   Montrose
Dunkeld   Forfar
Arbroath
TAY
Monifieth
Dundee
Perth
Firth of Tay

region owe their origin to a returning Jacobite of the '15, James Menzies of Culdares, who brought the first saplings from the Tyrol and presented them to the Duke of Atholl in 1737. James Drummond, 3rd Duke of Perth, who raised a mixed regiment of Highlanders and Lowlanders for Prince Charles, had been a leading light of the Society of Improvers of Agriculture in Scotland. In 1731 he rebuilt Crieff on a grid plan (which was the least he could do, since the Jacobites had burnt the place in 1716), and in 1739 he drew up the plans for the New Town of Callander, which was one of the first of its kind in Scotland. 'In order that the inhabitants should not dump their middens immediately in front of the house (as happened in the farmtouns) they made the front doors open directly on to the pavement. This normal absence of a front garden is one feature that can make a Scottish village appear singularly forbidding to English eyes.'[27]

The case of Drummond's Atholl neighbours is revealing, for Lord George Murray and the dispossessed Jacobite Duke William succeeded in forming a brigade of troops for the Prince, while their brother James, the official Hanoverian duke, failed miserably, an episode that demonstrates the power of leadership even in this borderland society.

Highland Way of Life
The style of life of the ordinary clansmen accustomed them from childhood to hardship, risk and the use of weapons. It is hard to imagine how the glens and straths – now for the most part silent and deserted – appeared in the 1740s. In summer time the hill pastures (shielings) showed scatterings of the herdsmen's huts, and of the diminutive black Highland cattle, which were different animals altogether from the great tawny, shaggy monsters of prehistoric aspect that appear on the present-day holiday postcards. The stone walls of the 'head dykes' separated the rough pasture from the lower infields, where the ground for the spring sowing of barley or oats was turned over by spade or the angular cashcrom, the scanty crops being pulled from the ground at harvest time, and the grain extracted from the ears by burning. This process left little straw for the winter feeding of the cattle, and by spring-time the people were subsisting on milk and a little meal, supplemented by the practice of bleeding the cattle to make blood cakes, which left the animals so weak that they could hardly stand.

The staple diet throughout the year consisted of mealed oats or barley, which were either made into bread or boiled with water. When the meat of cattle, sheep, goats or deer was available, the creature's own stomach was turned inside out, packed with meat, and the whole boiled over a fire. Hunting parties were accustomed to eat the venison raw after squeezing out the blood from the hunks of meat.

Root crops were scarcely known, and not many people bothered to fish the trout from the streams or lochs. After the '45 the Commissioners for the Annexed Estates noticed that the Highlanders would work hard enough when their masters told them to grow flax and run sheep, 'but they are averse to taking lint [linen] or wool to spin for others, and have no idea of buying the rough material and spinning it for sale'.[28] In any case, most of the hard work was left to the women, and the men were content to follow their herds over the hills, which left them with plenty of time to think deep thoughts and nourish grievances.

The settlements were strung out along the valley floors as collections of round cabins, barns and stables. The sides were built of rough stones, they were roofed over with turf, heather or reeds, and from a distance they looked like nothing so much as steaming manure heaps (as depicted in the film *Braveheart*). The open peat fires on the earthen floors were offset from the hole in the roof to prevent the flames from being put out by the rain, and so the smoke escaped through a process of seepage; 'They have no diversions to amuse them, but sit brooding in the smoke over the fire till their legs and thighs are scorched to an extraordinary degree, many have sore eyes, and some are quite blind. This long continuance in the smoke makes them almost as black as chimney-sweepers; and when the huts are not watertight, which is often the case, the rain comes through the roof and mixes with the sootiness of the inside, where all the sticks look like charcoal, and falls in drops like ink'.[29] A habitable cabin could be run up in three or four days, and an unattended one would revert to its natural elements in a couple of seasons. It is not surprising that none of them remains today.

The classic garb of the clansman was the plaid or *fèiladh-mor* of homespun wool. It was what its Gaelic name signified, a 'great wrap'. The intending wearer arranged the narrower part of the plaid around his waist in folds, so as to make a petticoat reaching down the thighs (most conveniently done when lying down), and he then brought the rest over his shoulder and fastened it with a fork, bodkin or sharpened stick. 'The plaid serves the ordinary people for a cloak by day and bedding by night: by the latter it imbibes so much perspiration, that no one day can free it from the filthy smell; even some of better than ordinary appearance, when the plaid falls from the shoulder, or otherwise has to be adjusted, while you are talking with them, toss it over again, as some people do with their wigs, which conveys the offence in whiffs which are intolerable.'[30] In battle the plaid was frequently cast aside, leaving the warrior clad only in his shirt, which he knotted between his legs to prevent it flapping about his person when he charged.

The headgear was the 'bonnet', which was not something tall with feathers but a floppy blue beret of wool; it kept some of the rain out of eyes and hair, and when it was totally sodden the wearer simply wrung it out like a sponge and replaced it on his head. A dirk was thrust down one of the woollen stockings (if indeed any were worn), and a tiny knife was secreted in an armpit, as was a highly flavoured little cake of meal. If the clansman chose not to go barefoot, his footgear consisted of crude shoes 'made of cow-hide, with the hair turned outward, which being ill made, the wearer's foot looked something like those of a rough-footed hen or pigeon: these are not only offensive to the sight, but intolerable to the smell of all those who are near them'.[31]

It will be evident that the present-day Scotsman in 'traditional' garb is wearing a highly sanitized version of the original, and that his kilt is not the *féiladh-mor*, but the neatly pleated variation of the skirt called the *féiladh-beg*, or 'little wrap', which was a newcomer in the 1740s. The company would run gagging for the door if an authentic Jacobite of 1745 were to appear at a modern Highland social gathering.

The incomprehensibility of the language was another barrier to the Englishmen's understanding of the Highlands, and Hanoverian interrogators had to employ interpreters if they were to make any sense of a good part of what their prisoners were saying.[32] The Highlanders who spoke English, or chose to speak English, did so not in the 'Rabbie Burns' accents of the Lowlands, but in a way they had learned from English officers, or others 'who could give them a good example of accent and pronunciation'.[33]

Although that was not the only evidence of civility, the Highlanders had acquired the reputation of being extraordinarily vindictive, grudge-bearing and quarrelsome. 'Every provocation was revenged with blood, and no man that ventured into a numerous company, on whatever occasion brought together, was sure of returning without a wound.'[34] Particularly numerous and dangerous companies came together at Crieff, which was the focal point of drove roads from the Highlands, and where the black cattle were sold on behalf of their real or supposed owners and from where they were driven into the Lowlands or England. In some respects the Union had accentuated the lawlessness of the Highlanders. Whisky distillers in the Lowlands were devastated by the Malt Tax, but the trade flourished in the Highlands where it was out of reach of the officers of the Excise. Likewise, the new demand for beef, hides and other by-products in the English market promoted the theft of cattle in the Highlands.

Just as cattle represented by far the most important source of cash for the Highlanders, so the work of thieving, guarding or retrieving the beasts was considered an eminently manly occupation. 'From habit it lost the appearance of criminality: they considered it as labouring in their vocation, and when a party was formed for an expedition against their neighbour's property, they and their friends prayed as earnestly to Heaven for success, as if they were engaged in the most laudable design.'[35] 'From this source the chieftains derived rewards for their numerous followers, and dowries sometimes for their daughters.'[36]

The clans most implicated in the business were reckoned to be the lawless MacGregors, the Breadalbane men, the MacDonalds of Glencoe, the MacDonnells of upper Glen Moriston, the MacDonnells of Keppoch, and the Camerons and their associates – the MacMillans of Loch Arkaig – who preyed on the herds of Sir Alexander MacDonald of Sleat as they were being driven from Skye to the market at Crieff. The Hanoverian authorities were at pains to identify the main cattle-thieving corridors and found that three of them led from the fat grazing in eastern coastlands of Banff, Aberdeenshire and the Mearns to their destinations in the Western Highlands:

❖ Northern Corridor, between the Spey and the Don: this ran through the broken country on the northern flank of the Grampians, from Banff and Strathbogie across Glenlivet and the River Avon to the ancient Abernethy Forest near the Boat of Garten

❖ Central Corridor, between the Don and the Dee: here the thieves took to the mountains north of the Dee, and exploited the cover offered by the forests of Morvern, Mar and Glenfeshie on their way to Badenoch. The isolated post Corgarff Castle was one of the few obstacles on the way (it is perhaps significant that both these corridors took the bands through Catholic glens)

❖ Southern Corridor: the cattle taken from south of Aberdeen and from the Mearns were driven up the converging glens on Esk and Tanar, and then across Glen Cova and upper Glen Shee to the neighbourhood of Atholl.[37]

Once they had passed Wade's road (today's A9), the raiding parties plunged into the Western Highlands, 'where dark woods, extensive wastes, high-forked mountains, and a coast indented with long winding branches of the sea, favoured the trade'.[38] Here the most favoured routes passed between lochs Ericht and Laggan, on by Loch Ossian, and finally around the head of Loch Treig into Lochaber. South of Loch Treig the passages intersected with the main north–south route of the cattle-thieving bands of the west, who were in the habit of resting their herds on Rannoch Moor, which was a hideous wasteland of lochans, bogs, heather, bracken and tussocky grass overlying a plateau of solid granite.

More was at stake than just the imposition of law and order, for cattle-thieving seemed to be 'a scheme artfully contrived to nurse and encourage the barbarism and idleness of these people, and may be called the principal spring of the rebellion ... this practice is a sure and known means of training up a number of men to the use of arms, who on the least prospect of plunder are ready to join in any rebellion or tumult'.[39]

In fact it seemed that virtually every habit of Highland life could be turned to military ends. Chiefs and gentlemen could use the pretext of a great stag hunt (tichel) to rally their supporters, as the Earl of Mar did in 1715. The ordinary clansmen needed no cover except their tartan plaids, which were dyed with infusions of herbs and blended in with the colours of the hillsides.[40] They had no call for tents and they had not much use either for bridges or ferries, since the only manly way to cross the streams and torrents was by wading. They had a practised eye for the rise and fall of the waters and they supported themselves against the current by sticks, or by clasping one another over the shoulders and pushing through en masse. Gillies considered it a matter of honour to be the first to make the crossing of a dangerous river, and their chiefs were happy to indulge them in their fancy.

With all of this, the Highlanders had traits which lifted them above the common herd. Edmund Burt conceded that they walked 'nimbly and upright, so that you never see, among the meanest of them, in the most remote place, the clumsy, stooping gait of the French *paisans*, or our own country-fellows; but on the contrary, a kind of stateliness in the midst of their poverty'.[41] Their real or supposed kinship with their chief in fact diffused a regal style through the clan:

> Every one of the superior clans thought himself a gentleman, as deriving his pedigree from an honourable stock, and proposed to do nothing un-worthy of his descent or connections ... The love, affection and esteem of the community [they] all aimed to procure by a disinterested practice of the social duties, truth, generosity, friendship, hospitality, gratitude, decency of manners, for which there were no rewards decreed in any country, but were amply paid among the Highlanders by that honour and respect of which they had a very delicate taste.[42]

CHAPTER 4

The White Cockade

WHEN PRINCE CHARLES CAME TO Scotland in 1745 his aim was to reclaim the British crown on behalf of his father, King James VIII ('The Old Pretender'). This statement will seem so obvious as to be scarcely worth setting down on paper, but a very great deal follows from it.

In the first place the Prince was staking a claim to conduct war as a lawful belligerent, and not a rebel. This consideration weighed heavily with men of the time, for it went to the heart of the issue of the just war, which revolved around two aspects: the *jus in bello*, which was the acceptable conduct in a declared war between legally recognized belligerents, and the more fundamental *jus ad bellum*, which was the right to resort to force in the first place.

Thomas Aquinas (1223–74) in his *Summa Theologia* indicated that the essential condition for a just war was 'the authority of a sovereign by whose command the war is to be waged. For it is not the business of a private individual to declare war'. In the sixteenth and seventeenth centuries the rights and wrongs of the case were debated further by Italian and Spanish theologians, and the Dutch jurist Hugo Grotius recast the arguments in secular terms (*De Jure Belli ac Pacis*, 1625). But the fundamental proposition of

---

A Jacobite soldier holding the famous 'Andrea Ferrara' sword

Aquinas remained unchallenged, and there was general agreement that a properly constituted state alone had the authority to wage war and that violence of every other kind was the work of thieves and brigands, who were not entitled to mercy. The middle decades of the eighteenth century are recognized as a period of unprecedented moderation in the conduct of war, and it would be reasonable to expect the foremost jurist of the age, the Swiss Emeric de Vattel (1714–67), to counsel some alleviation in the treatment of armed civilians. On the contrary, the old message of the *jus ad bellum* stood forward in all its harshness in his *Droit des Gens* (1758), for 'the sovereign power alone has the power to make war'.[1]

For these reasons Prince Charles was at pains to present the Jacobite cause as that of a sovereign power as it would have been understood by the jurists. He appointed lord lieutenants for local administration, he nominated bishops, he took to himself the tax-collecting powers of the London government. Thus the Jacobites persuaded or forced merchants, brewers and governmental officials to gather up the proceeds of the Cess (land tax) and Excise (purchase tax) from the Excise offices, or wherever else they were held, and James Ray saw Jacobite money-collectors roaming the country lanes for this purpose, with bags over their shoulders. When the cash finally ran out, Prince Charles commissioned the engraver Robert Strange to design a paper currency. The plates were completed and the press was about to go into operation when the cause suffered the catastrophe of Culloden.

Again, it is remarkable that we should be talking about a Jacobite 'army' in the first place, for the structure of the Jacobite forces was that of a conventional army, and not an insurgent peasant rabble. It was invested with all the apparatus of military routine, complete with orders of the day, duty rosters, passwords, courts martial and so on, and it was organized into companies, battalions, regiments and even a brigade (Atholl), and a full hierarchy of ranks with the appropriate rates of pay, for the Jacobites were not expected to live on enthusiasm alone.

At great effort the Jacobites dragged around with them their little train of artillery, and Prince Charles insisted that even the dangerous retreat from Derby must be conducted as befitted a proper army and not a defeated *chouannerie*. He halted for a day at Preston, and another at Lancaster. There were protests, 'but the Prince was inflexible in this point, he wanted to show the world he was retiring and not flying, and if the enemy came up he would give them battle'.[2] What made Culloden truly decisive was not the bloodshed on 16 April 1746, but the fact that Prince Charles was unwilling to prolong the fight in the Highlands with the 5,000 men who rallied at Ruthven four days later. Such a resistance would have had a guerrilla character, and everything in the conduct of the Prince during the rising indicates that he would not have sanctioned uncontrollable disorder. It is not too far-fetched to draw comparisons with the decision of Robert E. Lee to surrender at Appomattox in 1865.

The Jacobites invariably referred to the King George II as 'the Elector of Hanover', who had no legal authority in Britain, and strictly speaking Prince Charles ought to have kept the captured enemy officers and men under close supervision or simply killed them on the spot. Indeed, Chevalier de Johnstone observed that 'this was the only kind of warfare that we ought to have adopted, to infuse more terror into the enemy, and prevent us from having to combat the same individuals over and over again'.[3] That was politically impossible, and Prince Charles got around the logical difficulty by treating his enemies as misguided subjects who deserved every consideration.[4] In the course of the rising the Jacobites enrolled the captured Hanoverian soldiers in their ranks or simply let them go, while the officers were allowed to move freely around designated towns once they had given their word of honour not to escape.

When he returned to Edinburgh after Prestonpans the Prince set out a council that met every morning initially at Holyroodhouse, and consisted amongst others of the Duke of Perth, Lord George Murray, the principal clan chiefs, the Secretary of State John Murray of Broughton, Charles's old tutor Sir Thomas Sheridan, and the chief of staff John William O'Sullivan. By all accounts the proceedings were long and rancorous, with Lord John Murray leading the charge against the Prince's closest advisers and the Irish. Thereafter the council was convened less and less frequently, and on the last two occasions it reached decisions that were clearly against the Prince's wishes, namely at Derby to retreat to Scotland, and at Crieff to divide the army and retire towards Inverness. It was not in the power of Prince Charles to command obedience as sovereign, for he was nominally acting only for his father.

Prince Charles was also lacking in perceived military authority. 'One general of reputation in the world would have been of infinite service; besides the advantage that might have been expected from his knowledge in military operations, he would certainly have prevented all contests about power and command ... It must be acknowledged then, as one of the greatest oversights in the Prince's whole conduct, his coming over without an officer of distinction.'[5]

Command, Control and Discipline

It is true that Prince Charles's military experience was confined to having been a spectator of the siege of Gaeta in Naples in August 1734, but for the rest he stands out as a young man who had thought deeply about war, who had a strong strain of that essential attribute of luck, who kept himself in excellent physical condition, and who knew what was needed to motivate the ordinary men. He marched on foot at the head of the clans when he set out for England from Dalkeith on 3 November 1745:

> People thought it was only for a mile or two to encourage the soldiers at the beginning, and were surprised to see him continue all day, but it was the same every day after during the whole expedition; in dirty lanes and deep snow, he took his chance with the common men, and could seldom be prevailed upon to get on horseback to pass a river. It's not to be imagined how this manner of bringing himself down to a level with the men, and his affable behaviour with the meanest of them, endeared him to the army.[6]

A leader of a conventional military upbringing would have been unlikely to have generated the unique style of the Jacobite army, with its *élan*, impudence and opportunism. For counsel on matters military Prince Charles looked in the first place to his chief of staff, the Franco-Irish colonel O'Sullivan, then aged 45. In his youth O'Sullivan had studied for the priesthood, but he found that the calling did not suit him, and Marshal Maillebois finally persuaded him to take up a more active career:

> which he did with such success, that having attended his master to Corsica, when the French undertook to deprive these people of their liberties, he acted as his secretary. The Marshal, who was a bon-vivant, and used constantly to get drunk every day after dinner, was almost incapable of business the greater part of the twenty-four hours; during all which time the power devolved upon Sullivan, who executed it in such a manner as to do great honour to him and his master, having here gained a very high military reputation, as well as much knowledge in the art of making irregular war.

Later campaigns in Italy and on the Rhine enhanced O'Sullivan's reputation still further, and, so wrote a Whig in 1745, 'to the abilities of this man we may justly attribute the success with which a handful of banditti have long been able to overrun and plunder a large part of this opulent and powerful nation'.[7]

Lord George Murray soon emerged as the head of the avowedly Scottish party among the Prince's advisers and the leading general of the army.

He was a 'very active stirring man',[8] he was accessible to bold inspirations, he had an eye for practical detail, and like Prince Charles he knew that Highlanders must be led from the front. He opposed the chief of staff O'Sullivan's way of drawing up orders, which was simply to insert them in the orders of the day as was the routine in regular armies; Lord George knew how important it was to tell Scottish officers what they had to do, face to face, and then answer any objections on the spot.[9] He excelled in enterprises in which he exercised sole command, as witness his successful feint to Congleton, the well-managed rearguard action at Clifton, and the elaborate Atholl Raid. He would have done very well in place of Lord John Drummond as commander of the forces that were gathering in Scotland at the time of the Jacobite invasion of England.

With some rare exceptions (e.g. Stuart Reid), historians have been inclined to inflate Lord George's undeniable qualities into something altogether greater, and by the same token to deny military virtue to where it also belongs – to the physically and mentally tough Prince, the genuinely formidable Duke of Perth, and the professional and devoted O'Sullivan. The Jacobite army would not have achieved what it did without more than one good man at the top.

Lord George Murray's 'vast' experience of regular service was limited to his time as ensign in the Royals at the very end of Britain's involvement in the War of Spanish Succession, when he saw no action, having been laid up sick for most of the time. Two years of peacetime duties followed, then in 1715, when on leave in Scotland, he took command of a battalion of Atholl men in the Jacobite cause but was absent collecting taxes at the time of Sheriffmuir. He was 'out' again in 1719, and engaged in the 'scuffle' at Glenshiel, but the researches of Walter Biggar Blakie could find no trace of his alleged service in the army of Piedmont–Sardinia, and Lord George spent the years before 1745 managing affairs quietly on the Atholl estate.

Lord George remained ignorant of some standard military procedures, there were lapses in his highly praised judgement of ground, he mistakenly believed that the 'deserters' who left the army when it re-entered Scotland were gone for good, and he was badly informed when on 6 January 1746 he wrote to Prince Charles that all military operations must be determined by the majority vote of a standing committee or council of war. The Prince was right to reply that such a thing was completely unknown in regular armies, and, if had known about it, he could have cited the opinion of Frederick the Great of Prussia on the point: 'Prince Eugene once said that the only occasion on which a general should hold a council of war is when he has decided to do nothing. How right that is! Most of the opinions are always negative ... Besides, they invariably compromise that element of secrecy which is essential in war'.[10] In all likelihood the kind of council proposed by Lord George would have hardened into a council of regency, which would have deprived the Prince of political as well as military freedom.

In these and other debates it transpired that Lord George Murray was a vindictive man who was seeking to undermine O'Sullivan's authority as chief of staff and pursued feuds against the Irish and the Catholics in general. Lord George cited the Duke of Perth's Romish religion as the reason for relegating the duke from active field command shortly after the army crossed into England. Curiously, the desire to elevate Lord George into the all-Scottish hero has led the more nationalistic of the Scottish historians to caricature one of the best of their race, the Duke of Perth, as 'a silly horse-racing boy', in a phrase coined by an English Whig.[11] We shall encounter James, 3rd Duke of Perth, in a number of contexts which will give the lie to this canard, and it is enough for the moment to mention that he commanded the prettiest operation of the entire rising (the assault over the Dornoch Firth on 20 March 1746).

Lord George Murray was at least as responsible as his rival Murray of Broughton for sowing divisions in the original council from the time it first met at Holyrood, and Bishop Forbes heard 'some affirm, who had an opportunity of knowing them, that these were owing to the haughty, restless, unaccountable temper of Lord George Murray, some of whose blood-relations fail not to lay the blame upon him'.[12]

Unfitted to act as a member of a team, Lord George had an eye only for the troops under his immediate command, which he flung about with characteristic energy but without regard to what the rest of the army was doing, as witness the dash to Falside Hill before Prestonpans, the further attack of the right wing at Falkirk, and the way he disengaged his column from the march on the enemy camp at Nairn before the battle of Culloden. This was the same man who had led the call for the retreat from Derby and forced Prince Charles to forsake the eastern Lowlands in the retreat to Aberdeen. Lord George had a way of abandoning initiatives – and sometimes the ones he himself had launched. Full and convincing justifications can be assembled for his actions in each of these cases, but a pattern emerges when they are taken together that probably derives from his impulsive nature and underlying pessimism, which can be traced from the time he first committed himself to Prince Charles (p. 49).

Lord George was distrusted in the army,[13] and episodes like these lent colour to suspicions that he was a traitor to the Prince. O'Sullivan had been warned by Lord George's own friends and relations to be on his guard against him, and another source of unease was that Lord George had not at once declared for the Prince. Nowhere in the voluminous Hanoverian correspondence, however, is there the slightest hint that anybody in the high counsels of the Jacobite army was working in King George's interest.

We now have to ask how far the Jacobite forces were capable of responding to the directions that came from above. The answer is inevitably complicated, because the forces of Prince Charles were neither the witless savages of legend nor a uniformly schooled and settled army on the regular pattern. The Jacobite army was a new creation and it changed constantly in composition and character. Thus the ragged, cheerful and predominantly Highland band of 5,500-odd men and boys which marched into England was a different animal from the more balanced and much better-equipped army of about twice that number that came together later in Scotland. Altogether we encounter eight or so fully fledged clan regiments, three of mixed Highland and Lowland composition, two of Lowlanders, one of Manchester volunteers, four units of horse, and three sets of Scottish and Irish regulars who landed in 1746.

The clan regiments proper varied greatly in size, which was determined by imponderables such as local loyalties and the charisma of the leaders as well as by population base, and there could be no question of forming companies of uniform size as O'Sullivan had wished. Motives among the composite and Lowland units were mixed. Gentlemen and their servants formed the backbone of the respectable units of horse, while a distinct freebooter element emerged among the hussars. Some of the men came as volunteers, others were swept up by demands of levies that were made on the tenants of the gentry of the eastern Lowlands. The language used on such occasions could be forceful.[14] However, to judge these forces against the standards of the typical European army of the time is to be impressed by the generally high level of competence. It did not derive from any great reserve of experience among the generals and colonels, for only a handful of them had seen any kind of military service, and where they had, it was mostly at a junior level. It had more to do with a diffused military knowledge and a warlike culture. For generations there had been so little prospect of employment for the younger sons of the Jacobite gentry that many were forced

either to turn farmers at home under their eldest brother, or go abroad to serve in the French or Spanish armies. The first tends exceedingly to keep up the clanship, and the last produces still worse effects. These young gentlemen, when they are preferred to commissions, come privately every year to the country, and contract with some of the able-bodied young man of their neighbourhood clan, with whom they can have influence, for so many years service, and when that term expires, many of these choose to return home. And thus new levies are always made, and some of the bred soldiers are always returning. By this means, many are to be found among the inhabitants of the country, that have been disciplined in the French and Spanish armies.[15]

A few Whig observers were also right to detect the experience of service in the Independent Companies which the government in its wisdom had set up to police the Highlands. As early as 10 September 1745 a gentleman of Berwickshire commented how the policy of 'making the Highlands an academy for the art of war, displays itself notably on this occasion; for the fact is certain, that the west Highlanders, who first got together, had not been assembled a fortnight, when some of His Majesty's officers who had fallen into their hands, upon seeing them perform the manual exercise, were convinced that they did it with as much dexterity as any other regular forces could have done'.[16]

In one sense or another the Scots of the Jacobite army were all 'Highlanders', either by birth or at one remove by dress or emulation, and in that way the Highland spirit influenced the whole.[17] The typical Highlander was spared the time-consuming labours of domestic industry and working the fields, and it was 'perhaps owing to this idleness that the lower sort are more curious and inquisitive about news and politics, and better versed in their own history and genealogies than the common people of other countries'. Prince Charles happened to cross the historic valley of Glenshiel in the course of his escape, and his guide was able to provide details of what had happened there in 1719. 'The account was so rational, and the description so accurate, that the Prince could not help admiring the sagacity of his guide; who, though he had never served, spoke of these matters as an old sergeant would have done. That is the genius of the Highlanders; the feats of their ancestors is the common topic of conversation among them, and they have all some notion of military affairs.'[18]

A certain reputation preceded the Jacobite invasion force into England, where

the people … seemingly mightily afraid of the army … had abandoned all the villages upon their approach. When any of them was got, and asked why they ran away, they said they had been told that the army murdered all the

men and children and ravished the women, and when they found themselves well used, they seemed mightily surprised. There was an old woman
remained in a house that night where some officers were quartered. After
they had supped, she said to them, 'Gentlemen, I suppose you have done
with your murdering today, I should be glad to know when the ravishing
begins'.[19]

The old lady was left in frustrated peace, for by any reckoning the Jacobite
army must be reckoned one of the best behaved of its period, as supporters
of the government had to admit to themselves.[20] The MacDonalds of Glencoe
insisted on mounting a guard to protect a mansion on the banks of the
Almond at Kirkliston. This, as they well knew, was the property of the Earl of
Stair, who was commander of the Hanoverian forces in England at the time
and whose grandfather was the author of the massacre of Glencoe in 1692.
Such was the working of self-discipline and the regard for the honour of the
clan and for the authority of the clan chief or his representatives. Some of
their enemies were so deluded as to take the very lack of atrocities as evidence of a primitive state of mind. 'The poor wretches are entirely under
the command of their chiefs [wrote a Whig from Lancaster], for soon after six
at night the drum beat for them to retire to their quarters, which they did
immediately; when their officers went and locked them up.'[21]

The charges which are justly laid to the account of the Jacobite troops
relate to their vindictiveness on their retreat through England, and to offences
like stealing horses, poaching, killing hens and sheep, and the peculiar
Highland form of mass desertion which was really absence without leave – all
reprehensible, no doubt, but pretty mild when compared the plundering,
incendiarism and murder carried out under the authority of the Duke of
Cumberland in 1746.

Discipline was enforced by all the apparatus of the time, albeit tempered
by a regard for the genius of the army, as when on 9 October 1745 Prince
Charles announced a reprieve for seven of Lochiel's men who were due to
be shot.[22] The punitive measures were targeted in particular against the
hyaena-like stragglers and hangers-on who were a prime cause of the 'clamorous depredations' in the wars of the time, and on the march into England
the troops actually dispersed the camp followers by the drastic measure of
shooting at them.[23]

It was unwise for any junior officer to presume upon the good nature
of his superior. For example, a witness at Crieff noticed the treatment that
was meted out to Captain Alexander Buchanan of Auchleishie, who wished

to visit his father and applied for leave to the Duke of Perth, as the colonel of his regiment. 'I'll let you know, spark,' said Perth, 'that I have authority over you', and he forthwith delivered him prisoner to the captain of the guard. An ensign was taken aback at the severity, but Perth explained 'that it was not for any good or evil that Buchanan might do, but to show a better example to the rest'.[24]

The pipes were an important means of moving the troops in a more positive way. James Reid of Angus, a piper in the Regiment of Ogilvy, was captured along with the Jacobite garrison in Carlisle. He asked to be spared, as a simple musician, but the court ruled that 'no regiment ever marched without musical instruments such as drums, trumpets and the like; and that a Highland regiment never marched without a piper, and therefore his bag-pipe, in the eye of the law, was an instrument of war'. He was duly executed at York on 15 November 1746.[25] This was harsh but understandable, and James Ray complained that Carlisle had surrendered to the Jacobites in the first place on account of that 'bloody and inhuman weapon'.[26] The pipes likewise had the capacity of heartening the Highlanders after a hazardous task and worked equally well in battle, at least until the pipers cast their instruments aside and joined in the fray.

Details like this hint at the idiosyncrasies of command and control among the Highlanders. The clansmen would have been rallied to the cause by run-ners who bore the fiery cross through their territory (p. 89) and shouted the clan slogan at the place of rendezvous. Assembled in order of battle, the Highlanders occupied the first line, and the Clan Donald expected to take the place of honour on the right wing – a privilege said to have been granted by Robert the Bruce. It was difficult or impossible for an officer from another clan or from a Lowland regiment to assert his authority over a given body of Highlanders, and when combat was joined the generals and aides de camp might find it necessary to dismount, 'whereas they ought to have been on horseback, for generals' business in battle is more to command than fight as common soldiers'.[27]

The clan gentlemen in the first rank were responsible for hacking and hewing into the enemy with their broadswords, and if the clan chief or his representative happened to be killed the results could be disastrous, for by ancient Gaelic custom the fight ended with the fall of the leader. In such a way the conservative MacDonnells of Glengarry were demoralized by the acci-dental death of their war leader Colonel Angus, or Aeneas, after Falkirk, just as the heart went out of the Keppochs when their clan chief was killed at Culloden.

Logistics and Operational Mobility

Prince Charles fashioned his army for the offensive, and as long as he was dictating the pace of events the speed of his forces seemed miraculous to men who were accustomed to the ponderous tread of armies in continental Europe. When Wade's army was running itself into the ground his aide de camp Lieutenant Robinson wrote wonderingly to Lieutenant Colonel Joseph Yorke that their

> method of proceeding is quite military and good, but what we cannot, dare not practise. They turn everybody out of their houses and cover their men, and the country supplies them with everything gratis through fear ... Their field artillery in comparison with ours goes post, for they seize on 100 fresh horses every night and drive them at the head of the train, and as the horses grow tired, they put in fresh ones. Our train has suffered extremely this last march; nearly half our carriages are out of order and our horses almost all knocked up. I believe at last we must go upon their plan, if ever we intend to be up with them.[28]

By 3 December 1745 the Jacobites had succeeded in dodging between the armies of Wade and Cumberland and were on their way to Derby, which forced the Lord Lieutenant of that county to admit that he had 'no notion of an army being able to march at the rate these fellows have come'.[29]

On the move the Jacobites proceeded at 'a dog trot, or upon a half-run',[30] and they moved fast by the standards of Continental armies. Prince Charles's retreat from Derby was something of a coat-trailing exercise, which invited combat by the pursuing Hanoverians, yet he covered the 170 or so miles to Carlisle in fourteen days, or an average of just over 12 miles a day, which equates with the progress rate of Frederick's troops from Rossbach to Leuthen in November and December 1757. They were marching in better weather and over much better roads, but the episode was celebrated for its speed by Prussian historians.

The reasons for the Jacobite superiority in operational movement must lie elsewhere. In the first place, the standard of Jacobite staff work was usually very high, and was capable of bringing off a *tour de force* like the reunion of their three separate columns just outside Carlisle on 9 November 1745. On a smaller scale it was a technical feat which bears comparison with the way Frederick brought his scattered corps together inside the Austrian province of Bohemia in April and May 1757. The Jacobites dispersed and reassembled again in January 1746 when they retreated from Crieff to Inverness.

When the army was moving along a single line of march, as during the campaign in England, it usually did so by two major divisions, the Highland and the Lowland, which were separated by half a day's march. They travelled light, for the Highlanders could not be persuaded to use the tents which had been captured from Cope at Prestonpans (and were left behind with fifty or sixty carts at Lockerbie), and the Jacobites relied on local requisitions of food and fodder instead of the cumbersome system of trains and fixed magazines which sustained the conventional armies at that period. 'They march with droves of black cattle and sheep, three waggons of bread and cheese, they sit down at noon to eat; at night and morning get a little oatmeal which they buy up at their own price, or take away whenever they can get it, and constantly carry it in a little bag at their side.'[31] Edinburgh, Dumfries and Glasgow all had to submit to heavy requisitions of shoes and other commodities, and Manchester had to yield up 50,000 bullets.

Lord George Murray laid the foundation for the Jacobite style of logistics when he first arrived at Perth, and appointed proper commissaries,

> for otherwise there would be no keeping the men together, and ... they would straggle through the whole country upon their marches if it was left to them to find provisions, which, besides the inconveniency of irregular marches, and much time lost, great abuses would be committed, which, above all things, we were to avoid. I got many of the men to make small knapsacks of sacking before we left Perth, to carry a peck of meal each upon occasion, and I caused take as many threepenny loaves there as would be three days' bread to our small army, which was carried in carts.[32]

As for the important commodity of forage for the animals, Lord Elcho was put in charge of a specialized committee after Prestonpans: 'they issued orders in the Prince's name to all the gentlemen's houses who had employments under the government to send in certain quantities of hay, straw and corn upon such a day under the penalty of military execution if not complied with, but their orders were very punctually obeyed'.[33]

The much-maligned O'Sullivan was responsible for the overall planning of the movements by virtue of his post as quartermaster general, which at that period had nothing to do directly with stores and provisions (a cause of much misunderstanding among historians) but signified the army's chief of staff. By custom, however, everything that turned out well is attributed to the genius of Lord George Murray. The Duke of Perth (again underestimated in most of the literature) formed an effective pioneer corps of fifty men from the ranks of his own regiment to see to the repair of the roads on the army's route through England. Those who were positioned in front of the artillery and baggage were decked out with a sash and a white cockade, and they worked with pickaxe and spade to mend 'the roads between Macclesfield and Leek, about five miles from Macclesfield, and between Kendal and Penrith, about four miles north of Kendal on a mountain; and again about two miles north of Shap'.[34]

Prince Charles set his army in motion by daylight, or during the night if the moon permitted.[35] This by itself gave the Jacobites the advantage of an early start, and it was augmented whenever Prince Charles feinted in one direction and then jigged back in another, as on the retreat from Derby on 6 December 1745.

River obstacles counted for little in the face of an army accustomed to fording them in its stride, so it did the Hanoverians no good to break down the bridges over the Ribble and Mersey on the path of the Jacobites. On the subsequent retreat from Stirling, 'while the Duke of Cumberland had to wait a day for the repair of a bridge, and then could only drag his lumbering strength over the post-roads at a rate of twelve or fourteen miles in as many hours, Charles forded rivers, crossed over moors, and dared the winter dangers of a hill country with alacrity and promptitude'.[36]

Altogether, for the greater part of the rising the Jacobites were superior to their enemies in achieving a controlled and sustainable rhythm in their operations, or 'tempo', an advantage they retained so long as they were able to keep on the move and hold the initiative. When they were capable of doing neither, the balance turned decisively against the Prince.

Intelligence and Deception

The evidence concerning plots and spies is notoriously fragmentary, and its total absence can mean that an intelligence service was either very good or very bad. However, enough detail has survived to dissipate the curious notion that Prince Charles and the Jacobites gave this work a low priority. On the face of it, Prince Charles undertook his expedition to Britain on no more than a general understanding with the leading Jacobites that a French landing was a *sine qua non*. But that is not necessarily the whole story. By chance we have independent support for what the Hanoverian agent Dudley Bradstreet has to say about his part in the fateful council of war at Derby on 5 December 1745, and of the scheme to raise the nearly 1,500 weakly guarded French and Spanish prisoners who were being held at Plymouth and other places in the West Country. It would therefore be wrong to dismiss entirely his accounts of an elaborate plot to seize the Tower of London.[37]

Once he had embarked on his enterprise it was physically impossible for Prince Charles to have been involved in the many comings and goings between the coasts of northern France and south-eastern England. The travellers were mainly officers of the Irish Brigade or their associates and, according to one account, Colonel Lally himself, who embarked from Boulogne for Deal on a 10-ton fishing boat, 'disguised in a sailor's habit, to pass for a smuggler'.[38]

In France the duc de Richelieu attached considerable importance to the information gathered by one Laurence Wolfe, who set out from Paris at the end of November with the intention of making contact with Lord Dillon. Dillon, who was under close surveillance, was unable to see Wolfe in person but he contrived to pass on to him a list of the deployment of the governmental troops in Britain and overseas which Wolfe took back to France early in January, together with information on the progress of the rebellion and the public mood in Britain. Even then there were 'many private persons in London who only await the arrival of French troops to go to join them, but nobody dares to trust his neighbour'.[39]

Yet this kind of information at best merely helped to keep up a measure of interest among French military circles for a time after the most realistic chance for an invasion had passed. In Britain, meanwhile, Prince Charles's efforts to sound out the measure of his English support had initially been directed principally at the North-East (p. 71). His advisers had already ruled out on political grounds the idea of inciting the Catholic clergy of Lancashire, and the decision to invade England by the western route instead of the eastern was now taken at short notice. It should therefore come as no surprise that the attempts to establish contact with the gentry of the North-West and Wales were improvised and ineffective.

Yet the campaign intelligence of the Jacobites was usually much superior to that of the Hanoverian forces, despite their being caught badly by surprise on 18 December 1745 when the Duke of Cumberland nearly overhauled them at Clifton. As early as 1 September 1745 we find Jacobites stopping the Inverness postal coach, opening the letters and interrogating a passenger. The gentleman was brought before Prince Charles, who questioned him narrowly and sent him upstairs for further investigation. 'In the meantime a clergyman, whom he describes as having a white cockade in his hat, examined him as to any letters which were concealed, and told him he would hurt himself unless he made a full discovery ... some Highland officers offered to strip him, but on his offering to unloose his coat, the clergyman stopped them, but obliged him to put off his shoes, in case any letters were concealed in them.' The gentleman and the coach were sent on the way, though half the mail was retained for perusal.[40]

While Prince Charles was still at Holyroodhouse the work of examining correspondence fell to Ker of Graden, with James Stuart of Goodtrees as his deputy.[41] The Duke of Perth took over the responsibility for gathering and collating information, at least from the time the army entered England. He could look intimidating enough with his black cap and Turkish scimitar, and he emerges as an altogether sharper and more active individual than the sickly idealist who is depicted in the histories. He took up whatever newspapers were to be found in town or at the post offices, and interrogating suspects in person.[42]

The Duke of Cumberland was convinced that the Jacobite intelligence network was spread wider still. The Swedish ambassador Ringwicht reported that the duke had complained to King George that 'Your Majesty's orders would be put into effect much better than they are, if they were not known to the rebels twenty-four hours before Your Majesty's court'.[43] On this point the Duke of Newcastle was told by one of his informants that he was 'very sorry to hear and almost everywhere that the Duke of Cumberland complains that his instructions are discovered to the Pretender's Council, and that they know them, and from Your Grace's office, as soon as he. My Lord, I have been often at your office and have observed two people, that I know one to be a reputed papist, and the other a rank Jacobite ... they are frequently at your office asking for news'.[44] Once the campaign moved back to Scotland, the Hanoverian commanders were aware that their own sources of useful information had dried up and that they lived in an environment of hostile spies and informants.[45]

Prince Charles was obsessive on the issue of security. At the time that he was gathering his forces around Edinburgh and Prestonpans

> [an] abundance of people there, friends as well as enemies, had made it their business to find out the real numbers of the Prince's army, but to no purpose; great pains had been taken to conceal its weakness. Though the Prince was every day reviewing some of his men, he never made a general review. There were always troops at Leith, Musselburgh, some villages adjacent, when he reviewed the camp, besides the garrison that remained constantly in the city, and, lest people should reckon them in their different cantonments, they were eternally shifting their quarters, for no other reason than to confound the over-curious ... when any small party comes near Edinburgh, numbers of the

Highlanders go out in the night time and return with the fresh party, and then they give out as if they were now come from the Highlands, purposely to magnify their numbers. Their affairs are kept very secret ...[46]

Weapons

The classic fighting gear of the Highlander, or at least the Highland gentleman, was made up of the broadsword, the dirk, the target, the Highland pistol and the musket. The two-handed claymore had almost entirely passed out of use, and its place taken by the single-handed broadsword, which had developed gradually from the middle of the sixteenth century, and was fully fledged by the end of the seventeenth. The hilt was of Scottish manufacture, and its characteristic basket form not only provided excellent protection to the hand, but made this formidable weapon seem weightless. To grasp an eighteenth-century broadsword of the best kind is to understand the ancient belief that swords were living things. A Hanoverian officer explained that 'their swords are indeed manageable with much greater dexterity and smartness than ours; the three centres of motion, gravity and magnitude uniting in them, which the weight of our blades, and the lightness of our hilts, separate too much ... in a close engagement the broadsword and target seem to have much the advantage of the musket and bayonet; since the point of the bayonet may be received upon the target with the left hand, while the weighty broadsword does the business with the right, the fighter without a shield having no guard against the stroke'.[47]

In the skirmish at Clifton several of the Highlanders' broadswords shattered on the iron skull caps that the dragoons wore beneath their hats, and the broken or defective weapons were replaced by enemy weapons abandoned on the field. Thereafter swords of any kind were still in demand, as when the Chevalier de Stuart asked the duc de Richelieu to ship 5–6,000 from France, 'which should be easy enough for Your Grace, as You may obtain them from the arsenals in Flanders, and weapons which are useless for the French troops would be eminently suitable for the Highlanders, as the best swords for them are those which have a cutting edge, as long as they are straight and reasonably long'.[48]

The dirk is described as having a straight blade, 'generally under a foot long; the blade near one-eighth of an inch thick; the point goes off like a tuck, and the handle is something like a sickle. They pretend they cannot do without it; but it is a concealed mischief, hid under the plaid for secret stabbing; and, in a close encounter, there is not defence against it'.[49]

The target was a small circular shield, some 20 inches in diameter, formed of two layers of wood which were superimposed with the grains cross-ways. The exterior surface was clad in leather, and studded with nails driven home in circular patterns. It could serve offensive purposes if it were equipped with a central spike, and the owner might also hold a dirk in his left hand, with the blade projecting beyond the rim of the shield. The targets was nevertheless intended 'more for single combat than field fighting',[50] and most of them had been discarded by the time the Jacobites came to fight at Culloden.[51]

The traditional Highland pistol was manufactured at Doune and was of a distinctive design, being of all-metal construction, having a handle which ended in a fish-tail form and a knob-like trigger without a guard; and the Lowlanders and the second and third ranks of the Highlanders were equipped with muskets, or, *faute de mieux*, the long-shafted Lochaber axe. The Jacobites as a whole were badly armed at the outset of the rising:

> The most of people seems to be surprised that the Prince did not pursue the advantage of the victory [at Prestonpans] and march into England whilst they were still in such a consternation and panic; but if those people had known the state of his affairs at that time, their surprise might perhaps cease. 'Tis true that he got between 2 and 3,000 men together ill-provided with everything fitted for an army; notwithstanding the arms that was found in the city of Edinburgh there was a great number of his men at Gladsmuir (as it was called) that had nothing but pieces of old scythes fixed to the end of long poles for want of arms; and after the battle most of the arms that was taken there the Highlanders took the locks off and sold them, which rendered them of no service.[52]

In October 1745 the artillery officers James Grant and John Burnet landed from a French ship at Montrose and said afterwards to a drinking companion that they had brought with them 4,000 French muskets and as many bayonets and swords.[53] These, however, were retained for the Jacobite forces that were building up in Scotland, and the body which marched to Derby was observed to be 'in general but indifferently armed, few or none but the officers are what we call completely armed, their pistols are indifferent, but their firelocks are but very bad'.[54] This is a reference to pieces like the ninety-one ancient matchlocks which had been taken from Redbraes, the house of the Earl of Marchmont in Berwickshire.[55] This state of affairs was remedied when the army reassembled in Scotland, and thereafter there seems to have been no shortage of modern muskets and the requisite ammunition.

Tactics

The Jacobite way of combat was offensive, which is why a great deal hung on how they got their forces into a position to fight in the first place. One of the basic problems of tactics was how to answer the requirements of marching – best answered by moving in columns – with those of building up a fighting line.

British and Continental armies had worked out a compromise whereby the tactical building block was the platoon or the two-platoon division – units of about thirty-five and seventy of all ranks respectively – usually drawn up three ranks deep, giving corresponding frontages of at least ten and twenty-four files. The men were closed up almost shoulder-to-shoulder, with up to 3 feet being allowed for each file of infantry, and 3½ feet for each file of dragoons.[56] The marching formation was a stacked-up column of platoons or divisions, which diminished the length of the column in a useful way but demanded plenty of the lateral space usually to be found in the typically open country of continental European theatres of war. Upon the column approaching the enemy, the intervals between the platoons or divisions were opened up, which permitted a continuous three-rank line to be formed by simultaneous quarter-wheels of these sub-units. The army's foremost tactician, Major General Humphrey Bland, had expressed a clear preference for the column of platoons in the latest edition (1743) of his authoritative *Treatise of Military Discipline* (p.116).

This little digression will help to explain the advantage the Jacobites derived from the fact that they marched in a column only three files wide:

Marching columns compared

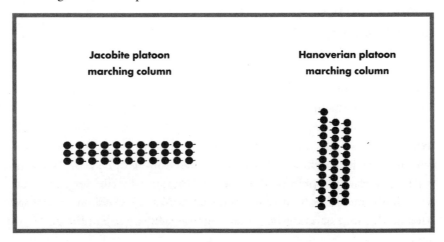

**Jacobite platoon
marching column**

**Hanoverian platoon
marching column**

The Highlanders have a very simple manoeuvre, well suited to a small army composed of undisciplined men. They formed themselves in line, three deep, and by facing to right or left, they formed themselves into a column for marching, three men in front; and, in the same manner, by facing to right or left, they were instantly in order of battle. It was deemed more advisable to allow them to adhere their ancient and simple manoeuvre, than to teach them, imperfectly, the more complicated movements of wheeling backwards to form columns of division, sub-division etc. and forwards to form into line.[57]

There was no reshuffling of the officers and men such as was involved in breaking down the companies into platoons, and the column frontage of just three men abreast permitted the Jacobites to pass along narrow tracks that would have been insuperable barriers to the redcoat columns marching in formations up to 30 feet or more wide (for the platoon), and up to 70 (for the division).

In such a fashion the Jacobite army was able to traverse the marsh at Prestonpans and thread its way across the Carron and up on to the moor at Falkirk. The penalty – a potentially serious one – was that the three-file column was inordinately long in proportion to its width and therefore liable to break apart. The effect at Prestonpans was not critical, but in the night march before Culloden the Highlanders and the Lowlanders lost contact altogether, with fatal consequences for the Jacobite cause.

Until just before the battle of Culloden there was a consensus as to the most desirable ground for the Jacobite way of fighting. The Welsh Jacobite David Morgan told his Hanoverian interrogators that 'the rebels wished to meet the King's troops rather in an open field, than in a close country; their reason for which was that they were for falling on at once, sword in hand, the King's troops having a great advantage over them in firing'.[58] The open stubble fields of Prestonpans met this requirement fully, while the ground at Falkirk answered reasonably well once the Jacobites had climbed the hill, although the attack by the left wing was disrupted by a steep ravine. Indeed, obstructions of any kind were believed to be damaging, for they would immobilize the troops under the superior Hanoverian fire. That was one of the good reasons why the Jacobites offered no real defence of the Spey on 12 April 1746. Here it is perhaps worth recalling that the Gaelic word *blair* or *blár* signifies both 'plain' and 'battlefield'.

In the middle of April 1746 Lord George Murray sowed much confusion for the Jacobites and for historians when he chose to abandon all tactical precedent. His notion of attacking the Hanoverian camp at Nairn by means of an overnight march was bold and 'Jacobite' in itself, but among the arguments he adduced was the unfamiliar one that 'I thought we had a better chance of doing it than by fighting in so plain a field'.[59] The 'plain field' was the flatter part of Drummossie Moor. The alternatives put forward by Lord George were to place the army either on Drummossie Moor behind a zigzag ravine near Dalcross House, or behind the substantial valley of the River Nairn.

The blame for the Jacobites' fighting where they actually did, on Drummossie Moor between the Culloden and Culwhiniach enclosures, is put on John William O'Sullivan as the army's chief of staff, yet O'Sullivan was against fighting in the first place, and the ground he chose corresponded much more to Highland precedent than did the positions advocated by Lord George. Concerning the Dalcross site, O'Sullivan asks us, as people

> that knows the Highlanders, whether a field of battle where there is such an impediment as that ravine was, which is impracticable for man or horse, was proper for Highlanders, whose way of fighting is to go directly sword in hand at the enemy? Any man that served with the Highlanders, knows that they fire but one shot, abandon their firelocks after. If there be any obstruction that hinders them going on the enemy, all is lost; they don't like to be exposed to the enemy's fire, nor can they resist it, not being trained to charge [i.e. 'fire'] as fast as regular troops, especially the English, which are the troops in the world that fires best.[60]

At Falkirk and Culloden there were some last-minute jockeyings for position in order to extract the last advantages from the direction of the wind or minor features of the terrain, and at Culloden a cannonade intervened, but once action was finally joined it was invariably violent and short. That is not the same as saying that the Jacobite attack was the product of fury and ignorance. The Jacobites as a whole were better shots than their enemy, but even so, their officers made them hold their fire until the closest possible range. There are few more impressive passages in eighteenth-century tactics than the coolness with which the Jacobites at Falkirk held their fire in the face of three advancing regiments of dragoons, and then, upon command, delivered an aimed salvo to devastating effect.

The first line would then cast its muskets aside, and the chiefs and gentlemen in the first rank would lead the charge with drawn broadswords, closing with the enemy in what are described as wedges or columns. The Chevalier de Johnstone is particularly informative:

When within reach of the enemy's bayonets, bending their left knee, they, by their attitude, cover their bodies with their targets, that receive the thrusts of the bayonets, which they contrive to parry, while at the same time they raise their sword-arm, and strike their adversary. Having once got with their bayonets, into the ranks of the enemy, the soldiers have no longer any means of defending themselves, the fate of the battle is decided in an instant, and the carnage follows; the Highlanders bring down two men at a time, one with their dirk, in the left hand, and another with the sword. The reason assigned by the Highlanders for their custom of throwing their muskets on the ground, is not without force. They say, they embarrass them in their operations, even when slung behind them, and on gaining a battle, they can pick them up again along with the arms of their enemies; but, if they should be beaten, they have no occasion for muskets.[61]

After a battle with the Highlanders there was a guarantee of plentiful grisly sights and horrid smells, what with cloven heads, severed limbs and spilled intestines, but the physical effects were less than would have ensued from an exchange of gunfire. In their battles the Highlanders cut with the edge of their broadswords, and did not thrust with the point – which would have been more lethal, and would have extended their reach. After Culloden the Duke of Cumberland's chief surgeon John Pringle saw 270 redcoat wounded who had been deposited in two malt barns in Inverness. 'There were many cuts with the broadsword, till then uncommon wounds in the hospitals; but these were easily healed, as the openings were large in proportion to the depth, as they bled much at first, and as there were no contusions and *échars* [fragments of cloth], as in gunshot wounds, to obstruct a good digestion.'[62]

What made the Highland charge unique and devastating was that it was initiated by warriors – essentially the chiefs, gentlemen and their relations in the first rank – who had the raw courage to come to close quarters with drawn swords. The contrast with combat on the European mainland was striking. There the battle was decided not by a single throw, but by a process of manoeuvre and attrition which might extend over several hours. There the charge with cold steel was effectively unknown. In all his campaigns against the Prussians, the experienced Austrian officer the Prince de Ligne saw only one episode of hand-to-hand fighting, which was at Moys on 7 September 1757, when the rival forces climbed opposite sides of the same hill and ran into one another at the top.

It is no exaggeration to say that, until the last phase of the rising, Prince

Charles lived on the capital of a few minutes of hand-to-hand fighting at Prestonpans. He and his men were imbued with new confidence, and their supporters in England maintained the psychological effect. On 6 February 1746 the Duke of Richmond commented to the Duke of Newcastle that the redcoats were sure to win if only they stood their ground, 'but indeed if our people run away at the sight of them, they must be beat even by the Westminster scholars. And what did that panic come from? – but from their hearing that these were desperate fellows with broadswords, targets, lochabers, and the Devil knows what, that was eternally preached up by the Scotch Jacobites, even at White's and St James's. Stuff actually fit to frighten nothing but old men and children'.[63] The Hanoverians were going to run away again at Falkirk eleven days later.

If the function of cavalry had been to fight other mounted troops, then the record of the Jacobite horse would have been accounted a dismal failure. The one opportunity of the sort came at Clifton on 18 December 1745, and the hussars declined it by running away. In terms of numbers the Jacobite horsemen were also insignificant, for they amounted to 800 at the most, and considerably less at any given time. The cavalry nevertheless served Prince Charles very well in other respects. His two troops of splendidly turned-out Lifeguards and his other mounted gentlemen gave him the desired element of regal credibility when he entered towns under the critical eye of the citizens. The cavalry as a whole scouted far and wide, brought large areas of territory under contribution in the course of his campaigns and projected panic well to either side of the army's actual line of march.

The story of the Jacobite artillery is probably best related in terms of 'generations'.

❖ Prince Charles had no artillery at all until he captured Cope's ordnance at Prestonpans, which amounted to six 1½-pounder cannon, two royal (full-scale) mortars and two coehorn (light) mortars. Afterwards Captain John Burnet of Campsfield was seen and heard in the park of Holyrood-house, testing the accuracy of the cannon against targets[64]

❖ In October 1745 the French succeeded in landing a mysterious 'octagon' gun of brass, and six light iron 4-pounders of French manufacture, the so-called 'Swedish' guns. On 17 November the Hanoverian informant Mr Alexander Spencer shared a bottle outside Carlisle with two Jacobite officers recently arrived from France, namely Colonel James Grant, and the Captain Burnet already mentioned, and he learned from them that their artillery consisted of 'thirteen pieces, six whereof were taken from

Sir John Cope, six 4-pounders that came from France, one piece that was brought from Blair of Atholl'.[65] From other sources we know that Cope's coehorns from Prestonpans were also taken into England. A little later the same Grant was seen at Lancaster, and was described as 'a serious sort of thinking man, and one would be surprised he should venture on this expedition; he is a Scotchman from somewhere to the north of Montrose, and says he was one of the twelve men sent by the French King a few years ago to ascertain the shape of the earth, he also says, that he fixed the train about seven weeks ago at Dunkirk intended for the expedition against England'.[66]

Lord George Murray had the unenviable responsibility of conveying the artillery over the Shap road during the retreat to Scotland, with the Duke of Cumberland close behind

❖ Meanwhile, on 24 November *La Renommée* grounded in Montrose harbour and landed a small French siege train of two 18-pounders, two 12-pounders, two 9-pounders, as well as a number of ship's cannon (which were formed into a shore battery). The Chevalier de Johnstone suggests that the difficulty of shifting this mass of metal helped to detain Lord John Drummond in Scotland with the forces he was building up there, instead of following Prince Charles into England[67]

❖ The Jacobites captured six pieces of light field artillery from Hawley at Falkirk, but shortly afterwards abandoned the French battering train when they gave up their siege of Stirling Castle. On the subsequent retreat towards Inverness the Jacobites took seventeen cannon with them by way of Blair, and three shots from one of these pieces were enough to reduce Ruthven Barracks on 9 February. Lord George Murray was meanwhile taking the coastal route. He shipped two 8-pounders from Montrose to Inverness, although, at least according to O'Sullivan, he had already been responsible for abandoning four more at Perth. Altogether, about thirteen 8-pounders had been left at that town, along with fourteen light swivel-guns which had been taken from the sloop *Hazard*[68]

❖ At Culloden the Jacobites fielded a reasonably strong and uniform train of eleven 3-pounders and one 4-pounder, which corresponded closely to the number of pieces presented by the Hanoverians.

Many loose ends remain to be tied up, and not just concerning the artillery abandoned at Perth, but the origin of the Jacobite batteries on the Forth at Alloa and Elphinstone Pans, and the kind of ordnance the Jacobites captured at Fort Augustus and brought to their siege of Fort William.

John Burnet stayed behind with the garrison in Carlisle, while James Grant did excellent service until he was disabled at the siege of Fort William. Otherwise the glimpses of the artillery personnel are fragmentary. Several witnesses were willing to accuse the coach-builder William Hall of Perth of making carriages for the Jacobite cannon. This solid craftsman was working in the same cause as the balletic Jean Baptiste Froment of Paris, who had performed at Drury Lane and Covent Garden, and was running a dancing school in Edinburgh in 1745. In the rising, Froment kept constant company with the gunners and the French officers, and was seen at the siege of Carlisle carrying a 6-pounder shot which had been aimed at him from the castle. Later in the campaign he assisted at the Jacobite attacks on Ruthven Barracks and Fort Augustus, and acted as aide-de-camp to Mirabelle de Gordon, a French officer of Scottish descent.[69]

There are also records of offers of specialized help in the early days of the rising. John Finlayson, a maker of mathematical instruments at Edinburgh, informed the Duke of Perth 'that he has made the Art of Fortification and Gunnery his particular study; therefore humbly craving that if it be thought proper to appoint him any officer within ... engineers, cannoneers or conductors he humbly requests to be appointed his charge ... and that he may have proper assistants appointed him so that he may have an opportunity of showing his zeal and readiness and application to His Majesty's service'.[70] The offer was taken up, and we encounter Finlayson again when he was siting the Jacobite artillery at Culloden. He had a respectable complement of cannon, as we have seen, and he positioned his pieces well, but he lacked the 'proper assistants' and was very soon outmatched by well-served pieces of the Royal Artillery. The Jacobite artillery might still have given a better account of itself if it had been commanded by Colonel Grant, who had managed the guns so well in his duels with the Royal Navy on the Forth in the second week of January, but in April was incapacitated by a wound he had sustained at the siege of Fort William.

The Chevalier de Johnstone probably went too far when he claimed that the ordnance was more trouble than it was worth, for a train of some sort was an attribute of a proper army, but he makes the telling point that cannon were useless against the high-perched castles of Edinburgh and Stirling and 'it is only by mortars or by famine that they can be reduced. It is surprising that the Court of France should have been so little acquainted with the peculiarities of Scotland, as to send us cannon instead of mortars, of which we had need for carrying on sieges'.[71]

After they retreated to Scotland the Jacobites put a great deal of effort into reducing the governmental strongholds which still held out there. They succeeded at Ruthven Barracks, old Fort George at Inverness and at Fort Augustus, but failed before Stirling Castle and Fort William. The short-coming again was of proper people to do the work. James Grant was almost the only person with adequate knowledge, and it was particularly unfortunate that the responsibility of besieging Stirling Castle was given to Mirabelle de Gordon, who made a number of inconceivable technical mistakes. The last of the sieges, that of Fort William, was abandoned after it was shown once again 'that it is hard to make Highlanders do the regular duty of a siege, though they are excessively brave in an attack, and when they are allowed to fight in their own way, they are not so much masters of that sedate valour that is necessary to maintain a post, and it is difficult to keep them long in their posts, or even in their quarters, without action'.[72]

CHAPTER 5

Government and Military Forces
in Hanoverian Britain

IN THE HANOVERIAN BRITAIN of the 1740s national leadership had
been largely reduced to the art of political manipulation, the latest instance
being the formation of the Broad Bottom Administration in 1744, in which
the Duke of Newcastle as principal Secretary of State, and his brother Henry
Pelham, had included some of their most persistent critics – Lord Granville
and his associates, and a number of Tories and opposition Whigs. Equilibrium was restored only after Newcastle and Pelham resigned in February
1746, promptly returning after the king (as they calculated he would) got
rid of the troublesome Granville. Meanwhile the response to the Jacobite
rising was less than decisive.

Beyond the capital, successive administrations in London had been
content to see the systems of control decay rather than fall into the hands of
potential political rivals. Many of the English counties were without a lord lieutenant, the individual immediately responsible for local security. Even when
the lord lieutenant (if he existed) and his deputy lieutenants called out the
country militia (p. 133), that body did not have a proper legal status until the

An elderly volunteer with the type of full-bottomed periwig fashionable in his youth

county had borne the expense for a month and Parliament had then agreed to repay the costs. This was a singularly awkward arrangement, in no way fitted to deal with an unexpected emergency and only partially remedied by a law which Parliament passed in November 1745.

By that year the friends of the Protestant settlement were also at a disadvantage in Scotland. For most of the century its interests had been represented effectively enough by the dukes of Argyll through their domi-nating influence over a State Council which sat in Edinburgh under the presidency of Duncan Forbes of Culloden, who was also the President of the chief judicial body (the Court of Session), and who was seconded most energetically by Sir Andrew Fletcher (the Lord Justice Clerk). Duncan Forbes had a thorough understanding of the Highland mentality and owned much credit among the chiefs. These comfortable arrangements were probably the best way of managing Scotland in the absence of the Scottish Parliament (which had voted itself out of existence in 1707) and the Scottish Privy Council (abolished in 1708). Scotland did not have lord lieutenants, such as had been appointed in England since 1715, and after a bitter lesson (p. 565) not even a duke of Argyll would now dare to assume military authority.

The dukes of Argyll counted as 'Opposition' Whigs, by no means devoted to the purposes of the Whig administration reigning in London, and their 'argethian' system was under challenge by the Scottish Whigs of the 'Squadrone' faction (see p. 565), who in 1742 persuaded the government to revive the office of the Secretary of State for Scotland – less to exercise effective control over that land than to deny that authority to the Duke of Argyll. In 1745 the post was held by a Borders laird, the Marquis of Tweeddale, who was gouty, resident in London, and knew nothing of the Highlands. He ignored the warnings that came to him from Archibald, 3rd Duke of Argyll, that the Jacobite rising was to be taken seriously, and by 28 September it was noted that he had 'laid himself open to the severest censures by the manner in which he treated the rebellion; for within this week he spoke of it to two gentlemen ... as a thing no more considerable than the desertion of the Highland Regiment [the Black Watch] in England the summer before last'.[1]

Tweeddale's already battered authority suffered when he put a bounty of £30,000 on Prince Charles's head and nobody came forward to collect it (p. 23). The pressure on him finally became so great that he was compelled to resign early in 1746. 'It is true that no evil intents have been laid to his account, but rather a considerable degree of sleepy complacency. Moreover he recommended a number of men, and especially the Provost of Edinburgh, to His Majesty, as being of unquestionable loyalty, whereas the contrary soon proved to be the case.'[2] Duncan Forbes and Andrew Fletcher were left to take charge of Scottish affairs until the Duke of Cumberland arrived in 1746 and effectively assumed political as well as military leadership.

In such a culture it is hardly surprising that the formal military command had taken so long to resolve. The first two leaders to try conclusions with the Jacobites had done badly. Lieutenant General Sir John Cope, who commanded the forces already garrisoned in Scotland, had left the enemy with an open door to the Lowlands, and was defeated at Prestonpans on 21 September 1745. The veteran Field Marshal George Wade now gathered considerable forces at Newcastle, but he was a burnt-out relic of his once genial and active self, and he was powerless to move his army from the 'wrong' side of the Pennines to stop Prince Charles marching through north-west England in November.

A further Hanoverian army was building up in the English Midlands, and the troops were much in need of the encouragement they received from the king's younger son, William Augustus, Duke of Cumberland, who was appointed to the supreme command in England on 23 November and reached the forces in the Midlands on the 27th. A bulky man, still only in his middle twenties, he had established his reputation for personal courage at Fontenoy and was now seen by the troops as their saviour. 'What contributes to keep up their spirits is the presence of the Duke, who is justly their darling; for they see he does whatever the meanest of them does, and goes through as much fatigue.'[3]

On 20 December the Jacobite army escaped to Scotland almost intact, after which the duke returned to London. In his absence the command passed to the quirky and sadistic Lieutenant General Henry Hawley, whom the Jacobites defeated in humiliating circumstances at Falkirk on 17 January 1746. Cumberland therefore had to mount a further rescue operation when he returned, and he initiated the period of training, planning and logistic preparation that helped to make the ensuing campaign of Culloden so short and decisive. Trooper Enoch Bradshaw of Cobham's Dragoons testified afterwards: 'I pray to God our Young Hero is preserved to be a second deliverer to Church and State, he being the darling of humankind ... I say, down on your knees all England, and after praising God who gives victory, pray for the Young British Hero'.[4]

The Question of Legality

The wavering of the Newcastle administration was notorious. It is interesting therefore to find it so firm on the central question of denying the Jacobites any right to be considered lawful belligerents. The issue was first raised by Field Marshal Wade, when in the middle of December he refused to allow the Jacobite Lord John Drummond to initiate a parley. The Duke of Newcastle wrote to congratulate him on his stance.[5]

On 30 December 1745 the first formed body of Jacobites fell into Hanoverian hands when Hamilton and Townley surrendered Carlisle. Still unaware of the outcome, the Duke of Newcastle wrote to Cumberland that it would be a sad waste to lose good troops to reduce such wretched men, and that the king therefore authorized him to offer them surrender 'on condition of their being all to be transported to the West Indies'.[6] This in itself would have been a virtual death sentence, and the letter crossed with one of Cumberland's which showed that he was not going to be at all backward in this respect: 'I wish I could have blooded the soldiers with these villains, but it would have cost us many a brave man and it comes to the same end, as they have no sort of claim to the King's mercy, and I sincerely hope will meet with none'.[7]

In such a way the Hanoverian political and military leaders had resolved the question of legality to their own satisfaction. They had to address the problem again when a powerful contingent of 6,000 hired Hessian troops arrived on the theatre of operations in March 1746. A Hessian hussar was captured on the 30th in the course of the skirmishing south of the Pass of Killiecrankie. 'He was a Swede by birth,' wrote Lord George Murray, 'and spoke very good Latin – was a gentleman, and had formerly been a lieutenant. As he said he did not expect any quarter (for hussars seldom give it), he was surprised when he found himself so well treated. I sent him back to the Prince of Hesse, desiring to know if he intended to have a cartel settled; but I had no answer. The Swede asked me if he must return [i.e. back from the Hessians] I told him not, except the Prince of Hesse sent him. He went away very well pleased.'[8]

In the message carried by the hussar, Lord George desired to know of Prince Friedrich of Hesse 'on what footing Your Grace proposes making war in these Kingdoms, and whether you would incline (as we do) to have a Cartel settled'.[9] He was referring to the civilized practices of war on the continent of Europe, where amicable exchanges of prisoners were negotiated by periodic agreements ('cartels'). Prince Friedrich forwarded the letter to the

Duke of Cumberland on 31 March, and desired to know how to reply. He mentioned that the hussar had been very well treated.[10] Cumberland was furious, and not just because in the course of his letter Lord George had referred to the king as 'the Elector', but because the Jacobites were putting themselves forward as belligerents within the understanding of international law. Cumberland continued to regard Jacobites who came within his power as rebels who were to be shot on the spot, or reserved for incarceration, transportation or later execution.

The Hanoverian thinking on legality was harsh, but it was only to be expected of a usurping dynasty which had been given a big fright, and could not afford to abate in the slightest its claim to lawful governance. Any weakening on that point would weaken the king's authority not only in the country at large but in the army itself. The Jacobite agent Laurence Wolfe reported in France that he had been 'personally assured that above 200 officers then in London were ready to throw up their commissions and go over to the Prince in case he advanced near London'.[11] Our first inclination must be to dismiss this assertion as being designed to bolster French support for the cause, but it has surprising support from the impeccably Whiggish Lady Jane Nimmo, who was in Edinburgh when the Duke of Cumberland stopped on his way to resume command in 1746. It made her tremble for his life when she considered 'how many of his own officers are Jacobites'.[12]

Signs of dissent in the other ranks drew down terrible punishment. News was sent from York on 21 October 1745 that the Royal Scots had arrived at Pontefract, and 'there was one of the soldiers had a thousand stripes given him … for drinking the Pretender's health, and for saying that half the regiment would run away and join him, if they were sent to engage; he was almost cut to pieces, none showing him any mercy'.[13]

All the same, a number of identifiable groupings within the British forces lent themselves more than willingly to putting Cumberland's desires into effect:

❖ Lieutenant General Henry ('Hangman') Hawley represented a pronounced strain of jocular savagery among the senior regular officers. When he had the remains of one of his executed deserters hanging in his tent (sources conflict as to whether this was the skeleton or the hide), as an example to his own soldiers, he was going to extend no particular leniency to real or suspected rebels. Old loons like Lieutenant General Joshua Guest or Lieutenant Colonel Sir Andrew Agnew actually excelled him in irascible eccentricity, though no outstanding atrocities were attached to their reputation

❖ The names of Battereau, Dejean, Durand and the two Ligoniers indicated
   how well officers of Huguenot descent were also lodged in the higher
   reaches of the officer corps. Like their counterparts in Prussia, many of
   them were even now inveterate enemies of anything that smacked of
   Popery. It was no coincidence that Major John Lafansille was responsible
   for devastating the Episcopalian meeting houses in Strathmore, and that a
   Captain Trapaud was a commander of the execution squads that roamed
   the field of Culloden after the battle

❖ Nothing, however, can compare with the enthusiastic ferocity displayed
   by a quartet of officers in the subjugation of the Western Highlands and
   the islands. The gentlemen in question were Major William Lockhart of
   Cholmondeley's 34th, Captain Caroline Frederick Scott of Guise's 6th,
   and two captains of the Royal Navy – John Fergussone, commander of
   the sloop *Furnace*, and Robert Duff of Logie, the commander of the
   sloop *Terror*. What is significant is that they were all Lowland Scots.

In contrast the greatest misgivings concerning the policy of repression were
expressed by the Scotsmen who knew the Highlands best, and had been the
most active in upholding the government's interests when they had been
the most under threat – Duncan Forbes of Culloden, Sir Andrew Fletcher,
Lord Loudoun and Major General Campbell of Mamore.

There are no grounds for the oft-repeated story that Captain James
Wolfe defied the Duke of Cumberland when he was ordered to shoot the
stricken Fraser of Inverallochy at Culloden. Compassion for the beaten enemy
was difficult to find among the English officers, but what concerned them
closely was their honour as individual gentlemen. The distinction between
public and private honour was well understood at the time, and the notion had
just been explained in its military context in the *Old England Journal*, which
drew attention to the 'importance of that *good faith*, to which an enemy as
well as a friend is entitled, and without which war becomes *butchery*, and its
seat only the *larger charnel-house of death*'.[14] From the day of Prestonpans
onwards Prince Charles had extended all possible consideration to the
Hanoverian officers who became his prisoners, the first batch of whom signed
an 'Obligation' on 28 September 1745 to repair to their first place of open
detention at Perth; they were to hold themselves there on their word of
honour, and afterwards a number of officers were left free to go to places of
their own choosing, as long as they remained north of the Tay. The same
freedoms were extended as a matter of course to the prisoners taken in later
actions.

Two officers of Lee's 55th nevertheless broke their parole and made their way to Berwick. The practice received official sanction from Wade in respect of the surrendered Hanoverian garrison in Carlisle, and from the Duke of Cumberland, who on setting out for Scotland for the last time sent word to all the captives that they were not bound by any pledges they might have given to the rebels. This applied most immediately to the officers who had been captured at Prestonpans, and were snatched by rescue parties from their place of abode in Glamis Castle, Leslie, Coupar Angus and other locations almost immediately after the battle of Falkirk.

Major Lockhart, already mentioned, who had been wounded and captured at Falkirk, was a personal enemy of the Jacobites, and it is not surprising that he considered himself free to break his parole a little later. However, the 'self-ransomed' prisoners also comprised men of seemingly good repute like the great piper Donald Ban MacCrimmon (again captured at Falkirk, and afterwards killed at Moy), and the Lieutenant Colonel Charles Whitefoord who is depicted in a virtuous light as 'Captain Talbot' in Scott's *Waverley*.

What troubled thinking officers the most was that they had been forced to break the promises they had tendered to their enemies, whether rebels or not. There had been a distinctly qualified welcome at Berwick for those two officers who had broken their parole after Prestonpans.[15] Major John Severin had been 'liberated' from Forfar against his will, and after he had been spirited back to Edinburgh he hastened to explain that he and many of his fellows feared that

> those who are not acquainted with the particulars may imagine it a contrivance of our own, and such a reflection would be equally unjust, and hurtful to us. It is a very nice point to know how some of us here are to behave, [having] been permitted to reside at places of our own choosing, on our paroles, without other guard, and in reach of being rescued at any time. I confess that I have and believe many more us have been rendered more uneasy for fear of the censure of the world, on this event, that we were during the time we were within their power.[16]

The Chevalier de Johnstone did not present the whole picture when he claimed that 'to the eternal disgrace of the English officers, there were only four who refused to accept the absolution of the Duke of Cumberland, viz. Sir Peter Halkett, lieutenant colonel of Lee's Regiment, taken at the battle of Gladsmuir [Prestonpans], and Mr Ross, son of Lord Ross, with two other officers, who replied, "That he was master of their commissions, but not of their probity and honour"'.[17]

The Land Forces

The Regular Army

In one way or another almost every problem confronting the British Army in the '45 turned on the entirely unfamiliar one of fighting a war in its own country. The issues concerned legality, as just mentioned, and also the deployment and character of the army, its intelligence, its logistics and its tactics.

The Hanoverian effort against the rising involved 13,000 British troops and 6,000 Hessians, not to mention the contingent of hired Dutch and Swiss which came and went without ever having come in sight of the enemy. As for the maintenance of public security in general, the government depended on the vigilance of its representatives on the spot; namely the country lord lieutenants and deputy lieutenants, the magistrates, the village constables, and even the postmasters – who in 1745 became London's first line of intelligence.

The control of violence – at least to a certain level – permitted the government to draw on the financial resources of the nation in a most efficient way. The principal sources of revenue in 1745 were the Customs (on foreign imports), the Cess or land tax (about 30 per cent of the total) which was collected through the agency of local men of standing, and the much-resented Excise (more than 40 per cent) which was raised on beer, malt, hops, soap, candles and leather, and assessed and collected by some ferociously busy government officials. Nobody expected that invaders would arrive on the scene, claim royal authority and exploit the apparatus for themselves.

The regular forces stationed in Britain in the late summer of 1745 were therefore in no way prepared to fight a shooting war. Out of Cope's army at Prestonpans, the two regiments of dragoons (Gardiner's and Hamilton's) had seen no active service since they had been raised in Ireland in 1715, and warlike experience among the infantry was confined to a few men in the two companies fielded by Guise's 6th. Experience was therefore at a premium, and on 31 December Lieutenant General Hawley urged how important it was to move the five veteran battalions of Barrell's, Pulteney's, Bligh's, Campbell's and Sempill's from Newcastle to Scotland, 'though 'tis true two of them are all Scotch men, and the Royals who are [already] gone are two-thirds Highlanders, whom I had rather have been without'. He was much in need of dragoons, for the regiments of Gardiner and Hamilton were recruited from untrustworthy Irishmen and were much depleted and demoralized by their experiences at Prestonpans and elsewhere.[18]

The unit strengths of the forces in any case ran below establishment, and thus the Duke of Richmond could write to His Grace of Newcastle from Lichfield on 25 November that the numbers available were not equal to defending the country, 'and I had always thought so, for I always reckoned that if we fight 500 men a battalion it is all that can be done'.[19] At Culloden the average reached just 427 of all ranks. It is also worth noting that the British regiments engaged in the '45 were effectively on a single-battalion establishment, and that the terms 'battalion' and 'regiment' were used indiscriminately.

The officer corps of the regular army was on the whole good at its work. The landed gentry predominated in the upper ranks, as was only proper in the society of the time. Commissions and promotions were normally obtained by purchase, but the practice was not universal; good men as well as bad could buy their way upwards, which made a useful foil to the deadening principle of advance through seniority. Professional competence was high, at least in the veteran regiments, and ambitious officers read avidly in the military literature that was on sale.

The ranks were filled largely by 'volunteers', if we can apply that term to people who were driven by the desperate circumstances of their civilian lives. They were supplemented by numbers of the notorious Vestry Men, who were criminals consigned to military service by the magistrates, and who lent themselves willingly to the atrocities authorized by the higher command in the course of the operations.

The Jacobite Highlanders had the inherent advantages of adroitness, and an acquaintance since boyhood with danger and the use of arms, and the men in the Jacobite regiments as a whole fought alongside relations and friends, or at least familiar faces, and under the direction of officers whom they had known as their masters in civilian life. By contrast, the redcoats were constantly moved between platoons. Their qualities came rather from subjection to discipline, habituation to set drills and attachment to a wider *esprit de corps*. Victory by a broadsword wielded by a Highlander was 'ascribed to personal valour', whereas 'the execution performed by firearms is too general to give the honour to any one agent'.[20] In almost Wellingtonian phrases Edmund Burt explains that the ploughmen from the English clays were lumpish creatures, 'but those very men, in a short time after they are enlisted into the army, erect their bodies, change their clownish gait, and become smart fellows'.[21] By the spring of 1746 there were no hiding places in the Highlands that were not accessible to the redcoats, who were now fully conditioned to rough going, a point worth considering when the debate turns to the possibility of the Jacobites maintaining a guerrilla-type resistance over the long term.

The English Militia and Volunteers

The difficulty of forming a coherent response to the Jacobite threat to England was augmented, if anything, by the plethora of ways in which assistance might be given to the regular army. Out of all these auxiliary units only a very few – like Kingston's Light Horse or Oglethorpe's command – took any direct role, while the others are usually glimpsed only when they were trying to put all the distance they could between themselves and the Jacobites.

Since Tudor times the county militia had been supposed to provide the first line of support to the regulars, and on 5 September 1745 it was decided to call out the militia of the four northernmost counties, namely Northumberland, Durham, Cumberland and Westmorland. Legal framework was one thing, practical arrangements quite another. The conservative 'county' interest among the squires had been attracted to the idea of the militia, as a counterbalance to the hated and distrusted standing army, but they had done little to keep it alive as an effective organization, and it was November before Parliament agreed to foot the bills for the mobilization – in the same month Prince Charles broke into England. The militias of Cumberland and Westmorland scarcely figure in the events, apart from the companies in Carlisle. In Lancashire two committed Whigs, Lord Derby and Sir Henry Hoghton, succeeded in mobilizing the county militia after a fashion, but Lord Derby disbanded it again in the face of the advancing Jacobites, whereupon the main concern of the authorities was how to keep its weapons out of the hands of the enemy. The heroes of the militia were therefore pulled back to Liverpool and their arms put on board ship for safekeeping.

Whiggish magnates and towns were in the meantime looking for a more immediate way of registering their enthusiasm with the government. This they found in setting up regiments of locally recruited volunteers, generally termed the 'Blues' after the colour of their coats, which were provided by their paymasters, while their weapons were supposed to be furnished by the government. The first proposal was made by the Duke of Devonshire as (confusingly) the Lord Lieutenant of Derbyshire, and the Derbyshire Blues became the model for the Blues of the North and West Ridings of Yorkshire (the largest county in England), and ultimately for all the regiments of the kind which were raised by the gentry, towns and loyal county Associations.

The Blues were no kind of troops to put in the direct way of the Jacobites, if the experience of the fleeing Derbyshire Blues was anything to go by, but where the danger was less acute, as in County Durham, the Blues made themselves useful by checking the credentials of travellers and searching the houses of suspected Jacobites. The units raised under the aegis of Brigadier General James Oglethorpe were a special case. As the founder of the colony of Georgia (and planner of the delightful town of Savannah), Oglethorpe had raised two troops of mounted rangers for service across the Atlantic, now available for use against the Jacobites. At a clamorous meeting in York on 24 September 1745 a number of fox-hunting gentlemen had the inspiration of forming a troop of horse.[22] The Yorkshire Hunters, Oglethorpe at their head, reached Newcastle on 25 October and 'on their entering the town they drew their swords, marched in good order with colours flying, trumpets blowing, and were welcomed to the town by the ringing of bells and other demonstrations of joy'.[23]

The Duke of Bedford gave the lead to fourteen or so peers in a far more grandiose enterprise, that of raising full regiments that were supposed to bear comparison with the regulars. A Jacobite agent reported that 'The army takes the raising of these new regiments very much amiss, for the officers who have been appointed to them have been placed on a footing with the regular officers, and because the recruiting has interfered with that of the army, due to the higher pay of the new troops'.[24] The first and effectively the only regiment of the new infantry to arrive with the field army was Bedford's, which came to Lichfield at the end of November 1745 and made an unfortunate impression, 'for this regiment was represented to be the forwardest of them, yet neither officers nor men know what they are about. So how they will do before an enemy, God only knows'.[25] Curiously, both Oglethorpe and Bedford were known to have Jacobite sympathies, which indicates how difficult it is to pin down allegiance in the England of the 1740s. The only one of the new regiments to make an impression was the Duke of Kingston's Light Horse (the 10th Horse). It was an excellent unit, recruited from Nottingham butchers who knew both how to keep animals in good condition and how to chop up meat.

In the England as constituted at that period there was no possibility of employing unformed countryfolk. When the Duke of Cumberland closed in on Carlisle in December 1745 'a great number of the people came out of the country to assist the King's army with clubs and staves, and such other weapons as they had: the game laws forbidding the use of firearms. The countrymen being most of them no use, and their number being about

10,000, His Royal Highness ordered all of them to return home, except a few who employed in cutting fascines for the batteries'.[26] In any case their enthusiasm was much exaggerated.

The Naval Forces

On paper the British Royal Navy in 1745 and 1746 ought to have been in a position to bring superior force to bear on its enemies, but was unable to bar completely the access to home waters to those France, Spanish or even New England skippers who were bent on bringing help to the Jacobites in various forms. Five main classes of Royal Navy vessels come under consideration:

❖ We hear little of the three types of line-of-battle ships, namely the three-decker First Rates (100 guns), the three-decker Second Rates (90 guns), or the Third Rates (three decks with 80 guns; two decks with 70 guns). These ships formed the backbone of the Western Squadron, which was stationed in Plymouth and anchorages in the West Country, and which acted as a check on the corresponding blue-water fleets of France and Spain. They were over-gunned even for their considerable bulk, difficult to man, and demanded deep water and considerable sea room, neither of which was available in the Channel narrows and the North Sea

❖ The largest British warships capable of operating in the narrow seas were the two-decker Fourth Rates (50 and 58 guns), typified by the *Gloucester*, a 58-gun ship on the Establishment of 1741, which served as Byng's flagship in the blockade of north-eastern Scotland

❖ The Fifth Rates comprised ships of 40 or 44 guns, like the 40-gun *Eltham* and *Milford*, which could outmatch even the largest of the French blockade-runners, though (as Captain Hanway discovered at Montrose) it was dangerous to pursue them too close inshore

❖ The last of the rates, the Sixth, took in two-decker 20- and 24-gun ships. Prominent roles were taken by the *Glasgow*, *Greyhound*, *Scarborough* and *Sheerness*, and the unfortunate *Fox* (wrecked at Dunbar). They were small and agile enough to venture among the Orkney Islands or the lochs and islets of the Western Highlands. They carried little of their armament on the lower gun-deck and it was the closing in of that deck that later produced the true frigate

❖ The workhorses of the Royal Navy in the inshore waters remained the two main types of unrated two-masted vessels – the sloops and the stoutly built adapted bomb vessels. They were tricky to handle, and (unlike the Sixth Rates) they had no continuous lower deck, but in compensation they had a large open deck space for their size and drew only between 9 and 12 feet of water. The record shows that the sloops could ground on sand or mud without coming to harm. The most celebrated of the unrated vessels in the '45 was to be the *Hazard*, a 12-gun snow-rigged sloop of the *Otter* class, and a sister-ship of the *Vulture* which was to do battle with the Jacobite shore batteries in the upper Forth. *Hazard* was captured by the Jacobites at Montrose, and enjoyed a brief but glorious career as *Le Prince Charles*. The unrated craft operated in conditions of general but not absolute British naval superiority, and Prince Charles's confidant Sir Thomas Sheridan indicated that 'if, instead of small craft they [the French] sent ships of 30 or 40 guns, they would be able to withstand anything, for the English never send large ones into these waters'.[27] Sheridan's point was proved on 3 May 1746, when two powerful French privateers defeated a small British flotilla in Loch nan Uamh (p. 365).

Intelligence

Major General Humphrey Bland was the author of the army's tactical bible, *A Treatise of Military Discipline*. The latest edition had been that published in Dublin two years before Cope's defeat at Prestonpans, and in the book the army could have read that there was 'not any thing in which an officer shows the want of conduct so much, as in suffering himself to be surprised, either upon his post, or in marching with a body of men under his command, without being prepared to make a proper defence, and not having taken the necessary precautions to prevent it'.[28]

The best safeguard against being taken unawares is good information, and this was rarely at the generals' disposal. By far the greatest effort of the Hanoverians concerning intelligence was directed at sniffing out disloyalty; in other words it was expended in a direction which was of little guidance in immediate military operations. When the Jacobites had still not ventured out of Scotland, the most consistently reliable channel of information was that initiated by John Goldie, a magistrate of Dumfries, who extracted whatever he considered of use from correspondence and newspapers and forwarded it to his friend, the Rev. John Waugh, Prebendary of Carlisle Cathedral, who sent it on to London. Once Prince Charles was marching through England the local postmasters and other well-wishers of the government forwarded a great mass of observations to the civil and military authorities. The information was trustworthy enough regarding the number and appearance of the Jacobites, but almost totally inaccurate when it concerned their likely moves. As for the directly employed spies, Roger Vere was captured by the Jacobites near Newcastle under Lyme, but Dudley Bradstreet worked to deadly effect when he intervened at a decisive moment at the Jacobite council at Derby on 5 December 1745.

The intelligence horizon clouded over once again when the theatre of operations returned to Scotland. Lieutenant General Hawley wrote to the Duke of Newcastle from Edinburgh on 7 January 1746 that 'all the intelligence I have yet learned by Lord Justice Clerk, and other gentlemen who are so zealous, is so unmilitary, the account varies so much every hour, and proves too often false, that I can depend on nothing'.[29]

The Hanoverian senior commanders were their own worst enemies in this regard, for their brutal ways were not such as to encourage reliable informants. The loyal schoolmaster Peter M'conachy had good grounds for believing that John Roy Stuart was planning a surprise. Lord Albemarle therefore placed his troops on alert for three days and nights, which came to Stuart's ears, but when no attack materialized Albemarle sent M'conachy to the Duke of Cumberland to determine his punishment. M'conachy was tied to a cart, 'stripped to the waist, with a label tied about his neck, specifying his crime, and … whipped for spreading false reports by the youngest drummer of each regiment, from the south end quite through the town of Strathbogie [Huntly]'.[30]

In a wider context the assessments were flawed because most of the hostile observers fell into the habit of regarding Prince Charles's army as a mob of degenerate Highlanders. The style was set by what was seen and told of Prestonpans. The Jacobite officers were described as fanatical and deluded individuals, like the mortally wounded Cameron whose father had been killed at Sheriffmuir, and who in turn asked for his sword to be put into the hand of his 12-year-old son, 'so deeply is this evil rooted in the Highlanders!'[31] The Jacobites accepted the offer of the local minister's son, Alexander Carlyle, to help to take care of the wounded, whom he describes as being in general 'of low stature and dirty, and of a contemptible appearance … this view I had of the rebel army confirmed me in the prepossession that nothing but the weakest and most unaccountable bad conduct on our part could have possibly given them the victory'.[32]

The last comment is significant, for it was difficult for many of the supporters of the government to reconcile themselves to the contrast between the reverses suffered by their forces and the appearance of the people who had inflicted them.[33] Denying all genuine military attributes to the Jacobites, their enemies could ascribe the defeats of the Hanoverian forces only to the failures of their own generals. These recriminations were damaging in themselves, and left their troops as open as ever to be caught at a disadvantage the next time, like Lieutenant General Hawley's army at Falkirk on 17 January 1746. He would have done well to read and heed 'Agricola' in the *Old England Journal*, who confessed that he and his friends had laughed at the presumption of the rebels before Prestonpans. What happened there should have taught them better, 'yet the fresh accounts we had in the papers of the dissensions and mutinies of the rebels kept us from being dismayed'. Now he was aware 'that nothing perhaps has so effectually aided the rebels' cause as those reports'.[34]

Logistics and Operational Mobility

The Hanoverian–British Army's experience and aptitude in warfare derived largely from campaigning on the European mainland, where its 'symmetrical' enemies employed much the same weapons and tactics. In matters logistic the generals took it for granted that they could rely on experienced contractors, ample and secure bases, an adequate road network (barring a few regions like the Spessart Hills), the facility of transporting bulky commodities by canal or along long stretches of navigable river, and a settled and compliant population which had been used to accommodating generations of soldiers. None of these conditions applied in Britain, where even the billeting of troops on private houses was prohibited by law.

The difficulties were compounded almost beyond measure by having to sustain what became a prolonged winter campaign. This point can hardly be stressed strongly enough, for conventional armies habitually went into winter quarters in November at the latest, and emerged into the field only in May, by which time the grass was growing, thus helping to alleviate the dependence on fodder, which was bulky and expensive, but essential to feed not only the horses of the cavalry, but those which transported the artillery and the supplies. Frederick of Prussia wrote on the subject: 'Winter campaigns ruin your troops for a number of reasons – the sickness they cause, and the never-ending action which prevents you bringing them up to strength, furnishing them with new uniforms, or replenishing the military stores and provisions'.[35] The Duke of Cumberland was therefore taking a gamble when

he took to the field in April 1746. That he finished his campaign victori-
ously just over a week later was impressive by any standard.

Cumberland's achievement must be measured against the logistic crisis
of the governmental forces earlier in the rising. As early as 3 October 1745
information came to the Duke of Newcastle that 'they [the Jacobites] want
a winter campaign, for their men are able to bear hardship'.[36] Over the weeks
justified concerns were raised for the army of Field Marshal Wade, which
was being ruined by marches and counter-marches in the snow east of the
Pennines, without ever getting to grips with the enemy. The Lord Justice
Clerk wrote from Edinburgh to the Duke of Newcastle that he was 'in great
pains about Mr Wade's army, exposed to bad weather, long and cold nights,
while the rebels are under cover'.[37]

The newly appointed Duke of Cumberland opened the campaign of the
second Hanoverian army from the fat lands of the English Midlands, but he
had to confess in 6 December that

> as this is my first winter campaign I can only judge by what others of more
> experience say and by what I have read, but this beginning has been as severe
> as it is possible to conceive, and every man has worn [out] one if not two
> pairs of shoes since the beginning of this march. I have been forced to
> promise them this day a pair of stockings and shoes each man, which I hope
> the King will not disapprove of. I have just received advice that the flannel
> waistcoats have arrived at Coventry.[38]

This happened to be the day when the Jacobites retreated from Derby and
thus conceded the initiative to him. Until then his dilemma had been that, by
ignoring the legalities, he could shelter his men well enough in the scattered
villages and little towns but would then be unable to concentrate them in
time to fight; conversely he could hold his men together in camp and see
them succumb to the intense cold. In this pastoral country there was no
straw available to spread on the ground inside the tents, and the troops had
no protection from the frosty ground except their coats.

Cumberland took over the command in Scotland from the luckless
Hawley early in 1746, but the difficulty of getting supplies together detained
him at Perth and then for a much longer time at Aberdeen. Indeed the move
to Aberdeen in the first place had been made possible only after Cumberland
had put pressure on the contractor Gomes Serra to lay in a full two-weeks'
worth of flour. Cumberland had to improvise a great deal on the spot, and he
was helped throughout by Andrew Fletcher, the Lord Justice Clerk, who
was 'of the utmost service to us here not only in obliging the country

to find us everything that may be necessary, but with his advice, and in being indefatigable in whatever may serve the troops'.[39]

For the final advance from Aberdeen in April the duke chose a route up the eastern coast, which enabled him to draw supplies from the squadron of Commodore Thomas Smith, and he arranged to have fresh bread baked for his army as it moved. He was rewarded by the brief and decisive campaign of Culloden. Trooper Enoch Bradshaw could say enough in his praise, 'for we had certainly been all lost for want of food, had it not been for his care to bring ovens and bakers with him'.[40]

Tactics

The British foot soldiers were schooled in the tactics which made for proficiency on the open battlefields of continental Europe, where infantry fights were resolved by a contest of attrition between rival lines which stood as little as 30 yards apart, and where discipline, steadiness and a high sustained rate of fire (up to three rounds a minute in the case of the British infantry) were the things that made for victory. The basics had been established in the wars of Marlborough and, when the veterans were leaving the service or dying out, Humphrey Bland committed the practical details to paper in his *Treatise of Military Discipline*, which went through many editions after its first publication in 1728 and was reproduced almost unchanged in the first official drill regulations.

In essence the British formed up for combat three ranks (rows) deep, the files being slightly staggered so that each man was supposed to have a clear shot at the enemy. For the purposes of fire the first ranks sank to the right knee, the second crouched forward, and the third stood upright. With very few exceptions the regiments consisted of a single battalion, a unit which could vary in strength from less than 400 to more than 600 of all ranks. The troops were broken up into eighteen tactical platoons (including the two small platoons of grenadiers), and these in turn were grouped into three 'firings' of platoons and a reserve. The platoons of each designated 'firing' were to discharge at the same time, so that volleys were supposed to thunder forth from different parts of the line every six or seven seconds. This amongst other things was intended to deter cavalry, which might have rushed in during the awkward interval of twenty seconds' reloading that would have supervened if everyone had fired simultaneously.

A number of details will strike us as being particularly awkward. The troops marched on a frontage which was inconveniently wide for broken terrain (p. 117), and which must have involved whole sets of files being detached from their sub-units, and reinserted when the going got better. Out of contact with the enemy, the men lived in ten administrative companies which were reshuffled for operations into platoons in the way just described. Except for the grenadiers (whose company was divided neatly into two platoons), the men therefore had no guarantee that they would be fighting alongside their everyday comrades.

Even the best of troops found it difficult to keep up more than a very few of the volleys by 'firings', and it was completely beyond men who were as untrained and frightened as were those of the Hanoverians in the early months of the rising. In August 1745 affairs were still in a state of tactical suspense, for 'they [the Jacobites] will not as yet, until they can gather more men, venture to fight with Sir John [Cope] on fair fields, and he is not able to attack them in their passes or strongholds, without Highlanders to flank them and climb the hills'.[41] Nothing prepared the Hanoverian troops for the experience at Prestonpans on 21 September. Such training as they had was for combat against a 'sensible' enemy, not one willing to cut his way through their ranks with cold steel. 'They were made to believe the Highlanders would only give one fire, and then run off, but when they saw their behaviour a panic seized the whole army ... Our men complain that they wanted their swords, which had all been left at Stirling; but if they could not defend themselves with screwed bayonets, the swords, or rather cutlasses, used in the army, would have stood them in little stead.'[42]

In times past the Roman consul Flaminius had been able to meet the onset of the wild Gauls by arranging his first rank in a kneeling posture behind the wall of their shields, while the veteran *principes* in the second rank thrust with their spears over the top. By 1746 the British too began to realize that they must take special measures against the northern warriors, and on 12 January, five days before the battle of Falkirk, Lieutenant General Hawley issued a tactical directive to the army which tried to persuade the troops that the sure way to demolish the rebels was to wait until the charging mass was just ten or twelve paces away, after which the third rank was to open fire, followed by the second and the first. That was asking a great deal of human nature, and Hawley could hardly have encouraged the men when he told them that if they opened fire any earlier they were as good as dead.[43]

The Duke of Cumberland's variant is well known. He offered the troops not just the resort of fire, but that of a new use of the bayonet, whereby the individual man thrust not to his front, which would have been turned aside by his immediate opponent's target shield, but diagonally to the right, whereby he would catch a Jacobite on the unprotected sword side. This tactic may not actually have been employed in the event, for it was complicated in itself, and most of the Highlanders had in any case cast aside their targets before the encounter. The true value of Cumberland's drill was probably in building mutual trust among the troops, for the bayonet, like the pike, was a collective weapon and deadly when wielded in concert. As employed by the redcoats for close-quarter combat at this period, the musket was held not in the later underhand style but chest-high with the right hand behind the butt. The posture was not easy to maintain for a long time, for the whole weight of the weapon was taken by the extended left hand; in compensation the redcoats had an important advantage in reach over the Highlanders with their broadswords, an advantage increased by the Highlanders' habit of hacking with the edge rather than thrusting with the point. Moreover the slim bayonet had great penetrating power, and if the blade did not kill the man on the spot its triangular section left a wound that was almost impossible to sew up.

The little Hanoverian regiments of horse were organized in six troops, grouped by twos or threes into two or three squadrons. When a full three squadrons were available, they were usually deployed with two up and the third in reserve. The cavalry worked to devastating effect at Culloden, where it was mostly a question of cutting down fugitive foot soldiers. Until then its showing had been dismal. It had been possible to blame the débâcle at Prestonpans on the fact that the two regiments of dragoons (Gardiner's and Hamilton's) had been raised in Ireland and were reputed to contain a large number of Irish Catholics. Further shortcomings came to light at Clifton on 18 December 1745, and one of them was that the British cavalry, almost alone in Europe, clung to the earlier concept of dragoons as mounted infantry, expected to fight on foot as well as horseback. The dragoons of 1745 did neither particularly well, and at Clifton they were at a disadvantage when they clumped forward in their heavy boots and were ordered to open fire at a range that was almost certainly too great for their carbines. Something much worse befell the horse at Falkirk early the next year, where the first attack was broken in the same style as at Prestonpans.

There were two underlying reasons for this consistently appalling performance. One was that only the dragoons and light horse had the speed to match the fast-moving Jacobites, and they consequently came up with them before the rest of the forces arrived. Moreover the practice of 'advancing the cavalry before the foot', as Bland put it, was part and parcel of the penchant of the fox-hunting British for flinging in their mobile forces with little or no support from the other arms, as witness the attack of Lord Uxbridge at Waterloo (18 June 1815), the charge of the Light Brigade at Balaclava (25 October 1854) and the advance of British tanks in Operation Goodwood (18 July 1944).

In 1746, at least, the high command finally drew the appropriate conclusions. In the final campaign the Hanoverian forces marched in a systematic and cautious way, as a coherent whole, and the horse were held back until artillery and infantry had done their work. Cumberland, unlike Hawley, understood that troops responded better to judicious praise than to hangings and floggings, and Trooper Bradshaw recalls how he and his fellows were heartened by the duke's way of calling them (with no good reason) 'Cobham's Heroes'.[44]

The story of the artillery is roughly comparable. To begin with both the Hanoverians and the Jacobites had to contend with the problems of putting together trains of artillery, moving them across difficult ground, and finding good men to direct and serve them. The Duke of Richmond had to write on 7 December 1745 that 'the carriages of the artillery are so disabled in these cursed roads that I am very much afraid we shall have little, or rather no help from it'.[45] This was from Coventry in the English Midlands, which was not even within sight of the southernmost outliers of the Pennines. There was no artillery at hand at Clifton, while at Falkirk the guns were abandoned on the hill slopes without having fired a shot. Even at Culloden the cannon were puny 3-pounders and 1½-pounders, and did not begin to compare with the firepower that could be brought together on the Continent (Frederick of Prussia had fifty-five howitzers and 12-pounder cannon in a single battery at Burkersdorf on 21 July 1762). The genuine advance, and the one which gave the crucial advantage over the Jacobites, was in the matter of personnel. At Prestonpans and again at Falkirk both the artillery trains and the gun detachments were improvised, whereas at Culloden the ordnance was directed and served by the Royal Artillery.

One technical curiosity relates to the British habit of using siege mortars for action in the open field in their Scottish campaigns. The weapons in question were little coehorns (devised by the Dutch engineer Menno Van Coehorn in the seventeenth century). Originally intended to be set up in the forward trenches, the Hanoverians used them in the howitzer role at both Glenshiel in 1719 and Culloden in 1746. Such an employment of the coehorns was unknown on the continent of Europe, but it made a lot of sense in difficult country, for these stubby little weapons were

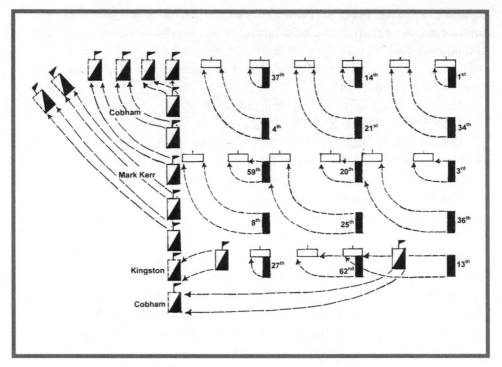

Cumberland's advance to Culloden in multiple columns

economical in powder, and with their flat beds could be transported readily on ordinary carts and lifted by a handful of men. Lord Cathcart's map of Culloden shows that on that field the coehorns were deployed in the second line, and were lobbing their bombs clear over the heads of the first line; a strikingly early application of indirect fire. When it came to moving the army as a whole through hostile country, the Hanoverians at last came to realize that they must be prepared at any time to confront a mobile and unpredictable enemy. The practices they adopted there-fore resembled less the marching formations of Western Europe at that time than the ways of the Russians and Austrians when they were cam-paigning against the Turks or Tartars. The army's leading theoretician, Humphrey Bland, now happened to be a major general with Cumberland, and he wrote to the duke's aide-de-camp on 29 March 1746 to explain how he had devised the march of one of the columns from Oldmeldrum to Strathbogie (Huntly). His sketch has not been preserved, but his text describes how, every time the troops approached a ford, a party of 100 horse and a few men of the Argyll Militia split up to pass the stream above and below the crossing, while the massed grenadiers advanced against the passage frontally. These forces constituted the advance guard, and a number of battalions were detailed to support them in case they got into trouble:

> I look upon the vanguard as a body of troops designed for the first attack, and so composed as fit to pursue the enemy when they have forced them. If more are wanted for the pursuit, Kingston's Light Horse can move up from the rear for that purpose: for, considering the misfortune that has lately happened by advancing the cavalry before the foot, I have placed but very few in the attack, in order to fall on the foot when disordered by our fire, or to pursue them when they are broke, or to charge the horse that should come against them, but not to attack foot, unless they could gain their flank, or catch them unawares after a long march, or making a wrong movement; but it must be by officers of judgement and experience, which are rarely met with in the cavalry, that know how to lay hold of those lucky opportunities.[46]

Bland was almost certainly responsible for the design of the ultimate advance across Drummossie Moor, where the Duke of Cumberland adopted a formation of widely spaced columns – three of infantry, and one of cavalry on the left – which reconciled the needs of forward movement (by battalion columns, on a Jacobite-style three-man frontage) with the ability to form lines of battle and in particular to guard against a flanking movement of the enemy from the valley of the Nairn over to the left. In the event the army was able to form into battle order and back again into column three times before the encounter. Unlike Cope and Hawley, who had pulled their forces off balance by throwing in their horse unsupported, Cumberland was content to see the enemy suffer under the fire of his artillery and let them come to him.

Scotland in Particular

Military Presence

More Scots were under arms against Prince Charles than for him. That does not apply to the field of Culloden, but to the balance of forces as a whole. For some time the regular army had owned regiments which could be counted as Scottish in whole or part – the 1st of Foot (St Clair's, later the Royal Scots), the 13th (Pulteney's), the 21st (Campbell's or the Royal North British Fusiliers) and the 25th (Sempill's). The 43rd (Black Watch) was a recent creation (below), and Loudoun's 64th Highlanders were still being formed. To these must be added the militia (even if only the Campbells made any kind of showing) and the loyal volunteer regiments of Edinburgh and Glasgow.

In peacetime the thinly spread regular forces in Scotland were deployed only to garrison the forts and barracks and to stamp out public disorders such as had erupted in Glasgow in the Malt Tax Riots of 1725, and in Edinburgh in the Porteous Riots of 1736.

The history of the locally raised security forces in Scotland was not particularly happy. The troops in question began life as the Independent Highland Companies, which were first raised in the reign of William III to keep a military presence in the Highlands. They were recruited by outwardly loyal clan chiefs, who saw them primarily as a means of protecting their herds and bolstering their local power. The companies were abolished in 1717 after the corruption had got out of hand. In 1724 the devious Simon Fraser Lord Lovat petitioned to have the units reconstituted.[47] They would give of their best when the high local offices in Scotland were bestowed on reliable men, by which he understood people like himself.

The government in London had every reason to be suspicious of this reasoning and accordingly sent the experienced General George Wade to investigate on the spot. Wade submitted his report to George I on 10 December 1725. He had verified what Lovat had written concerning the lawless state of the Highlands, and concluded that one of the measures indicated was to revive the Independent Companies. Six companies of sixty men each were accordingly established and they became known as the Black Watch, from the dark hues of their tartan. One of Wade's associates was rightly uneasy about the diffusion of military knowledge among the Highlands and foresaw that 'a time may come when the institution of these corps may be thought not to have been the best policy'.[48]

In November 1739 the establishment of the Black Watch was increased to an establishment of ten companies and it became a full regiment (the 43rd; the 42nd from 1749). The men believed that they would continue to serve only in the Highlands, but in 1743 they were ordered down to London, on which their lieutenant colonel, Sir Robert Monro, asked a Minister: 'But suppose there should be any rebellion in Scotland, what should we do for these 800 men?' 'Why, came the answer, there would be 800 fewer rebels there!'[49] On being ordered to make ready to go overseas (actually to Flanders), they conceived that they were going to be consigned to the West Indies. More than 100 broke free and began to make their way back to Scotland, but they were pursued by dragoons and got no further than the fringes of Rockingham Forest, where they ensconced themselves in a moated compound near the shell of Lyveden New Bield House. Having been persuaded to surrender by fair promises, they were placed under arrest. Out of the 107 men who were court-martialled, three (two of them MacPhersons) were shot and the rest transported to Georgia or the West Indies. The remainder of the regiment sailed to Flanders and did well enough at Fontenoy, but the episode left a bitter taste among the clans of the eastern Highlands.

Later in 1745 the Black Watch was brought back to England after the outbreak of the rising, and deployed not against Prince Charles but in Kent to guard against a French invasion. 'When it is estimated that more than three hundred soldiers of the Black Watch had fathers, brothers, or near kinsfolk taking part in the Jacobite rebellion, the wisdom and humanity of keeping them aloof from such a struggle between duty and natural affection is obvious.'[50] In other words, they could no longer be trusted.

The history of the militia opened soon after the rising broke out, when Major General John Campbell of Mamore (later the 4th Duke of Argyll) was commissioned to raise eight companies in Argyllshire, though on 12 November his men were still devoid of suitable clothing, and lacked all muskets except 400 or so old weapons which had been rusting at Inverary since 1715. As some consolation they were given iron caps and pieces of armour hanging down the back as protection against the broadsword, and furnished with 'poignards, the blades whereof about four inches long, an inch and a half broad, sharp as a razor on both sides, with a short handle and two cross bars of iron. These instruments, they confessed, had been invented to be worn in their left hands under the cuffs of their coats, that they might, if they came to close quarters with the Highlanders, have stabbed them unawares, and were termed by the Highlanders "Presbyterian dirks"'.[51]

Loyal chiefs were also recruiting on their own initiative, and Norman MacLeod asked for broadswords to be sent from Glasgow to Skye, 'as a Highlander does not think himself properly armed without his broadsword'.[52] In due course the Highlanders from Skye were pitted in the far north of Scotland against the forces of the Jacobite Earl of Cromartie, whose Mac-Donalds were 'much perplexed in the event of an engagement how to distinguish ourselves from and our brethren and neighbours the [Sleat] MacDonalds of Skye, seeing that they were both Highlanders and both wore heather in our bonnets, only our white cockades made some distinction'.[53]

It was not just appearances that made it difficult to distinguish one kind of Highlander from another. Major General Campbell reached the army at Perth on 9 February 1746 with four of his companies from the west, and assured Cumberland that his men would show no favouritism to the Jacobites. 'As he knows them best,' noted the duke, 'he must answer for it, for myself I suspect the men greatly, for those who were here before we came absolutely refused to plunder any of the rebels' houses, which is the only way we have to punish them.'[54]

Further experiences confirmed Cumberland in his beliefs, and he had to write to London on 19 March that he thought it 'more for the honour of His Majesty's troops and of the Nation to finish this affair without any further use of the Highlanders than plundering and sending of parties'.[55] Having earlier refused to gut the houses of confirmed Jacobites, the Highlanders proceeded to sack the house of Mrs Gordon of Cooberedie, who had a specific protection from Cumberland. Major General Bland was unable to recover any of the goods, 'so dextrous are they at concealing what they steal, and, being informed it was done by the Argyllshire men, I ordered Colonel Campbell to make a strict search among his people; but nothing could, or would be found'.[56]

Cumberland and Bland had been expecting altogether too much of those people. The last big clan battle had been the one between the MacDonnells of Keppoch and the MacPhersons at Mulroy in 1688, and after that the inter-clan conflicts began to take on a ritual character, in spite of the happenings in Glencoe in 1692. 'When Highlanders came up against each other there was very little actual fighting. The campaigns were like those of the Italian condottieri in the fifteenth century.'[57]

The good Whigs of Edinburgh and Glasgow had meanwhile raised one regiment each in the English 'Bluecoat' style. Both cities had been under Jacobite occupation, and the loyal townsmen were now careful to distance themselves from any appearance of complicity. The Edinburgh Whigs kept their regiment on foot even after Cumberland gave them leave to disband on March 1746,[58] while those of Glasgow could, with more justification, declare that their community had 'always been remarkable, even in the worst of times, for their steady adherence to the Protestant religion and their zeal for the liberty of the subject'.[59]

Military Engineering

Forts and Barracks

Among the instruments that were employed by the London government to control Scotland, military engineering of various kinds was one of the most important. Its purpose was to maintain and support a permanent armed presence in key locations, and its legacy is visible today.

Cromwell began by planting citadels at Ayr, Perth, Inverlochy, Inverness and Leith. The works fell into decay under the Stuarts, and thus by the eighteenth century the pentagonal earthen fort at Inverness (1652) had its landward ditch almost filled with rubbish, and the grassy ramparts made a pleasant walk on summer evenings.

In July 1689 Major General Hugh MacKay of Scourie, the Williamite commander in Scotland, brought construction materials from Greenock to the uppermost end of Loch Linnhe, and began to build a stronghold he called Fort William, after his master. The place would figure soon in history as the base for the party that carried out the Glencoe Massacre on 13 February 1692. Fort William was the first of a new generation of forts, and it remained one of the most prominent, thanks to its situation at the south-western end of the Great Glen fault and in the heart of Jacobite Lochaber: 'It was in great measure originally designed as a check on the chief of the Camerons, a clan which … was greatly addicted to plunder, and strongly inclined to rebellion'.[60] Fort William was moreover the only one of the strongholds that could be supplied and reinforced by sea. All of this helped to justify further expenditure on the establishment. The civil settlement of Maryburgh sprang up just to the south, 'originally designed as a sutlery [i.e. supplying goods and services] to the garrison in so barren a country, where little can be had for the support of the troops. The houses were neither to be built with stone nor brick, and to this day [the 1730s] composed of timber, boards and turf. This was ordained, that they might the more suddenly be burnt, or otherwise destroyed by order of the governor, to prevent any lodgement of an enemy that might annoy the fort, in case of rebellion or invasion'.[61] The original earthen ramparts were revetted in stone early in the eighteenth century, and in July 1708 work began on a substantial barrack block to accommodate 432 men.

The abortive Jacobite expedition to the Firth of Forth in March 1708 had alarmed Queen Anne's government to a surprising degree, and the new barracks at Fort William were just part of a wider programme of work that involved strengthening the castles at Edinburgh and Stirling in a modern

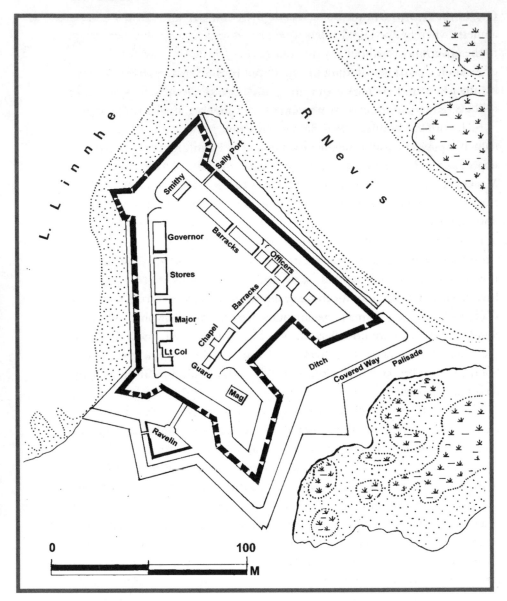

Fort William

artillery style. A further heavy investment at Edinburgh Castle in the later 1720s and the 1730s resulted in the zigzag walls that embraced the northern and western sides of the castle, and which are still so prominent when viewed from below.

The '15 threw a still mightier fright into the new Hanoverian regime.

One of the consequent measures was the Disarming Act of 1716, an arms amnesty whereby the Highlanders were invited to deliver up their weapons to the government without any questions being asked. The measure, like all of its kind, caused law-abiding people to put themselves at a disadvantage by abandoning their means of self-defence, while the malcontents and robbers yielded up some rusty wrecks but retained their usable weapons.

The other response was to launch a further scheme of fortification, namely a constellation of fortified barracks. The building of Inversnaid on upper Loch Lomond was, amongst other things, a gesture of triumph over the MacGregors, for it was sited on land which had been confiscated from Rob Roy. The barracks at Kiliwhimen were built on Fraser land but served a more obvious military purpose, for they were positioned near the south-western end of Loch Ness. The levelled-off top of a drumlin on the upper Spey provided a ready-made site for a substantial barrack block at Ruthven in Badenoch. It was an important strongpoint on the natural route from the Lowlands to Inverness, and would have been more useful still if, in due course, General Wade had been able to make his intended road down Glenfeshie to upper Strathspey. Lastly, a remote barracks was established on MacLeod land in the Western Highlands at Bernera. It covered the short crossing over the Sound of Sleat to Skye, and helped to protect a community of loyal Presbyterians at Glenelg.

The question of fortifications was one of the issues that was addressed by General Wade in his famous memoranda of December 1724 and April 1725. He argued that it was a good idea to have a strongpoint at the south-western end of Loch Ness, 'and this appears to be more necessary from the situation of the place, which is the most centrical part of the Highlands – a considerable pass equally distant from Fort William and Inverness, and where a body of a thousand men may be drawn together from those garrisons in twenty-four hours, to prevent any insurrection of the Highlanders'.[62] However, the site of the existing barracks at Kiliwhimen was badly chosen, for it was situated several hundred yards up from the loch and Wade was adamant that a new work must be planted next to the water, where amongst other advantages it would be supported by a galley which he intended to base on a little harbour at the nearby mouth of the River Tarff. His *Highland Galley* was launched by April 1725. It was capable of mounting up to eight little guns, and a cargo of either sixty soldiers or 20 tons of freight.

Captain John Romer, Wade's favourite engineer, finally began work beside Loch Ness in August 1729. The place was now designed as a stronghold and not just a barracks, and the construction dragged on until 1742.

At a casual glance it appeared to be a fully fledged four-bastioned fort, and it was named Fort Augustus after George II's favourite son, Augustus William, Duke of Cumberland (who in fact looked upon it with a jaundiced eye).

Romer was likewise the architect of Fort George at Inverness which was founded in August 1727 and named (with more presumption still) after George II himself. Wade had decided to let the old Cromwellian fort decay in peace, and Romer instead added a fortified barrack complex to the medieval castle which stood on a steep hill just to the south of the town.

Although it was not included in the original scheme, Dumbarton Castle was strengthened substantially in 1735 by a ravelin sea battery, complemented by a most handsome governor's house. Dumbarton sat on the north side of the Firth of Clyde and was going to prove a most convenient staging post for operations in the Western Highlands and islands in 1745 and 1746, and for receiving prisoners afterwards.

Fort William at Inverness and the strengthened castles at Edinburgh and Stirling were genuine fortresses, which could be reduced only by formal siege by a powerful and well-equipped force. Dumbarton Castle, too, was a difficult nut to crack for the landward side was barred by defences which crowned a great double plug of basalt. The other forts and barracks were little more than defensible patrol bases, which could beat off a casual attack by a raiding party but were vulnerable to any foe that approached them with serious intent. In a number of places the outer walls of accommodation blocks did double service as ramparts, which was a bad idea as they were inherently thin. Old castle sites were pressed into service at both Inverness and Ruthven. As a general rule, therefore, too much regard had been paid to cutting costs, and further defects came to light in the course of time, not least for the fact that the works at Inverness sat on a bank of loose gravel.[63]

At Ruthven the barracks crowned a narrow and steep-sided drumlin mound, which had served well enough for the castle that originally stood on this feature, but permitted only a feeble flanking fire to be brought to bear on the approaches. Moreover the whole site was overlooked by high

Fort Augustus

ground which rose well within artillery range to the south-west. Three cannon shot were enough to persuade the garrison to surrender to the Jacobites in 1746.

Captain Romer at least laid out Fort Augustus on a bastion trace with proper flanking, but he undid the good work by planting a curious and highly visible circular pavilion on each of the four bastions. These held vital internal features: powder magazine, provision store, well and latrines. In 1745 and 1746 the roofs of the fort were still covered by nothing more substantial than straw, which leaked badly in wet weather and was highly combustible when dry. Not long before, a soldier had described the fort as 'a new thing where the public money has been thrown away profusely. They say it cost £30,000 on spacious buildings, a governor's house, etc., but it is no fortress and one would be amazed at the folly and profusion that appears there'.[64]

Nothing short of a strong and mobile field force could have prevented an insurrectionary Highland army from emerging into the low country through the Perth and Stirling gaps – a danger of a magnitude not foreseen by the London government. By 1745 the forts and barracks were not even capable of answering their limited purposes, for the garrisons had been run down to well below their designated strengths.

Roads

Until the late 1720s the only carriage roads that were built and maintained to presentable standards were routes like the solitary turnpike which had been authorized near Edinburgh in 1713, and two stretches of the discontinuous eastern coastal route – the one from Berwick to Edinburgh, and the Causey Mounth from Stonehaven to Aberdeen. The Highlands were scarcely penetrated at all, until General Wade was commissioned to begin work on his celebrated system of roads, which were intended to facilitate the movement of troops between the isolated strongpoints. He knew the difference a good road could make to military operations, having seen how they enabled heavy guns to be hauled over the rugged island of Minorca in 1708, though oddly enough road-making does not figure at all in his reports of 1724 and 1725. William Caulfield took over the responsibility in 1740, but he had done virtually nothing before he was overtaken by the '45.

By 1730 Wade had a respectable annual budget of £30,000 and the routine was well established. The first people to arrive on the site of a projected road belonged to the survey party – no more than a civilian surveyor, an NCO and half a dozen soldiers, equipped with theodolite, measuring chains and other gear. They staked out the line of the intended route by two rows of camp flags, and from the beginning the rule had been to choose the most direct lines possible. Five hundred or so men of the garrisons and Independent Companies carried out the donkey work, and Wade kept his 'highwaymen', as he called them, in good heart by laying on festive ox-roasts and a generous allowance of beer.

The standard road width was 16 feet, and the road was built up of successively finer layers of stone and topped off with gravel. On each side of the road there was a bank and an outer ditch, and at intervals the road was traversed by large flat stones to enable rivulets and flood water to drain across. It is easy to imagine how the Highland terrain dictated many departures from the norm. In hilly country the line of the road curved around the slopes rather than following the valley floors, which were mostly obstructed by bogs, lochs and falls of stones. Across marshy ground the surface gravel was laid across a foundation of logs and bundles of brushwood, which before long became iron-hard in the soggy and airless peat. Conversely, sizeable rocks were moved out of the way by jacks or crowbars, or drilled and blasted, like the Black Rock beside Loch Ness.

It proved impossible to establish permanent fords across streams or rivers, for new boulders came tumbling down the beds every winter and obstructed the passage. Therefore there was no alternative but to build bridges, and ultimately Wade was able to take as much pride in these as in his roads. The system of communication was complemented by the simple inns called 'King's houses', which offered the first accommodation of any kind in most parts of the Highlands.

A crude but useful way to grasp the layout of the road system as it existed in 1745 is to picture it as a weightlifter who is struggling to hold a bar above his head. The bar in this case is the first and most important of the roads, the 60-mile route which connected the 'weights' at either end, namely Fort George at Inverness, and Fort Augustus at the south-western end of Loch Ness. The road was finished along most of its length by 1727, then prolonged to Fort William in the 1730s. The original road, as built by Wade in 1725, corresponded among most of its length with today's B862, and wound through the hills and straths to the south-east of the lake.

By 1733 the route had been supplemented by another road (the B852) which was driven along the immediate lochside from Dores to Foyers. (The tourist-ridden A82 on the north-western shore of the lake was built very much later.) The new road stretch was pioneering in every respect. For 12 miles on end it formed a terrace that had to be cut into the rock, and 'the fragments are cut into a loose wall at either side, with apertures left at very

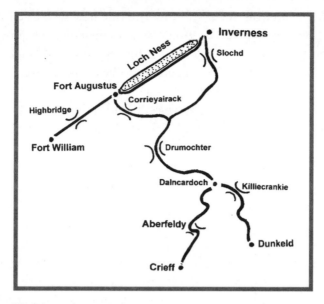

Wade's road system

short spaces, to give passage to the wintry currents'.[65] It was impossible to find a way around the Black Rock, which was much too hard to be tackled with picks and crowbars, and so 'the miners hung by ropes from the precipice over the water ... to bore the stone, in order to blow away a necessary part of the face of it, and the rest likewise was chiefly done by gunpowder'.[66] The stupendous effort enabled the rare travellers to enjoy 'a most romantic and beautiful scenery, generally in woods of birch or hazel mixed with a few holly, whitethorn, aspen, ash and oak, but open enough in all parts to admit a sight of the water'.[67]

A mile beyond the 'General's Hut' the way was obstructed hopelessly by the foaming chasm of the Falls of Foyers, which 'obliged General Wade to make a detour from its banks, partly on account of the expense in cutting through so much solid rock, partly through an apprehension that in the case of a rebellion the troops might be destroyed in their march, by the tumbling down of stones by the enemy from above; besides this, a prodigious arch must have been flung across the Glen of Foyers'.[68] The road turned away from the lake, ascended through moorland to reach Wade's first road near Whitebridge, continued along the original route over the the craggy Carn na Dreamaig and finally twisted down towards Fort Augustus, 'leaving on the right Loch Tarff, a small irregular piece of water, decked with little wooded islands, and abounding with char'.[69]

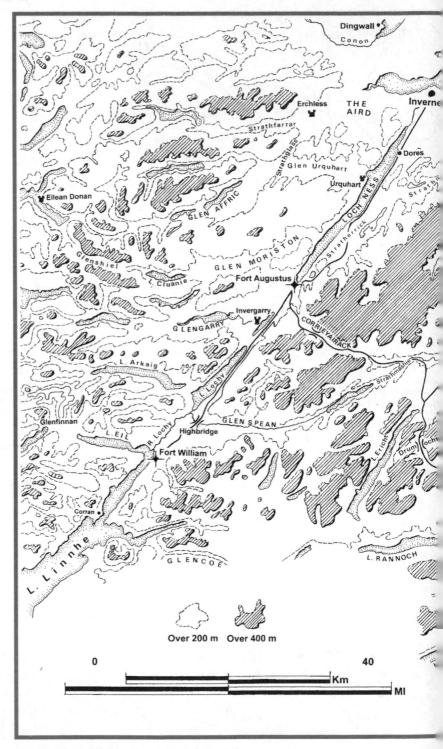

The Southern Highlands, with Wade's roads

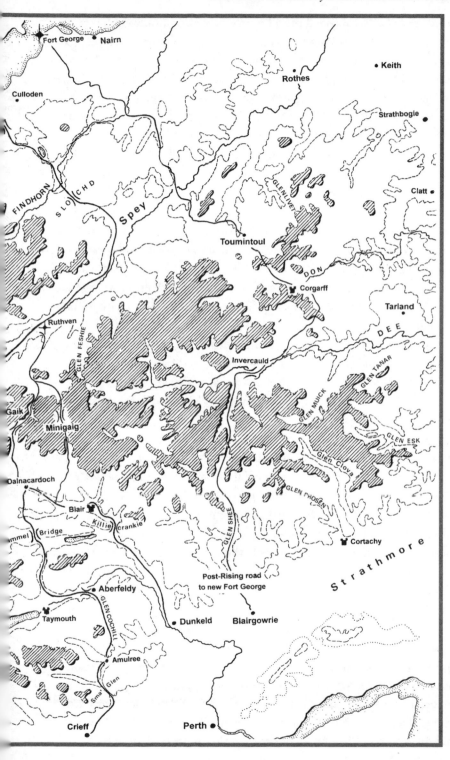

Once Wade had established the all-important communication between Inverness and Fort Augustus he prolonged his route down the Great Glen all the way to Fort William. His road down the south-eastern side of the gloomy and narrow Loch Oich replaced a perilous track that had been accessible only by the boldest Highlanders, and then by dint of clinging on to rocks and bushes. The glen at Loch Lochy was of much more open aspect, but the road had to be driven along the lakeside at the foot of the steep south-eastern slopes, a business which required 'a great deal of gunpowder'.[70] The bold bridge spanning the gorge of the Spean at Highbridge (1736) enabled the link to be completed to Fort William.

Wade penetrated the Highlands from the south along two routes, the two 'legs' of our weightlifter. The present A9 corresponds with the line of one of the roads, which carried the easterly route from Dunkeld (and therefore from Edinburgh and Perth) by way of the Killiecrankie Pass and Blair Atholl to Dalnacardoch. The engineering in this case was relatively easy, except where the road followed the precipitious left bank of the Garry through the Killiecrankie narrows.

It was highly desirable to open an alternative route well to the west, even at the cost of traversing two Highland massifs and two rivers. The road will here be described in a little detail, since it features so strongly in the history of the '45 and is by far the most rewarding of Wade's routes for the visitor to retrace at the present day.

The 'new' road in fact followed the line of the old drove route, down which cattle had long been driven from Dalnacardoch to the market at Crieff. The road left the Lowlands at Crieff and climbed through moorlands before making a first descent through the grimness of the Sma' Glen, with its screes and rocky outcrops. After a further descent the road passed Amulree, dipped into the head of Strathbraan, and climbed Glen Cochill to one of the finest views in the Highlands: half-left the distant peaks of Carn Mairg and Schiehallion; ahead the dark ragged ridge on the far side of Strathtay, with the volcanic knob of Farragon Hill rising beyond.

The new road descended steeply through birch woods to Aberfeldy in Strathtay, which was one of the most important transverse avenues of the Highlands, for it linked the lands of the Breadalbane Campbells in the west with Atholl to the east. The region itself was the homes of the clans Robertson, Stewart and Menzies, whose loyalty could not be taken for granted. It was important for Wade not only to bridge the Tay at Aberfeldy, but make something of a show about it. The river here was 62 yards wide, and Wade spanned the water in 1733 by the most splendid of his bridges, which was

87 yards long and extended over five arches. The material was the local light grey chlorite schist, and the designer, William Adam, topped it off with ornamental pinnacles. The bridge was grossly over-engineered, which is why it still bears the heaviest traffic, even though Thomas Telford announced in 1819 that it did not have long to live.

On the far side of the river the new road bordered the flat and fertile Strathtay, passing the site for a new king's house at Weem, the nearby Castle Menzies and the house of Archibald Menzies of Shian at Farleyer. Just beyond Comrie Castle the route swung to the right past the exit of Glen Lyon and made its next major ascent along the eastern edge of the gorge of the Keltney Burn, and thence to the top of the hill of Tophubil, where the labourers were rewarded with another stupendous view, with the quartzite dome of Schiehallion (the 'Fairy Mountain') rising to their left. A descent by rocky slopes brought Wade to the valley of the Tummel, which was accessible to the wild MacGregors of Rannoch Moor, and here much under the influence of the traditionally Jacobite Stewarts of Kynachan. Wade carried the road across the Tummel by a bridge (more modest than the affair at Aberfeldy), and drove it half-right by way of Bohespie to reach Glen Errochty at Trinafour. From there a stiff climb and a long gentle descent led due north to Dalnacardoch, where the route joined Wade's original road (the one by way of Killiecrankie).

The road just described, passing from Crieff by way of Aberfeldy to Dalnacardoch, was the one that was to be taken by the luckless Cope on his push into the Highlands in August 1745, and by Prince Charles and the Highland division after the council at Crieff on 2 February the following year.

Wade in the 1730s was satisfied to have provided alternative avenues across the southern Highlands to their meeting place at Dalnacardoch. From there he built a single new road (the weightlifter's trunk) across the wastes of the Drumochter Pass to upper Strathspey in the neighbourhood of Ruthven, where it branched in two to form the outstretched arms. Drumochter was dismal on all but the finest day, but much preferable to the two historic routes which lay further to the east:

❖ The Gaick passage ascended beside Edendon Water, crossed the Gaick proper, and descended to Strathspey by way of Glen Tromie. The Gaick route lay only 5 miles or so to the east of the Drumochter, and was only 100 feet higher, but the passage had an evil reputation and had accounted for many deaths through exposure and avalanches

❖ The Minigaig was high and bleak, but before Wade did his work it
   had served as the main passage between Atholl and Strathspey. It
   climbed Glen Bruar, crossed the summit to the Allt Bhrain, and joined
   the Gaick route in Glen Tromie. The Minigaig was still in use as a short
   cut to Strathspey in 1745 when it was said to have killed a party of the
   government's soldiers.

Wade's new road system, having arrived in Strathspey, reached out to
the north-east. The route followed the flat-bottomed valley of the Spey to
Aviemore, from where it extended painfully to Inverness across the ridge of
the Monadhliath Mountains by way of Slochd, once a notorious haunt of
thieves who, according to Burt, 'lay in wait within that narrow and deep
cavity, to commit their depredations upon cattle and passengers [i.e.
travellers] ... The first design of removing a vast fallen piece of rock was
entertained by the country people with great derision ... A very old wrinkled Highland woman, upon such an occasion, standing over-against me,
when the soldiers were fixing their engines, seemed to sneer at it, and said
to an officer of one of the Highland companies ... "What are these fools a-
doing? That vast stone will be here for ever, for all of them." But when she saw
the vast bulk begin to rise, though by slow degrees, she set up a hideous Irish
yell, took to her heels, ran up the side of a hill just by, like a young girl, and
never looked behind her while she was within our sight'.[71] On 29 August 1745
Cope made all possible speed over the Slochd road in case the Jacobites got
there first and blocked his way to Inverness.

The last connection in Wade's programme was the other branch, which
forked left from Dalwhinnie. The road then crossed the western Monadhliath
Mountains and reached the south-western end of Loch Ness at Fort
Augustus. Wade had to build a bridge to cross the upper Spey at Garva, but
his *tour de force* was the passage over the 2,500 foot-high Corrieyairack Pass,
which involved constructing a sequence of zigzags to overcome a particularly steep climb of 500 feet. Wade spanned the pass in 1731 and completed
a useful transverse route from Catlodge to the first route in 1735.

On 27 August 1745 Cope shrank from the prospect of forcing the
Corrieyairack Pass against the Jacobites whom he supposed to be already in
position there, and he scurried away by Ruthven and Slochd to Inverness,
leaving Prince Charles with a free passage from the north-western Highlands.
That episode was typical of the way the Jacobites were able to fasten on the
Hanoverian security system in an almost biological manner. It was they, and
not the forces of the government, who derived the most advantage from

Wade's roads in Scotland, just as in England they proceeded to collect the Excise and the land tax *de jure regio*, and directed their advance along the new Lancashire turnpikes:

> *For so it is that man who has laboured, wisely, skilfully and successfully must leave what is his own to someone who has not toiled for it at all. This too, is vanity and great injustice.*
>
> *For what does he gain for all the toil and strain he has undergone under the sun?* (Ecclesiastes, 2:21–22).

PART TWO

THE RISING

CHAPTER 6

From the Western Isles to the Corrieyairack,
22 July – 29 August 1745

ON 23 JULY 1745 PRINCE CHARLES first set foot on Scottish ground in a cove of white sand on the western side of the isle of Eriskay, a location that became known as 'The Prince's Beach' (Coilleag a' Phrionnsa'). Before setting out from France he had collected seeds of a seashore convolvulus, which he now scattered on a rocky hillock nearby, and the plant is said to have flourished there ever since. Less romantically, Charles was carried ashore piggyback in driving rain and spent the night in a turf-roofed cottage belonging to the island's tenant.

But the sense of purpose that had guided Prince Charles to the shores of Scotland in the high summer of 1745 was the Stuart belief in the God-given mission of their house that had brought Charles I to the scaffold in 1649, and provoked the Glorious Revolution of 1688. The same sense of purpose gave Prince Charles the strength to overcome – or rather ignore – the setbacks and disillusionments that would have sent a more reasonable man back to France.

The plans of the Prince had already been shattered twice before his first sight of the British coast. One of his main supporters had been arrested, and

'Duncan Mcgregor of Dalnasplutrach'

on 9 July his ship encountered HMS *Lion*, which forced his supporting vessel *L'Elisabeth* to put back to France with the bulk of the military stores and with the 700 troops of the Irish Brigade. The invasion was now reduced to a gamble, in which the only companions of the Prince were the 'Seven Men of Moidart' – 'a most extraordinary band of followers, no doubt, when we consider the daring enterprise on which they were entering, which was no less than that of attempting to wrest the crown of Great Britain from the House of Hanover, that had been so long in possession of it'.[1] The Prince's companions were the Franco-Scottish banker Aeneas MacDonald, an alcoholic and irascible Franco-Irish cavalry officer Sir John MacDonald, the Protestant Irish clergyman George Kelly, the English gentleman Francis Strickland, Prince Charles's old tutor Sir Thomas Sheridan, a Franco-Irish staff officer John William O'Sullivan, and the Jacobite Duke William of Atholl, as well as an Italian valet who presumably did not qualify to be counted among the seven.

The first landfall was presumed to be the northern Irish coast, and so the *Doutelle* ('a good sailer') was turned towards the chain of the Outer Hebrides, whose humps soon showed along the eastern horizon. On 22 July the vessel rounded the southernmost of the islands, little Berneray, then sailed north-east past a succession of further islets until she came to Barra. Here, at the Castle of Kiessmul, the longboat put Aeneas MacDonald ashore to search for his brother-in-law, the absent Roderick MacNeil of Barra. His piper undertook to pilot the *Doutelle* to the anchorage of An-t-Arcasaid Mhor, between rocky Eriskay and the much more considerable island of South Uist, landing the Prince on Eriskay the following day.

Much had been expected of Alexander MacDonald of Boisdale, a powerful man in South Uist, and half-brother of the chief of the MacDonalds of Clanranald, the most significant of the Catholic clans. On 24 July Boisdale set out from his castle of Kilbride (Cille Bhrighde) and was rowed across the Sound of Eriskay to meet the Prince. He did not hesitate to tell him that there was no question of coming out in support, for Charles had brought with him none of the French troops who alone would have given the rising some hopes of success.

Prince Charles's thoughts again turned to the Clanranald country on the mainland, where there might be a better chance of finding people who were prepared to 'come out'. The *Doutelle* left her anchorage on the night of 24/25 July with as little commotion as possible, for an unidentified ship was still in the offing, and she took advantage of a favourable westerly wind to make a swift passage past the islands of Canna, Muck and Eigg to anchor

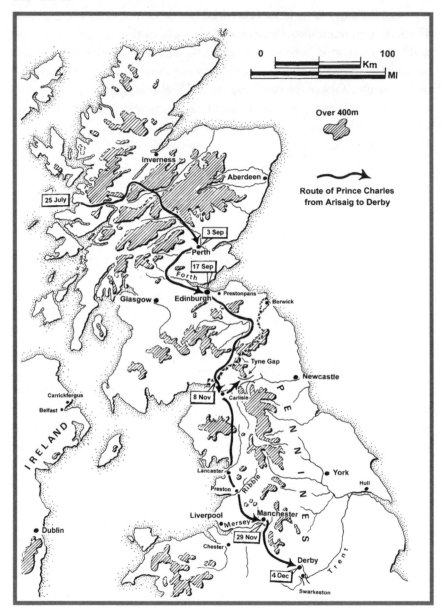

From Arisaig to Derby

early in the afternoon off the northern shore of Loch nan Uamh ('the Loch of the Caves') in Arisaig. Here a windblown landscape of stunted oaks reached down to a shoreline of shelving beaches and rocky excrescences, and Prince Charles took up his quarters in the respectable but secluded Clanranald farm of Borrodale.

Insurrections are never more vulnerable than in their earliest stages, and it is highly significant that Arisaig belonged to a part of the Highlands shaped by the 'Moine Thrust', a zone of metamorphic rocks that have been folded and crumpled by tectonic forces against and over an immovable barrier of Lewisian Gneiss – some of the oldest rock in the world. The process has been likened to snow piling up in front of a snowplough, and the effect in the present context was to raise tortuous mountains which isolated this part of the western coastlands from the rest of the Scotland to the east. Altogether, Arisaig

> was a place suitable above all others for the circumstances and designs of the Prince, being remote and difficult of access, and in the centre of a countryside where Charles's surest friends resided. It belongs to a tract of stern mountain land, serrated by deep narrow firths, forming the western coast of Inverness-shire. Although in the very centre of the Highland territory, it is not above 180 miles from the capital [Edinburgh]. The MacDonalds and Stewarts, who possessed the adjacent territories, had been, since the time of Montrose, inviolably attached to the elder line of the royal family; had proved themselves irresistible at Kilsyth, Killiecrankie and Sheriffmuir, and were now, from their resistance to the Disarming Act, perhaps the fittest of all the clans to take the field.[2]

The anchorage at Borrodale was open to a south-west wind, and on 29 July the *Doutelle* made the short passage across the Sound of Arisaig to a new and more sheltered anchorage off Forsay on the northern coast of Moidart. The Prince was visited there by one of the small delegations of the Highland chiefs and gentlemen who came to pay their respects and weigh up the state of affairs. Charles was passing himself off as an English clergyman, visiting the Highlands out of curiosity. He was agreeably modest in his demeanour, and had on 'a plain black coat with a plain shirt, not very clean, and a cambric stock fixed with a plain buckle, a fair round wig ... a plain hat with a canvas string having one end fixed to one of his coat buttons; he had black stockings and brass buckles on his shoes'.[3]

The very isolation of this coast made it unsuitable as a place to rally larger numbers of the clans of Lochaber, which lay beyond the impassable mountains to the east. Prince Charles had no alternative but to circumvent the massif by its southern flank, making what use he could of water transport. The anchorage of Forsay was in any case unsuitable for the landing of stores, and so on 11 August the Prince shifted his base southwards yet again. He was rowed ashore in Glenuig Bay, and trekked over Glen Uig to the shore of the muddy and seaweedy Loch Moidart, where another short trip by water brought him to Kinlochmoidart.[4] The Clanranald MacDonalds had to get there by marching all the way around the head of Loch Ailort.

The northern shore of Loch Moidart widened into a stretch of level pastureland and the *Doutelle* was unloaded a mile from the Prince's quarters in the house of MacDonald of Kinlochmoidart (one of the brothers of the banker Aeneas MacDonald). This spot was just 2 or 3 miles distant from the long inland water of Loch Shiel, 'by which he might transport his stores and heavy baggage within twelve miles of so of Fort William'. Prince Charles's first concern was to get the gear moved to the house of Kinlochmoidart, 'which notwithstanding his continual care and industry, was a great while of being accomplished, so superiorly indolent and idle are the people of that part of the country'.[5]

On the Prince's command Captain Walsh set off back to France with the *Doutelle*. The gesture was dramatic, for it signified that the Prince had committed himself to the goodwill of the Scots. It also had an unforeseen and happy consequence, for on the same day Walsh encountered three merchantmen off Skye, laden with altogether 400 tons of barley and oatmeal.[6] Walsh put prize crews on board the craft and sent the welcome windfall back to Loch Moidart.

Prince Charles had already designated Glenfinnan at the far end of Loch Shiel as the rendezvous for the well-affected chiefs, and he ordered the precious stocks of arms, ammunition and pioneer equipment to be carried on clansmen's shoulders along the lake, 'for there was no possibility that loaded horses could cross them mountains'.[7] Thus spoke O'Sullivan. Probably the stores were carried no further than the nearest stretch of Loch Shiel, from where they were transported the rest of the way to Glenfinnan by water. The Clanranald MacDonalds were distinctly unwilling to be employed as pack animals, and much of Walsh's barley and oatmeal got no further than where it was first unloaded on Loch Moidart.[8]

All the time Prince Charles had been striving to widen his following beyond his immediate control, which was not the least of the ways in which his time in Arisaig and Moidart resembled the creation of a revolutionary base such as that would have been understood by Mao Zedong in the 1930s. The greater chiefs of the Long Island and Skye could be counted out of the reckoning, for they could see no evidence of direct support by the French and two of them (Norman MacLeod of Dunvegan and Sir Alexander MacDonald of Sleat) were under threat of blackmail from the Whiggish Lord President, Duncan Forbes of Culloden.

It is quite likely that nobody would have moved at all had a lead not been given by a headstrong young gentleman, Ranald MacDonald (another brother of Banker Aeneas), who declared that he at least would draw his sword for the Prince. His example brought out MacDonnell of Keppoch and his wild clan, MacDonald of Glencoe, and young Clanranald and all the MacDonalds of his clan. Just as welcome in its way was the coming of the old and bent John Gordon of Glenbucket, for he was the first of the eastern lairds to declare himself. 'He kept his bed for seven years,' writes a hostile commentator, 'but hearing his ged wife talk about a muckle Prince coming to Scotland, readily concludes that some revolution was contriving, and in great hurry calls her to bring him his hose and breeks, "for ged," quoth he, "I must away to my ... Prince once again, and welcome him to the North."

From Arisaig to Glenfinnan

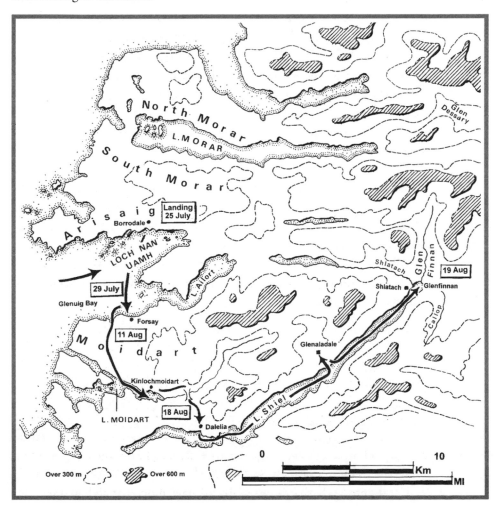

Now here reigned a true spirit of rebellion in this greyheaded sinner, that the thoughts of war and destruction should put a new vigour into his old soul, and bring him out again to lend a helping hand in the destruction of his country.'[9]

Commitment of that order was rare, and the case of Donald Cameron of Lochiel was more typical of the chiefs and gentlemen who ultimately came out. The manner in which he received the summons of the Prince at Achnacarry was nevertheless worthy of an ancient saga, for he abandoned the row of beech saplings he had been setting out in a temporary trench by the Water of Arkaig (they are now a row of venerable trees), and at once made his way to Charles. Lochiel met the Prince on 30 July, but left without having given any firm pledge, and Charles could not be entirely sure of the part he would take until he saw the Camerons at Glenfinnan on 19 August. This alone made it possible to expand the rising beyond its base in the widest of the Western Highlands, for Lochiel's example weighed heavily among the other chiefs, and his Clan Cameron controlled the south-western end of the Great Glen. The considerations that probably weighed most heavily with Lochiel were the strong Jacobite traditions of his fathers, and a number of assurances that were given by Prince Charles, not the least of which being that, if the worst came to the worst, Lochiel would be compensated by the Stuarts for any losses.

On 18 August Prince Charles left Kinlochmoidart for the first stage of his journey to Glenfinnan. He walked a couple of miles up the right bank of the River Moidart, then crossed at Brunery to take the track which led to Loch Shiel at Dalilea, where he and his escort embarked on small boats. The Prince landed to spend the night at Glenaladale. The party re-embarked at 7 a.m. on the 19th, and arrived at 1 p.m. at the head of the loch at Glenfinnan, at the meeting of the three glens of the Shlatach, the Finnan and the Callop:

> No more suitable place could have been found in the West Highlands for such a gathering than the fine stretch of level ground at the head of Loch Shiel, which forms a natural amphitheatre of about half a mile square, surrounded on all but the loch side by huge mountains ... and to the southwest, as far as the eye can reach, Loch Shiel, embosomed among the mighty cloud-capped hills which rise precipitously from its dark blue waters, stretches for 15 miles into the hazy distance.[10]

There, if anywhere, Charles would know whether his enterprise had a future, for he had arrived at the extremity of the Catholic Rough Bounds and brought with him little more than a bodyguard of 400-odd MacDonalds of Clanranald and Morar, along with a number of MacGregors and Glenbucket's Gordons.

Until well into the afternoon of 19 August the only inhabitants of the valley were the Prince and his escort, and some grazing cattle and the people who followed them. At some time between 3 and 4 o'clock the sound of bagpipes was heard from the east, and then 800 Camerons swarmed over the hills in a scene that would have been too theatrically embarrassing to record if it had not been true. The Prince then ordered the Duke of Perth to carry the standard 'to the other side of the River Finnan', with an immediate escort of 100 of the MacDonalds, and accompanied by 300 more. Lochiel's men were stationed 'on the other side of the river'.[11] Other sources add that the little army now gathered to witness the Catholic bishop Hugh MacDonald bless the standard of King James VIII. It was then spread to the wind – a red silken flag with a white square inset, sewn by the ladies of Kinlochmoidart.

The precise location of this remarkable event is still in dispute, for it all depends on which side of the Finnan the Prince first came ashore. If to the east, then 'the other side of the Finnan' indicates the western side of the little river, somewhere in the triangle formed with the Shlatach stream. If, however, the Prince landed at Shlatach, the location must have been on the eastern side of the Finnan near today's Visitor Centre, and quite possibly on the little rocky hill just behind. The latter case gains credibility when we consider that Prince Charles is mentioned as having returned to his quarters, when the only building in the locality was probably the little Shlatach House. The site of the early nineteenth-century Glenfinnan monument can be ruled out altogether for it was much too boggy.

Among the gentlefolk who witnessed the scene was the Jenny Cameron who had brought 200 of the Camerons of Glen Dessary. 'She is a genteel, well-look'd, handsome woman with a pair of pretty eyes, and hair as black as jet. She was a very sprightly genius, and is very agreeable in conversation.'[12] The crowd was augmented at 6 p.m., when MacDonnell of Keppoch arrived with 350 of his men, together with two bemused companies of redcoats captured three days before, whose presence served as a reminder that the first armed clashes of the rising had already taken place.

Highbridge, 16 August 1745

By 13 August Major Hugh Wentworth at Fort Augustus was already aware that serious trouble was brewing in the Great Glen:

The people in general in this neighbourhood seem mightily rejoiced to find the Chevalier so near them, and within these two days all the gentlemen of figure in this part of the world are gone off. One Glengarry said yesterday, before he left home, to the blacksmith that was shoeing his horses, that both these barracks would be in his possession before Saturday night ... Our men have very hard duty, having both the old and new barracks to defend; but I thank God, in very good spirits. Here is a very good train of artillery; but I cannot find one man who knows how to point a gun, or ever saw a shell fired out of a mortar.[13]

The first response of the Hanoverian military authorities in Scotland was to dispatch reinforcements in the direction of Fort William, the most isolated of the major strongpoints. Prince Charles sent word to his supporters in Lochaber to stop them, and on 14 August an initial party of sixty soldiers under Captain John Sweetenham was captured by the Keppoch MacDonnells.

Two days later disaster also befell Captain John Scott and the untrained troops of two depot companies of the 1st Foot (the later Royal Scots), who were on the march from Fort Augustus. The total distance was 28 miles, and on 16 August the reinforcement was approaching Highbridge, just 8 miles, or some three hours' marching-time, from their destination. The present line of the A82 jinks away from Wade's road to cross the Spean upstream at the little tourist town of Spean Bridge, where the river passes almost unnoticed beside the main car park. Only from one of the minor roads to the west can the significance of the Spean valley be fully appreciated, as it falls from both banks with increasing steepness to a rocky gorge, down which the Spean tumbles on its way to the River Lochy. In 1736 Wade spanned the gorge by a bold triple-arched bridge, one of the last items in his scheme of road-building, and when travellers peered over the edge they could see the brown water stirring far below.

On 16 August Donald MacDonnell of Keppoch set about gathering what clansmen he could, and sent his cousin Donald MacDonnell of Tirnadris with eleven men and a piper to devise some means of holding up the troops at the bridge. What happened next is a well-known story of the '45. On approaching the bridge Captain Scott glimpsed figures flitting among the trees and mossy boulders on the far bank, and the disturbing groans of a bagpipe carried to his ears. He sent his servant and one of his sergeants to investigate. They were snatched up immediately by the unknown enemy, an experience that unnerved Scott's little force, which fell back the way it had come. 'Had they forced their way through this handful, they might soon have reached the fort [Fort William], the road being plain and open. But they unadvisably retreated towards Fort Augustus, which was eighteen [sic] miles distant; a part of the way lined with rocks, and all through the enemy's country.'[14]

Summoned by messengers, or drawn by the noise of the firing, Jacobite reinforcements hastened to the scene of the action. The arrival of Keppoch brought the party to about fifty, but for a time at least the retreating red-coats had the advantage of the terrain, for the road back to Fort Augustus was compressed between the spectacular Loch Lochy and an inaccessibly steep ridge. The Highlanders did not dare to close with the sword, so broke off the immediate pursuit and hurried along the far side of the ridge by way of Glen Gloy, emerging to confront Scott's party on the heavily wooded little plain of Laggan, which separated Loch Lochy from narrow Loch Oich. Lochiel and a party of his Camerons were still on their way along the far side of Loch Lochy, but Keppoch and Tirnadris now had the support of a body of Glengarry's people from the village of Laggan Achandroom, and the redcoats were cut off before they could throw themselves into the only possible refuge: Invergarry Castle.

Scott's force was out of ammunition as well as surrounded. He himself was wounded in the shoulder, he had lost a sergeant and up to six men killed, and another dozen were casualties. Keppoch demanded and received Scott's surrender and then had his defeated enemy's wound dressed at Lochiel's house of Achnacarry.

'The young brat is landed'[15]

By early August 1745 many letters had reached London to confirm that Prince Charles had succeeded in putting an expedition together and setting sail. On 2 August the Duke of Newcastle wrote to the Duke of Cumberland in Flanders to warn him that it might be necessary to make a detachment from the British army there, though he hoped that the need would not arise. Four days later the Swedish ambassador reported to his king in the same vein:

> Although all the letters from abroad make a great deal of the embarkation of the Young Pretender, there appears little trace of any concern here, especially because every report from Scotland verifies that everything in that part of the world is peaceful. However all the officers belong to the regiments which there have been ordered to return to their posts without delay.

In past times the troubles there found their origin and chief support among the mountain Scots, the 'Highlanders', but nowadays the whole country is traversed by broad and respectable roads, and redoubts and fortifications have been established on nearly all the passes, which means that the malcontents can be kept in constant check, and rebels brought to book in short order.[16]

News of the actual landfall was slow to arrive. On 3 August Norman MacLeod of Dunvegan noted that a single ship bearing Prince Charles and his small party was hovering off the Western Highlands, but he was persuaded that 'no man of any consequence benorth the Grampians will give any sort of assistance to this mad rebellious attempt'.[17]

The Presbyterian minister of Ardnamurchan, Lauchlan Campbell, had observed for some time that his congregations were in a state of badly concealed excitement, and on the 4th one of their number finally admitted that Prince Charles had come ashore on the mainland. The Duke of Argyll's factor conveyed the information to his master at Inverary, and the news reached London on 13 August.[18]

The Duke of Newcastle, at least, was inclined to take the danger of a rising seriously. Orders were sent to Lieutenant General Cope to bring his scattered forces together, and the duke had thirty suspects confined as the first step in a much bigger programme of arrests. The Swedish ambassador reported that 'some people say the landing was effected at Inverary, an estate belonging to the Duke of Argyll; others indicate Mull, which is a Scottish island facing the coast of Ireland. No great consequences are foreseen, and especially because the enterprise is supported neither by foreign powers nor regular troops, but it has had some effect on commerce, by causing a fall in the stocks. However a bounty of £30,000 has been put on the head of that gentleman [Prince Charles], which makes it unlikely that he will get very far in his undertaking'.[19] In the event nobody ever came forward for the bounty (p. 125).

The Earl of Stair, as commander-in-chief in England, believed that the 6,000-odd troops in the kingdom offered adequate security, especially when reinforced by seven battalions of Dutch which were now being summoned by the British by virtue of a treaty of 1713. A further battalion of the Dutch troops was sailing direct to Scotland, where Lieutenant General Sir John Cope had up to 3,850 men under his command, the main force consisting of two regiments of dragoons and five regiments of foot, namely: Gardiner's 13th Dragoons and Hamilton's 14th Dragoons in the Central Lowlands,

East Lothian and eastern Borders; Guise's 6th Foot, shortly to be moved from Aberdeen and split up among the Highland garrisons; Lee's 55th Foot, five companies only (the rest were in Berwick), distributed over the western Lowlands; Thomas Murray's 57th Foot being extricated from Highland garrisons; Lascelles' 58th Foot around Edinburgh; and the Earl of Loudoun's 64th Highland Foot still in early formation. Nine 'Additional Companies' of depot troops helped to make up the nominal 3,850 men, but they were little more than temporary holding units for drafts of recruits. Two such companies belonging to the 1st Foot (the main body of which was elsewhere) were forced to surrender to the Jacobites at Highbridge on 16 August (above). The standing garrisons of invalids in the fortifications were totally unfit for service and the forts and barracks generally were in a state of neglect.

The Race for the Corrieyairack Pass, 20–30 August 1745

A small pernickety man, Lieutenant General Sir John Cope was a veteran of the War of the Spanish Succession, and had done creditably enough in the battle of Dettingen in 1743 before he was appointed to the Scottish command in February 1744. Now in August 1745 he lacked not so much experience, or even mobile troops, as proper support from the big men who were supposed to be the government's friends in Scotland. On 7 August Cope received reliable news that Prince Charles had landed in that country. Cope's instinct was to take decisive action to destroy the rising before it could gather strength, and on the 10th he deliberated in Edinburgh with the Lord Justice Clerk (Andrew Fletcher), the Lord President (Duncan Forbes of Culloden) and the Lord Advocate (Robert Craigie), as the main instruments of civil government in Scotland. On the strength of the assurances that he would receive local support, Cope resolved to strike from the Lowlands to Fort Augustus, near the seat of the rebellion, and carry 2,000 muskets to be thrust into the hands of the Whiggish clans which had dutifully delivered up their weapons under the Disarming Act of 1716.

Cope's expeditionary force consisted of the five available companies of Lee's 55th, Thomas Murray's 57th, the greater part of Lascelles' 58th, and two additional companies of the 43nd (Black Watch) who soon deserted. He left the two regiments of dragoons in the Lowlands as being of no use in the northern wilds.

On 19 August Cope joined his troops at Stirling, and on the 20th he completed the first stage of his march, north to Crieff, where he encamped to the east of the town on the site of the present eighteen-hole golf course.

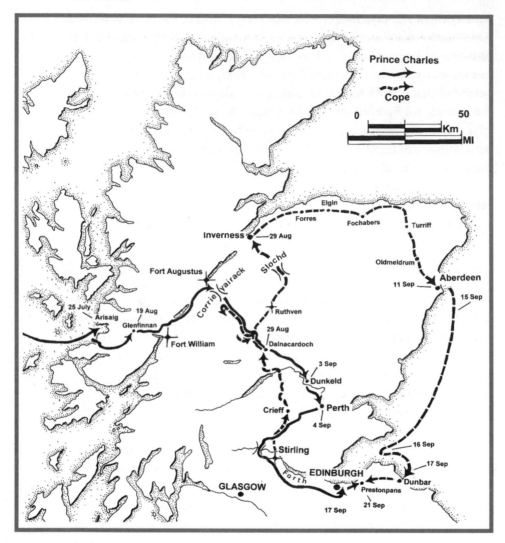

Cope outwitted

He was now at the starting point of by far the more difficult of the two roads
leading into the Highlands, the one over to the west by way of Aberfeldy
(p. 158). He had already found it difficult to obtain biscuit and bread, and
only the promise of meeting loyal Highlanders on the way could have made
him commit himself in this direction.

In the event, the Duke of Argyll washed his hands of the whole affair
and made off to London, while the other Whig magnates were unable
to raise any of the clansmen in the Hanoverian interest. Lord Glenorchy
(representing his father, the Campbell Earl of Breadalbane) was one of the

people who let Cope down, but claimed afterwards that the general should have stayed in the Lowlands at Stirling, for in that case the rebel Highlanders 'must have separated before now from want of provisions, meal being excessively scarce of which they make their bread in the Highlands; besides, the people of that country dislike coming southward and fear dragoons more than double the number of foot. If they had ventured forward, Cope might have met them on ground where both his cannon and horse would have been of vast service; whereas he was forced to leave his dragoons behind for want of forage on the road'.[20]

Cope had planned to meet the enemy in the Lowlands, but considered himself bound to continue north as ordered by the Marquis of Tweeddale, the Secretary of State for Scotland, who was trying to dictate strategy from distant London.

On 22 August Cope marched from Crieff and negotiated the twisting Sma' Glen to Amulree. He had relieved himself of some dead weight by sending 700 of the spare muskets back to Stirling, but 'having a greater demand for horses than could easily be provided, from the weakness of them, and the backwardness of the country people, who used to rip up the sacks, destroy the provisions, and run off with horse loads entire, into the woods … the days' marches were short at first'.[21] At each night's halt the horses were put out to graze in the wild country on account of the lack of fodder, and the animals had to be rounded up before the next march could begin in the morning.

Cope reached Taybridge on 23 August. An imminent clash with the Jacobites could not be ruled out and he made arrangements accordingly. Lieutenant Colonel Whitefoord testified that 'here on giving orders again to lighten the baggage, part was left, and you made a disposition for your army in any case of being attacked by the rebels; and on your march kept the Highlanders always advanced, extended to the left and right, with trusty officers who were to make signals, in case of the enemy's lurking in the hills, whose quick motions in that ground would not admit of your forming in the ordinary way'.[22] Cope thereby counted on being ready for action in just three minutes.

On 25 August Cope reached Dalnacardoch, where the two routes north joined. His tedious and unproductive diversion by way of Aberfeldy was now at an end, and he made good progress along the single road to Badenoch, arriving at Dalwhinnie on the 26th. He was near the point where the ways further into the Highlands diverged, for one of Wade's roads inclined to the right (as he saw it) towards Inverness, and the other to the left and over the

Corrieyairack Pass to his intended destination at Fort Augustus. At Dalwhinnie he learned, on seemingly good authority, that the rebels were ensconced on the Corrieyairack 'in hollow ways or watercourses, [where] they had bodies of men posted to flank you as you was attempting to mount the hill, which required seventeen traverses to make it accessible. These were also lined with men and sleeping [concealed] batteries of twenty-four 1-pounders, brass guns; on the top of the hill they had another body, and at the foot 800 were to lie concealed, as were all the rest till you entered on the mountain. These numbers were believed to amount to 2,500; besides, the bridge between Corrieyairack and Snugburgh was said to be broken down, where they had another body of upwards of 500'.[23]

The terrain under review was that of the Monadhliath ('Grey Wolf') Mountains, one of the great watersheds of the Highlands. Their backbone was a series of granite knobs which intruded through the sedimentary rock, and which were prolonged to the south-west to reach their highest point at Ben Nevis. The Corrieyairack had attracted Wade's attention as the only remotely passable saddle on the western Monadhliaths, and he completed the 28-mile passage in a single season of road-building between April and the end of October 1731. The 'seventeen traverses' were the zigzags on the near side which lifted the military road towards the summit. 'Snugburgh' was a name conferred by Wade's soldiers, and was a tiny patch of level ground on the far side by the stream called the Allt Lagan a' Bhainne. Here Wade had treated them to an ox-roast on the king's birthday, on 30 October, when their work was done.

Cope called his senior officers together and they agreed at once not to attempt to force the pass. Not only did the ground favour the Jacobites, but they supposedly outnumbered Cope's 1,400 remaining effectives by a wide margin. The council also rejected the option of waiting for the enemy on the near side of the passage. Cope had only enough rations to feed his troops for another three days, and while he was still committed to the military road the nimble Highlanders would be able to get around him by the wild country to the west and cut him off from Stirling. One of his officers wrote:

> the rebels could march to Stirling a nearer way than we could, by their marching down the side of Loch Rannoch, they would get to the bridge of Kynachan before us, they'd break it down and thereby cut off our retreat. This is a bridge upon Tummel, a water so rapid that it is not fordable in any place that I could hear of. To stay where we were, and thereby pretend to stop their progress southward, was a folly; they could, without

coming over Corrieyairack, go south by roads over the mountains, practicable for them, utterly impracticable for regular troops.[24]

A retreat to Stirling would in any case have signified that Cope had abandoned the friends of the government in the north-east Highlands. The converse would evidently hold true if the army made off down the Spey and over the Slochd Mor Pass to a new base at Inverness. By establishing himself there Cope was confident that he would bringing over the waverers in those parts to the government's side, promote the recruiting of Lord Loudoun's new Highland Regiment (the 64th), and rally the Presbyterian clans of the Grants, the Munros, the Sutherlands and the MacKays. With due account has been taken of all the pros and cons, it is still difficult not to conclude that Cope and his officers were influenced principally by some of the sights about them – the view of the grim, hostile and continuous wall of the Monadhliath Mountains to the front, and the green flat-floored valley of the Spey which extended invitingly to their right.

On 27 August Cope pushed his forces up the approaches to the Corrieyairack Pass as far as Garvamore, so as to fix the Jacobites in their supposed positions above, but then doubled back by a forced march to Ruthven. Overnight he received false reports that the enemy intended to anticipate him at the death trap of the Slochd Mor passage on the way to Inverness. This had to be prevented at all costs. Cope left a sergeant, a corporal and twelve men in Ruthven Barracks with orders to tip the stores of oatmeal into the well, and he then executed a further forced march on the 28th as far as Dalrachnie. On 29 August a final march brought Cope over the eastern edge of the Monadhliath ridge and safely to Inverness. His force was tired but intact – and the way to the Lowlands was open to the Jacobites.

To put together a balanced assessment of Cope's conduct we have to turn to the doings of Prince Charles and his Highlanders after they raised their standard at Glenfinnan on 19 August. On the next day the Prince had marched his little army east to Kinlocheil at the head of the long and narrow Loch Eil, which was an eastward extension of the sea loch of Linnhe. It was a decisive move in its own right, for it indicated that Prince Charles was leaving the base area where he had been building up his strength for so long, and was making for the southern end of the Great Glen. The march itself was scarcely 5 miles but the path was bad and the horses were few, and the Highlanders were notoriously unwilling to address themselves to hard and patient work – activity of a kind they had left to women in peacetime. They buried twelve of the swivel guns from the *Doutelle* only about a mile from the spot where the standard had been raised, and they dumped most of the musket ammunition and the shovels, hatchets and pickaxes at the head of Loch Eil (from where they were later retrieved by the garrison of Fort William).

On 23 August, despite having learned that Cope intended to reach Fort Augustus, Prince Charles covered only a short distance along the northern shore of Loch Eil, a sign perhaps that his army was still shaking itself down, or of the total absence of any road. The Prince turned away from the loch and lodged for the night in Fassifern, the house of John Cameron, a younger brother of the famous Lochiel. John had slipped away before the party arrived, but Charles 'made as good cheer as he could anywhere, and God knows he wanted it, as did all those that were with him, for he himself ate but very little bread for a long time before, and always marched a-foot at the head of his men as he continued all the time he was in Scotland, as well as in England, which prodigiously encouraged the men'.[25] Tradition has it that the bush of white roses that still stands outside the house was planted by the Prince.

The 24th brought the problem of how to get the Highlanders and their surviving cannon to the Great Glen safely out of the reach of Fort William and a warship seen to be lying offshore. William Drummond Norie describes the force continuing up Glen Suileag, turning behind the great ridge of Druim Fada, and descending Glen Loy to reach the Great Glenn at Errocht – a very long way around indeed. However, a more specific local tradition relates that the Prince followed the north shore of Loch Eil as far as the Annat Burn (Allt Dogra, near today's paper mill) where he, Lochiel and two other officers applied for help to a cottager at Annat. The man guided the column up the right bank of the Annat Burn then east to Gleann Laragain, a route which brought the Jacobites to the Great Glen just 4 miles above Fort William.[26]

A bout of illness confined Prince Charles for two nights to the house of Moy, beside the racing River Lochy and not far from his exit from the Western Highlands (not to be confused with Moy Hall to the south of Inverness). The Jacobites were on the move again north-east along the Great Glen on a very wet 26 August. They forded the Lochy at Moy, and crossed the Spean gorge at Highbridge (the scene of the clash ten days before), where the Prince learned that the redcoats were approaching the far side of the Monadhliath Mountains. The clansmen prolonged their march along Wade's road beside Loch Lochy and bivouacked on the plain of Laggan after trudging 25 miles through the rain. Prince Charles and his party put up at Invergarry Castle, an historic but much decayed stronghold of the MacDonnells of Lochgarry.

At Invergarry the Prince received an invitation from Fraser of Lovat to continue along the same axis all the way to the neighbourhood of Inverness, where the Frasers and other clans were in a receptive mood. Charles, however, was determined to settle affairs with Cope and anticipate him on the Corrieyairack Pass.

The 27th brought the Jacobites to the far end of the narrow Loch Oich at the settlement of Aberchalder, where Prince Charles established his headquarters in the farmhouse, and where his force was swelled by parties of the MacDonalds of Glencoe, the MacDonnells of Glengarry and the wayward Grants of Glen Moriston, but diminished when numbers of the temperamental MacDonnells of Keppoch chose to desert their chief. That day's march had been short, probably to give the reinforcements time to arrive and to enable the men to recruit their strength for the great enterprise of the 28th, which was the dash for the Corrieyairack.

The Prince expected to have to battle for the passage, and he confirmed that in such an event the Clan Donald was to have the right wing, 'according to the established custom in the Highlands, a privilege given them by the most ancient of Scots kings, and never was disputed with them'[27] – or at least not disputed until just before the battle of Culloden.

The Highlanders left their bivouacs at 3 a.m. on 28 August. There could be no question of taking up Wade's road where it ascended from the Great Glen, for that point was only a mile from Fort Augustus. Instead, as was noted by the garrison, the column turned hard right from Aberchalder and disappeared up Glen Buck. This route was not only concealed from Fort Augustus but enabled the Jacobites to take a short cut to Wade's road, possibly making a stiff initial climb beside the Allt a Ghlinnhe. They then traversed a broad saddle and descended to meet the road in the hollow of the Allt Lagan a' Bhainne at Snugburgh. There or nearby the Prince and his higher officers sat down to eat at 'Prince Charlie's Table', a circle of turf around which the Highlanders had cut a circular trench for their comfort. The pause must have been one of the few respites on that fine and exceptionally hot day, for the Prince was walking so fast that he wore out one of his brogues and the clansmen moaned at the unrelenting pace.

> Nothing could exceed the wildness and grandeur of the scenery by which the Prince was surrounded. In front, barring his way to the south-east, were … four mighty hills … their majestic cloud-wreathed peaks rising nearly three thousand feet into the sky, and standing out all dark and awesome against the rising sun. Among these stupendous mountains the road wound and twisted,

here crossing a foaming torrent, which roared and tumbled over lichen-covered boulders, there spanning a deep ravine ... To the north-east Loch Ness, a sea of silver light from which the morning mists were slowly rising, glittered and shone between the hills of Glen Moriston and Stratherrick, with Fort Augustus obtruding its ugly grey walls in mid-distance; on all sides mountains, lochs, and streams, and everywhere, save on the grey scarred summits, the glorious purple heather wearing its summer robe of royal colour as if in honour of the Prince's visit.[28]

The column had gained a useful amount of height in the first haul from Glen Buck. Some altitude had been lost in the descent to Snugburgh, but now the Jacobites had the advantage of Wade's road, which climbed left to reach the summit of the pass. There was nobody there to stop them. They made the jarring descent on the far side by the zigzags, and continued down the valley of the Upper Spey to the King's House at Garvamore. Prince Charles and his senior officers discussed what to do next. They had learned that Cope had backed away from the confrontation, and that he was now making for Inverness, which prompted one of the party to suggest that 500 picked men should dash along the length of the Monadhliath ridge and down Strathdearn (the valley of the upper Findhorn), so as to anticipate the redcoats at the Slochd Pass. It was a good idea, but it had to be dismissed, for the distance amounted to 24 miles of difficult going and Cope had a clear lead.

The instincts of many of the clansmen still drew them towards Inverness, as much on account of the plunder to be had there as to finish off Cope. However, Prince Charles had set his sights on the larger objective of exploiting down the military road to Atholl, and so to Perth and the Central Lowlands. The Prince still could not afford to leave the narrower world of Highland politics entirely out of account. Considerations of this kind had certainly worked in his favour when Donald MacDonald and Duke William of Atholl had supported the initial move over the Corrieyairack – Lochgarry because it would give additional security to his country, and Duke William because it would be a step on the way to evicting his Whiggish brother James from the family property. There was another gain on the 29th, when a raiding party of Camerons brought in the MacPherson clan chief's eldest son, Ewan, who had more or less allowed himself to be taken prisoner. But the same day saw a useless diversion of effort at the behest of old Gordon of Glenbucket, who wished to secure the oatmeal and weapons which Cope had abandoned in the allegedly undefended barracks at Ruthven.

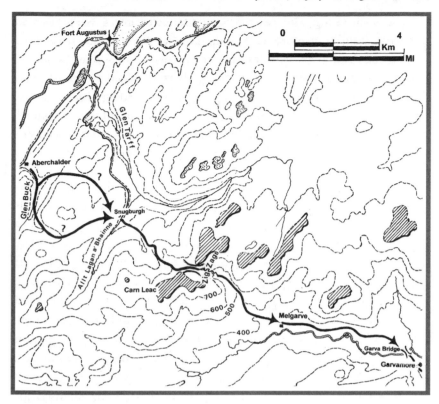

The Corrieyairack, 28 August 1745

   The Jacobite chief of staff John William O'Sullivan was now forced
to call off a reconnaissance in force towards Atholl, and much against his
judgement (as he makes clear from his memoirs) he had to join his party of
thirty-five or so officers and men to a body of Camerons under Archibald
Cameron (another of Lochiel's brothers) and make off down the Spey to
Ruthven. This gave rise to the spectacle of one Irishman, O'Sullivan,
approaching the barracks in Highland dress to investigate, while another,
the red-coated Sergeant Terence Molloy of the 55th, disposed his corporal and
twelve men to defend the rambling complex as best he could. O'Sullivan
verified that the barracks were garrisoned, as he had suspected all along, and
he improvised a two-pronged attack. He himself with one of the parties was
to take advantage of the cover afforded by the new stable block, and plant
a barrel filled with combustible materials against the door of the north-
western end of the main black. When the barrel took fire a force of thirty of
the Camerons was supposed to reach the opposite end of the block by means
of the access ramp, and then scale the wall by ladder.

It all went wrong. The redcoats poured musketry into O'Sullivan's men, who were unable to manoeuvre their flaming barrel into a satisfactory position against the door, which was sited at the top of three steps. On the far side of the barracks the steep access ramp likewise defied all the efforts of the Camerons to bring up their ladder. Late in the evening Molloy allowed the Jacobites to pick up their casualties (about two dead and three wounded) and carry them away unmolested. He had lost one man, who had been shot through the head when standing dangerously high above the parapet, contrary to orders.

While this nonsense was going on, Prince Charles and the rest turned their noses to the south, and the first episode of the campaign of the '45, what might be termed the 'Corrieyairack phase', was at an end. On the Jacobite side Prince Charles had succeeded in raising the kernel of his force in the Western Highlands, and then brought it on to the wider Scottish stage. However, neither he nor Sir John Cope was entirely liberated from the baleful influence of local interests.

A comparison of dates and places will show that when Cope turned back from the Corrieyairack route on 27 August the Jacobites (and only 1,400 of them) were still on the far side of the Monadhliath ridge down at Aberchalder. In other words, it had been in Cope's power to reach the summit virtually unopposed, which would probably have given rise to an action under the blazing sun of the 28th in the neighbourhood of Snugburgh. The outcome would have been doubtful at best, and when Cope was called to account long afterwards, the court martial concluded that he had been right to turn his back on Prince Charles. With all of this it is difficult to grasp how Cope, having discovered how empty the promises of the Whiggish Scots had already been, should have trusted in the assurances that were now given him that the Presbyterian clans of the north-east would rally to his support at Inverness. Meanwhile the way to the Lowlands stood open to Prince Charles.

CHAPTER 7

Edinburgh and Cope's Last Challenge,
30 August – 30 October 1745

ON 29 AUGUST PRINCE CHARLES AND the main force of the
Jacobites had marched from Garvamore to Dalwhinnie and reached the head
of Wade's road to the south, the Monadhliath Mountains having given way
to rounded, peat-covered hills. The Jacobites were on the move again early
on the 30th, and followed the new road as it wound up the narrowing plain
of the Truim towards the Pass of Drumochter. Beyond the watershed of the
'Drumochter Dome' the route inclined to the east and followed the left
bank of the infant Garry on its way through Dalnacardoch, where the army
halted for the night after a respectable but untiring march of 17-odd miles.

The first day of September saw the Jacobites leave the sub-arctic environment of the Highlands and reach Blair Castle in the Vale of Atholl. Here
the reconstruction of the celebrated castle had only just begun, for the
Hanoverian Duke James of Atholl dwelt mostly at Dunkeld and the old place
was still like 'a prison in appearance, having the windows covered with iron
bars, and walls five foot thick'.[1] A resolutely Jacobite neighbour of the Murrays, Lady Lude, nevertheless put the castle in a fit state to receive Prince

'A seceding minister exercising his militia' in Edinburgh

Charles as well as his companion William, the Jacobite Duke of Atholl. Here, Prince Charles was able to familiarize himself with some of the customs of his would-be kingdom in the two days he spent at Blair,[2] including, on 2 September, repairing to Lady Lude's house nearby, where he tasted his first grouse and took the time to dance a number of reels and a Highland minuet.

The army set out again on 3 September. If there had been anybody to oppose Prince Charles the march would have come to a halt within the first couple of hours, for he had to negotiate the formidable Pass of Killiecrankie. On the far side the army descended Strathtay to Dunkeld, a traditionally royalist and Jacobite town where the Prince stayed overnight in Dunkeld House (demolished in 1830), the new residence of the Dukes of Atholl. The youthful Neil Gow, later a celebrated fiddler, helped with the generally successful entertainments (though the servants of Duke James had taken care to hide all the silver plate).

On 4 September the army strode across low ground to Perth on the River Tay, the first sizeable place they had so far encountered.[3] An advance party of 900 Highlanders had arrived on the morning of the 3rd and proclaimed King James VIII at the cross. With the town already secured, Prince Charles stopped to dine on the way at Nairne House, a great mansion (demolished in 1759) near Auchtergarven. An enthusiastic Jacobite barber was ringing the bells when the Prince rode into Perth on 4 September, by way of the North Port. As the sun was setting he passed through streets lined with joyful or merely curious townspeople, and the merchants who had come to town for the Fair. He lodged in the house of the vintner John Hickson in South Street.

Charles's style of leadership was already set, and it was noted in Perth that 'the Young Chevalier affects the example of Charles XII of Sweden. He marches the whole day on foot, and every river they have to cross, he's the first man that leaps into it. He dines with his soldiers in the open field; and his soldiers pay ready money for what they take … The Pretender makes himself greatly popular: he is dressed in a Highland coat of fine silk tartan, red velvet breeches, and a blue velvet bonnet with gold lace round it, and a large jewel and St Andrew appended; he wears also a green ribbon, is above six foot, walks well and straight, and speaks the English or broad Scots very well'.[4]

Prince Charles's army remained in quarters in Perth and on the North Inch until 11 September. A correspondent of Lord Chesterfield claimed that the Jacobites extorted contributions to the value of £500 from the town, but he admitted that 'they had many friends there and treated them well'.[5] This corresponds with O'Sullivan's statement that 'the town in general was not well disposed, but there were some honest people that gave good intelligence. The stay we made in Perth gave us some leisure to accustom our folks to a little regular duty, of mounting of guards, and of occupying of posts, and visiting of them, which was still forming 'um'.[6]

Prince Charles laid on a ball to please the well-affected ladies of the neighbourhood. Lady Lude was 'so elevate while she was about the Young Pretender that she looked like a person whose head was gone wrong'. Miss Threipland of Gask was moved to write: 'Oh, had you beheld my beloved hero, you must confess he is a Gift from Heaven … in short … he is the Top of Perfection and Heaven's Darling'.[7] With that social obligation out of the way, the Prince threw himself into his duties, for this was a period of important change in the character of his army.

The march into Perthshire had brought his troops into a region where the clan culture of the Highlands merged with the feudal structures of the south, and Prince Charles thought it expedient to reward three of the grandees with the rank of lieutenant general. One was James Drummond, the Duke of Perth, who was a Catholic nobleman of great abilities and high local credit. William, the Jacobite Duke of Atholl, another of the newly minted lieutenant generals, had accompanied the Prince from France. There was much greater surprise when the same rank was awarded to the duke's younger brother, the restlessly ambitious Lord George Murray, who was known to have met Cope on the general's way north at Crieff on 20 August. Prince Charles never overcame his doubts concerning Lord George's loyalty, but the man bore the Murray name, and he now used his influence to support the work of bringing in the Atholl tenants and the men of the southern clans – Farquharsons, MacGregors, Stewarts, Menzies and Robertsons. Young Ewan MacPherson of Cluny cast off his pretence of being a prisoner of the Jacobites and went north to raise his clan for the Prince.

News then came that Lieutenant General Cope had sent word to Edinburgh to have shipping dispatched to Aberdeen, designing to march his troops there from Inverness, and then bring them by sea to the Firth of Forth. The Prince and his advisers debated whether they should try to intercept Cope when he was still on his way to Aberdeen, but they decided instead on the bolder course of anticipating him at Edinburgh. The Jacobites set out from Perth on 11 September. Geography dictated a route to the southwest and well out of the direct path to Edinburgh, for the army had to circumvent the steep igneous ridge of the Ochil Hills as well as clear the head of the Firth and the redoubtable stronghold of Stirling Castle.

Early that day Prince Charles is said to have made a sentimental visit to the House of Scone, next to the coronation site of the old Scottish kings where his father had stayed thirty years before. After this act of piety he took the Roman road that led west from the neighbourhood of Perth along a wooded ridge, with views to the Highlands on the right, and over fertile Strathearn to the grim Ochil ridge on the left. The Prince was in the country of the Oliphants of Gask, Jacobites through and through, and breakfasted at the ancient, stone-built House of Gask a little way down the slope towards Strathearn.

Leaving the Roman road, the Prince followed a winding route across Strathearn, lunched with Lord George Murray at his House of Tullibardine, and, very well fed indeed, continued hard under Sheriffmuir to reach the little cathedral town of Dunblane. He lodged for the next two nights with the noted Jacobite MacGregor of Balhaldie, who was, or liked to think he was, the head of the clan MacGregor.

The army was supposed to have reached Dunblane on the same 11 September and was probably assigned to the main road by way of Auchterarder. However, the troops did not trail in until the 12th, 'and in general the men seemed extremely fatigued with this march, which could only be imputed to the good quarters and plentiful diet which they had at Perth, and their being so many days without exercise. Upon which it was resolved, that henceforth they should encamp in open fields, and be kept constantly in motion'.[8] At the special request of their chiefs, who felt deeply shamed, the men were made to bivouac outside the town in the area of the present Keir Gardens to the south.

The chastened clansmen got to their feet again on 13 September and marched by way of Doune towards the flats of the upper Forth above Stirling. A number of redcoat prisoners were deposited for safekeeping at the Castle of Doune, and the ladies of the area of Menteith gathered close by at Newton House to see Prince Charles pass. The owner, Mr Edmonstone of Cambus, was another committed Jacobite, and the Prince, without dismounting, accepted a glass of wine and drank to the health of them all.

Prince Charles left a small garrison in Doune Castle, both to guard the prisoners and to hold this important little strongpoint. It was stoutly built of the distinctive purple sandstone of the locality, and stood on one of those heavily dissected gravel banks that had been of military importance in the Forth valley since Roman times. For the immediate purposes of the Jacobites it commanded the access to the only practicable means open to them of crossing the upper Forth, Stirling Bridge being dominated by the cannon of the Hanoverian garrison in Stirling Castle.

The Prince now led his troops out of Doune through undulating

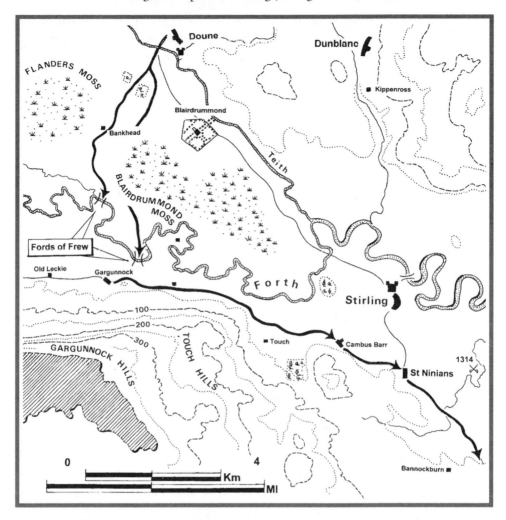

The Fords of Frew, 13 September 1745

pastureland, then took to the tracks which struck across the marshy levels, where great spreads of peat overlay the silts and clays of ancient tidal flats. The Trossachs were in constant view beyond Flanders Moss to the front, peak upon peak, and most prominent of all was the cone of Ben Lomond, the last mountain of the Highlands. The paths swung to the left to approach the Fords of Frew, where the sediment cast by the Boquhan Water made convenient crossings.

The channel was narrow and no significant obstacle except to wheeled vehicles, or generally in time of spate. However, the marshes on either side confined troops using the passage to predictable avenues, which made the crossing potentially vulnerable to the dragoons whom Cope had left behind when he left for the Highlands. One of the regiments, Gardiner's 13th, was close by, and the Jacobites were consequently 'expecting to have been opposed there by Colonel Gardiner's dragoons ... who we heard were threatening to cut us in pieces if we attempted to cross the water. The dragoons however upon our approach galloped away in a great hurry and lay that night at Falkirk'.[9] Prince Charles drew his sword, descended the low bank, and was the first to wade the water.

The water was not particularly deep, for the recent weather had been fine, but those few steps were of great symbolic and military significance, for they denoted that Prince Charles had crossed his Rubicon, the boundary between the Highlands and the Lowlands. 'Hitherto he had been in a land where the Highlanders had a natural advantage over any troops which might be sent to oppose him; but he was now come to the frontier of a country where, if they fought at all, they must fight on equal, or perhaps inferior terms ... various less decisive measures were proposed ... but Charles was resolved to make promptitude and audacity his sole tactics and counsellors.'[10]

The next few hundred yards were of scarcely less interest, for the direct way further south was barred by the great basalt tableland of the Gargunnock Hills. The whole had once been overlain by a glacier, and the impassable near slopes had been worn into spectacular horizontal striations by the ice as it pushed down the Stirling Gap. The Jacobites continued on their way to the foot of the hills, where a shelf of slightly higher ground offered the Prince the option of turning westwards towards Glasgow, or eastwards towards Stirling and Edinburgh.[11] Prince Charles in person, and probably by calculation, turned to the west, calling first at the nearby tower house of Leckie. George Moir, the proprietor, was not at home to welcome him, for he had been seized by the dragoons the night before and whisked off to Stirling Castle, but the Prince stayed long enough to dine and to write a summons to the Provost of Glasgow, requiring him to deliver up all the arms in his town, together with a contribution of £15,000 pounds. All of this indicated a march to the west, but in fact the Prince had already launched the army in the other direction, to the east. This eventful day's march came to an end when the troops bivouacked just 2 or 3 miles short of Stirling under the Touch Hills – the eastward prolongation of the Gargunnocks. The Prince 'posted the guards in person, and lay out all night with the men'.[12]

In reality Prince Charles had no means of putting his demands on Glasgow into effect, for he was now going the wrong way, but his mere threat of coming in this direction was enough to throw the town into a panic:

The tumults of the honest people grew then higher, they had offers of aid from Paisley and Kilmarnock of 300 militia from each, like offers from Clydesdale. But the Magistrates having found upon inquiry that there were not above three hundred firelocks in the town, and two hundred of them fowling pieces, thought the town incapable of any effective defence, and that taking of arms would only provoke the enemy to plunder: and thus we are left (the populace say, betrayed) by our governors to be the spoil of our enemies, and not only we but the whole west country, the best subjects the King has in his dominions.[13]

The alarm spread beyond Glasgow to the Whigs of Dumfries, who were persuaded that the 'business has been strangely conducted, some fatality seems to attend us. What we do here we know not, or how to secrete our arms. Some have proposed to send the few we have to you [Carlisle] where we hope they might be assured and out of the enemy's reach, but we have resolved on nothing'.[14] The Duke of Newcastle already assumed that the Jacobites would march without halt into England, and that they would arrive by a westerly route.[15] Prince Charles had already outmanoeuvred Cope, and this was the first of the many times he was to make deliberate use of bluff and deception, almost always to good effect.

The Prince had his sights set firmly on Edinburgh, and he had no intention of crossing swords with Major General William Blakeney and his garrison of redcoats who were perched in Stirling Castle. Prince Charles still had to squeeze his troops through the space between the extremity of the Touch Hills and the castle rock, which brought them within range of Blakeney's artillery, but they accomplished this in excellent order early on 14 September, with pipes playing and colours flying. The Prince's place was in the centre, by the royal standard, and 'General Blakeney, who commanded Stirling Castle, fired at the white flag, hoping to hit the Chevalier, but the bullet lighted about twenty yards from him. He fired four times, but did no execution, the cannon being only 6-pounders, at a mile and a half's distance'.[16] The people of Stirling then emerged in silent crowds to see the Highlanders march through St Ninians on the far side of the narrows.

Having traversed St Ninians, the Highlanders paused to eat on the historic battlefield of Bannockburn, while Prince Charles called at Bannockburn House, the home of Sir Hugh Paterson, 'a gentleman attached in the most enthusiastic manner to his cause'.[17] The march terminated just to the west of Falkirk, where the army bivouacked among the fields of broom that extended between the town and Callendar House, the home of William Boyd,

4th Earl of Kilmarnock. This highly strung young nobleman was not a dyed-in-the-wool Jacobite, like the gentry Prince Charles had met over the last few days, but he was very hard up, and the present turmoils could just as easily ruin his finances altogether as give him the chance to set them on a new footing. Having accompanied the dragoons when they made off at speed to the west, he became concerned for the wellbeing of his house, which he had left at the mercy of the Jacobites. He returned there on the evening of the 14th and became the host of the Prince overnight. An enemy informant learned that they dined together, and that 'after drinking freely, he [Charles] came out with these expressions: That he could have a great many forces from France, but that he rather choosed to throw himself into the arms of his subjects, and that he proposed to march for Wales (if he did not meet with obstruction in the way) where he expected to meet with his brother [Prince Henry] and the Duke of Ormonde'.[18] The Prince almost certainly intended these remarks for public consumption.

Another item in the conversation at Callendar House was the whereabouts of the only mobile forces available to the government in this part of the world, namely the 13th Dragoons, under their highly eccentric colonel James Gardiner. As a young officer Gardiner was notorious for his foul language and licentious life. One night in July 1719, while waiting for an assignation with a married woman, out of curiosity he picked up a book entitled *The Christian Soldier, or Heaven Taken by Storm*. He was glancing at the book with no particular interest when all of a sudden the pages were illuminated by a blaze of light, and Christ appeared to him and reproved him for his evil conduct. Gardiner (who had recently suffered a nasty fall from his horse) resolved at once to amend his ways, and began to set himself up as a religious warrior – a type that became known as a 'Blue Light' in the next century.

On 15 September 1745 Colonel Gardiner was struck by a still more terrible vision, that of being attacked by the Jacobites in Linlithgow. Early that day he took off at speed with his dragoons, and arrived at Corstorphine just to the east of Edinburgh. What had been going on? Kilmarnock had told Charles that the dragoons intended to make a stand at the bridge over the Avon in front of Linlithgow, and the Prince had detached Lord George Murray and 1,000 men to ford the river 1½ miles upstream and take Gardiner in the rear. Lord George made good time on his expedition, but he found that the enemy had already left. The Jacobites were therefore able to take peaceful possession of Linlithgow in the morning, and Prince Charles spent the day quietly by himself in the great sandstone palace of his ancestors overlooking Linlithgow Loch. In the evening the army bivouacked out on the Edinburgh road 3 miles to the east of the town, and Prince Charles lodged for the night in Champfleurie House (since rebuilt).

'Bell of ominows sound' – Edinburgh falls to Prince Charles

By now Edinburgh could no longer doubt that it was the next item on the Jacobites' menu. On paper the forces now available to the friends of the government were quite respectable. Gardiner's 13th Dragoons had arrived not far from the town, and Hamilton's 14th were at Leith; if the two regiments had joined at the Fords of Frew they might have been able to prevent the Jacobites getting across. By the very specific statement of Richard Jack, the other men in and about Edinburgh amounted to 3,464 – 1,000 men of the historic Edinburgh Trained Bands, 600 just raised for a newly authorized Edinburgh Regiment, the 114 of the standing Town Guard (tough old armed watchmen), 400 ultra-Protestant Seceders of Gibb's Meeting House at Inveresk, 750 further volunteers from the Lothians, and a separate corps of 400 Volunteers from the professional men and gentry, as well as 200 of Lascelles' regulars under the command of Lieutenant General Joshua Guest up in Edinburgh Castle.[19] The castle itself could be reckoned as virtually impregnable, for it sat on the tactically commanding position of a basalt plug, 250 yards in diameter, which had formed in the mouth of a long-vanished volcano. The artificial defences had been strengthened over the generations, and most recently in two intense bouts of building (after the scare of 1708, and again in the 1720s and 1730s).

In the middle of September 1745 the forces available to the Jacobites amounted to probably no more than 1,800 not very well-armed men. This was to reckon without the panic and confusion which reigned in Edinburgh, the obstruction and delays put up by the Lord Provost Archibald Stewart ('there was not a Whig in town who did not suspect that he favoured the Pretender's cause'),[20] and the significant elements of Jacobite support among the citizens and the visitors, 'and now being harvest the Heighlanders of there partie, man and woman, had been sent up a good number under the pretext of harvest work'.[21]

Outside the town the Whiggish sadler and ironmonger Patrick Crichton was alerted to the approach of the Jacobites. However, the 15th was a Sunday, and John Wilson, the Presbyterian minister of Glencorse, was in full flow, detaining his people in the kirk 'with a long sermon and ane ill-timed exhortation after which I had not patience to hear owt, considering the enemmie was at the gaits'.[22] Inside Edinburgh nobody could determine whether the local forces ought to emerge and join the two regiments of dragoons. Alexander Carlyle, son of the minister of Prestonpans, was numbered among the 400 Volunteers who mustered in the College Yards at the eastern end of the Cowgate, and from where they made their way up to the Lawnmarket to await the arrival of the other irregular companies. They raised a cheer for Hamilton's Dragoons as they clattered their way across the square from Leith to join Gardiner, and 'while we remained there, which was the great part of an hour, the mob in the street and the ladies in the windows treated us very variously, many with lamentations, and even with tears, and some with apparent [i.e. open] scorn and derision. In one house on the side of the street there was a row of windows, full of ladies, who appeared to enjoy our march to danger with much levity and mirth. Some of our warm Volunteers observed them, and threatened to fire into the windows if they were not instantly let down, which was immediately complied with'.[23]

The Volunteers then marched down the narrow and winding Bow to the Grassmarket near the West Port. They had to endure another wait, relieved only by a party of clergy headed by Dr Wishart, the Principal of the College. There were many students among the Volunteers, and Wishart 'called upon us in a most pathetic speech to desist from this rash enterprise, which he said was exposing the flower of the youth of Edinburgh, and the hope of the next generation, to the danger of being cut off, or made prisoners and maltreated without any just or adequate object'.[24] After these heartening words the Volunteers were dismissed, and told to return in the evening to furnish the guards for the town walls.

Edinburgh's static defences were in no way able to make up for the lack of effective forces. The castle on its rock to the west was proof against assault and any artillery the Jacobites were likely to bring against it, but the stronghold was too isolated to be of much help in defending the town. The walls mentioned by Carlyle were those of the Flodden Wall, which had been thrown up by the town authorities in the emergency following the defeat and death of King James IV of Scotland at Flodden on 9 September 1513. The rampart was of crudely dressed stone, set in lime mortar, and was primitive even by the standards of that time, being a simple battlemented wall which stood between 15- and 20-feet high. Its so-called 'bastions' were just feeble little towers, and it had no provision for mounting cannon or bringing down a crossfire to bear on the approaches.

The line of the wall followed the southern and eastern limits of the old town, from the castle by way of the West Port to the axis of the present

Lauriston Place and so to the south-eastern corner at the Bristo and Pot-terow Ports. It then turned north by way of Netherbow Port to reach the foot of Calton Hill. The near-stagnant lake of the Nor' Loch was believed to offer sufficient cover to the northern side of the town. These arrange-ments isolated the Canongate, which was considered a separate entity from Edinburgh proper.

The Flodden Wall was mostly complete by 1518, but was beginning to fall down as early as 1557, and underwent intermittent repairs thereafter. Two extensions (1620–28, and 1636) took in respectively Heriot's Hospital and its grounds, and the South Greyfriars Yard, and sprouted a small and primitive bastion at the junction of Heriot Place and Lauriston Place, but otherwise added little to its strength. The elections to the Crafts of the Masons and Wrights delayed work in the new emergency of September 1745, and the wall was 'neglected to such a degree, that it was impossible for the town to stand out six hours, though within it there would be thrice the number of the rebels. The principal defect was that the parapet of the embra-sures was so low, as not to cover any man of middling size above the thighs, and were above two feet wide, so that the whole chest of a man was exposed as a mark to the enemy, and before he possibly could have time to present his firelock, he must necessarily have been shot by the besiegers'. The town authorized Colin MacLaurin, Professor of Mathematics at the College, to devote his talents to putting the wall in order. Richard Jack, a private tutor in mathematics, was deputed to help and

> got more above fifty cart-load of turf thrown up and completed the Potterow Port and part of the Bristo Port, which were the two principal places first to be put in a good posture of defence. On Sunday morning [15 September] we began our work, and completed the Bristo Port, both in the embrasures and merlons (their parapet not being above breast high) as also the next adjacent bastion to the south of that port. These ports with that bastion being finished, I was setting about the repairing of all the other bastions to the south, when I was desired by Mr MacLaurin ... to view the wall towards the north part of the town, lying between the New Port and Trinity Hospital which, he said, he was informed was also too low in the parapet.[25]

On the 16th Jack collected a hundred labourers and set to work there, too. A number of cannon were borrowed from the ships in Leith harbour, but Provost Stewart refused to allow the sailors to man them, claiming that their shooting would be too wild.

By this time events were gathering their own momentum. Early in the morning of 16 September Brigadier Thomas Fowke reviewed the two regiments of dragoons, a handful of the Town Guard, and the new Edinburgh Regiment on a field near Coltbridge. Hamiltons' Dragoons (the 14th) were in good shape, though their Irish accents gave cause for concern. Both the horses and the men of Gardiner's (the 13th) were in a bad way, and Colonel Gardiner himself was scarcely recognizable as a military man, being enveloped in a blue surcoat, and having his hat secured by a handkerchief which ran over the top and was tied under the chin. He declared that he did not have long to live – and he was right. On the recommendation of Lieutenant General Guest the dragoons were ordered to make their way around to the west of the town to Leith. On the way the rearguard took fright, and soon the people of Edinburgh could see what became known as the 'Coltbridge Canter', with the dragoons streaming from left to right across the Lang Dykes – the high ground beyond the Nor' Loch (now covered by the New Town). The flight continued east along the coast as far as Prestonpans, leaving the way strewn with pistols, swords and other gear. 'It was an unlucky dragoon ... who fell into a coal-pit, not filled up, when his side-arms and accoutrements made such a noise, as alarmed a body of men who for two days had [already] been panic-struck.'[26] Upon this fright the wild career began anew.

Crichton records that 'the city was in a fay upon the military going off ... The Provost ordered his dolefull alarme by bell of ominows sound, and this was ane unconcerted signal to call the inhabitants under ther pannick to see if they wowld defend or surrender'.[27] The Volunteers reassembled on the Lawnmarket and sent two of their lieutenants to find out what was going on. 'While they were absent, two Volunteers in the rear rank (Boyle and Weir), just behind, quarrelled, when debating whether or not the city should be surrendered, and were going to attack one another, one with his musket and bayonet, and the other with his small sword, having flung down his musket. They were soon separated without doing any harm, and placed asunder from each other.'[28] The Volunteers were sent to the castle to deposit their arms there, and it was clear that Edinburgh had been given up for lost. Alexander Carlyle and his 15-year-old brother decided to make their own way out. They left by way of the Netherbow Port on the eastern side of the Flodden Wall, giving on to the Canongate and Holyrood, and continued by way of the shore to reach their home in Prestonpans, where they had every reason to think they would be left in peace.

Early on 16 September Prince Charles and his army began a measured advance on Edinburgh. They set off early from their bivouacs east of Falkirk and marched on by way of Winchburgh to the crossing of the River Almond at Kirkliston. As a matter of honour the Glencoe MacDonalds volunteered to safeguard the nearby Newliston House, the home of the absent Earl of Stair (p. 107). There was a two-hour halt at Todshall (Foxhall), and early in the afternoon the army reached Corstorphine, from where the Prince sent a summons to Edinburgh. The Jacobites now took up the anti-clockwise route to bring them around to the south-east side of the city the next day. The Prince stopped for the night of the 16th at a mill on the left bank of the winding River Leith just below Slateford, while his army bivouacked outside.

Overnight Lochiel and O'Sullivan set out with several hundred picked clansmen straight for Edinburgh. They were making for the Netherbow Port and their aim was to take it by a *coup de main*. The City Guard refused to admit one of their number who pretended that he was a servant, but their chance came at 5 a.m. on the 17th, when the gates were opened to allow a coach to return to its stables in the Canongate. Thirty of the High-landers rushed in unopposed and opened the way to the rest of the party. All of Richard Jack's work on the Flodden Wall had gone for nothing, and he was reduced to being a spectator when the Jacobites secured the city: 'They were in two parties, which I carefully numbered from my window. The first consisted of fifty ranks three men each, the second of fifty-three ranks six men each including officers … so that the whole army that entered the town consisted of 468 men, some of them altogether unarmed, others with a broadsword, some with corn forks, and many with muskets without locks, in a word the number of guns that reasonably might be supposed to fire, did not exceed 200'.[29]

The good news was conveyed to Prince Charles and the rest of his army at Gray's Mill on the morning of 17 September. The Jacobites continued along the same circuitous route that they had adopted the day before, this time with the aim of keeping as much high ground as possible between them-selves and Edinburgh Castle:

> This march, though short, was not altogether free of danger, for he could see from his present position the flag of defiance flying on the battlements of the Castle, and apparently daring him to venture within the scope of its guns. The eminent position of that fortress was such as to command nearly the whole country for miles around, and it was a matter of difficulty to dis-cover a path which should conduct him to the city without being exposed to its fire. Some of his train, however, by their acquaintance with the locali-ties, enabled him to obviate this petty danger.[30]

The Jacobites took up a stretch of turnpike at Morningside (later a famously genteel quarter), but before approaching too close to Edinburgh they turned off east again along the foot of the Braid Hills and worked their way north-east to the King's Park at Prestonfield, which they entered by a gap in the enclosure wall. Lord George Murray tucked the troops away for a time in the hollow known as the 'Hunter's Bog' between Salisbury Crags and Arthur's Seat, before leading them to a bivouac site by Duddingston. The Jacobites were by this time outnumbered many times over by cheering townspeople. Prince Charles was mounted on a fine bay which had been given to him by the Duke of Perth, who knew about horses, and 'he ... continued ... always followed by the crowd, which were happy if they could touch his boots or his horse furniture. In the steepest part of the park going down to the Abbey, he was obliged to alight and walk, but the mob out of curiosity, and some out of fondness to kiss his hand, were like to throw him down, so, as soon as he was down the hill he mounted his horse and rode through St Anne's yards into Holyroodhouse amidst the cries of 60,000 [sic] people, who filled the air with their acclamations of joy'.[31]

Even the enemies of the Prince had to concede that the behaviour of the Highlanders was 'more regular than had been expected'. Their bivouacs were established behind Holyroodhouse in the direction of the King's Park, and only the security guard was allowed in the town until, on 18 September, 900 men marched in to attend the proclamation of King James VIII and his son as Regent at the Mercat Cross. 'The young man, who stood on the street all the time the ceremony lasted, had his hand kissed very passionately by great numbers of old women on their knees.'[32] The Edinburgh Whig Magdalen Pringle was drawn by curiosity, and tried to pretend to her sister Tib that she was unmoved, describing how 'the windows were full of ladies who threw up their handkerchiefs and clapped their hands and showed their loyalty to the Bonny Prince. Don't imagine I was one of those ladies, I assure you I was not'.[33]

The Reckoning with Cope

By the end of August 1745 the contending forces in Scotland had drawn apart in a curious fashion. Prince Charles had left the Highlands and was turning towards Perth and Edinburgh; Lieutenant General Cope, declining to venture over the Correiyairack Pass, had hastened north-east as if pursued by demons. He reached Inverness on the 29th, and he or one of his officers could write the next day that 'if our intelligence is to be depended upon, we are just now lying within two or three miles of them ... If we had them in plain muir [sic] we should be able to thrash them, but as they are placed just now behind two hills it would be impossible to make anything of them'.[34] That was at a time when the nearest respectable body of armed Jacobites was nearly 50 miles away, and going in the other direction.

The one positive motive for Cope's retiring to Inverness had been to rally the Presbyterian clans of north-eastern Scotland, but this at once proved to be a fantasy, for no contact could be made with either the Sutherlands or the MacKays, and the 120 Munros who put in an appearance did so only on condition that they must return home in two weeks to gather in the harvest. On 31 August Cope established that the Jacobites were making for the Lowlands, and he now bent all his efforts towards anticipating them at Edinburgh. Major Whitefoord later declared in Cope's defence that 'as you saw the necessity of being soon in the south, and the impossibility of getting to Edinburgh before the rebels by land, you resolved to send to Leith [the port of Edinburgh] for a number of transports to carry your army by sea, that being the only means left to get there before them'.[35] He would not wait for the transports to round Fraserburgh and sail all the way up the Moray Firth to take him off, but instead marched diagonally overland to Aberdeen to embark there.

Cope's army set out from Inverness on 4 September and marched to Aberdeen with all possible speed, reaching Nairn on the same day, Elgin on 5 September, Fochabers on the 6th, Cullen on the 7th, Banff on the 8th, Turiff on the 9th, and Oldmeldrum on the 10th. The troops arrived at Aberdeen on 11 September, and to the concern of the local farmers they encamped amid ripe standing cereals on Dove Cote Brae (the site of the later Union Street). Cope declined an offer from the local Whigs to put his troops on fishing craft, preferring to embark on the ships from Leith which arrived off the town on the same day. A malevolent combination of winds and tides prevented the force from sailing until the evening of the 15th, and a succession of calms and adverse winds made it impossible for Cope to reach the Firth of Forth until after dark on the 16th. The Jacobites were already outside the town on the landward side, and quite possibly the sight of the boats in the Firth triggered the *coup de main* which gained Edinburgh for Prince Charles early on the 17th.

Cope made eastwards along the coast to Dunbar, the nearest secure port. He arrived on 17 September and completed his disembarkation the next day. Since leaving Inverness he had shown no lack of urgency, for he had marched to Aberdeen without a day's rest, and failed to anticipate the

Jacobites at Edinburgh by only a matter of hours. At Dunbar he met Gardiner's and Hamilton's Dragoons, but found them so badly shaken that he had to remain there overnight so that they could put themselves in some kind of order. The delay must have been galling, for he was determined to bring the Jacobites to combat and allow them no more time to savour their outrageous success or to build up their forces.

Cope had his battle. It was at Prestonpans on 21 September, a day that ended with his troops being totally routed and the survivors streaming over the Lammermuir Hills to the south.

Edinburgh the Princely Residence, 22 September – 31 October 1745

On 22 September the Jacobite forces returned to the neighbourhood of Edinburgh in triumph. In arid scientific perspective the site is a classic crag-and-tail formation, where the eastward push of the glaciers of the Ice Age had been resisted by the basalt plug of the castle rock, and the sheltered sedimentary deposits behind fell as a 'tail', a long, steep-sided ramp. The tail became in due course the site of Edinburgh town, with the Royal Mile crowning the uppermost edge as it descended toward the Netherbow Port and the Canongate. In this cramped environment the stone-built houses, or rather the teeming tenements, could attain a height of ten storeys, and they were jammed so close together that the steeper slopes to either side of the crest (down to the Nor' Loch to the north, and the Cowgate and Grassmarket to the south) could be negotiated only by means of dark and narrow alleys.

In eighteenth-century Edinburgh curious contrasts could be observed between, say, the pretensions of the Writers of the Signet (the lawyers), or the measured diction of the ladies' speech, and the squalid conditions of everyday living. 'I was invited to a tavern,' wrote one of Wade's surveyors. 'The cook was too filthy an object to be described; only another English gentleman whispered [to] me and said, he believed if the fellow would be thrown against the wall, he would stick to it.'[36]

Every morning the water had to be carried in pails up the multiple stairways of the tenements, but much worse happened when the liquids or semi-liquids were disposed of in the evening. They were cast out of the windows with a perfunctory warning, and 'it is Fortune favours you, if a chamber pot with excrements etc. is not thrown upon your head'.[37] Your only refuge from the stink was to retire into a corner of a room and burn paper under your nose.

Prince Charles had good reasons not to overburden Edinburgh with his army's presence. Such of his troops as entered the town were on their best behaviour, but it was wise not to test the tolerance of the citizens too far, and in any case the sight of a Highland plaid was enough to draw down a storm of 9-pounder shot from the dominating half-moon battery of the castle. The cantankerous 85-year-old governor, Lieutenant General Joshua Guest, was ensconced up there with the original garrison of invalids, together with two companies of Lascelles' 58th and a few runaways from Prestonpans.

Prince Charles was content to have the defenders bottled up by Lochiel's Camerons, who kept watch on the castle from their station on the Lawnmarket and lived in an indoor camp which they established in the Parliament House. On hearing that the garrison was short of provisions, Prince Charles ordered the Camerons in the Weigh House at the head of the Lawnmarket to stop all communication from the town. On 1 October Guest retaliated in style, pouring down 'small shott from muskets and pertreg [partridge] shot from the cannon when any of them dars peep owt. 'Tis said Lochiell was behind some howse in the hill and the fall or flying of some stons hurt his showlder. 'Tis not safe being in the Lawn or Grassmarkets. I saw a musket ball battered upon the stones in Grassmarket and a gentleman missed it narrowly'. A maidservant, less lucky, was hit in the foot as she was standing with her pitcher beside a cistern, while a cannot shot 'went through a window in Haddock's Hole Kirk, so that the inhabitants were excessively alarmed, and obliged to keep close in their houses'.[38]

On 3 October a party descended from the castle by ropes and captured an outpost which, as Lord George Murray alleged, O'Sullivan had placed rashly in the West Kirk In the course of a still more ambitious sortie on the night of 4/5 October the troops contrived to dig a great ditch 14 feet wide and 16 deep, half-way down the esplanade – the open space descending to the nearest houses of the town. The fire continued on the 5th, and on looking along the northern side of the High Street our informant Patrick Crichton saw 'a tradesman in a blew frock had just been shot his brains dashed owt and in his blood'.[39] Prince Charles lifted the blockade, though the garrison continued to take pot shots at anybody in tartan.

The Prince's people could move more freely beyond the Netherbow Port in the Canongate, which was a separate burgh with its own town guard, prison, tolbooth, and a handsome kirk (built in 1688), which held redcoat prisoners for a short time after the battle of Prestonpans. The Canongate was admittedly decayed from the days of its glory at the time of the old Scottish kingdom. The dignified abodes of the old nobility were somewhat run down, and the quarter was now remarkable for 'a great number of bawdy-houses … which amongst the frequenters of them, it is a common question to ask, if they have got a pair of Canongate breeches, meaning the venereal disease, which rages here as well as in other places of note'.[40]

Beyond the Canongate again the royal palace of Holyroodhouse became the symbolic residence of Prince Charles in his Scottish capital. The Palladian pile been commissioned by Charles II from the diplomat and Architect Royal Sir William Bruce. Oddly enough King Charles himself never set foot there, and its one occupant of note was his brother the Duke of York (the future James II), who functioned as Viceroy of Scotland from 1679 to 1682.

Edinburgh

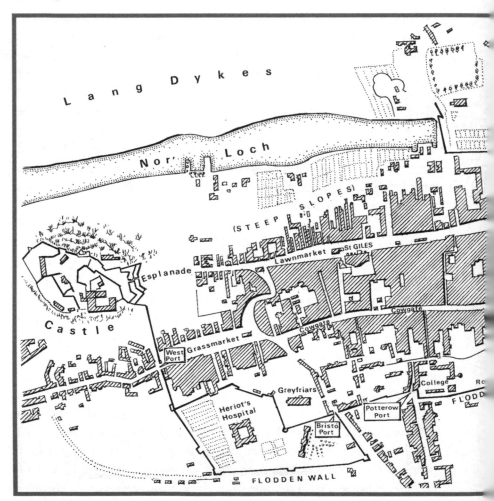

As the Hereditary Keepers of the palace, the Dukes of Hamilton kept the Queen's Apartments in good repair for their own use during the long period of neglect which followed, and it was there, and not within the king's range, that Prince Charles held court during the five weeks he spent in Edinburgh in 1745.

Probably the most frequently used of these chambers was the ante-room in the James V Tower, where the Prince received visits and conducted his official business. The Great Dining Room was by far the largest enclosed space in the whole palace, and was adorned with a new William Adam fireplace, mahogany furniture of Edinburgh manufacture, and portrait upon portrait of Stuart monarchs, their features recreated for the most part in

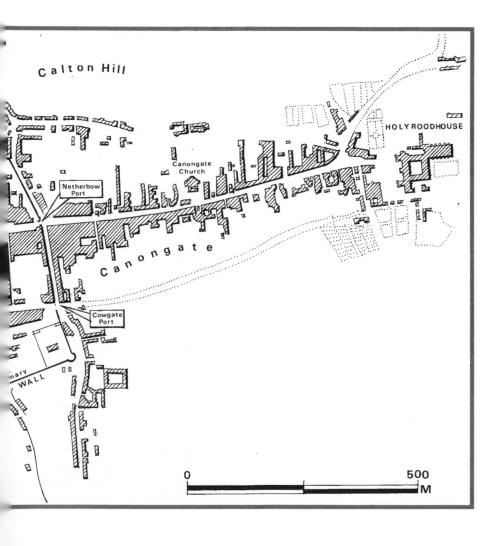

the imagination of the painters. However, at this stage of his enterprise Prince Charles lived the life of a military monk, shunning social engagements, and he had to be persuaded to attend a ball which his wellwishers had laid on for his entertainment.[41]

The Prince began most days by receiving a number of his officers in the ante-room, where he then convened his argumentative Grand Council at about 10 a.m. He lunched in the palace in public view (an obligation of traditional monarchy), then rode out in the afternoon to inspect the troops. He was back at Holyroodhouse in the evening to dine and receive Jacobite ladies and other social guests, but he never danced, and he then retired quietly, or rode out to spend the night with his army. One of his more distant excursions is said to have taken him to Traquair House, and tradition has it that on his departure the Earl of Traquair cast the keys of the great Bear Gates into the Tweed, declaring that they would never be opened until the lawful Stuart line returned. They are still shut, and the original avenue leading to the house is covered with grass.

The local tradesmen were alert to the opportunities opened to them when the Prince's entourage and officers arrived in their midst. William Cheape, a weaver of Bonnymills, inserted an advertisement in the *Caledonian Mercury*, pointing out that 'the Royal Scots Thistle Pattern being often chosen, he has, for the benefit of his customers, drawn a beautiful new figure of the same, supported at the root by a Flower de Luce [Lys], with crowns, motto, etc. in their proper places'.[42] The friends of the government were lying low, but after the paper published a particularly effusive letter in praise of the Prince, one of the Whigs pencilled on his copy that 'The joy of the wicked is like the crackling of thorns under a boot'.[43]

The Prince's most frequent goal on his outings was the standing camp just on the far side of Arthur's Seat at Duddingston, to where he had removed the main body of his troops from their billets and bivouacs in Edinburgh. In this more military environment he sought to accustom his growing forces to the routine of a regular army, complete with drill, orders of the day, and daily challenges and passwords (e.g. *Taffy* to be answered by *Wales*, and *Patrick* by *Ireland*), and the apparatus (if not the full reality) of formal discipline: 'His Royal Highness is informed of the little notice the officers, especially the majors, take of his orders ... His Royal Highness will not forget those who are exact, as he will not those who neglect their duty'.[44]

Overcoming her political principles, Magdalen Pringle went out to see the Prince take a parade:

He was sitting in a tent when I first came to the field. The ladies made a circle around the tent, and after we had gazed our fill at him he came out of the tent with a grace and majesty that is inexpressible. He saluted all the circle with an air of grandeur and affability capable of charming the most obstinate Whig, and, mounting his horse in the middle of the circle, he rode off to view the men … He was dressed in a blue grogram [coarse-spun] coat trimmed with gold lace, and a laced red waistcoat and breeches. On his left shoulder and side were the Star and Garter, and over his shoulder a very rich sword belt. His sword had the finest wrought basket ever I beheld, all silver. His hat had a white feather in it and a white cockade, and was trimmed with an open gold lace. His horse was black and finely bred (it had been poor Gardiner's). His Highness rides very finely, and indeed in all his appearance seems to be cut out for enchanting his beholders and carrying people to consent to their own slavery in spite of themselves.[45]

The Jacobites had all the captured equipment of Cope's army at their disposal, but nothing could persuade the Highlanders to pitch their tents in military style. On 14 October, with the approach of winter, a number of troops were moved back to Edinburgh and the Canongate, though the Athollmen, the MacLachlans and the followers of Stewart of Ardsheal remained at Duddingston, and a number of large detachments were deployed on outpost duty – Lochiel at Leith and Clanranald at Newhaven to secure the coast, Keppoch at Inch on the road to the south, and the Duke of Perth at Restalrig. 'There was a party of them entered Inveresk … when the Minister, who is a young man, was about to begin the last prayer, and prayed for King George. Upon this they stopped him and ordered him to pray for their King, but he proceeded, and they held a piece to his breast. He told them they had no power to hurt him at that time, upon which they dragged him out of the pulpit, which bred much confusion, and no wonder.'[46]

Young Glengarry led a party into Berwickshire to snatch horses and other desirable articles from the Whig gentry. On 9 October he arrived at Redbraes, the home of the absentee Earl of Marchmont. Warned in time, his sister Lady Jane Nimmo and his steward John Hunter had spirited away the horses, but there was nowhere to hide a great portrait of George I. On arriving at this place, Glengarry kept his men on the bowling green outside and sent only six of his officers inside, where they behaved, according to Lady Jane, 'with the greatest civility, laughed egregiously at Johnny Cope (as they call him), and talked with the three girls for two hours at the dining room fire, and gave them apples they had brought from Nisbet'.[47]

One of the reasons why Charles redeployed his forces was to prevent spies from identifying the changes in the character of his army, which not only swelled to 7,287 infantry and 300 horse, and acquired some formal ways, but became more representative of Scotland as a whole with the arrival of more of the gentry and recruits from the east. That was partly owing to the example set by the respected 68-year-old Lord Pitsligo, who returned looking 'like an old carrier',[48] partly to the impetus given by the victory at Prestonpans, but not least to the capture of the considerable port-town of Aberdeen by James Moir, 4th Earl of Stoneywood.

Stoneywood had delivered his coup on 15 September. He had slipped away from the army to raise recruits, and was accompanied, it was alleged, by only a handful of street porters and bankrupt merchants. 'The well-affected people in town seemed only to make a jest of Stoneywood and his procession, and the Magistrates found it convenient to overlook it, since any ill-usage of him might have been avenged by a very small party, for as Cope had carried off the town's arms, lest the rebels should have seized them, a very few armed men might have come and plundered the whole town; but from this small beginning thus neglected, the rebels very soon became masters of his place in reality.'[49] The Jacobites were to capture Manchester in the same style.

Young Lord Ogilvy then arrived in Edinburgh with 300 men from Angus, venerable Glenbucket with a further 300 from Aberdeenshire, and (just before the campaign began) a body of the Athollmen collected by the young MacPherson of Cluny. They were ferried across the Forth, and one of Cluny's clansmen wrote to a friend that he was now on the 'south side of the water of Forth, opposite to Alloa, sitting on a slimy bank, my feet in the ugliest slime, my target my table, waiting [for] the rear, I being one of the first men crossed of my regiment'.[50] MacKinnon had contrived to bring 120 of his clan all the way from Skye, and redcoat sergeants, corporals and privates of Cope's army arrived in such numbers that the Jacobite clerks were almost overwhelmed.

Lord Strathallan's troop of horse was now supplemented by the two troops of the Lifeguards, Lord Kilmarnock's Horse Guards, the middle-aged gentlemen of Lord Pitsligo's Horse, and the younger and much less well-behaved hussars.

Prince Charles had put together his expedition and sailed to Scotland without the knowledge of the French king and ministers, but in the hope that they would be impelled into action when they were presented with a *fait accompli*. Between 9 and 19 October four French privateers reached Montrose and Peterhead, bearing some £5,000 in gold, together with 2,500 muskets, six light field pieces, and twelve French artillerymen under the direction of the Franco-Scottish lieutenant colonel James Grant. On 14 October one of the passengers, Alexandre de Boyer, Marquis d'Eguilles, presented himself at Holyroodhouse as the personal representative of Louis XV, and when the Athollmen came at the end of the month they brought the French artillery with them across the Forth.

With hindsight we can pick up clues which indicate that the French had not yet decided how far, or in what form, they should commit themselves to the rising. Thus the equipment and personnel had been carried on commissioned privateers, not warships, and d'Eguilles had come essentially to find out what was going on. The support was nevertheless tangible, and the decision to send it had been sent before news of the victory at Prestonpans had reached Versailles (it took Burgoyne's surrender at Saratoga in October 1777 to induce the French to support the rebel Americans). At this juncture nothing could have been more welcome to Prince Charles and his supporters in their daily battles with the sceptics in his Grand Council.

The Council comprised the grandees, the most eminent gentlemen of the north-east and the leaders as the clan regiments, together with the immediate circle of the Prince. He had to allow his principal supporters some kind of collective voice, but the Grand Council was an obstacle to the making of speedy and resolute military decisions, and it institutionalized the divisions in the leadership, with Lord George Murray ranging the majority against Prince Charles, the Catholic Duke of Perth, the Earl of Kilmarnock, the lords Nairne and Pitsligo, the Secretary of State Murray of Broughton, and John William O'Sullivan the chief of staff. The presence of O'Sullivan was cited by Lord George that Irish companions still exerted undue influence over the Prince.

Only the first demonstrable proof of French help, together with some powerful arguments marshalled by Prince Charles, could have induced the Council to reach the resolution it did on 30 October 1745, which was to invade England. Towards the end of this month Colonel John Roy Stuart had summoned Allan Ramsay to make a portrait of Prince Charles at Holyroodhouse. The work could hardly have progressed beyond the preliminary sketches before the sittings were interrupted.

CHAPTER 8

Invasion: The Bid for a Kingdom, 31 October – 22 November 1745

THE DEBATES IN THE GRAND COUNCIL had come to a head on 30 October 1745. For a time Lord George Murray and the majority of the clan chiefs argued the case for remaining in Scotland. In their homeland they could eliminate the recalcitrant areas and isolated redcoat strongpoints, recruit and consolidate the Jacobite forces, and wait in security for cash, arms and reinforcements to arrive from France by sea.

Prince Charles and his supporters urged that, on the contrary, the Jacobites were made for movement, for the Highlanders had a way of going to pieces if they were kept waiting about, and all the acceptable ways of raising revenue had been exhausted, even though the Royal Bank of Scotland had made no difficulty about turning its notes into gold coin to pay the troops. By carrying the fight into England the army could provide the Highlanders with all the action they wanted, collect the public monies, and live off the country. Prince Charles could not say in public that it was only through a full-blooded invasion that he could reclaim the British crown for the

Murray of Broughton's Hussar showing scimitar sword and pistols

Stuarts and that he had no particular interest in sustaining a long-drawn-out uprising in Scotland.

As for particulars, the Prince argued that the Jacobites must advance boldly into Northumberland and beat Wade's hastily collected army (p. 214) before his troops could pull themselves together after their long marches and voyages. Again, it would not have been prudent for Charles to mention that all the effort of establishing active contacts with the English Jacobites had been directed along this eastern route.

The Council decided to embrace the principle of the invasion by a single vote, and then only because Lord George Murray persuaded enough of the members of the merits of advancing into England from the north-west. He argued that a western route would offer a more secure communication with Scotland, take the army through the supposedly sympathetic county of Lancashire, and enable the Jacobites to receive help from French landings on the western coasts of England or Wales. In addition, the pronounced slant of the border meant that an advance by the western avenue would bring the army much more readily into the heart of England than a march to the east, the only obstacle being the decaying walls of Carlisle. The matching fortress-town to the east of the hills was Berwick-upon-Tweed, which was a tougher proposition and not worth the expenditure of time, 'which was then so precious. I proposed marching into England [by] the other road, but, to conceal the design, that the army would march in two columns, the one by Kelso, which would be supposedly designed to go in by Wooler-haughhead, and the other to march by Moffat, so that both columns could join, the day appointed, near Carlisle'.[1] Thus writes Lord George. The matter was finally settled the next day when Prince Charles, although still believing the eastern route to be better, told Lord George that he would comply with the majority.

On balance the dangers were increased rather than lessened by his concession. Not only had the Jacobites abandoned the opportunity of bringing Wade to battle while they still held the moral advantage, but they put at risk their holdings in Scotland which were patchy and insecure. After three or four marches they must abandon Edinburgh and the Lothians, which were untenable against a sortie from Edinburgh Castle and a thrust from the advanced elements of Wade's army at Berwick.

The core area of the Jacobite forces remaining in Scotland inevitably moved to the eastern counties of Aberdeenshire, Banffshire, Angus, the Mearns and Atholl, or in rough geographical terms the tract of Scotland lying between the Moray Firth to the north and the Firth of Tay to the south.

Here a comprehensive military and civilian administration was now organized under the authority of Brigadier General the Viscount Strathallan (succeeded by Lieutenant General Lord John Drummond after he landed on 26 November). The chiefs and gentry prosecuted a forceful programme of local recruiting, and the ardent Jacobites of the eastern ports rendered all possible help in getting ashore the equipment and reinforcements that continued to arrive from France (p. 366).

As the army of Prince Charles moved west then south into England, the connection with the forces building up in Scotland became tenuous in the extreme, in spite of what Lord George had said, for it had to pass through the no-man's-land of the 'wasp waist' of the Central Lowlands. The enemy still held the well-nigh impregnable Stirling Castle in the middle, while the Jacobites never penetrated the country further to the west, where the Whigs held Dumfries, Glasgow and the lands of the Campbells. The Jacobite presence was reduced to the passage of couriers, the battery which commanded the Forth downstream of Stirling at Alloa, and the Castle of Doune near the Fords of Frew 7 miles upstream.

John MacGregor of Glengyle remained at Doune with a party of his clan, and 'he was governor of that castle all the while that the rebels was in England'.[2] He took charge of the prisoners (beginning with forty-five captured at the barracks at Inversnaid on Loch Lomond), and he had to be on his guard both against Blakeney's garrison in Stirling Castle to the east, and against the Campbells beyond Menteith and the Trossachs to the west.

The Jacobites north of the Tay soon had preoccupations of their own, for an active Hanoverian front opened in the north-east on 14 October, when John Campbell, Earl of Loudoun, disembarked at Inverness with weapons and money and the commission to command all the sympathetic forces in that part of the world. He succeeded, when Cope had not, in raising the Presbyterian clans for the government, and by the end of November he was in a position to put 2,000 militiamen into the field. In such a way north-eastern Scotland was overtaken by a civil war which bore no relation to the campaign south of the Border (pp. 348ff).

A Jacobite force of some 6,000 was available at the start of November for the great adventure in England. The staff work provided for a brief initial concentration 6 miles east-south-east of Edinburgh at Dalkeith, after which the troops were to march in two columns in the way outlined by Lord George, and reunite just inside England at Carlisle.

On 31 October the main body of the army marched from Edinburgh to Dalkeith, where the men bivouacked between the Newbattle Water and Melville Burn. Prince Charles arrived on 1 November, went to the magnificent Palladian palace of the absent Duke of Buccleuch, 'and there fixed his headquarters, which lay conveniently for sending his spies to see what was doing in the North of England'.[3] These people were being sent even now into the north-eastern counties. The army was busy rearranging itself into two columns or divisons, namely:

Lowland Division of the Dukes of Perth and Atholl (west)

(Total about 2,640)

Consisting mainly of heavy-footed Lowlanders, and encumbered by the artillery, this division was to set out first and take the easier and more direct route out to the west by way of Auchendinny, Peebles and Moffat.

❖ Atholl Brigade

❖ Duke of Perth's Regiment

❖ Gordon of Glenbucket's Regiment

❖ John Roy Stuart's Regiment

❖ Lord Ogilvy's Regiment

❖ Lord Pitsligo's Horse

❖ Lord Kilmarnock's Horse Guards

❖ Hussars

❖ Army Train of six 1½-pounder cannon, six French 4-pounders, one unidentified cannon and four coehorn mortars. The Train was commanded by Colonel James Grant, assisted by the Chevalier James de Johnstone, and escorted by three or four companies of Perth's Regiment which did service as the Pioneers. De Johnstone had been glad to resign as aide-de-camp to the spiky Lord George Murray, but his new task proved to be 'almost as fatiguing as the one I had quitted'.[4]

Highland Division of Prince Charles and Lord George Murray (east)

(Total about 2,250)

Lightly equipped and fast moving, the Highlanders were to take a route to the eastern Borders as if making for Newcastle, then jink to the right at Kelso, cross the high watershed of the Central Uplands and descend Liddesdale to reach the lower Esk and Eden near Carlisle.

Clan regiments of:

❖ MacDonnells of Glengarry

❖ MacDonnells of Keppoch

❖ MacDonalds of Clanranald

❖ Cluny's MacPhersons

❖ Stewarts of Appin

❖ Lochiel's Camerons

❖ Lord Elcho's Lifeguards (branching out to the west by way of Hawick and Langholm, and rejoining the route of the main column at Canonbie).

Hanoverian Preparations

King George II returned to London on 31 August. After a few days it was clear that the government could no longer rely on the assurance of the Earl of Stair that the rising in Scotland could be put down by the forces at hand. On 4 September the Duke of Newcastle wrote to the Duke of Cumberland in Flanders, warning that he must call on ten of the battalions of British troops that were serving alongside the Dutch and Austrians there:

> Though I have constantly seen the reality and danger of this attempt to invade His Majesty's dominions, I did not imagine that, in so short a time, the Pretender's son, with an army of 3,000 men, would have got between the King's troops and England, and be within a few days' march of Edinburgh, where, some think, we shall soon hear that he is; and that he may attempt to call a Parliament there. Others rather suppose that he will proceed with his army through England, where there are no regular troops to oppose him, 'till he comes towards London.[5]

But by the middle of September the Swedish ambassador could report that 'the ruffians who have collected in Scotland include many men who have been brought along by force. They run off again as soon as they can, so that the remaining force is not reckoned to exceed 3,000. Added to this reports say that there is disunion in their counsels as to what they ought to do next'.[6]

Then came the news of the rout at Prestonpans, which reached London on the 24th. The shock was palpable. The Hon. Charles Yorke could not conceive how Prince Charles, a man of no particular character or gifts, should have landed with a few friends in a corner of Scotland and been allowed to accomplish so much in such a short time. 'It is indeed a dreadful and amazing consideration to reflect … that a fabric of so much art and cost as the Revolution [of 1688] and its train of consequences, should be in danger of being overwhelmed by the bursting of a cloud, which seemed, at its first gathering, no bigger than a man's hand.'[7]

Not surprisingly, however, the summoning of reinforcements (which mostly had to be disengaged from the campaign against the French in Flanders) proceeded by fits and starts. In essence it proceeded in three stages and helped to build up two armies. The relevant strategy was sketched at a council of war on 4 October. One of the armies, under the 72-year-old Field Marshal Wade, was to gather in the far north and confront the Jacobites. The second, under Cumberland's deputy, Lieutenant General Sir John Ligonier, was to keep a watch on the western approaches to the English Midlands – initially to hold a position at Chester and along the Dee, and then more generally the area between the Severn and the Trent. If no Jacobite force turned up in this part of the world, Ligonier was to move east by way of Nottingham and join the army of Wade.

The Reinforcements
First Lift: the auxiliary Dutch and Swiss
The first resource available to the government was the 6,000 Dutch troops and Swiss troops in the Dutch pay, summoned from the Continent on the strength of a treaty dating back to 1713. One of the Dutch battalions was sent directly to Cope, and reached him at Berwick after his defeat: 'They seem mostly Papists, use the Romish ceremonies, and ask where they may have Mass'.[8] On 19 September the three battalion-strong Swiss regiment of Hirtzel disembarked on the lower Thames. Four battalions of Dutch arrived there on the next day, and two of them were forwarded by sea to Newcastle.

Second Lift: the initial British reinforcement from Flanders
They came in answer to the Duke of Newcastle's request of 4 September (above), and landed in the Thames on the 23rd at Grays, Gravesend and Blackwall. The tidings of Prestonpans arrived on the next day. The Duke of Newcastle, at least, was convinced that the Jacobites were 'determined and well-disciplined', and he wrote to Cumberland on the 25th that 'had not that reinforcement providentially arrived the day before the news came of Sir John Cope's defeat, the confusion in the City would not have been to be described, and the King's Crown (I venture to say) in the utmost danger'.[9]

Third Lift: the further British reinforcements from Flanders

The government now ordered the Duke of Cumberland to come to Britain in person, and nearly all the remaining British forces were retrieved from Flanders under the Earl of Albemarle. All but one of the battalions sailed from Hellevoetsluis on 13 October, and were directed straight to Newcastle.

The Armies and Detachments

(infantry regiments were single battalions (bn) of about 500 each, unless otherwise stated)

The Army of Field Marshal Wade in north-eastern England

(Approx. 4,500 Dutch and Swiss infantry; 4,950 British infantry; 1,500 British horse. Total: 10,950).

Wade's army was put together from a variety of sources – a small field force which Major General Wentworth had assembled in London by 21 September, together with two battalions from Ireland, nearly all the Dutch and Swiss, and nearly all Albemarle's reinforcement. The first troops gathered at Doncaster in the middle of October, when Wade was ready to move to either side of the Pennines. He then changed the rendezvous to Newcastle upon Tyne, where he could receive reinforcements by sea directly from Flanders, and protect the rich north-eastern coalfields upon which London depended for its fuel, and which seemed to be the part of the kingdom most threatened by the Jacobite concentration at Edinburgh. The coalfields had indeed featured as a Jacobite target in 1708, and Prince Charles would have come this way by preference in 1745. Albemarle's battalions reached the Tyne after a stomach-churning voyage on 26 October, and Wade arrived three days later with the forces that had marched overland.

Dutch–Swiss Division under Lieutenant General Schwarzenberg

❖ Regiment of Hirtzel (Swiss, 3 bn)

❖ Regiment of Villatre (2 bn)

❖ Regiment of Holstein-Gottorp (2bn)

❖ Regiment of Patot (2 bn)

❖ Regiment of La Rocque (1bn)

> (N.B. one of the bns of Villatre, Holstein-Gottorp, Patot or La Rocque was with Cope/Handasyde).

Division of Lieutenant General William Keppel, Earl of Albemarle
(Major General John Huske, Brigadier General James Cholmondeley,
Brigadier General John Mordaunt, Brigadier General James Oglethorpe)

❖ Infantry

❖ Howard's 3rd

❖ Barrell's 4th

❖ Wolfe's 8th (200 only)

❖ Pulteney's 13th (from the initial British reinforcement)

❖ Price's 14th

❖ Blakeney's 27th (5 coys only, brought by Wentworth)

❖ Cholmondeley's 34th (from the initial British reinforcement)

❖ Fleming's 36th

❖ Munro's 37th

❖ Ligonier's 59th

❖ Battereau's 62nd (from Ireland)

Cavalry (Lieutenant General Henry Hawley)

❖ Montague's 3rd Horse

❖ Wade's 4th Horse

❖ St George's 8th Dragoons

❖ Oglethorpe's Georgia Rangers

❖ Royal Yorkshire Hunters

Lieutenant General Handasyde's Detachment at Berwick-upon-Tweed

(Represented the remains of Cope's command. Later reinforced by Price's
14th and Ligonier's 59th from Wade's army)

❖ Murray's 57th

❖ Lascelles' 58th

❖ Gardiner's 13th Dragoons

❖ Hamilton's 14th Dragoons

❖ One Dutch bn arrived after Prestonpans

Command of the Earl of Loudoun in the North-East Highlands

(In process of formation)

❖ 64th Highlanders

❖ clan militia

The Army of Lieutenant General Sir John Ligonier in the English Midlands

(Commanded by the Duke of Cumberland from 27 November)
(Approx. 8,500 infantry, 2,200 cavalry. Total: 10,700)
Formed around eight of the ten battalions of the further British reinforcements from Flanders. The regular regiments of foot were good; the 'new' regiments raised by the nobility (68th, 69th, 71st, 74th) very bad. Among the 'new' regiments of cavalry Montagu's Light Horse (9th) was passable and Kingston's Light Horse (10th) excellent.

Brigade of Guards (Brigadier General George Churchill)

❖ 1st Foot Guards

❖ 2nd Foot Guards

❖ 3rd Foot Guards

Regiments of Foot

❖ Sowle's 11th

❖ Skelton's 12th

❖ Howard's 19th

❖ Bligh's 20th

❖ Campbell's 21st

❖ Sempill's 25th

❖ Bragg's 28th (?)

❖ Handasyde's 31st

❖ Douglas's 32nd

❖ Johnston's 33rd

❖ Bedford's 68th

❖ Montague's 69th

❖ Granby's 71st

❖ Halifax's 74th

Cavalry (Lieutenant General the Duke of Richmond)

❖ Ligonier's 8th Horse

❖ Bland's 3rd Dragoons

❖ Cobham's 10th Dragoons

❖ Kerr's 11th Dragoons

❖ Montagu's 9th Light Horse

❖ Kingston's 10th Light Horse

Forces at Chester

(Approx. 1,450)

❖ 220 of Bligh's 20th

❖ 5 coys of Blakeney's 27th

❖ Cholmondeley's 'new' 73rd (to be distinguished from his regular 34th)

❖ Gower's 'new' 77th

At this stage it will probably prove useful to summarize all the above:

Jacobite Forces

Main army: Lowland and Highland Divisions invading England by way of Carlisle.
Forces in Scotland: Lord Strathallan (later Lord John Drummond) raising recruits, receiving French assistance, facing the forces of the Earl of Loudoun.

Hanoverian Forces

Army under Field Marshal Wade assembling in north-east England, with the reinforced former command of Cope at Berwick-upon-Tweed.
Earl of Loudoun recruiting in north-eastern Highlands.
Army of Lieutenant General Ligonier (later the Duke of Cumberland) assembling in the English Midlands.
Small force based at Chester.

To the Border, 1–8 November 1745

The brief concentration of the Jacobite army at Dalkeith broke up at the beginning of November, when its divisions set out on their respective paths to north-western England. In their first marches they climbed from the Lowlands to the broad belt of dissected high land that is known in sterile geological terms as the Southern Uplands, but famed in history and epic as the Borders. There were very few crossings of the central border spine of the Cheviot Hills, but on the Scottish side the grain of the country – very usefully for Jacobite purposes – favoured lateral movement, whether sliding by way of Kelso, Coldstream and Wooler to turn the Cheviots by their north-eastern flank, or taking one of the long valleys trending south-west and south to arrive at the head of the Solway Firth.

For the sake of clarity we shall follow two principal columns along their respective routes until they joined near Carlisle.

The Lowland Division (western route)

The Lowlanders left the rest of the army at Carlisle on 1 November, and their invasion force covered only very short distances on their first couple of days on the road, perhaps out of regard for the condition of the men after their long stay in quarters. They marched in the lee of the Pentland Hills by way of Roslin and Auchendinny Bridge, and reached the neighbourhood of Penicuik on the 2nd. The pace picked up considerably on 3 November, when the division struck due south and reached Peebles amid the Border hills. The troops evidently enjoyed being free of the restrictions of the old standing camp, and it was 'recommended to all the officers to take care that the most exact discipline be observed, as they are to be answerable for their respective corps [i.e. regiments]. It is forbid above all things to shoot sheep, hens etc.; or break open the country people's houses, or cause any disturbance'.[10]

At 6 a.m. on 4 November the Lowlanders assembled in a large field outside Peebles, then followed the Tweed upstream. They crossed the river repeatedly, passing by Neidpath Castle, Stoke Castle and Polmood, then rested for the night beside the upper Tweed after a march of some 10 miles. The country thereabouts and for most of the rest of the way was a grand but unthreatening landscape of rounded, grassy hills, and the road leading south was well trodden and in a generally good state.

On 5 November the column recrossed the Tweed for the last time, and marched up the right bank of the dwindling stream by way of Tweedsmuir to reach the watershed that gave rise to the Tweed, the Annan and the Clyde. From the Devil's Beef Tub the troops saw the deep valley of Annandale stretching to their left front, with a gibbet crowning the hill to the north. They now descended the west bank of the Annan towards the spa town of Moffat, 'where there is famous wells which are much frequented by ladies and gentlemen'.[11] There were two springs, rising from a rock by the Annan, the lower with a curiously metallic taste, which 'purges like those of Scarborough, and is very good against Cholic and Nephritic pains, by powerfully removing the Obstruction of the Bowels'.[12]

On 7 November Ogilvy's Regiment pushed ahead to Lockerbie.[13] Observers took particular note of a 'gentleman richly mounted, [who] called himself an Englishman but that has been eleven years in the French service, that he was in all the campaign in Flanders and came over in the ship that landed at Montrose, that he brought over with him 100,000 guineas with twenty pieces of brass cannon that fires several times in a minute, he also tells that they are marching straight for London and that the party that was at Jedburgh last night are to meet them in the west'.[14]

Other reports told of an apparent threat to the Whiggish town of Dumfries, even though it lay well to the west of the actual line of advance. On 8 November a mounted messenger returned to Carlisle, reporting 'that before he came from thence a quartermaster with a drawn sword in his hand attended by four Highlanders came there and asked for the Provost, that one of them said there was 2,000 men encamped all night at the Carse of Kinnoll, a place eight miles distant from Dumfries'.[15] This impression was confirmed by two further reports, and by Lieutenant John Kilpatrick, of the Light Horse of the Cumberland Militia, who captured the man in question later on the 8th. He proved to be James Brand, lieutenant and quartermaster of Kilmarnock's Horse Guards. Brand was taken to Newcastle and interrogated by Wade in person, but 'behaved very insolently, and said he did not value if he was shot immediately. He was dressed in a Highland plaid and bonnet, and on one side of which was a plaid cockade; he had two cases of uncharged pistols, and a backsword, and had about him a very remarkable cap, worked round with iron chain, which also covered his neck, shoulders and breast, and was a sufficient defence against any sword. After examination he was committed to Newgate'.[16]

There was now some urgency about making the rendezvous with Prince Charles and the Highlanders, and on 8 November the rearward units made an exhausting march down Annandale, and passed by Johnstonebridge and Lockerbie to reach Ecclefechan at 9 p.m., all plastered with mud.

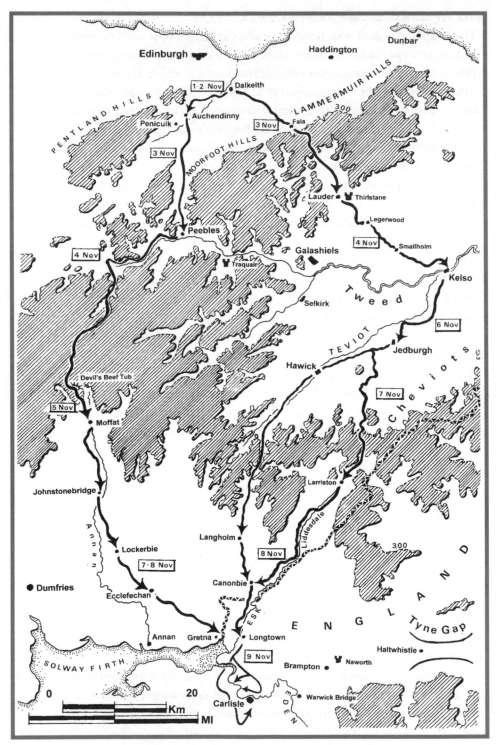

Through the Borders

The Highland Division (eastern route)

The Highlanders had waited for two days at Dalkeith while the Lowlanders and the artillery made their way towards the upper Tweed. During this time Prince Charles was reminded of how much he was giving up in Scotland when, on 2 November, the garrison of Edinburgh Castle debouched from its rock and took possession of Edinburgh town. The troops wrecked the apartment which the Prince had occupied in Holyroodhouse and made their way to the infirmary, where they tortured the Jacobites by tearing open their wounds or twisting their recently set limbs. The army was powerless to respond, for it was committed to the invasion, and the Highland Division had not only to rejoin the Lowlanders at Carlisle at the time appointed but also make the enemy believe that the Jacobites would come at them around the eastern flank of the Cheviots.

The Highlanders set out from Dalkeith on 3 November 'in good order and in top spirits'.[17] Elcho's troop of the Lifeguards led the way, and the Prince was marching just behind at the head of the clans. The route lay southeast over the Lammermuir Hills, a sprawling ridge of boggy pasture. A bend in the road beyond Fala gave a last glimpse of the lowlands beside the Forth, and then the column traversed the summit and descended the widening valley of the Leader Water to a first camp site at Lauder. Prince Charles lodged to the east of the road in the tall sandstone pile of Thirlstane Castle, the home of the absent Earl of Lauderdale, now bare and deserted; the Prince put himself up modestly at the back of the building, in a small circular room on the second storey of the north-west turret.

The previous day's march (about 14 miles) had been rather ambitious when we bear in mind that the troops had just left quarters, and on the morning of 4 November Prince Charles had to ride back 6 or 7 miles to chivvy the lagging rearguard before he could order a general advance to the lower Tweed at the market town of Kelso. The river at this point was far wider than upstream near Jedburgh. It was also swollen by rain, and altogether had a restless and nasty look that gave an added importance to this traditional crossing point, which lay on the most direct road between Edinburgh and Newcastle. John Rennie's great bridge was not complete until 1803, and the only way to get across was to pay extortionate sums to the insolent ferrymen, or to trust oneself to the ford: 'the Tweed is so dangerous a river, and rises sometimes so suddenly, that a man scarcely knows, when he goes into the water, how it shall be ere he gets out at the other side; and it is not strange to them at Kelso, to hear of frequent disasters in the passage, both of men and cattle'.[18]

Lord George Murray knew how important it was to let curious eyes see that respectable forces were crossing there as if on their way to England, and when even the bold Highlanders hesitated to plunge in, he led the way with two companions. When they had braved the deepest and fastest part 'they leaped and danced in the river to show the soldiers that there was no great danger, and to encourage them to follow, which they instantly did ... After fording the river each man got a glass of gin and a half-penny roll'.[19] Prince Charles slept in Sunlaws, a house (since much rebuilt) of the Kerrs 3 miles out of town to the south, but he held his division in and about Kelso until the 6th, to fix the supposed threat to Newcastle firmly in the minds of his enemies.

On hearing that three of the Highlanders had ventured as far as Coldstream, five of the Berwick Volunteers descended on the inn where the Jacobites had halted. 'One of the Volunteers immediately ran to the room door, where he was met by one of the Highlanders named Randle, who snapped his pistol at him, and clapped to the door; the Volunteer then fired his pistol through the door, but did no execution. The Highlanders then got out of the house a back way, but as they were getting over a dyke two of them were taken, who delivered up their broadswords and pistols; but the third made his escape, however they got all their horses.'[20]

Early on 6 November the Highlanders swung out of their previous line of march and made south-south-west up the right bank of the Tweed towards Jedburgh, as the first stop on their way to the rendezvous at Carlisle. It was important to keep up the impression of the lunge towards Newcastle, and so Lord George's highly competent aide-de-camp, Colonel Henry Ker of Graden, took a party of horse across the nearby border and around the Cheviots to Wooler, which was the station of the enemy dragoon regiments of Gardiner and Hamilton. These gentlemen were still in a state of shock from their experiences at Prestonpans, and they galloped off to Whittingham.

The main Jacobite force meanwhile made its way over the little Jed Water by the hump-backed Canongate Bridge, and entered Jedburgh just beyond. James Hilson was then a 13-year-old lad, and long afterwards he told how 'all the men, who were opposed to the rising, left the town to avoid being compelled to join the rebels, but as he was a boy, he, with the curiosity of his age, made his way down to Bonegate and walked alongside of the Prince and his troops as they came up and entered the town'.[21] The womenfolk without hesitation flocked into the street to kiss the Prince's hand, and the sturdy farmer Davidson of Carlieshope came panting up to join the Jacobites, though it is uncertain whether he ever caught up with them, since he was one day behind and laden with weapons. The town was replete with the traditions of Mary Queen of Scots and other Stuart monarchs, and Prince Charles's lodgings in the Castlegate (No. 11) were just around the corner from the magnificent though roofless ruins of Jedburgh Abbey. But despite its past splendours Jedburgh had suffered along with the other towns of the Borders from the Union of 1707, and the historic road (the A68) which climbed to the border at Carter Bar had declined in importance, possibly explaining why it was never considered as an invasion route in 1745.

There was justifiable reason to suspect that Field Marshal Wade would not be deceived by the feint towards Newcastle, but would try to cut westwards across England by the shortest route, namely the Tyne Gap, which was the corridor lying immediately south of the Cheviots.[22] The urgency explains why Lord Elcho's troop of Lifeguards was detached along the fast route (A7) south from Hawick to Longtown, and why the march of the Highlanders on 7 November represented by far the most strenuous effort of any of the Jacobite forces during the advance to England.

In 1826 a very ancient lady related having seen the Highlanders set out from Jedburgh and climb Dunion Hill to the south-west. On the far side they descended the narrow and dank valley of the Rule, then made their way diagonally along the densely wooded eastern side to emerge in a tract of open grassland under the volcanic saddle of Rubers Law. The further route took them up a valley leading between grassy hills (now blanketed in Wauchope Forest); they were now marching parallel with the border, which ran to their left along the bleak limestone plateaux of Hartshorn Pike and Peel Fell. A final climb brought them through moorland to the watershed of the Note o' the Gate Pass, from where they descended a V-shaped valley to the more gentle scenery of pastoral Liddesdale. After a march of a good 25 miles the Highlanders encamped along the Liddle Water. A party went in search of William Armstrong, the virulently anti-Jacobite minister of Castle-ton (now Old Castleton), but that gentlemen had fled across the border.

Prince Charles stayed overnight in the farm of Larriston (Haggiehaugh) off the path to the left, and he paid one Charlie of Kirndean half a guinea to slaughter and dress ten sheep for his party. A number of Highlanders observed what had passed, tracked Charlie until he was out of sight of the Prince and then robbed him in safety.

By now the two divisions were converging fast. On 8 November Prince Charles hastened ahead of his main body, escorted only by Lochiel's Camerons and the hussars, and made his first footing on English soil when he crossed to the left bank of the Liddle Water near Canonbie. 'It was remarkable that being the first time they entered England the Highlanders, without any orders given, drew their swords with one consent upon entering the river, and every man as he landed on the other side wheeled about to the left to face Scotland again.'[23] Lochiel cut his hand when drawing his broadsword, which was not the best of omens. The Prince sent the hussars to scout several miles ahead, and established his quarters for the night at Riddings Farm (the original building demolished 1818), which was then tenanted by David Murray, a wealthy Jacobite.

Into England – Carlisle and Brampton, 9–18 November 1745

The Jacobites might have entered England by a crossing of the lower Tweed over to the east, or by Carter Bar in the high Cheviots, with its vast horizons. They instead made the passage over what is still one of the most inconsequential transits from one country to another, the marshy flats where creeks and little rivers oozed their way to the shallows of the Solway Firth.

> These sands lie at the mouth of the River Esk, eight miles from Carlisle, and in the direction of the road from Carlisle to Dumfries. At low water they are very hard and firm, but as soon as the tide flows they are soft and spongy, or quicksands, so that any weight easily sinks down in them irrecoverably. Their breadth is from three to four miles, and in neap tides one may ride across them at leisure, but in spring tides a prudent man, who is acquainted with them, will make the best speed he can; for the tide rushes in like a torrent.[24]

A report reached London to the effect that the Jacobites had lost all of their artillery and most of their baggage in the crossing, but nothing so dramatic had taken place.

The main body of the Lowland Division set out from Ecclefechan on the morning of 9 November, and just beyond Gretna the troops crossed the legal border at the narrow River Sark. Here, according to one commentator, the river 'affords good fishing, but all here about which are called "Borderers" seem to be very poor people, which I impute to their sloth; Scotland this part of it is a low marshy ground where they cut turf and peat for fuel'.[25] However, the symbolic passage into England was that of the Esk a couple of miles further on. The Lowlanders forded without difficulty, though one of the guns became irretrievably bogged down in the mud.

Prince Charles meanwhile left Riddings Farm with the blessing of David Murray, who presented him with a bag of gold and ten horses; the Prince reciprocated by giving a golden ring to each of the daughters of the house.

The leading troops of the two divisions now came together on the last reaches of the sinuous Eden, between Carlisle and the head of the Solway Firth, and from 2 p.m. they forded the river at Kingmoor, Cargo, Rockliffe and Peat-wath. Nobody drowned, though the passage was potentially more hazardous than that of the Esk, since the river was wider, and there was only a short interval of slack water before the tide began to flow. The reconnaissance party of hussars had already ridden ahead to Stanwix Bank, from where they saw the ground falling steeply to the Eden, the two successive bridges that

The advance on Carlisle

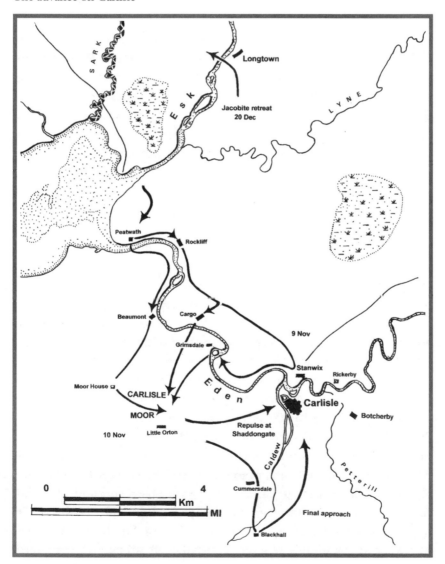

spanned the river, and the sandstone walls of Carlisle crowning the far bank.

Carlisle was an unusual survival in the England of the time, for it was a walled garrison town with hardly any suburbs to speak of. Every night the 4,000 inhabitants were confined within the walls when the guards shut the three stout gates – the Scottish Gate (8 miles from the border), the Irish Gate (leading to Whitehaven and Cockermouth) and the English Gate facing south. The town occupied a mudstone plateau which rose between three valleys – that of the winding Esk to the north, the Caldew to the west and the little Petteril to the east. Its defensive potential had been recognized since Roman times, and indeed a stretch of Hadrian's vallum ran immediately in front of the castle.

The fortifications as they existed in 1745 owed their origins to Henry I of England, who commissioned the first works in 1122. They were not strong enough to keep out the Scots, and both the keep and the town walls were completed by King David I before the place was handed back to the English in 1157. But it was not until 1538 that Henry VIII, faced with an unprecedentedly powerful coalition of Scotland and the major powers of Catholic Europe, had to catch up rapidly with the changes that artillery had wrought and bring the fortifications up to date. The works undertaken at this time were soon outdated by further developments in fortification, but they made feasible the defence of Carlisle against artillery attack. Carlisle was strongly Royalist in the Civil War (a fact not without relevance a hundred years later), and withstood a siege of eight months from October 1644, surrendering only after the battle of Naseby. The city was now of consequence only as a market town, and even then could not compete in trading prosperity with Whitehaven on the coast. However, something of the old glories remained, in the very style of 'city' – in the spacious market square, the houses of the doctors, the Dean and Treasurer of the cathedral, and in the cathedral itself, 'high and very eminent to be seen above the town'.[26]

On 9 November 1745 the prospecting Jacobite hussars grabbed a countryman and sent him across the river with a summons requiring Carlisle to provide quarters for 13,000 infantry and 3,000 cavalry upon pain of seeing the town reduced to ashes. The reply came in the form of a number of cannon shot from the walls, whereupon the hussars retired over the crest of Stanwix Bank and the landscape disappeared in mist. The Whiggish Archbishop Herring of York, writing to a friend on the same date, shrewdly observed: 'You see ... that these ruffians are marching to England, and probably are, by this time, as far as Carlisle; for their horses' hooves are of flint and their wheels like whirlwind. It is most certain that they are strong, well-disciplined, dauntless and united ... I am far from thinking that victory is infallible, but you may imagine I don't propagate this doctrine'.[27]

Carlisle's display of resolution was entirely misleading. On 25 September, when the Jacobite threat was still distant, Lord Lonsdale, the Lord Lieutenant of Cumberland, had called out the county militia. Moreover, 'a good number of the inhabitants have formed themselves into companies to assist the garrison in defending the town and castle, and I had letters yesterday from the commanding officer that he had directions to deliver arms to the associated inhabitants'.[28] It was nevertheless a bad sign when the Duke of Newcastle declined Lonsdale's request to have two battalions of reinforcements diverted to Carlisle, saying that the cost of sending an express messenger was too great.

All Lonsdale could do was to procure the services of an experienced professional soldier, Lieutenant Colonel James Durand of the Foot Guards, who arrived on 11 October and was appalled by what he encountered. The eighty regular invalids who constituted the standing garrison were willing enough to do their duty, but were by definition in poor physical shape, and Durand as the military governor had no authority to command the county militia or the citizen gunners and volunteer companies. Although he was able to borrow ten small ships' cannon from Whitehaven to add to the twenty 6-pounders in the castle, the obstructive town authorities refused to demolish the outlying shacks and houses which obstructed the fields of fire from the walls, and declined even to muster the town's artillerymen for his inspection, pleading that the gunners were poor working folk who could not afford to lose a day's pay.

The Jacobite columns executed a grand converging movement on Carlisle towards 10 a.m. on 10 November. The Duke of Perth arrived on Stanwix Bank to the north, and the rest of the available Lowlanders under the Duke of Atholl came together with the Highland division on Carlisle Moor to the west of the town. 'We were very much surprised,' wrote de Johnstone, 'on finding ourselves all arrive almost at the same instant, on a heath in England, about a quarter of a league from the town of Carlisle.'[29] The dramatic effect was diminished by the continuing fog, but the gunners took advantage of the cover to establish a battery in what seemed to be a good position on the road called Shaddongate outside the Irish Gate. The fog dispersed in the middle of the day and revealed that the guns had been planted only 50 yards from the bridge over the little river Caldew, and in the one site where the feeble ordnance of the castle could be concentrated against them. The four-gun battery by the south-western corner of the outer castle yard opened fire, while the eight-gun battery on the north-eastern wall of the inner castle opened up against Stanwix Bank. The Jacobites recoiled so quickly that the defenders persuaded themselves that they had worked a massacre, and the deputy mayor Thomas Pattinson penned a report which enumerated his heroic deeds. The chastened Jacobite army settled down for the night in the neighbouring villages, and Prince Charles put up at the well-built Blackhall Farm, where he could look down the Caldew valley north to the town.

The report came to Prince Charles that Field Marshal Wade was on the march against him from Newcastle, as had long been anticipated, and the Prince now lost no time in moving all his disposable forces to Brampton in order to confront Wade when he emerged from the Tyne Gap, 'it being of the highest importance to us to give battle before we advanced into England, in order to preserve a free communication with France'.[30] A victory over Wade would also be valuable on its own account by confirming the moral ascendancy that the Jacobites had gained by beating Cope at Prestonpans.

At 11 p.m. on 10 November a party of four typically ebullient Jacobite quartermasters and their escort entered the neat little sandstone town of Brampton. An aged inhabitant of Cumrew recollected in the next century that 'her father drove the cattle from his small farmstead into the neigh-bouring woods to be out of the way, while her mother collected such valuables as they possessed and hid them under the clothes in the child's cradle'.[31] The great fear was that of the infants being eaten by the Highlanders, and many other children were sent to a secluded spot near Nether Denton.

The main Jacobite force arrived at Brampton on 11 November, and from then until the 18th Prince Charles had his quarters just off the Market Square in the Joiners Arms in High Cross Street, his bedroom, on the first floor at the back, being little more than a respectable cupboard.

Prince Charles liked the look of a potential battlefield on the high ground extending to the east of the town, and Ogilvy's Regiment and Elcho's troop of Lifeguards took station there at Naworth Castle. They were well-dressed and well-behaved people, and they were appalled to see Captain Hamilton arrive there on the 12th, demanding quarters for 12,000 men, 'upon which the [Life]guards began to look blank, and secure their portables. About noon several hundreds, described as a wretched, ill-looking, shabby crew, armed with targets, broadswords, muskets etc., arrived, and seemed very angry that no deference was paid to their flag. That afternoon and the next day they spent in shooting sheep, geese etc., and robbing on the highway. Their chiefs expressed great dissatisfaction but could not restrain them'.[32]

This demand for quarters for hugely exaggerated numbers was a typical Jacobite bluff, for Prince Charles had already summoned his council and decided to move his army back towards Carlisle to mount a serious attack on the town. The reason was that one of his patrols had reached Haltwhistle, and discovered that the snow in the Tyne Gap was so deep as to make it impossible for Wade to come that way until it cleared.

On 13 November Prince Charles accompanied Lord George and the army back to Carlisle. In the lead were two hussars

> in Highland dress, and high rough caps, like pioneers; next, about half a dozen of the chief leaders, followed by a kettle drum; then the Pretender's son, at the head of about 110 horse called his Guards, two and two abreast; after these a confused multitude of all sorts of mean people, to the number (as was supposed) of about 6,000. In this order they advanced to Warwick Moor; where they halted about half an hour, and took an attentive view of the city; from thence the foot took the lead, and so marched to Carlisle about three in the afternoon.[33]

The Prince turned back towards Brampton, and it may have been on this day that Prince Charles was entertained in Warwick Hall. His hosts were Mrs Warwick and her kinswoman Mrs Howard of nearby Corby Castle, both committed Jacobites, and, the Prince declared, the first civilized company he had encountered in England. The park and the country thereabouts were loud with the noise of fir trees being felled to make scaling ladders for the siege of Carlisle.

Back in the city, one of the roving parties was led by Captain Donald MacDonald of Kinlochmoidart. On the night of 14 November he took his band to Rose Castle, the official residence of the Bishop of Carlisle, where it was feared that he and his wild men were bent on plunder. They stopped in their tracks when an aged servant told them that the bishop's daughter had given birth to a girl, who was about to be christened:

> The Captain enquired when the lady had been confined. 'Within the hour,' the servant replied. MacDonnell stopped. The servant added, 'They are just going to christen the infant.' MacDonnell, taking off his cockade, said 'Let her be christened with this cockade in her bonnet; it will protect her now, and later if any of our stragglers should come this way. We shall await the ceremony in silence.' Which they accordingly did; and then went off into the courtyard where they were regaled with beef, cheese and ale. They went off without the slightest disorder.[34]

The child was christened Rosemary, and as Lady Clerk she wore the cockade when she was presented to the Prince Regent in Edinburgh in 1822, some seventy-seven years later (p. 546).

The fate of Carlisle hung on the issue of morale, like nearly all the turning points of the rising before the battle of Culloden. The winter weather which had closed the Tyne Gap gripped the Solway Firth on the night of 13/14 November, just when the Highlanders were opening the siegeworks, complete with Colonel Grant's battery of 4-pounders. The range was very long, at 300–400 yards, but the attack was directed against the long eastern wall, which was the most vulnerable side of the town, being unprotected by any of the rivers. Lord George Murray commanded the thinly spread blockading force from his headquarters at Harraby. He remained remote in every sense from the prosecution of the siege, and refused to release any of his troops to relieve the exhausted diggers in the morning.

By the standards of continental European siege warfare the attack on Carlisle was little more than a demonstration of ill-will. In the mood prevailing in the town it proved to be enough. At 5 p.m. on 13 November a messenger reached Colonel Durand to say that Wade would be unable to come to his relief in the foreseeable future, and the morning of the 14th showed not only Grant's battery but a trench which the Jacobites had made under cover of a hawthorn hedge only 200 yards from the wall, 'on which the fire from the garrison was renewed; but the rebels made no return, only in derision, with their bonnets, holding them up on the end of their spades, except one musket that was fired from behind a haystack'.[35]

However, the fire from the walls was lively enough to persuade some of the diggers to abandon the trench and flee to the Duke of Perth's quarters in a village close by, and 'being awakened, he immediately got up and ran to the trench with his whole regiment, and directed the men in what manner to carry on the trench, and took a spade himself to show them'.[36] The Duke of Atholl joined in the work, and the sight of the two dukes labouring without shirts both encouraged the men, and acted as a reproach to Lord George Murray.

The garrison had assumed that the Jacobites were gone for good, after their supposed repulse on 10 November, but now it was clear that they were set on a siege. Out in the countryside 'so many persons have this morning fled from the villages on the south and west sides of Carlisle, as affords us sufficient evidence that the whole rebel army are endeavouring to surround Carlisle. They shoot at everybody that flees them; we hear of one person killed, and they are now actually putting the country under military executions. They seize all able-bodied men, horses and carriages, and declare that they will force them to carry their ladders to the walls of Carlisle'.[37] The violence was exaggerated, but the general talk of taking Carlisle by storm served the Jacobites very well.

The spirit of the garrison collapsed in an atmosphere of dissension and terror. There was goodwill among the leading clergy and the companies of town volunteers, but the officers of the county militia came together and voted in favour of surrendering. Colonel Durand went to the King's Arms Inn and tried in vain to reason with them, and the Cathedral Chancellor, the Rev. John Waugh, commented that the town volunteers were just as tired as the militia, and needlessly so, for the militia officers were constantly calling false alarms.[38]

There was a further crumpling of resolve when the town council also voted in favour of giving up. Durand thereupon ordered the cannon on the town ramparts to be nailed up, and withdrew into the castle with the invalids and 400 of the militia. A Mr Dobinson accordingly began to hammer home a spike in the vent of one of the cannon in a drum tower of the Citadel. He had forgotten to check whether the piece was loaded, and a spark from the friction touched off a live round inside and burst the barrel. The siegeworks were now within 80 yards, and one of the fragments nearly decapitated the Franco-Irish engineer officer Dalton, who had climbed out of the trench to jeer at the garrison. The Highlanders were infuriated, which put the defenders in an even greater fright. Overnight the militiamen deserted over the walls of the castle, and by 8 a.m. on the 15th none of the heroes was left.

A messenger had been sent to Brampton to discover what terms Prince Charles might offer. The Prince, recalling how Edinburgh Castle had continued to hold out after the Jacobites had captured the town, now insisted that any agreement must embrace the castle at Carlisle as well as the town. At 10 a.m. on the 15th the town fathers told Durand that they saw no alternative but to comply, and they proceeded to negotiate a surrender on terms that were not ungenerous, for they permitted the defenders to march free on condition only that they were not to serve against the Jacobites until after a year had elapsed, and that the militiamen must deliver up their arms. Durand had to acquiesce in the deal, though he refused to put his signature to it.

On 16 November the mayor, John Backhouse, went forth with a deputation to deliver the keys of Carlisle to Prince Charles at Brampton. The party travelled unescorted, which later laid Backhouse open to the suspicion of treason.[39] The garrison made its way out of the castle on the same day, and the Jacobites snatched the muskets from the arms of the invalids, contrary to the capitulation. As a patriot the Rev. John Waugh found it impossible to remain: 'I was on foot and in a deep snow, and got a fall which gave me a little fit of gout in the hand'.[40]

The Duke of Perth on campaign was a determined character, and we find him in Carlisle on 17 November pointing a pistol at the head of the town clerk, John Pearson, and threatening to blow out his brains unless he proclaimed the return of the Stuarts. Pearson, although protesting 'that he had never proclaimed a king and knew no form for it',[41] thought it best to comply.

On 18 November Prince Charles entered Carlisle in impressive style, mounted on a white charger and accompanied by 100 pipers. The streets were lined with cheering Highlanders, there were salutes of cannon and musketry from the castle and the walls of the town, and 'the bells [were] ringing all the time'.[42] He took up his quarters for the next four days in the Earl's Inn, in English Street, in the house of a lawyer and his wife who continued to live there, enjoying the generous rent and the free meals provided by their guests. The townspeople, after their recent terrors, were so reassured by the good behaviour of the Scots that they came out to them with free beer. Inside the town the Jacobites had found 1,500 muskets, 160 barrels of gunpowder, 500 grenades and 120 or so good horses.

Carlisle had not been an immediate barrier to the Jacobites in the physical sense, for the rivers were passable both above and below the town, but they could not have left it unreduced in their rear if they were to continue their advance. In a wider sense the capture represented a staking of their claim to England. The Duke of Cumberland complained that 'the surrender of Carlisle to the rebels was the source of all the distress this part of the kingdom has felt from them, and it of so scandalous a nature that it deserves the strictest enquiry and punishment'.[43] These matters call for some explanation.

The First Hanoverian Response

It is easy enough for us, with all the advantages of hindsight, and with a small-scale map in front of us, to dictate 'obvious' moves and countermoves to the rival forces as they existed in the early winter of 1745. It is less easy to fulfil the obligation of reading ourselves back into the minds of the men of the time, and in particular to grasp the dilemmas of the supporters of the Protestant Succession, who had to confront an enemy who had seized the initiative in a most dramatic style, and who had a wealth of options open to him. The regime, its generals and its local representatives were able to focus only very slowly on the nature and direction of the dangers to Britain south of the border. This is interesting in itself, for it shows that the government had no highly placed informants in the Jacobite councils in Scotland.

The North-East

The almost inconceivable defeat of Lieutenant General Cope at Prestonpans on 21 September made its most immediate impact in north-eastern England, which was the most exposed part of the kingdom. Cope was at Berwick-upon-Tweed during the final days of his command, a town situated on the lowest and most important passage of the Tweed, just 3 miles from the Scottish border. Until 1603 this had been England's only land frontier with a foreign power. In 1558 Henry VIII's daughter Queen Mary commissioned the fortified perimeter that surrounded the town, but the ramparts were low-lying and Cope complained that they were 'of a larger compass than I have either troops, or burghers in arms to line them with in case of attack … I am endeavouring, in concert with the Magistrates, to bring in a number of men from the country, armed with scythes, pitchforks and such like weapons, which I hope will be of some use'.[44]

However, the only specific threat came in the form of probing by Jacobite parties east from Edinburgh to Haddington, Dunbar, North Berwick and the neighbourhood of Berwick itself.[45] There was no weight behind any of these forays, and Lieutenant General Handasyde (who took over the command at Berwick) read nothing of significance in the concentration of Jacobite forces at Edinburgh.[46] He was strengthened in his opinion by the news that the Jacobites had planted a battery of five cannon at Alloa, on the Forth below Stirling. 'Had they no intention of returning to the Highlands that way, why should they leave near five hundred men to defend this pass? Then consider the Highlanders were never fond of passing the Borders, and great desertion – should they do it – will certainly be the consequence.'[47] The Duke of Newcastle took due note of Handasyde's comments, but he was well aware that the rebels would 'undoubtedly use their utmost endeavour to conceal their real designs'.[48]

The alarms spread unabated down the north-eastern coast. A refugee Scottish Whig, Sir John Clerk, found that the news of Prestonpans had put Newcastle upon Tyne 'in such a terrible consternation, that if the rebels had followed their blow I believe this important city had surrendered to them … I must here observe in general that where I stayed and travelled in England a most terrible panic had possessed all the people to such a degree that many rich people around Newcastle, Durham and York had sent off a great deal of their effects to Holland and Hamburg, and all their silver plate, jewels, money and such like necessities were hid under ground'.[49] However, the Whiggish magistrates of Newcastle were determined to keep a grip on affairs, and Major General 'Daddy' Huske reported from there on 4 October that the gates in the town's medieval walls had been blocked up, and that cannon (taken from the ships in the Tyne and the abandoned Clifford's Fort) would be planted about the town.[50] By 12 October it was possible to record that 'several sentry boxes are set at convenient places on the walls, a vast number of sandbags are to be hung over them, and palisades near them, to hinder the access of the enemy; and several parts of the river are to be palisaded to prevent the enemy from crossing at low water'.[51] However a Jacobite sympathizer noted that there was grave suspicion of the 1,500 Scottish keelmen (lightermen) who dwelt just outside the walls, and that little confidence could be placed in the 700 Dutch auxiliaries 'who would not be equal to withstanding the desperate Highlander's trusty broadsword and target, headed by a person who can lie on straw, eat a dry crust, dine in five minutes, and gain a battle in four'.[52]

The Whigs of the Yorkshire coastal town of Scarborough also felt ill at ease, for they feared that the Jacobites might hold them to account for the £350 pounds they had raised for the government as a loyal subscription. On 22 November a committee of twelve gentlemen was elected to determine how the money should be spent, and it was decided that there could be no better way than by fortifying the town,

> which they immediately set about with so much alacrity, and without distinction, under the direction of Mr Vincent, their engineer, that in three weeks' time, with the labour of 1,000 hands daily, they raised breastworks and batteries before the avenues leading to the town, from the south to the North Sea, and planted thereon 91 pieces of cannon, which were taken from the shipping in the harbour, and had in readiness 2,000 small arms, and plenty of ammunition; which with the assistance of the sailors, who seldom fail in their undertakings, were determined to defend the town for the honour of the government and their own safety.[53]

There were close parallels with the case of the Whiggish port of Hull, where measures were taken to flood the surrounding countryside[54] and more than 2,000 townspeople went voluntarily to work on the ditches, 'and on the bastions and ramparts, and have so far completed them, that we have nothing to fear from these rash desperadoes'.[55]

Just how far the alarm spread is shown by the fear of King's Lynn, a trading port in a notoriously Whiggish enclave of Norfolk, where 'it being apprehended that the rebels may come this way, towards the eastern coast, where a French invasion from Dunkirk is threatened, the mayor and inhabitants have armed 1,000 able sailors and others, and have taken the command of them to defend this place; which by the gates being kept shut, and a strong wall and ditch which fortifies it, being put in good condition, will be able to make a sufficient stand against the whole force of the rebels. The access to it over the River Ouse is also prevented by German's, Magdalen, Stow and Downham bridges all being broke down'.[56]

The North-West and the Scottish Borders

Meanwhile the Scottish Borders remained in a state of entirely justified fear. The 'poor town of Jedburgh' was 'in great terror', and had set out observers along the route from Lauder.[57] If the Jacobites arrived in force nearby at Kelso, 'it may be very well apprehended that their design is to take the same route into Lancashire that the rebels did in the year 1715, with an expectation of the French landing some troops upon that coast to join them. This [wrote an English Whig] I rather believe, because to my certain knowledge persons ... have within a month past been sounding the coast ... from Lancaster to the next town of Liverpool.'[58] The Provost of Dumfries, John Goldie, was the most industrious and reliable of the government's sources of information in Scotland, and on 1 November he sent word that the Jacobite artillery and baggage were on the move from Edinburgh to Dalkeith, and that the whole army would follow and march south, giving out 'that they were to go by Kelso and were resolved to meet Marshal Wade and give him battle'.[59] On 8 November foreign diplomats in London reported that the capital was buzzing with speculation. Most people were inclined to think that the Jacobite army would veer to the west of the Pennines and gain four marches on Wade, who was concentrated beyond those 'mountains' at Newcastle. However on 8 November both the Austrian and Swedish ambassadors noted the theory (probably originating with Handasyde) that the Jacobites had no intention of invading England, and were just manoeuvring to conceal their real design, which was to fall back to the Highlands.[60]

By 13 November it appeared in London that the Jacobites were advancing from Carlisle, and were most probably committed to invading England by the western avenue. A party of about 200 descended on Appleby and for several days proceeded to roam the neighbourhood, which gave the Duke of Newcastle reason to think that the main force might swing east into Yorkshire by way of Appleby and the Stainmore passage (A66) over the Pennines,

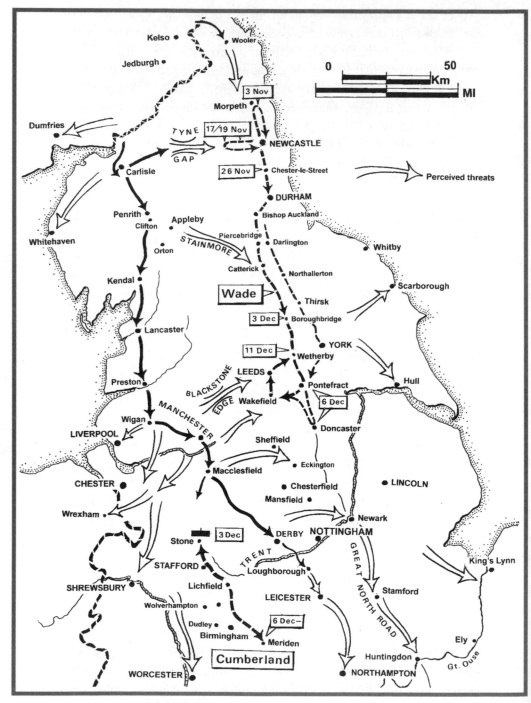

The invasion of England, with feints and panics

'however as this route is very uncertain, it is necessary to be as well prepared as possible, everywhere, and I am still of opinion, they will go to Lancashire, Cheshire etc.'.[61] It nevertheless seemed curious to Lord Lonsdale, the Lord Lieutenant of Cumberland, that the Jacobites had returned to besiege Carlisle after having been 'repulsed' from there on 10 November, and he concluded that the rebels were just interested in raising contributions in the neighbourhood, and did not have it in mind to advance any further into England.[62]

All doubts as to the fact of a serious invasion disappeared after the loss of Carlisle, when the Jacobites pushed down England west of the Pennines, most obviously threatening Lancashire and the line of the Mersey. But the further direction of the invasion was unclear, and the Jacobites were still at dangerous liberty to turn in any direction in an arc that extended from Yorkshire to Wales. On 22 November all that the Duke of Newcastle could do was to send word to the 'western' army gathering in the English Midlands that, in view of all the uncertainty, it should commit itself no further north than Stone in Staffordshire,[63] a disturbing order considering that Stone was 150-odd miles as the crow flies from the nearest point of the Scottish border.

Wade's First Failure, 31 October – 22 November 1745

The prime responsibility for crushing the despised Jacobites, or at least stopping them well short of the heart of England, had fallen to Field Marshal Wade's 'eastern' army, which had finally come together at Newcastle upon Tyne on 31 October. His subordinate George Keppel, Earl of Albemarle, was all for crossing the border and extirpating the rebellion without further loss of time, and with some misgivings the old field marshal decided to march thither by way of Morpeth and Berwick: 'the greatest of our wants is to supply the men with shoes, which, from the badness of the roads, are torn to pieces in this long march. The English regiments have found a supply in this town [Newcastle], with some they have picked up on the road, but the Dutch General [Schwarzenberg] came to me this morning, and told me there were so many of their men barefoot that they could not march till they had supply'.[64]

On 3 November Wade halted the northward march at Morpeth, for he had learned that the Jacobites had set out from Dalkeith for Peebles (i.e. the Lowland Division), and he deduced correctly that the enemy were bound for Carlisle. He pulled his army back to the old camp at Newcastle, from where he would have the facility of moving west across the Tyne Gap. He was again right to suspect that any Jacobite moves towards north-eastern

England would be merely feints 'calculated to amuse us, by magnifying their force, and to give us apprehensions, as if their design was to march towards us'.[65] However, his generals were evidently not of the same opinion, for on the 6th a council of war decided to 'continue in our present camp till we are more fully informed of the rebels' intentions, and to be equally in a readiness to march as soon as it shall be necessary'.[66]

The generals returned to the scheme of the offensive into the Lothians, this time no longer by the main army, but by the command of Lieutenant General Handasyde at Berwick, where the remains of Cope's old force were reinforced by two regiments of infantry which came directly by sea. The Jacobites had abandoned Edinburgh when they moved to Dalkeith on 31 October (p. 221), but Handasyde needed to be convinced that the way was clear before he finally moved on 12 November. 'The field marshal sent me discretionary orders for that purpose; but I did not, for fear of being cut off, think it prudent to execute the same until now.'[67] The redcoat garrison of Edinburgh Castle had long been in possession of the town by the time Handasyde arrived there on the 14th, but he packed his troops into the place as if it had been a hostile town now under occupation (which was not altogether far from the truth), and a state of 'anarchy' continued in the civil administration.[68]

Morale and health suffered badly in the soggy camp at Newcastle, where Wade's disparate British, Dutch and Swiss regiments remained until 16 November, the day the field marshal finally set them in motion towards the Tyne Gap to intercept the Jacobites in Cumberland. Lord Harley (later the Earl of Oxford) had travelled the same route in a milder season, and described it as 'a way which no coaches are hardly ever known to pass but those of the Judges, who are necessitated to go through it once a year, and where persons of a less share of wisdom than those learned gentlemen would hardly travel over twice without some urgent occasion'.[69] The route was totally unfitted for an army, with its cannon and carts, and indeed the last people to build 'strategic' roads in England had been the Romans.

The destination of the first day's march was Ovington, 17 miles away, and an early start was necessary if the troops were not to find themselves stranded overnight on the frozen and rutted road, or in the 3-foot-deep snow on either side. The Swiss regiment of Hirtzel at the head of the column refused to move until 10 a.m., while the Dutch remained as unpopular as always: 'The dogs not only grumble, but plunder everywhere with a heavy hand'.[70] Parties of villagers had to go out by torchlight to guide the men who were still short of Ovington after dark, but this failed to prevent a number of them dying from the cold, since the ground was frozen too hard to pitch tents, and Wade, untypically miserly in his old age, had begrudged spending money on straw and firewood.

The march was resumed on the following day, and the last troops straggled into the town of Hexham at midnight. Patrols had penetrated across the snow as far as Haltwhistle, and reported to Wade that Carlisle had already surrendered to the Jacobites. As Wade had no artillery with which to retake the town, even if his troops had not already marched themselves into the ground, he held his army at Hexham until the 19th, when he learned that the Jacobites (Elcho's troop) had already reached Penrith, and had gained a head start on their way to the south on the opposite side of the Pennines. He wrote to the Duke of Newcastle that there was no means of getting at them 'by any other road than that of Newcastle to Boroughbridge if the rebels should proceed to Lancashire, and even in that way they will be there long before us; and we must expect a great diminution in our forces, from the numbers that fall sick every day by the severity of the weather, and badness of the roads. I am sorry to tell Your Grace that, in all the service I have seen since my first coming into the army, I never saw more distress than what the officers and soldiers suffer at this time'.[71]

The army was back at Newcastle on 22 November, after a march of unrelieved misery. Everything to do with transport, supply and shelter had collapsed, and Wade's aide-de-camp concluded that in these respects the army had a great deal to learn from the Jacobites.[72]

CHAPTER 9

Invasion: The Bid for a Kingdom, 18–30 November 1745

From the Eden to the Ribble, 18–27 November 1745

CARLISLE HAD FALLEN, AND ON 18 November Colonel Grant and Captain Burnet of the Prince's artillery had time on their hands at Carleton, a village 2 miles south of the town. One Alexander Spencer, pretending Jacobite sympathies, engaged them in conversation, and after sharing a bottle with him the pair entered into some detail as to their system of operations. They explained that the practice of their army was to march as far as possible under cover of darkness, to conceal both the numbers of the troops and the road they were taking. Four thousand of their infantry were Highlanders,

> being the choicest of their clans, the rest not so good, but [they] were of opinion they would fight ... I asked them which way in their opinion they would now take. Answer was that every hour they expected an account of the Pretender's youngest son [Prince Henry] landing in England with a body of

---

Jacobite soldiers with fixed bayonets

French troops. I asked if they knew in which part they expected to hear of their landing. Mr Grant answered now as near London as they could, their embarkation was to be from Dunkirk and Ostend, and it was upon that account which had induced them to march into England that they might draw all the troops from about London [a point also made by the government spy Dudley Bradstreet], and as they were informed they were very well assured they had a great number of friends, especially about the City of London that were to join the French army.[1]

Neither Grant nor Burnet or indeed anybody else in the body of the army was aware that their high command was prey to divisions and doubts. At a turbulent meeting of the council on 15 November there was a falling-out between Lord George Murray and the Duke of Perth, precipitated by the fact that Perth had not included Lord George in the negotiations for the surrender of Carlisle. On a more fundamental issue Lord George insisted that the Catholic duke must abdicate his rank as lieutenant general, now that the army was in England and subject to English laws. Lord George threatened to resign unless he got his way, whereupon Perth stepped down rather than cause trouble. Lord George's position was enhanced as one of the three surviving lieutenant generals; the Duke of Perth was now officially relegated to the command of the baggage and artillery, although he continued to take an active role in collecting intelligence.

On the 18th Prince Charles took formal possession of Carlisle. On the same day a further and still more critical meeting of the council debated the army's next move. Lord George and his party reasoned against proceeding any further with the invasion, for the army had shrunk to 4,500 effectives and there was so far no sign of the English Jacobites rising in support or the French actually landing. Prince Charles nevertheless argued that the army must continue to march into England, from where he had letters of support from sympathizers. Lord George and his friends gave way, but they were to hold the Prince to his promises.

It is impossible to establish what was in the Prince's mind when he gave those assurances. He mistrusted Lord George, and perhaps he was hiding the identity of English friends and plotters who relied on his confidentiality. It is more likely, and the surviving documentation suggests, that the Prince had put his efforts into establishing contacts in north-eastern England rather than the north-west, where, prompted by Lord George, the army was now entering. He dared not disclose how little thought had been given to preparing the ground in that part of the kingdom before 11 November, when he was already at Brampton and casting around for people to carry messages to his potential supporters.

One of the couriers was intercepted when apparently on his way to the Welsh magnate Sir Watkin Williams Wynn. Another couple of messages were entrusted to the Cockermouth grocer Peter Pattinson (not to be confused with Thomas Pattinson, the deputy mayor of Carlisle), who had come to Brampton to offer his services. Sir Thomas Sheridan showed him to the Prince's house, and Pattinson 'put his head into the room and saw the Pretender's son ... sitting at breakfast with some gentlemen in plaid waistcoats very richly laced ... [he] well remembers they were breakfasting upon a couple of ducks and a hot breast of mutton'.[2]

Pattinson is much criticized by historians, but he and his companion John Newby succeeded, at great risk, in making their way on 16 November to Marbury Hall in southern Cheshire, the seat of the aged but influential Jacobite James Barry, 4th Earl of Barrymore, who had unfortunately gone to London to attend Parliament. Barrymore probably could not have acted even if Pattinson had reached him, however, for he was suspected by the authorities and was being detained in London by the moral pressure of his friends (p. 64). In all good faith Pattinson and Newby delivered the relevant message to his Whiggish son, Lord Buttevant, who burnt the paper and put them under arrest.

Cumberland and Westmorland, the north-westernmost of the English counties, were dominated by the Whiggish and immensely wealthy Lord Lonsdale. Lancashire, the next county beyond, was on the face of it much better disposed, for Stuart Royalist traditions persisted, along with sizeable minorities of Catholics in the countryside, and peculiarly militant Non-Juring Episcopalians in the town of Manchester. However, the Prince's advisers had set themselves against calling upon specific Catholic support (p. 67) long before Lord George's outburst on 15 November, and the Lancashire Catholics had never recovered in spirits after the failure of the rising of 1715, which they blamed on the lack of support from the Episcopalians. For years afterwards Preston was in a state of shock.[3] The Scottish Jacobites had come back to themselves much more quickly, but the River Ribble at Preston remained in their 'cognitive maps' as a symbolic barrier, reinforced by the stories of how Cromwell had defeated the Scottish forces there in 1648.

In terms of physical geography, the coming theatre of operations was dominated by the hills of the North Country, and more particularly the chain of the Pennines, a high, broken plateau which reached in places to more than 2,000 feet, and which extended down the central axis of England for some 150 miles from the Tyne Gap in the north to the valley of the Trent in the south.

The Pennine crossings as they existed in 1745 were largely the work of great glaciers which worked their way generally south or east from southern Scotland and the Lake District, scouring passages like those of the Tyne Gap, the Stainmore Pass, Airedale and the other long, south-east-trending Yorkshire dales. The descents on the eastern side of the Pennines were on the whole gradual, but those to the west were more abrupt, for the watershed lay closer to this flank of the range and many of the hills presented steep and rocky 'edges' to the setting sun. The regimes of the westward-flowing rivers were consequently short, and they had a way of combining with cloudbursts to create flash flooding downstream. A traveller might paddle across the few yards of the upper Mersey one morning, and return early in the afternoon and be presented with several hundred yards of swirling brown water.

These features were to bear directly or indirectly on the course of the campaign of 1745 in England. It so happened that in the middle of November the Jacobite army at Carlisle was reshaping itself in a way which enabled it to take the best possible advantage of them. The arrangements had as much to do with necessity as with any foresight. The Highlanders had never had much use for tents, and in spite of their lengthy stay around Carlisle made no attempt to retrieve these or the other gear that had been left with the fifty or sixty carts of the baggage train which, through the lack of horses, they had abandoned at Lockerbie. With winter coming on, even the tough Highlanders would have to be given shelter overnight in the towns, villages and farms along the way. Skilful staff work had enabled the Jacobites to converge on Carlisle by separate columns, but now the two divisions would be marching along the same route and it was important to prevent overcrowding in the limited accommodation.

The army was accordingly divided into three main elements. Lord Elcho was to take the lead with his Lifeguards, scouting ahead and issuing deliberately inflated demands for food and quarters. At the same time he sent out patrols and circulated wild rumours which projected panic and confusion well to the sides of the army's actual axis of advance. Lord George came next with his Lowland Division, and after each night's rest he set off early the next morning to clear the accommodation for Prince Charles with the Highland Division and the rest of the cavalry. 'Undoubtedly both Charles Edward and Lord George relished the days out of each other's sight.'[4] The two divisions were not to rejoin until they reached Preston. In such a way a given locality might see parties of Jacobites trailing through the streets over the course of three or four days.

The Duke of Perth brought up the artillery and the remaining baggage, if needs be along an alternative route, and when the advance reached deeper into England he formed a corps of Pioneers to help to clear the way. The army obtained its food, fodder and other necessities from the places along its route, whether by outright purchase, promissory notes or (in the case of recalcitrant Whigs) the occasional use of threats. Field Marshal Wade and the Duke of Cumberland, on the other hand, never came to such successful terms with either the terrain or the season at any time during the campaign in England.

Lord Elcho and his 120 Lifeguards took the Roman road south from Carlisle on 18 November. They passed through the rich red ploughlands of the Vale of Eden, probably then mostly under snow. The high ground began to close in again after 10 miles of marching, and as the Lifeguards approached Penrith they could see the ridge to their left rising to the wooded hill of Penrith Beacon, which took its name from the square tower accommodating the brazier that alerted the whole district in time of danger. The structure was now topped by a pyramid to commemorate the defeat of the rising of 1715, and the veterans on Elcho's troop were no doubt prompted to relate how the Penrith militia had fled at their coming and how hostile a reception the Jacobites had been given.

Nothing had changed. No kind of opposition was offered to Elcho when he approached Penrith in the afternoon, and once again the coldness of the townsfolk stood in curious contrast to the welcoming look of the place – a manifestly prosperous market town of blood-red sandstone. Elcho now required Penrith to provide quarters for his '250' men and for the '800' infantry to be expected the next day, and he ordered 1,000 bales of hay and ten cartloads of oats to be delivered up by each of the great houses of Greystoke Castle, Dalemain, Hutton John, and Lowther, Edna and Hutton Halls.

Elcho directed the march of the 19th no further along the Roman road (which now inclined left from Penrith towards the Stainmore Pass), but south-south-east over the fine bridge which spanned the Eamont, just outside Penrith, a river in which 'are great falls of water called cataracts by reason of the rocks and shelves in it, which makes a great noise'.[5] There was no point in pressing too far ahead of the army, and Elcho and his people availed themselves of free quarters in Lowther Hall, the house of the Whiggish Lonsdales, which had failed to comply with his demand for fodder.

The respite ended on 21 November, when the Lifeguards made for Shap Fells. The first stage of the route lay through lanes lined with dry stone walls, and brought the Lifeguards to the straggling village of Shap. After a couple of miles the enclosed pastureland gave way to the high Shap Fells, which even at the best of seasons presented a picture more 'dreary and melancholy than any of the Highland hills, being not only very barren, but destitute of every picturesque beauty'.[6] The fells were covered with snow, and the Lifeguards did well to be able to descend into Kendal early in the evening.

Lord George's Lowland Division marched from Carlisle on 20 November, and struggled through ice and snow in the wake of the Lifeguards. They reached Penrith at 2 p.m., and the men began to make their way to their assigned billets in that singularly handsome town. The troops were on their best behaviour but their reception was as icy as the climate. The march through the unforgiving weather was resumed on the 21st and took the column by way of Eamont Bridge, Clifton and Thrimby to a comfortless night at Shap.

Captain MacLean entered in his diary how on the 22nd the Atholl Brigade crossed Shap Fells, then descended to the Kent, 'a beautiful water and large too passing through a part of Kendale, which is a large and handsome town where we quartered that night. We marched twelve miles that day having deep snow in the moor, passing through wreaths [sic] of snow and it happened to be a thow [thaw]'.[7]

Early on the 21st Prince Charles's Highlanders left Carlisle by the English Gate, and a hostile watcher reported from Penrith at noon that 'the Highland army is swarming in here all this day like bees, those we had last night [i.e. the Lowland Division] are all gone the Lancaster road. The Prince is expected every minute; his quarter's in Simpson's'.[8] Another observer noted that 'by the best reckoning I could make by persons at Eamont Bridge and Falconfield Bridge in the town the Highlanders might be about 3,000, they have odd straggling parties which makes any account difficult ... the whole body together is not above 6,000 besides women and boys'.[9] The men accumulated in Penrith numbered 2,846. Prince Charles took up his quarters at the George Inn off the Market Square (still standing as the George Hotel in Devonshire Street), from where he required the High Constable to 'cause all the shoemakers within the village of Penrith and the neighbourhood thereof to bring to our Secretary's office ... all the men's shoes in their custody for which they shall receive the usual prices, and this our order you and the said shoemakers are to obey under the pain of military execution to be done against you and your persons and effects'.[10]

That night Prince Charles learned that Marshal Wade was retiring to Newcastle. The news was welcome in itself, and all the more encouraging because it was brought by a lieutenant and up to a dozen soldiers who had deserted from Wade's army.[11]

The Highlanders remained at Penrith on 22 November to await the arrival of the Duke of Perth with the artillery and the surviving baggage train of sixty carts, which had taken the easier but roundabout route out to the east by way of Warwick Bridge. The Highlanders strode out again on the 23rd, and Prince Charles hoped to cover the 18 difficult miles to Kendal by nightfall. At 5 p.m. an observer was able to report from Penrith that 'we are now clear of the Highland army ... their forces is [sic] far from formidable, they are poor shabby fellows most of them'.[12] By that time Prince Charles was in a state of collapse, for he had halted only briefly at Lowther Hall and insisted on making the trek over Shap Fells and down to Kendal on foot, where he arrived in a near-coma.

The artillery and baggage were making another detour to the east, by way of Orton, but the Lowland and Highland divisions were now concentrated in and around Kendal. A person who saw the Jacobites arrive at the town over the course of these days described the cavalry as being 'armed with blunderbusses, some with muskets, and one, two, three or four pistols apiece, the foot with muskets, broadswords, targets, and some with dirks ... there was about 2,000 of them good-like men, but the rest as poor a set of wretches as one could desire'.[13]

Kendal was welcoming, all the more so after the hostility of Penrith and the rigours of Shap Fells. The town sat in a gentle limestone landscape and there was much to remind the Scots of their homeland – the green woollen 'Kendal cotton' on sale in Scotland for plaids, the alleys and the covered passages which reached on the one side up to the fells, and on the other down to the Kent, and the river itself, which was 'pretty large, but full of rocks and stones, that makes shelves and falls in the water, it's stored with plenty of good fish, and there are great falls of water partly natural and added to by putting more stones in the manner of weirs, at which they catch salmon when they leap with spears'.[14] Kendal was also celebrated for its tanneries and leatherware, and no doubt some of the footsore Jacobites fitted themselves out with new shoes. Prince Charles himself lodged in No. 98 Stricklandgate, a comfortable enough house built in 1690, which in 1745 was owned by Justice Thomas Shepherd.[15] More and more of the Highlanders were gathering in Kendal, but were soon outnumbered by the country folk, who fond of a raree-show, flocked to the town in such vast numbers, that, by their assistance, we outstared the whole Highland army, some of which walked the length of a street, and others stood together in large numbers in several places of the town, to show themselves to the best advantage … Should 2,000 of their best be drafted out of this brave army, the rest would be such a poor, lousy, miserable pack, that any man who did not know their errand, and if they had not arms, would imagine some great famine to be in Scotland, and that these poor creatures were come into England to beg their bread. They have several young men in close plaid waistcoats, and huge fur caps, which they call their hussars; but they have such scurvy horses, that I have seen several of them exert all their vigour to bring them to a gallop; in spite of which the poor beasts immediately fell into a pace more suitable to their age and infirmities.[16]

The Jacobite army was now concentrated, and ready to irrupt from the remoter north-western corner of England into Lancashire. All the leading elements were in motion on 24 November. The Lifeguards and the fur-hatted hussars were out ahead, and over to their right the sandy bay of Morecambe gave them their first glimpse of the sea, or what passed for sea, since the muddy flats of the Solway Firth hardly counted. Daniel Defoe had been this way some time before, evidently at high tide, and writes that the route was 'as it were locked in between the hills on one side, high as the clouds and prodigiously higher, and the sea on the other, and the sea itself seemed desolate and wild, for it was a sea without ships, here being no seaport or place of trade, especially for merchants; so that, except colliers passing between Ireland and Whitehaven [actually the other way around] with coals, the people told us they should not see a ship for many weeks together'.[17]

The Lifeguards having turned aside, the hussars were the first Jacobite troops to enter Lancaster, at 11 a.m. on the 24th. The ancient county town lay 'as it were, in its own ruins'.[18] It had neither the busy prosperity of Penrith and Kendal which had been left behind, nor the graces of Preston that lay ahead. However, the splendid bridge (an important tactical feature) over the River Lune drew approving comments from travellers, and they found it worth their while to make the long trek up the grassy hill to the castle and ascend to the top of the square tower and take in the view.[19]

Lord George Murray reached Lancaster three hours after the hussars with the leading troops of the Atholl Brigade, having marched from the neighbourhood of Kendal by way of Barrows Green, Endmoor, Farleton and Burton-in-Kendal, 'a long stripe of a country town which had a good church in it'.[20]

The Lifeguards had left the main road at Burton and were making a sweep out to the east by way of Hornby Castle, where they were met by one of Yorkshire's leading Jacobites, the physician and antiquarian Dr John Burton, who had come to greet the army and renew his acquaintance with the Duke of Perth. The irascible Lord Elcho placed him under arrest and took him prisoner to Lancaster, where Lord George Murray set him free.

The rest of the Lowlanders reached Lancaster during the night. The carefully planned staging of the advance had gone somewhat awry, because the Lowland Division was getting too far in front, as if to hog all the glory, but, as Lord George explained to O'Sullivan, priority was given to speed, 'having no earthly intelligence of the enemy, and as they may possibly be nearer than we think'. In any case the army would soon be together again at Preston, and the proper routine reinstated.[21]

Prince Charles and the Highlanders remained on 24 November in Kendal. It was a Sunday, and the Prince encouraged his officers to attend the local church services and give generously to the collections, though (to avoid offence to one religious party or the other) he invented an excuse for staying away. On the 25th the Division embarked on the easy march to join Lord George in Lancaster, passing by way of the rocky knoll of Farleton Knot. Prince Charles and his men were seen on the road by a Whiggish physician of Lancaster, Dr Henry Bracken, whose description, although partisan, is probably the most closely observed to have survived from the campaigning of the Jacobites in England in 1745. To him the Prince appeared to be a young gentleman who was

> about five foot eleven inches high, pretty strong and well built, has a brown complexion, full cheeks, and thick lips that stand out a little, he looks more of the Polish than the Scottish breed, for he is nothing like the King they call his grandfather [i.e. James II]. He looks very much dejected, not a smile being seen in all his looks, for I walked a quarter of a mile with him on the road and afterwards saw him in his lodgings among company.

As for his followers, 'I believe one might single out about 1,000 fresh-looking fellows among their officers and soldiers; the first, I find, are of desperate fortunes (in general) and might as well be shot or hanged as go back; there are several very old fellows who were at the battle of Sheriffmuir in the last rebellion, and have brought their sons and grandsons along with them.'[22]

Another physician, the Jacobite Dr John Burton, was now at liberty, and had secured himself a viewpoint in an upper room of Jane Strangeway's public house,[23] and looked on the Prince and the Highlanders with a much more favourable eye when they crossed the bridge and entered Lancaster. Prince Charles made his way along Bridge Street and China Street to a gathering in the Market Place, and Captain MacLean records that 'all the cavalry and infantry we had there were turned to a parade at the Cross, and the Provost and Baillies were called and the Provost appeared in his velvet gown and black rod with a silver head. And upon the Cross they proclaimed the King'.[24]

The Prince slipped away to his quarters in the house of a Mr Edward Martin in or near Church Street, where he was visited by Alderman William Bryer.[25] Some time during the night the Prince felt the need to relieve himself, and 'his Guards were in a terrible pother … thinking they had lost him, but he had only gone to the little house'.[26]

The townsfolk of Lancaster were more friendly than those of Kendal, who again had been more amiable than those of Penrith, but in none of those places was there much inclination to sign on with the Jacobite army. However there were indications that the support out in the country was wider, and in Ormskirk, at least, it was barely contained by the local Whigs. Here on the night of 25/26 November 'a body of men, 200 of the Roman Catholics near Ormskirk, assembled in that town with a drum, beating up for volunteers to enter into the Pretender's service, and openly … proclaimed him King. But the townsmen rose upon them and fought them stoutly, took ten or twelve … the which were taken were put into their crib [prison], and should if possible be removed to some other gaol more remote than Preston. There are great number of them who have in that part always publicly professed the Romish religion and many others that will not oppose the Scotch army'.[27] The Duke of Cumberland dismissed the 'Ormskirk Rebellion' as the only manifestation of its kind in Lancashire, though King George was disturbed to see in it 'a disposition in the Roman Catholics to rise'.[28]

Bracken had meanwhile made it his business to dine in company with Duke William of Atholl, whom he had known in Paris, and 'what I observed from their discourse was, that they designed to push on for London with all speed, but did not themselves know the route, the Marquis of Tullibardine [Duke William] went so far as saying, it would be time for Don George [Lord George Murray] to march off very soon, I observed also that they magnified their numbers exceedingly and told confounded lies about their proceedings'.[29]

'Don George' and Lord Elcho had already stationed the Lowland Divison and the Lifeguards at Garstang on the road to the south, and they set off for Preston on the morning of 26 November. At 11 a.m. Elcho and the Lifeguards secured the place without opposition, and the infantry came up behind. The Atholl Brigade was nearing the town when 'we met two violers with their fiddles playing *The King Shall Play his Own Again* ... for several of our officers threw money to them. That day we met several men and women on the road that wished us success and many huzzas as we passed.' Lord George rushed his men through Preston and across the bridge leading over 'a beautiful water named Ribble'[30] to gain a good foothold on the far side. This was good psychology as well as good tactics, for it exorcized the ghosts of 1648 and 1715, and Lord George had to show the Scots that it was possible to overcome the barrier of the Ribble.

Another important destination was Hoghton Tower, the home of Sir Henry Hoghton, who was the most rabidly anti-Catholic of all the Whig leaders of Lancashire. Now he 'had but just time to mount his horse, and take his lady behind him. They [the Jacobites] made themselves, however, very welcome, and drank out all the wine, beer and other liquors that were in the cellar, after which, by way of paying the reckoning, they talked of burning the house, which one of their chiefs prevented by threatening to put them to death if they did'.[31]

Prince Charles led the main force along the 20 miles of good road between Lancaster and Preston. A young Lancashire gentleman, John Daniel, saw the troops on the stretch from Lancaster to Garstang, 'the brave Prince marching on foot at their head like a Cyrus or Trojan hero, drawing admiration and love from all those who beheld him, raising their long-dejected hearts, and solacing their minds with the happy prospect of another Golden Age'.[32] A little later Daniel was drinking with some friends at a public house beside the road when the Duke of Perth dropped by and invited him outright to join the army. Daniel accepted on the spot, and was given the first task of distributing Jacobite proclamations. He gathered up forty recruits and distributed the pamphlets at Eccleston, Ingleton and other familiar places in the Fylde – the tract of level and low-lying ground which extended between the Lune, the Ribble and the sea.

Prince Charles was still short of the town of Preston when he learned that the Hanoverian authorities were breaking down the bridges along the middle and lower Mersey. There was not enough time to send Lord Elcho to interrupt the work, but the news that the enemy were resorting to such desperate measures was seen as 'an argument of their weakness, at least of their fear, and gave great encouragement'.[33] The Prince entered Preston to a genuinely warm reception, and put himself up on the northern side of Mitre Court at the entrance to Strait Shambles (a site now occupied by the Guild Hall). The army headquarters was established in what is now the Old Bull Inn, standing in Church Street.

A Whig clergyman of the West Riding of Yorkshire had disguised himself as an agricultural labourer, and came to town to spy on the newcomers. After he had seen the Prince conducted to his lodging, he went to an inn, 'where soon after a lieutenant came into the room. He asked a great many questions about General Wade and General Ligonier, whom he seemed to be very anxious about, and wished much to learn where they were; and then enquired how far it was from the sea, how far to Wales, and how far to London'.[34]

The 27th of November was declared a rest day, and now that the army was concentrated, the chiefs took the opportunity to meet in council. Prince Charles was set on continuing the advance as far as London, and declared that he had assurances of support from leading Jacobites along the way. The French ambassador, the Marquis d'Eguilles, backed him up by saying that French forces had already landed on the south coast of England, or were about to do so, and for the time being at least the rest of the council swallowed its reservations.

In such a way a gulf in perceptions began to grow between the Prince's council, which was beset by doubts, and the ebullience of the army. One of the junior officers wrote:

> we have left Wade and have stretched long marches to get before him, we expect to meet with Sir John Ligonier first and so go to London, and if we beat him we have great hopes of seizing London by the assistance of our friends there who may join after another victory, and also the French landing which we think would secure all. The people in Lancashire are much more our friends, the country people blessing him [the Prince] as he goes along, and we are getting recruits, some English gentlemen (of small estate) have joined us, and two from Wales ... The weather has been desperately cold, but now is turned very mild again. I have held out thank God very well, for we are now coming into great towns and lodge well, which was not the case at first.[35]

If Kendal had brought reminders of Edinburgh in the physical sense, Preston resembled that town in its society. 'Here's no manufacture; the town is full of attorneys, proctors and notaries, the processes of law being of a different nature than they are in other places, it [Lancashire] being a duchy and county palatine … The people are gay here, though not perhaps the richer for it; but it has by that obtained the name of "Proud Preston".[36] More than any place the Prince had so far encountered in England, this town gave him a notion of what it might be to live in a kingdom that was restored to the Stuarts.

Altogether sixty men enlisted at Preston on the 27th, and the army was joined there by the Catholic gentleman Francis Townley and by the Welsh lawyer David Morgan and his servant – the 'two from Wales'. Morgan betook himself to Lord Elcho's lodgings at the Joiners Arms, and in the course of a lively dinner he told Elcho that there was little to stand in the Jacobites' way, 'speaking with great earnestness and warmth, and reinforced what he said with significant shaking of his head, and motions of his hand'.[37]

The rightful king was proclaimed at the Cross. Three or four regiments were drawn up around the site, and one of the soldiers of Perth's was 'very near the person that read the proclamation, and heard the person's voice, but could not hear the words distinctly by reason of the noise, and as soon as the paper was read the persons standing by pulled off their hats and bonnets and waved them over the heads and made three loud huzzas'.[38] After the ceremony Charles rode a mile out of town with his Lifeguards to visit Lord George at the outposts, and to view the ground of the battle of 1715.

The Kingdom Invaded: The Immediate Local Response

The reports of the breaking of the Mersey bridges were the first indication to reach Prince Charles of any kind of organized response to his progress. Wade's army was isolated on the far side of the Pennines, Ligonier's was forming in the Midlands; they began to come under effective direction only when the Duke of Cumberland arrived at Lichfield on 27 November. In the absence of any coherent command, a state of alarm or exultation (according to one's political sympathies) gripped Britain from the Clyde to beyond the Mersey, and from the North Sea to the Irish Sea.

Up in Scotland the Glaswegian Whigs were the first people to recover their equilibrium.[39] The boldness or otherwise of such people depended entirely on whether or not the Highland army seemed to be coming in their direction. In such a way the alarms at Dumfries subsided from 9 November when it became clear that the Jacobites had veered aside and were concentrating inside England, at Carlisle and Brampton. The militant anti-Jacobites of Dumfries were headed by the Seceders, the members of a radical new Protestant sect, and on 14 November a party of these marched the 16 miles to the neighbourhood of Lockerbie and Ecclefechan and made off with the baggage which the Jacobites had abandoned there and never bothered to recover.

In England the town of Whitehaven was situated where the coast of Cumberland reached furthest into the Irish Sea, and was one of those west-coast ports that had prospered under Hanoverian rule, in this case by shipping coal from the Lonsdale family mines to Dublin. The people felt accordingly grateful. Self-interest was also involved, for the timber merchants were in debt to Donald Cameron of Lochiel to the tune of up to £12,000, and they feared that he might pay them a visit with his clansmen to collect what was owing. The town raised ten companies of fifty men apiece for its defence, and set up breastworks on all the approaches. However, the resolution collapsed when news arrived that Carlisle had surrendered, and 'Whitehaven being an open town, it was thought advisable to dismount the guns, and put them aboard the ships, that they might not fall into the enemy's hands; and many of the houses and shops were disrobed [sic], so that all the horses and carts, with many people, were employed for day and night in carrying and putting goods on board the ships to be sent to Dublin, the Isle of Man etc. So low was the rebels' credit in Whitehaven,' writes James Ray, 'that I saw an old woman carrying away a large basket full of empty bottles, rather than trust them to Highland civility'.[40]

Patriotic resolution began to return to the far north-west when it became clear that the Jacobites were marching south by way of Penrith. That place was clear of the rebels by the evening of 23 November, and on the 27th a party of the townspeople mobbed the Earl of Kilmarnock's third son and a number of companions who were on their way to join the army. The young nobleman and his friends galloped off, but then most unwisely stopped to dine at Lowther Hall. The Whigs caught up with them again, and in the course of a firefight drove them from the Porter's Lodge, through the ornamental garden and into the kitchen and stables. The surviving Jacobites broke free, but they left one of their people dead and ten or eleven as prisoners.

The first part of England to take fright had been the north-east, on account of the shock of Prestonpans and the long continuance of the Jacobite army at Edinburgh, which had disturbed the supporters of the government in Northumberland and Durham and along the Yorkshire coastlands as far south as Scarborough (p. 234). The Whigs of York were by no means reassured to learn that Prince Charles was advancing to the west of the Pennines, for they feared that he could at any time direct his army over the hills into the north-eastern counties, if no longer by the Tyne Gap, at least by the Roman road across Stainmore (the A66) and the other routes further south – the valleys of the Swale, the Ure and the Wharfe, or from Rochdale over Blackstone Edge and on by way of Halifax.

No more than 350 militiamen could have been assembled at Richmond to block the way of the Jacobites if they had chosen to cross the North Riding of Yorkshire to the rich plains of the East Riding and thus to the city of York, where the Jacobites and the Catholics were among the most assertive of the North Country, and where inspection showed that the town walls and Clifford's Tower were untenable. For a time spirits were buoyed up in the textile towns of the West Riding by the news that 'there hath been an action between General Wade and the rebels at Carlisle and he hath slain 2,000 of the rebels and taken a great number of them prisoners and the rest are fled away. And they were ringing the bells at Barnsley this day for joy of the victory'.[41] That was succeeded on 23 November by equally unfounded reports that the Jacobites were moving on Leeds and Wakefield. 'They say the rebels in Carlisle took the women and children and bound them hand and foot and chained them together and set them in the forefront of the castle so that they could not shoot at them, but they would kill their wives and children and so took the castle. They say General Wade is going back to Newcastle … A cold dark rainy day. Sleet in the morning.'[42] The clothiers were still removing their stocks from Leeds and Halifax on the 25th, but they recovered from their alarms on the next day when they learned that the Jacobites were continuing south through Lancashire.

That county stood squarely in the path of the Prince as he advanced by way of Penrith and Kendal. On 12 November Lord Derby, the Lord Lieutenant of Lancashire, mustered the militia on his own authority rather than await permission from Parliament as required by the Mutiny Act of 1662. He raised the necessary funds by a 'voluntary' subscription, but he was aware that a number of towns had paid up only with reservations and that the men were 'very unfit for service, without an officer capable of commanding, and without most of the conveniences and necessaries of an army'.[43]

Parliament legitimized the raising of the militia on 14 November, but ten days later the Jacobite advance guard reached the county town of Lancaster, and Lord Derby and his Deputy Lieutenants decided to disband the force and sent the arms away to Liverpool to be put safely on board ship. He explained that the men might have been of some use if the king's troops had arrived on the scene before the Jacobites, but he thought it could 'scarcely be expected by anybody, that a raw indisciplined militia, consisting of foot,

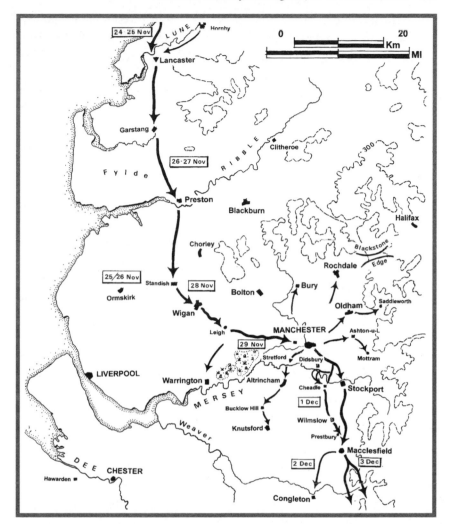

Lancashire and North Cheshire

without anyone that knows how to command, should be able to prevent the advance of an army seven or eight times this number'.[44] The government in London was taken aback, and Major General Humphrey Bland claimed that the Lancashire Militia was 'a very fine body of men, well armed and tolerably well disciplined, and very willling to join the King's troops everywhere. They did not give up above 200 of their arms, saying they durst not return home without them for fear of their Papist neighbours'.[45] Major Stanley, a recently appointed deputy lieutenant, was so angry at what had been done that he rounded up 300 horses belonging to the Catholics and brought them across the Mersey into Cheshire.

If the Jacobite army had now veered to the south-west there would have been nothing to stand in its way before it came to Liverpool, a place bursting with civic pride as the grandest of all the Whiggish ports.[46] It owned the second wet dock in England (the first being the East India Company's dock at Blackwall on the Thames), and was well placed for the trade with Ireland, Wales, the American colonies and the West Indies.

On 22 September permission had arrived from the government for the town fathers to do something entirely novel, which was to raise a regiment of their own by voluntary subscription. On the 28th a meeting resolved to rig out the men in blue coats, hats and stockings, and the regiment of the Liverpool Blues became the model for the many further 'Blues' that were raised by local initiatives elsewhere. The 800-strong force was drilled by a complement of regular officers and retired NCOs, and the home-grown officers were 'a set of soldier-like gentlemen, though they had never been bred in a military way, being mostly gentlemen, tradesmen etc. yet had acquired a very good discipline, having thrown up their trade and mer-chandise for a time, and ventured their lives, their fortunes, and everything that was dear to them, in defence of their King and country. Such men ought to be had in the greatest esteem, by all true lovers of our happy Establishment'.[47]

None of this counted for much when, on 30 November, Liverpool was overtaken by such a panic that

> there is scarce a woman stays in the town, all fly to the other sides of the river in Cheshire, where great numbers have been this fortnight, and their most valuable effects are on board ships, which lie under the cannon of two men of war lately built here, which are now in the channel. On this occa-sion lodgings are raised so prodigiously in all the villages on the other side of the water that a single room will fetch ten shillings a week. Nothing can equal the horror and fright of the population; all last night carts were taking goods away, carpenters are also at work making boxes for packing, and all furniture is pulling down. There is hardly any shop goods, plate, linen or clothing left in the town: in a word, Liverpool is stripped almost entirely.[48]

The reason was that the Liverpool Blues had been whisked across the Mersey to Cheshire on the 29th. That county was the most likely avenue for the advance of the Jacobites from Lancashire, whether they were making for the Midlands and London, or south-west into Wales. They had said in October that they were expecting 'a rising in Wales in their favour, and say the Welsh are by far the best militia in England'.[49] This last (usefully for Jacobite purposes) promised to divert a great deal of attention to the defence of

Chester, and this delusion was encouraged by the fact that the Lord Lieutenant, the Earl of Cholmondeley, was also Governor of Chester Castle. Rather than summon the country militia, as in Lancashire, Cholmondeley and his fellow Whiggish magnates decided to raise a 'Blues'-type regiment by voluntary subscription. Cholmondeley was able to report on 8 November that he had already recruited the considerable number of 600 men, in spite of all the difficulties made by the Tory gentlemen. But Cholmondeley was worried about the state of Chester Castle, where ten to fourteen days' work would be needed to make it habitable, 'and indeed if the rebels bring any cannon with them, 'tis a place of no defence'.[50] He had not yet sealed his letter when he learned that the Jacobites had reached Moffat, only 36 miles short of Carlisle.

Cholmondeley was made acutely aware of what still had to be done when a regular officer, Brigadier William Douglas, arrived at Chester in the middle of November. Douglas was already in a bad temper, for he had made a difficult journey through snowdrifts, and when he reached Chester he found that Cholmondeley was technically superior to him by virtue of his rank as a lieutenant colonel of the county, and that the sandstone walls dated back to medieval or even Roman times. He wrote to the Duke of Cumberland how

> my zeal for the public service would incline me to get over this, as I think this is no time for punctilios of command, but I see very plainly that I can be of no manner of service here; with the tools I have to work with I pronounce the place quite defenceless, and the ramparts, walls we should call 'em, are commanded in many places by the best houses in the suburbs and are to be got over in several others; the castle is a very weak place and tho' it has some guns, not a manner of gunner that can point one; and the regiment here, a parcel of ragged youths and some old men; the first of 'em got arms but on Wednesday last [the 13th] and the last of 'em on Saturday, so they don't know at all the use of 'em, and I am thoroughly convinced if an enemy should appear they would throw them away.[51]

By the 23rd Chester was in the grip of a panic similar to the one that was going to overtake Liverpool.[52] Five companies of Blakeney's 27th had been stationed in Chester since September, and by 4 November Cholmondeley had assembled there about half of his own 'new' regiment, the 73rd. The Duke of Newcastle had tried to bolster confidence by hastening the march of 220 further regulars, from Bligh's 20th, together with another of the 'new' regiments, Gower's 77th from Birmingham.

The forces in Chester now amounted to less than one regiment's-worth of regulars, together with two of the lordly but well-nigh useless 'new' regiments. It was an unstable assemblage, and Cholmondeley had to report that 'there is a great deal of difference between such raw men as ours who have never had their arms until within these nine days ... and well-disciplined troops'. Cholmondeley was overtaken by the general panic of 23 November, and, when he contemplated the courses open to him if the Jacobites ever bore down on Chester, he believed that he must send the two new regiments to safety on the left bank of the Dee, break an arch of the bridge behind them, scuttle the ferries, and retire into the castle with the regulars.[53] This scarcely amounted to a resolute defence of the Dee, let alone the forward line of the River Mersey.

The Mersey was formed by the meeting of two streams of the western Pennines, the Tame and the Goyt, which came together just above the market town of Stockport. Emerging from the sandstone narrows, the river first described a looping course through the flat and marshy borderlands of Lancashire and Cheshire by way of Didsbury, Stretford and other places to the south of Manchester. There were standing bridges at Stockport and Stretford, and a multitude of lanes snaked through the poplar-grown wetlands to reach no fewer than forty fords along this stretch of the river,[54] not to mention the bridges and ferries. Highlanders in any case scorned artificial crossings as effeminate, and it was observed that 'after the Prince passed Preston all the bridges where he was to pass were broke down in order to hinder his passage, but that was a needless precaution, for Highlanders give themselves no trouble about a bridge, if the water be in any way fordable'.[55] However, not even these folk could tackle the Mersey when it was subject to one of its numerous and unpredictable floods.

Between Stretford and Warrington the obstacle value of the Mersey was enhanced by bogs which went by the local name of 'mosses' and which were formed of a great depth of compacted cotton grass. The most notorious of the morasses was Chat Moss, which extended to the north of the river, and which, by Defoe's calculation, measured between 5 and 6 miles from east to west, and up to 8 from north to south. It looked black and dirty from a distance, as the water that drained from it was 'of a deep brown, like stale beer'.[56]

Warrington stood on the northern, or Lancashire, side of the river, and was a large and populous market town which had an important trade in textiles. The handsome bridge there was the lowest permanent crossing of the Mersey and carried the main road connecting Scotland with London west of the Pennines. For those reasons it was always reckoned to be 'a pass of the utmost importance. It was found to be so on several occasions in the time of the late Civil War, and had the rebels advanced thus far in the late Preston affair [of 1715], so as to have made themselves masters of it, it would have been so again; and, on that account, the King's forces took special care by a speedy advance to secure it'.[57]

The river widened steadily below Warrington, and from Runcorn to the final narrows at Liverpool it formed a banana-shaped inland sea. The banks of sand and mud were as much an obstacle as the water, and when at low tide a passenger grounded far from the shore, the passenger would be retrieved by 'some honest Lancashire clown' and carried piggyback to dry land.[58]

The Mersey signified little in the cultural sense, for the adjacent parts of Cheshire belonged to the North Country rather than the Midlands, but in the second half of November 1745 it grew large in the thinking of the friends of the government, for it stretched from the foot of the Pennines to the Irish Sea, and constituted the only barrier of any kind between the Jacobite army poised at Manchester and the English heartland. The Austrian ambassador noted that the Ministry put a good deal of trust in the ability of loyal persons to destroy the bridges over the 'considerable rivers' which stood in the Jacobites' way, and hoped thereby to win the few days that were needed for the two English armies to do their work.[59] This was asking a great deal, for the two armies in question were still far distant at the crucial time, and the only forces available to the government were the Liverpool Blues. The few regular officers were alive to the importance of their task, but the same urgency was not always shared by the local interests.

The notion of destroying the bridges over the Mersey first comes to light in a letter which the Duke of Newcastle wrote on 13 November to Lord Cholmondeley, as the Lord Lieutenant of Cheshire. In his vaguely worded reply Cholmondeley mentioned that the River Weaver, which ran up through central Cheshire to Runcorn, had lost all its defensive worth after it had been canalized in the 1730s; something could still be made of the Mersey, but he pleaded that the Crossford Bridge at Stretford ought to be spared as 'the great pass of this country for all the salt trade of this county [Cheshire], and the linen and cotton trade of Ireland, Wales and Manchester'.[60]

Cholmondeley and his deputies were content merely to barricade the bridges until, on the evening of 23 November, he received an order from the Duke of Richmond, as the commander of the leading elements of the 'western' army, to destroy the bridges in the way of the Jacobites, beginning with the bridge over the Irwell between Salford and Manchester, 'as this is the first step to be taken in order to prevent the passage of the rebels into Cheshire'.[61] Brigadier William Douglas and the other regular officers reported at the same time how important it was to cut the bridge at Warrington, 'and I perfectly agreed with them,' wrote Cholmondeley, 'as it will retard the march of the rebels, which is a material point, in the present situation of the Duke's [Cumberland's] army, so many corps being at a distance of several marches'.[62]

On 25 November Brigadier Douglas and the Liverpool Blues demolished the two central arches of the Warrington bridge, and raised a considerable breastwork of rubble on the near side. Douglas left two companies of Blues to guard the fortification, and on the 26th he sent five more companies on a forced march upstream to tend to the bridge at Stockport. This was at the insistence of the Duke of Richmond, being 'so necessary a work for the defence of this part of the Kingdom'.[63] The testy Douglas arrived at Stockport ahead of his troops and found that Sir Peter Davenport and other bigwigs hesitated to see their beautiful sandstone bridge disappear into the Mersey. As Douglas put it, 'when I came there, I found the Justices of the Peace and others concerned, assembled to answer the Duke of Richmond's letter for that purpose, which they did with many representations about fords in several places of the river, which made the breaking of no avail. As there was a pretty large fresh [i.e. high water level] in the river, I thought their reasoning not quite just and that they proceeded from a great deal of tenderness to their bridge, and therefore resolved with myself what to do as soon as my people came up. They came that night having made a great march of twenty-two miles'.[64]

The blue-coated Liverpudlians demolished the bridge at Stockport early on 26 November. On the same day Lieutenant Colonel Gordon with the two companies of the Blues from Warrington proceeded to break down a number of the crossings which carried routes from Manchester over the Mersey – Barton Bridge (near the crossing of the later Bridgewater Canal), the wooden Carrington Bridge, and the economically important Crossford Bridge at Stretford. Orders to spare the Crossford Bridge had come too late, and Douglas was glad to learn that the demolition had progressed so far that the structure was now supported only by a single battered pillar which was on the point of collapse.

Altogether the authorities had done all within their power to deny the passages of the Mersey from Stockport all the way downstream to Warrington. The river would become a barrier in the absolute sense only if it were subject to one of its floods, but it would at the least compel the main force of the Jacobite army to make special arrangements for the passage, and these in turn might well betray the direction in which their further ambitions were tending.

Manchester, 28–30 November 1745

It is time to return to the actions of Prince Charles and his army, the cause of all these commotions. The Jacobites had taken the road from Preston on 28 November. By design the first day's march was directed not along the obvious route south-east by Bolton towards the real objectives (Manchester and the upper Mersey) but due south through Standish to Wigan. In the last century the intervening 15 or so miles had been very difficult going on account of the bogs and meres, and the numerous little streams which were liable to flash flooding. It could now be traversed along a road which had been turnpiked in virtue of an Act of 1726. A march down the turnpike would also, as Lord George Murray insisted, help to persuade the enemy that the Jacobites intended to cross the middle Mersey and press on to Wales. In such a way Ligonier's army would be thrown out to the west, and the Jacobites would have a clear passage over the upper Mersey and through north-eastern Cheshire.

Elcho's Lifeguards and the infantry of the advance guard set out from Preston at 6 a.m. on that day. They held to the turnpike for the first 8 miles, after which Elcho and his troopers veered to the left and made their quarters at Leigh on the Manchester side of Wigan. The lead was now taken by Pitsligo's Horse, and behind them Prince Charles and the main force of the army kept to the turnpike all the way to Wigan itself. The Prince lodged in the Old Manor House in Bishopsgate (a site now occupied by Walmesley House), while his officers made their way to the Eagle and Child and whatever other inns the small market town had to offer. The bluff was working well, assisted by stirrings by the local Jacobites at the Red Lion Inn and the Old Coffee House in Warrington, and panic spread down the lower reaches of the Mersey.

On 28 November Manchester was claimed for the Prince in a manner that was almost ridiculous. 'Manchester was taken by a sergeant, a drum, and a woman about two o'clock in the afternoon, who rode up to the Bull's Head, on horses with hempen halters (a just emblem of what they deserved) where they dined; after dinner they beat up for recruits, and in less than an hour lifted about thirty. They were likewise joined by several others, some of desperate fortunes who were modelled into what they called the

"Manchester Regiment", mostly people of the lowest rank and vilest principles."[65] So writes a Whig.

The sergeant was a Scot called John Dickson, who had been recruited into Perth's Regiment from among the prisoners at Prestonpans. He had been less successful than the other sergeants in attracting recruits in Preston and he had set out on his own initiative to see if he would have any better luck in Manchester. The girl was his companion Peggy, 'Long Preston Peggy', who came from the village of that name near Settle in Ribblesdale. She had a fine singing voice, and she set her own words to the tune of *Chevy Chase* to explain how she had joined the Highland army:

> *Long Preston Peggy to Proud Preston went,*
> *To see the Scotch rebels it was her intent;*
> *For in brave deeds of arms she did take much delight,*
> *And therefore she went with the Rebels to right ...* [66]

The trio passed through Salford, and found that the bridge spanning the Irwell to Manchester was intact. The hump-backed sandstone structure (demolished in 1837) consisted of three pointed arches resting on massive piers, and was narrow enough to be eminently defensible, as had been shown in an episode of the First Civil War in 1642. It was typical of the Lancashire bridges in that it had been built to cope with a river which, 'though not very great, yet coming from the mountainous part of the country, swells so suddenly, that in one night's time ... the waters would frequently rise four or five yards, and the next day fall as hastily as they rose'.[67] The far, or Manchester, bank, was lined with a jumble of sandstone rocks, which was a further obstacle. The bridge at Salford had therefore been the first item in the authorities' scheme of demolitions (p. 260), but the local Jacobite mob had other ideas, and succeeded in preserving it for the use of some particularly welcome guests.

There was no opposition of any kind, and in any case more than 100 of Pitsligo's Horse arrived in the evening to reinforce Dickson and his friends.[68] The Lancashire militia had already been dissolved, and the weapons of the Manchester Militia Horse had been left in the keeping of Trooper Samuel Lightbourn. He had been embarrassed to know what to do with them until the Clerk and a choir member of the ultra-Jacobite Collegiate Church took them into helpful safekeeping.[69]

Manchester was known as 'the largest village in England', a phrase which gives a clue to a multitude of paradoxes, and helps to explain these extraordinary events. Already prosperous from the manufacture and trading of textiles, the population of Manchester had reached some 20,000 and was rising fast. Half-timbered houses still predominated in the Market Square, along Deansgate, and up the narrow, winding and muddy Market Street lane, but here and there they were giving way to the showy detached mansions of prosperous merchants, and an elegant new quarter had sprung up in the shape of St Ann's Square, which was lined with plane trees and dominated at one end by St Ann's Church (1708–18), and towards the other by the Palladian Exchange (1729, demolished 1792).

The passions and ideologies of 1740s Manchester harked back to the Civil War. The defence of the bridge over the Irwell had been the most overt action so far taken by a local community on behalf of Prince Charles, and was the product of a century or more of violent antagonisms in this part of the world between militant Presbyterians and equally militant High Church Episcopalians who equated the Hanoverian usurpation in 1714 with those of Dutch William and Cromwell. The people of Rossendale to the north of Manchester were willing to oppose the Jacobites by force (p. 318). In the little places to the south, Didsbury and Northenden traditionally favoured the Stewarts, while Cheadle had supported Parliament in the Civil War and was (and is) Low Church.

In Manchester itself the Presbyterians congregated at Cross Street Chapel, and the Low Churchmen at St Ann's, while Dr John Clayton of the Collegiate Church and the Non-Juring bishop Dr Thomas Deacon promoted Jacobitism as a semi-religious creed (p. 65), and had a devoted following among the leading citizens and neighbouring gentry, some of whom were going to venture and lose their lives in the cause.

For John Byrom (author of the words of *Christians Awake!* and the first Pitman-style shorthand) Jacobitism remained an intellectual exercise.[70] His 23-year-old daughter Elizabeth ('Beppy') had no such reservations, her enthusiasm being shared by her friend Hugh Stirling of Calderbank, who was apprenticed in Manchester but had gone to join the Highland army. After the news of Prestonpans came to town Elizabeth bought herself a gown of blue and white in celebration, and she noted that 'the Presbyterians are sending everything that's valuable away, wives, children, and all for fear of the rebels'. Upon the advance of the Jacobite army into England 'everybody is going out of town and sending all their effects away, there is hardly any family left but ours and our kind'.[71] The night of 28 November was fine and moonlit, and when Pitsligo's horse clattered into the Market Place she saw young Stirling in their ranks.

It was typical of Manchester that it still had no mayor and corporation, and ranked only as a parish, its day-to-day affairs being managed by

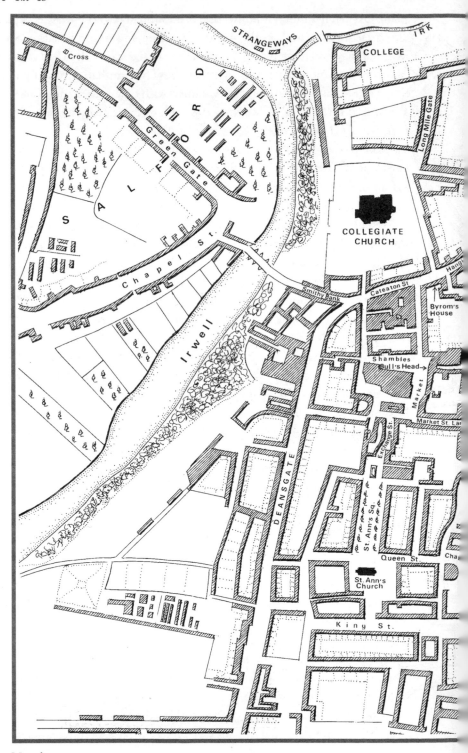

Manchester

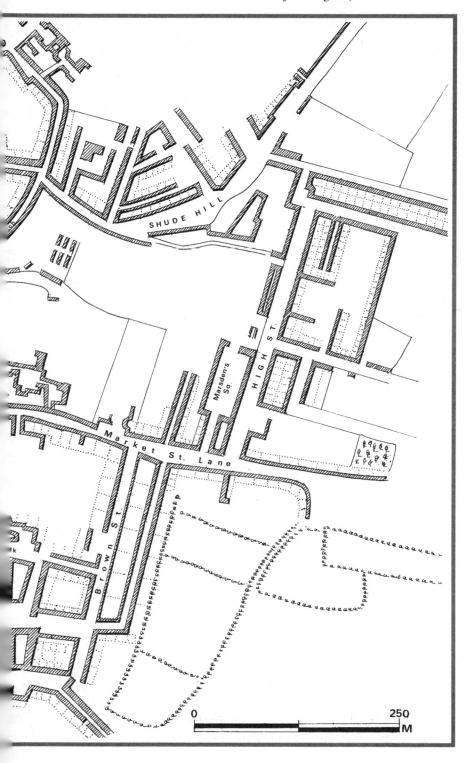

two unpaid constables, the unfortunate William Fowden and Thomas Walley. On legal advice they now kept quietly to themselves, but they were not to be left in peace for long. At 9 p.m. Fowden was hauled from his house by a party of Jacobite officers armed with pistols and swords, and was taken to the headquarters at the Bull's Head in the Market Place. 'The prisoner then demanding by what authority he was sent for, the commanding officer drew his sword and said, "Damn you – by this", and then told the prisoner he must obey all the orders of their prince, as they called him, upon pain of military execution.'[72]

On 29 November Prince Charles and the main army turned east from Wigan and embarked on the 14- or 15-mile march along poorish roads to Manchester. The way was lined with friendly or curious people, and the excitement grew as the column neared the town. The Rev. John Clayton, Jacobite ideologue and preacher at the Collegiate Church, had his house at Salford. He was waiting at his door, decked out in gown and cassock and sporting a white cockade in his hat. At the sight of the Prince, Dr Clayton pressed through the crowd, and 'coming up to the said Pretended Prince who was on horseback the said Clayton gathered up his gown, pulled off his hat, and knelt down on one knee before the said Pretended Prince and … the said Pretended Prince smiled on the said Clayton'.[73]

The leading troops of the main army turned into St Ann's Square just as the first Rector of the new church, Rev. Joseph Hoole, was being buried. The officers stood quietly at the graveside until the ceremony was over, and then attended to their duties. Their men were reported to be 'but a despicable body, many boys and old people among them; of this number about 2,000 were well armed, the rest very indifferently, the horse [probably the hussars] for the greatest part shabby, equipped with blunderbusses, hangers, and two or three pistols each'.[74]

The two constables were taken under guard to the Market Cross, 'where a rebel officer tendered the proclamation [of King James III] to Mr Walley, who absolutely refused to read it, and it was then tendered to the prisoner, Mr Fowden, who made a like refusal, but, upon being pressed, he told them he could not see without his spectacles. Then Mr Walley, being demanded to repeat the proclamation after one of the rebel officers, said he had a hesitation in his speech and could not, upon which they obliged Mr Fowden to repeat after them, which he did unwillingly and in great fear'.[75]

Prince Charles dismounted at or near the bridge over the Irwell, and at about 3 p.m. he entered Manchester under a white banner, and to the accompaniment of cheers and the ringing of bells he made his way up Market Street

Lane to his quarters with John Dickenson, a prosperous Jacobite linen draper. The house was typical of the new Manchester rich, as a brick-built mansion with stone corners, a stone balustrade, a central doorway approached by a flight of steps, and a railed-off garden forecourt. The Duke of Atholl stayed nearby in the new house of Mr Marsden, a still more elaborate affair adorned with pilasters, statues and a cupola.

The working headquarters of the army was already in operation at the Bull's Head Inn in the Market Place, where the barber–surgeon Whitlock collected a great quantity of freshly printed proclamations, and

> after he had cut the said declarations in two (for there were two in one sheet) folded them up, and threw them out of the window of the said room to a great number of people that were at that time assembled in the Market Place, and before the said Bull's Head Inn ... the said Whitlock was employed at least four hours in cutting and distributing the said declarations, and giving whole handsfull at a time ready folded that they might not separate, to several gentlemen who were in the said room at the time, for them to dispense of.

Whitlock then went out to buy ribbons, and came back to the Bull's Head, where he and his fellow-Jacobite Alexander Dawson made them up into white and blue cockades.[76]

Colonel John William O'Sullivan was working from the Saracen's Head in Market Street Lane and arranged for the troops to be billeted in the Market Place, Market Street Lane, King Street, Deansgate and Ridgefield. Colonel James Grant as commander of the artillery established his headquarters at the Spread Eagle in Hanging Ditch, and parked his train in view of the admiring public in Camp Field (site of the later Artillery Street), an open space which led down from Deansgate to the Irwell. Other places of popular resort for the newcomers were the Sign of the Anchor in Cockpit Hill, and the Golden Goose in Key Street.

In the evening Prince Charles held a grand reception at Dickenson's house. John Byrom was unwilling to declare himself for the Prince outright, and appeared at the affair under armed guard. Parson Clayton had no such reservations, and he both kissed the Prince's hands and pronounced grace at the meal. A number of the senior officers also entertained nobly at their respective quarters, but

> most of the common men lay upon straw. Many of them were very lousy, and in many houses they made nasty work; some shitting out of the

windows where they lodged, and others in the streets. Some of the officers bespewed and beshit their beds. Others when they were shown to a house of office instead of sitting on them got upon them with their feet. In general they behaved civilly, excepting to those they imagined to have either horses or arms; and several of the town Volunteers, who knew almost everyone's circumstances, came to such with drawn swords, threatening to fire their houses if they did not discover where they were.[77]

The suspected friends of the government were in fact going about at their peril. John Dickenson's eldest son Samuel was roaming the town with a number of tartan-clad Scots, and identified Robert Jobb as a Whig who had contributed ten pounds to a loyal subscription. Late at night he took him to his father's mansion, 'and upon the same being demanded of him, he laid down four pounds fifteen shillings, telling them it was all that he had in his pocket, pleading at the same time poverty and badness of trade, on which the said Samuel Dickenson answered that he was surprised he should talk after that manner, being reputed to be worth ten thousand pounds, or words to that effect'. Dickenson senior then entered the room and resolved the impasse by lending Jobb what was needed.[78]

As a member of the recently dissolved militia, the weaver John Taylor was singularly ill-advised to linger in Manchester, just out of curiosity to see the Highlanders. He was identified, taken at a house in Fennel Street for interrogation, then on to the house of Dr Deacon, where, after the party had drunk spirits and ale, 'the said Dr Deacon said to this informant that he was glad he … would go with them (the said rebels) as one of them. "Don't be afraid young man, your case is as good as a great many [who] have joined them" … and that he hoped a great many more would'.[79]

Detachments from the army were now ranging over wide tracts of country to spread the good news, and to gather in horses, fodder and the proceeds of the Excise. They made the known Whigs their main targets, and they could usually find local sympathizers to show them the way. We find these enterprising people calling at Bury and Bolton to the north and northwest of Manchester, and riding down the Mersey as far as Warrington, where two of them were bold enough to cross the bridge to the south bank and were captured by the Liverpool Blues. The line of the Mersey south of Manchester was tested by parties that penetrated Cheshire, and called respectively at Altrincham, Gatley and Cheadle, Stockport, and even as far as Macclesfield (p. 271).

There was particular activity towards the Pennines and Yorkshire. One of the patrols reached Oldham in the evening of 29 November, and on the next day it went about its business with the help of the plumber John Whitehead and the merchant Theophilus Ogden the Elder. With their directions the raiders managed to find their way to objectives such as the house of the Whiggish innkeeper Zachary Fielding, a location they would never have found otherwise, 'it standing in such an odd place'.[80]

Later investigations into the case of John Appleton brought a great deal to light concerning the little towns of east Lancashire. He earned his bread as a labourer, but his gentleman father had lost his estates as a consequence of the '15, and John was bent on winning them back.[81] On 30 November a townsman saw 'John Appleton at the head of a parcel of rebel Highlanders ... coming to Ashton-under-Lyne with a Scotch cap on his head ... and Henry Andrew a poor collier called out "Damn thee Appleton!" and immediately added "God Bless King George!" Upon which the said Highlanders were very angry and drew their swords and pistols, and threatened to do the inhabitants of the town great mischief'.[82]

Appleton kept guard on the weapons of the Highlanders while they gathered in the Excise at the house of the Collector, Mrs Finlow, and he told them that they would find an excellent young horse in the possession of a Mr John Stopford. That gentleman's servant, Joshua Wardle, explained afterwards that he had told them that he did not know where the beast was, 'to which the said John Appleton said "damn you, you lie!" and ... pulled out a pistol, when this informant was so frightened that he began a-crying, and one of the rebels said "damn you, we will have none of your crying!"'.[83]

New waves of panic spread through the West Riding of Yorkshire and well beyond. On the 29th the expedition to Oldham, a foray to Mottram and the appearance of forty horse at Saddleworth gave rise to tales that 'a very great mob was risen and plundering all before them, and would be in Huddersfield this day, and they sent from Huddersfield in the night to go to the clothiers and fetch away their pieces, and they are gone for them this morning. They are in a terrible consternation at Huddersfield, Holmfirth, Wooldale, Scholes and all places hereabouts, and are securing their best effects'.[84] On the same day twenty-three further Jacobite troopers arrived at Rochdale, which seemed to betoken an advance over Blackstone Edge to Halifax and (by a great leap of imagination) on to York, where it was reported that 'people run about the streets crying "We are ruined!" and we who had not packed began to secure a few of our best effects, every coach in York was hired to carry the women out of the present danger'.[85]

Down in Manchester the main Jacobite force celebrated 30 November as St Andrew's Day and there was much wearing of the white and blue cock-ade by the Scots and their local supporters. Beppy Byrom and her friends had spent the morning putting cockades together, and towards noon she went to the house of Mr George Fletcher to see Prince Charles getting ready to show himself once more in public. 'And a noble sight it was, I would not have missed it for a great deal of money; his horse stood for an hour in the court without stirring, and as soon as he was got on he began a-dancing and capering as if he was proud of the burden, and when he rode out of court he was received with as much joy and shouting almost as if he had been King without dispute, indeed I think scarce anybody that saw him could dispute it.'[86]

The Prince was escorted by the Lifeguards, and the show made a most favourable impression as it toured the streets. Services were then held in the churches, after which the Prince reviewed the Manchester volunteers, or rather the new Manchester Regiment, in the precincts of the Collegiate Church (now Manchester Cathedral). The largest single elements were the thirty-nine raised by John Daniel in the neighbourhood of Garstang, and the ninety-odd recruited by Sergeant Dickson on the 28th. After some debate the command had been entrusted to Francis Townley (1709–46), a short-tempered individual who nevertheless commanded authority in virtue of his services as a regular officer with the French (p. 66).

Both the Hanoverian commentators and the more nationalistic of the Scots had an interest in decrying the calibre of the Manchester Regiment. However, the workers and small craftsmen among the other ranks were typical of the proletarian supporters of the cause in England. Most of the officers were people of high local standing, and 'though it is often objected to them, that they were not men of an extraordinary rank, yet they behaved so as to make those of nobler birth blush; for, from the time they had the honour of joining the Prince's standard, they never sought payment either for themselves or their men, honourably maintaining the supporting of the Regiment themselves'.[87]

In comparative terms response of the English to the appearance of the Jacobite army was by no means contemptible (p. 53) but it fell well short of what Prince Charles had promised the chiefs, and when he reconvened his council on the 30th he had to go to the limits of his credit to persuade them to continue the invasion. The bad-tempered meeting finally settled on a number of compromises (mostly on the initiative of Lord George Murray), whereby the army would continue the march to make a fair trial of English support, and, if the further advance on London were indicated, it should be by way of Stafford, Birmingham and Oxford. 'Their design of going to Oxford was in hopes the students would join them and thereby attach their respective families, and their march to London was in hopes the Irish and Scotch Papists would join them.'[88]

In the course of the day a number of patrols made forays across the upper Mersey into Cheshire (p. 268). At 4 p.m. a body of ten, 'the scum of the whole',[89] forded just above Stockport, called for a dozen of ale at the Angel, and went back the way they had without ever dismounting. Colonel Henry Ker with another fifty-four crossed at Gatley Ford, turned east to Cheadle, and returned to Lancashire by way of Cheadle Ford.[90] Colonel Ker was Lord George's aide-de-camp, and it is likely that both these probes were essentially reconnaissances.

The main concern of the Jacobite high command was to support the impression that the army would pass the Mersey further downstream by the Crossford Bridge at Stretford, as if intending to make for Wales or the upper Severn. The Jacobites therefore compelled Fowden and Walley to assemble timbers, planks, ropes, chains, nails and the like, and have them carted to the river at Stretford, where conscripted labourers were working to repair the bridge. A Whiggish gentleman of Cheshire sent one of his retainers to discover what was going on, 'and he observed that there were about forty or sixty men at work; that they begun as soon as the moon gave light; some with pickaxes and shovels were felling high poplars that grew by the river to be formed into a bridge. The labourer (they being his fellow workmen) entered into discourse and stayed with 'em some time, said there were ten or twelve officers (as he called them) overseeing and attending the workmen, but how long they would be in completing their work he could not guess'. When the bridge was completed the Jacobites 'raised a rejoicing shout'.[91]

CHAPTER 10

Invasion: The Bid for a Kingdom, 1–30 December 1745

Across the Mersey and into Cheshire, 1 December 1745

ON THE SNOWY 1 DECEMBER the Jacobite army passed the upper Mersey on a frontage of 6 miles, which was more like 11 if all the meanders are included. The objective for the day was the market town of Macclesfield in the hill country of eastern Cheshire, 12 miles from Manchester as the crow flies. In the process the Jacobites had to prevent their forces from piling up at the river, and they had to keep up the impression that they intended to strike south-west as if for Chester and Wales. For these reasons the Mersey was to be crossed at five different points, namely (from east to west):

❖ Prince Charles with the Highland Division at Stockport

❖ the artillery and baggage at Cheadle Ford

❖ Lord George Murray with the Lowland Division at Gatley Ford

❖ some of his cavalry at Northenden Ford (to throw the enemy off the scent)

❖ the Lifeguards and the Manchester Regiment by Crossford Bridge

---

A fierce Highlander with a turcaich blade

The necessary staff work was complicated but efficient, and took into account the reports of the most recent patrols, which indicated that the water was not unduly deep. The only obstacle was presented by the canal-like banks, which rose 10 feet or so to the level of the water meadows, and made it necessary to build a further bridge at Cheadle Ford of poplar logs to enable the artillery and baggage to pass.

The two divisions of the main army set out from Manchester at 4 a.m. Prince Charles was seen progressing along Market Street Lane at 6 a.m., the town being free of the infantry by 10.30. The news spread through the North Country: 'It hath oft been affirmed that the rebels leave abundance of lice behind them where they come, and that Manchester is very full of lice, and that a great number of the rebel army are such lousy tattered creatures as never was seen. Cornelius Bower's wife buried at Lydgate this day'.[1]

Prince Charles and Lord George at first followed a common route that led south-east from Manchester by the genteel suburb of Ardwick Green, and on through dairy farms through Longsight to the neighbourhood of Rushford Bridge and Slade Hall, where their paths diverged. Prince Charles took a fork to the left, or east, and marched through Levenshulme and Holmes Chapel to arrive at the valley of the infant Mersey at Stockport (a route corresponding with the A6 Stockport Road, and then with the left-branching A626 Manchester Road). At that period the scene was of considerable beauty. The low sandstone cliffs on either side of the demolished bridge were clothed in vegetation, and on the far side timber-framed houses crowded around the foot of a triangular sandstone bluff. The summit was crowned by the quaint little town of Stockport, complete with market place, parish church and castle ruins.

As there was no crossing at the site of the bridge, the division crossed a short distance upstream by a narrow ford which followed a fault of very hard conglomerate sandstone.[2] Prince Charles (dripping from the waist downwards) was met on the far side by a number of Cheshire gentlemen, and by the aged Mrs Skyring, who as a child in 1660 had seen Charles II disembark at Dover to reclaim his kingdom; every year she had sent half of her income anonymously to the Stuart court, and now, having sold all her valuables, she laid the proceeds in a purse at the Prince's feet: 'Straining her dim eyes to gaze on his features, she exclaimed with affecting rapture, in the words of Simeon: "Lord, now lettest thou thy servant depart in peace!"'.[3]

After the notoriously dismal landscapes of the flatter part of Lancashire, Prince Charles and his troops now marched through one of the most splendid parts of the kingdom, where the foothills of the Pennines gave way to

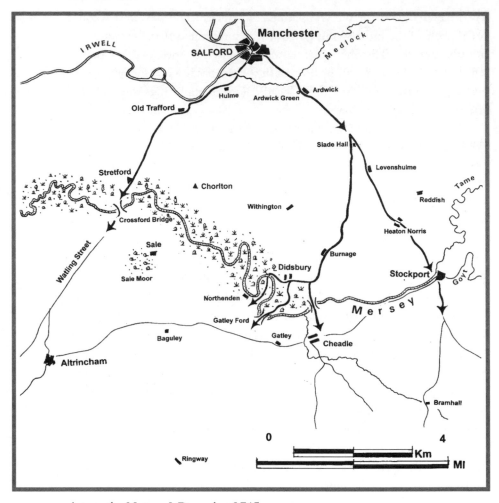

Across the Mersey, 1 December 1745

the lush, undulating pasturelands of north-eastern Cheshire. The route lay along winding lanes through Woodford, Adlington and Prestbury.[4] The long ridge of the Bow Hills rose to the left, and the boxy tower of Lyme Cage stood at the top of an outlying height. Lyme Hall lay in a hollow close by, out of view.

The estate of Lyme was that of the Leghs, a family well known to the Stuarts. Very soon after the Glorious Revolution of 1688 the Leghs had convened the first meeting of the Jacobite Cheshire Club in the hall (p. 65). In 1715 the Club nevertheless failed to support the Jacobites of neighbouring Lancashire, and it served so little purpose that it was disbanded five years later. The Club came together again in 1745 on the initiative of a number of

Cheshire squires who were eager to join the Prince, but they were unable to persuade Sir Peter Legh XIII, who had inherited Lyme the year before. He now cast his vote against the enterprise. The outcome was more than one disappointment among many, for nothing could have been more welcome to the Prince at this moment that the proof that a substantial body of English gentry was on his side.

We left the division of Lord George Murray just south-east of Manchester. When the route of the Prince's division diverged to the left, he continued south towards the Mersey to the vicinity of Parr's Wood (i.e. down a short stretch of the modern A34, then down the whole length of Burnage Lane). Here he turned west, or right, and detached the train of artillery and baggage carts to cross the bridge of felled poplars that had just been built at Cheadle Ford. He continued on his way as far as Didsbury, a tradition-ally Royalist village, and seems to have halted for a time at the 'Scots Croft' (now an area of tennis courts, gardens and office buildings). The troops in general behaved well, though they commandeered the horses in the local-ity, and a number of villagers had to yield up their shoes. (Years later one of these people told his granddaughter how a soldier had taken his wooden clogs, found them uncomfortable and threw them into the river, which floated them out of view.)

The infantry then descended a muddy track (the present Millgate Lane), and cut across the boggy woods to reach the Mersey at Gatley Ford. The crossing was stony and reasonably firm under foot, but the water reached to the chest – higher than at Stockport – and it was fortunate that nobody was swept away. A force of Jacobite cavalry (probably Kilmarnock's) had made to the right down Stenner Lane and was crossing at Northenden Ford, while the Lifeguards and the Manchester Regiment traversed the repaired Cross-ford Bridge at Stretford.

The task of the last two detachments can only have been to draw the attention of the gathering Hanoverian army to central Cheshire, while Prince Charles and Lord George were making for Macclesfield. At Sale Moor the Manchester Regiment encountered a party of twelve Hanoverian dragoons who were on patrol from Congleton: 'the officer was an old man and coura-geous, standing his ground till the enemy was very near, and then retreated and went back to Congleton to give information to the regiment there'.[5] At 10 a.m. 200 Jacobite infantry (almost certainly the Manchester Regiment) reached Altrincham. They stayed there until early in the afternoon, when, having learned that a large enemy force was positioned at Knutsford, they asked for a guide and set off for the rendezvous of the main forces at

Macclesfield. Altrincham was left in peace until a body of the Jacobite cavalry arrived in the evening. Twenty-one of them scouted from there through Bucklow Hill and at least some of the way to Knutsford beyond. Two Jacobite troopers lost their lives in all the comings and goings. One was dispatched by the sword of George Barlow, innkeeper of the Old Bleeding Wolf at Ashley Heath near Altrincham, and the other by a farmer who was shooting from behind a hedge at Ringway.[6]

Having crossed the Mersey by Gatley Ford, Prince George's Lowlanders reunited with the train, artillery and baggage in the vicinity of Cheadle before continuing south to Wilmslow. From there Thomas Deacon (a son of the famous Dr Deacon) guided the column through the close-set countryside, passing over or close under the wild hill of Alderley Edge to reach Macclesfield.

The Highland and Lowland Divisions joined outside the town. 'Macclesfield, or Maxfield, gives its name to a spacious forest on the edge of Derbyshire, which is watered (besides other rivers) by the Bollin, on which the town stands. 'Tis an ancient, large town, one of the fairest in the country ... The church, or rather chapel (it being in the parish of Prestbury) is a fair edifice, with a very high tower steeple, and a College adjoining to it ... Their chief manufacture is buttons ... There are several good inns, of which The Angel is the best, for good entertainment and civil usage.'[7]

On the previous night an advance party of redcoat dragoons had reached the town, whereupon Samuel Cooper, the mayor, 'went to the commanding officer to give him all the intelligence and assistance he could, and at the officer's request procured him a spy [probably the Samuel Salt mentioned below] to go out and gain intelligence on the motions of the rebels'.[8] Now on 1 December the spy was snapped up by the swiftly advancing Jacobites. The officer of dragoons was dining with the mayoress ('Never fear, madam, we'll protect you'),[9] when the report came that the Jacobites were just outside the town. The officer and his troopers fled, but Mayor Cooper did not have the time to get his wife and family away, and by his own account he thereafter complied with the Jacobite demands in a state of panic and confusion.

The first Jacobites to arrive were twenty quartermasters, who enquired after the residence of Sir Peter Davenport. He was a supposed Jacobite, and he had in fact opposed the demolition of the bridge at Stockport. The quartermasters made their way to his brick-built house in King Edward Street. He was away from home, which made them curse, and without further ado they chalked the word 'Prince' on the door. They were followed by about one hundred cavalry, mounted on 'shabby horses and of different colours'.[10]

In the second or third rank was a local man, Samuel Salt, who had been caught spying, and was now 'guarded by four terrible fellows with their drawn swords'.[11]

Four of five regiments had entered Macclesfield by the time Prince Charles arrived on foot. He happened to pause for a couple of minutes in Jordangate below the house of the lawyer John Stafford, who observed: 'he was in Highland dress, with a blue cap on, and was surrounded by about forty who appeared to be his Guard. He is a very handsome person of a man, rather tall, exactly proportioned and walks very well'. Parliamentary and Whiggish traditions were strong in this corner of north-east Cheshire, and 'there was nothing but profound silence and nothing to be seen on the countenances of the inhabitants but horror and amazement'. The newcomers forced Mayor Samuel Cooper to proclaim King James III at the Market Cross and put on a display of enthusiasm, and 'endeavours were made to have given 'em a peel on the bells, for fear of insults, but four ringers were all that could be got and they rung the bells backwards, not with design, but through confusion'. Closer examination showed that 'many of the officers appeared very well. Some few indeed were very old, in particular Glenbucket who seemed to be eighty at least and bended almost double on horseback'.[12]

The Old Field Marshal and the Young Hero

The skirmish on Sale Moor on 1 December represented the first contact between the Jacobite army and the regular forces of the enemy since Cope's dragoons had fled from Wooler on 6 November. This is all the more surprising because all the troops of the government had now been withdrawn from Flanders, and the two armies, the 'eastern' and the 'western', were actually present in England.

The eastern army (numbering 6,876 on 1 December, but falling rapidly) was under the command of the much-decayed Field Marshal Wade. The weather had forced him to turn back from the Tyne Gap on 19 November, and now that the Jacobites were moving south he was unable to keep pace on his side of the snow-covered Pennines. His generals argued that the infantry ought to march by successive divisions, so that the soldiers could find shelter in the towns and villages (which was the standard procedure of the Jacobites). However, the places along the way were so small that the householders would have to be evicted to provide space for the men, 'rendering them liable to be pillaged by our troops (too much addicted to that practice)'.[13] The Jacobites, unlike the redcoats, had the capacity to cut across the

Pennines, which Wade saw as another argument for keeping his infantry together and hugging the eastern flank of the hills. Among these foot soldiers the Dutch auxiliaries had 'suffered extremely by distempers, to which no doubt the drinking of brandy frequently has much contributed, as they march along. The battalions of Swiss and Dutch appear very weak, they straggle much, and the country people complain of them, but are very kind to the English troops, and invite them into their houses, and treat them without suffering them to pay'.[14] The heavy cavalry had an absolute need for better going and accommodation, and was assigned a route through the flat land to the east by way of Northallerton, Thirsk and York.

Wade's army set out from Newcastle on 25 November, and a spell of milder weather enabled it at first to make good progress by way of Chester-le-Street (the 26th), Durham and down the old Roman Dere Street to Piercebridge, where shortages of food and clothing once more began to tell. Wade wrote from there on the 27th that the only way by which he could traverse the Pennines to intercept the Jacobites would be to continue south to Wetherby, where he could pick up the route (corresponding with the modern A58) which led south-west by way of Leeds, Halifax and over Blackstone Edge to Rochdale and Manchester in Lancashire, that being the only way he could bring any of his artillery with him. As it was, he had been forced to abandon four of his 3-pounder cannon at Newcastle, 'the roads in our last march to Hexham were so broken, the carriages were damaged, and half the drivers deserted, which occasioned our leaving them behind'.[15]

By 29 November there were already doubts as to whether it would be possible to overhaul the Jacobites, for 'this quickness of their march comes from the natural conveniences their manner of life and clothing give them; they have no need of tents; can bear cold; stay not for breaking bread, but scatter the barley and oats on the ground, fire it and pick up the ears, and eat the parched corn; they drive cattle along with them, and kill and eat as they want; they keep the coach-horses they have taken to draw the cannon and carriages; therefore they march in two days, what we can hardly make in three; but if once we come up to them, they will then feel that they have no chance against regular disciplined troops'.[16]

On 30 November Wade's first march took him the 14 miles from Piercebridge to Catterick. It was hard work. After further stages the exhausted troops had to rest at Boroughbridge on 3 December, and by the time they trailed into Wetherby on the 4th about 670 of their number had fallen out. At Wetherby the field marshal learned that the Jacobite advance guard was already at Ashbourne; in other words very far ahead of him on the opposite side of the Pennines. Wade and his generals therefore gave up all hope of crossing the hills and resolved instead to continue their southerly course to Doncaster – tacitly conceding that the Jacobites would reach the Midlands before them. Wade remained in the camp at Wetherby on 5 December in order to fit out the troops with clothing and bring up the bread which had been deposited on the now-abandoned line of march at Leeds. As a defeated and infirm man he wrote to the Duke of Newcastle that he must decline the offer just now made to him, which was to command the government's forces in eastern Scotland.[17]

For some days the London government and its leading military men had been forced to recognize that only the exertions of the 'western' forces could halt the progress of Prince Charles's forces towards the English heartland. It was not a question of a marching a formed army to confront the Jacobites. In the first place the forces would have to be put together in the north-west Midlands out of troops coming from Flanders and Ireland, and the amateur 'new' regiments of unknown quality that had been raised by prominent noblemen. The season of the year moreover dictated that the governmental troops must be distributed under cover in the little towns (in 'cantonments', in the jargon of the period), which would make it difficult to bring them together to head off the Jacobites, who would have a multitude of options open to them if they succeeded in passing the Mersey.

As for the higher direction, Lieutenant General Ligonier was of a generation with Wade, and, although he was better preserved, he was suffering from a bout of malaria. The Duke of Cumberland was designated supreme commander on the 23rd, but with all possible speed it would take him four days to reach headquarters from London, and meanwhile the responsibility of collecting the forces and countering the Jacobite advance rested with the cautious and pessimistic Duke of Richmond. In a confidential note Richmond asked the Duke of Newcastle: 'for God's sake don't think of sending [Lieutenant General] Hawley from us. Indeed he is equal to anybody, and will speak his mind. Ligonier is a good man but in my poor opinion too complaisant, besides that, one of his legs was numb the other day, and I don't think his life is to be depended upon … I am sorry to say we are in a strange irregular way, and if the rebels had attacked us at Stone … as we thought they would, we had been undone, and Ligonier said [so] himself'.[18]

The town of Lichfield was to be the focal point of the cantonments, which Richmond hoped would be the means of 'gathering the troops as fast and as far forward as possible, still keeping them together'.[19] On the 23rd two battalions arrived at Stone and Stafford respectively, as the forward elements of the infantry, though the duke feared that the forced marches would render the troops incapable of fighting. In the experience of one of the officers it was taking about two weeks for a typical regiment from Flanders to reach the rendezvous from a landing place in the Thames.[20]

The two 'new' cavalry regiments (Montagu's 9th and Kingston's 10th) were to scout ahead, but Richmond had no real hope of being able to hold the line of the Mersey, even if the bridges were demolished. The possibility of delaying the Jacobite advance north of the river vanished entirely when the Earl of Derby disbanded the Lancashire militia. On 25 November Richmond wrote that the four regiments so far arrived in the area of Lichfield amounted to only 2,325 of all ranks, and he ventured to say that 'the success of this little handful of men is of so great importance that, if we are not ... attended to, this Kingdom may be undone in a fortnight'. The cantonments extended from there northwards to Newcastle under Lyme, in northernmost Staffordshire, but he intended to consolidate himself in the centre of the county just to the west of Stafford town. He went that day to reconnoitre a site for an encampment within a mile of the town, which lay 'between the two rivers of Penk and the Sow, and they say a fine dry piece of ground, and extremely well guarded by these two rivers, that are deep and now overflowed, and I am not at all ashamed to say that till all our troops are assembled, I should be glad of a secure camp, then, when we are once got together, I shall be desirous as any to march up to the rebels'.[21]

Two days later, on Richmond's orders, Brigadier Bligh found enough empty houses in Stafford to quarter Sempill's 25th and Johnston's 33rd, and he investigated the defensibility of the place further. He found that 'about two-thirds of the town is very well secured by the little rivers that cover it, but the side next Stone lies open, and before the East Port of that side, there is a hill that commands the whole town, which would be necessary for us to secure by having some work thrown up there, with a few pieces of cannon, if we are to defend it; we have no intelligence of where the rebels are at present. P.S. There is no wall about the town'.[22] Sempill's Regiment, just named, was pulled back from Newcastle under Lyme, much to the alarm of the people of that town. All of this indicates that Richmond had given up the Mersey and the county of Cheshire for lost, and that he was thinking about fighting defensively at Stafford.

The king's younger son, the 25-year-old William Augustus, Duke of Cumberland, arrived at Lichfield from London late on the night of 27 November. 'The journey hither was a little fatiguing, and though I stopped nowhere from my first setting out, I was one and thirty hours coming hither.'[23]

Cumberland stood high in the esteem of the troops and well-affected people, and the gathering forces were much in need of the encouragement he brought. The Duke of Richmond wrote to London to justify his cautious conduct, but he was now 'as desirous as His Royal Highness's young blood can be to march on and attack them ... I fancy the Duke will send you food for Tyburn soon'.[24]

At the end of November the Duke of Cumberland took stock of the state of affairs, and was reasonably satisfied with what he saw. On the 29th the forces available to him across the cantonments, at Chester, and in the outposts stood at very approximately 12,000 men. The six 'new' regiments of foot raised by the nobility were useless. However, the Duke of Kingston's 'new' regiment of light horse, the 10th, was doing good outpost duty in Cheshire; the First Battalion of Foot Guards was awaited on the 30th, and the remaining two were expected to arrive on the following day. The Jacobites had lost the chance of striking at the Duke of Richmond when his forces were still weak and scattered, and it appeared to Cumberland on the 28th that his army was equally well placed to counter the likely moves of the enemy – whether east towards Derbyshire, or west towards Wales. Perhaps the Jacobites had run out of impetus altogether: 'by our latest advices the rebels, who were already marched as yesterday to Preston, and who seemed to have a mind to remain there, may give us time to collect our whole body together, and then to advance directly up to them, in which case I flatter myself the affair would be certain in our favour, but should they be mad enough to march forward to Manchester and Stockport, then it will be impossible to say how soon there may be an affair, as I must move forward to hinder them their slipping by me, either way'.[25]

There had been some anxiety lest the Jacobites should side-step from Manchester and dodge out of sight behind what Ligonier called 'a ridge of impracticable hills called Bow Hills, which part this country from Derbyshire'.[26] The route in question was the excellent road (turnpiked by an Act of 1725; it is now a succession of lanes to the east of the later A5004) which ran by way of Buxton to Derby. However, the Duke of Devonshire, as the Lord Lieutenant of Derbyshire, was using local labour to make three cuts along the section of the turnpike between Whaley Bridge and Buxton, and another on the road which ran from Whaley Bridge to Chapel-en-le-Frith. These labours appeared to bar the ways through Derbyshire, and it was odd that reports were still arriving to the effect that the Jacobites might be coming through the county after all. It did not occur to Cumberland or Ligonier that Prince Charles might choose to march there by way of the *near* side of the Bow Hills, and still be covered from view by the close country and further outlying ridges.

The Duke of Cumberland looked forward to advancing in concentrated force to the Mersey at the beginning of December, and he was willing to accept the penalty of encamping the troops in open country, in spite of the bitter weather. Meanwhile he was confident that he would receive timely news of enemy movements from the Duke of Kingston, who based his regiment of light horse at the nodal point of Congleton in Cheshire, and established outposts at Nantwich, Knutsford, Macclesfield and a number of smaller places. Major Chiverston Hartopp reinforced Cornet Brown's exposed post at Cheadle, due south of Manchester, by six men, and he wrote from there that he had 'also dispatched two men by the assistance of the honest gentlemen of this town to Bullock Smithy two miles on this side [of] Stockport and within seven miles of Manchester where the turnpike road to this place and Derby parts, so that I shall have information from one of them (the other being ordered to stay) which way the rebels are marching, which I will immediately send word of to the Duke of Cumberland'.[27] He did not foresee that the Jacobites were going to advance from Manchester on a much broader front, which gave no clue as to their further intentions.

On 1 December the Hanoverian forces at last abandoned their waiting posture and began to move forward. Thomas Anson wrote to his brother (the famous commodore) that everybody was 'in spirits and jollity, impatient for action, and no fear but that the rebels might slip into Derbyshire, Wales, or return by the way they came'.[28] Cumberland was about to transfer his headquarters from Lichfield to Stafford, a place where Catholicism and Jacobite sentiments were strong, but which was much nearer the scene of likely action. His secretary wrote to Wade that the duke had urgent need to hear from him, and outlined the dispositions for the following day, which provided for a full squadron of Kingston's up at Cheadle, two more squadrons of horse in support at Congleton, and the rest of the army about Stoke and Stone, or on the way there.[29] The ink was not dry before news arrived that the Jacobites were across the Mersey near Stockport and were advancing on Macclesfield, but Wade was assured that the arrangements just outlined would stand.

It was nevertheless difficult to identify the axis of the principal Jacobite effort. On the same 1 December a lieutenant from Colonel Honeywood's troop arrived at speed at Congleton from Macclesfield to report that the main Jacobite force was actually entering the town,[30] which seemed to confirm the threat to the eastern flank. Conversely, the Jacobites had completed the Crossford Bridge near Stretford, and parties were roaming through central Cheshire: 'Joseph Butcher of Major Hartopp's Troop says that about two miles on the Congleton side of Northwich he was fired on by two men, one in a Highland dress, and that he returned the fire'.[31] He could say no more, being drunk, but Cornet Smith reported soberly enough from Northwich itself that 'one part of the rebels will be at this place in a few hours, another the same time at Middlewich, and the third part at Nantwich', and that Cornet Graham was about to withdraw the outposts thereabouts to Chester.[32] The Duke of Kingston forwarded the reports to his superior officer Major General Humphrey Bland at Newcastle under Lyme, who concluded that the Jacobites were aiming to reach North Wales by way of Shrewsbury or Wrexham, and that he must pull back all the cavalry first to Stone, and then if necessary all the way to Stafford.[33] The Jacobites' bluff was working magnificently; but how long would they be able to sustain it?

The Feint to Congleton and the Advance to Derby 2–5 December 1745

The Duke of Cumberland hoodwinked

The Duke of Cumberland had yet to familiarize himself with the Jacobites' mode of progression, whereby they would periodically stop for a day or two to rest and gather their wits and then execute a forced march and disappear from view. The 2nd of December was one such halt, which the main force spent in Macclesfield. The townspeople of all classes were sullen and hostile. One Alexander Kelloch had business in the town and afterwards denied that he had any dealings with the Highlanders, being 'not in company with them, save only in the public shit house, where he did speak to one of them in an open public manner'.[34] Lawyer Stafford's response to finding fifty Highlanders sleeping on straw in his barn was that they seemed like a pack of hounds in a kennel.

The Jacobites troops in Macclesfield spent their waking hours preparing for battle. They fired off the old loads in their muskets and pistols, lest they should have become damp, before cleaning and reloading the weapons. The noise of the discharges echoed mightily over the countryside, where a great deal was going on. Parties went forth to search for horses, fodder and weapons at Thorneycroft, Birtles New Hall, Pott Shrigley, and the house of the Whiggish Colonel Legh at Adlington. Jacobite sentiments began to be heard in the villages. Robert Hamilton was a Scottish merchant then living in Nether Knutsford, and was known as 'a reserved man in discourse and of a morose temper, and seldom cared to answer any questions on a frivolous matter in his way of common conversation'.[35] He now spoke with unaccustomed animation about the failure of the Lancashire Catholics to rise. 'No God damn 'em for a parcel of scrubs for that they had not risen and joined the rebels as they ought to have done.'[36] He turned on a neighbour, Martha Brown, who complained of the Jacobite exactions, telling her 'the rebels want their rights and ... the Cheshire people might do well to repent of their lives, for they had not above two or three months to live'.[37]

Hamilton informed a young gentleman who was bent on riding north to join the Jacobite army that he might as well wait for it where he was, and 'upon such advice the said gentleman's horses were unsaddled and he did not go at that time ... Hamilton spoke of several gentlemen without naming them, and expressed himself in such a manner as if he knew of several who intended to join or who were in favour of the rebels' undertaking'.[38]

Hamilton had in mind people like John Cupid of Lymm, who went to Wilmslow on 1 December to see his close friend Captain Moss, who had thrown in his lot with the Prince, and who had lent him a horse, a laced hat and a pair of pistols. Cupid rode on to Macclesfield on the 2nd, and, as he later told Hugh Leech, a neighbour,

> having desired to see the Prince ... he was introduced to him and stayed an hour with him, and had a glass of wine given him there by the Duke of Perth, and that whilst he was in the room with the Prince the company was looking at a map of the roads which showed the road the plainest that he ever saw, upon which this examinant [Leech] said 'it is a wonder that they would let you stay so long in the room where they were looking at such things, as you was a stranger', upon which the said Mr Cupid replied, 'Oh I was in all their secrets', and the said Mr Cupid told this examinant that when part of the rebel army was drawn up in Macclesfield the said Mr Cupid offered to enter the rank[s] with the common men, but that some of the rebel officers came up to him and told him he was designed for a better post.[39]

Among the other arrivals that day were the Nottinghamshire gentleman Edward Graves and his friends from Newark. They had left their horses at Chapel-en-le-Frith, probably on learning that parties were breaking up the road beyond, and they had come the rest of the way on foot. Lord Elcho with his Lifeguards and the Manchester Regiment likewise came up by way of Wilmslow, after their useful foray to Altrincham and beyond. However, Henry Ker of Graden (the eyes and ears of the army ever since the eve of Prestonpans) returned from reconnaissance with disturbing news. Very early in the day the Prince and his advisers had abandoned any remaining notions of turning into Wales, and had fixed instead on making a dash for London by way of Leek, Ashbourne and Derby, but Ker now had to tell them that they did not yet have a clear run in that direction. Lord George Murray therefore proposed that the attention of the Hanoverians could best be drawn away to the west if the Jacobites sent a diversionary force to Congleton. This was in fact going to be the best kind of feint – one which reinforced the existing fears of the enemy – and it was to be executed in a full-blooded manner by Lord Elcho's Lifeguards, Kilmarnock's Horse and the Atholl Brigade – 1,200 men in all. Meanwhile the main army made ready for the march to Derby, and the Duke of Perth's useful Pioneers made the first 5 miles of the road to Leek practicable for the artillery.

Lord George and his powerful diversionary force set off from Broken Cross to the west of Macclesfield after daybreak (we are still on 2 December). At 10 a.m. they were passing by Gawsworth, and a Mr Furnivall sent word to the military authorities that 2,000 infantry were on the march from Macclesfield. 'I heard great firing all the way I rode from Congleton, and I am told it is on cleaning and trying their pieces.'[40] The message reached Cumberland's headquarters at 4 p.m., and must have given additional credibility to the diversion. The outposts of Kingston's Light Horse were in a high state of tension, which suited the Jacobite purposes, and the commander of the principal base at Congleton was under orders to 'keep his men and officers very alert, and to relieve his detachments every twenty-four hours. If he receives certain intelligence from his officers detached, that the enemy advances, he is to call in his out parties, and (leaving a captain and fifty men as a rearguard) is to retire to Newcastle'.[41]

The 'certain intelligence' duly arrived, whereupon the cavalry made off, leaving Congleton to Lord George, who went through the formalities usually practised in a hostile town, forcing the mayor to proclaim King James III and making inordinate demands for billets and forage. Mr John Kent, having come to Congleton to see the Jacobites, was decked out by one of the officers with his own tartan sash, 'and said he looked very well in it, and asked him to go along with them'. Kent later told the Hanoverian authorities that he had refused, yet reports claimed that he had been seen marching with the Jacobites, wearing both sash and white cockade.[42]

Lord Kilmarnock and Colonel Ker set out from Congleton with a mixed

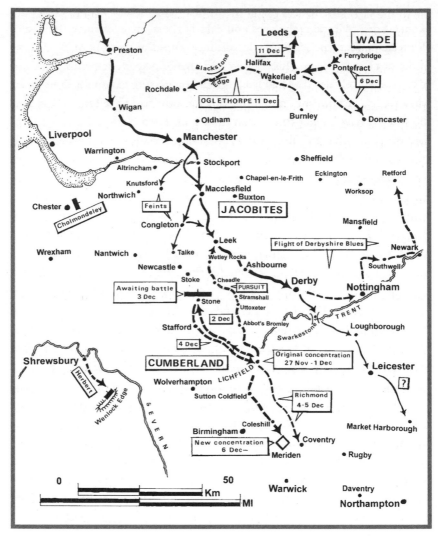

Cumberland deceived

body of fifty or so horse and foot, and probed south by way of Astbury and Church Lawton towards Newcastle under Lyme. They passed close by Mow Cop, which was almost the southernmost outlier of the Pennines, and, guided by Mr William Vaughan, they penetrated as far as Talke o' the Hill, where a party of enemy cavalry had been dining at the Red Lion Inn. The red-coated troopers dived through the windows to safety, but the Jacobites found a notorious spy, John Vere, hiding under a bed, and hauled him off in the reasonable expectation that he was going to be hanged. Vere was spared at the instance of Prince Charles, and, like more than one Hanoverian who owed his life to the Jacobites, he was going to purge his sense of obligation by helping to send them to the scaffold.

The Duke of Richmond, as commander of the cavalry outposts, was just 5 miles away at Newcastle under Lyme. He wrote to Cumberland at 9 p.m. that large numbers of the Jacobites were present at Congleton, where 'they have been firing their artillery' (in fact cleaning their weapons); he had a party just north of Newcastle at Chesterton, which relieved him of immediate anxiety concerning the Jacobite party advancing from Congleton, and which he put at about thirty men (the infantry probably having been left on the way at Astbury). The Duke of Richmond nevertheless shared the almost universal misconception of the Hanoverians that the Jacobites could reach Derby only by way of the turnpike beyond the Bow Hills, and from the reports that the rebels had a large party at Leek (most probably the Pioneers) he concluded that they had it in mind to cut him off from the main army. He was prepared to make a stand close under Newcastle, but he admitted to the Duke of Cumberland 'that by all I can learn of the Duke of Kingston and Major General Bland, there is not one spot of ground except just out of town, where a squadron can be drawn up between this [place] and Congleton, the whole country being nothing but small enclosures, very deep, and all the lanes narrow defiles'. He had with him the first squadron of Kingston's Light Horse, the dragoon regiments of Bland (3rd) and Kerr (11th), and the battalions of the Sowle, the Royal Scots and Sempill. Even this post might well prove untenable 'if the whole corps [of the Jacobites] should come upon us as they may, in two columns from Congleton and Leek'.[43]

One of the battalions had marched that day to Newcastle from Stone, 'and just as we had settled ourselves, got some refreshment, and many in bed, our drums beat to arms, the common cry along the streets was that the rebels were entering the town, the women and children all over the streets were running about like mad people, crying and fainting for fear, and flying into the country amongst their friends to seek shelter from the rebels. Our regiments were all drawn up on the parade, and rested there under arms for some time'.[44]

At 11 a.m. on the same 2 December the Duke of Cumberland was riding north from Stafford to Stone. He was still responding to the supposed Jacobite threat to Wales, and his secretary, Sir Everard Fawkener, wrote that 'just before he departed he received the two latest pieces of intelligence, by them one would imagine there would be an action tomorrow at, or near Stone. God prosper the good cause, and give His Royal Highness the success the nation so much wants'. Fawkener could not entirely conceal his misgivings, for by committing itself so far to the north-west the army was no longer in a position (as it had been at Lichfield) to be able to move to counter the threats to either Derbyshire or Wales, 'if the motion westward was a feint, then indeed we shall by our advancing be less in reach of keeping them out of Derbyshire. What is most apt to perplex, is that often people mistake a small party for the body'.[45]

Just to the north of Stone the duke found an excellent potential battle-ground on the great open space of Stonefield, and he returned to a well-earned dinner at Stafford. He had just finished eating when he was told that the Jacobites were within 9 miles of Newcastle, which is to say sooner and closer than he had expected, as if they were bent on reaching Wales. His own forces were on the march to join him from Newcastle and the scattered can-tonments, but the duke could count on being at Stonefield very early the next morning with eleven veteran battalions, Ligonier's and Cobham's Dragoons, and at least the second squadron of Kingston's Light Horse.

From 4 a.m. to 11 a.m. on the frosty and snowy morning of 3 Decem-ber the Hanoverian army was drawn upon on bleak Stonefield. Cumberland was ready for his battle, but the enemy failed to turn up. The duke had to recognize that he had been deceived, and that the way to Derbyshire and far beyond was open to the Jacobites. Cumberland hoped that some of his cav-alry would be able to head off the enemy at Northampton, but Kingston's Light Horse had been run into the ground, and the infantry would have to rest overnight in Stone after their forced marches. Some of them had gone twenty-four hours without eating, and endured several cold nights in suc-cession without a roof over their heads: 'Victuals and lodging here were extremely scarce. We were glad of a little straw, strewed on the floor (for many officers), and bread was so scarce that it was rare to get a loaf; and beer, in its turn, was as difficult to procure, for this little town was so full of soldiers that it was impossible to pass by one another'.[46]

In such a way Lord George Murray had fixed the Hanoverian army 15 miles to the west of the route of the Jacobites' march to Derby. Early on 3 December he sent word of his success to Prince Charles, and moved directly from Congleton to pick up the intended line of march at Ashbourne ahead of the main army. The frozen ground was hard on the feet of the troops, but they made rapid progress, passing closely under the Cloud to cover the 7 miles to Leek by 9 a.m., and then the further 10 miles to Ashbourne. They were overtaken by darkness before they arrived, but a captain of the Atholl Brigade writes that 'when we came within a mile of it we heard their bells

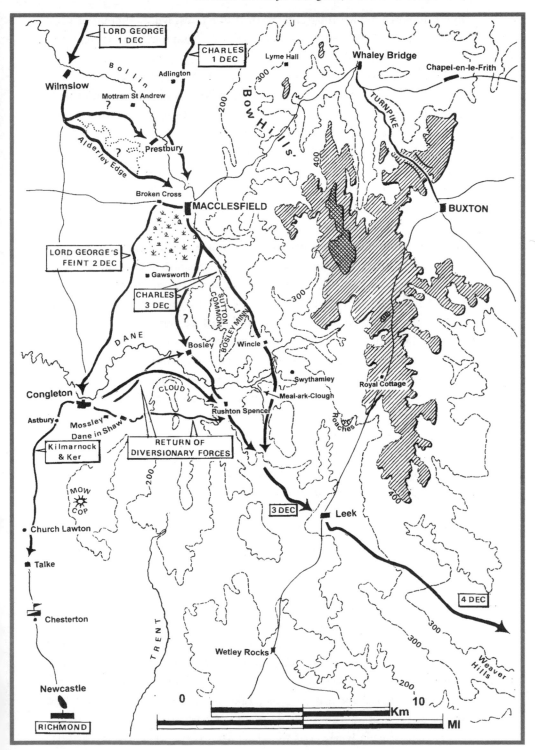

LORD GEORGE
1 DEC

CHARLES
1 DEC

Lyme Hall

Whaley Bridge

Chapel-en-le-Frith

Bollin

Adlington

Wilmslow

Mottram St Andrew

?

'Bow Hills'

TURNPIKE

Alderley Edge

?

Prestbury

Broken Cross

MACCLESFIELD

BUXTON

LORD GEORGE'S
FEINT 2 DEC

Gawsworth

CHARLES
3 DEC

SUTTON COMMON

BOSLEY MINN

DANE

?

Bosley

Wincle

Swythamley

Meal-ark-Clough

Royal Cottage

Congleton

CLOUD

Rushton Spencer

Roaches

Astbury

Mossley
Dane in Shaw

RETURN OF
DIVERSIONARY FORCES

Kilmarnock
& Ker

MOW
COP

200

3 DEC

Leek

Church Lawton

Talke

4 DEC

Chesterton

TRENT

300

Wetley Rocks

Weaver
Hills

Newcastle

200

0

10

Km

RICHMOND

MI

Into Derbyshire

loudly ringing, and when we entered the town it was wholly illuminated and a bonfire upon the street. We crossed the bridge and the water of Dove and we entered Derbyshire'.[47]

The troops of Prince Charles assembled at Macclesfield at 4 a.m. 'The colonels are to recommend to their officers that the soldiers are to provide bread and cheese for two days, not knowing but we may be in the enemy's presence tomorrow. The officers will take care that the arms may be in good order.'[48] Headed by the hussars, the army took the winding roads which led south from Macclesfield through the intricate country where Cheshire, Staffordshire and Derbyshire meet. The routes had been discounted entirely by the Hanoverians, and were in any case concealed by a series of heights and ridges – The Cloud, Bosley Minn, Sutton Common, Biddulph Moor and, towards Ashbourne, the Weaver Hills. Prince Charles probably marched by way of Bosley, while the baggage and others climbed to an upland pasture to the east, then descended a steep and twisting track which took them through Wincle and to the wooded valley of the little River Dane, which marked the border between Cheshire and Staffordshire.

The Duke of Cumberland and his army were ignorant of what was going on, but the farmers of Swythamley and Heaton knew every inch of the landscape and hid their cattle in the secluded dell of Meal-ark-Clough which led off the Dane valley. They were acting wisely, for the borderlands were being traversed by no less than three columns – the two of Lord George and Prince Charles, as we have seen; and the little command of the intrepid Lord Elcho, whose party divided after the thrust to Talke, and rejoined the main army in Leek by way of Bosley and Rushton, and Mossley and Dane in Shaw. 'All the way the people seemed much afraid of the Prince's army, and the tops of the hills were crowded by men on horseback, who were often pursued, but never came up with, as they were well mounted.'[49]

The baggage was delayed by the passage of the upper Dane, but Prince Charles and the main body made good time to be able to reach the neat little hill town of Leek early in the afternoon. Mr Toft, the Quaker, invited the Highlanders for a meal of boiled beef at his house in Hareygate, and Prince Charles rested for a few hours in the seventeenth-century Greystones House down Stockwell Street. By the account of local Whigs the place was 'vastly filled with a multitude of ruffians, being the main body of the rebels, with their baggage and cannon, which are said to be fourteen or sixteen pieces. All along as they have travelled they take all the horses, saddles, bridles, boots, armour or anything else they can carry off. … They … used many people ill, particularly Mr Lockett, whom they tied neck and heels, because he would not discover where his son was, who by his diligence had given them great offence.'[50]

The enemy could not be far away, and the men took advantage of the pause to sharpen their broadswords and practise their marksmanship on the stumps of the Norman crosses in the parish churchyard. The army was on alert to be ready to leave at midnight, for which end the officers were to be 'very vigilant', and 'visit their posts and the soldiers' quarters, that they may not sleep but keep themselves in readiness at the least hour's alarm … Manchester's Regiment will follow the baggage'.[51]

The column actually set out at 1 a.m. on 4 December. The road was hard frozen, which helped progress, and the moonlight showed that the army was marching through a high pastureland of open aspect. Beyond Swinscoe the road fell to the valley of the Dove and the substantial town of Ashbourne – an important-looking place, with a gigantic parish church (St Oswald's) and fine new houses of red brick springing up among the earlier structures of grey limestone. The troops entered at daybreak, and found Lord George's corps waiting for them. The combined force pushed on immediately for Derby, and encountered almost the first friendly faces seen since Manchester:

> We marched from Ashbourne and passed through Brailsford, a country long town, and at several houses we saw white flags hanging out such as napkins and white aprons, and in gables of some houses white cockades fixed. And after that we passed another town called Mackworth and they had a bonfire in the middle of the town, and as often as a captain passed by, the whole crowd of the town who were gathered there about the fire gave an huzza and the men waved their hats. And as we were out of the town, a jolly hearty man met us who wished us good success, and said we would see him the morrow with five hundred men [a bit of an exaggeration] not one among them worse than himself.[52]

That genial individual was James Sparks, a framework knitter of Dayson Lane in Derby, who had come with some friends to greet the Jacobite vanguard in Mackworth Field. He jumped a ditch, and shook the first officer by the hand, 'saying, "I am glad to see you, I have long wished for you, I care not who the devil knows it!"' He took the white cockade, and chatted with his deliverers all the way to Derby.[53]

There are also accounts of hospitality being extended by Squire Hugh Meynell of Bradley Hall, and the villagers of Kirk Langley, just outside Derby, who regaled the troops with food. The gentry of this part of the world were on the whole sympathetic to the cause, and probably took their lead from Sir Nathaniel Curzon, 4th Baronet, whose wealth and influence challenged the domination of the ultra-Whig Cavendish Duke of Devonshire. A party of the Prince's army called at his house at Kedleston, but, like so many Jacobite gentlemen, Sir Nathaniel was away from home.[54]

Derby saw its first Jacobites at 11 a.m on 4 December. They were two quartermasters who demanded accommodation for 9,000 men, and had lists of billets drawn up for them at the George Inn.

> In a short time after, their whole vanguard came in, consisting of about thirty men (besides officers and their servants); they wore gold-laced hats, with white cockades, were clothed in blue, faced with red, had on scarlet waistcoats trimmed with gold lace, and most of them likely young men, made a handsome appearance. They were drawn up in the Market Place, and sat there on horseback near three hours, during which time they ordered the bells to be rung and bonfires made, which was done accordingly, to prevent any mischief which might have ensued on a refusal.
>
> About three in the afternoon Lord Elcho, with the Lifeguards (as they were called) and many of the chiefs also arrived on horseback, to the number

The march through Derbyshire

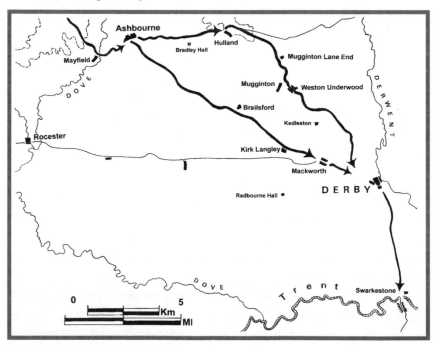

of about 150, most of them clothed as above [these descriptions suggest that Balmerino's Troop of the Lifeguards made up the 'vanguard', and that Elcho was accompanied by his own troop]; these made a fine show, being the flower of their army. Soon after their main body also marched into town, in tolerable order, six or eight abreast, with about eight standards, most of them were white flags with a red cross [i.e. the English St George's cross]. They had several bagpipers, who played as they marched along, and appeared in general to answer the description frequently given of them, and with their plaids thrown over their shoulders ... they appeared to me [writes a Whiggish townsman] like a parcel of chimney-sweepers rather than soldiers.[55]

Derby was regarded at the time as 'a large handsome town',[56] but was still largely confined within its medieval limits on a tongue of gently rising ground between the Markeaton Brook and the Derwent. Prince Charles arrived on foot with a large escort at 6 p.m., having made a not particularly productive detour to visit the Jacobite squire German Pole at Radbourne Hall. 'It is justice to say that he is a fine person, six foot high, a very good complexion, and presence majestic. He had a Scotch bonnet with a white silver rose, which needs no further explanation ... tall, straight, slender and handsome, dressed in green bonnet laced with gold, a white bob-wig the fashion of the day, a Highland plaid, and a broadsword.'[57]

The Prince approached along the Friar Gate suburb, crossed the Brook by a bridge, progressed up the narrow and curving Sadler Gate and finally walked across the market place to his lodgings in Exeter House on a corner of Full Street. Exeter House was an old building, remodelled in a modern style, and faced not towards the town, but towards a long garden that gave on to the Derwent. The river was already losing its rustic character, for the waters were retained by a weir, and just upstream from Exeter House they powered the great water wheel of Lombe's celebrated silk mill, which was one of the first purpose-built factories in the world.

There was plenty of accommodation for the senior offices in the town houses of Derbyshire gentlemen and civic worthies. The Duke of Atholl was guided to the residence of Mr Thomas Gisbourne in Bridge Gate, Lord Perth to Miss Rivett's, Lord Pitsligo to Sir Hugh Meynell's, Lord George Murray to that of the lawyer Mr Heathcote, old Glenbucket to Alderman Smith's, and Lord Nairne to Mr John Bingham's. Lord Kilmarnock at first lodged badly at the Nag's Head in the parish of St Peter, but his outraged valet soon arranged for him to move to the genteel house of Mrs Bayley next door.[58] The prominent Manchester Jacobites Thomas Syddall and Peter Moss stayed with the maltster Joseph Sykes, who afterwards testified 'that he had asked Syddall how he could leave his wife and children, at which Syddall said he left them without a tear'. Syddall nevertheless left £20 with Sykes, asking him to forward the sum to his wife in Manchester, which was duly done.[59]

Elsewhere 'some common ordinary houses had thirty and forty men each, some gentlemen's one hundred, and others none at all; which irregularity was occasioned by their giving out, and ordering billets for some thousands more than there were'.[60]

One of the Whigs thus imposed upon described how forty Highlanders crowded into his residence looking like 'so many fiends turned out of Hell to ravage the kingdom and cut throats, and, under their plaids nothing but a various sort of butchering weapons were to be seen.' All the same he was amused to note 'these desperadoes, from officers to common men, at their several meals first pull off their bonnets, and then lift up their eyes in the most solemn manner, and mutter something to themselves by way of saying Grace, as if they had been so many pure primitive Christians. Their language seemed to be as if a herd of Hottentots, wild monkeys in a desert, or vagrant gypsies had been jabbering, screaming and howling together'.[61]

At this crucial stage of the campaign the most significant achievement of the Jacobites was to secure the ancient (1192) Swarkestone Bridge, which spanned the Trent 6 miles beyond Derby. The Trent, a deep and restless stream, was 65 yards wide here (the Mersey at Gatley was only 25), and it was bordered by wide water meadows over which the road was carried by a causeway of pointed arches. The bridge and the causeways together extended for nearly a mile, and the Duke of Cumberland had ordered the bridge to be destroyed, for there were (and are) few crossings of the Trent, which formed a great loop around the southern end of the Pennines and offered the only natural barrier standing between the Jacobites and London. The word came too late to prevent an eighty-strong Jacobite party securing the bridge on the night of 4/5 December, and a Jacobite spy reckoned that 'the Prince by his position there could have marched to London and reached that capital three or four days before either the Duke of Cumberland or Marshal Wade'.[62]

The episode was typical of the way the Hanoverian forces were being overtaken by events. On the 4th Cumberland had written to the Duke of Newcastle to tell him how confident he was of being able to anticipate the enemy at Northampton, while advising him to assemble infantry north of London on Finchley Common, just in case a small party happened to slip by.[63] The Duke of Richmond had the responsibility of taking the lead with

Bland's and Mark Kerr's Dragoons, and he was supposed to traverse the 27 miles from Coventry on the 5th, and the further 31 to Northampton on the 6th. On 4 December he already doubted whether he would have the time or the forces to fulfil his task.[64] Early the next day came news that Swarkestone Bridge had been lost, and he wrote to Cumberland's headquarters at 8 o'clock that morning:

> I am just going to march to Coventry today, and Northampton tomorrow, according to His Royal Highness's orders, but I have no other orders of any kind. I know very well what I am to do if the enemy comes up to me, but what am I do if I am advised of their approach? For as to sending out guards for outposts, it will be impossible after two such days' march from thence to Northampton, as they might do it, but the horses absolutely cannot; and now they have got over the Trent, there is no pass to defend. And if they please to cut us off from the main army they may, if also they please to give us the slip and march to London, I fear they may, even before this avant guard come up with them.[65]

An hour later we find him writing to the Duke of Newcastle: 'As a general I don't presume to advise, but as one of His Majesty's Council, I do advise a camp be formed immediately upon Barnet or Finchley Common or somewhere thereabouts, and immediately, else you will be too late, if the rebels think proper to advance'.[66] These words are remarkable, for they confirm that the thinkable scene of campaigning had moved from the North Midlands to London.

Dire consternations were spreading even where the Jacobites were not physically present. Shrewsbury stood in the way of two of the possible avenues of enemy advance – to central Wales, and down the Severn valley to the West Country. Lord Herbert wrote in near-panic from that place to Major General Bland in Staffordshire, and he could not have been reassured by the reply which Bland sent by return of post on 1 December, advising him to abandon Shrewsbury rather than put his men at risk.[67]

At the same time a curious chain of events was transmitting terror down the eastern side of England. A Midlands gentleman, Mr Thornhagh of Hilton, learned that the Liverpool Blues had demolished the bridge at Warrington, and he concluded that the Jacobites, thwarted at the Mersey, might well march east across the Pennines by Sheffield or Chesterfield, and on by way of Newark, which was where the Great North Road crossed the lower Trent on its way to London. Thornhagh wrote of his fears to the Duke of Newcastle, and on 30 November he sent one of his servants to his old friend

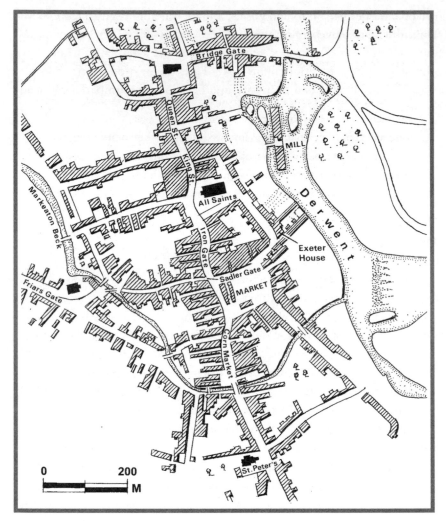

Derby

Rev. Dr Griffith, rector of Eckington in the south-eastern Pennines. On the way the servant encountered great numbers of Sheffield townspeople, fleeing before three heavily armed Jacobites who had been seen coming across the moors. Five hundred rebels were reported to be behind.[68] This message, and nine others, convinced Dr Griffith that the rebels were on their way to Worksop. (Only later did it transpire that the fantasies were occasioned by three military contractors who were on their way across the Pennines to reach Field Marshal Wade.)

At these alarms a Mr R. Sutton and other Whiggish gentlemen of Nottinghamshire took themselves to Newark, where at a meeting of the mayor and aldermen Sutton proposed sending a humble representation to the Duke of Cumberland, informing him that

> there are three bridges within a mile of this place and three or four fords which at high water are not to be passed, and at other times may be defended by a small body of men, so that if Your Royal Highness upon the nearer approach of the rebels to this place should judge proper to order a body of horse and foot to demolish or guard the said bridges and defend the fords, the march of the rebels might be obstructed till Your Royal Highness might have an opportunity of attacking them with all that bravery which is inherent in you, and with all that success which the justice of our cause deserves.[69]

However, 'after three meetings [we] could not prevail upon them to take any step towards making any defence for themselves or anyone towards showing loyalty or affection to the best of Kings and the best of governments'.[70]

Mr Charlton objected that a message of this sort would seem like telling the Duke of Cumberland what to do, while Mr Heron pointed out that 'if it should be known by the rebels, it would be a means to exasperate them against the town of Newark should they make it a visit'.[71] It is quite possible that Sutton and the other Whigs were encountering deliberate obstruction, for Newark was proud of its attachment to the Stuarts, having withstood two sieges by Parliamentary forces in the Civil War, and surrendering in a third only after receiving a direct order from Charles I.

By now the Duke and Duchess of Norfolk had fled from Worksop Manor, and the Nottinghamshire roads were 'crowded with gentlemen and ladies from all the considerable families of that country ... so that the inns could not contain them, and many obliged to sit by the fireside all night for want of beds'.[72] Yorkshire took fright anew, and one of its wealthiest merchants, Mr Wilkinson, sought refuge in London, and then, not considering himself safe there, fled to The Hague in Holland.

The Derbyshire Blues and the county Lord Lieutenant, the Duke of Devonshire, stood briefly in the actual path of the Jacobites at Derby. On 3 December the duke wrote to his only potential support, the Duke of Montagu's 'new' regiment of horse (the 9th, the counterpart of Kingston's much better 10th), then standing at Loughborough, that a small party of the rebels – marching with incredible speed – had reached Ashbourne.[73]

This note of panic was soon converted into action. At the further news that 3,000 Jacobites had reached Ashbourne, the Duke of Devonshire led the Blues in a hasty retreat overnight by way of Borrowash to Nottingham, hoping, as a Jacobite satirist put it, to find his way to Field Marshal Wade, 'then behold we shall be safe, for he is a peaceable man'.[74] He arrived at Nottingham at 5 a.m. on 4 December, and at once took himself to bed.

The Duke of Cumberland was now alarmed for the safety of the arms and military stores in Nottingham Castle.[75] The castle was held only by a steward and a few troops, and the man complained that no support was forthcoming from the Duke of Devonshire, who 'for good reasons (as I suppose and doubt not) [had] withdrawn both his own regiment and the troops of the town of Nottingham at some distance'.[76]

These last guarded words refer to the further retreat, or rather flight, of the duke and his Blues from Nottingham. After night fell on 4 December they were making their way north from Sherwood Forest towards Mansfield when they encountered a herd of cattle being driven nearby. The noise was enough to convince them that the Jacobite army was nearly upon them, and one of their drummers dropped his instrument in his fright: 'And Gr..tt … n the Lieutenant, came riding furiously, and he whipp'd his horse cruelly, saying, flee swiftly, for on thy speed dependeth my Life. And saw not the drum, but rode upon it and burst it; and the Noise thereof was like the Report of a Great Gun; and the Beast was in a Fright, and threw his Rider to the ground, and he roar'd terribly, crying, Oh! I am slain and the stench of this Man was grievous to be borne'.[77]

Montagu's Horse arrived at Mansfield at midnight, only to be infected by the general terror, and on the 5th the cavalry and the Blues alike ran for Southwell and Newark amid scenes of ludicrous confusion. The Blues did not consider themselves safe even there, and did not draw breath until they reached Retford.

The 5th of December 1745 was the high tide of the Jacobite cause, and the army of Prince Charles spent the day in and about Derby in a state of almost unalloyed happiness. Money was being taken in by the Jacobite Collector of Excise, who installed himself at the Virgin's Inn, and Whiggish gentlemen were being relieved of sums equivalent to their donations to the Loyal Subscription to King George. The troops 'were to be seen, during the whole day, in crowds before the shops of the cutlers, quarrelling about who should be the first to sharpen and give a proper edge to their swords'.[78] Reports of thievery were circulated in the hostile press,[79] but all of that was belied by Samuel Kirkman of Coventry, 'a substantial man of silk', who informed Cumberland's headquarters that the Jacobites had behaved politely all day.[80] No damage was done to the great silk mill, and it was noted that when one of their parties searched the farm of George Mellor for arms, they opened a box, but would not take the bank bills and the two gold watches they found there. Large contingents of officers were present at the morning service and evening prayers at the handsomely rebuilt Church of All Saints, which rang with the eloquence of 'Parson Cappoch of Manchester', and the notes of the new organ as played by Thomas Chadwick, another Mancunian. The optimism extended to the letters that were written that day to ladies in Scotland:

> At every town we were received with ringing of bells, and at night we have bonfires and illuminations. I hear General Wade is behind us, and the Duke of Cumberland and General upon one hand of us, but we are nearer London than any of them, and it is thought we are designed to march straight there … But though both these forces should unite and attack us, we do not fear them, for our whole army is in top spirits, and we trust in God to make a good account of them … even what has happened already must appear to posterity like a romance rather than anything of truth.[81]

None of the happy throng could have believed that even now one of the agents of their ultimate destruction was pushing his way through their midst, in the shape of a gentleman who was clad in an expensive gold-laced brown suit and mounted on a fine gelding.

CHAPTER 11

The Council at Derby, and the Retreat to Scotland, 5–30 December 1745

DUDLEY BRADSTREET, ALIAS 'OLIVER WILLIAMS', was a gifted spy and confidence trickster. Born to a minor Protestant Anglo-Irish family in County Tipperary in 1711, he had spent his adult life as one of the most accomplished spinners of fraudulent schemes in Hogarthian England. Now his services as an agent and trouble-maker had been accepted by the Duke of Newcastle's secretary, Oliver Stone, who fitted him out with a false identity and the necessary papers. Bradstreet's account of his subsequent doings, once dismissed as a picaresque novel, can now be confirmed in many incidental details from official documents. He posted north from London on 2 December, met the Duke of Cumberland at Lichfield at 3 p.m. on 5 December, and rode into Derby after nightfall, announcing that he was a gentleman come to join the Prince.

Bradstreet arrived in the interval between two tense meetings of the Prince's Council, which, unknown to the rest of the army, were deciding whether the army should advance from Derby or retreat. It is not the purpose

Edinburgh militia

of the present work to recapitulate the details of the sessions, which are recounted at length in every serious biography of the Prince and study of the '45. In the broadest outline, Lord George Murray and the senior Lowland officers took Prince Charles to task for having failed to produce any credible evidence that the French would land, or that any substantial numbers of the English were willing to come out. The Highland chiefs in general supported the Prince, or at least hid their reservations, but Charles was already losing ground by the time the first meeting broke up.

Dudley Bradstreet was brought before the Council in the course of the evening session, and declared that the Duke of Cumberland was about to cut across their path of retreat from Lichfield with 8–9,000 men, while the Duke of Richmond harried their right flank with his cavalry, and – a total fiction – that Ligonier or Hawley would oppose them frontally with a third force at Northampton. The remaining support for Prince Charles was overborne, and Lochiel now threw his authority behind the retreat.

Bradstreet was to remain with the army on the march back through the north of England, and, on passing through Standish in Lancashire, left a report with Edward Smalley, the curate. Smalley forwarded the account to the Duke of Newcastle, and added: 'Mr Williams [i.e. Bradstreet] did in my hearing, I assure Your Grace, appeal to several of the rebel officers, if he was not the cause of their present march towards the north; and they readily acknowledged that he was, much against their inclinations, which were strong for London'.[1]

Generations of historians have argued about whether or not Prince Charles and his army would have succeeded in reclaiming the crown of Britain for the Stuarts if, instead of turning back from Derby, they had continued their advance on the capital. I do not intend to re-plough already well-turned furrows, but rather to examine the evidence in terms of some perhaps unfamiliar specifics, before venturing a few comments.

The Balance of Evidence: Material

The main force of the Jacobite army was physically capable of marching 28 miles in a single day, as on the dash from Leek to Derby on 4 December. Rested and refreshed as it was at Derby, the army would have been fully up to executing four or so days of marching at a rate of 20 miles a day. Allowing for a further day's halt, it would have been well within the capacity of the foot soldiers to have covered the remaining distance to London in a further two days. The distance from Derby to London was about

120 miles. If we allow a generous six days for the march, and one for the rest, by setting out from Derby on 6 December the Jacobite infantry could have arrived in London on 12 December. Colonel O'Sullivan, who would have been responsible for the planning, believed that Prince Charles would have reached London sooner still,[2] and it is perhaps worth bearing in mind that on 5 December Jacobite out-parties were already ranging well beyond the Trent.

How well placed were the two Hanoverian armies to intercept Prince Charles before he was fairly on his way? On 6 December Field Marshal Wade's forces were scattered – his cavalry just arrived in Doncaster, and his infantry at Ferrybridge – and totally out of the reckoning in a race for London. The troops of the Duke of Cumberland were somewhat better positioned. The crucial place was Northampton, and the crucial day was 8 December, when the Jacobite infantry would probably have been passing through after covering the 61 miles of poorish road from Derby on the third day of their march.

On 4 December Cumberland's headquarters had drawn up a provisional plan for a general movement of his forces on Northampton, which would have had his leading forces arriving there on the following dates:

❖ 6 December: Bland's 3rd and Kerr's 11th Dragoons

❖ 7 December: Cobham's 11th Dragoons, and elements of Ligonier's 8th Horse and Kingston's 10th Light Horse; also the three battalions of Foot Guards (but only if they had been able to procure horses to serve as mounted infantry)

❖ 8 December: Sowle's 11th Foot (after 22 miles of marching from Rugby), and Handasyde's 31st Foot and the train of artillery (after the 14 miles from Daventry).

This remained a paper exercise, for it is doubtful whether any credible forces could have reached Northampton in time. Cumberland learned of the Jacobite march from Derby (the retreat, as it turned out) in the course of 6 December, but his forces were in no condition to respond. We have already seen the Duke of Richmond, as commander of the cavalry, pointing out early on the 5th that the horses of Bland's and Kerr's Dragoons would not have been up to executing the march from Lichfield to Coventry (27 miles) on that day, or the further march (31 miles) from Coventry to Northampton on the 6th (p. 295). In any case it would have been a recipe for disaster to send in unsupported light cavalry against the Highland army. As it was, the

Duke of Cumberland had to set aside 7 December as a day of rest for his entire army, for it was badly weakened by forced marches and the lack of food and shelter in freezing conditions.

The capabilities of the redcoat infantry also deserve to be examined. When the army of Ligonier and Cumberland was gathering in the Midlands, a good march to the rendezvous could be reckoned as 13 miles a day, but the average was a good deal less when account is taken of the rest days, and the first, very slow progress through the Home Counties. A regiment could put in an exceptional effort on a particular day, to cover, for example, the 24 miles from Daventry to Coventry, or the 27 from Coventry to Lichfield, but the distance on the next day would be correspondingly less, say the 6 miles from Lichfield to Rugeley.[3]

What was Cumberland now asking of his foot soldiers? The scheme of 4 December was calling for average daily marches of more than 17 miles. On 8 December, the first day on which the army was at all fit to move, the two concentrations of infantry would have been faced respectively with marches of about 40 miles from Meriden to Northampton, and about 47 from Coleshill to the same place, or a good three days of sustained marching, which would have brought them to the town at best late on 10 December, or at least two days after the Jacobite infantry.

The only force capable of moving at speed would have resembled the flying column which Cumberland actually put together to pursue the Jacobites on their way north. It comprised two regiments of horse and 1,000 mounted infantry (p. 321), and executed two successive marches of 28 and 23 miles. However, it would have been able to move only on the morning of 9 December, by which time the Jacobites would have been well on their way to the capital. The well-informed Jacobite agent Laurence Wolfe calculated that they would have arrived there three days before either the duke or the marshal.[4]

It is therefore likely that the Jacobite army would have had a free run to the neighbourhood of London. What forces might have awaited them there? The marching orders in the War Office papers do not tell us much, because they were so soon overtaken by events.[5] Better indications are given by a memorandum which the Duke of Montagu submitted to the Duke of Newcastle on 3 December,[6] and a report drawn up by Lieutenant General St Clair at the command of George II:[7]

UNITS	STRENGTHS

Foot ❖ Seventeen grenadier companies
of the Foot Guards — 1,200

❖ 1st Bn of St Clair's 1st (Royal Scots) — 660

❖ Mordaunt's 18th — 623

❖ Huske's 23rd — 611

❖ Bragg's 28th — 641

❖ Beauclerk's 31st — 490

❖ Richbell's 39th (8 companies only) — ?

❖ Murray's 43rd (Black Watch) — 616

A further foot regiment (Harrison's) was expected at the Tower 'on Wednesday next', probably 11 December. On this reckoning the regular infantry available about London to meet the Jacobites would have reached at the least about 5,325 (taking account of the reduced establishment of Richbell's), but around 6,000 if Harrison's arrived in time, and his regiment accorded with the average strength.

Horse ❖ Horse Guards (2 troops) — ?

❖ Horse Grenadiers (1 troop) — ?

❖ Ligonier's 8th Horse (2 troops) — 110

❖ Hawley's 1st (Royal) Dragoons
and Rich's 4th Dragoons — 431 together

The strength of the regiments varied wildly, and it should be pointed out that Rich's Dragoons had lost all their horses in Flanders. If, from the example of Ligonier's Horse, the rough average troop strength is to be put at 55, then the strength of the cavalry in the neighbourhood of London stood at about 700, not all of whom were mounted.

Artillery

An artillery train of 33 or 34 field pieces, together with 48 covered carts, 20 boxes of weapons, and 240 gunners, was assembled in the Tower and ready to march on 9 December for Finchley Common 'under the command of Captain John Speedwell, an old officer who served in both King William's and Queen Anne's wars'.[8]

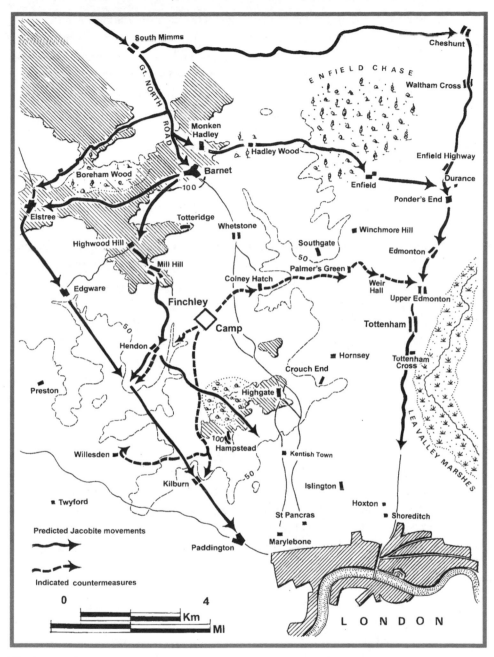

The contest for London – presumed Jacobite thrusts and planned countermeasures

For good reasons (p. 311), no account is taken of the London Militia, which on paper might have fielded four regiments of foot and one of light horse.

Although the figure of 6,940 regulars has been reached with some guesswork, it corresponds remarkably closely with Laurence Wolfe's 'number of about 7,000'. At the lowest possible estimates the redcoats were much stronger than appears in the neo-Jacobite histories, and in all probability they had a numerical advantage over the forces of Prince Charles, whose effectives are usually put at about 5,500. Wolfe found that his Jacobite contacts believed 'that the Prince acted the most prudent part in not risking such a march, whereby his army must certainly have been very much harassed, and that in a such a condition he must have fought the army that was assembled on Finchley Common that was fresh, and though attended with success, in three or four days after, another superior army composed of the best troops in England under the command of the Duke of Cumberland and Marshal Wade'.[9]

As for the ways by which the Jacobites might have come at London, the Duke of Cumberland had written on 3 December that the enemy, on finding the turnpike to Derby broken up, might well turn east across the Pennines by way of Sheffield and advance down the Great North Road (the A1). The Duke of Newcastle was reinforced in this impression by a mistaken report that reached him on the afternoon of 6 December, that the Jacobites were in possession of Nottingham. If this were true, then the rebels might seek to evade Cumberland's army either by marching all the way down the Great North Road by way of Stamford, Biggleswade and Welwyn, or branching off at Huntingdon and taking a route further to the east by way of Royston and Ware (the A1198, then the A10). He informed Cumberland that the king had ordered a camp to be established between Highgate and Whetstone (i.e. on Finchley Common, below), and magazines of provisions to be formed at Dunstable, St Albans and Barnet.[10] This last was a strange decision, for these exposed depots were asking to be snapped up by the Jacobites, who would then have been well fed for the final advance on London.

For the close defence of the capital, the government adopted St Clair's proposal to establish an encampment 12 miles to the north-west of the City on Finchley Common, with the right extending towards Colney Hatch, and the left to the 'white house belonging to Mr Fotheringall', presumably a prominent building that stood in open country. Finchley is now engulfed by housing, but a local street name, 'Gravel Hill', reminds us that the area is a geological anomaly, an isolated spread of gravel rising proud of the surrounding London clay. The Common was therefore both good camping ground, and a central position from where the Hanoverian forces could counter the most probable moves of the enemy.

St Clair assumed (not necessarily correctly) that the Jacobites would not dare to mount a direct assault on the encampment, but would instead seek to reach London around one or another of the flanks.

❖ He outlined the most likely routes to the west under the heading *Motions towards London, which the rebels might make upon their right.* Here the intention of the Jacobites would be to leave the Great North Road at one point or another, and gain the Edgware Road, which ran towards the capital from the north-west. The turn-out points might be: 2½ miles short of Barnet, and then by way of Boreham Wood to Elstree; from Barnet itself by the direct route (A411); or across Barnet Common, then by Highwood Hill and Hendon to reach the Edgware Road at a point only 6 miles from London.

By now the Jacobites would be on the deep flank of the encampment on Finchley Common, and they might choose to strike directly from Hendon to London across Hampstead Heath. 'All of these roads are hard and good; but it is not probable that the rebels will take the road that goes by Hendon, because they must in that case necessarily expose their flank for a considerable way to His Majesty's troops, and that at no great distance.'

The best counter, according to St Clair, would be for the forces from Finchley Common to march by way of Hendon to come at the Edgware Road 3 miles south of Edgware, and 7 miles from London. Alternatively, they could still reach the Edgware Road further south by way of Highgate and Hampstead in the direction of Willesden, or to 'a place called Kilburn' 4 miles or so from London.

❖ By the *Motions towards London which the rebels may take to their left,* St Clair understood the potential turn-offs from the Great North Road to the east. By leaving the highway at South Mimms, 5 miles north of Barnet, the Jacobites could reach 'the great road leading from Ware to London' (the A10) at Cheshunt. This transverse road (running just to the north of the M25 between Junctions 23 and 25) was only 7 miles long, but bad. Otherwise the Jacobites could turn aside just 1 mile short of Barnet at Monken Hadley, and cross Enfield Chase to reach the 'great road' beyond at Enfield, 10 miles from London. The route was shorter still than the first, at only 5 miles, but deep in mud where it crossed Enfield Chase.

The indicated countermove by the governmental forces would be from

Finchley Common by way of Colney Hatch, Palmer's Green and Weir Hall, arriving at the Old Bell at Edmonton, south of Enfield, a road 5 miles long and in good condition.[11]

St Clair did not specify exactly when the troops would concentrate on Finchley Common, and meanwhile they were to be sheltered in villages over an arc to the north of London, the average distance from the encampment being more than 3 miles. The Duke of Montagu had already been alarmed by the policy of dispersing the troops in billets. He believed that the advance of the Jacobite army on London was sure to be concerted with malcontents in the capital and that 'a sudden rising of the disaffected people in the night must carry their point, even before the troops could be alarmed, assembled and march to the relief of the town, though from so small a distance as the above places'.[12] When the Council rose at St James's Palace on the morning of 6 December – London's 'Black Friday' – the orders went forth for all the grenadiers of the three regiments of Foot Guards to march directly to Finchley, where the encampment was being marked out. The Horse Grenadiers and the Horse Guards probably arrived there on the 7th, the day the City saw Hawley's Royal Dragoons pass through on their way to Barnet, and the Black Watch (the 43rd) on their way to Enfield. As far as can be established from the confusion of countermanded orders, Mordaunt's 18th was positioned at Highgate and Hampstead, between the encampment and London, and Richbell's 8th in front of the encampment, at Totteridge and Whetstone, and in Finchley village itself. King George in person was prepared to take up his station on Finchley Common, accompanied by his standard and his son and heir Prince Frederick, 'whose Princess and the rest of the family were ready to be sent to Portsmouth'.[13]

On 8 December the necessary horses were sent to the Tower to draw the train of artillery to Finchley, but it was reported on the 9th that 'the order was countermanded on the arrival of an express ... that the Duke's army, having by extraordinary marches got the rebels into such a situation, that they must either fight or run, chose the latter, and accordingly retreated to Derby ... and are endeavouring to return the way they came'.[14]

The Balance of Evidence: Morale

London's 'Black Friday' earned its name from the leading citizens' panic on that day. There was a classic run on the Bank, and indeed the town was 'in such an uproar as cannot be expressed, and is scarce to be imagined'. By this time the lie had been given to the propaganda that denied all military virtue to the Jacobite army and its leader, and indeed 'My lord Cobham's expressions in this respect before a numerous assembly is very remarkable. "It must be owned," says he, "that this young man is a most glorious fellow; it is a pity he is a Catholic." And again His Lordship discoursing about the Pretender's operations in England, "I don't know who has the conduct of those people's affairs in the military, but this I can assure, that they have not committed one mistake since they came into the kingdom"'.[15] The patriotic bluster of the Whigs was faltering, and three years later William Pitt conceded that 'if they [the Jacobites] had obtained a victory and made themselves masters of London, I question if the spirit of the population would have taken a very different turn'.[16]

It is important to ask how far the prevailing mood in the capital affected the high political leadership. In spite of wishful thinking on the part of the Jacobites afterwards, King George was preparing to position himself at Finchley, and did not have his bags packed ready to flee the realm. Again, there is no evidence to support the Chevalier de Johnstone's much-quoted statement that he been assured, 'on good authority, when I was in London some time after our unfortunate defeat, that the Duke of Newcastle remained inaccessible in his own house, the whole of the 6th of December, weighing up in his mind the part it would be the most prudent for him to take, and even uncertain whether he should not instantly declare himself for the Pretender'.[17] On the contrary, documents show that Newcastle was busy that day dictating orders and official letters, whether useful or not is another question.

The reports of foreign ambassadors paint a fairly consistent picture. On 15 November the Austrian Wasner noted that the Jacobites were besieging Carlisle in earnest. He was inclined to think that the London government was exaggerating the dangers, in order to exact more money from the king's subjects, and he could not understand why the Ministry was unwilling to turn its mind to urgent questions of foreign policy.[18] By 19 November news had come that Carlisle had fallen, and the Jacobites had the liberty of various courses of action. 'Otherwise matters here, whether internal or foreign, remain in their old state of indecision and confusion.'[19]

On 3 December Wasner began to write that the days of the rebellion seemed to be numbered. He was interrupted by the news that the Jacobites were in possession of Manchester. Even then he could not bring himself to believe that the rebels would have the temerity to slip between the armies of Wade and Cumberland and leave them in their rear, but that is just what the Jacobites proceeded to do. On the 6th Wasner assessed that the objective odds seemed to be against the rebels, but 'they [the Ministers] make no attempt to conceal their astonishment and alarm'.[20] At the same time the Swedish ambassador noted that an encampment was to be formed to the north of London, but he could detect no sign of the 'appropriate measures and swift implementation which the situation demands'.[21]

Instead, Newcastle's attention was taken up by the threat he conceived was coming from secret enemies. On 6 December he informed the Lord Mayor of the king's wishes for the internal security of London. He was to list all the horses available for hire in the City, and order the Trained Bands to set out alarm posts and to be on their guard against disorders. The Master General of the Ordnance was to see how the various ways into London could be obstructed, and the king was ordering the Lord Mayor to give all possible encouragement to the people who had offered to lend armed support. His Majesty was assured that His Lordship would exert his 'utmost endeavours in opposition to the bold and dangerous attempts, now making by the Pretender and his adherents, which threaten the peace and tranquillity of this great and flourishing City'.[22] In the event of a rising in London the alarm would be given in the daytime by a flag hoisted on St Paul's Cathedral, to be answered by a flag on the spire of St Martin's in the Fields; the corresponding signal at night took the form of seven cannon fired at the Tower, answered by seven more at St James's Palace, repeated every half minute.[23]

Newcastle's next priority was to enforce the existing Acts of Parliament (dating from the time of Elizabeth I and James I) against the Jesuits and other Popish priests, who were now deemed more dangerous than ever. They were to depart from London by 9 December, and a reward of £100 was held out to every person who detected a priest within 10 miles of the capital from that date. At the time when the government needed all the support it could get from abroad, it acted with the full force of the law against the English and Irish priests who officiated at the embassy chapels of the Catholic powers. The ambassador of the Venetian Republic concerted the protests, and on 10 December the ambassadors of the Catholic states delivered their respective complaints to the Duke of Newcastle, as Secretary of State for the Southern Department, and to Lord Harrington, his counterpart in the Northern Department.[24] The government received the remonstrances politely enough, but proceeded to arrest a chaplain of the Portuguese embassy and clap him in irons in the criminal prison of Newgate.

Looking back in the New Year, the Swedish ambassador, Ringwicht, reported to his king that 'I do not believe I am mistaken when I say that the Ministers themselves do not know what they are about ... They live in a state of false security, without even thinking of what measures might be needed to confront an enemy. Now that a designated committee has got to work, it acts more often than not at cross purposes, whether on account of the magnitude of the task at hand, or because it is not up to it. On top of this, the decisions become known to the enemy before they can be put into effect'.[25]

When considerations of morale and capability are put into the scale, they serve to redress the numerical preponderance of the government's forces. The Jacobite spy Laurence Wolfe knew that Wade's army had been 'prodigiously reduced by death and sickness',[26] but he was unaware of just how badly Cumberland's troops had been affected by their experiences on shelterless Stonefield and Meriden Heath.

As for the forces in and about London, the militia would have had to perform miraculously better than any of the local forces so far put into the field, if it was to be reckoned of the slightest account, and the Lord Mayor himself admitted later that no more than 500 citizens would have been willing to serve. Chief Justice Sir John Willes aroused nothing but derision when he recruited an Associated Regiment of Law: 'the story is a very strange and ridiculous one … The grave and eminent part of the profession are much scandalised at being so exposed'.[27] The London Trained Bands were at best good for containing the much-feared disorders by the Scottish and Irish workers in the capital.

Among the regular troops the grenadier companies of the Guards were less formidable than their designation might suggest, for they included a large number of raw recruits raised by the local parishes, such as the men who responded to the bounty of £5 which was on offer by St Martin's. On these matters Laurence Wolfe carries some credibility, for he was convinced that the Jacobite high command had been right to turn the Highland army about at Derby. At the same time he was alive to the strength of the counter-arguments, and not least the evidence of disaffection in the Hanoverian army as represented most immediately by the case of the Black Watch (the 43rd Foot), which was assigned an important post on the eastern flank of the forces in front of London. There had long been doubts as to the regiment's loyalty, and Wolfe learned that 'in so desperate a situation King George was in a strange dilemma how he should dispose of the Highland Regiment then near London, but upon Lord Stair's offering to be security for their behaviour, they were likewise ordered out to Finchley camp … His Lordship had been very much mistaken, for numbers of the Highlanders declared to their friends that if they were ever within twenty miles of the Prince and their brave countrymen, nothing should hinder them from going over to him all to a man'.[28] There had been similar talk in the ranks of the Royal Scots (p. 128).

The Balance of Evidence: the Verdict

> *To speculate on what might have occurred if Prince Charles had continued his*
> *march on London is, after the lapse of more than a century and a half, to indulge*
> *in an interesting but unprofitable speculation.* (William Drummond Norie,
> *The Life and Adventures of Prince Charles Edward Stuart*, 1901, II, 205)

As century succeeds century it becomes more and more difficult to take issue with Norie's conclusion. To have followed Charles thus far is to be aware of how difficult it was to predict the Prince's actions from one day to the next. Would he necessarily have continued his advance by way of Northampton, as we all suppose? Might he have attacked the encampment at Finchley by direct assault, or might he have surprised the redcoats in their billets before they had time to assemble? Would the government's advantage in numbers have been sufficient to outweigh the superiority of the Jacobites in leadership and morale? Questions like these are impossible to resolve, and the outcome might well have hung on something as trivial as a MacPherson in the Black Watch recognizing a fellow-clansman in the opposing ranks.

Should Prince Charles have continued his advance on London? When it is put in that form, the question becomes easier to address. At first glance it would appear that Lord George Murray and the majority of the Council were justified in committing the army to the retreat, for they were balancing the uncertain outcome of an advance on London with what seemed the danger of being taken between three converging forces. In the long term, however, and with the advantage of hindsight, we can see that Lord George and his allies doomed the army anyway.

The real damage was cumulative and slow to manifest itself, but none the less fatal on that account. The news of the retreat was a further setback to the efforts of the duc de Richelieu, who was the only senior French commander still pushing for an invasion of southern England. Prince Charles, once the abstemious and inspired warrior leader, was overtaken by depression and open to self-indulgence. The troops continued to fight hard, and Lord George and the other commanders still had the capability to spring some nasty surprises, but by turning back at Derby their army began to forfeit the impetus of its horror-inducing moral superiority, which was its chief weapon against numerically superior forces. (It was the kind of superiority enjoyed by Guderian's Germans in France in 1940, or Yamashita's Japanese in Malaya in 1942.)

The decision of the Jacobite high command on 5 December 1745 had less to do with the circumstances as they existed at the time than the culture of the Council, and the deep-rooted opposition of Lord George Murray and his circle to the enterprise in England. The onus was now on them to provide a realistic strategy for the upholding of their cause in Scotland. The council of war at Crieff on 2 February 1746 revealed that they had nothing to offer, and set the seal on what had been decided at Derby. Concerning the resolution of 5 December one of the Jacobite officers wrote:

> One thing is certain, never was our Highlanders in greater spirits notwith-
> standing their long and fatiguing march; they had indeed got good quarters
> and plenty of provisions in their march, and were well paid; so that we judged
> we were able to fight double our numbers of any troops that could oppose
> us; and would to God we had pushed on though we had all been cut to
> pieces, when we were in a condition for fighting and doing honour to our
> noble Prince and the glorious cause we had taken in hand, rather than to
> have survived and seen that fatal day of Culloden when in want of money,
> provisions etc. we were obliged to turn our backs and lose all our glory.[29]

Yes, Prince Charles should have advanced from Derby, for that course offered a realistic, if incalculable chance of success, as against the near certainty of the destruction of the armed Jacobite cause.

From Derby to Kendal, 6–15 December 1745

Although Swarkestone Bridge is taken symbolically as the furthest point of the Jacobite advance, some parties had ranged from there over the East Midlands in the course of 5 December, to reconnoitre the routes and spread reports of the coming of great forces. Nearby Melbourne was required to pro-vide billets for 2,000 men for the following night. A fishmonger travelling to Birmingham encountered another detachment, which was on its way to pay a visit to Loughborough.[30] Two of this party were said to have ridden on to Leicester to commandeer quarters for the whole army,[31] and they may have been identical with the two Highlanders who were said to have ordered accommodation for 12,000 men at Market Harborough. Leicester was only about 100 miles from London, and Market Harborough not much more than 80, which indicates how swiftly the forward elements of the Jacobite army could have reached the capital. As things were, these efforts counted as no more than a diversion, for the army was heading in the opposite direction.

Once the Council had taken the momentous decision to retreat, it seemed reasonable to get on the move as quickly and secretly as possible. The Duke of Cumberland was too far behind to be able to catch up in the short term.

As for Wade, the Jacobites could win one march on him, even if the elderly gentleman tried to intercept them on his own initiative, which was unlikely. A gain of two days over him would be certain if he attempted to cross the Pennines by way of Skipton, which would enable the Jacobites to get to Lancaster before him. 'The only thing to be apprehended from Wade was, that he might march his army straight to Penrith in Cumberland. As the road [Stainmore, the A66] was exceeding good, and hardly any detour, he might have got to Penrith at least a day before the Prince, and by taking an advantageous post, put the Prince under great inconveniences.'[32]

All of this was the logic of the calendar and the map, and put on one side the effect of the retreat on the army of Prince Charles as a living organism. The leading elements left Derby at about 7 a.m. on 6 December. The darkness for a time concealed from the men the reality of what was happening. Sparkes, the excitable Derby Jacobite, was 'flinging his arms about and shouting, and one of the rebels drew a backsword and gave him into his hand ... Sparkes, as soon as he had got it, flourished it about and said "I'll do some execution with this before it be long"'.[33]

The Highlanders were in the highest spirits, believing reasonably enough that they were on the march to attack the army of the Duke of Cumberland, 'but as soon as the day allowed them to see the objects around them, and they found that we were retracing our steps, nothing could be heard throughout the army but rage and lamentation. If they had been beaten, the grief could not have been greater'.[34] Wild reports about the dissensions in the high command began to circulate in the army, and Captain 'John McAnsey' (James MacKenzie?) of Glengarry's Regiment believed that Lord George Murray had been found in possession of correspondence with his brother, the Whiggish Duke of James of Atholl, and that he had been deprived of his sword and was being kept under close watch.[35] As for Charles, 'the pretended Prince, in a Highland dress, mounted upon a black horse (said to be the brave Colonel Gardiner's, who was killed at the battle of Prestonpans) left his quarters at about nine o'clock, and riding across the Market Place, attended by some of his chiefs, went up Rotten Row, then turned down Sadler Gate towards Ashbourne'.[36]

Whiggish gentlemen calculated the number of their departed guests at 6,620, including the accompanying women and children, a figure they reached by touring the vacated billets in the town and the neighbouring villages: 'most of the houses of the inhabitants looked like stables or pigsties, and stunk much worse, from the loathsomeness of many of their fellows, which were so nauseous, that to publish the particulars would be indecent, and were there nothing else we disliked them for, this would be sufficient to turn the stomach of any Englishman against them'.[37]

Taking the most direct route to Ashbourne, the Jacobites 'marched very fast, and ... the horses which drew their artillery and baggage went upon a trot'.[38] The main force covered the 13½ miles to Ashbourne without incident, and the Atholl Brigade crossed the River Dove to Mayfield on the far side. Three hundred troops were packed into the Talbot Inn at Ashbourne, but the quartermasters chose more spacious accommodation for the Prince and his party at Ashbourne Hall to the east of the town, and chalked the appropriate names on the doors – 'Perth', 'Atholl', 'Elcho' and so on. One of the doors still existed in 1906, when varnish obliterated a chalked name that had been legible until a short time before, 'Sir Tamas of Cheridon' (i.e. Sir Thomas Sheridan).

The departure of the army from Ashbourne on 7 December was a protracted affair, for the leading troops set out at 1 a.m., and Prince Charles with the main body from 7 a.m., while a rearguard of cavalry lingered till noon. A countryman, still living in 1835, recalled the Weaver Hills being covered with 'them Scots rabils as thick as leaves in Vallambrosia'.[39] The Hanoverian spy Dudley Bradstreet was riding with the Prince's party. The nearby troops marched with colours flying, drums beating and pipes playing, for it was important to keep up appearances, but Charles shot many bitter glances in Bradstreet's direction.

The march of the main body terminated at Leek, which now seemed a small and hostile place. A forward party of 1,500 men (Elcho's Troop, Pitsligo's Horse and the regiments of John Roy Stuart and Ogilvy) continued all the way to Macclesfield, arriving between 5 and 6 p.m.: 'the town was very thin of inhabitants, and very dismal were the countenances of those who were left in it [they had been expecting Wade's army], the only comfort ... [was] to find the rebels looked full as dismal as ourselves'.[40]

Some important changes in relationships were taking place. Prince Charles was slow to leave his quarters in the mornings, and where he had once marched with springy step at the head of the army he now rode in the middle or rear. The new station was where action was the most likely, but it also corresponded with the downcast mood of a Prince who had been turned back within a matter of days of the capital. There was a fretful, snappish feeling among the troops, who shot three local men in or near Ashbourne, as well as the landlord of the Hanging Bridge Inn on the way to Leek. Successive parties looted Okeover Hall, and there was further plundering in Leek itself. Lord George noted that his great difficulty was 'to bring up stragglers, who could not be kept from going into houses and committing abuses. I found it necessary to have, every day, a clever officer out of each battalion, to assist in this, for whatever regiment happened to have the rear, they had only authority over their own men'.[41]

The Jacobites began to file out of Leek at 6 a.m. on 8 December, a day of snow and ice. The princely party had put up in the house of Mr and Mrs Mills, who were not free of their guests until 11 a.m., when a coach bearing some of the ladies (probably Lady Ogilvy and Mrs Murray of Broughton) departed with an escort of seventy cavalry. When Mrs Mills entered the room which had been vacated by the Prince, she found that the pillow was saturated with tears. That day Charles followed the route of one of the columns up the steep road leading to Buxton, but he stopped after less than 5 miles to spend the night in at a lonely farmhouse to the left (the 'Royal Cottage').

The Jacobite columns were moving in a generally northerly direction, though dispersed widely over the landscape. The main force made its way to Macclesfield, arriving at about 3 p.m., while the vanguard under Lord Elcho pushed on for Stockport. Out to the west a party of cavalry marauded in the villages between Leek and Newcastle under Lyme, which produced a powerful but altogether unintended diversion. On the night of the 8th Newcastle was a scene of 'confusion and dismay ... Lights were ordered to be set in every window in the town, and nothing was to be heard but noise, tumult and lamentation'.[42]

The alarm spread to Shrewsbury in Shropshire. Lord Herbert was standing there with his regiment of locally raised men, and 'this town, were my regiment to stay in it, being in no condition to make any stand against the rebels ... orders were given for it to be ready on Monday morning [the 9th] to march and join the army under His Royal Highness; and instructions, likewise, for securing the vessels on the River Severn'.[43] In fact Herbert's Regiment fled to Wenlock Edge.

That was one of the few occasions on which the Jacobite army in England was still capable of inspiring a fright of that kind. Now that the rebels were on the retreat, a new-found patriotism became evident among the Whigs along the way, and 'Then you might see heroic valour displayed among cocks that never crowed but among hens and on their own dunghill'.[44] Two Highlanders were taken near Ashbourne, and put in view on the camp at Meriden, where they appeared 'such miserable poor objects that one would think it impossible for an army consisting of such to penetrate into the very heart of so powerful a kingdom as England, if they had not had many friends along the roads'.[45] Individuals were at even greater risk. On 8 December a young English recruit (such people still existed) had his throat cut while resting by the roadside ahead of the main column. Conversely one of the Highland stragglers, Alexander MacLean, lagged so far behind that a couple of days later he called at the inn at Wincle to eat and was overpowered by the burly proprietor, Joseph Cunliffe, who snatched his musket and delivered him up to the redcoats. However, the inn (now called 'The Ship') preserves an alternative version, whereby the Highlander simply exchanged a huge antique gun for the landlord's musket, and left a piece of a Manchester newspaper as a keepsake.

Cumberland was allowing his troops to have their way, without the slightest pretence at legal formality. On the way to Macclesfield they captured three Highlanders 'whom they tied to their horses' tails, and made them go at a full trot'.[46] Another prisoner had been delivered up by the villagers of Cheadle (Staffordshire), and was hanged by the troops in Macclesfield itself. A surgeon of the town bought the body for four shillings and sixpence.[47]

Meanwhile the leading troops of the Highland army were nearing the Lancashire border. When they approached Stockport on the 8th, Lord Elcho and the vanguard were involved in at least two exchanges of fire with the newly bold local men, and the troopers burned a number of houses by way of retaliation. The events were witnessed by Martha, a girl of 10 or so, who was able to talk about them lucidly until the year of her death in 1823.

Manchester was in various states of turmoil. The Whigs had gained a temporary ascendancy in the town, but four officers of the Manchester Regiment (captains Deacon and Bretlargh, Lieutenant Holker and Ensign Syddall) had been given a rough reception when they arrived on a recruiting expedition on the night of the 7th, being chased by a mob down Market Street Lane and into St Ann's Square. They all escaped by one means or another, Syddall by abandoning his horse and making his way to his house on foot.

On the morning of 8 December the Bellman (town crier) went about Manchester to summon loyal subjects to turn out with pickaxes and the like to break up the roads and Mersey fords, but when some 10,000 collected, 'armed with scythes, hedge-stakes etc., who seemed very hearty to have a brush with the rebels',[48] the magistrates took fright, realizing that such enthusiasm was likely to cause death and destruction. The merchant Abraham Howarth noted the incongruity of 'calling people to arms by the Bellman one hour, and reading to them the Riot Act at the next'.[49]

Another gathering place was St Ann's Square, where the miller James

Tomlinson had just arrived from the country, and 'though far advanced in years, and being furnished with no such weapons, yet being zealous and willing to stand by and defend King George and Country, did join the said armed persons and go along with them to their rendezvous in St Ann's Square'. A little later Booth and his assistants arrived on the scene and called out: 'Disperse! Disperse!' Tomlinson protested, whereupon the magistrate raised his horse whip as if to strike him, and consigned him to the House of Correction.[50]

A number of the frustrated patriots collected under the command of a Captain Hilton, and went out to Cheadle Ford, with the frustrated intention of breaking it up. It was the same story to the north of Manchester, where 500 volunteers from Rossendale were on the road from Bury to Manchester on 9 December before they were turned back, much to the amusement of the Lancashire Jacobites, for "tis thought proper not to oppose the rebels'.[51] The Whiggish Dr Richard Kay received a copy of a mock recruiting notice for the 'Regiment of Rossendale Plunderers'. Recognizing himself as the colonel in this satire, he wrote in his diary 'Lord, suffer us not to be a reproach, and let us hope in Thy salvation'.

In their original advance the Jacobites had passed the Mersey by multiple columns, but they now took an easterly path, crossed the river by the ford at Stockport, and arrived at Manchester on 9 December, after a 19-mile march from Macclesfield. Prince Charles had sent two battalions and two squadrons ahead to disperse the hostile mob, and laid a fine of £2,500 on the town. He later reduced the sum by half, perhaps influenced by his warm reception from the local Jacobites. The Prince seems to have stayed at Mr Dickenson's house, as before, while Bradstreet and a number of the officers were accommodated in quarters not far out of town, 'where this night we were all magnificently entertained by a beautiful lady, whose husband was abroad for some time before. She had the greatest desire to kiss the rebel Prince's hand, and had been promised by one of the gentlemen that he would introduce her to him next morning'.[52]

Prince Charles would have liked to have stayed two full days in Manchester, but Lord George Murray emphasized that the army must be on the move again so as to reach Lancaster before Wade could cross the Pennines from Yorkshire. The departure of the troops on 10 December extended from 9 a.m. until the light faded at 4 p.m. The army was making for Wigan and the villages thereabouts, an average march of about 15 miles. The route had proved difficult on the outward journey, and now it was made worse by the ice and snow, and some sniping from the bolder Whigs. However, there was no sign of the Hanoverian regular forces and the army settled down for the night in cantonments which extended on either side of Wigan from Leigh to Standish. One of the parties made a detour out to the west by way of Ormskirk, where they collected a great number of bottles from a glassworks and smashed them on the road behind them to deter pursuit.

On 11 December the scattered units had between 8 and 17 miles of easy marching to reach their destinations in and about Preston. The bridge over the Ribble was luckily found to be intact, and the Prince and his party were able to reach Preston at 2 p.m. In a letter, much reproduced in the press, a Whig lady reported that 'the Young Pretender seemed very faint and sick, and is very assiduously ministered unto by Jenny Cameron. O'Sullivan, on the Young Pretender's Council, and a very likely fellow, made free with our house, and we were under an obligation to treat him civilly. He returned it obligingly enough ... This wild rabble ... look all like hunted hares, and had rather hear the name of the Devil than of the Duke'.[53]

For both symbolic and practical reasons Prince Charles insisted that the army must stay at Preston throughout 12 December and into the early hours of the following day. He sent out parties to gather in all possible fodder from the country thereabouts – the most fertile part of the country the troops were likely to encounter for a long time – and it took some effort on the part of Lord George Murray to wean the Prince, the Duke of Perth and O'Sullivan from the notion of standing and fighting in the vicinity.

This protracted debate explains why it was only on the evening of the 13th that the Duke of Perth set out on the important mission to find out what was happening in Scotland, where reinforcements from France were bolstering the Jacobite forces. Precious time had been lost and the ailing duke was travelling in a carriage with Lady Ogilvy and Mrs Murray of Broughton, which was a considerable drag on the mobility of the escort (Colonel Bagot and his 120 hussars), and made a tempting target for the local Hanoverian levies. The column had the misfortune to reach Kendal on the morning of the 14th, which was a market day. One of the hussars was killed by a shot from a window, and the hostile mob dragged two of Perth's servants from their horses and beat them so severely that one of them died. The hussars in their turn shot down three of their attackers. The Duke of Perth intervened to prevent a wholesale massacre, and 'the Magistrates protested their innocence, and laying the blame upon the country people as the scuffle happened on the market day, the chiefs were pacified and no resentment shown against the town'.[54] The party trailed slowly out of town then made the stiff climb from Kendal over the hills to Shap, from where eight of the hussars raced ahead to discover what hostile forces might be in Penrith, and what was meant by the firing of Penrith Beacon, 'which was then flaming and can be seen for ten miles around'.[55] The Duke of Perth wisely resolved to spend the night in Shap, for Penrith (the capital of far north-western Whiggery) held armed levies, together with a Captain Wren and 120 of Wade's troops who must have made forced marches over Stainmoor.

On 15 December, a day that became known as 'The Sunday Hunting', the Jacobite party made enquiry after discreet roads to Carlisle, and succeeded in working some way around to the east of Penrith by way of Cliburn, then down the right bank of the Eden through Temple Sowerby and Culgaith. They would have got through safely if a force of mounted levies from Penrith had not hastened ahead of the infantry and intercepted Perth's party at Langwathby Moor.

The carriage having been abandoned, the Jacobites scampered back through Culgaith, and then by the narrow lanes through Newbiggin, Milburn, Kirkby Thore and across the Eden, and then through Bolton, Morland and Newby before they lost their pursuers after nightfall on the way to Orton. The Whigs had picked up Perth's portmanteau, and one Fitzgerald, 'bookkeeper to Messrs Thornbarrow and Tufton, druggists in Minories London'.[56] The Jacobites had a prisoner of their own in the shape of 'a country boy who had discharged his pistol two or three times at them, and [they] seemed determined to shoot him; but Perth dissuaded them, saying he was a pretty boy, and "twould be a pity to kill him'.[57]

The Jacobite army had meanwhile resumed its measured retreat. The troops filed out of Preston from 4 a.m. on 13 December, the artillery in the lead, and marched in good order along the easy road that skirted the nearby coast to Lancaster. Lord George Murray was all for pressing north on the next day, 'but the Prince was inflexible on that point, he would show the world he was retiring and not flying, and if the enemy came up he would give them battle'.[58]

The Jacobites had made a clean break from the Hanoverian regular forces, and for a full week, from 6 to 13 December, the rival armies were entirely out of contact. When Prince Charles turned about at Derby on 6 December, the Duke of Cumberland was facing in what was now the wrong direction, with his cavalry at Coventry and his infantry encamped at Coleshill and on Meriden Common near his headquarters at Packington House, the residence of the Earl of Guernsey. In the course of the 6th he learned that the Jacobites were marching back at great speed towards Ashbourne. His reponse shows understandable confusion (after all, the Jacobite troops had

Prince Charles Edward Stuart.

TOP The ancient bridge spanning the Esk at Musselburgh. The Jacobites crossed from left to right, as we see it.

BELOW The 'impractible' Bow Hills, as seen from Alderly Edge.

ABOVE Dumbarton Castle.

ABOVE Wade's bridge at
Aberfeldy.

RIGHT The Flodden Wall,
Edinburgh.

OPPOSITE Wade's Garva Bridge,
crossing the infant Spey at the
foot of the descent from the
Corrieyairack Pass (beyond).

James, 3rd Duke of Perth.

OPPOSITE TOP The Mersey marshes at Didsbury.

OPPOSITE BELOW Jordangate, Macclesfield. Prince Charles halted at this spot under the hostile scrutiny of lawyer Stafford, whose high-perched Cumberland House rises in the background.

LEFT The house of the Byroms in Manchester.

BELOW The rock-lined Mersey at Stockport.

ABOVE The Ship Inn, Wincle, where
Alexander MacLean, willingly or not,
deposited his gun.

RIGHT Macclesfield.

LEFT Prince Charles Edward Stuart.

BELOW Blackstone Edge. Oglethorpe's final climb before the descent to Rochdale.

ABOVE Castle Stalker at low tide, with the hills of Appin beyond.

RIGHT Under the gun. Stirling bridge from Stirling Castle.

OPPOSITE TOP William Augustus, Duke of Cumberland.

OPPOSITE BELOW Clifton, the view south from the village over Town End Farm Cottages to Brackenber Hill. The present road is much wider than the original, but follows the same axis.

ABOVE Falkirk. Looking north over Abbot's Moss towards Muir. The Clan Donald advanced (from left to right) over the wall to the left of the view, and engaged the dragoons on the high ground to the right.

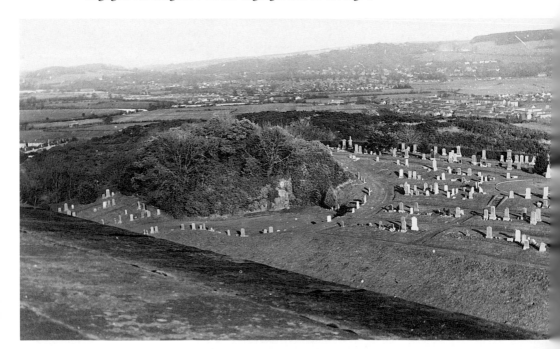

ABOVE The Queen Anne Battery at Stirling Castle.

LEFT The Gowan Hill, as seen from Stirling Castle.

OPPOSITE TOP Stirling Bridge. The garrison broke the central span, which impeded the Jacobite supplies during the siege, but delayed the subsequent pursuit by Cumberland.

OPPOSITE BELOW Ruthven Barracks, with the stable block to the left.

ABOVE Castle Menzies.

LEFT The tower of St Ninians. The sole remains of the church destroyed by the great explosion of 1 February 1746.

TOP Corgarff Castle, target of Lord Ancrum's raid. The surrounding barmkin was built after the rising.

BELOW Lord George's proposed battle site at Dalcross – the high ground to the centre and left, as seen from the east.

themselves been taken by surprise), but it also indicates how little chance he would have had of catching up with Prince Charles if the Jacobites had made for London.

Cumberland's first message was to Field Marshal Wade, telling him that affairs were 'now strangely altered by the rapid motions of the rebels, who are again moving westwards, as we have certain accounts of this by people who saw them on the Ashbourne road. Their intention at present can in my opinion be only for Wales, as they cannot flatter themselves with hopes of passing by you to Scotland. Our troops here are so excessively harassed with the continued marches and countermarches we have made, that they must have a day or two's halt here or hereabouts'.[59]

The whole of 7 December was therefore spent in giving the army its essential rest, and the Duke of Richmond exclaimed: 'I don't swear thousands in London now sit upon their arses, and say "why does not the Duke march up to them?" as if it was all Hounslow Heath between us; it would be a shame if he did not, but it is not to be conceived what a cursed country this is for marching, as we can move but so slowly that I fear they will have always time to escape'.[60]

By the afternoon of 7 December Cumberland seems to have been better informed about the line of the Jacobite march, and the next day he set off north-west with 1,000 volunteer infantrymen who were planted on local horses: 'our foot soldiers, not being accustomed to riding ... looked odd on horseback, with their muskets and knapsacks flung over their shoulders; but their desire to come up with the rebels was visible on every one of their countenances, with so much pleasure they rode along, and the countrymen with fresh horses coming up to remount our soldiers, running themselves on foot very cheerfully, that it really afforded a most pleasant prospect'.[61]

The flying column reached Lichfield on the night of 8 December, joining Bland's and Mark Kerr's Dragoons who had already arrived there under the command of Major General Bland. The troops set out on the morning of the 9th for what Cumberland knew was going to be a difficult 28-mile march along twisting roads through Abbot's Bromley, Uttoxeter, Stramshall and Tean to Cheadle (Staffordshire): 'I fear our march will be fruitless, for they [the Jacobites] marched at such a rate that I can't flatter myself with the hopes of overtaking them ... It is impossible regular forces should move with the expeditious rabble, and who take by force whatever they want, which we can't always come at, though I sometimes use means I would rather leave alone'.[62] Concerning the disparity in the rates of marching, the Swedish ambassador commented that 'a couple of lightly-mounted regiments of hussars would unfailingly have brought the whole matter to an end within twenty-four hours … which the heavily-mounted English horse is incapable of doing'.[63]

The next day was another day of hard riding, in which the column traversed the 23 miles from Cheadle to Macclesfield. Here the duke lodged comfortably enough in the house of the Whig lawyer John Stafford in Jordangate (now known as Cumberland House), but was disconcerted to learn that the Jacobites had already reached Wigan, instead of remaining at Manchester as he had been informed, and that he must now rein back his forces so as to be able to deal with the imminently expected French invasion of southern England. An aide-de-camp wrote from Macclesfield on the 11th that he had hoped that the army would have caught up with 'these lousy, nitty rebels, but they never stop. We marched from Packington to Lichfield, from thence to Cheadle and yesterday arrived at this place, thro' as difficult a country as cavalry ever went thro', and the snow froze on the ground made it impossible to keep our legs'.[64]

After this wasted day, an advance party under the Duke of Kingston set out on the 12th and secured Manchester for the Whigs. The main body of Cumberland's flying column, knowing it could be recalled south at any moment, executed a forced march all the way from Macclesfield and across the Mersey to Wigan in Lancashire. The troops marched in two columns, an eastern column by way of Wilmslow and Holling Ferry, and the other under Cumberland's personal command, passing the river at Warrington by the bridge. On the way 'one of the turnpike men endeavoured to put them out of the road the rebels had taken, which was soon discovered, and the man was instantly taken and hanged on a tree for his treachery'.[65] The Jacobite landlord of the Red Lion Inn in Warrington had already been hanged under martial law, and it is significant that the same treatment was being meted out to a further Englishman.

These dramatic moves, it must be emphasized, relate only to the flying column. The main force of infantry had remained under Ligonier's command on Meriden Heath for a number of comfortless days and nights: 'the ground was at that time exceeding wet, and the air extremely cold and windy, so that I believe many of us would have dropped off here, if it had not been for the great plenty of coals the country produces, for our firing; and the strong beer, at the Bull's Head, of which we soon made an entire consumption'.[66] The infantry then lumbered north by way of Stafford and Macclesfield to Stockport, 'a town of good entertainment, lying in a valley by the River Mersey; the bridge over this river was blown up, to prevent the rebels' retreat, so our men were obliged to ford it up to their middles; the soldiers' wives did the same, which afforded much diversion, both to ourselves and the inhabitants of Stockport who came to gaze at us.' A march of 6 miles across a fine and fertile country brought the troops to Manchester: 'here we halted two days, and find three parts in four of the inhabitants to be Jacobites. Our soldiers did not spare to tell them often of it'.[67]

The first contact with the receding Jacobites was made not by the young Cumberland, the hero of all loyal subjects, but by troops of old Field Marshal Wade, who had spent the previous weeks marching up and down to the east of the Pennines. The news of the Jacobite retreat reached Wade surprisingly early, on 6 December, the day he arrived in Doncaster with three regiments of horse, and when his infantry reached Ferrybridge from Pontefract. His army turned about in a typically ponderous way, and by the night of 10 December had got only as far as Wakefield, just 20 miles from Doncaster and 12 from Ferrybridge. Here Wade learned that the Jacobites had been making much faster time on their side of the Pennines and were three or four marches ahead of him. There was, he decided, no hope of catching them up with his main force, which could be better used to cover Newcastle. However, on 13 December he detached Major General Huske with 4,000 of the fitter men to cross the northern Pennines by the Stainmore route to Penrith, and, more immediately, he sent Major General James Oglethorpe to come at the rebels directly by passing the range further south with a mobile force of 500 men. Oglethorpe was under orders to 'pursue them [the rebels] with all expediency, to attack any small parties that are sent to raise contributions in the country, to pick up stragglers and such as fall behind, and to take all other advantages to distress them in their defeat, or rather flight'.[68]

On 11 December Oglethorpe's command rode from Barnsley to Huddersfield along the eastern flank of the Pennines. On the 12th the horsemen traversed the hills by the ancient route of Blackstone Edge, with its successive false crests, and 'noted all over England for its dismal high precipice and steep in the ascent and descent at either end; it's a very moorish ground all about and even just at the top, though so high that you travel on a causeway, which is very troublesome as it's a moist ground, so as is usual on these high hills they stagnated the air and hold mist and rains almost perpetually'.[69] The passage was a bleak experience at the best of times, and now the wind whipped the riders' cloaks about their heads, and the horses' shoes gave out on the ice, stones and ancient cobbles. A last, steady ascent brought the column through the tussocky moorland to a bluff which overlooked the town of Rochdale. The troopers descended to the relative shelter of the Lancashire valleys and reached Preston by 1 p.m. the following day, 13 December, having completed a creditable but exhausting march of more than 100 miles in seventy-two hours.

Both the Hanoverian high command and Prince Charles were hankering for a resolution of their quarrel inside England: 'the Prince having acquired a strong relish for battles, from the facility with which he had gained the victory at Gladsmuir [Prestonpans] at so small an expense, was always for fighting, and sometimes even reproached Lord George for his unwillingness to incur the risk of an engagement'.[70] On a dark and rainy 14 December the Jacobite army rested in and about Lancaster, while Lord George Murray, O'Sullivan, Lochiel and Lord George's aide-de-camp, Colonel Henry Ker of Graden, went out with an escort to prospect a battlefield for the Prince.

O'Sullivan was attracted by a site just half a mile out of town to the south. 'From this ground we had a fine sight on the high road, so that nothing could approach us that way without being discovered, but there was a hill on our left, that the reverse of it was thought necessary to be examined, fearing lest the enemy may steal a march on us that way, as they did at Preston [1715], which could easily be prevented.'[71] On the way there the escort captured seven or eight of Oglethorpe's green-clad Georgia Rangers, who belonged to a detachment that was also on reconnaissance, but mounted on horses that had been exhausted by their crossing of the Pennines.[72]

After this excitement the party completed its prospecting of the hill, which Lord George then said he preferred to the previous site.[73] Nothing had therefore been settled before he and O'Sullivan returned. Their report could not have inspired the Prince with any great confidence, nor could the misleading information from one of the Rangers that a large part of Wade's army had joined the Duke of Cumberland, and that Oglethorpe's main force was just 3 or 4 miles away.[74]

Prince Charles gave up the idea of standing and fighting near Lancaster, and left for Kendal early on 15 December, thus losing his first and last chance of doing battle with the Duke of Cumberland, while he was not only inferior (by about 3,000 men), but had a badly balanced force made up half of infantry and half of cavalry. The column had scarcely left Lancaster when the town bells began to sound, 'and soon after the word went from the rear to the front that the enemy were appearing, upon which orders were given for the Prince's army to form, which they did with a great deal of cheerfulness'.[75] Charles himself exclaimed 'I am very glad, let them come on, I am prepared. Give me my fusee!'

The alarm proved false. The column continued its march on Kendal, the advance guard dispersing a force of the Westmorland Militia who had been persuaded that the defeated Jacobites were running for their lives. Elcho's troopers snapped up a number of the fugitives, and 'those that we took made a most pitiable figure, crying in a most lamentable manner'.[76] The army arrived in Kendal over the course of several hours, the men 'pretty fatigued, the horses more so and badly shod, and they had endeavoured to get the smiths to shoe them, but they would not be obliged, which retarded their march'.[77]

The Jacobites learned from a captured militiaman that Wade's army was after all on the far side of the Pennines, but Lord George represented that the artillery and heavy baggage should be abandoned, observing that 'the country is mountainous between Kendal and Penrith, and the roads in many places difficult for such carriages, but the Prince was positive not to leave a single piece of his cannon; he would rather fight their [i.e. Cumberland's and Wade's] armies than give such an argument of fear and weakness'.[78] Lord George argued that the Jacobites should at least commandeer the local two-wheeled carts to replace the cumbersome four-wheelers, and issue the men with a one-day ration of bread and cheese as there would be little to eat at Shap. By his account O'Sullivan was at supper with the Prince, savouring his favourite muscatel wine, and by 11 p.m. he had still not issued the necessary orders.[79]

The Duke of Cumberland was standing at Preston with his flying column of horse and 1,000 mounted infantry. He was paralysed and chagrined by an order which reached him this 15 December, telling him that he must march back to London, for 12,000 French had landed at Hastings (a report that proved to be entirely erroneous). He complained to the Duke of Newcastle that he was 'very sorry that Mr [Admiral] Vernon's frights should have saved the rebel army near Lancaster, where we had drove them, and where I had hoped to have kept them at bay till I could have had the assistance of Marshal Wade's army utterly to have destroyed them'.[80]

Skiteraluch younger

CHAPTER 12

Shap, Clifton and the Defence of Carlisle, 16–30 December 1745

Shap, 16–17 December 1745

THE JACOBITE ARMY LEFT KENDAL on the morning of 16 December, 'a very foul and bad day, and a bad road'.[1] The preferred route out to the east (the A685) by way of Orton had been barred by the country people, who had dug up the surface and formed obstructions of boulders, and the Shap road actually taken (A6) was as 'slippery with a fall of rain after a great frost' and 'very narrow and steep in places'.[2] The Pioneers had done useful work on the first 4 miles of the road from Kendal, but the surface deteriorated on the further climb across the bare fells, and something of the old spirit of Prince Charles could be seen in his efforts to animate the troops, being 'always afoot, and forded those torrents as the men did, but none went off, nor stayed behind, only that were really sick or old'.[3]

It became evident that there was no hope of reaching Penrith in this wretched weather, and that the march would have to come to a halt in the neighbourhood of Shap. Captain MacLean records that the Atholl Brigade

---

'Skiteraluch younger', the title a parody of the Highland style of name

was still marching seven hours after nightfall before it 'came at last to Shap, and our regiment having about forty prisoners in charge was very late and gave them to the guards, standing on the dirty street. And after all our regiments was billeted three miles out of town, I, being abundantly wet to the skin and exceeding cold, two officers and myself missing our regiment and company by darkness of the night, proposed to stay in the town. We were put off several houses. At last we were glad to be allowed to sit in our wet shirts and clothes, only sometimes come to a fire'.[4] Prince Charles was lodging nearby.

Shap was every bit as crowded as MacLean suggests. A villager reported, 'we had 200 in our house … They broke open every lock, and ransacked the house twenty times over … breaking open the door of the room where I was lying sick of the gout [they] dragged me out of bed, stripped me quite naked, took my flannel waistcoat and drawers, and searched every place about me. They took two guineas my wife had put into my hand just before to hide; but she had the good fortune to toss nineteen shillings into the ashes, which were saved'.[5]

For the march on the 17th the Pioneers were able to patch up only the first 2 miles from Shap. There was a delay when the troops reached 'a little country town' (possibly Hackthorpe, or one of the Stricklands) and were told that the enemy were formed in line of battle just ahead, 'and our men having their guns (at least many of them) much damaged by the day before's great rain, fell to briskly fire their pieces or draw their shot and prepare for an engagement, but it was found false'.[6] The fells had been left behind, and Penrith, which lay ahead, was a sizeable town, and one more to invite marauding on account of its Whiggish behaviour. The troops reached shelter by nightfall, and groups went to plunder Lord Lonsdale's Lowther Hall and in Penrith itself, where Charles restored order by having the pipes played as if for a general review.

Lord George Murray meanwhile had charge of the artillery and the ammunition carts, which were coming up behind the army so as not to impede its march. The train and its escort (the Glengarry MacDonnells and the Manchester Regiment) had left Kendal on the morning of 16 December. The convoy crossed the plain of the Kent and the Mint, then rose gradually through a hillocky pastureland, to the range of heights that connected the south-eastern Lake District with the Pennines.

Lord George was then stopped by what he had feared – a narrow turning across a stream, followed by a steep ascent. 'It is not easy to express the trouble we were at. The horses of two waggons were yoked to one, besides

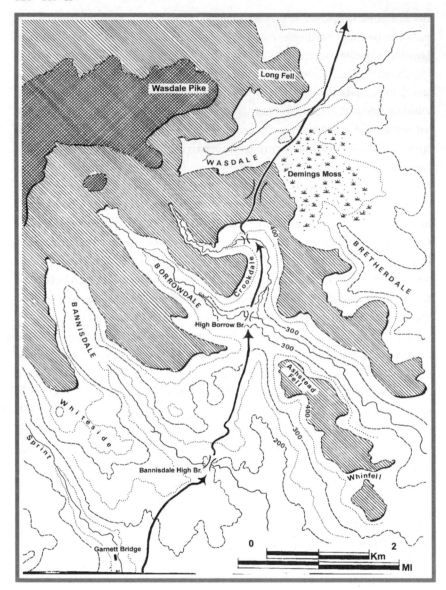

Shap Fells, 16–17 December 1745

at least forty hands. Two or three of the Manchester officers were vastly useful, and, entirely of their own accord, they were up to the middle in water for an hour … It was the Glengarry men in the rear that day; they are reckoned not the most patient, but I never was better pleased with men in my life, they did all that was possible.'[7] The column had to stop for the night among the nearby fells, and Lord George and most of the Glengarry men

sheltered in a spread of farm buildings beside the road. None of these locations can be fixed with any certainty, but one is possibly the steeply banked
Bannisdale Beck at the site of the present Bannisdale High Bridge.

On the 17th, 'as soon as the day began to break, we got all the small
carts (they had timber wheels, or wheels of one piece of wood, as none other
could be had) we could purchase, and sent even two miles off the road and
got some. We unloaded the waggons, and put the things into those small
carts'. Lord George was surprised to discover how little the cumbersome
waggons contained, and 'found two barrels of biscuit, which had travelled
from Edinburgh to Derby, and back again, which I gave amongst the men'.[8]

Along the road the column encountered a still more formidable combination of stream and slope. The water was too deep to ford on account of
the overnight rain, and one of the drivers contrived to steer his four-wheel
waggon over the side of the bridge, 'which was got out with great difficulty,
but the horses so spoiled that they were fit for nothing. And in order to make
everything as easy as possible, what things was fit for use was put in the small
carts that had cannon ball (which was by no means to be left behind) and
twelve pence offered by Lord George for every cannon ball that should be
brought to him at Shap ... by which most of them was carried forward and the
money paid'.[9]

The crossing was possibly that of the Borrow Beck in Borrowdale, but was
more likely that of the Crookdale Beck further on, where Crookdale Bridge
is today. By far the steepest part of the climb lay ahead, from where the pack
road left a bend in narrow Crookdale and made for the summit across boggy
and open moorland. In geological terms Lord George was traversing a zone
of igneous intrusions – lava and tuff, and a knob of granite at the highest
point of the fells – and all under a leaden sky and driving rain (see p. 386)
and snow. There was some respite when the convoy reached the far side, but
on reaching the straggling village of Shap it was found that all the food had
been eaten by the main army. A reinforcement was waiting there, in the
shape of John Roy Stuart's Edinburgh Regiment, which in fact incorporated
some Atholl men from Strathbraan, as well as the townsmen, but Stuart
himself was no friend of Lord George.

The progress of the artillery train had been no more than 18 or so miles,
but it would still have been impossible for Lord George to have made greater
speed, even if he had known how close the enemy was on his tail. On 16
December the Duke of Cumberland literally jumped for joy when he learned
that the report of the French invasion had been false and that he was free to
resume his chase. Lieutenant General Ligonier and nine battalions were still

on their way to London and beyond immediate recall, but Cumberland advanced his command of horse and mounted infantry to Lancaster, and unleashed Oglethorpe's detachment in close pursuit. By 6 p.m. on the 17th Oglethorpe had arrived just three-quarters of a mile to the east of the unsuspecting Jacobite troops in Shap, but the intervening ground being snow-covered and pock-marked with pits, and both men and horses being in a bad way, Oglethorpe directed them back to Orton for the night.

Clifton, 18–19 December 1745

Unsuspecting, Lord George spent the early morning of the 18 December commandeering carts from the fell villages, and transferring the loads from his overburdened waggons. The train had hardly set out from Shap village before unprecedented quantities of mounted militiamen appeared over the heights to right and left, and hovered just out of musket shot. Lord George detached forty of the best men of the Glengarry and John Roy Stuart regiments to either side of the road to prevent the enemy sneaking up from the rear, and two companies of the Regiment of Perth arrived under the command of the Franco-Irish lieutenant Ignatius Brown of the Regiment of Lally. Towards noon the column began to ascend the broad swell of Thrimby Hill, and 'we instantly discovered cavalry, marching two by two abreast on the top of the hill, who disappeared soon after, as if to form themselves in order of battle behind an eminence which concealed their numbers from us, with the intention of disputing our passage. We heard, at the same time, a prodigious number of trumpets and kettle-drums'.[10]

Without waiting for orders, Brown threw the troops of Perth and John Roy Stuart directly at the summit. The Glengarrys cast off their plaids, made extraordinary speed through the enclosures, and arrived at the crest almost as soon as Brown's men, who had had the advantage of the road. The intimidating force of cavalry proved to be just 300 of Bland's 3rd Dragoons and Oglethorpe's light horse, who at once fled in disorder, 'and of whom we were able to come up with one man, who had been thrown from his horse, and whom we wished to make prisoner to save him from the fury of the Highlanders, who cut him to pieces in an instant'.[11] From the sight of the abandoned trumpets and drums the Jacobites concluded that the enemy had intended to persuade them that the whole of Cumberland's army lay just beyond the summit.

Such was the first episode of the prolonged action of Clifton, the interest of which greatly transcends its small scale. It was the last armed clash ever to be staged in England, and afforded the Duke of Cumberland a chance of eliminating the rebels before they could escape into Scotland, and before winter brought operations to an entire halt. He was at his last logistic gasp, and if he failed to gain a decision here and now, the Hanoverian regime would be faced with the prospect of a war extending indefinitely into 1746.

One of the ammunition carts broke down irretrievably less than half an hour after the column resumed its march, so the Chevalier de Johnstone, the bold Sergeant Dickson and six or seven of the men went to a farm lying over to the right of the road, where they were fortunate enough to find an acceptable replacement standing in the yard. 'In returning from the farm, Dickson called our attention to something which appeared blackish to us, on a hill about a league to our left; and he alone, contrary to the opinion of everyone else, maintained that he saw it moving, and that it was the English army, advancing towards us. As we took what we saw for bushes,' writes de Johnstone, 'I treated him like a visionary.'[12]

The new cart took its place in the column, but the march continued for only a couple of miles before the Glengarry Regiment in the rear was assailed by a combined force of Bland's Dragoons, Kingston's Light Horse, Oglethorpe's Georgia Rangers and Yorkshire Hunters, and probably also Cumberland's personal escort of Austrian hussars (who had attached themselves to him in Flanders, and were now rigged out in crimson and green). The cavalry was being spurred on by the duke himself, furious to find that Oglethorpe had failed to engage the enemy at Shap.

Lord George knew the neighbourhood well, from his visits to the Lonsdales at the nearby Lowther Hall. On hearing that a part of militia was ensconced there, he asked the exhausted Glengarrys if they would volunteer to clear the building. They responded enthusiastically, and when denied access at the locked gates a number of the Highlanders swarmed over the wall, at which the house disgorged a green-clad mounted Ranger and one of Cumberland's mounted footmen, who made a vain attempt to escape. The footman told the Jacobites that the duke was just a mile away with a mass of cavalry. 'It was very lucky the taking of the footman, for otherwise the duke might have marched into Penrith without being perceived, for till then there had not been the least notice of his being so near at hand.'[13] The little expedition was doubly valuable, for not only did it yield this important news, but Cumberland's advance lost some of its momentum when he sent a detachment to clear the Jacobites out again.[14]

Lord George was helped by the fact that the high fells had given way to the hedges and enclosure walls which lined the narrow approach road to the village of Clifton. It was typical limestone country, though Clifton itself (again helpfully for Lord George) stood on a low ridge of millstone grit which cut in from the south-east. The main body of the enemy advance guard (Bland's Dragoons, the Georgia Rangers and Kingston's light horse) now approached the outlying houses of the village, unaware that the Jacobite rearguard had been reinforced, and that Bagot's Hussars, Pitsligo's Horse and the Regiment of John Roy Stuart were secreted in ambush.

Some of the hussars were hidden beside the barn at Town End Farm Cottages, which lay towards the bottom of a gentle slope 320 yards from the nearest houses of the village. The owner, the Quaker Thomas Savage, saw the Hanoverian commanders appear on the crest of the low Brackenber Hill, another 700 yards or so to the south of his farm,

> whereupon my very heart was in pain, for believing that a great number might be cut off before they were aware; so our care was to give the King's men notice, for which my son [Johnathan] ventured his life and gave them notice about 300 yards before they came to the place, when, in the meantime, a second ambush was laid about 100 yards nearer the King's men, and the King's hussars, with some of the Yorkshire Hunters, came down, and so soon as they came opposite the first ambush, the rebels fired upon them, but did no execution, and then issued out of the ambush at my doors, and a furious firing they had, the King's men acting in the quickest and nimblest manner that ever my eyes beheld, not one of them receiving any harm. Some horse followed the former, so that in a few minutes the rebels ran away like madmen.[15]

A Jacobite account nevertheless has Cumberland dispatching down 'one who by his dress seemed to be an officer, and was brought down by a shot from one of the Highlanders'.[16]

The Jacobite hussars and the other would-be ambushers crowded back through the narrow village street, and the Edinburgh lawyer Captain George Hamilton of Redhouse found himself stranded in a cottage in the confusion. One of the Austrian hussars is supposed to have forced him out by firing through the window, then engaged him in hand-to-hand combat, cut him on the head and made him prisoner. The Hanoverian volunteer James Ray states that 'one Ogden of Manchester was likewise taken by an hussar, who after he had begged for his life, privately drew a pistol and shot at the hussar but missed him; he in return cut Ogden down the side of the head: I have since been informed that he died in Lancaster Gaol'.[17]

It was now about 2 p.m., and the prolonged skirmishing was building up

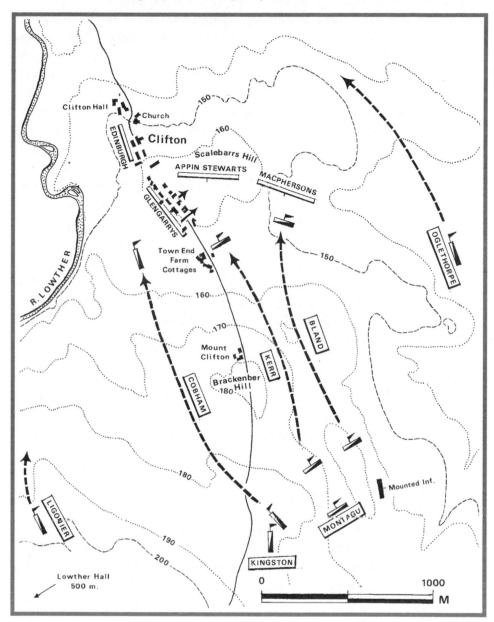

Clifton, 18 December 1745 (positions and movements conjectural)

on a scale that threatened to overwhelm Lord George and the rearguard. Prince Charles was bringing his army together for a general review on the moor north of Penrith, but he was alerted to what was happening by reports from below, and he detached successive reinforcements. In a reversal of the usual roles, the Prince was against bringing on a full-scale battle, while Lord George was warming to the prospect of action in the close-set neighbourhood of Clifton, where the available Hanoverian force (effectively all cavalry, with a couple of companies of militia out on the right) would be at a disadvantage. The Duke of Perth accordingly stationed the Atholl Brigade in deep reserve on the northern side of the Lowther at Lowther Bridge, with the main army guarding the Eamont above Penrith, for 'some peoples well inclined in the town (though there were but few) assured the Prince that there were fords eastwards of the town, where man and horse could easily pass; the Prince marched immediately towards those places and set himself in battle, and was very well posted'.[18] After some complicated comings and goings, occasioned mainly by the deceptive pause in the Hanoverian advance, the regiments of Cluny MacPherson and the Appin Stewarts continued all the way into Clifton and put themselves at the disposal of Lord George.

Clifton village consisted of 'one street with poor houses and enclosures all about made with dry stone walls and thick hedges'.[19] The locality, as exploited by Lord George, now made it, in the Duke of Cumberland's words, 'one of the strongest posts I ever saw'.[20] Lord George took advantage of the fact that the zone of enclosures and ditches reached further down the western side of the road than the eastern, thus forming a useful salient. He posted the Glengarry Regiment there as his right wing, not just to hold ground (which was relatively easy), but to bring a flanking fire to bear across the 20-foot wide road against the redcoats attacking his left wing.

The left wing was positioned to the east of the road, and was held back, or 'refused' in the technical jargon of the time, in order to take advantage of the enclosures on this side, and allow the Glengarrys a clear field of fire across the front. Lord George posted the MacPhersons on the left of this wing among the hedges, and the Appin Stewarts on its right, where they were covered by a swamp or boggy ditch. Finally, the troops of John Roy Stuart's Edinburgh Regiment were held back towards the centre of the village, and could have been the people who were seen 'plundering our town, leaving nothing they could lay their hands on, breaking locks and making ruinous work, even to all our victuals and little children's clothes of all sorts'.[21]

The Jacobites deployed in the lull that followed the collapse of their intended ambush. Thomas Savage was at first deceived by the silence.

Looking south he saw the Hanoverian forces drawn up reassuringly on Clifton Moor, but when he turned about he saw the Jacobites filling the village street, and lining the hedges and walls which extended towards him down the road. A second ambush was in prospect, and he was in 'great pain for the Duke and his men, it beginning to grow darkish; but I ventured my life and stood a little off, and waved my hat in my hand, which, some of them discovering, one of them came down towards me, and I called to him, bidding him cast his eyes about him, and see how the town was filled and the hedges lined, after which he returned'.[22] Possibly the man was one of the Austrian hussars, who, by another account, conveyed the warning to the duke.[23]

Lord George had about 1,000 men in position. Cumberland believed that his enemies had only about half that number, but, duly forewarned of the ambush, he drew 250 men from his three regiments of dragons and threw them into a dismounted assault – Bland's 3rd on the right; Mark Kerr's 11th in the centre; and Cobham's 10th on the left. The overall command was entrusted to Lieutenant Colonel Sir Philip Honeywood, a much-wounded veteran of Dettingen. The light horse of Montagu (9th) and Kingston (10th) were held back as a reserve, with Ligonier's 8th circling well out to the west from Lowther Hall, and the 1,000 mounted infantry tucked away on their right. The short day had come to an end, and the evening was 'generally dark, for masses of sombre clouds now rolled across the sky, and when the winter moon did shine forth, she seemed to do so with unaccustomed lustre. The lonely heath of Clifton Moor looked dark and weird. The alarm fires were burning redly on Skiddaw and Helvellyn'.[24]

The action opened at about 5 p.m. in something of an encounter battle to the east of the road, for, in a piece of fine adjustment, Lord George ordered the MacPhersons and the Appin Stewarts to leave their position and advance to a further hedge which was situated in a hollow. The MacPhersons duly hacked through the first hedge with their dirks, 'the prickles being very uneasy, I assure you, to our loose-tailed lads',[25] but they were anticipated at the second hedge by Bland's Dragoons who, according to Cumberland, opened fire with their carbines at 150 paces (100 yards),[26] which was a long range for accurate shooting. The MacPhersons responded, and Lord George,

> as soon as we had given our little fire, ordered us to draw our broadswords, which was readily done, and then indeed we fell to pell-mell with them. But the poor swords suffered much, as there no less than fourteen of them broke on the dragoons' skull caps [of iron strips, worn under their tricorn hats]

> … What, I think, indeed must have contributed to our safety, was the great hurry with which we went down towards the hollow towards them, by which means they were so suddenly mistaken of us that much of their fire went over our heads, and were at their muzzles before they got all their fire given.[27]

The dismounted troopers took to their heels and were shot up in their turn by the Glengarrys, who were firing into their flank. A number of the men 'had endeavoured to pull off their boots to fly the easier, and some of them were killed with one boot off and another on, and some with a boot only half on'.[28] The swords were being discarded wholesale. Among all the heroism Colonel Honeywood slipped on a turd and was assailed by the Highlanders, but he was retrieved from the fray with three or four cuts in the head (he had neglected to wear his skull cap), and later recovered.

Little is related of the action of Mark Kerr's 11th and Cobham's 10th, committed in the direction of Clifton village. Here the Glengarry Regiment was strongly placed, and MacDonnell of Lochgarry (commander of the Glengarrys) records that 'it then being quite dark, they coming very close to us, we only heard the noise of their boots, and could plainly discern their yellow belts. We received their first fire, which did us little damage. We immediately gave ours, and then attacked them sword in hand, and obliged them to retreat'.[29]

Lord George knew that he had done enough to ensure that the rearguard could disengage cleanly from the village, and after scarcely thirty minutes of fighting he directed his troops along the road to Penrith to rejoin the army. They were undisturbed, and 'nothing can be a plainer proof of the falsity of the Highlanders being driven out of Clifton than that of Mr Ferguson, ensign in Glengarry's Regiment, bringing off his colours with one man in company, who went with him to look for them in the field where he laid them down, when he was ordered not to keep flying them, to prevent the dragoons knowing their post'.[30]

The Duke of Cumberland occupied Clifton at about 6 p.m. and launched Oglethorpe's command on a wide outflanking movement to the east to cut off the Jacobite retreat at Eamont Bridge. Oglethorpe once again arrived too late, and encountered nothing more than a small Jacobite party, which opened fire then withdrew. So ended what from the Jacobite perspective was a little action which would have done credit to 'the oldest and best-disciplined troops'.[31]

The casualties on both sides had been surprisingly light. The Jacobites had 'but few men killed; for it was dark, and they had the advantages of the walls and hedges and their dirty dress into the bargain; they could not be distinguished from the hedges but by the flash of their firelocks, whereas our men being tall and cross belts made them easier perceived'.[32] Cluny MacPherson notes that one sergeant and twelve of his men lost their lives, and the five Jacobite dead who are buried at the southern edge of the village by the 'Rebel Tree' are almost certainly members of his clan. A number of the bodies were discovered by 'some frolicsome soldiers' who 'dug a deep hole in the ground, and put one of them into it with his feet downwards, and so filled the earth about his body that nothing but his head and shoulders were above the earth, and in that position left him'.[33] The losses among the Appin Stewarts, the Edinburgh Regiment and the well-protected Glengarrys must have been minimal.

The only prisoners recorded as being lost during the action were Thomas Ogden of Manchester, and George Hamilton of Redhouse, captain in the Jacobite hussars, who was brought to the Duke of Cumberland in a bloody condition. The duke 'told him he was sorry to see him engaged in such bad company, "but I will endeavour to save your life", and ordered him to be carried to York ... This Hamilton had two years before been a companion of the duke's in his youthful frolics, but missing a position in the army, and being encumbered with debt, took refuge among the rebels to avoid his creditors, and was made a captain by the Young Pretender'.[34] He was duly executed on 1 October 1746.

Lord George had borrowed old Glenbucket's target, and he writes that the shield was 'convex, and covered with a plate of metal, which was painted; the paint was cleared in two or three places with the enemy's bullets, and indeed, they were so thick about me that I felt them hot about my head, and I thought some of them went through my hair, which was about two inches long, my bonnet having fallen off'.[35]

Ten dragoons are listed in the Clifton parish register as having been killed, and they are probably the men who rest in the communal grave in the yard of the little church of St Cuthbert's, to the north of the village. However, Cumberland's aide-de-camp reckoned the Hanoverian dead at between twenty and thirty, all common troopers,[36] and a man told the Jacobites that he had seen 'forty wounded being dressed in a single room'.[37] Fifty or more dragoon swords were abandoned on the field and taken up by the Jacobites, and 'in the morning we found that they belonged, not to one regiment, but to detachments from all the dragoons there, and Cluny himself was possessed of one that was really a very valuable sword ... but who was master of it none of us can tell'.[38]

More significant than the bloodletting or the ironmongery was the delay imposed by Lord George on the Duke of Cumberland, who was now uncertain of the strength of the Jacobite rearguard, and did not dare to commit his force on this murky night in the very broken country between Clifton and Penrith. All but a few of his troopers spent the night in the open on Clifton Moor, but Cumberland himself was able to find shelter at Town End Farm Cottages. On hearing a great beating at the yard door, Thomas Savage hastened to open it, and 'the first words said to me were, "Could the Duke lodge here tonight?" To which, with pleasure, I answered, "Yes", and a pleasant, agreeable company he was – a man of parts, very friendly, and no pride in him. Much I could say, if it would not be tedious to thee, yet I shall mention one thing more to thee, which was, our cattle were all standing among the slain men, and not one of them was hurt'.[39]

The dim light of 19 December found Cumberland's men and horses almost paralysed with the cold and wet, and the Duke was able to bring all his forces together in Penrith only on the following day. The Jacobites meanwhile marched undisturbed through the appalling rain of that day, and arrived in Carlisle from noon onwards.

The Passage of the Esk and the Defence of Carlisle, 20–30 December 1745

Prince Charles called his council together in Carlisle on 19 December and took what in retrospect was called 'perhaps the worst resolution the Prince had taken hitherto'.[40] This measure was to withdraw into Scotland, but leave Carlisle garrisoned by up to 400 of all ranks, together with most of the artillery train – the cannon captured at Prestonpans, and three of the six 'Swedish' pieces from France. The garrison comprised the surviving 20 officers and 93 men of the Manchester Regiment; 256 Scots (mostly eastern Lowlanders); Lieutenant Ignatius Brown, another officer and three privates of the Franco-Irish regiment of Lally; Captain Sir John Arbuthnot of the Royal Ecossais; and a complement of French gunners to serve the artillery.

At the council the Prince had enjoyed the support of O'Sullivan, who argued that Cumberland had no heavy cannon with him, and that the possession of Carlisle by the Jacobites would force him out to the east by way of Brampton, and cost him two days' march. Lord George Murray represented in vain that Cumberland could obtain heavy cannon from the port of Whitehaven (which he did), and that if the Jacobites wished to invade England again they could always go by way of Brampton. The rival positions made complete sense only in a wider context. Lord George wished to be free of English entanglements. Prince Charles on his side had just received important dispatches from Lord George Drummond which told him for the first time of the powerful Jacobite forces that were building up in Scotland, together with regular troops and siege artillery from France. 'We hope,' wrote Sir Thomas Sheridan, 'that within a few days we shall have reduced the fortresses which are still holding out for the Elector, after which we shall pay another visit to England.'[41] Carlisle would therefore offer a convenient bridgehead to the south, or at the least remain a symbol of the Stuart claim to England – a view which seems to have been shared by the officers of the Manchester Regiment, if not by their luckless soldiers.

On 20 December the Jacobite army addressed itself to the passage of the rivers that still stood between it and Scotland. The margin was tight, for the waters were swollen by the recent days and nights of rain, and the Duke of Cumberland hoped that they would prove to be an impassable barrier, and so give him a chance even now to bring the rebels to book inside England. The heavy carts and three of the remaining 'Swedish' cannon were sent on a detour to the east to take advantage of the relatively easy crossings towards the hills. This column passed the Eden at Warwick Bridge, with the loss of a waggon which stuck fast in the ford of the Cairn stream just below the mill (the vehicle was later fished out by the miller, who was then observed to be a man of great wealth). The train then crossed the upper Esk at Canonbie or Langholm.

Prince Charles was unable to take his troops back by the way they had come. 'The River Esk being very high, and the Dumfries people having destroyed the ferry boats, he was obliged to march several miles higher than the ordinary passage before they could ford the river.'[42] The chosen spot was about 300 yards below Longtown. The banks were low, and the river only some 60 yards broad, so the passage bears little comparison to the French crossing of the Beresina in 1812, for example, but the waters were already 4 feet deep over the bed of brown rock, and were rising fast.

The army arrived from Carlisle by way of the old road which led by Arthuret. There was already talk of the river being unfordable, but Prince Charles obtained guides and sent them out to test the water on the tallest horses in the army:

> The men seeing the horses got over, though with a great deal of difficulty, cried out that they would pass it, as they did, which was one of the most extraordinary passages of a river that could be seen. The Prince stopped them, and went in himself with all the horse we had, to break the stream,

that it should not be so rapid for the foot; this was of his own motion. The foot marched in, six abreast, and in as good order as if they were marching in a field, holding one another by the collars, everybody, and everything without any loss but two women belonging to the public [i.e. camp-followers] who were drowned ... The interval between the cavalry appeared like a paved street through the river, the heads of the Highlanders being generally all that was seen above the water ... The deepness and rapidity of the river, joined to the obscurity of the night, made it most terrible; but the good Prince here in particular animated the men; and how noble it was to see these champions, who had refused him nothing, now marching breast-deep supporting one another, till wonderfully we all passed safe. The Duke of Perth here signalised himself much by his goodness; for, crossing the river several times on horseback, he betook behind him several of the common soldiers, whose strength was not sufficient to bear up against the current.[43]

Prince Charles himself made a soldier get up behind him on his horse, but the Lancastrian John Daniel was nearly drowned when he tried to save the two girls who were being swept downstream. They would not let go, and he himself would have been drowned if he had not been rescued by another rider. The pipes began to play on the far side, and the men danced reels until they were dry.[44] A couple of miles further on, the crossing of the little River Sark signified the actual return to Scotland.

The Defence of Carlisle

At 4 a.m. on 21 December the Hanoverian forces set out for Carlisle in three columns, with the infantry and artillery taking the post road in the centre, one of the cavalry columns making its way to the right by way of Armath-waite, and the other to the left by Hutton Hall.[45] At about 1 p.m. the redcoats came within sight of Carlisle, and the Duke of Cumberland sent out detach-ments to invest the town on all sides. His aide-de-camp writes that 'His Royal Highness does not think fit to summon them [to surrender], because he is for giving them no quarter, and therefore chooses to wait patiently in a vile cantonment till everything is prepared to attack 'em ... I shall not be sorry when it is over, for we are miserably off now, in worse villages than I ever saw in the mountains in Germany, but as the Duke is as ill off as other people, nobody can repine'.[46]

Events had taken an unexpected turn, for the Jacobites had withdrawn their main force out of reach but left a garrison in Carlisle, and Cumberland was now particularly glad to have received an offer from the loyal citizens of the port of Whitehaven, namely to put at his disposal ten 18-pounder cannon, twenty barrels of gunpowder and an initial 400 shot – with an unlimited quantity available upon request from a private forge near the town.[47] Cumberland had taken up the invitation, even though he had thought the rebels 'will hardly venture what may be called a garrison there, knowing it must fall into our hands without any loss'.[48]

James Ray, a Whitehaven Whig, claims that great numbers of local people arrived to help in the siege,[49] but another acount noted that 'the Duke has found such great difficulty in bringing the country folk to work, that he is almost inclined to use severities to them; his designs have been retarded by their backwardness to serve in the trenches'.[50]

Most of Cumberland's original infantry had been retained deep inside England to confront the expected French invasion. He had chased after the Jacobites with a mixed force of cavalry and mounted infantry, and the forces with him gradually built up to a strength of some 4,000 with the help of what other troops could be spared. Four regiments are known to have been on the march to the North at this time – Campbell's 21st, Sempill's 25th, and four of the 'New' regiments. One of the officers was agreeably surprised to find that the reason the Lancashire women were called 'witches' was 'by reason of their great beauty, which I think they really deserve'. On the further march into Westmorland there was nothing to be seen 'but mountains and stone walls for hedges, the country not so populous, and the Lancashire witches all lost, the women here being the most ugly I have ever seen, and the houses so desolate and solitary, that I thought I was sometimes in Flanders, sometimes on the borders of Spain … they also burn turf in this country, which makes us smell a town at a great distance'.[51]

During the enforced lull the garrison of Carlisle had time to put itself in order. All of this time the place had been held for Prince Charles by a small garrison and a governor, Captain John Hamilton of Sandstown. He had invaluable military experience, for he had served in both the Dutch and Russian armies in the 1700s, and he had maintained tight discipline in Carlisle, but he now had to share his authority with Colonel Francis Townley of the newly arrived Manchester Regiment. On 22 December the senior officers convened the first of their councils under the chairmanship of Hamilton, and established the details of the routine, each of the regiments being ordered to detach one-third of its complement to furnish the guards on the castle and the city gates, together with the intermediate patrols. Townley planted *chevaux de frise* (barricades of pointed stakes) at all the gates and entrances, and 'did all that he could in defence of his place. The garrison being in great want of provisions, he ordered a party to sally out and bring in sheep that was feeding not far off in the fields, and at the same time mounted the walls with a pistol in his hand, that if he should see the King's forces bending that way, he might give his party timely notice to retreat'.[52]

The Jacobite artillery defence was concentrated in the castle, where they had a four-gun battery at the north-western angle of the outer castle yard, and another battery of four guns at the southern end of the yard's western face; the fire was supplemented by two 4-pounders which were installed on the wall of the inner castle yard just north of Haschenperg's roundel, while a further battery of eight guns lined the north-eastern wall of the inner castle yard facing Stanwix Bank.

John Burnet of Campsfield fired the first cannon shot at the Hanoverians, and the Duke of Cumberland had to admit that 'they endeavour to appear resolute, and have fired their cannon upon everybody who has shown himself'.[53] By the evening of 27 December the Jacobites had still failed to kill a single man by their eight-gun battery facing towards Stanwix Bank, and very few by the cannon elsewhere on the walls. A Whig gentleman wrote on that day that 'these balls I am apt to think from what happened yesterday, are thrown too high; for as I was riding towards Rickerby, a village pretty much exposed to Carlisle, a ball whistled over my head; this action occasioned me to enquire at Rickerby, and likewise at Stanwix, what had been the effect of their batteries, everyone assuring me nothing at all ... were not their gunners execrably bad, I don't see how they could avoid dislodging our men both at Stanwix and Newtown'.[54]

The initial instalment of six cannon for the besiegers arrived from Whitehaven on 26 December, drawn by horses from the estate of Lord Lonsdale, and by some less impressive nags which had been furnished by the country people. It was turning out just as Lord George Murray had feared, and the guns were formidable 18-pounders, which were among the heaviest pieces employed by either side during the whole rising. The cannon were assigned to a battery which was being built on Primrose Bank, an elevated pasture 400 yards from the north-western end of the city wall, while a party of Dutch bombardiers from Wade's army moved into position near the foot of Stanwix Bank with some light coehorn mortars.

At about 8 a.m. on 28 December the cannon opened fire against the Jacobite four-gun battery on the north-western angle of the castle yard wall, and the two-gun battery mounted in the keep behind. Our gentleman noted that the Jacobites recovered from their initial surprise, and at first their fire from the town considerably exceeded ours, owing perhaps to the smallness of their pieces in proportion to the Duke's, but at twelve they failed prodigiously, some of their guns being dismounted. General Bligh said in my hearing he saw one fly from their battery, and others declare that the slackness of their fire ... proves that three guns of the four-gun battery were absolutely silenced. I was near enough to observe several balls strike the walls, and likewise to discover a small breach which the soldiers love to magnify, affecting to be seven yards wide. The soldiers are all in good spirits, and have only lost one gunner, not another.[55]

In the succeeding darkness the Dutch bombardiers lobbed coehorn shells into the castle, so that altogether more than eleven hundred cannon shot and shell were fired by the besiegers in the course of that day.[56] It would have required 24-pounder cannon to breach the ramparts of a proper fortress, but the 18-pounders with Cumberland were more than enough to dominate the light cannon of the defenders, burst through the parapets, and begin to breach the old walls, as the soldiers had detected. One of the shot ricocheted off the north-west angle of the wall of the outer castle yard, and

Carlisle under siege

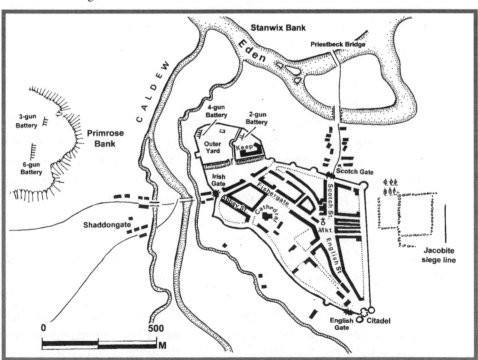

still had the force to strike in succession the two abutments of the distant Priestbeck Bridge.

The Jacobite council met had met at 4 p.m. in an atmosphere of crisis. Colonel Townley proposed to set up scaffolding behind the targeted sector of the wall, so that the defenders would have somewhere to stand, and be able to use the body of the wall as protection instead of the vanishing parapet. Captain Burnet objected that the necessary labour was not at hand, and that the 5-foot-thick wall would still offer no real cover, and the troops would suffer unnecessary casualties without being able to hit back, because the cannon could not be mounted on Townley's scaffolding. The council settled on a compromise whereby ladders would be brought up from the castle stores and set up behind the city wall, so that sentries could at least keep the besiegers under observation.

The fire of the besiegers abated considerably on 29 December, for they were running short of cannon shot, and a replenishment did not arrive until the following night, carried on horses organized by the Whitehaven volunteer James Ray. The garrison was able to use the time to undertake some repairs, and to demand the withdrawal of the Dutch, who had come from the surrendered garrison of Tournai; according to the terms of that capitulation, therefore, they could not be used against troops in the French service (like the Irish officers in Carlisle). On that point alone Cumberland was willing to give way, and the Duke of Richmond commented that the episode showed 'how useless these damned Dutch troops are; I actually think they should not be paid, but transport themselves home again; for it will be very odd to pay troops that we know will not fight for us'.[57]

The defence was nearing its end. Two great rents showed in the north-western city walls, and an ominous crack opened in the wall of the castle itself; some of the Hanoverian artillery officers were convinced that three of the cannon shots fired from the castle that day were blank rounds, which suggested that the defenders were low on ammunition.

At the garrison's daily council meeting Townley was in favour of retiring to the castle for a last-ditch stand. Captain George Abernethy, the next to speak, argued that 'the thing was impracticable both on account of the badness of our men, the want of arms, and no relief to be expected from the army'; the garrison should therefore seek terms as soon as the crack in the castle wall opened into a proper breach (which, by the conventions of the time, would show that a continued defence by the Jacobites was impossible). Abernethy was still farther of this opinion considering that yesterday, after Captain Burnet of the artillery stood on one of the batteries in order to fire upon the enemy, and was deserted by his gunners and matrosses [artillery assistants] on account of the enemy's fire, and that in the evening of the same day, when I and several officers commanding detachments in the garrison went to order our men upon the walls to oppose the enemy, who had approached so near the foot of the wall that they were firing with small arms upon the French gunners, neither he nor any of his officers could get a single man to go with them, and on this day, when planted on the wall, several of the sentries came off their post on account of the enemy's fire.[58]

The great majority of the officers agreed with Captain Abernethy, but no firm resolution was reached before the Hanoverians decided the matter for them. On the morning of 30 December the Duke of Richmond was writing to London that the defenders 'want extremely to capitulate, but to be sure the Duke cannot treat with them, yet if they put out the white flag I really can't see how he can put them to the sword after it. Though to be sure they ought all to be hanged ... P.S. The rebels have just hung out the white flag'.[59]

What had happened was that the Jacobites had sought to capitulate immediately the original six-gun battery reopened fire. Cumberland sent word that all the terms he would grant were 'that they shall not be put to the sword, but be reserved for the King's pleasure'. Everyone familiar with the language used on such occasions knew that this signified that the garrison would not be massacred on the spot (much to Cumberland's frustration), but still subject to every punishment up to and including death thereafter.

The officers of the garrison were consigned to the city gaol and the other ranks penned up in the cathedral without any provision made for water, food or sanitation. The men would have died of thirst if they had not broken open an ancient well in the building, and they had nothing to eat until one small biscuit per man was issued on 4 January. Major General Howard reported two days later that the city fathers had refused to give the prisoners bread, and had given way only after he had promised that the government would compensate them. By that time four or five out of the 349 prisoners in the cathedral had died, and more would follow if they were not removed.[60] On the 10th the men left under the escort of Mark Kerr's Dragoons, and more than eighty died in a further period of confinement in Lancaster Castle, where their food was rotten offal. The fate of most of the survivors was to be transported or hanged.

Carlisle set about cleaning and washing its cathedral, but this proved 'of very little use, for the flags being old, spongy and ill-laid, the earth under them is corrupted, and till it is removed the Cathedral Church will not be sweet, nor will it be safe to have service in it'.[61] The first service was held in February, after much burning of sulphur and tar.

The Jacobite North Country after the Retreat

The Duke of Cumberland was determined to take his revenge on Carlisle for having surrendered to the Jacobites on 15 November and its equivocal conduct thereafter. He actually put in a claim for the church bells (an ancient perquisite for the artillery after an enemy town was taken by storm) and he encouraged the 'puppies' among his officers to ill-treat the citizens. Nothing more was heard of the demand for the bells, but the duke instituted a campaign of persecution against individuals. The mayor, the town clerk and other leading citizens were placed under arrest, and there was a purge of one of the humbler families, the Hewitts. On 13 January James Hewitt writes of his father as being imprisoned for having acted as postmaster for the Jacobites, albeit under duress, and adds, 'I am so much afraid that our troubles are only beginning, for with confinement and our father's unreasonable fretting I fear it will bring some illness up him; at this time his legs swell to such a degree that he is scarcely able to walk over the floor'.[62] A little later four more of the Hewitts were behind bars, along with James himself. He was accused of having gone to fetch the Jacobite baggage from Lockerbie, and he protested in vain that he had gone about armed with a pistol only 'for fear of the Highlanders' cruelty and displeasure'.[63]

The treatment of one Major Farrer, a recently retired officer of dragoons who had given long service to the Crown, 'made great noise in the country', his cause being taken up by Lord Lonsdale. Farrer protested that during the original defence against the Jacobites 'for seven days and nights I never pulled off my clothes, and visited the walls and spent in treating the men a great deal of money'. After having had a bad time under the rebel occupation it was now hurtful to be so appallingly used by Cumberland's soldiers in 'breaking down upon me doors and windows, and plundering my house the first night and carrying away above £300 in goods and things of value, which we miss every day more and more, and using my wife ill by dragging her out of the house above five hundred yards in only a petticoat and without shoes, and myself and three daughters in only petticoats barefoot and bare-legged, myself in only my breeches barelegged and without shoes'. After this visitation Farrer had thirty dragoons and forty-two infantrymen billeted upon him, and the troops helped themselves to 140 cartloads of hay from his barn, leaving it empty.[64]

Elsewhere in the north country the genuine Jacobites refused to be intimidated, even though the Duke of Cumberland had retaken all of England for the king, his father. The city of York had been polarized throughout the rising, and on the night of 11 December a symbolic shot was fired at the soldiers guarding the Michelgate Bar, the bullet passing between two of the men and clipping the wig of a third. The first two believed that the shot came from the area of the house of the notorious Jacobite Mr Selby, and the third thought he saw a flash from one of Selby's windows. The wad in any case fell into the middle of the street in front of Selby's house. The magistrate Dr Jacques Sterne, a sworn enemy of the local Jacobites, protested to the Duke of Newcastle that the city recorder had refused to take any action: 'My Lord, if the Papists and some of the magistrates go on in the manner they have done, it will not be safe for the King's friends and good subjects to walk in the streets without a guard'.[65] It came to nothing, for the Lord Mayor of York reported to London that there was no foundation in the charges, and the guard on Selby's house was therefore stood down.[66] Trouble on a much greater scale was brewing in the far north-east, however, where the Northumberland Jacobites had designs on the town of Newcastle (p. 72).

When the Duke of Cumberland was pursuing the Jacobite army on 12 December he had bypassed Manchester to the west, and the leading people tried to convince the government that 'it was to the mortification of the people of that town that he did not honour them with his presence as he went to Lancaster'.[67] It is possible to read into this plea both an anxiety on the part of the Whigs to distance themselves from their Jacobite neighbours, and fears for their safety at the hands of the same people, Manchester being another of the faction-ridden towns. After Carlisle was taken, 'the King's friends in Manchester' specified the misdeeds of the Jacobites in the captured garrison, and begged humbly 'that His Majesty would be graciously pleased to order the heads of the rebels as mentioned … be fixed up in the most public places in Manchester'.[68]

a Penicuik volunteer

CHAPTER 13

Meanwhile, in Scotland ...

HISTORICAL EPISODES HAVE A WAY of compressing themselves in the imagination. Just as we are tempted to make a leap from Culloden to the Highland Clearances, so it is natural to pass directly from the Jacobite army's about-turn at Derby to the final battle at Culloden – the two events are connected, but a great deal was going on in the meantime, much of it concerning happenings in Scotland when the Prince was still south of the border. Probably the best way to make sense of a complicated state of affairs is to identify the main groupings of the rival forces. There were three on the Hanoverian side – the Central Lowlands between Edinburgh and Glasgow, the territory of the Campbells in the south-west, and the area around Inverness in the north-east. In contrast there was a single area of Jacobite predominance, along the eastern coastlands from the Firth of Tay to the Moray Firth.

Hanoverian Scotland

From the map Field Marshal Wade's forces on the north-eastern Borders would seem to have been well placed to pounce on Edinburgh after Prince Charles abandoned the city, and swung towards England by a westerly path.

A Penicuik Volunteer

However, Lieutenant General Roger Handasyde, who commanded the forward concentration at Berwick, took a long time to convince himself that the way was clear, and not until 12 November did he set out with Price's and Ligonier's regiments of foot, and the remains of Cope's two regiments of dragoons – the 13th (the late Gardiner's) and Hamilton's 14th. Handasyde reached Edinburgh on 14 November after just two days of hard marching through wintry weather. The task facing him would have been much more difficult if two strongpoints had not been held by Hanoverian forces throughout. 'The King owes the safety of this part of the Kingdom to the two castles of Edinburgh and Stirling, and the governors ... should not be forgot.'[1]

The regular forces were supplemented by 180 men recruited in Paisley and Renfrew, and on 30 November Handasyde dispatched a consignment of muskets to arm the volunteers in nearby Glasgow. Over the next nine days 600 Glaswegians enlisted, and on 10 December the Earl of Home marched the new Glasgow Regiment to the main concentration of force at Edinburgh, where the priorities seemed to be 'to relieve our prisoners at Perth, before they can be put out of our power ... To prevent any more rebels from passing the Forth; to free the counties of Angus, Perth, Fife etc. from the great oppressions they now labour under'.[2] Altogether the mobile forces available to the Hanoverians in the Central Lowlands stood at about 2,100 men.

The 3rd Duke of Argyll had gone to London. For a time the security of south-west Scotland therefore lay in the hands of the able Lieutenant Colonel John Campbell of the 64th Highlanders, who was succeeded in overall command on 22 December by his father, Major General John Campbell of Mamore. Their forces at this period comprised a company of the Black Watch (the 43rd), sent by Cope, and three new Independent Companies, who could call on the services of the Argyll tenants, and were supported by a constellation of strongpoints (pp. 559–63).

The Campbells kept a close watch on those known to be on their way to join the Jacobite army, but there was only one armed clash before the end of the year, occasioned by a party of the Glengyle's MacGregors, who penetrated between Loch Fyne and Loch Goil to support some of their friends in the south. On 10 November, on their return journey, they had been ambushed in a pass by Lieutenant Colonel John Campbell and lost eighteen of their men as prisoners.[3]

There was no permanent contact between the Hanoverian forces in the Central Highlands and the Campbells, and none between either grouping and the troops that were being built up around Inverness by Duncan Forbes

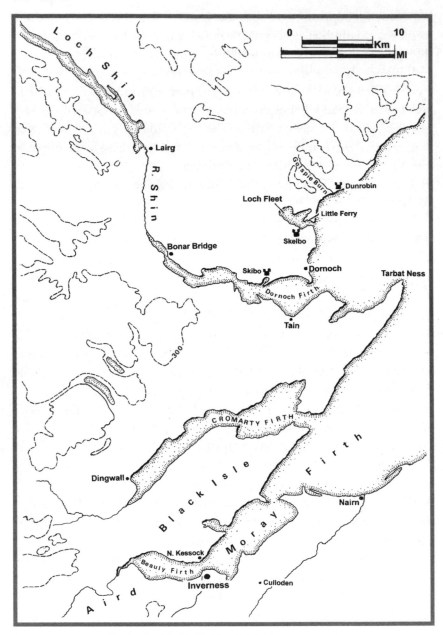

Operations in north-east Scotland, 1745 and 1746

(Lord President of the Court of Session) and by Cope's former adjutant general – yet another John Campbell, more usefully known as the Earl of Loudoun, who arrived to take command on 11 October 1745. When Cope had marched from Inverness on 4 September he had left behind some weak companies of the 43rd (Black Watch) and 64th Highlanders who, supplemented by men raised from the loyal northern clans, by February 1746 ultimately made up eighteen fully recruited Independent Companies.

The important thing about the troops at Inverness was not what they did (which never amounted to very much), but where they were. They impeded the movement and recruiting of the Jacobite Highlanders,[4] and they encouraged noblemen as far distant as the Earl of Sutherland and the Skye chieftains Sir Alexander MacDonald of Sleat and Norman MacLeod of Dunvegan to raise their clansmen in the governmental interest.

The Jacobite East

When we turn to the Jacobites, we find that they devoted their efforts almost entirely to consolidating their rule and building up their forces along the eastern coastlands. Here they brought together the men of the sympathetic eastern and western clans, recruited the Lowland regiments of Lord Lewis Gordon and Ogilvy, and in the course of October received the first of a series of shipments from France, which brought help in the shape of muskets by the thousand, the equivalent of £5,000 sterling in gold, and a train of six 'Swedish' cannon and the accompanying French gunners (p. 366).

The muskets were entrusted to the care of the uncommonly determined Lord Lewis Gordon, the younger brother of the Whiggish Duke of Gordon and an ex-officer of the Royal Navy, who took charge of them at Brechin, inland from Montrose, and set about distributing them where they were the most needed.[5]

The artillery train was ferried across the Forth downstream from Stirling at Alloa, and reached Edinburgh on 30 October with an escort of 600 Atholl men (p. 206). This was the last reinforcement from the north to have reached Prince Charles before he set out for England. His troops took the road on 1 November, and from then until well into January the army under the Prince and the Jacobite forces in Scotland may be regarded as entirely separate entities. By 4 November the cannon guarding the passage at Alloa had been removed to the Castle of Doune, the only outpost remaining to the Jacobites in the Central Lowlands and one which enabled them to use the passage of the upper Forth at the Fords of Frew.[6] Prince Charles appointed

John MacGregor of Glengyle as governor, with a standing garrison of sixty men (p. 210).

Altogether more substantial shipments were sent from France in the course of November (p. 366). Some got into Montrose on 24 November, 'protected by a violent but rather useful storm'.[7] Other vessels reached Stonehaven and Peterhead, and helped to bring the accession of regular forces to a total of some 800 men (mostly Royal Ecossais, together with three picquets from the Irish regiments of Dillon, Lally and Roth) and the train of six heavy pieces (two 18-pounders, two 12-pounders and two 9-pounders).

Lord John Drummond (colonel of Royal Ecossais) was a tall, sunburned and more obviously soldierly individual than his elder brother, the under-estimated Duke of Perth. Harsh and imperious, Drummond believed that he had come as the saviour of Scotland and went without delay to the town of Perth, the headquarters of Lord Strathallan, whom Prince Charles had left in charge of affairs north of the Forth. Lord Strathallan, at least by Drummond's account, was then shut up in a tiny corner of Scotland with just 1,500 men. Drummond claims that he took over the direction from Strathallan in response to a general demand, and 'by dint of sending out letters, some of them enticing, others threatening ... I prevailed upon a number of considerable persons to join me, and others just to send their men ... It was by no means easy to bring around people of such diverse mentalities, for, depending on the case, too little or too much severity would have been equally harmful'. He was at the same time recruiting for the second battalion of his own regiment, the blue-bonneted Royal Ecossais, and by force of necessity had to give the command of the companies to 'men of influence in the locality'. By 12 December he reckoned that 'our army amounts to 6,000 excellent men, and the numbers are growing daily'.[8] A Hanoverian commentator claims that 'this desperado' had 'sent his men through the country, with lighted faggots in their hands, who called at gentlemen's and farmers' houses, inquiring how many men servants they had; and if they did not immediately send out whatever number they demanded, they set fire to their houses'.[9]

The Jacobites at the same time set up a complete alternative administration in their eastern realm. Lord Lewis Gordon was appointed Lord Lieutenant of the shires of Aberdeen and Banff, and he in turn made William Moir of Lonmay Deputy Governor of Old and New Aberdeen, and Baird of Auchmeeden Deputy Governor of Banff. Up in this north-eastern corner of Scotland the little ports of Fraserburgh, Peterhead and Stonehaven could be counted as reliably Jacobite. The temper of Aberdeen was uncertain. The

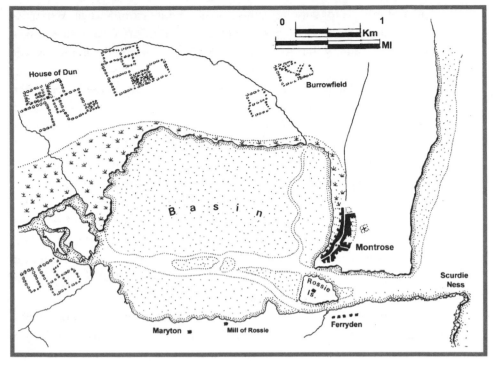

Montrose

local credit of the 4th Laird of Stoneywood helped to recruit a large contingent for the Regiment of Lewis Gordon, and afterwards it transpired that 'while the rebels were here Alexander Bannerman, merchant in Aberdeen, was very active in assisting them in everything, and particularly went express himself both to Montrose and Stonehaven and assisted in getting the French landed, and was active in going about the country getting horses for them to carry off their ammunition when landed, and kept close company with the French and other rebel officers, and was always looked upon in this place as inclined that way'.[10]

Old Aberdeen was nevertheless hostile, and when a Dutch merchant ship ran aground on the sands William Moir could not immediately set out for the rescue, for he could not risk dividing his troops. Lord Lewis Gordon sent reinforcements, and on 27 November Moir rendered thanks, for 'we are now out of hazard from mobs, and are going on successfully with the taxation of the town, and I reckon it will be wholly paid up in a day or two. We are to begin tomorrow to send out greater parties on the shire'.[11]

Further south Montrose was of the first importance to the cause of the Prince, for he had a large and active following there and it was the main port of ingress for supplies and reinforcements from France. When the Hanoverians eventually repossessed the place they drew up parallel lists of informants, and of thirty-one prominent Jacobites who came under investigation. The suspects included David Carnegie, the Laird of Craigo, the town clerk John Spence and John Scott as the Substitute Lord Lieutenant. Cummings, the Collector of Customs, had the distinction of figuring in both lists, because 'tho' a rogue, he may yet be useful'.[12] Local Whigs protested in vain that he had been hand in glove with the Jacobites and the French.[13]

Dundee on the Firth of Tay was in the charge of Mr David Fotheringham, who did not have the easiest of tasks in a place where allegiances were very difficult to pin down. It had been sacked by the troops of the Marquis of Montrose in the 1640s, which inclined it against the Stuarts, and in the first half of the eighteenth century its loyalties were divided. At the time of the '45 the hinterland was under the sway of Jacobite gentry, who had houses and interests in town, while Sir James Kinloch collected taxes in the neighbourhood and recruited for Ogilvy's Regiment.

None of this impressed the Presbyterian clergy or the recalcitrant council, and on 30 October (the king's birthday) a riot ensued. When order was reimposed the Jacobites took care to keep the town under the guard of the second (Kinloch's) battalion of the regiment. The battalion had an important role in assisting the landings of troops and equipment from France, and in honour of the disembarkations at Montrose in 25 November 'it was proclaimed that every house should testify their joy by illuminating their windows, or be subject to a fine of £20 Scots, a notable way of pointing out to the Highland executioners the families who would not rejoice on this event. The Presbyterian ministers, it seems, could not on that point temporise with them; the effect was like to be unhappy, their windows were broke, and at last they fired sharp shots into their houses'.[14]

A short distance up the River Tay the town of Perth stood at the junction of important roads from the Highlands and the Episcopalian eastern coastlands, and served as the Jacobite forward base. The local population was divided in much the same way as in Dundee, and the royal birthday was the signal for malcontents to flock into Perth and ring the church bells, in defiance of the Deputy Governor, Lawrence Oliphant of Gask the Elder. Oliphant ordered the patriots to desist, but they answered '"that they would continue ringing till ten at night", and in the evening there were bonfires in the streets, and the windows were illuminated. Such as refused to illuminate their houses had their windows broke'.[15]

Oliphant feared for the safety of the ammunition and 400 French muskets which had arrived from France and were now stored in the Town House, and between 9 p.m. and 10 p.m. he sent fifteen armed men to disperse the mob by firing at them. A number of the rioters were killed or injured, but the Whigs returned in force, disarmed the fifteen men and beat them up, and besieged the Jacobites in the Town House. However, Oliphant contrived to send word to Margaret, the Dowager Lady Nairne, who resided nearby, and who was of the typically formidable style of Jacobite old ladies. She conscripted a number of her servants and tenants and sent them to the Five-Mile House, where they found Lady Margaret's three daughters and a daughter-in-law, who 'put white cockades into the bonnets of such of the tenants who would allow them to do so'.[16]

A mysterious Frenchman issued the men with muskets, and they made their way to the Town House, where the defenders had meanwhile received a message, seemingly from the Dissenting Minister, offering them protection if they would lay down their arms, 'but the whole body of gentlemen thought the arms was the best protection they could get, and afterwards at about twelve o'clock at night there came again a body of men down the streets in purpose to attack them, upon which the guard fired on them, and the mob continued firing at the windows but did no execution, excepting the killing of Captain O'Gallon a Frenchman who was shot through the head'.[17] The mob drew back, and Lady Nairne's people helped the defenders to stand guard the next day.

The violence on 30 October was at least in part the work of outsiders. Something of the nature of Jacobitism in Perth itself came to light in February 1746, when the provisional Whig administration cited more than thirty Jacobite activists. The spread of occupations resembled that of the Manchester Jacobites rather than that of the seaport town of Montrose, for it included six merchants, one lawyer, two fully fledged surgeons, one barber-surgeon, three glovers and six or seven journeyman craftsmen. The investigators singled out the vintner John Hickson, who had gone forth as a spy (and turned king's evidence), John Carmichael of Baglie and John Balfour, who had taken the lead in collecting the town's Cess, Sir John Wedderburn, who had gathered in the Excise, and seven individuals who had worked in the civil administration and acted as 'tools of oppression to the rebel governors of Perth'. Others included one who had stored requisitioned oatmeal, another who had acted as postmaster to the rebels, and procured them horses and weapons. Among the professional men the writer (lawyer) John Rutherford 'threw off the hats and insulted some of the inhabitants in the open streets, for not bowing to the Pretender as he passed out of Perth 11th September

1745', and the surgeons James Smith and George Stirling, committed Jacobites, having both been 'out' in 1715, attended the Prince when he was in Perth, consorted constantly with lords Strathallan and Oliphant of Gask, and helped to put down the riot of 30 October.[18]

The Action at Inverurie, 23 December 1745

Active operations between the rival forces were on the smallest possible scale, and tinged with farce. The hinterland of Loudoun's concentration at Inverness was the home of the Frasers and their wily and semi-criminal chief Simon Fraser, Lord Lovat. He for a long time held back from committing himself, but he commissioned one of his leading clansmen, James Fraser of Foyers, to kidnap Duncan Forbes of Culloden, the soul of the Hanoverian cause in the northeast. On the night of 15/16 October 1745,[19] some 200 of the Stratherrick Frasers duly approached the battlemented Culloden House, but scampered off as soon as they came under fire. Having every reason to suspect the loyalty of Simon Fraser, Loudoun mounted a little expedition to Castle Downie in Stratherrick on 11 December, and brought the protesting clan chief back prisoner to Inverness, 'after abundance of shilly shollie stuff'.[20] Lovat escaped on the night of 19 December, being carried to freedom on the back of a servant.

The foray to Stratherrick was a diversion of effort from what was, in concept at least, the far grander enterprise of recovering the shires of Aberdeen and Banff from the Jacobites, and eliminating their base at Aberdeen. For this purpose Norman MacLeod of Dunvegan led five of the newly formed Independent Companies of the Skye MacLeods from Inverness, and marched by way of Fochabers (15 December) and Oldmeldrum (20 December) without encountering any opposition. He became understandably cautious when he learned that regular troops from France were at hand to bolster the Jacobites, and was glad to meet two Independent Companies of the Munros under a professional soldier, Captain George Munro of Culcairn. However, no more reinforcements were forthcoming, and Jacobite parties dominated the hinterland of Aberdeen from Kintore to Inverurie.

In this state of uncertainty MacLeod and Culcairn distributed their troops in billets in and around the string of houses which made up Inverurie. The little place lay in the angle between two waters, the River Don, which ran to the south, and its tributary the Urie, flowing about 500 yards to the east. The total force numbered about 700 men, of whom 400 of so (four of MacLeod's companies) were available for action at short notice, all the rest being scattered in farmhouses to the west.

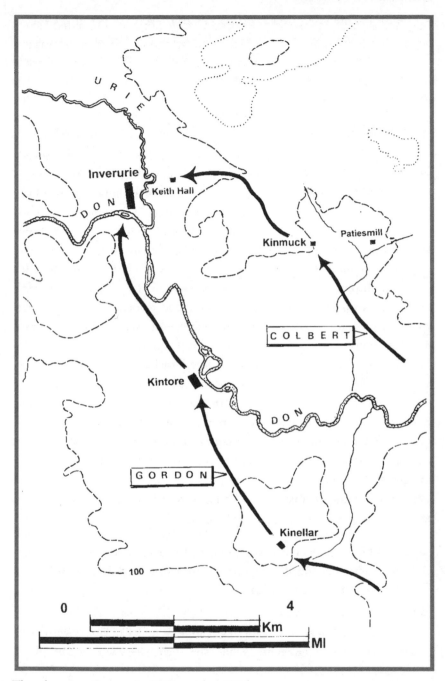

The advance on Inverurie, 23 December 1745

Blind and immobile, MacLeod and Culcairn were dangerously close (at 15 miles) to Aberdeen, where Lord Lewis Gordon 'took all proper measures, and provided so well to give them a warm reception if they should attack either by the Bridge of Don or the Kintore road, or by both, disposing his men so that, wherever the attack should be made, the different posts might be conveniently supported one from another'.[21]

On the Jacobite side, on 22 December Captain Alexander White and Lieutenant Robert Sinclair left their base at Aberdeen to reconnoitre the quarters of the MacLeods at Inverurie, and on their way back to Kintore they took into custody the Aberdeen lawyer John Bartlett, who had been travelling to Inverurie to act as a guide to the MacLeods. Captain White returned to Aberdeen with Bartlett and a number of further people who had been taken on the road, while Sinclair continued the reconnaissance.

In the evening of the 22nd Lord Lewis learned from Captain White that the enemy had not moved from Inverurie, while a letter of Loudoun's, intercepted at Turriff, told him that Loudoun was too preoccupied with the hunt for Lord Lovat to be able to send any help to the MacLeods. Lord Lewis resolved to go over to the attack.

The force consisted of some 1,400 men, mainly Lowlanders, together with two companies of the regulars of the Royal Ecossais. The expedition set out at 9 a.m. on 23 December. 'As they had all along guarded the avenues from the town very carefully, they did it now so effectually that there was no possibility of sending any intelligence of their march ... While they were marching they all along kept advance parties before their main bodies came in sight, so that when they were observed, these parties prevented any persons getting past with information.'[22] The Jacobites had devised a two-pronged attack:

❖ The left-hand column, under Major John (?) Gordon, an officer of Royal Ecossais, was to advance directly along the main road, ford the Don and come at the place from the south

❖ Major Lancelot Colbert (another officer of Royal Ecossais) commanded the right-hand column, which was to set out from Bridge of Don downstream, continue on the left bank of the Don, then swing back, and ford the Urie to attack the village from the east.

The whole stood under the command of Lord Lewis Gordon, who accompanied the right-hand column, but as an ex-naval officer he deferred in matters of execution to Gordon and Colbert.

The left-hand or western column comprised the 300 men of John Gordon of Avochie's Strathbogie battalion of Lord Lewis Gordon's Regiment, and the 200 of Sir James Kinloch's battalion of Ogilvy's Regiment. They had much less far to go than the right-hand column, and so they bided their time out of sight in the church and churchyard of Kinellar about 6 miles from Inverurie, and sent an advance party to lie in wait in a number of houses along a low-lying stretch of the road near Kintore. The Presbyterian minister of Kintore walked along the road to investigate what was going on. He could see nothing, but on his return journey he was taken into care when the Jacobites emerged from the houses. Major Gordon resumed the march when he judged that the other column must be well on its way.

The right-hand or eastern column was made up of the 200 men of Monaltrie's battalion, the further 200 of Stoneywood's battalion, 200 assorted volunteers in two parties, and, crucially, two companies of Royal Ecossais. The force actually got to its forming-up point ahead of time, and a number of men took the opportunity to view the prospect of Inverurie from the higher ground of the Earl of Kintore's plantation (in the neighbourhood of

Inverurie, 23 December 1745

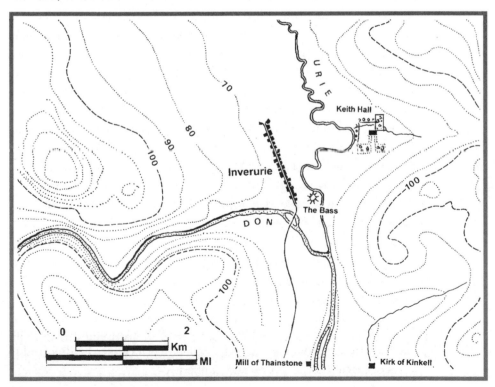

Keith Hall). They were spotted from the village, and MacLeod and Culcairn were duly informed, but neither sent anyone to investigate.

The Jacobites advanced to their respective fords one hour after sunset on the moonlit night of 23 December. We first take up the story of the right-hand or western column. Colbert directed the advance over the mill dam at Mill of Keith, and in the process captured an outpost in full view of the amazed MacLeods on the far side of the Urie. Norman MacLeod and Culcairn were dining with some Presbyterian ministers at the time but they at once organized counter-measures. Colbert made for the only available ford, the exit of which lay hard under the Bass, a steep-sided mound of a vanished Norman castle, which lay close by a walled churchyard. The regulars of Royal Ecossais marched resolutely to the crossing, 'but many of the common men ran off and skulked'.[23]

Pundits claimed afterwards that the MacLeods should have concentrated against one or another of the Jacobite columns – preferably by anchoring themselves on the churchyard and the Bass, which commanded the ford over the Urie and from where it would have been difficult to dislodge them, for the only Jacobite artillery was made up of two rusty old ship's cannon which were lagging far behind.[24] There were shots fired at the Jacobites when they were passing the ford, but they brought down just one man. Arrived on the far side, Colbert arrayed his force with Royal Ecossais on the right, Monaltrie's battalion on the left, and Stoneywood's battalion and the volunteers in the centre. A well-informed Jacobite gives credit to the MacLeods for now being 'very well posted, with a dyke on their right, the Urie on their left, and the town in their rear'. However, they were fatally disadvantaged by having the Jacobite left-hand column coming at them across the Don, and their leaders had not set them the best of examples. 'A little after the engagement began, the lairds of MacLeod and Culcairn (according to the report of prisoners), having scarce a sergeant's command keeping together, given secret order to some of their officers to retreat if they were attacked, privately left their men, and sent off the military chest with the money. But MacLeod, who had not time to bridle his horse, his men flying and so hotly pursued into the town by the whole of Lord Lewis's army, was obliged to ride off with a halter on his horse's head instead of a bridle.'[25]

The Royal Ecossais advanced up Inverurie, keeping up a regular 'street fire' by rotating their successive platoons around the head of the column. They had been rejoined by their 'skulking' companions, but one of their senior officers (probably Colbert) conceded that the MacLeods had fought 'more like regular troops than militia, and that were it not for the few

Irishes [i.e. Royal Ecossais] he commanded, the rebels would not have stood the second fire'.[26]

The action ended with the MacLeods and Munros fleeing over the stubble fields to the north of Inverurie. They turned about and fired just once, upon the false report that Norman MacLeod had fallen into the hands of the enemy, but they then resumed their flight, accompanied by the men who had been billeted in the distant farmhouses. The Jacobite forces were unable to catch up, 'but seeing a ridge with a few furrows in it, amidst a great deal of unploughed stubble ground, and taking it in the moonlight for a row of men, they fired once or twice into it very successfully'.[27]

Nine of the Jacobites had been killed, mostly from the Royal Ecossais. Some twenty men were wounded on each side, and the Jacobites took about sixty prisoners, including the highly significant figure of Donald Ban MacCrimmon, who was hereditary piper to the MacLeods of Dunvegan, and indeed the most famous piper in the whole of Scotland. He was released on parole, which he broke, and survived to be killed at the Rout of Moy on 16 February 1746. It was impossible to establish the number of MacLeod and Munro dead because a sympathizer had flung a number of bodies into the river to prevent them being counted by the Jacobites.

On 24 December John Innes and the other Jacobites of the little town of Turriff tried to capture some of the fleeing officers, who had taken refuge in the house of the Collector of Excise, John Urquhart. They were thwarted by Urquhart and his wife, who refused to admit them. The Jacobites then took it into their heads to seize the town drum, which was in the keeping of the brewer Alexander Panton. His wife heard of what was afoot, and was able to conceal the instrument by covering it with a cloth and hiding it under a bed. When it was all over Brewer Panton explained that 'John Innes's design was not against the MacLeods, but against Captain Munro of Culcairn, he having done something to his father in the year 1715, which he was now to resent'.[28]

Inverurie was one of those little actions which were much more important than their scale suggests. The Independent Companies did not draw breath until they were over the Spey. Loudoun now abandoned the shires of Aberdeen and Banff entirely to the Jacobites, no longer daring to venture far from his base at Inverness, while Lord Lewis Gordon was now free to move all but two of his battalions south to reinforce Lord John Drummond. A volunteer with Prince Charles observed that the episode had turned out 'very luckily for us; for if Loudoun had not met with a check, he would probably have been able to collect a strong army to cut off our retreat, or at least give us a warm reception on our return to Scotland. This news therefore gave us great comfort'.[29]

Everything else which has been reviewed over the last few pages took place without the slightest reference to the Jacobite army that had invaded England. As early as 21 November Lord Strathallan had written that the Hanoverian forces based at Edinburgh had interrupted all communications, and that nothing had been heard from Prince Charles since the time he had marched south from Carlisle.[30] The perspectives of his self-appointed successor, Lord Drummond, were entirely Scottish, as emerged in a detailed report to Paris which he compiled on 12 December. He made only passing allusions to Prince Charles, who was said to be continuing his march on London 'with sublime courage and skill'. Drummond now intended to force the passage of the Forth, capture the castles of Stirling and Edinburgh and 'regain possession of the whole of Scotland'.

Otherwise Lord Drummond had his eyes on the capture of Inverness, which would reopen the communication with the Highlands,

> where there are four or five thousand men just waiting for the opportunity to take up arms and join us. For that reason I proposed to send a large detachment to the north with four cannon to take the Castle of Inverness and facilitate the junction with our forces up there, but some of the leaders of our army failed to agree, claiming that the only thing that mattered was to go and join the Prince in England. They did not consider that a march of this kind is totally impossible; besides, we could not do it without abandoning the cannon [i.e. the six heavy pieces landed in November] and the ammunition which the King of France sent them, which I could not do without an order from the King or the Prince. This reasoning made them consent to the siege of Stirling, though affairs would have been on a much better foundation if we had begun by laying siege to Inverness.[31]

CHAPTER 14

The Elements: The Seas and the Skies

The Seas

THE CONTESTS IN THE HINTERLAND of Aberdeen and Inverness
had already shown how much the control of the ports of north-eastern
Scotland was to become the issue on which the outcome of the whole Jacobite
enterprise depended. The north-western coasts and islands also feature
throughout the rising from the time Prince Charles first set foot on Eriskay.
By December 1745 the grand strategy of the Jacobites and the French –
improvised as it might have been – turned on placing the centre of Hanoverian power under two threats: first, that of the army of Prince Charles from the
north, and second, an army of the French poised to invade south-east
England. All of this underlines the influence of the maritime setting.

North-Western Seas

On 29 November 1745 a naval tender from Liverpool reached the Campbell
capital of Inverary with a much-needed cargo of arms and ammunition. The
20-gun *Greyhound* arrived at the same place on 21 December, having sailed

A Volunteer farmer, with fowling-piece

from Spithead (the roadstead of Portsmouth) with more weapons, a supply of cash, and Major General John Campbell of Mamore. *Greyhound* had stopped on the way in Carrickfergus Loch, and her voyage underlined how convenient it was for the Royal Navy to be able to 'stage' its operations by way of convenient and friendly ports or anchorages. The three major ports of north-west Britain – Liverpool, Whitehaven and Glasgow – had all done well out of the Union and the burgeoning trade with America, and their Whiggish sympathies were thereby confirmed.

Liverpool now resumed its Cromwellian role of logistic support, while Whitehaven amongst other services supplied the battering cannon and gunpowder with which the Duke of Cumberland reduced Carlisle. On the south-western Scottish mainland the Firth of Clyde offered the new Port Glasgow, Greenock, and the facilities of Dumbarton Castle as a secure repository for prisoners and military stores. All the time Irish meal was being brought in by way of Belfast.

The long, north-east-trending sea lochs of the Scottish West gave access to operational bridgeheads whose influence might extend deep into the hinterland. One such bridgehead was the foundation of Campbell power at Inverary towards the head of Loch Fyne, which could be reached from the Firth of Clyde by a short voyage in relatively sheltered waters. The other was Fort William at the head of Loch Linnhe, which from February 1746 was given immediate assistance by the *Baltimore* sloop and *Serpent* bomb vessel. The last leg of the voyage of the reinforcements and supplies was in fact the most dangerous, for the craft had to wait for a favourable combination of wind and tide to be able to run the Corran Narrows, which were commanded by the Jacobites, and where the tidal current reached 5 knots. However, there were plenty of staging posts on the way there – the isle of Kerrera, with the White Horse anchorage, the bay of Duart on Mull, the seaweedy and shallow harbour behind Dunstaffnage Castle, and Castle Stalker on its little island off the coast of Appin.

The Sound of Mull offered the most convenient passage and shelter for the vessels of the Royal Navy on their way to and from the far western waters, those of the Inner Hebrides, Skye and the Outer Hebrides. Operating in those seas, the craft obstructed the passage of Jacobite reinforcements to the mainland, mounted punitive expeditions among the islands and peninsulas, and engaged in the abortive hunt for Prince Charles after Culloden. In the Sound of Mull itself the British made frequent use of the deep-water anchorages in the bays of Scallastle and Aros, and established an important base at the harbour of Tobermory. The one notable disadvantage of the Sound showed when the waters were whipped by a north-westerly wind blowing down its length, such as the blast that sank three craft of a Cromwellian expedition off Duart Point on 13 September 1653.

At Isleornsay at the base of Skye the Royal Navy commanded the short passage of the Sound of Sleat, and supported the troops and the Protestant population on the mainland bridgehead of Bernera and Glenelg. The Isle of Canna was a stepping stone on the way to the Outer Hebrides, where in turn the warships could find shelter at Lochboisdale on South Uist, and Stornoway on Lewis.

Despite its many advantages the Royal Navy got the worst of its only engagement of note, when on 2 May 1746 Captain Thomas Noel brought the Sixth Rate *Greyhound*, the *Baltimore* sloop and the *Terror* bomb vessel to attack the substantial French privateers *Mars* and *Bellone* which had been landing arms and gunpowder on the rocky shore of Arisaig, so giving rise to a prolonged duel. The French, as was their custom, concentrated their fire on the masts and rigging, which was a particular danger to the British because the battle was staged so close to the shore. As a result *Baltimore* and *Terror* lost most of their mobility at the outset,[1] and the British finally broke off the engagement after the pounding match had lasted six hours. The French were free to make away with an important consignment of Jacobite fugitives, though not with Prince Charles himself, who was stranded on the Long Island and had to watch the two privateers pass by.

North-Eastern Seas

Conditions were radically different on the north-eastern coasts of Britain. A glance at a map shows at once that the shoreline on that side was much 'smoother', with the exception of the indentations formed by the Humber estuary, the firths of Forth and Tay, the Moray Firth, and the firths of Cromarty and Dornoch. By sweeping up most of the shipping in the Forth and Tay at an early stage of the rising the Hanoverian authorities forced the Scottish Jacobites to make long inland detours on their way to the south. Conversely, Cope's army was able to take ship direct from Aberdeen to Dunbar and present itself in reasonably good order to be beaten at Prestonpans. Afterwards the Royal Navy was able to take advantage of easterly winds to escort successive waves of Swiss, Dutch, British and Hessian troops to support the effort in Britain.

Otherwise the indentations generally turned to the disadvantage of the government. In murky weather it was easy to lose one's bearings along this

generally low-lying coast, and a convoy bearing a final batch of reinforcements for the army in 1746 entered the Humber by mistake, and was unable
to land the troops before the campaign was over. Even when craft entered
an estuary or firth on purpose, they might be marooned there for weeks on
end until a favourable wind could whisk them out again, like the supply ships
intended for the Duke of Cumberland at Aberdeen. Meanwhile the Moray
Firth helped to isolate Lord Loudoun and the locally raised loyalist forces
in the far north from any possible support, while the Dornoch Firth proved
to be no barrier to the Duke of Perth in his bold amphibious stroke on
20 March 1746.

An asset of almost incalculable value to the Jacobites was the 150-odd-mile
stretch of north-eastern Scottish coastline from Portsoy to Arbroath, the
home of people like the brewer Daniel Barclay, who 'hoisted a white flag on
the shore of Arbroath and apprehended one of the *Hazard*'s crew making
his escape, and caused him to be severely whipped'.[2] Opinions in Aberdeen,
Dundee and some other places were divided, but the population in general
was Episcopalian and the most committed single element in Britain. Their
harbours, too, presented by far the most important channel for troops and
supplies coming from France (pp. 353–4), and 'the principal ones are Arbroath,
Montrose, Stonehaven and Peterhead'.[3] Navigation was no particular problem,
for the French had at their disposal the long string of friendly ports, and
knew the coasts well from centuries of trading.

From September 1745 the difficult task of blockading this coastline fell
to Rear Admiral Byng, who normally held his principal concentration off
Montrose, and assigned his other craft to cruising stations off Peterhead, off
Aberdeen, between Stonehaven and Buchanness, and between Redhead and
the mouth of the Tay. The flotilla was frequently blown offshore, and between
9 and 19 October 1745 the French succeeded in landing some particularly
valuable consignments of gold, arms, artillery and specialist personnel at
Montrose and Stonehaven. A further sailing of two frigates and six privateers left Dunkirk on 14 November, and ran into the same spell of bad weather
that scattered Byng's squadron to the winds and wrecked the *Fox* at Dunbar
with heavy loss of life. The frigate *La Renommée* reached Montrose on
24 November at an eventful time on shore.

The story began on 16 November when Captain Thomas Hill RN
anchored the *Hazard* opposite Montrose, at Ferryden, on the far side of the
channel that led to the spacious inland basin. His purpose was to 'protect
His Majesty's good subjects in the town of Montrose',[4] and to that end he
installed a puppet administration in the town under the Excise Supervisor

Cumming, and seized four 6-pounder cannon and two 4-pounders which the Jacobites had installed in a rather elaborate battery further towards the sea on the Ferryden side. The guns were placed for safekeeping in a merchant vessel.

These proceedings drew the attention of Captain David Ferrier, who was both a particularly enterprising officer in Ogilvy's Regiment and the Jacobite deputy governor of nearby Brechin. In fact 'His Majesty's good subjects' were few, and Ferrier proceeded to march to Montrose, incarcerate Cumming and his fellows, and go in person to the water's edge, 'where we dared the master and crew of the *Hazard* sloop to come on shore. Captain Ferrier had his piper playing all the time, but these gentry thought proper to lie snug. Captain Hill's cabin boy deserted him, and went away with Captain Ferrier, and assures that the whole want likewise an opportunity to desert on account of the severe treatment they meet with'.[5]

La Renommée arrived on 24 November and broke the deadlock. Having been signalled to come straight in, she sent ashore 150 troops of Royal Ecossais, landed an additional six medium cannon which she had been carrying as cargo, and then beached in a little bay 2 miles south of Montrose. On the following morning the French raised two batteries on the Ferryden side of the channel, while Ferrier retrieved the town cannon from the merchant ship (braving *Hazard*'s fire), and installed them in a battery on the Montrose side on Dial or Horloge Hill, near the site of the later Hill Street. *Hazard* was now trapped further up the channel. The French and the Jacobites maintained fire from 8 a.m. until about 11 p.m., by when they had raised two more batteries on the southern side and one more on the northern. After a pause all the batteries opened fire together, and by 10 a.m. on 25 November they had 'torn to pieces and destroyed all her rigging, and rendered her incapable of making any successful resistance'. In response to a summons Captain Hill sent his lieutenant, Michael Burgess, to the northern shore. He was received by a party of about fifty French and Scottish Highlanders commanded by Nicholas Glasgow, who showed Burgess a 'stove with coals going to be set on fire, [and] declared that [it] was [his] intention to heat red hot balls to set the sloop on fire and sink her'.[6] Burgess reported this encounter to Captain Hill and his officers, who agreed unanimously to surrender; *Hazard* was about to enjoy a new life as *Le Prince Charles*.

On the night of 26 November a second and larger frigate, *La Fine*, approached Montrose, bearing Lord John Drummond in person and several hundred more of Royal Ecossais, who were landed on the open beach (by the present golf links) behind Scurdyness. The captain anchored with some difficulty at the entrance to the channel, but was unwilling to venture any further on account of the difficult navigation. He was soon presented with no choice, however, for early on the 27th the 40-gun HMS *Milford* presented herself and 'assailed the frigate with such speed that the local pilots decided that the only way to save her was to bring her into the river, where she had the ill-fortune to be lost'.[7] She had grounded on a gravelly bank on the north-eastern shore of Rossie Island, on the southern side of the entrance to the basin.

Milford's appearance was no accident, for Captain Hill had contrived to send word of his plight to Byng at Leith, and the admiral had at once ordered Captain Hanway and his *Milford* to Montrose.[8] *Milford* too ran aground, but Hanway was able to haul her off before the tide fell, and had the satisfaction of seeing *La Fine* break her back on the shoal. Some at least of her guns were rescued, but she was now an authentic wreck, around which the sand accumulated over the years to form the Scaulp Bank (dredged in 1875). On 28 November *Milford* took to the open seas again, and by chance captured the transport *Louis XV*, which had been making for Montrose with detachments of the Franco-Irish regiments of Bulkeley, Clare and Berwick.

Altogether Montrose figured so prominently in the rising that the Duke of Cumberland wrote from London to Hawley on 11 January 1746 to enquire if it were possible to land a small force to seize the place, 'and so cut the rebels off from their communication with France, which would be one of the effective and speediest ways of destroying them'.[9] Byng was asked at the same time for his opinion on the naval aspects of the enterprise. His reply was generally discouraging, but he confirmed how important it was to take Montrose, since 'All the ports on the north coast of Scotland from Inverness to the River Tay are all open to the sea, and are bars and dry harbours at low water, except Montrose ... This being the only port capable of securing their ships from our cruisers, they make a point of keeping it at all events, and have erected five batteries to prevent any of His Majesty's small ships putting in there'.[10]

As things turned out, the Jacobite high command abandoned Montrose and the other ports of the east coast as a direct result of their council of war at Crieff on 2 February 1746. The problems which faced the Duke of Cumberland in his advance up the coast were therefore primarily logistic, and for this he looked to the support of the flotilla of warships and supply vessels commanded by Commodore Thomas Smith. 'Since Commodore Smith's arrival in these parts,' wrote the duke from Aberdeen on 19 March, 'I have neither seen him nor heard from him, but by all that I can hear of his character, I am convinced that it proceeds from a sea education, rather than want of attention'.[11]

Cumberland had no further cause for complaint, for Smith not only kept the army provided, but helped it by way of observation and fire support. If we except the fire support, there is a direct parallel with the flotilla that sustained Gnaeus Julius Agricola, the governor of Roman Britannia, when he moved up the east of Scotland against the Caledonii in AD 83. The comparison would undoubtedly have occurred to the duke's very well-read secretary, Sir Everard Fawkener.

The interpenetration of the marine and land environments does a great deal to explain the circumstances of the Battle of Culloden. A later passage (p. 463) will describe how *Le Prince Charles* (formerly the *Hazard*) was chased into the Kyle of Tongue on 25 February 1746, and how, after a prolonged pounding-match, Captain Talbot and a party of his officers and men got ashore with a consignment of gold destined for the pay of the Jacobite army, but were hunted down by MacKay clansmen and a body of the 64th Highlanders. By the middle of April significant Jacobite forces were still locked up in the far north of Scotland, nominally at least in search of the lost gold, while the unpaid troops of Prince Charles about Inverness were weakened by hunger and desertion. Prince Charles was reduced to recompensing his demoralized troops with meal from the dwindling magazines at Inverness, which he believed he must defend even at the cost of a battle. The battle was fought at Culloden.

The Narrow Seas

Schemes of Invasion

The French had devoted considerable thought and resources to the project of invading England early in 1744. The plan was conventional, in that it involved (like the Armada of 1588) co-ordinated action between fighting fleet and troop transports; it fell apart for the traditional reasons, namely an over-elaborate plan and a terrible storm (in this case the tempest of 24 February). To all appearances the principle of invasion was now abandoned altogether. When, altogether unexpectedly, news arrived of the battle of Prestonpans and the spectacular progress of Prince Charles, a design for a new invasion was put together in a scramble from the middle of October 1745.

None of this augured well, but the scheme that emerged was simple and realistic. The army of Marshal de Saxe had captured the port of Ostend in the Austrian Netherlands, which enhanced the options open to the French while giving the British ships and agents a longer stretch of coast that had to be watched. The French for a time contemplated a descent on Bridlington Bay in Yorkshire, to cut the supposed land communications of the British forces operating in the North, but they finally settled on an operation that was to be limited to the Channel narrows. Some 15,000 troops (with a large contingent of redcoat Irish) were earmarked for the invasion. Spies and observers would be sure to notice the initial build-up of the fishing, privateering and smuggling craft at Dunkirk, but this might work to the advantage of the French, who planned to move the flotilla along the coast to Boulogne and launch the invasion from there. A wind from the south or south-east would carry the boats in a matter of hours to the coast of south-eastern England; there was to be no escorting fleet, but the long nights of winter would provide the necessary cover, and the Kent and Sussex smugglers would pilot the craft to their destinations. The craft in question were mostly open-decked, but eminently seaworthy.

The expedition was in the charge of Louis François Armand du Plessis, duc de Richelieu, who was genuinely committed to the notion of invading Britain. In his comprehensive instructions he laid down that absolute silence must be observed during the passage. Once the troops were on shore, they were to form up in front of their respective boats and await orders, which depended in turn on the reports of the patrols that were pushing inland. Richelieu was right to expect that there would be little immediate opposition (p. 375) and he believed that the greatest danger was likely to come from 'friendly' fire, especially because of the presence of the Irish in their red coats. Richelieu told his generals to impress this upon the troops, 'who must wind about them something which is white and stands out, like shirts or handkerchiefs, which are easier to see than cockades'. Discipline was more important than ever,

> bearing in mind that we are coming to that country as friends, and we count
> on being joined there by some of the local people. Every soldier and driver
> is forbidden on pain of death to leave his unit on any pretext whatsoever,
> and, without the express permission … of the officers, they are likewise for-
> bidden, under the same penalty, to enter any of the villages, private houses,
> hamlets or barns, or to cut any trees or forage. Arrangements will be made
> with the people of the country to provide the firewood, straw and other

necessities of the troops during the march. The duc de Richelieu forbids any kind of altercation with the local people, and any argument on the matter of religion.[12]

Edward Vernon, Admiral of the White, was in charge of the naval defence of Britain from 4 August 1745 to 2 January 1746. It is significant that for most of the period of his command his attention was taken up with perceived dangers on the outer maritime flanks, and diverted away from the coasts of Kent and Sussex. To the west he had to counter the Brest fleet, which might gain the open Atlantic and reach Ireland or other places of interest to the French. The immediate responsibility for acting against this threat lay with the Royal Navy's Western Squadron. However, the Squadron's lumbering First, Second and Third Rates were altogether unsuited to the shallow waters at the meeting of the English Channel and the North Sea, where the squadron under Vernon's personal command had its principal anchorage in the Downs, the roadstead between Deal and the Goodwin Sands.[13]

Winter both made the Downs totally unsuitable for the three-deckers, and furnished the long nights which might enable the French to execute what Vernon identified as the other threat, over to the east, where the most likely target seemed to be Orford harbour in Suffolk, where 'you have a narrow bar entrance, and from the entrance, a like secure harbour as secure as the Thames, from thence passing by Orford quite up to Aldborough, all within land, and a bold landing anywhere. And I have even heard it said that this was the place where Marshal Saxe had pointed out to the King of France as the most proper for it, having a breadth of heath or four or five miles between it and the enclosed inland country. And this was one of my reasons for advising a squadron to be kept in Hollesley Bay'.[14]

In the throat of the Channel in the Downs Admiral Vernon typically had two 50-gun ships, two of 20 guns, and a number of smaller craft. There were usually a couple of Sixth Rates on the Dogger Bank, a sloop off Ostend, and another out in the Channel to the west. This was not much of a barrier to set against what Richelieu actually had in mind, which was a descent on the coast of Kent between Folkestone and Dungeness.

Richelieu reached Dunkirk on 17 December, but found that delays in embarking the artillery made it impossible to take advantage of the favourable wind blowing on that day. News came from the 18th that Prince Charles had turned back from Derby, which was a disappointment, but not a death-blow to the scheme, which was still being supported actively by Louis XV. However, the options open to the French were now closing.

Vernon at last awakened to the danger of a south or south-easterly wind immobilizing him in the Downs, or driving him from there, which would open a long stretch of the coasts of Kent and Sussex to a French descent. He wrote of his concerns to the Admiralty on 16 December, and alerted Sir John Norris (Governor of Walmer Castle) who assembled 4,000 local volunteers at Swingfield Minnis. Vernon, like everybody else, had assumed that the invasion would be launched from Dunkirk, but on the 18th two hired Dover privateers (an excellent investment) sighted sixty coast-hugging craft which were making their way from Dunkirk to Boulogne with ammunition and military stores. Seventeen of the vessels were driven aground or captured, and the privateers gained the vital information that the French had instead concentrated at Boulogne. An important element of surprise was therefore lost to the would-be invaders. On the same day the west wind carried to the Downs the first three of the 50- and 60-gun ships which the Admiralty had ordered from Admiral Martin's Western Squadron in Plymouth. Martin himself arrived on the *Yarmouth* on 21 December. By the 26th the redeployment of forces to the Channel narrows was complete, giving Vernon five handy ships of the line, and a strong complement of small craft.

Vernon conceded that the project of the dash across the Channel had been realistic, and that he could not have stopped it if it had been launched with a favourable wind as late as 23 December. London had been in a prolonged panic, augmented by a report that the French had actually come ashore at Pevensey, and on 15 December the Duke of Cumberland had been held back at an interesting stage of his pursuit of Prince Charles.

It is not true, as has been claimed, that the interception of the shipping on 18 December set 'Marshal Richelieu's face against any further attempts, and ... put an end to all hopes of a successful invasion'.[15] On 2 January he received an order from Louis XV telling him to invade without further loss of time, and Richelieu now suggested a diversionary descent on Cornwall. This county was remote from the main concentration of Vernon's ships and the British land forces, and its geography was such that 'it would favour a defensive contest between a small number of troops and a much larger one, and I believe that in England's present situation a landing there by some troops, no matter how few, would be enough to reduce affairs there to total confusion.' A landing in Ireland was a possibility (and one which held a particular appeal to the influential Pierre André O'Heguerty), though it would be attended with more difficulties, and would not attract the same attention from the enemy.[16]

Lieutenant Nagle of the Irish Brigade regiment of Lally was smuggled from Rye to France on 9 January. His report confirmed what the Jacobite spy Wolfe had already written about the state of affairs in England, and he brought the news that Hawley had taken over from Wade and was marching on Edinburgh, and that Prince Charles would shortly be joined by the forces which had been gathering under the command of Lord John Drummond. On this basis Richelieu wrote to his War Minister in more specific terms, suggesting that an expeditionary force should be embarked on the numerous and powerful St Malo privateers and land in Ireland or on the tip of Cornwall. The scheme was not taken up, mainly because the ministers were interested in other projects – recapturing Louisbourg on the far side of the Atlantic, or sending help direct to the Jacobites in Scotland.[17]

The Invasion Coast and the Southern Rebels

Out of all the intended invasions of England, the one devised by the French for December 1745 had a better chance than most of getting troops ashore. To investigate what might have happened next is to see the topography of Kent and Sussex, and its dominating feature, the Weald, in a perhaps unfamiliar light.

The Weald formed a distinct entity which stretched for about 70 miles along its east–west axis, and for up to 30 between the North and South Downs, with the eastern side reaching the sea in a zone of marshes. The chalk Downs to north and south were an open landscape of sheep-cropped grass, which offered good going, even if the paths could become slimy in wet weather. However, the intervening Weald was a region of steep little hills, isolated valleys, small clearings and marshy-banked streams. The characteristic ground cover was dense coppiced woodland (which produced charcoal for the declining iron industry), and the lanes were sunk so deep into the soft earth that along many stretches the trees closed over the top to form bosky tunnels. The Weald in the eighteenth century was thus hard work for wheeled vehicles in summer, and was almost impassable to them in winter.

In broad terms the Weald as it existed in the 1740s served to isolate the coastal areas of Kent and Sussex from the centre of governmental power in London, and (given the facility of seaborne transport) to bring them closer to the Continent. Everything seemed to ensure that the most typical cross-Channel relationship must be smuggling. The traditional trades and occupations of Kent and Sussex were in decline, for the iron-working in the Weald was almost extinct, along with cloth-making, and the harbours were

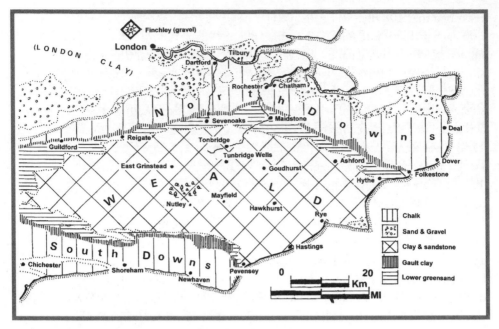

The invasion coast – geology

silting up. Sheep still abounded on the Downs and the coastal marshes, and yet a long-standing ban was in place against the export of wool to France, where the cliffs could be seen in clear weather along the horizon. The Whiggish Sir Robert Walpole was prime minister from 1721 to 1742, and the taxes imposed on tea, alcohol and other desirable commodities during his term of office not only sharpened the incentive to smuggling, but helped to identify Whiggery in general with self-enriching officiousness, which established an important ideological connection.

One of the features of the Kent and Sussex style of smuggling was that it was organized by large and powerful gangs that specialized (like the Hastings Outlaws) in bringing the goods ashore, or in the equally important business of transporting them to the neighbourhood of London. Among the inland smugglers the avowedly Jacobite Mayfield Gang was smashed in 1721, but its most important successor, the Hawkhurst Gang, was in operation by 1735 and flourished in the early 1740s. Not only predominantly Jacobite in sentiment, the smugglers were numbered among the few Englishmen who had firearms and were willing to use them.

The scale of the smuggling operations, and the declared allegiance of those engaged in them, made these activities more than just a symbolic protest against the irksome presumptions of Whig rule. Admiral Vernon reckoned that 400 men were engaged in the smuggling trade at Dover, and 300 each at Ramsgate and Folkestone. The Duke of Richmond, the most influential Whig landowner in west Sussex, urged on the campaign against the smugglers from his residence at Goodwood, but the dragoon patrols and the riding officers of the Customs ventured at their peril along the lonelier stretches of the coast, and were incapable by themselves of taking effective action against the concentrations of smugglers inland. Thus in late January 1746 it was found necessary to redeploy three companies of the 30th Foot to Lewes, and the troops 'took tents and camp equipment as if for a campaign'.[18] That was a wise precaution, for the smugglers were capable of bringing together 500 armed men at short notice.

More alarming than the loss of revenue, or the challenge to public order in general, was the clear evidence of the political inclinations of the Kent and Sussex smugglers, who linked themselves with the cause of Prince Charles by declaring themselves to be the 'Southern Rebels', and even taking oaths of allegiance to King Louis. The Duke of Richmond was convinced that the matter was more than bravado, and 'a much more serious thing than people seem to apprehend in London'.[19]

In terms of specific action the smugglers assisted recruits for the Irish Brigade to make their way to France, and helped Jacobite spies and agents in their passages across the Channel. The matter became more urgent as 1745 wore on, for accurate information on the whereabouts of the Royal Navy might determine the timing of an invasion. Admiral Vernon complained that 'this smuggling has converted those employed in it, first from honest industrious fishermen to lazy, drunken and profligate smugglers, and now to dangerous spies on all our proceedings for the enemy's daily information'.[20] The British consul at Flushing received a report on 20 December that the French had hired the men of the smuggling cutters to Boulogne as pilots, and he commented that 'it is a pity such pernicious vermin cannot be destroyed ... they keep up to my certain knowledge a daily correspondence betwixt England and France, so that there is not the least thing ordered or done but the enemy immediately know it by their means'.[21]

The smugglers were hired to pilot the French to their destination, and they would probably have advised them of the best routes to London, which is where the expertise of people like the Hawkhurst Gang was relevant. This, however, is where the real difficulties would have begun for the French, at least according to a pair of officers of the British Army who were tasked to make the appropriate topographical studies.

One report was probably by a Major General C. Ellison[22] and focused

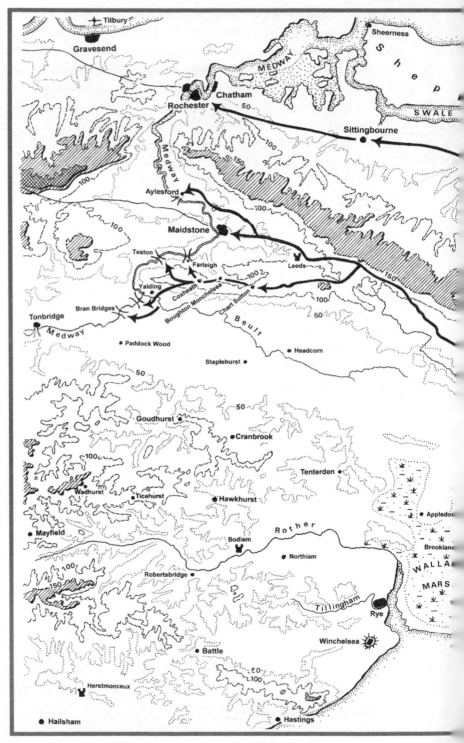

The invasion coast, with presumed avenues of French invasion

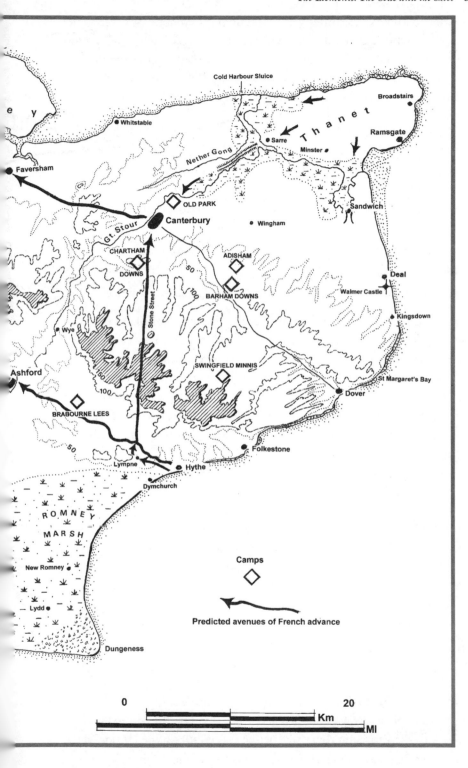

Camps

◇

Predicted avenues of French advance

0   20

Km

MI

primarily on Sussex; the other was by Lieutenant General St Clair [23] (the same officer who had planned the defences of the approaches to London against the Jacobites in December) and focused on Kent. Although neither seems to have known what the other was doing, the two officers managed none the less to agree on the fundamentals, namely

❖ The coasts of Sussex and Kent were envisaged as an arc extending rather more than 60 miles from London, which they assumed to be the target

❖ with the exception of beetling cliffs like those of Dover or Beachy Head, there were few places where the French could not get ashore with a favourable wind, which made it unrealistic to think of stopping the enemy on the beaches

❖ The Hanoverians must therefore turn their attention to the routes leading to the capital

❖ These routes were limited by the natural barrier presented by the Weald.

It was thought that on the western flank the French might land between Selsey Bill and Shoreham. They would then enjoy an initially easy passage of the South Downs, but then have to contend with difficult country to within a few miles of Guildford in Surrey, from where a good road (the A3) led to London. The enemy might be tempted to open up a central axis from the coast at Newhaven by way of Ashdown Forest. Here too there was bad going, on the initial stretch as far as Nutley, and again on the approaches to Tonbridge.

Kent was reckoned correctly to be a much more likely target. The pebble cape of Dungeness could be approached by both easterly and westerly winds, and 'that being a bold beach, they can land on either side of it, and so steep-to, that they can lay their boats' sides at high water'.[24] However, the cape gave way inland to the Walland and Romney marshes, and in common with all this length of coast it was assumed to have no access through the Weald.

The French might make a dash for Thanet in the far north-east of Kent. Getting ashore presented no difficulty, but getting off Thanet would not be easy, for in medieval times this bare plateau was literally an island, and even in the 1740s it was separated from the hinterland by a wide belt of low marshy ground. The path along the immediate north shore by Cliffsend and the Cold Harbour Sluice (the exit of the Nether Gong) could be ruled out, as being impassable to artillery and wheeled vehicles. The Roman road (A28) south-south-west to Canterbury was better going, but on the far side of the stone bridge at Sarre it ran for 1½ miles across the marshes on a causeway which was no more than 20 feet wide. The southern exit from Thanet was also easy to defend, for it had to cross the loop of the Stour at Sandwich, where the ford was narrow and passable only at the lowest of low tides.

By process of elimination St Clair was left with the shore from Folkestone (where the North Downs receded from the coast) to a point a couple of miles beyond Hythe. The French could land on the gravel beaches with ease, and a climb of a few hundred yards would bring them to one of the crests of the Downs. They now had two courses open to them:

❖ They could reach the route across north Kent from Canterbury to London by marching due north up the Roman Stone Street (B2068) to Canterbury, and then turn at right angles to the west along one of the principal highways which led to London (in this case the A2). Much depended on the speed with which the French gained ground along Stone Street, which ran arrow-straight, and was 'a hard and a good road, but mostly through woods and coppices, where a small body of men properly posted might easily obstruct the march of an army'[25]

❖ Alternatively the enemy could make north-west direct for London along the axis of the highway (A20) which ran by way of Ashford and Maidstone. This took advantage of the strip of firm ground (corresponding with gault clay and greensand) which lay between the North Downs and the Weald, where the French could march along both the main road and the minor lateral routes to the south, and where there were no obvious blocking positions short of the Medway.

St Clair proposed to block the first route by encamping troops in a constellation of sites about Canterbury, and the second by a corresponding camp at Brabourne Lees. The French indeed intended to land in the neighbourhood of Folkestone, but also along the coast much further towards Dungeness, and their smuggler friends were familiar with the ways through Romney Marsh. In that event the proposed concentrations of Hanoverian troops to the east would have been outflanked. The government must then have had to fall back on St Clair's plan for a last-ditch defence of the line of the River Medway, which hung on defending the bridges from Bran Bridges down to Rochester (see map). That was where the Romans under Aulus Plautius and Vespasian had broken through the defences in AD 44, and opened the way to the conquest of Britain.

The Skies

(See also Appendix IV, *Scotland's Weather, 8 July 1745 – 16 April 1746*)
Periods of global warming and cooling are an inherent part of the earth's
history. Why this is has never been fully explained. At the time of the '45,
the world-wide 'Little Ice Age' that had set in from 1314 had still far from run
its course. Between 1690 and 1728 Eskimos in their kayaks appeared among
the Orkney Islands, one even venturing into the Don at Aberdeen. The tops
of the Cairngorms lay under snow all year round, and even the hardy oats
failed in all but one of the harvests between 1693 and 1700, making Scotland's 'Seven Ill Years'.

The Scots drew differing interpretations for this, depending on their
political and cultural persuasions. A number of the Whigs lost confidence in
the ability of their remote northern land to survive as an independent entity,
and sought to link themselves more closely with England. The Jacobites, on
the other hand, and especially those of the Gaelic tradition, knew that pleni-
tude and good weather were associated only with the rule of a lawful king,
without which 'Every day is cold and rainy, every night dark and stormy.
Miserable and grim is every day, oppressive and heavy with mist. But waken
up people, and banish your dejection. Cast away your sorrow; Aeoleus and
Neptune are about to make a pact covering sea and sky, and every sort of
ease will attend it. Fair weather will come with the [rightful] King, snow and
ice will retreat from us; hurtful storms will be proscribed, solace will come
and pain will go'.[26]

Indeed, even Daniel Defoe, after the opposition he encountered when
trying to drum up support for the Union, believed that 'the final passage of
the Articles of Union through the Scottish Parliament was in large part due
to the fortuitous outbreak of wet weather which discouraged those people
"that thought and contriv'd the Mischief of Rabbles and Arms"'.[27]

The weather in Britain in the 1730s proved to be deceptively mild, but
a run of very cold easterly winds set in during the winter of 1739/40 and
marked a return to adverse conditions which lasted into 1742, and returned
intermittently thereafter. There was severe famine in Ireland, food riots in
Edinburgh and the Scottish burghs, and a markedly reduced growing season.
A bad, wet harvest in Scotland in 1744 was succeeded by the coldest winter
in living memory, with an iron frost obtaining in January and a great depth
of snow in February. An assiduous diarist, Thomas Barker of Lyndon Hall
in Rutland, noted in 1745 that 'a hard frost all February lasted even into
March, in which time I never remember a settled frost before'.[28] The Vale

of Atholl was spared the worst, but Lord George Murray wrote from the Highlands in April 1745 that

> the losses by the hard winter are greater in the North than you can well imagine ... Good substantial tenants six months ago are now reduced to want. Many are throwing up their tacks [leases] and will either go to service or list for soldiers who were in good circumstances last year. The greatest part of the cows in calf are lost in most of the Highlands, and their other stock is in great distress, being in want of fodder ... The cold is so nipping that weak and starved cattle are not able to withstand it. A few days longer of such weather will destroy the whole cattle where there is no hay or straw.[29]

In England too the now familiar frosty weather continued into the March of 1745, and the summer brought no alleviation. Any hopes of recovery were put back by the wet and squally weather which overtook England on 5 August. The price of hops soared on account of the ruined crop,[30] and to cap it all a distemper set in among the cattle, possibly due to the beasts 'feeding too plentifully on grass, which this year, from the wetness of the season, has been more juicy than [is] common'.[31]

Scotland was not spared these afflictions, and the people who understood such things knew what to read into the coming of the lawful Prince, who seemed capable of providing a substitute for the failed harvest.

Uniquely for such a distant period we know a great deal about the weather during the Rising. First, the basic material is at hand in comments entered in civilian diaries, in remarks made by officers of the land service, and, most abundantly, in the daily logs in the ships of the Royal Navy. The warships acted as so many weather stations posted around the British Isles, their logs telling us about the direction and velocity of the wind, the cloud cover, the precipitation, the visibility, and sometimes also the state of the sea. Secondly, no campaign is ever immune to the influence of climate, but again the '45 is unusual in that its operations were peculiarly susceptible to the impact of weather, for they constituted in effect a prolonged winter campaign, and one that was conducted over high or otherwise difficult terrain.

On 9 July 1745 gentle northerly breezes prevailed when Prince Charles's expedition so unfortunately encountered HMS *Lion*. High pressure prevailed for most of the month, and a shifting of the wind to the west facilitated the last stages of the Prince's voyage past the northern Irish coast and the Hebrides to the mainland of Scotland. He landed with a light westerly wind at Loch nan Uamh on the sunny 25 July. When Antoine Walsh set out for

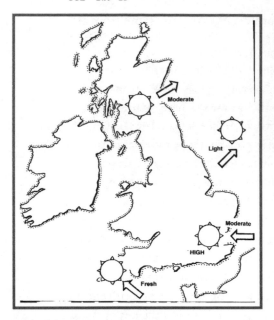
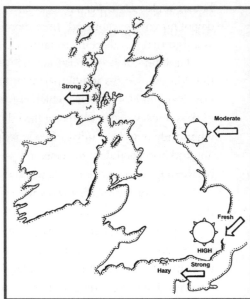
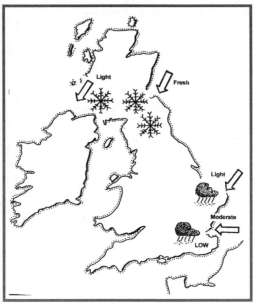
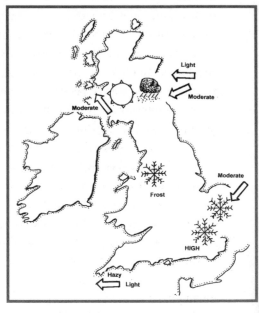

Weather retrospects and key dates (1)

ABOVE LEFT   13 September 1745 (passage of the Fords of Frew)

ABOVE RIGHT   23 September 1745 (first lift of reinforcements from Flanders)

BELOW LEFT   November 1745 (Tyne Gap snowed in)

BELOW RIGHT   8 December 1745 (Jacobites on the retreat; Hanoverians affected by severe weather)

France on his *Doutelle*, having seen the Prince safely ashore, and on the first day of his voyage captured three merchantmen laden with meal, it was taken as a sign that 'God seems to favour them in all things'.[32]

God did not seem to favour them quite so well in terms of weather when the Prince raised his standard at Glenfinnan on 19 August, for the west wind now brought cloudy skies, which continued with brief intervals for a number of days. Heavy rain was driving into the backs of Charles and his Highlanders when they marched along the Great Glen on 26 August, but the day was fine and hot when they traversed the Corrieyairack Pass two days later and got between Cope and the Lowlands.

September's weather was inconstant. However, a short spell of rain in the Central Lowlands had ceased by the 8th, and the waters in the Fords of Frew were conveniently low when the Jacobites traversed the upper Forth in the sunshine on the 13th. Cope, meanwhile, was detained at Aberdeen by contrary winds. The redcoats finally sailed from there on the 15th, but a south-west wind prevented them from making the port of Leith on the following day, and they finally disembarked at Dunbar on the 17th, by which time Prince Charles had been given a free run to Edinburgh. In the cold vapours of the early morning of 21 September the Highlanders emerged from the marsh near Prestonpans and routed their enemies. The Gaelic bard Alexander MacDonald sang of the Prince that 'His appearance is like the stormy close of Winter; the chill breeze before a squall, a glimpse of a storm-riven rainbow; a slender blade in his hand to make carnage, scything through bodies like oats in a field'.[33]

The main force of the British Army had been deployed in Flanders, along with its hired auxiliaries, and only a succession of favourable winds could convey the troops across the southern North Sea to England to meet the emergency, which was developing fast. The wife of the Lord Chancellor was able to write on 17 September that 'the wind has been easterly for several days. I hope good from that quarter if time is not neglected'.[34] Three battalions of Swiss disembarked in the Thames on the 19th, four battalions of Dutch arrived there on the 20th, and the Lord Chancellor noted on the following day that 'the wind continues as far as it can blow, and we expect the 6,000 British in the River [Thames] today ... God send them well here. I shall then believe that we shall soon, by His blessing, crush this insolence'.[35] These men, constituting the first wave of the British troops proper, actually arrived on the 23rd.

The second sailing of the British reinforcements left Helvoetsluys under the Earl of Albemarle, and was making direct for the Tyne when a strong south-westerly wind swept over Britain and the North Sea on 18 October. It was eight days before the vessels got together again in the Tyne, and meanwhile a further lift of seven battalions of foot and three regiments of horse had to be postponed due to the lack of transports.

There had been hopes that an invasion of north-western England could be delayed, at least, by the swollen rivers of Esk and Eden,[36] but in the event the Jacobites marched through the Southern Uplands of Scotland in dry and hazy weather, and they waded the rivers with no difficulty on 9 November. When, however, the columns concentrated in front of Carlisle on the 10th, the fog was so dense that they inadvertently halted within cannon shot of the walls of the castle and town (p. 227).

The rival forces were now on opposite sides of the Pennines – the army of Prince Charles to the west, and that of Marshal Wade to the east. Both commanders were keen to get to grips – the Prince in order to finish things there and then, and Wade because he wished to save Carlisle – and the resulting battle would probably have been staged in the Tyne Gap. Nature now supervened, for a cold and strong east wind blocked the Gap with snow on 12 November. By the 16th the snow lay a foot deep around Carlisle, and 3 feet deep in the Gap itself, and in some parts the drifts reached 12 feet, for 'the storm in the north of England had been the severest ever known'.[37] Prince Charles's way was blocked east of Brampton, while Wade's army struggled only as far as Hexham, the troops literally perishing from the cold. Carlisle fell to the Jacobites on 15 November, but the news was slow to reach the Whigs in Edinburgh, one of the Sir Andrew Fletcher's messengers taking five days to reach him, and the other six, for 'the weather is so bad, and the snow lies so deep, that they were obliged to quit their horses and walk afoot, which makes me in great pains about Mr Wade's army, exposed to bad weather, long and cold nights, while the rebels are got under cover'[38] (p. 139).

Fletcher was right to be concerned, for the marshal's troops had to fall back to the shelter of Newcastle under appalling conditions. Wade's army had set out for the Gap at a time of intense frost, which had turned the roads iron hard, and the only cheering sight to be seen through the blizzards had been that of lanterns of the country folk, who had been summoned out to help the benighted soldiers. The food had been running out, the waggon drivers had been deserting, and the train of artillery was ruined.

A lieutenant and his men deserted to Prince Charles and brought him news of Wade's retreat to Newcastle. Later in the campaign Major General Oglethorpe was to lead his mounted column across the Pennines by way of Blackstone Edge, and so become the only significant element of Wade's army to make contact with the Highlanders on their retreat. With these exceptions, the hills remained an impassable barrier between the two sets of forces.

The weather between 20 November to 4 December 1745 (when the Jacobites advanced from Carlisle to Derby), was marked by extremes. The fells were covered with snow when Lord George Murray led the Jacobite advance guard from Carlisle to Penrith on 20 November. A Whig, writing in Perth on the previous day, however, noted that 'we had a vast fall of snow last night, but as we had a thaw wind this day, it's considerably gone, in so much that if the wind continues, it will be quite removed before tomorrow this time. I am wishing a speedy and happy end to this present unnatural war'.[39] The snow was still deep when Lord George's troops were traversing Shap Fell on the 21st, but it was melting fast when they descended to Kendal on the 22nd.

A dark 24 November was succeeded by a cold but fine 25th, and on that day and the next Wade was able to make deceptively fast progress south from Newcastle via Chester-le-Street to Piercebridge. The 27th was mild, which helped the Jacobites to enjoy the amenities of Preston. Sharp weather returned on the 28th, which was the frosty day on which the leading Jacobite troops entered Manchester, and the cold weather prevailed with intermissions until Prince Charles reached Derby. The Mersey was subject to sudden floods, but the river allowed the Jacobites an unhindered passage into Cheshire on the murky 1 December, being just waist-deep at Stockport, though somewhat higher at Didsbury. Moonlight and hard-frozen roads facilitated the final push from Leek to Derby early on 4 December.

By that time Wade had given up all hope of intercepting the Jacobites on their march south. Meanwhile another Hanoverian army was building up in the Midlands, under the command of the Duke of Cumberland. One of the battalions of reinforcements had landed at Gravesend in the Thames on 5 November, and marched north-west to the rendezvous at Lichfield, from where an officer wrote that 'at our first setting out from London we had gentle frosts, but the weather soon turned into great rains and wind, which continued daily, making the roads and travelling extremely bad; and sprained ankles were a common complaint amongst us'.[40]

Deceived by a Jacobite bluff, the Duke of Cumberland held his army on comfortless Stonefield on the frosty 3 December, and then moved his troops to equally bleak encampments in the heart of the Midlands by the 6th, where the men suffered so badly that they were incapable of moving until the 8th. The Jacobites had been resting in comfort in Derby on 5 December, with the regimental officers and the troops looking forward to the final advance on London. Wider strategic considerations, and not the weather, determined the high command, rightly or wrongly, to turn back towards Scotland on the 6th.

These contrasting experiences, under what were essentially the same conditions of weather, emphasize that the impact of climate on military affairs is not a scientific absolute, but is shaped by influences as varied as terrain, march formations, clothing, and habituation to hardship. The Jacobites, at least as long as they were on the offensive, held some important advantages. Their staff work was very good, and they had moved the two component divisions of their army by separate routes as far as Carlisle, and then further into England, by carefully judged intervals along single or parallel roads. The Jacobites were housed and fed in the towns and villages along the way, and so the progress of their army took the form not of a headlong rush, but of sudden moves in unexpected directions by fresh and rested troops, who were marching in handy columns just three files wide. The Highlanders were accustomed to wading rivers in their homeland, and their soft and ungainly brogues gave them a good purchase on those frozen ruts which were so taxing to the Hanoverian troops in their hard and stiff shoes.

The Hanoverian commanders had scarcely begun to address the problems of a winter campaign. Uncertain as to which way the enemy might be heading, they had to concentrate their troops in encampments, without straw to spread on the ground inside the tents, and without winter clothing – indeed, without waistcoats, until those items were donated by some Quaker merchants. In all probability the Jacobites would have enjoyed an almost unresisted advance from Derby to the neighbourhood of London if their leaders had decided to make the attempt. Instead, and incomprehensibly to the troops and the regimental officers, the high command decided that the army must retreat.

The Jacobites turned north on a dark and cold 6 December. They encountered ice and snow on their march across the Derbyshire moors, and thence by way of Stockport into Lancashire. The 13th was felt to be the most severe day of the winter so far, on account of a cutting wind which blew steadily from the south, a direction from which better things might have been hoped. The Highlanders were inured to adverse weather, but it would have been surprising if their culture had not inclined them to draw parallels between the hostile skies and the turn in their fortunes.

Both the weather and the continuing threat of a French invasion contrived to prevent Cumberland setting after the Jacobites with the main force of his army. Instead the duke himself took up the chase with a picked

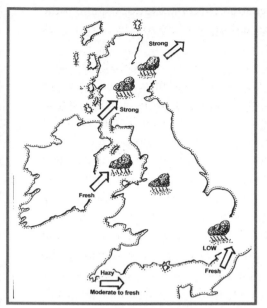
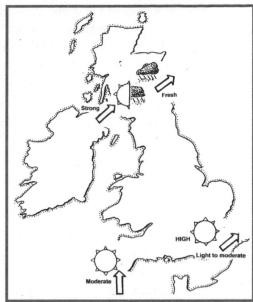
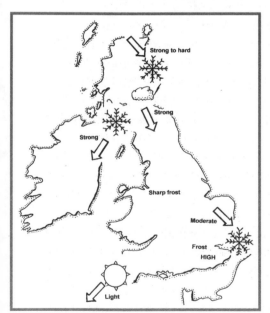
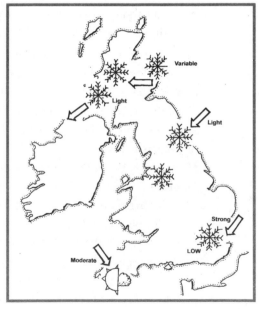

Weather retrospects and key dates (2)

ABOVE LEFT 20 December 1745 (Jacobites ford the fast-rising Esk; Vernon immobilized in the Downs)

ABOVE RIGHT 17 January 1746 (the day of Falkirk)

BELOW LEFT 17 February 1746 (the Jacobite retreat from Aberdeen)

BELOW RIGHT 8 March 1746 (the Great Snow)

column of horse and mounted infantry, while Oglethorpe crossed the Pennines from the east by way of Blackstone Edge with his exotic volunteers. The Hanoverians would probably not have caught up with the Jacobites at all if it had not been for some deliberate delaying on the part of Prince Charles. He was cutting his margins fine, and the rearguard under Lord George Murray began to be in some peril on account of the dark and wet weather which set in on 14 December.

Particularly heavy rains overnight on 16/17 December added to the travails of Lord George Murray when he was bringing the artillery train across the swollen streams on the eastern flank of the Lake District. The pack road over Shap Fells was particularly difficult going, for a wet wind had set in from the south-west, and the frozen ground was now overlain by mud. Lord George negotiated the Fell successfully, but he was forced to turn and confront his pursuers at Clifton as night was falling on the 18th. The action was unusual for more than one reason, for it was the last engagement ever fought on English soil and was staged in a darkness pierced only by bursts of moonlight and the flashes of muskets and carbines.

On 19 December the reassembled Jacobites prosecuted their retreat through the continuing heavy rain and strong south-westerly winds to Carlisle. The Duke of Cumberland's sodden troops were in no state to move from Clifton Moor, but he had reason to hope that the swollen River Esk would trap the Jacobites on the near side, and so put them at his mercy before they could escape to Scotland. The Jacobites crossed the river successfully on the 20th, and only in the nick of time, for the Esk was rising fast, and a number of unfortunates were swept away. On the far side Prince Charles and the Highlanders proper turned towards Dumfries, while Lord George and the Lowland Division took the muddy paths to Ecclefechan.

The little campaign of Falkirk sits chronologically in 1746, but it was really a prolongation of the events of the previous year. The morning of the battle of Falkirk (17 January) was fine and fresh, but was succeeded in the afternoon by a strong south-westerly wind which blew hail and rain into the faces of the Hanoverian troops as they struggled up the slopes of Falkirk Muir. Many of their muskets were rendered useless, while their artillery was abandoned on the slippery hill slopes without ever coming into action. The counter-attacks and resistance of the redcoats literally fizzled out, and the day ended with the Jacobites victorious, though unable to exploit their success.

On 2 February 1746, under pressure from Lord George Murray and the chiefs, Prince Charles assented with deadly reluctance to a general retreat towards Inverness and the Highlands. In this context some of the happenings later in the month are particularly interesting. On 10 February Byng's flag-ship *Gloucester* was churning in the seas off Montrose, and the admiral cursed 'the violent gales and N and NNE that we have had for these last three days'.[41] He did not know that the Jacobites had already resolved to abandon this whole stretch of coast. Their retreat from Aberdeen began the next day. The wind had shifted to the north-west, and they were marching in the teeth of blizzards which brought about the near-ruin of the cavalry troops of Pit-sligo, Kilmarnock and Balmerino. At the same time a number of ships, laden with flour and bread for Cumberland's army, were detained at Leith by the headwinds, while the transports bearing 6,000 miserable Hessian merce-naries were bucketing up and down offshore, unable to make harbour.

In these conditions it was impossible for the Royal Navy to maintain an effective blockade. A French privateer reached Aberdeen on 22 February, and succeeded in landing 130 of FitzJames' Horse. The leading ships of a convoy arrived offshore on the 27th, but the French learned that the last of the Jacobite troops had just left, the Jacobite high command having thrown aside the last opportunity of receiving substantial help from France. There-after the survival of the cause depended as much as anything else on the weather.

The Duke of Cumberland installed his army in Aberdeen and the hinterland, and he had to reconcile himself to the prospect of being unable to move until the spring arrived. The winter had come late to Scotland, but it was hitting very hard, and it was as difficult as ever for the transports of provisions and reinforcements to claw their way up the coast to him. Brief and deceptive thaws (16 and 24 February) did nothing to break the grip of the winter, and the Lord Justice Clerk wrote in the relative comfort of Edinburgh on 1 March that 'we have very cold weather, frost and snow, which must be very hard on our army; at Aberdeen I hope our army will find better cover, as when they proceed further they will not meet with such accommodation. I hope the weather will mend as the days grow longer, and thereby disappoint the rebels' expectations of destroying our army by long marches in bad weather without cover'.[42]

He was writing a little too soon. Scotland came under a northerly airflow on 2 March, with snow falling in the east from the 6th. On the 8th a stu-pendous blizzard exceeded anything that had been known all winter. It seemed impossible that the adverse conditions could last, and on the 9th Cumberland dared to hope that 'as soon as the great fall of snow which fell last night has a little run off, we shall march from hence'.[43] Colonel Campbell

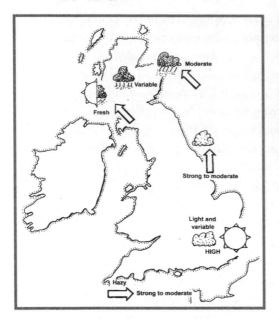
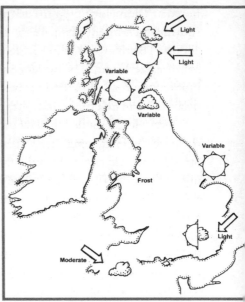
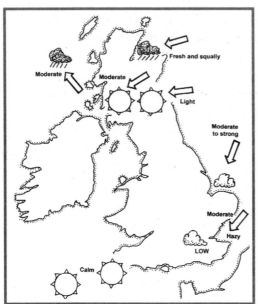
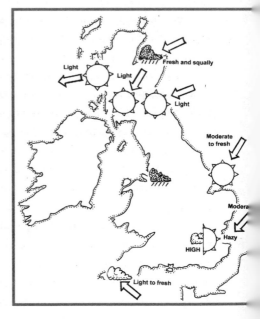

Weather retrospects and key dates (3)

ABOVE LEFT 15 March 1746 (the thaw)

ABOVE RIGHT 13 April 1746 (the Duke of Cumberland on the march)

BELOW LEFT 15 April 1746 (the march on the Camp of Nairn)

BELOW RIGHT 16 April 1746 (the day of Culloden)

noted at Oldmeldrum on the 13th that the wind had moved a little to the south, which might dissipate the snow that blanketed the country thereabouts. The thaw was in full evidence on the 15th, under the influence of a south-easterly wind, bringing cloud and rain; over to the west, landslips blocked the road at two points beside Loch Lochy and Letterfinlay, which delayed the march of the Jacobites' artillery to their siege of Fort William.

Heavy fog shrouded the Hill of Foudland on 17 March, which helped to frustrate the Hanoverian *coup de main* against the Jacobite detachment at Strathbogie, and generally murky weather, with rain, hail and fog, prevailed until the end of the month.[44] The Duke of Cumberland had to report on the 31st that 'the continued ill weather we have had here for this month has raised the waters of Spey so high that I fear it will retard me still a week longer; I propose now to march on Inverness without halting as soon as ever the waters will allow us'.[45] He was writing about the violent but short season when spring rains and melt water combined to give the Spey the force to bear great tree trunks down to the sea, and scour new channels through the boulders and gravel.

The duke had judged correctly. April brought fine weather, along with favourable winds which wafted the transports carrying provisions and Bligh's Regiment of foot to the army. On the 4th Cumberland learned that 'the Spey is now so low and fordable in so many places, that the rebels have guards everywhere'.[46] Four days later 'His Royal Highness marched from Aberdeen, with six battalions of foot, and Mark Kerr's Dragoons, in order to seek the rebels. It being fine weather, our transports at the same time moved along shore with a gentle and a fair wind'.[47]

After two days of marching under hazy skies the redcoats forded the indefensible Spey near Fochabers on 10 April. A moderate wind with rain was then blowing from the east and east-south-east, which would have acted to the disadvantage of the Jacobites if they had chosen to make a stand. Sunny weather prevailed on the 11th, 12th and 13th, with the continuing easterly winds bringing a return of cloud and rain on the 14th. The weather deteriorated further on the 15th, with the Jacobites having to contend with a wet and squally wind gusting from the east-north-east as they attempted a night march to Nairn. This was singularly unlucky, for the rest of the kingdom was enjoying good weather. The same conditions prevailed on 16 April, the day of Culloden, when the rain and smoke blew relentlessly in the faces of the Jacobites, and, as John Roy Stuart remarked, 'a third of our misery came from the skies'.[48]

PART THREE

FALKIRK TO CULLODEN

CHAPTER 15

The Campaign of Stirling and Falkirk, 20 December 1745 – 1 February 1746

Through the Scotland of the Whigs, 20–30 December 1745

WE LEFT THE TROOPS of Prince Charles on 20 December, capering around to dry themselves after fording the border rivers. The pursuit by the Duke of Cumberland was over, and the Whigs of Scotland were thereby much chagrined 'considering how easily this wicked rebellion might have been suppressed and extinguished, had the King's forces given chase to the rebels immediately after the siege of Carlisle'.[1]

The news that Prince Charles was back in Scotland arrived speedily in Edinburgh, which the Lord Justice Clerk now believed to be between two fires and untenable by the 1,250 regular forces there.[2] That was a mistaken but entirely natural conclusion, and it helps to explain why the Jacobites made their march back through Scotland initially by two separate columns: one to the east under Lord George Murray, who would incline the Whigs in Edinburgh to a state of panic; and the other under Prince Charles, who was to sweep through the untouched Whiggish country further to the west. No

---

Carlyle's Volunteers at drill

active provision was made to support the defenders of Carlisle, and it is impossible to establish when they ceased to figure in the calculations (p. 338).

Immediately after the army passed into Scotland on 20 December, Lord George and the Lowland Division forked to the right along the muddy paths to the Welsh-sounding Ecclefechan. Lord George writes that 'those that went to Ecclefechan had a very bad march, mostly through mossy ground, and our guides led us off the road. I found that it was to shun houses, that our men might not go into them, and when they did not pass near them they would not see them'.[3]

The next day's destination was the elegant spa town of Moffat: 'we went off from Ecclefechan', writes an officer of the Atholl Brigade, and 'passing through the town of Lockerbie we were alarmed by some of our own that returned, telling they saw a company of light horse coming towards us. We alighted and strived the best we could to order such men as we had, which was not easy done, as they were some out of each regiment and company, and would not obey but their own commanders'.[4] It was fortunate that the alarm proved to be groundless.

On 20 December Prince Charles with the Highlanders had taken leave of Lord George and followed the route leading along the boggy northern shore of the Solway Firth. Prince Charles stayed briefly in the Buck Hotel (1700, remodelled 1903) in Annan, but the troops marched on through the night, 'though it had never ceased raining since the affair at Cliftonhall. Highlanders alone could have stood a march of two nights of continual rain in the midst of winter, and drenched as they were in crossing the river; but they were inured to fatigue, frequently marching six or seven leagues a day [a league being 3 miles], on ordinary marches in England, without leaving any stragglers behind'.[5] The troops reached hostile Dumfries at about 10 a.m. on the 21st. They were in very good spirits, and much amused to see candles lit and bonfires burning in the place to celebrate their supposed annihilation by the Duke of Cumberland.

Dumfries was 'a very neat and well-built town', but 'full of fanatical Calvinists'.[6] A party of Seceders there had made off with thirty cart-loads of baggage which the Jacobites had left at Lockerbie on their way south, which was enough to justify the Prince now demanding 1,000 pairs of shoes and a fine of £2,000 (of which £1,100 was actually raised). However, there were well-affected people in and around the town, in spite of its reputation, and Prince Charles took up quarters in the house of the prominent Non-Juror Richard Lowthian (on the west side of the High Street). Lowthian (a timid soul) made himself too drunk to be presented, but the Prince was made most

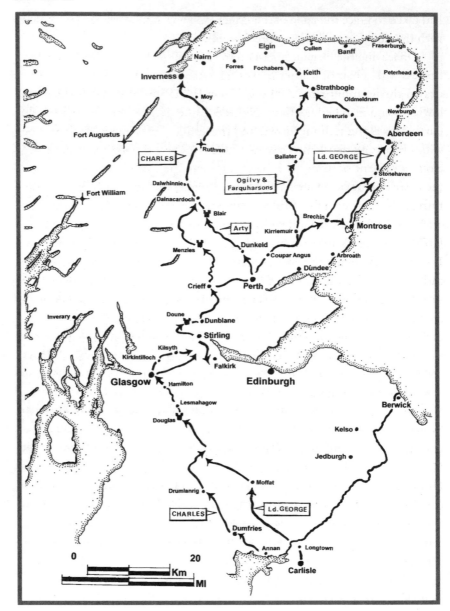

The Long Retreat, from the Borders to Inverness

welcome by his wife and the women of the family of Carnwarth, which had suffered greatly for its attachment to the Stuarts in 1715. Robert Chambers wrote that 'when the author was in Dumfries in 1836, he saw, in the possession of a family, one of a set of table napkins, of the most beautiful damask, resembling the finest satin, which the ladies Dalzell of Carnwath had taken to grace the table of the Prince, and which they had kept ever after with the care due to the most precious relics'.

On leaving the elegant house on the 22nd Prince Charles presented his hostess with a pair of leather gloves 'so extremely fine, that they could be drawn through her ring'.[7] The Highland Division now left the Solway lowlands and marched north up Nithsdale, 'the river meandering with bold curvatures along rich meadows, and the country for some space adorned with groves and gentlemen's seats ... the river keeps its beauty, wandering along a verdant bottom, with banks on each side clothed with wood; and the more distant view hilly'.[8] After some 18 miles on the road Prince Charles turned left, crossed a fine bridge spanning the deep glen of the Nith, then after a long ascent through parkland arrived at Drumlanrig, a great house (1679–91) of pink sandstone belonging to the Douglas dukes of Queensberry. It was a square building 'with a square tower at each corner, and three small turrets on each. Over the entrance is a cupola, whose top is in the shape of a vast ducal coronet: within is a court, and at each angle a round tower, each containing a staircase: everywhere there is a wearisome profusion of hearts carved in stone, the Douglas coat of arms. Every window, from the bottom to the third storey, is well secured with iron bars; the two principal doors have their grated guards; and the cruel dungeon is not forgot: so that the whole has the appearance of a magnificent state prison'.[9]

The Douglas family had been the most devoted of the supporters of Robert the Bruce, and the castle of Drumlanrig and the later house on the same site passed without interruption from father to son from 1388 to 1778. However, James, the 2nd Duke of Queensberry, had become known as 'The Union Duke' for promoting the connection with England, and his son Charles, the cultivated but equally Whiggish 3rd Duke, was away from home. The retreating Jacobites now treated the estate as hostile land. Prince Charles rested for the night in some state in a gloomy, oak-panelled bedroom, but, contrary to his usual custom, he felt under no obligation to pay for his accommodation. His men held a barbecue of slaughtered cattle in the forecourt, rode their garron ponies up and down the great oaken staircase, and are said to have slashed Godfrey Kneller's equestrian portrait of William III.

On 23 December the Highland Division wound for a further 10 or 12 miles up Nithsdale, then struck half-right at Mennock, crossed the open Lowther Hills, and descended the far side to join the Lowlanders in Clydesdale in the neighbourhood of Douglas Castle, a stronghold famous as the home of 'The Good Sir James Douglas', to whom Robert the Bruce had presented his sword on his deathbed in 1329. One of the Jacobite soldiers now put the weapon to good use by taking it for himself (and carrying it at Falkirk and Culloden).

On the 24th the main body of the combined force waded the deep and swift Douglas Water, and had 12 miles of 'very clatty travelling'[10] to the vicinity of Hamilton Palace, the seat of the dukes of Hamilton, and a Whiggish pile on a still grander scale than Drumlanrig.[11] Something of a party atmosphere was again in evidence. Prince Charles himself marked Christmas Day by shooting in the Duke of Hamilton's celebrated parks, 'in which he behaved to the admiration and surprise of all present, killing or hitting everything he shot at, so that, without flattery, he was looked upon to be the best marksman in the army'.[12]

On the same 25 December the advance guard made its way to 'one of the prettiest (but most Whiggish) towns in all Scotland, viz. Glasgow'.[13] The Covenanting tradition lived on there, and 'this city had always been considered as the headquarters of the Whigs in the reigns of Charles and James II, and was thereby exposed to very indifferent treatment'. In those two reigns its population fell by 2,700. It still lay within range of raids from the Highlands, and to compound its misfortunes it was laid waste by a fire in 1677. The fortunes of Glasgow began to revive with the usurping

Glasgow

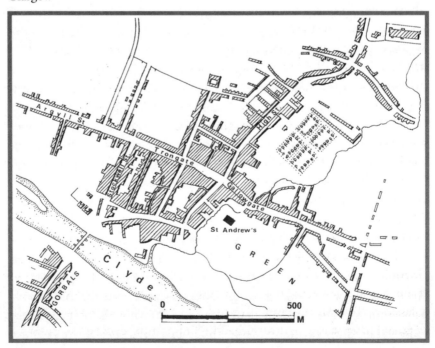

dynasties. Port Glasgow was laid out down the Clyde in 1690, at a time of general misery elsewhere in Scotland, and the Union of 1707 opened a lucrative trade with the West Indies and the North American colonies. The new constructions were now of stone: 'they are well washed, all of one model, and piazzas run through them on either side, which give a good air to the buildings'. The development of linen and jute manufactures combined with the flourishing trade to bring the population to some 25,000 by 1745, and that of neighbouring Paisley had already reached 4,000.

The ways of Glasgow nevertheless remained 'but coarse and vulgar. Very few of the wealthiest gave dinners but to anybody but English riders [travellers], or their own relations at Christmas holidays. There were not half a dozen families in the town who had man servants; some of those were kept by the professors who had boarders. There were neither post chaises nor hackney carriages in the town, and only three or four sedan chairs for carrying midwives about in the night, and old ladies to church, or to dancing assemblies once a fortnight'.[14]

With the approach of the Jacobite army through northern England the Glasgow regiment of 600 loyal volunteers made off to Edinburgh, and the town authorities shipped the governmental stores of weapons and ammunition down the Clyde to Dumbarton Castle. The main force of the army arrived on 26 December, and Prince Charles entered on foot in the afternoon. A Whig was observing from his lodgings on the Gallowgate, and wrote that 'the men are many of them bad, being some very old, others weak, others young. I assure you I had a much greater opinion of the Highland army before I saw them, than since I have seen it. They have no artillery but three small cannon. They are of brass and they called them 4-pounders'.[15]

Prince Charles stayed in Glasgow for a week, but 'he and his rebel followers were never able to procure from the loyal community the least mark of approbation or compliance, no bells were rung, no acclamations to be heard, nor even the common civility of a hat given'. There was no point in trying to conciliate people like these, and the Jacobites forced the Magistrates to supply 6,000 short coats, 12,000 linen shirts, 6,000 waistcoats, 6,000 pairs of shoes and 6,000 blue bonnets.

The soldiers were lodged among the people and in the almost-complete St Andrew's Church (1739–46), while Prince Charles took quarters off Trongate in Shawfield House, then owned by the wealthy merchant Mr Glassford. Townspeople were free to see him when he dined with his officers, and he took care to dress elegantly, 'but nothing could make the Whigs of Glasgow regard him with either respect or affection ... To such a height did this feeling rise, that an insane zealot snapped a pistol at him as he was riding along the Saltmarket. He is said to have admired the regularity and beauty of the streets of Glasgow, but to have remarked, with bitterness, that nowhere had he found so few friends'. Among the few ladies who brought themselves to the Prince's attentions was Clementina Walkinshaw, his future mistress and the niece of the dedicated Jacobite Sir Hugh Paterson.

> The army having been here provided with clothing and other necessities, of which they were very much in want, the Prince resolved to make a general inspection and review of them. Accordingly orders were issued for that purpose, for all of us to repair to a place a little distance from the town. So we marched out with drums beating, colours flying, bagpipes playing, and all the marks of a triumphant army to the appointed ground, attended by multitudes of people, who had come from all parts to see us, especially the ladies, who before were much against us, and were now, charmed at the sight of the Prince, become most loyal.[16]

The day was 30 December, and the location was Fleshers Haugh on Glasgow Green by Bridgton. The muster was unusual in that the Prince had never before brought his army together in public, but he knew that any figures put together by the Whigs would soon be irrelevant, for he was to be joined by the still greater numbers that were coming to him from the north-east.

The Massing of Forces

Almost by consent, the available troops of the Jacobites and Hanoverians converged in a confrontation in the Central Lowlands in the middle of January 1746. The Jacobites, as will be seen, had the advantage in concentration, if not numerical superiority:

JACOBITE FORCES

❖ Prince Charles with the army which had invaded England, and was now on its way back through south-western Scotland (about 5,500)

❖ Lord Drummond coming from north-eastern Scotland with the locally raised troops, and the Franco-Scots and Franco-Irish regulars landed from France (together about 6,000, of whom 4,000 were available to join the Prince).

THE HANOVERIAN FORCES

❖ The army of Field Marshal Wade (replaced on 27 December by Lieutenant General Hawley). Made up of two elements – the main force moving up through north-eastern England (below), and Lieutenant Handasyde with an advanced detachment at Edinburgh, comprising Price's 14th Foot, Ligonier's 59th, the Edinburgh and Glasgow volunteer regiments, the Paisley volunteers, and the shaken regiments of Cope's original force – Lee's 55th Foot, Murray's 57th, Lascelles' 58th, and the 13th and 14th Dragoons

❖ The Campbells. The strength of the Campbell militia was building up in the far south-west of Scotland, and twelve of their companies reached Hawley just in time to take part in the Battle of Falkirk

❖ Lord Loudoun. After the repulse at Inverurie at 23 December, Loudoun was immobile in the area of Inverness with his newly raised 64th Highlanders, the companies of the 43rd, and the growing militia of the loyal far northern clans

❖ The Duke of Cumberland. He had arrived at Carlisle with his flying column of horse and 1,000 mounted infantry, well ahead of the rest of his army. He had taken Carlisle, but nearly all the main body had turned back to confront the danger of a French invasion of southern England. Only Campbell's 21st Foot and Sempill's 25th, and the 'new' 68th, 69th, 71st and 74th, had continued their march to the north, though it is uncertain when they arrived. Cobham's 10th Dragoons and most of Ligonier's 8th Horse joined Wade; otherwise, as already indicated, all the rest of Cumberland's army was out of reach in England and had no part in the campaign of Stirling and Falkirk. The Duke himself repaired to London.

Field Marshal Wade was well aware of how slowly his troops were moving north. He had turned his army around from its southward path at Doncaster and then, realizing that the bulk of his forces would be unable to cross to the western side of the Pennines in order to intercept the retreating Jacobites, he had dispatched Major General Oglethorpe with the light horse to pass by way of Blackstone Edge on 12 December (p. 323). By the 14th the army had progressed no further than Boroughbridge, 44 miles from Doncaster, and Wade sought to repeat Oglethorpe's performance on a larger scale by detaching Major General John 'Daddy' Huske with 4,000 of the fittest infantry to cross by the ancient Stainmore passage to Penrith. He changed his mind the next day, and redirected Huske to Newcastle. The rest of the army was to follow, 'which can be but slowly from the extreme hardships they have endured by being constantly encamped in this rain and cold weather, which occasions great numbers to fall sick, who we are obliged to leave in the towns and villages through which we pass'.[17]

The army would have been destroyed altogether if he had continued to encamp overnight in the open air, and Wade was forced to break it down into separate divisions in the Jacobite style, so that the men could be accommodated under cover in the places along the way. In such a manner Wade's forces straggled towards Newcastle along three roughly parallel routes:

❖ Huske out to the east by way of Northallerton, Darlington and Durham

❖ The Dutch and Swiss in the centre up the Great North Road by Leeming and Piercebridge

❖ The main force of the British by a roundabout route by way of Bedale, Richmond, Barnard Castle and Bishop Auckland.

The government would have had no forces capable of taking the offensive in the Central Lowlands if it had not been for the energy of Lieutenant General Henry Hawley, highly professional soldier, sadist, and man of very strange private habits, who was appointed commander-in-chief in Scotland on 20 December. Hawley arrived in Newcastle on 27 December and was annoyed to find that the march of eight designated battalions for Scotland had been halted for no reason he could identify. He got them on the move the next day, which would give him ten serviceable battalions in Edinburgh in ten days' time, though for the time being the only horse would be the almost useless 13th and 14th Dragoons, the heroes of Prestonpans. He set down his impressions in his usual way, as the thoughts came to him, with little regard for punctuation or coherence, and he asked the Duke of Newcastle to pardon his 'rough military style'.[18]

Hawley left Newcastle on 2 January 1746, the same day that the first two battalions of reinforcements reached Edinburgh. The following troops were fed across the border in batches of two battalions at a time, much aided by the horses provided by the local people. Hawley arrived at Edinburgh on the 6th, by which time the forces were building up well, though (as a devotee of floggings and executions) he was disconcerted to find no document in the castle authorizing him to hold courts martial.[19] Once the men were executed, their bodies, if not buried on the spot, could be put to a variety of good uses, Hawley, for example, hanging the remains of one such in his headquarters.[20]

By the time he marched on 13 January, Hawley had at his disposal twelve battalions of regular foot, the Glasgow and the Edinburgh Volunteers, the Paisley militia, and even a contingent of the Yorkshire Blues. Ligonier's 8th Horse and Cobham's 10th Dragoons arrrived to supplement the disgraced 13th and 14th Dragoons, who were removed from their quarters 'to make room for the other troops, who ridiculed and scolded them unmercifully'.[21] Hawley had a good team of senior officers with him in the form of brigadiers Cholmondeley and Mordaunt, and Major General Huske, who provided a useful foil for the asperities of the commander-in-chief.

As for the likely Jacobite objectives, Hawley learned on 7 January that 'Lord Kilmarnock is fortifying by pallisades and entrenchments a strong camp at his own camp at Callendar by Falkirk to cover the siege of Stirling Castle; it is nine miles on this side (a new way of covering a siege). The main body of desperate men (as they call them here) have left Glasgow, and are about Stirling'.[22] Influenced by a letter he then received from the Duke of Cumberland, Hawley believed by 15 January that upon his army approaching the beleaguered fortress 'they will go off or they are mad'.[23] This corresponded with the general opinion of the friends of the government that the Jacobite siege of Stirling was 'a farce, considering what a force will march against them'.[24]

The Opening Moves

The Jacobite March on Stirling

The rival Jacobite concentration in the Central Lowlands had taken the form of a converging movement on Stirling by Lord John Drummond, marching south-west from Perth by way of Auchterarder and Dunkeld, and Prince Charles, moving north-east from Glasgow. The Prince's army left Glasgow at first light on 3 January 1746, and took with them 'two of the most substantial burgesses, one of them a present Magistrate, along with them as hostages. Although all imaginable occasions of delay were contrived, even to expose the town to the risk of being plundered, the inhabitants were at last obliged to furnish by far the greater part of the demand, which, according to tradesmen's accounts, amounted to above £5,000 sterling'.[25]

One mile out of town the army split into two columns. Lord George Murray inclined to the right with six clan regiments and Elcho's Horse Guards, and marched along the short and easy route (the axis of the M80) to Cumbernauld. The route of Prince Charles and the rest of the army was to the left, or west, and took it through Kirkintilloch, a place still deep in Whig country. The Prince restored a stolen plough horse to an indignant woman, but two of Lady Lochiel's servants were murdered in the town and a straggler was shot dead by the Cross Stone by a local lad called Dalton, who was aiming from the concealment of a barn. A dozen miles' march along difficult and winding roads (corresponding to the modern A803) brought the column to Kilsyth, in the shadow of the Campsie Fells. Prince Charles lodged at a mansion which was then owned by Campbell of Shawfield, but was part of the forfeited estate of William Livingstone, Lord Kilsyth, who had been 'out' in 1715.

On 4 January the columns of Lord George and the Prince came together in the neighbourhood of Stirling. The troops were assigned to cantonments nearby, and Charles made his quarters near Bannockburn in the house of Sir Hugh Paterson, where he was able to make the closer acquaintance of that gentleman's niece, Clementina Walkinshaw. His military priority was to seize Stirling Castle, which from its rock commanded the high-arched Stirling Bridge, the lowest permanent crossing of the Forth before that river widened dramatically into tidal loops.

The Hanoverian commentator James Ray defined the apparent objectives of the Jacobites in general terms. 'First, it would have given them reputation at home and abroad, as Stirling Castle is famous, and reputed a place of greater importance than it really is. Secondly, if they could have got this place, and fortified Perth, they might have secured the country behind them for the winter. Thirdly, it would have afforded them means of maintaining themselves along the coasts, on both sides of the island; which would have facilitated their supplies from abroad.'[26] The Chevalier de Johnstone, a disillusioned Jacobite officer, who was to be engaged closely in the operation, conceded that Stirling was the 'cause of much annoyance to the Highlanders, by annoying them in their coming and going from their country', but for that very reason 'the possession of this petty fort was of no essential importance to us, on the contrary, it was of more advantage to us that it should remain in the possession of the enemy, in order to restrain the Highlanders, and prevent them from returning, when they pleased, to their own country, from the fear of being taken prisoners in passing this castle, for they were constantly going home, whenever they were possessed of any booty taken from the English, in order to secure it'.[27]

Both Ray and de Johnstone conceived of Stirling as a barrier of one kind or another, and missed the fact that it was the only avenue by which Prince Charles could ever have maintained a presence both north and south of the

Forth, and ultimately have carried operations beyond the Central Lowlands and into England. For the Hanoverians, its loss would undoubtedly have been 'of very ill consequence'.[28]

The walls of Stirling town were in a still worse way than those of Carlisle, and an unofficial committee of the citizens opened the gates on receiving assurances that the Jacobites would not plunder the place or exact contributions.

> And consequently [writes an officer of the Atholl Brigade] the 8th January we were ordered to march into town, but with a guide that would bring us safe without being exposed to the castle cannon. However we marched and passed through Cambusbarron and St Ninians, and it seems they did not think they had any need of a guide, but went on and passed through the carses and came all open and exposed to the castle, and as well the castle did fire upon us four cannon and some of them came near a yard length of some of our men, but mercifully escaped and entered the town.[29]

Here 'the great street ... looks very grand, the houses are exceeding high, and there are several antique buildings in the highest part of the town, but greatly decayed by being neglected'.[30]

The regular garrison of Stirling had been depleted in order to bolster the forces gathering at Edinburgh, but the old and wily Major General William Blakeney as governor could call on the services of the remaining regulars, 320 (eight companies) of militia, his Volunteer Battalion of 200 men and a number of armed townsmen. The castle was strong both by nature and on account of its recent programme of refortification, and nothing short of the attentions of a battering train of heavy cannon would give the Jacobites a good chance of cracking it open. The enterprise would have been unthinkable if the French had not landed a consignment of such artillery at Montrose (p. 366, two 18-pounders, two 12-pounders and two 9-pounders). Lord John Drummond was bringing the cannon with him from the north-east, but their great dead weight 1¾ tons in the case of the 18-pounders) still had to be brought from the north side of the Forth to the south. Two of the pieces were dragged, with enormous difficulty, across the soft Fords of Frew above Stirling, but the rest would have to be ferried across the tidal Forth below the town. This requirement gave rise to a little amphibious campaign in which the Jacobite gunners got the better of the Royal Navy.

The Amphibious Operation, 7–12 January 1745

The original consignment of French artillery (the six 'Swedish' cannon) had been ferried over the Forth before the invasion of England, and the Jacobites had assured its passage by setting up batteries on the last stretch of the river before it widened into the Firth. Colonel Richard Warren, 'ane Irish man and ingeneer', had boasted 'abowt his battery he had erected at Alway to defend the pass and of his red hot ball he was to burn the men of war with'.[31] The French guns had got safely across, but Warren's battery seems to have been wrecked or dismantled early in November.

The Forth between Elphinstone Pans and Alloa once more came into prominence at the end of the last week of January, by which time the army of Prince Charles had returned to the Central Lowlands, and it was a question of transferring the French siege train across the river. The Royal Navy now had a flotilla of sloops and smaller craft operating from Leith and other ports down the Firth, but the captains looked for guidance and inspiration to Walter Grossett, late Collector of Customs at Alloa, who had an expert knowledge of the middle Forth, where the tides still flowed strongly and alternately covered and exposed the banks of grey mud.

Grossett had prided himself on his alacrity in moving all the craft on the Forth to the south bank when Prince Charles had first arrived from the Highlands, but he was not prepared for what happened in January 1746, when the Jacobites occupied both sides of the relevant stretch of the river. Lord Elcho knew something of the ground on the southern bank, having paid court to a lady of the locality the year before. He took up his quarters at Kersie Mains House, and Pitsligo's Horse and his own Lifeguards were deployed further down the bank. One of his detachments, the Regiment of Perth, did very well to seize a merchant brig (a kind of two-masted vessel) at Airth on 7 January; the Jacobites at once brought it upriver to Alloa on the north bank, for it gave them the means of ferrying even the heaviest guns across the river.

The Royal Navy put in its first appearance on 8 January, in the shape of Captain Faulkener's sloop *Vulture*. His longboats succeeded in burning two small vessels which had been beached for the winter on a slipway on the Pow, a creek on the south bank just below Airth. Faulkener was able to retrieve his longboats, but the falling tide left *Vulture* herself stranded in midstream. This was at a time when Jacobite field artillery was on its way to battery sites on both banks of the river. By the end of the day Colonel Henry Ker had planted six 6-pounders from the captured sloop *Hazard* (p. 367) on the quay at Alloa. The town of Stirling surrendered to the Jacobites on the same day,

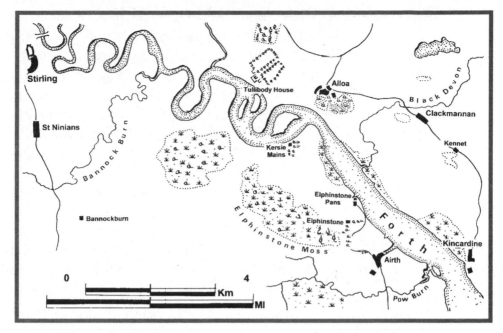

The Forth below Stirling

which freed the expert gunner Colonel James Grant to bring up three 4-pounders to the south bank.

Grant arrived on the Hill of Airth at 8 a.m. of 9 January, and had the agreeable experience of seeing both *Vulture* and her companion the *Pearl* lying aground in front of him. The crew of the *Vulture* fired 190 rounds and persuaded themselves that they had dismounted the Jacobite battery. Grant on his side states that 'we fired about 20 shot at 'em and probably pierced one, for they were pumping for a considerable time after; their firing was very hot but to no purpose'.[32] The contest ended with the vessels re-floating and making their way downriver.

Grant was not altogether satisfied with the performance of his battery, for the river at Airth was too wide (1,100 yards at high tide) for his 4-pounders. He accordingly moved them up the south bank and overnight he established them – and a further 4-pounder from Falkirk – in a good battery site at the old palace of Elphinstone, where the river narrowed to a more reasonable 600 yards. Three more guns were meanwhile added to the existing battery at Alloa on the far bank.

Later in the night the batteries opened fire on the indistinct shapes of three enemy craft which, extraordinarily enough, were passing them from upstream. They were two of the boats from the sloops, and a merchant vessel from Kinghorn that had been decked over with a platform; the sloops' boats were each jammed with fifty armed sailors, and the Kinghorn craft was bearing fifty troops of Blakeney's 27th. The expedition had been organized by Grossett, who had hoped to capture Elcho at Kersie Mains, upstream on a great bend of the river. The expedition had slipped past the Jacobites unseen and the soldiers were duly landed, but it transpired that Elcho had left the house half an hour before. There was still some hope of burning the Jacobite brig at Alloa on the return journey downstream, and the enterprise might have succeeded if one of the boats had not run aground and taken some time to refloat. It was now a question of escape, and the three craft had to brave the fire of the 200 men of Cromartie's Regiment lining the north bank, and the successive batteries at Alloa and Elphinstone, 'but Mr Grossett having by order of Lord Justice Clerk taken two hundred mats of flax from on board a Dutch ship in the Road of Leith, and placed these along the sides of the boats, there was only one man killed and another wounded on this expedition'.[33]

On 10 January the attention of both parties shifted to the north bank, and the opposing moves took on the dimension of a miniature campaign. The Jacobites acted first, by ferrying 300 of Lochiel's Camerons from the south bank. The operation was lengthy, for the troops had to be sent on relays on a single punt, but the reinforcement arrived in time for the Camerons and Cromartie's men to advance together down the bank to confront Colonel Francis Leighton and 300 men of the 27th, who in their turn had been ferried to Kincardine and were marching upriver. Grossett was scouting ahead, and from an 'eminence' (possibly the hill by Kennet) he espied that the reinforcements had reached the enemy, giving them a near two-fold superiority. The redcoats re-embarked in haste.

Leighton's men came on again on 11 January, in four boats, and this time on the spring tide behind the shelter of *Vulture* and *Pearl*, which had been anchored opposite Grant's battery at Elphinstone from 1 p.m. 'And after about three hours' close cannonading within less than a musket shot of the battery, all their [Jacobite] cannon but one were silenced. But the *Pearl* having her cable cut asunder by a cannon ball, she was forced from her station by the strength of the ebb tide, and the two pilots of the *Vulture* ... having each of them at this time lost a leg by another cannon ball, and by which accident they both died, they were obliged to quit the battery.'[34] The defeated flotilla slipped down the river with the tide, and so ended the fourth and last attempt of the Hanoverians to dispute the passage.

The Jacobites were able to ship the heavy French guns across the Forth, the issue on which the whole confrontation had turned. The brig had transported the two 18-pounders from Alloa to Polmaise on the morning of the 11th, before the enemy appeared, and ferried the rest of the train after the sloops had been beaten off. The margins all the time had been narrow, and not least because the Jacobite land forces had been so badly stretched. Prince Charles had feared that the landing at Kincardine had been a feint to draw his troops to the 'wrong' side of the river, while even after the final repulse Lord George wrote from Falkirk that 'It weakens us here very much (and we are God knows few enough when together) that I am obliged to send a battalion at least every day three or four miles to the riverside, to hinder the enemy landing and taking possession of the Carse of Stirling, and the country so useful to us'.[35]

The Landward Operation and the Battle of Falkirk, 13–17 January 1746

The first encounter in the new land campaign was occasioned by the curious fact that the Hanoverian authorities had positioned a depot of bread and fodder at Linlithgow, a town which stood between Hawley's concentration at Edinburgh and the Jacobites at Stirling. Linlithgow was located close to Lord George Murray's covering force of five clan regiments and Elcho's horse at Falkirk. On 13 January Lord George pounced on this tempting target, and by 9 a.m. he had secured the town and could begin loading the provisions on carts.

By chance Lord George's coup coincided with the opening move of the campaign, for Major General Huske was advancing west from Edinburgh with the first division of Hawley's army (Price's 14th, Munro's 37th, Cholmondeley's 34th, Ligonier's 59th, the 13th and 14th Dragoons, and the Glasgow Militia), or about 4,000 men altogether. On the way Huske was told by Walter Grossett that 1,200 of the enemy were in Linlithgow, and the place 'lying in a hollow upon the south side of a large lake which cuts off all communication or access to the town from the north, and Mr Grossett having acquainted the general of this and the situation of the country, the general in order to surprise and cut off the main body of their army … sent a strong advance party forward with orders to halt, and remain upon a rising ground another way, till they came near the West Gate thereof; and the rebels having no suspicion of the main body's advancing upon them, while the advance guard stood still in sight, their communication with the main body of the army would by this means have been cut off'.[36]

It came to nothing. Elcho's cavalry gave timely warning of the redcoats' approach. Moreover operations like these in populated areas were a great attraction for the local people, and one of the spectators rode off and told Lord George what was afoot. At 4 p.m. Lord George withdrew his force from Linlithgow, crossed the Avon by its only bridge, and held his troops some way back from the bank, hoping to lure some of the enemy force across and to attack it with its back the river. Huske's dragoons were too cautious to be drawn into the trap and the day ended with an exchange of insults from the opposite ends of the bridge.

The confrontation at Linlithgow on 13 January was useful to the Jacobites in two ways. It enabled Lord George to get clean away with the captured provisions. It also confirmed the enemy generals in the belief that the rebels would never stand their ground.[37] Hawley should have known better, for he was aware that the enemy were stronger than they had ever been. The veteran forces of the MacDonalds, MacDonnells, Camerons and Stewarts were reinvigorated with fresh blood from the clan recruiting grounds. Also Lord John Drummond had arrived with some 4,000 of the troops which he had been building up in the north-east, bringing with him the clan contingents of the Frasers, MacPhersons and Farquharsons, Lord Lewis Gordon's Regiment from the eastern coastlands, Lord Cromartie's men from the far north, and, most significantly, the picquets of the Irish Brigade and elements of Royal Ecossais. None of this made any impression on Hawley. He was 'resolved to strike while the iron is hot', and he believed that 'with everything they have brought from the north they are now 7,000 men, but that's nothing, they are Scotch, and only so many mouths which must be fed'.[38]

The Hanoverian generals feared only that the Jacobites might slip away before there was a chance to bring them to battle. Otherwise the impending operation appeared to represent little more than an administrative exercise, in which the most pressing problem (and the bugbear of the redcoat army), was how to move and accommodate the troops in wintertime.[39]

Prince Charles left the regiments of Perth and John Roy Stuart and most of Royal Ecossais at Stirling to maintain the siege of the castle, and on 15 and again on 16 January he assembled the rest of the army in battle order south-east of Stirling on Plean Muir. The ground had been reconnoitred closely, and the respective flanks were secured by coal diggings, and by the Torwood – an ancient growth of beech and fir. Hawley moved more slowly than had been expected, and only on the afternoon of the 16th did he march his troops through Falkirk, and encamp them (well short of Plean Muir) on low-lying ground between the town and the Carron Water.

The site of the Hanoverians' camp was chosen for convenience, not for tactical purposes, and Hawley and his staff had so little sense of urgency that they took up their quarters to the east (or far side) of Falkirk in Callendar House. The house was 'an old building, of no great consequence, but has a noble fir wood on the backside upon a hill. Fronting this house you have a vast space of ground, the Forth keeping its course in the middle. The prospect is most delightful and entertaining, by reason of the great number of gentlemen's seats sited on either side the banks of the Forth. These houses are of white stone, and the roofs covered with blue slate, which makes a most agreeable impression in glistening sunshine weather, which we then had'.[40] Callendar House was the residence of Lord Kilmarnock, who was away with the rebels, but Lady Kilmarnock had Whiggish sympathies and the welcome she gave to Hawley and his officers was probably genuine. Nothing was further from the minds of those people than the possibility that the Jacobites might come out to attack *them*. In any case they had a large post of dragoons ahead at Larbert Bridge, which was the only permanent crossing of the Carron Water.

The Jacobites had assembled in battle order twice over, which was an exhausting business even for the hardy Highlanders, and so Prince Charles and all the senior officers fell in with Lord George Murray's proposal for the army to make a right-flanking move through Torwood, across the upper Carron Water and over the Muir of Falkirk, an uneven rolling plateau that dominated the enemy encampment. This upland was in fact an ancient coastal bluff, dating from post-glacial times when the plain of the Forth had been an arm of the sea. Its military potential had already been recognized by the Romans, and a stretch of the Antonine Wall ran along one of the nearby raised beaches. The vegetation of the Muir in 1746 was predominantly heather and bushes, relieved by dry stone walls and patches of rough grazing around the scattered farms. The most striking single feature was a steep-sided ravine (an ancient coastal chine), which ran from near the summit to the low ground to the south. The term 'ravine' was used loosely in eighteenth-century military writing, but this was one which lived up to its name, being impassable to troops of all kinds.

The odds in the coming battle were approximately equal. The Hanoverian forces probably had a small advantage in numbers (below), but a number of the regiments of the infantry of the line were not as solid as they ought to have been, for the Edinburgh and Glasgow Regiments and the newly arrived Argyll Militia were untried units, raised recently from civilians, and among the three regiments of dragoons only Cobham's 10th were 'troops that may be depended upon'.[41] Little trust could be put in Ligonier's (late Gardiner's) 13th or Hamilton's 14th, both of which had failed at Prestonpans.

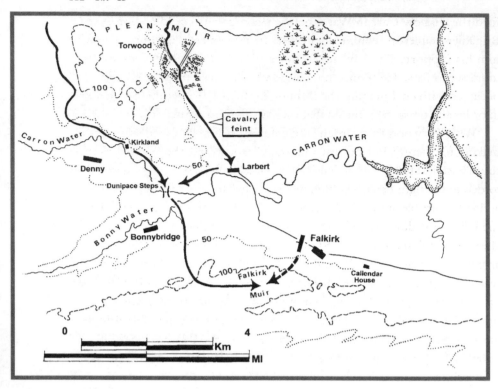

To Falkirk, 17 January 1746

On the morning of 17 January Prince Charles once more reviewed his army on Plean Muir. The muster was completed in the usual style, but instead of standing on the moor for the third day in succession, the troops, to general mystification, were formed into two parallel columns 200 yards apart and directed to their right along side paths.[42] Lord John Drummond was detached with the cavalry to the north of Torwood to make a show along the road from Stirling. As a further eye-catcher the Prince's white standard was left flying in the camp, and fires were lit along Torwood ridge. Lord George Murray sent the military chest and the records under escort to Dunblane, and if the same precaution had been observed at Culloden in the coming April 'things might have remained a secret to this day, that were partly discovered by neglecting to secure the papers concerning the enterprise'.[43]

The relations between O'Sullivan and Lord George broke down after only about half a mile of marching, when the Irishman rode up to say that the movement must surely have been seen by the enemy, and that the Jacobites must postpone their further advance until after dark. Lord George replied that nothing could now stop the progress of the army, which was certain to ford the shallow Carron Water before the redcoats could respond, and Brigadier Stapleton (commander of the Irish picquets) came up and gave him his support. The advance went on: 'We had very bad sloughs and morasses to pass. The Prince was always where he was most necessary, was occupied with encouraging the forming of them … to get them to march in order and press them on, so that there would be no interval'.[44]

With Torwood to their left, the columns at first marched south, as if making for Denny, but on reaching the Carron Water they veered to the south-east and followed the left bank as far as Dunipace Steps, where they forded to the right bank. The Bonny Water a few hundred yards beyond was an inconsiderable stream, and on the far side the Jacobites began to climb the hills in the direction of Falkirk. Colonel Henry Ker of Graden scouted ahead, while Kilmarnock guided the troops, using his local knowledge. The artillery train was lagging behind, and was still short of the Carron when it reached a fork in the path and halted in perplexity. The Duke of Perth drove up in his chaise, for a boil made it impossible for him to ride, and he was driving back to join Glenbucket in the trenches before Stirling. He told the gunners that there would probably be no need for the cannon that day, 'and upon this they marched very cheerfully and with such dispatch to the river that they arrived in time to share the victory'.[45]

Both O'Sullivan and Lord George had been in the right: O'Sullivan because the army had been seen by the enemy, and Lord George because he was justified by events. Hawley (contrary to legend) left the comforts of Callendar House commendably early, at 5 a.m., and over the following hours both Lord John Drummond's diversionary force and the main Jacobite columns were sighted a number of times. But the Hanoverians did singularly little about it. After one of the earlier alarms, when the Jacobites were glimpsed on a hill 4 miles away, 'the regiments turned out and drew up in front of their camp, and the artillery was in readiness for any command, this about nine in the morning, but the rebels soon disappeared again, the soldiers were ordered into camp and the artillery horses, by order, sent to their pickets to feed; Captain Cunningham [of the artillery] went to Falkirk to shave and shift himself, for he had no tent in the camp, having been obliged to leave that at Newcastle when he came post from thence'.[46]

The first countermove of any kind was executed towards 2 p.m. by the ailing Colonel Francis Ligonier (brother of the lieutenant general), who led the three regiments of dragoons past the eastern walls of Bantaskine House and up the slopes of the hill. It is quite possible that Hawley even now had not guessed what the Jacobites had in mind for him. The Edinburgh

Volunteer John Home writes that 'it is said, and generally believed, that General Hawley, when he heard the Highlanders were about to cross the Carron at Dunipace, did not think they were coming to attack his army, but imagined that they were going to give him the slip, and march back to England: that in this conceit, he ordered the dragoons and foot to march up the hill, intercept the rebels, and force them to come to an action. Hence the conflict happened upon a piece of ground which he had never viewed, and was a field of battle exceedingly disadvantageous to his troops'.[47]

The Hanoverian infantry trailed out of the camp and addressed itself to the climb in the face of a strengthening south-west wind. As for the cannon, Captain Cunningham was finally able to obtain orders 'to march the artillery up … the hill in the rear of the front line of the army. The roads here were so very bad and intricate, that it was not only out of his power to keep up with the first line, but the rear line also passed by the train, and were both forming before he could possibly bring up the artillery. Then two of his largest guns [probably 6-pounders] in the front stuck in a bog, from which he could not disengage any of the guns that were behind except two 4-pounders, and one 1½-pounder'.[48] The cannon had been borrowed from the armament of Edinburgh Castle, and the personnel were also improvised, being a party of sailors to serve the guns, and a number of the Yorkshire Blues who were supposed to help to move them.

There ensued a jockeying for position around the southern flank of Falkirk Muir. A number of Hanoverian dragoons came down as if to gain the Jacobite right, but the onrush was checked when Lord George advanced a column to head them off. A party of MacGregors under Colonel John Roy Stuart were in the lead, and plunged into the Abbot's Moss along the Glen Burn, an obstacle that henceforward gave the Jacobites a secure flank protection. Prince Charles for his part was pushing his army as a whole out to the right, to win the greatest advantage from a change in the weather, 'for now the day, from being an exceeding fine one, became on a sudden obscure; the sun which till then had shone upon us, was now as if it were eclipsed, and all the elements in confusion so that the heavens seemed to fulminate their anger down upon us'. It was important to have the 'impetuous storm of hail, wind and rain' at their backs, and driving in the faces of the enemy.[49]

Both armies began to form up in two lines and a small reserve. The Jacobite first line had on its right the three Clan Donald regiments of Keppoch (400), Clanranald (350) and Glengarry (8–900), which had been the first to arrive on the field. Then came in succession the Stewarts of Appin (300), Lochiel's Camerons (8–900), the Farquharson of Monaltrie's battalion (150)

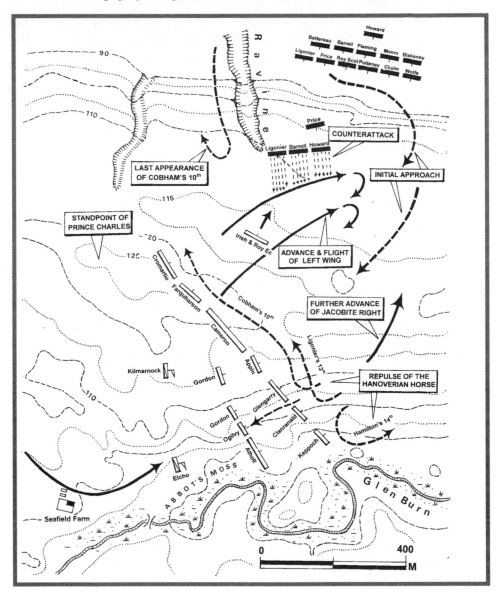

Falkirk, 17 January 1746 (positions and movements conjectural)

and the regiment of Lord Cromartie (200). The Jacobite second line (again reading from its right to its left) was formed entirely of Lowlanders, namely the Atholl Brigade (three battalions, 6–900), Ogilvy's Regiment (two battalions 5–900), and the recently arrived regiment of Lord Lewis Gordon (two battalions, 4–800). The units of the smaller clans were attached to those of their larger neighbours. The reserve of up to 250–300 troops consisted of the three picquets of the Irish Brigade, and the grenadier company and a fusilier company of Royal Ecossais. Now that there was no further need for deception, Lord John Drummond brought up the cavalry by the direct route from the east of Torwood and across the Carron Water by Larbert Bridge. All the horsed units were present (the regiments of Elcho, Balmerino, Pitsligo, Kilmarnock and the hussars: 360–440), and they were deployed in two groups, one on either flank.

Every investigation of the battle has thrown up wide variations in the figures given for the Jacobite forces,[50] with the grand totals varying between 6,160 and 8,200.

The three regiments of dragoons (Cobham's 10th, Francis Ligonier's 13th and Hamilton's 14th) had been the first units of Hawley's army to arrive on the Muir. Behind them the infantry was forming up in two lines. The first comprised Sir John Ligonier's 59th, Price's 14th, the second battalion of the Royal Scots, Pulteney's 13th, Cholmondeley's 34th, Wolfe's 8th. In the second line we find Battereau's 62nd, Barrell's excellent 4th, Fleming's 36th, Munro's 37th, and Blakeney's 27th. Howard's 3rd was in close reserve behind the right. The Scottish irregular forces were tucked away in locations where they ought to have been at no risk. The Glasgow Regiment and Paisley Volunteers took up stations on the left and well to the rear of the dragoons. From the loyal south-west Lieutenant Colonel John Campbell of Mamore had brought up one company of the Black Watch (43rd), three of Loudoun's 64th Highlanders, and twelve of the Argyll Milita. They were posted down the hill on the far right to guard the camp.

The numbers (with the usual reservations) came to about 5,850 of the line, 800 dragoons (though the Jacobites estimated 1,200), 650 of the Glasgow and Paisley volunteers, and 800 of the men of the Highlanders and militia of Campbell of Mamore, with a grand total of some 8,100. Taking both sides together, the totals can be put at between 14,260 and 16,300, which most probably makes Falkirk the largest engagement of the rising.

Neither side brought any artillery into action, the Jacobites because they had left theirs behind the Carron Water, and the Hanoverians because Cumming's guns were still stuck down the hill. Another curiosity was that the Hanoverian right wing much outflanked the Jacobite left, an accident which the redcoats could not put to any use, at least for offensive purposes, on account of the intervening ravine. A greater crowd of spectators than ever was gathering to see the show.

At 3.30 p.m. the combat opened for the Hanoverians in the style of Prestonpans and Clifton, by an unsupported action by their three regiments of dragoons, in this case against the most ill-chosen of opponents, the Clan Donald. Both Lord George Murray and young Angus MacDonnell (war leader of the Glengarrys) had ordered the men to hold their fire in the face of advancing horsemen, 'although they were horrendous to behold with grey blades unsheathed'.[51] John Daniel records that

> when I saw this moving cloud of horse, regularly disciplined, in full trot upon us down the summit, I doubted not but they would have ridden over us without opposition ... but I soon found myself mistaken ... The brave front line of MacDonnells suffered the enemy to come ten or twelve paces of them without firing. [They] nobly altogether presented, and sent their benediction upon them, so that in the third part of a minute that rapid and impetuous torrent, which seemed in rolling to lay all waste before them, was now checked and stemmed in such a manner that it was made to retake its course faster than it had proceeded.[52]

Most of Daniel's fellow-Jacobites remembered the event in the same way, but there is a touch of realism in de Johnstone's account when he writes that 'the English began the attack with a body of about eleven hundred cavalry, which advanced very slowly against the right of our army, and did not halt till they were within twenty paces of our first line, to induce us to fire. The Highlanders, who had been particularly enjoined not to fire till the army was within musket shot of them, the moment the cavalry halted, discharged their muskets, and killed about eighty men, each of them having aimed at a rider. The commander of this body of men, who had advanced some paces before his men, was of this number'.[53]

The slain officer was Lieutenant Colonel Shugborough Whitney of Ligonier's 13th Dragoons. His men, or at least those nearest to him, closed up their depleted ranks, put spurs to their horses, and

> rushed upon the Highlanders at a hard trot, breaking their ranks, throwing down everything before them, and trampling the Highlanders under the feet of their horses. The most singular and extraordinary combat immediately followed. The Highlanders, stretched on the ground, thrust their dirks into the bellies of the horses. Some seized the riders by their clothes, dragged them down, and stabbed them with their dirks; several again used their pistols; but few of them had sufficient space to handle their swords ... The resistance of the Highlanders was so incredibly obstinate, that the English, having been for some time engaged pell-mell with them in their ranks, were at length repulsed and forced to retire.[54]

A body of the dragoons had nevertheless succeeded in breaking clean through the Highlanders, and became hotly engaged with the Lowlanders standing behind. Ogilvy's Regiment was for a time in a bad way, but the Irish major Nicholas Glasgow was able to retrieve one of the colours, which had been dropped, and the horsemen were finally repulsed with the help of the Menzies of the Atholl Brigade.

The beaten dragoons made off in diverse directions. Hamilton's 14th were the first to run, and the Clan Donald chased after them with its broadswords, having ignored the injunction of Lord George to stand fast. One of the officers of the Keppochs, Major Donald MacDonnell of Tirnadris, mounted a riderless horse, but the beast took off after its fellows and carried him off. He reached Barrell's Regiment, mistaking it for the red-coated Irish, and when he discovered his error he tried in vain to pass himself off as a Campbell. Hawley reported that 'one Major MacDonald [sic], who blundered up to the head of one of the two battalions where Huske was, and when he was found out and ordered to be seized, pulled out a pistol and had shot Huske if it had not been for [Brigadier] Cholmondeley'.[55] Another account explains in more detail that Huske was in an unusually savage mood, with his sword encrusted with blood and hair, and would have had MacDonnell shot down if Lieutenant Colonel Robert Kerr had not inter-vened by beating down the raised muskets, and showing himself willing to accept his surrender. 'When the major was pulling his pistol from his belt he happened to do it with such an air that Huske swore the dog was going to shoot him. To which the major replied, "I am more of a gentleman, Sir, than to do any such thing. I am only pulling off my pistol to deliver it up".'[56]

Meanwhile the flight of the 14th Dragoons continued unchecked. They rode over a company of the Glasgow Regiment and probably also a large number of the spectators. A number of the Glaswegians opened fire in self-defence, but their commander, the Earl of Home, galloped all the way to Linlithgow and safety.

As for the rest of the horse, Cobham's 10th and Ligonier's 13th were in a still worse state, for they broke to their right, a direction which carried them across the front of the Jacobite left wing, which shot them up as if they had been 'running the gauntlet, exposed to the fire of all the line'.[57] Cobham's Dragoons ended up among the Argyll Militia at the bottom of the hill.

Now that the left wing of the Highlanders had expended its fire, the Camerons and the Stewart Appins cast their muskets aside and charged broadsword in hand; 'this was perhaps one of the boldest and finest actions that any troops in the world would be capable of'.[58] The impact carried away the four first-line regiments of Wolfe, Cholmondeley, Pulteney and the Royal Scots, and the panic was transmitted to the second line, some of which fled in its turn. Most of the surviving details concern Munro's 37th, which was not the regiment of the Presbyterian clan of Munro, but an English unit (late Ponsonby's) recently taken under the command of Sir Robert Munro of Foulis. There was therefore no blood connection between Munro and his men, and

> Sir Robert alone, who was so corpulent a man that he had been obliged at Fontenoy to stand upon his feet when all the rest of his regiment lay down on their faces to avoid the enemy's fire, boldly faced the charging High-landers. He was attacked at once by six antagonists, two of whom he laid at his feet with a half-pike, but a seventh came up, and discharged a shot into his body, by which he was mortally wounded. His brother, an unarmed physician, at this juncture came to his relief, but shared in the indiscriminate slaughter which was then going on.[59]

Captain George Fitzgerald commanded the last 'hat' (fusilier) platoon on the left of the regiment, and

> Blakeney's Regiment being put into some disorder on the left of ours, by being attacked on their flank by the rebels, occasioned ours likewise to give way. It was at this time that I was knocked down by a musket ball which went through my hat and grazed my head, but I rose again, being only stunned by it, and perceiving the left wing of both lines broke and retreat-ing down the hill, I observed the army still formed on the right and was endeavouring to make that way, but was surrounded again by a party of the rebels who cut me in the head and knocked me down a second time, when they began to rob me and, as I imagined, would have afterwards murdered me, but I called out to a French soldier going by and desired he would not suffer these villains to kill me, and he immediately came to my assistance and prevented their doing me any further mischief, but they said I was their prisoner and they would carry me to their Prince.[60]

The army was saved from destruction largely by 'those honest battalions of Barrell and Ligonier'.[61] Barrell's 4th had Brigadier Cholmondeley with it, as we have seen, and also Brigade Major Captain James Wolfe from Hawley's staff, and no doubt the presence of these officers helped to bol-ster the resistance. The troops stood firm when the fleeing Royal Scots surged around their flanks, and then advanced to plug the consequent gap in the first line. Ligonier's 59th also stood its ground, under the command of

Lieutenant Colonel George Stanhope, and Cholmondeley was able to anchor the two regiments firmly in position – with their left flank abutting a farm-house, and their right flank protected by the providential ravine. Howard's 3rd moved up in reserve, and Huske brought up bits and pieces of Price's 14th and Battereau's 62nd.

The redcoats formed what O'Sullivan called 'that accursed hollow square',[62] and poured volleys into the left flank of the Highlanders as they chased after the disintegrating left wing of the Hanoverians. In the recriminations long after the battle Lord George Murray claimed that the issue would have been decided there and then if Lord George Drummond had been where he was supposed to be, in command of the Jacobite left wing, where he could have ordered up the second line in support. However, Elcho puts the blame on the failure of the Jacobites to bring up their right wing, which was nobody's fault in particular, for 'the badness and darkness of the weather prevented the Prince's right from seeing what had passed on the left, and then all the generals and aides-de-camp were on foot, whereas they ought to have been on horseback, for generals' business in battle is more to command than to fight as common soldiers. However it is certain the Highlanders must have good example shown then, and that was the reason for it'.[63] Lord George was responsible for this part of the army, and he was busy directing the Atholl Brigade as it exploited the victory of Clan Donald.

Prince Charles's standpoint on the highest part of the hill was distant from the combat as it was now developing, and the only attempt to exercise control was the person – either Lord John Drummond or John Roy Stuart – who suspected an ambush, and called the advance to a halt. The effect was unfortunate, for 'the cry of "stop" flew immediately from rank to rank, and threw the whole army into disorder'.[64] The Lowlanders of the second line gained the impression that the day was lost, and some of them carried the news of the supposed disaster back to Bannockburn and Stirling. Thus at this stage of battle large numbers of the rival armies were fleeing in opposite directions, leaving the plateau somewhat bare.

The respite encouraged Major General Cholmondeley to organize a counter-attack. Almost everything that we know about this episode comes from his own pen:

> During this time General Huske was rallying the other troops that had been broke, then I told these two battalions [Barrell's and Ligonier's] that if they would keep their ground, I would go back and rally the dragoons [probably Cobham's], they promised they would, and kept their word. Accordingly

I went to the dragoons and rallied about one hundred of them, and told them that I had repulsed the enemy with two weak battalions, and that if they would march up I would head them, and that I would order the two battalions to march up briskly at the same time, and give them their fire, and that they should fall in, sword in hand. They were greatly pleased with this, and, with many oaths and Irish exclamations, swore they would follow me. I marched them up to the two battalions, but when we were to advance they kept at least one hundred yards behind me; with some difficulty I got them to the top of the hill, where I saw the Highlanders formed behind some houses and barns (where I was forced to fire a pistol among them before I could get them to do this), I then returned to the two battalions, to march them up. Here General Huske joined me, and I told him that if we could get some more battalions to join us, we might drive them, but as night was drawing in he ordered me to retire.[65]

The shyness of the dragoons was occasioned by the decisive move of the battle, which was the bringing up of the unengaged deep reserve of the Jacobites, namely the Irish picquets and the men of Royal Ecossais, who were now advanced by Brigadier Stapleton. The credit for this brilliantly timed initiative has been assigned variously to Prince Charles, O'Sullivan, or Lord George Murray acting through his aide-de-camp Colonel Henry Ker of Graden. Some 600 or 700 men rallied on the French troops, and the sight of the red- and blue-coated regulars advancing against them persuaded the dragoons to fall back on the intact Hanoverian infantry, whereupon the combined force executed a disciplined retreat towards Falkirk.

The rest of Hawley's army was streaming to the town in a state of disintegration. Duncan Ban MacIntyre, a paid substitute in the ranks of the Argyll Militia, writes that none of Hawley's army had thought it possible that they were the ones who were to be 'driven, like sheep before a dog', when 'Prince Charles and his Frenchmen' charged downhill.[66] Captain Cunningham takes up the story of the artillery, whose bogged-down cannon were abandoned by the sailors, the Yorkshire Blues and the locally recruited civilian drivers.

In such a situation, deserted by his men, and the rebels within paces … he thought it prudent to order them down the hill where perceiving every-thing in confusion, after having endeavoured with several officers to rally the flying soldiers, but in vain, the report running that the whole army was broke, he retired with the multitude to Falkirk, whose gates were so crowded with officers and soldiers that he could scarce get entrance. He went to his quarters where his cloak bag was, and in which there was £120 of the government's money, which he thought it his duty to secure lest it should fall into the rebels' hands.[67]

Major James Lockhart of Cholmondeley's 34th had joined the retreat, but was ordered back to the camp to save the tents. His servant William King gave him his horse, but before Lockhart had ridden 20 yards 'the horse fell with his master and tumbled over him, whereby he was so bruised as to become insensible ... he [King] ... hearing a cry that the Highlanders were coming through Callendar Wood and would be immediately down to the highway where his master lay, was afraid the enemy would cut him to pieces, and therefore ran to Callendar House and begged assistance to carry his master to that place ... and on carrying him to Callendar House his master had great woundings and cried he was a-dying'.[68]

Ideally the Jacobites should have been in a position to convert their more than creditable victory into a battle of annihilation. There was much talk afterwards of Lord George Murray having thrown away the chance by ordering a new halt, but he explains that 'our vast loss was that not a pair of pipes could be got. The pipers, whenever a battle begins, give their pipes to their boys, who take care of them; and the pipers, who are commonly as good men as any, charge with the rest'.[69] It would in any case have been very difficult to exercise effective command in the conditions then obtaining – the darkness, the storm, the broken ground and the disordered state of the troops. Many of the senior officers had lost contact altogether with what was going on. When the redcoat captain Fitzgerald was being led prisoner to the rear he encountered first Prince Charles 'with a number of horsemen about him with his back to a hut to shelter him from the weather, it raining and blowing excessively hard'. Further on at Dunipace were to be seen a number of chiefs, 'as Lewis Gordon, Cluny MacPherson, one Farquharson etc. who seemed to be apprehensive that some of our dragoons were pursuing them, nor did they know till next morning the Pretender's son was at Falkirk, by several things I heard them say'.[70]

In the general confusion 'it was Lord Kilmarnock who first discovered the flight of the English. Being well acquainted with the nature of the ground, as part of his estates lay in the neighbourhood, he was sent by the Prince to reconnoitre the enemy; and, having approached the great road to Edinburgh, beyond the town of Falkirk, passing by by-paths and across fields, he saw the English army panic-struck and flying in the greatest disorder, as fast as their legs would carry them'.[71]

The most disciplined bodies available to the Jacobites – the Atholl Brigade, the Irish and the Royal Ecossais – now took possession of Falkirk. The only show of opposition was put by a rearguard along Cow Wynd in the east, and in the fighting Lord John Drummond had his horse shot under him and received a ball in the arm. Many of the other troops now took the opportunity to plunder the abandoned camp, while Prince Charles was led by torchlight to the house of Madam Graham, widow of a physician, 'and a woman whose intelligence and superior manners are still remembered with veneration at Falkirk'.[72]

All the officers who were not on duty spent the next day, 18 January, in Falkirk town under cover from the streaming rain. In the dim light something of both the scale and the nature of the victory could be seen on the higher ground to the south, and 'especially in a hollow towards the foot of the hill where the cornfields were thickly strewn with bodies'.[73] Overnight they had been

> stripped so effectually, that a citizen of Falkirk, who next morning surveyed the field from a distance, and who lived till recent years to describe the scene, used to say that he could compare them with nothing but a large flock of sheep at rest on the face of the hill ... The ... day, during which it continued to rain with little intermission, was spent at Falkirk by the insurgents in securing the spoils and burying the slain. They employed the country people to dig a spacious pit upon the field of battle, into which they precipitated the naked corpses. The rustics who stood around easily distinguished the English soldiers from the Highlanders by their comparative nudity, and by the deep gashes which seamed their shoulders and breasts – the dreadful work of the broadsword. The numbers of slain inhumed in this pit was such, that some years after the surface sank down many feet, and there is still a considerable hollow in that part of the battlefield.[74]

The pit towards the bottom of the hill was the site of the later High Station, and the bodies came to light again when work started on the railway tunnel in 1839. The other slain still rest in the upper pit, the one with the sunken surface, which is now ringed with trees, and located by Dumyat Drive.

It is impossible even to guess at the mortality on either side. The number of the Jacobite dead could conceivably be no more than 50, which is difficult to believe. Some estimates at the time reached more than 1,200,[75] which is quite impossible, given the numbers still at the disposal of the Jacobites afterwards, and the usual ratio of wounded to dead of three to one. Two of the authenticated losses affected the Clan Donald in particular. The Major

MacDonnell of Tirnadris who had fallen into the hands of the enemy was renowned as the officer who had got the better of the redcoats at Highbridge on 16 August, which was the first action of the rising. He was condemned to death and executed at Carlisle on 18 October 1746. On the day after the battle a clansman of the MacDonalds, who was cleaning his gun in Falkirk, killed Angus MacDonnell, who was the war leader of the Glengarrys. It had been a pure accident, but the Glengarrys could not reconcile themselves to the death of their war chief, and the execution of the wretched MacDonald did nothing to assuage their anger.

The initial Hanoverian return listed 12 of their officers and 55 of their men killed, and 280 others missing, which is possibly a grievous underestimate. 'Of General Hawley's army were killed (according to the report of Colonel MacLachlan of Lachlan, who by orders surveyed the field in the morning after the action) above 800, besides those who, in their flight, running towards the river of Forth in hopes of getting aboard some vessels, were drowned in the River Avon, besides many buried in the night time by the country people, and some who fell into the coal pits and were too far down to be got up'.[76]

What was immediately clear was that the number of senior officers killed was very high in proportion, and Hawley rightly suspected that it was because they had been deserted by their men during the general disintegration of the left wing. The tally was headed by Colonel Sir Robert Munro of Munro's 37th, and the lieutenant colonels Maurice Powell of Cholmondeley's 34th and Shugborough Whitney of Ligonier's 13th Dragoons. Another victim was Colonel Francis Ligonier himself, who dragged himself to the battle half-dead, and expired afterwards at Edinburgh of aggravated pleurisy. He was commemorated on his tomb as *A zealous Protestant and subject of England, sacrificing himself against a Popish Pretender at the Battle of Falkirk 1746*.

The two brothers Munro had been found lying together in a pool of water formed by the rain. Colonel Sir Robert 'was heard much to blaspheme during the engagement, and as a punishment for which his tongue was miraculously cut asunder by a sword that struck him across the mouth. His brother, a physician, was likewise killed at his side'.[77] More sympathetic observers noted that as a sign of Sir Robert's warrior spirit, 'his right hand still clenched the pommel of his sword, from which the whole blade had been broken off. The corpses were interred in one grave in the parish churchyard'.[78] The monument still stands.

More than 300 Hanoverians had been taken prisoner, and they included, revealingly, several Presbyterian ministers, and a number of Hawley's prized hangmen. The surgeon of the Irish picquets, John Crosbie, was now 'at great pains and expense in dressing the wounded and applying medicines to the wounded of the King's troops left at Falkirk and Stirling'.[79]

Material trophies counted highly in the military point-scoring of the time. The Jacobites seized the carts and waggons in the abandoned camp, picked up muskets by the hundred on the field, and had captured two infantry colours, a kettledrum and three dragoon standards. One of the standards was that of Ligonier's 13th Dragoons, bearing the motto *Britons Strike Home*; the Jacobite volunteer John Daniel, as an Englishman, saw no reason why he should not put it to use in a good cause, and he carried it at Culloden. The Chevalier de Johnstone was sent with a sergeant and twenty men to search for the abandoned artillery:

> The sergeant carried a lantern; the light was soon extinguished, and by that accident we immediately lost our way, and wandered a long time at the foot of the hill, among heaps of bodies, which their whiteness rendered visible, notwithstanding the obscurity of a very dark night. To add to the disagreeableness of our situation from the horror of the scene, the wind and rain were full in our faces. I even remarked a trembling and strong agitation in my horse, which constantly shook when it was forced to put its feet on the heaps of the dead bodies and climb over them. However, after we had wandered a long time amongst these bodies, we at length found the cannon.[80]

There were seven of the pieces.

Although the battle of Falkirk had been given under circumstances vastly different from that at Prestonpans, a number of the essentials remained remarkably unchanged. Once more the Hanoverian dragoons had been engaged regardless, once more the Hanoverian artillery had amounted to nothing, and yet again the enemy had been underestimated. The recriminations that followed were of much the same kind. The 13th and 14th Dragoons were the same units that had run away at Prestonpans, though Cobham's 10th, an English regiment, had remained under some kind of command, and now escaped censure. Worst of all in Hawley's view was the misbehaviour of leaders, like the officer of Blakeney's 27th who was seen galloping away with a colour in his hand. Hawley therefore placed five of his officers under arrest, as well as setting his hangmen to work among the rank and file.

The most prominent victim was Captain Archibald Cunningham of the artillery, who had come to Hawley's notice when the army was on the retreat, and the general applied to the artillery train for a fresh supply of gunpowder.

He now learned that Cunningham had fled towards Edinburgh, and left no powder in the barrels. 'For this treachery, when General Hawley returned to Edinburgh, he had him seized, and would have shot him, had he not, the night before it was to be done, with a penknife cut the arteries of his arm and bled to death.'[81]

Major Lockhart survived with his reputation intact, for he was able to bring together an impressive number of witnesses. He had been unable to bring off the tents from the camp, having been crushed by his horse in a fall (p. 422) and then carried to Callendar House. From there, according to his testimony, Lady Kilmarnock delivered him up to the Jacobites.[82] He fell into an abusive argument with John Roy Stuart when he was being taken under escort to Stirling,[83] and survived to become one of the most relentless persecutors of the Jacobites.

Unlike Cope, Hawley himself escaped a court martial, but right-thinking men pronounced their own verdict. 'General Hawley ... had neither knowledge nor conduct (whatever may be his personal courage) to command in a general battle; nor had he that room in the affections of officers or soldiers that could make him hope for success. Kindness, civility and an affable courtesy will inspire resolution and fortitude, but bad usage begets contempt'.[84]

The Jacobites had seen the Highland charge work its old magic, though a significant number of the Hanoverian infantry had for the first time stood and fought, and the breakdown of the Jacobite command and control had been remedied only when the 'French' regulars were fed into the action. However, these reservations did not detract from the magnitude of what had been achieved. 'Thus,' wrote the Whiggish Sir John Clerk of Penicuik, 'our brave army of regular troops which amounted to about 8,000 men, and which had behaved well in Flanders, fled before an army of no greater force than our own, to the shame and disgrace of all military discipline'.[85]

The Lost Victory: The Siege of Stirling Castle and the Advent of Cumberland, 18 January – 1 February 1746

For the Jacobites everything now hung on whether or not they would be able to exploit their astonishing tactical success on the operational and strategic planes. Prince Charles had been ill during his stay with Sir Hugh Paterson at Bannockburn House, and it is possible that his sickly state accounts for two extremely questionable decisions. The first was to return to Stirling and continue the siege of the castle, regardless of the changed conditions that obtained after the battle of Falkirk, when a sustained pursuit might have completed the rout of Hawley's army before it could come to its senses and gain reinforcements. Among the troops of Prince Charles the Highlanders were made for the offensive, and the *élan* and impetus of the chase – and the prospect of booty – would have helped to keep them with the colours. In that event the castle would have been isolated without any foreseeable prospect of relief, and it would probably have surrendered anyway, 'being in want of stores and many other things, quite scandalous to the people who have the management of those affairs'.[86] Instead, on 19 January Prince Charles left Lord George Murray on guard at Falkirk with the clan regiments, and brought the Lowlanders back to Stirling to reinforce the siege.

In any other context Stirling Castle would certainly have been a major prize for the Jacobites on its own account, whether for offensive or defensive purposes, for it was situated at the narrowest point of the British mainland (p. 38), and at the intersection of the principal axes of Scottish communications, from north to south, and from east to west. Its importance had been underlined repeatedly in Scottish history, not least when William Wallace defeated the Earl of Surrey at Stirling Bridge on 11 September 1297, and Robert the Bruce beat King Edward II himself at Bannockburn nearby on 24 June 1314. At that time the castle had been the only stronghold still held by the English in Scotland, and it surrendered immediately after Bannockburn. Towards 1500 the old timber bridge across the Forth was replaced by a fine new structure of stone about 60 yards downstream. The bridge remained the lowest permanent crossing of the river, which was here 74 yards wide, and the connection between bridge and castle was if anything strengthened by developments in artillery which brought the bridge within distant cannon shot of the crag. The castle occupied the highest point of this volcanic crag standing proud of the denuded lower ground, which until the nineteenth century was covered with great expanses of peat bog extending up the plain of the upper Forth to the west. Stirling town occupied the sheltered 'tail' to the south-east.

The castle was first adapted to the demands of artillery fortification in the 1550s. Between 1708 and 1714 a more thoroughgoing transformation was undertaken to the designs of Captain Theodore Drury, who razed or trimmed a number of the old defences, and in particular strengthened the townward side by means of a zigzag outer rampart and a ravelin-like projection. If the attack were to have any prospect of success it would have to be on this side, where the ground sloped gradually up from the town and modern siege artillery gave the means of effecting practicable breaches. The

Parliamentary lieutenant general Monk had used this approach when he laid siege to the castle in August 1650, and the scars of his strikes are still to be seen on a gable of the Great Hall and the lower part of the Elphinstone Tower. The great strength of the castle remained in the precipices which bordered all the other sides, and the sense of superiority imparted by the command of 'the finest view in Scotland',[87] extending east over cornfields and the meanders of the lower Forth to the Ochils, north to the entrance to the Grampians by Dunblane, and to the west over Drip, Blairdrummond and Flanders Mosses to the Trossachs.

Colonel James Grant's brave and brilliant handling of the field artillery had just defeated a flotilla of the Royal Navy and enabled the French siege train to be brought across the Forth, and he now proposed that the castle should be attacked from the classic direction of the town cemetery, where the siege guns would be most nearly on a level with the fortifications. Prince Charles preferred to give an ear to the townspeople, who were afraid that Stirling would be wrecked by the return fire from the castle, and he fell in with the alternative offered by the incompetent Franco-Scottish engineer Mirabelle de Gordon, who had come with Lord John Drummond. Mirabelle de Gordon advocated an attack from the little Gowan Hill, which lay hard under the north-eastern side of the castle, totally dominated by whatever cannon the besiegers might choose to bring to bear against it. The bedrock lay only 15 inches under the surface, which would make it difficult for the besiegers to throw up effective cover, and as a final disqualification the ramparts on this side crowned a stretch of the near-vertical cliff, which would make it impossible even for the agile Highlanders to scale any breach that might still be made.

Accepting Mirabelle's advice was the Prince's second miscalculation, and probably no other tactical mistake can be pinned so firmly on him. It is difficult to account for the blunder in this case, unless he was affected by his

Stirling Castle from the Jacobite battery on Gowan Hill

illness or distracted by his love affair with Clementina Walkinshaw, for he ought to have been able to make an informed judgement on the proposals that were now being put to him. An acquaintance with the principles of siegecraft and fortification were part and parcel of a gentleman's education at the time, and what Charles had seen of the siege of Gaeta in 1734 had given him the opportunity of seeing how theory was put into practice.

The garrison had cut an arch of Stirling Bridge, which prevented the country people from bringing produce to the Jacobites from the rich plain of the lower Forth, and so the resources of the Lowlanders, who formed the greater part of the besieging force, were depleted by having to send out parties to gather in provisions.[88] Another consequence was that the labour and danger of building the siegeworks on the Gowan Hill fell chiefly on the Irish picquets, who suffered daily casualties from sniping and the bombs of coehorn mortars. 'What a pity that these brave men should have been sacrificed to no purpose, by the ignorance and folly of Mirabelle! These picquets, who behaved with the most distinguished bravery and intrepidity at the battle of Falkirk, preserving the best order, when the whole of the rest of the army was dispersed, and keeping the enemy in check by the bold countenance they displayed, ought to have been reserved for a better occasion.'[89]

Mirabelle's mistakes did not end there. An eighteenth-century siege battery consisted of two main elements – a thick protective breastwork or bank (in this case built up with sandbags and wool sacks), and the embrasures or holes through which the cannon barrels projected when the decisive moment came to open fire. It was important to have all the pieces able to operate simultaneously, so as to have the best chance of gaining the superiority of fire, but Mirabelle was lulled by the lack of response from the castle (old Major General Blakeney was just biding his time) and he opened up on 29 January with just three of the intended six embrasures completed. 'It was of short duration, and produced very little effect on the batteries of the castle, which being more elevated than ours, the enemy could see even the buckles on the shoes of our artillerymen. As their fire commanded ours, our guns were immediately dismounted; and in less than half an hour we were obliged to abandon our battery altogether, as no one could approach it without meeting certain destruction; while our guns, being pointed upwards, could do no execution whatsoever.'[90] Afterwards one of the cannon barrels was found to have been hit no fewer than nine times, some of the gouges being of a surprising depth.

Some of the moral credit which had been derived from the last battle was already ebbing away. The operations were boring and static, and many of the clansmen took the opportunity to wander among the neighbouring villages, or pay visits to their families in the Highlands. Moreover the Jacobite concentrations at Falkirk and Stirling took the pressure off the parties of loyalist militia north of the Tay, and on 18 and 19 January the inventive Walter Grossett directed a series of raids on Glamis Castle, Leslie and Coupar Angus which retrieved a large number of the officers who had been captured at Prestonpans and were now living at ease on parole. The morality of the rescue was a different issue, and a number of the more thinking officers were uneasy at having broken their word of honour to the Jacobites not to escape (p. 130).

Meanwhile the lull in active field operations gave time to the enemy to collect themselves. Immediately after the battle of 17 January, when Hawley had seen his defeated troops at Linlithgow, he found that all the cartridges in their ammunition pouches were sodden and useless and that the army, having lost all its camp equipment, could not be accommodated in that small town. He fell back all the way to Edinburgh, and set about gathering in 'our flock of sheep that run away. Some few are gone off and joined the rebel flock … I am told they are Scotch and Irish sheep, we are getting ready as fast as we can in hopes to catch them again'.[91]

The redcoats left behind 'vast number of arms, hats, wigs, caps, swords and several pieces of furniture belonging to officers, of which last many were advertised in the Edinburgh newspapers, which caused a great deal of laughter among the disaffected who read the newspapers'. Holyroodhouse was turned into a barracks for some of the fugitives, 'who exercised the fury of their swords upon the fine pictures of many of the kings of Scotland for the defeat they received at Falkirk from their lineal descendants: but for what reason they spared the picture of King Robert the Bruce is hard to account, unless his Highland dress made them afraid to venture too near'.[92]

Reinforcements were coming to the beaten army (Sempill's 25th arrived at Edinburgh on the day of the battle, Campbell's 21st Scotch Fusiliers on 18 January, Lord Mark Kerr's 11th Dragoons on the 23rd, and a train of sixteen cannon and forty gunners and assistants on the 26th). The government in London had been shocked by the news of the defeat at Falkirk, for the rising had seemed to be all but over. The Duke of Cumberland left the capital very early on 25 January and drove north with all possible speed, pausing only briefly on the way to acknowledge the greetings of the townspeople at Durham, Newcastle, Morpeth, Alnwick and Berwick. He arrived at Edinburgh in his coach at 3 a.m. on the 30th, and ordered the gunners of the castle to delay the customary salute until he returned victorious from his campaign against the rebels.

For his temporary quarters the duke chose Holyroodhouse, and the same room which Prince Charles had occupied in the previous September and October – a point that was not lost on the Edinburgh Jacobites. The tailoring contractor Robert Barclay and his wife had been among the most enthusiastic of their number, and their maidservant claimed that Mrs Barclay and five other ladies now went to Holyroodhouse and tried to set fire to the ammunition carts which stood in the palace yard, 'but that their design was prevented by the many people that were standing about them. She saith ... that the writers of all the signets [the solicitors] are a parcel of Jacobites, and as strongly disaffected to the present family upon the throne'.[93]

Inside the palace Cumberland spent nearly all the 30th in conference with Hawley and the other senior officers. Only with difficulty could his aide-de-camp Lord Cathcart prevail upon the Duke to say some words to the sixty Whig ladies who wished to make their mark with him. They 'paid their compliments at the time appointed, very richly dressed; His Royal Highness received them with great familiarity, saluted each of them, and made a short speech to them. One Miss Carr, or Keir, made a very fine appearance; at the top of her stays, on her breast, was a crown well done in beagles and underneath, in letters extremely plain to be seen, as *William Duke of Cumberland*; on the right side of the Crown was the word *Britain's*, and on the left, *Hero*'.[94]

Stirling Castle was in danger of succumbing to a lack of provisions, if not to Mirabelle's siege, and with a commendable sense of urgency Cumberland set his army in motion at 5 a.m. on 31 January. In order to make a show, the Duke departed in a coach and twelve, presented to him by the Earl of Hopetoun.

> As he passed up the Canongate and the High Street, he is said to have expressed great surprise at the number of broken windows he saw; but when informed that this was the result of a recent illumination, and that a shattered casement only indicated the presence of a Jacobite, he laughed heartily. His coach was followed by a great number of persons of distinction, and by a vast mob. On reaching a place in the suburbs called Castlebarns, he left the coach, and mounted his horse. The state officers and others then crowded about him to take leave, and the mob gave him a hearty huzza.[95]

On his further progress to Linlithgow the Duke made a point of marching on foot at the head of the army, almost certainly to show that Prince Charles was not the only person who could set an example in that respect. He and many of his troops took up quarters that night in the Renaissance palace of Linlithgow, crowning a height between the town and the loch. When they left the next morning the pile was burning down behind them. If they had not set it on fire deliberately, they made no attempt to retrieve the contents or put out the flames, which left nothing standing but the sandstone walls.

On learning of Cumberland's arrival, Prince Charles looked forward to a second and probably decisive clash, and sent his Secretary of State Murray of Broughton to Lord George at Falkirk to ask him to prepare a plan of battle.[96] The answer came in a form the Prince could have least expected. On the night of 29 January he received a letter from Lord George and the clan chiefs which told him that his army, weakened by desertion, was in no state to meet the enemy, that it must retreat to the Highlands, where it could spend the rest of the winter in a purposeful way, by reducing the governmental forts and recruiting itself to a strength of 10,000 men to open a new campaign in the spring. The demand was an ultimatum, verging on a mutiny, and Prince Charles did not have a following in the high command which would have enabled him to resist. He consented with a deathly reluctance:

> Shall we make the retreat you propose, how much more will that raise the spirits of our enemies and sink those of our own people? Can we imagine, that where we go the enemy will not follow, and at last oblige us to a battle which we now decline? … what will become of our Lowland friends? Shall we persuade them to retire with us to the mountains? Or shall we abandon them to the fury of our merciless enemies?[97]

All was going to be fulfilled to the letter. Whatever the outcome of a new battle near Falkirk might have been, the army was never again to have the opportunity of confronting the Duke of Cumberland on remotely equal terms.

The heavy guns on the Gowan Hill were spiked, and before daybreak on 1 February the Jacobite forces at Stirling and Falkirk streamed towards their assigned rendezvous at St Ninians, where the ammunition for the siege was stored. The wounded Hanoverian captain George Fitzgerald had been taken to the village under guard, and

> on the morning of the flight Lord Lovat's son came into the room where I lay and told me they were going over the Forth, and that I must ride and go with them. I told them I had taken physick, and that it was not possible for me in the condition I was to stir. But that if I must go they should dress me, and throw me over a horse, for I was not able to do it myself. The

Pretender's son came at that time and sat on horseback at the door talking to Mrs Jenny Cameron [i.e. an unknown female], till about five minutes before the Church of St Ninians was blown up, when he and his own rabble galloped away.[98]

The main body of the church was wrecked completely, and only the free-standing tower (refurbished in 1734) was left.

The local Presbyterians believed (and some still believe) that the church was blown up deliberately by the retreating army, though it is more likely that the explosion was caused when the powder was being removed. Curiously enough, one of the Jacobite Protestants, John Cameron, the minister to the Regiment of Lochiel, was passing by the church in an open carriage when the magazine blew up. He was in the company of the young wife of Murray of Broughton, who was thrown from the chaise and concussed when the horses were startled by the falling stones. A number of the Jacobites were buried in the ruins, along with nine of the townspeople.

O'Sullivan and Lord George blamed one another for the lack of proper directions, and the appalling crash accentuated the disorder among the men, who had broken into small groups. It would have been worse if a party of Hanoverian horse under one Captain Campbell had succeeded in their design of depositing sackfuls of caltrops (iron tetrahedron spikes) at the principal crossing of the Fords of Frew on the evening before. The Jacobite farmer at Wester Ross on the northern side of the river was able to misdirect Campbell to a little-used ford upstream, and then 'secretly rejoicing at the service he had done to the Prince, crossed the water the next day, along with his son and servants, and remained near His Royal Highness all the time he was at dinner. When their meal was finished, the party took the proper ford, all except Charles, who, not thinking any information necessary regarding fords which he had [already] used, rode through one different from either of the above mentioned, and in which the farmer had seen one of Campbell's men drop a single caltrop. The Prince's horse picked this up, and was wounded'.[99] In fact it was difficult enough to cross the fords anyway, and after several hours of effort the Jacobites had to abandon an 8-pounder cannon which had stuck in the mud. Prince Charles lodged for the night in Drummond Castle, and his troops took up quarters in Doune and Dunblane. The horizon to the north was rimmed with the outlying peaks of the Highlands.

CHAPTER 16

The Retreat to the Highlands

The Fatal Council at Crieff, 2 February 1746

THERE ARE REASONS FOR IDENTIFYING 2 February as the day that doomed the rising, and more so than the retreat from Derby or the defeat at Culloden. The Lowlanders and the French regulars had marched to Perth; Prince Charles with the Highlanders and the chiefs had marched to Crieff – both of these locations stood on the Highland/Lowland divide and both offered strategic options.

Prince Charles chose Fairntower House (demolished in 1962) for his quarters, and his horse was taken for shoeing in Crieff. When the Highlanders were now reviewed in the 10-acre Market Park (later Morrison's Academy and its grounds) it transpired that Charles had known the clansmen better than did their chiefs, for the desertion proved to be much less than had been represented and 'the Prince, who had reluctantly consented to retreat, upon the supposition that he had lost one-third of his army, was affected, as one may imagine, on this occasion'.[1] The comings and goings of the Highlanders had amounted to absence without leave rather than desertion, and they had returned to the ranks after satisfying their curiosity or securing

John Gordon of Glenbucket

their loot. 'This was always their way when they fought under the Marquis of Montrose, in the reign of Charles I, and under Lord Dundee and Buchan at the Revolution.'[2]

The council reconvened at the Drummond Arms Inn in Crieff. Prince Charles was angry, and with every reason, but he was once again overborne by the majority. The retreat was to continue, and 'Lord George proposed to divide the army, that he would take the low road with the regular troops, the horse and the low country peoples, and that the Prince would go by the mountains with the clans and artillery. His Royal Highness was not of that opinion at all, and would have the whole march by the coast side, and keep at Montrose and those ports as long as possible, where he expected daily succours from France. Lord George pretended there was no possibility to keep to the coasts'.[3] In detail, the army was to divide into three columns, and take the following routes, east to west:

❖ Lord George Murray with the French troops and most of the Lowlan-ders, skirting the eastern coast by way of Perth, Dundee, Montrose and Aberdeen

❖ Lord Ogilvy's Regiment and the Farquharsons in the middle, marching by their own country by way of Coupar Angus, Glen Cova, Glen Muick and Speyside

❖ Prince Charles and the Highlanders making more directly to Aberdeen by Wade's roads. For the initial march the Highlanders were assigned to a left-hand route through Tummel Bridge and Trinafour, and the carts and the artillery the easier road by Dunkeld and Blair Atholl. They were to reunite at Dalnacardoch, and continue by way of Badenoch.

The rendezvous of all three columns was in the neighbourhood of Inverness.

Lord John Drummond had argued the case for a Highland-based strategy still more consistently than had Lord George, and was delighted by the out-come: 'If we were to resume on a solid foundation, it was absolutely essential to make ourselves masters of the north, where Lord Loudoun and about 1,500 men were in possession of the Castle of Inverness [Old Fort George], keeping the whole region in subjection, and cutting the country completely in two, which prevented a large number of the Prince's friends from join-ing him'.[4] A spy took due notice of the talk among the Jacobite leaders, and reported that

> they are to unite all the clans in the north and west among 'emselves, and to
> their party, and to compel all the north by fire and sword to join 'em, and

then give battle to the Duke of Cumberland … As for Lord Loudoun, they are either to draw his men to their party, or to destroy 'em. And indeed they are talking very confidently that let the Duke of Cumberland hasten his march northwards as fast as he pleases, they'll be masters of Inverness and all the other forts in the north before he can bring his army to that country. And their officers are of opinion, that if they get all the clans, and the north to join 'em, they'll carry all before 'em, and be too hard for all the force in Britain. To speak the truth, they either really are, or seem to be in very high spirits. Their officers declare that they shall never ask quarter, but resolved all to die. I had almost forgot one part of their scheme, which is to draw the King's forces to remote places, and get many advantages over 'em.[5]

The Highlanders did indeed recover cohesion and energy when the theatre of operations approached their straths and glens, and in the early spring they were able to go over to the offensive. However, it remains difficult to conceive what kind of future the victorious Highland party envisaged for the armed Jacobite cause. The retreat to Inverness brought with it the abandoning of two essential props: the Episcopal eastern coastlands, with their faithful and active people, and the seaports by which alone help from France could arrive in any strength. Indeed, French transports bearing 650 troops arrived off Aberdeen on 27 February, only to be told, by a man walking his dog along the shore, that the Jacobites had left and that the enemy were a matter of hours away. The ships had no recourse but to sail off, and the reinforcement that was due to follow was inevitably countermanded, for it had nowhere to land. 'In abandoning the coast thus, the Prince lost many in Clare's and Berwick's regiments, which had joined, and others who would have followed, if those had landed.'[6]

For the sake of clarity we shall trace the course of the two main columns separately, that of Lord George (with the Duke of Cumberland coming up behind), and that of Prince Charles and the Highlanders.

Lord George's retreat, 3–27 February 1746

William Drummond, 4th Viscount Strathallan, and other Jacobite notables of the eastern shire had long occupied quarters in Perth as the main permanent base towards the Central Lowlands, and it came as a shock when the town was suddenly abandoned on 4 February. The Whig merchant Henry Fife had taken due note of all the comings and goings, and a little after Strathallan 'with other rebels had fled over Tay, he saw an old man servant to the

Viscountess on horseback on the streets of Perth, and the Viscountess talking to him, and at parting heard her say to him, "well you are going away, the Lord benith [bless] you all", and then saw the Viscountess and her daughters go out of Perth westwards towards Machan, their country seat'.[7]

Prince Charles delayed the move of the Highland column in order to facilitate the evacuation of Lord George's train of artillery, especially the four 8-pounders which were needed to lay siege to the northern forts, and he sent Murray of Broughton to help out. It is still uncertain what pieces were or were not taken by Lord George, and O'Sullivan claims that such a chaotic retreat had never been seen, 'and all those that were with him says, no orders given, never halted a day, until he arrived at Nairn'.[8]

On 5 February the Jacobites from Perth were found streaming through Glamis[9] and Kirriemuir to an initial rendezvous at Brechin. From there one of the columns took an inland route direct to Stonehaven, while the other marched to the nearby coast to spend two or three days at Montrose, 'a fine loyal seaport town, and looked upon … to provide men of the highest wisdom in Scotland'.[10] Montrose too was abandoned, from 8 February. Rear Admiral Byng commanded the squadron of the Royal Navy offshore, and wrote to Cumberland's headquarters, for having

> no doubt as His Royal Highness is so sensible of the importance of having Montrose in the possession of the King's troops, he will order a strong detachment from his army to secure that place, which is the only convenient port they have in all Scotland to land their troops, arms and ammunition in, and I hope in time to see it fortified in such a manner, and garrisoned by the King's troops, as will ever put it out of the power of that most rebellious Jacobite town giving any favour or assistance to the French, for the time to come … I hope very shortly the Duke will be in possession of all the places along the coast, where the rebels have received all their supplies, and will effectually prevent any landing for the time to come, and the principal ones are Arbroath, Montrose, Stonehaven and Peterhead.[11]

The Jacobites had spiked all the cannon emplaced at Montrose except four medium cannon (6-, 8- or 9-pounders), which they intended to plant at the Bridge of Dee in front of Aberdeen. A boat succeeded in escaping with two of the cannon, but the presence of the hostile ships forced the other craft to bring back the remaining two pieces to the shore. On the 11th Byng accordingly sent fifty marines ashore to take possession of the town, while one of his lieutenants supervised the spiking of the two guns on the beach and disabled the boats in the harbour.[12]

The Jacobites began to evacuate Aberdeen on 11 February, the first marches being executed under terrible conditions:

> When we marched out of Aberdeen, it blew, snowed, hailed and froze to such a degree that few pictures ever represented Winter, with all its icicles about it, better than many of us did that day; for here men were covered with icicles hanging from their eyebrows and beards. An entire coldness seized their limbs, it may be wondered at how so many men could bear up against a storm, a severe contrary wind driving a little cutting hail down upon our faces in such a manner that it was impossible to see ten yards in front of us. And very easy it was to lose our companions, the road being bad and leading over large commons, and the paths being immediately filled up with drifted snow.[13]

Lord George with the main column marched by way of Oldmeldrum to Huntly, while the Irish picquets and Royal Ecossais halted for a day at Inverurie and Kintore, then set off in that direction by an exceptionally snowy and difficult route further inland. Lord George waited in his turn until he knew the French troops were well on their way, then left Huntly in order to make room for them in the town. Lord George's progress took him through the land of the Grants, whom he ordered, under threat, to yield up money, transport and men.[14]

By chance the last of the Jacobite forces had still not left Aberdeen when, on 22 February, the privateer *La Sophie* (the survivor of a sailing of three vessels) was able to land 130 officers and troopers of FitzJames' Horse, the heavy cavalry unit of the Irish Brigade. They came with all their equipment and weapons, but their horses were lost and as an élite unit they were given the mounts of the Pitsligo and Kilmarnock Regiments, such as they were, which from then on did service on foot. Aberdeen was finally abandoned on the 23rd, by when the rest of Lord George's column had reached its assigned quarters along the coastlands of the Moray Firth between the Spey and Aberdeen.

Lord George had never intended to stage a rearguard action, except possibly at the Bridge of Dee at Aberdeen, so when the Hanoverian forces took control of the great tract of abandoned territory it was by a process of occupation, not conquest. The Duke of Cumberland had not been able to shoot off in immediate pursuit of the Jacobites on the far side of the Forth, since the gap in Stirling Bridge had first to be repaired. 'At the time our men halted here [Stirling], which was two days, they were continually digging in the trenches to find dead men for their clothes, sandbags etc., and others seeking out where cannon balls had razed the earth, then they dug for them and by this means they got much money in selling them; which made it a sort of carnival all over the town, this money making them first drunk, then mad.' Many Jacobites were being brought in from their hiding places, and 'some of these our men, as soon as taken, stripped off their clothes, and dressed themselves up in the captive Highlanders', with their tartans, etc ... Their strutting about in this manner made a very comical appearance, and was very diverting'.[15] Other parties were rummaging through the ruins of St Ninians, likewise bent on plundering the dead. The explosion had broken the windows of all the dwellings, 'so that they appeared like so many bawdy houses'.[16]

On 4 February the Duke of Cumberland was across the river and on his way to Dunblane. The allegiances in the cathedral town were known to have been divided, and now the Baillie, Mr Russel, and the minister (a Presbyterian but a secret Jacobite) led the people across the bridge of the Allan Water and some way up the hill of Skelly Braes to meet the duke, hoping to impress him with their loyalty. At a given signal the crowd raised a dutiful cheer. Russel led Cumberland down to his own residence, Allanbank House at the north end of Millrow. He was disconcerted to find that his guest, in justifiable fear of assassination plots, brought all his own linen and table service with him, and posted five sentries outside his bedroom and four inside.

The army set out from Dunblane on the 5th, but Cumberland tarried a little to supervise the punishment of thieves who had been at the baggage. One of them, a certain MacNiven, was duly hanged. On his way out Cumberland passed under Viscount Strathallan's town house, and a Jacobite servant girl took the opportunity to aim a containerful of boiling water or oil at him from an upper window. The seething liquid only just missed the Duke and landed on the haunches of his horse, which threw him to the ground. The girl escaped, and it was only with difficulty that he could be dissuaded from visiting his vengeance on the town.

When the duke was approaching Crieff 17 miles or so further on, there was another alarm when five well-meaning local lads hid themselves behind a hedge and made the advance guard welcome by firing pistols and striking pots and pans together. However, Crieff was known to be a place of generally Whiggish sympathies, albeit lying on the estates of the Duke of Perth. Cumberland threw the boys some coins, and inside the town he was greeted by a loyal address.

On 6 February the army turned east for Perth, and the march thither proved to be 'a very long one, and very bad roads, but then we had agreeable fir woods, which are mighty solitary and amusing, and are the only beauty of these mountainous places, being always planted very close and regular, and affording an entertaining scene to a wearied traveller'.[17]

The main force of the army reached Perth on 6 February and remained there until the 20th. Cumberland wrote to the Duke of Newcastle on the 14th that he was 'sorry and almost ashamed that I am forced to date my letter from this place, but greater difficulties than we have, it is scarcely possible to encounter. No contract, or any sort of agreement for bread, but all turns on one Gomes Serra, a Jew, who is provider of bread for the army and has a warrant from the King for that purpose, a man no way of an equal capacity for such an undertaking, though I hope honest'.[18] Serra was operating from Edinburgh, and the bread and flour, even when assembled, still had to be shipped across the Firth from Leith.

Cumberland was also influenced by repeated reports that Prince Charles was trying to escape to France by the western coast, and by the divergent directions of the Jacobite retreat, which made him 'very apt to believe I shall soon hear of their total separation'.[19] Persuaded that he had 'already as much foot as more than sufficient to finish this affair',[20] he was embarrassed when a contingent of hired Hessians – some 5,500 infantry and 500 hussars – arrived at Leith from Holland on 8 February. He agreed reluctantly to let them come ashore, after the miseries of ship-borne life, and he wrote to London that 'the Hessians coming here just at this time, puts the finishing hand to the confusion we are in about bread, as they are utterly useless here; I have quartered them about Edinburgh till I may receive His Majesty's orders to re-embarking them, and sending them where they are so much wanted [i.e. for the war in Flanders]'.[21]

Meanwhile, the work of holding important posts could be left to detachments. On 8 February Cumberland ordered Lieutenant Colonel Sir Andrew Agnew to secure Blair Castle with 500 infantry and 120 Argyll Militia, and Lieutenant Colonel Leighton to occupy Castle Menzies. They were then to send out parties to annoy the Atholl Jacobites and seize their cattle, and 'if you are attacked you will defend yourself to the utmost, as the rebels have no artillery but 3-pounders to annoy you, and as succour will be sent to you. If any officer or soldier shall refuse to defend the house to his utmost, you will let them know that you have His Royal Highness's orders and power from him to inflict punishments even death for such disobedience without a court martial'.[22]

Agnew's march to Blair lay by way of Dunkeld and Killiecrankie, and one of his people gives us a unique vision of the Highlands as they first appeared to the redcoats:

> no sooner had we got over one high mountain, and into a pleasant valley, but another hill, higher, presented itself for our next labour. Between and upon the declivity of these hills we had most solitary fir woods, all regularly planted, and oftentimes a perfect sugar-loaf mountain was chosen for this purpose, which, as it was a Roman Catholic country, no place would be more acceptable for the fixing of a crucifix, or saint, to worship. After you have passed a ridge of mountains, and come into a valley, you are sure of meeting a most agreeable river, with noisy purling streams, occasioned by large rock stones lying in every part, and the river in most places being exceeding shallow, so that the stones are frequently higher than the water; the sides of the banks being as often lined with the same rocky substance, make the stream glide most swiftly ... We did not see Dunkeld till we just came upon it; it then seemed to be a very neat and agreeable small village, but enclosed with most high mountains on every side, and having the ... beautiful River Tay winding almost round it, and is very broad, so that we are always obliged to be ferried over, to go into the town ... the river is exceeding deep, and the water looks quite black from a distance.[23]
>
> We had a continual view of rocks, mountains, woods, plains, flats cultivated, and rivers; and on the mountains we saw frequent great herds of cattle, such as oxen, sheep and goats. This Pass of Killiecrankie is situated at the foot of a vast mountain near a mile long. Next, there is a river called the Tummel which divides it from the mountains, still higher on the other side, which are covered with woods. The road through it is very narrow and dangerous to retreat for [on account of] the river, which is close to you in a vast hollow. From the woody mountains here run frequent streams of the purest water, which are obstructed now by the hard frost, and makes most romantick winter-appearances, by the congealed streams of icicles which hang pendulous over the rocky banks of these rivers.[24]

On 15 February Cumberland paid a flying visit to Edinburgh in order to settle a number of details concerning the intended advance, and not least a guaranteed two weeks' supply of bread. He was back in Perth the next day and the march finally began on the 20th. As a kind of afterthought he assigned the Hessians to security duties on the lines of communication, namely two of the battalions in Stirling and four to replace the army when it vacated Perth. Naval parties had already secured Montrose, and on 27 February loyal or apprehensive crowds applauded the duke as he entered Aberdeen.

The Retreat of Prince Charles, the Rout of Moy and the Capture of Inverness, 3–21 February 1746

The routes of Prince Charles and his Highlanders led more directly northward than did Lord George's dog-leg, and were the guarantee of some excitements when they brought the Prince to Lord Loudoun's concentration at Inverness.

If the passage of the Fords of Frew marked a symbolic farewell to the Lowlands, Prince Charles began to enter the Highlands proper when he crossed Wade's great bridge at Aberfeldy on 4 February and took up quarters at Castle Menzies, the residence of Sir Robert and Lady Menzies. A Miss Isabel Stuart, who accompanied the army in an unknown capacity, saw Lady Mary and her two sisters Lady Grace and Lady Jean introduced to the Prince, 'but they surprised me for you never saw any creatures so much dashed as they were. For Lady Mary, who should not have esteemed the Prince, it was not in her power to speak one word for some hours, but after supper she recovered a little, and next night she had a good deal to say. Sir Robert was not seen'.[25]

Sir Robert was indeed not to be seen, for he was a man of pacific temperament, and he tried to persuade the Hanoverian Lord Justice Clerk that he had removed himself as soon as he had known the Jacobites were on the march from Crieff, and had nothing to do with the Jacobite chiefs' choosing to lodge in his castle.[26] It did him no good, for parties of the 21st North British Fusiliers and the Argyll Militia were going to descend on the castle, eject Sir Robert and Lady Mary, and inflict £6,000-worth of damage.

Prince Charles enjoyed a day's shooting at Castles Menzies before making his way on 6 February through the Pass of Killiecrankie to Blair Castle, the seat of the rival dukes of Atholl, where he was to stay until the 10th. An informant told the Hanoverian Duke James that his brother, the Jacobite Duke William, was 'very unwilling to leave Blair, otherwise they had gone north before now. It is said he is determined to keep Blair Castle or die in the defence of it, as he is in a very bad state of health and cannot think of marching north'.[27] The spy could find nobody who was brave enough to go to Blair Castle itself, but he put the Jacobite force there at 2,000 at the most, for Lochiel had gone to Lochaber and Cluny MacPherson to Badenoch to stir up their respective clans, recruiting parties were out in Atholl, and a strong detachment would set out shortly for Strathmore (p. 481).

Prince Charles and his party left Blair Castle on the 10th for a lodging at Dalnacardoch on Wade's road to the north. The move was said to have been prompted by a servant of Duke William, who reported (erroneously) that a mixed force of 4,000 cavalry and 2,000 Argyll Militia had arrived at Dunkeld. 'Upon the first information of the troops marching to Dunkeld, Duke William proposed to the Prince to oppose them at Killiecrankie, but the Prince said this was impracticable, for the Campbells were Highlanders, and could climb hills. When the certain accounts of their being at Dunkeld arrived, the Prince looked grave and immediately retired to his own room, and the baggage was soon after ordered to move northwards ... and the whole company were to follow immediately after dinner.'[28]

Most of the column had already traversed the waste of the Drumochter Pass. Cluny assembled his MacPhersons in Badenoch, and the next day they were joined by parties of MacDonalds, MacGregors, MacKinnons and Camerons. Isabel Stuart had intended to take her leave of the army there, but 'the storm was too great. I could not venture the hill road, and all the way was the terriblest cold frost with snow I ever felt, though I walked one day fourteen miles (which indeed was the most I ever did) yet I was never warm. Mrs Murray [of Broughton] was riding ... but we really thought she would have died, but after she got a chus [chaise], for she turned occasionally tender and is able to bear very little'.[29]

The immediate focus of interest was Ruthven Barracks, where Terence Molloy (now commissioned as lieutenant) and his tiny garrison had all the time been holding out for King George in hostile Badenoch. The Jacobites had one cannon with them, probably a 6-pounder, and 'it was the same evening [9 February] levelled to the barracks there. And fired three shots and made as many holes, which made them surrender that night',[30] Molloy and his men being allowed to march free. Inside the barracks the Jacobites found a hundred bolls of oatmeal and a quantity of malt. Prince Charles gave the bedding and all the other contents to Cluny's people, after which the main block was burned down on 14 February, and the stables the next day.

Prince Charles spent the nights of the 12th, 13th and 14th close to the barracks, by tradition in Ruthven Farm. On 15 February he moved to Inverlaidnan near Carrbridge, the home of the Whiggish Grant of Dalrachny, and then on the 16th to the more welcoming surroundings of Moy Hall, the residence of the militantly Jacobite 'Colonel Anne', who was the effective leader of Clan MacKintosh now that her husband Aeneas had taken service with King George. Moy Hall was 'pleasantly situated at the head of a small but beautiful lake of the same name, full of trout and char ... This water is two miles and a half long, and half a mile broad, adorned with two or three islands prettily wooded. Each side is bounded with hills clothed at the bottom with trees; and in front, at a distance of thirty miles, is the great mountain of Karn Goran [Cairngorm], patched with snow'.[31]

After the check at Inverurie on 23 December (p. 361), Lord Loudoun had concentrated the loyalist Highlanders of northern Scotland at Inverness. The Duke of Cumberland wrote to him that the Jacobite sympathizers had 'given out that the clans proposed to fall on you, but I have not been under any apprehensions that in their present condition they have spirits for any attempt of the sort, but rather imagine the people will be for returning home and concealing themselves, and that their chiefs will try to get off by sea'.[32] By the middle of February Loudoun concluded that the Jacobites were not only weak but careless, for Prince Charles and a number of the leaders had laid themselves open to a *coup de main* by taking up quarters at Moy, which was only 7 or 8 miles from Inverness.

Abandoning his habitual caution, Loudoun slipped out of Inverness on the night of 16 February to deal the blow with 1,500 men of the Independent Companies and his 64th Highlanders. He was confident that he had escaped detection, but word of his design was carried speedily to his intended target. The circumstances are still obscure, though the accounts (not necessarily contradictory) attribute the warning variously to the daughter of Mrs Baillie, who overheard officers talking of the scheme at her mother's inn, and ran all the way to Moy barefoot, or to the Dowager Lady MacKintosh, who lived in Kirk Street in Inverness, and deduced that something was wrong when so many troops were on the move at that time of night. According to Isabel Stuart, the old Lady MacKintosh sent two messengers, one a Miss Taylor, 'the loyalest lassie in the world', and the other 'a man … who went two miles on his hands and feet for it was moonshine in case they would see him, and came first to fourteen men, advanced guards the Prince had, and put them on their guard, and went on to the house some hours before daylight'.[33]

When the news came, Colonel Anne ran about in a panic, and the alarm was 'such that the Prince was shaken forcibly awake. He was urged to escape as soon as he could, but [referring to an episode in the War of the Polish Succession] he declared that he had no intention of behaving like Marshal Broglie, and leave his shoes behind; when he left, it would be dressed and armed. But the danger had already passed'.[34] Matters had been taken in hand by the village blacksmith of Moy, Donald Fraser, who was confident that he and a few of his friends could stop the enemy in their tracks. What transpired is one of the most curious but best-authenticated episodes of the '45.

After 3 miles of marching from Inverness, Loudoun had detached an officer and thirty men who were to secure the expedition against prying eyes, and wait in position until the main force opened its attack at daybreak on 17 February. By Loudoun's frank account,

> we marched to the heights above the water at Nairn, when to my infinite mortification, saw and heard about a mile on my left, a running fire from the whole detachment [i.e. the officer and his thirty men]. They saw, or imagined they saw, four men [the blacksmith and his companions], on which they made this fire. But the consequence on the main body was very bad, for it threw us into the greatest confusion. I got my own regiment [the 64th], at the head of which I was in the front, saved from falling out of the road. All faced to where they saw the fire. They were ten men deep, all pressed [together], and a good many dropping shots, one of which killed a piper at my foot, whilst I was forming them. The rest fell all back out of this road in a considerable way. It was utmost confusion, and it was a great while before I could get them brought up and formed; and the panic was still so great that it was with the greatest difficulty when the party came in, in twos and threes, that I could, standing before the muzzles of their pieces, prevent their firing on them.

When Loudoun counted his force he found that the five companies in the rear of the column had made off. The first of these companies had been composed of MacKenzies, who deserted their officers. The next was under the command of an officer, 'a very good man, but very short-sighted', who marched his company after the MacKenzies in the murk, followed by the third and fourth companies, who imagined that the people in front knew where they were going. The fifth company, together with the spare ammunition, never came up at all.[35] Now that the hostile countryside was thoroughly alarmed, Loudoun collected his force and retreated to Inverness, thus completing what became known as 'The Rout of Moy'. The dead piper was the great Donald Ban MacCrimmon, and Isabel Stuart confirms that he had been killed by the Jacobites.

If the casualties among Loudoun's force had been minimal, he lost 200 men by desertion over the next few hours, which left him with a total force of just 1,700 men after he had provided for the garrison of Inverness Castle (the original Fort George). He took counsel with Duncan Forbes, Norman MacLeod and the others senior officers, and they agreed that it was impossible to make a stand at Inverness. They were probably right, and in the event the little army escaped disaster by the narrowest of margins.

On the morning of 18 February Loudoun began to march his available troops over the bridge to the left bank of the River Ness, and hastened towards Kessock, where the frigate *Sheerness* had collected boats for the short passage to the Black Isle. Prince Charles's troops had meanwhile advanced to the forward slopes of Drummossie Moor, facing the town. Isabel Stuart had never been 'in the least uneasy till then, that our folks gave me some of their watches and purses and other things their pocket books, and anything they thought most valuable, for they never doubted they were immediately to engage, but behold in less than half an hour what do we observe but a great number of boats below the town ferrying them all over to Rosshire'.[36] The Jacobite advanced guard at once swept down, but it was impossible to reach the enemy, for the bridge was commanded by the castle and the tide was too high to permit the crossing of the ford downstream.

The frustrated pursuers had to be content with running a 6-pounder and two 3-pounders at a full trot around to the north of the town, and cannonading the departing boats from the neighbourhood of the Cromwellian citadel, 'which, though it did no damage, yet having thrown sundry shot over and among us, it struck a most unaccountable terror into the Highlanders, which appeared by many deserting that night, and more soon after'.[37] The main force of the Jacobites was meanwhile making ready to march into Inverness. One of Lord Glenorchy's spies 'could not learn their numbers, but ... as they were drawn up in a line three deep before they entered town, he judged their line to extend near half a mile'.[38]

Loudoun now stood on the Black Isle, which was actually a fertile peninsula of gently rising ground. It was no kind of refuge for his depleted force, because the Jacobites could still reach him, if not by crossing the Kessock narrows, then by making the short overland circuit through strongly Jacobite Fraser country around the head of the shallow Beauly Firth. On 19 February Loudoun therefore withdrew his troops to Easter Ross on the northern side of the Cromarty Firth, some by means of the short transit by ferry and the others marching around the head of the firth. He did not feel safe even there, for he feared that he had 3,000 men on his tail and that they could once more take the landward route and turn his position. He was confident that this would not hold true for the third and last water barrier at his disposal, however, the Dornoch Firth, for this substantial inlet constituted a continuous water barrier with the River Shin and its associated lochs, which reached far to the north-west into the remotest Highlands, and converted Sutherland into a strategic redoubt where Loudoun could gather support from the loyal Munro, Sutherland and MacKay clansmen. He accordingly ferried his troops across the Dornoch Firth from Tain, and explained his thinking in a long letter to Lord Stair. He asked him to look at the map, and what you see, like a large river, is what they call a 'kyle', and is a narrow arm of the sea, and runs up about fifteen miles above this [Dornoch], and is easily defended, if they don't bring a great many boats from Moray, which is not very easy; but to prevent that, I have 600 men in this neighbourhood; in the neighbourhood of Bana [Bonar Bridge], another ferry, I have 300. And ten miles above this, where the Sinn falls in, which river is four miles long, and has three fords in it, I have 400 MacLeods and 200 Sutherlands; and 300 more Sutherlands I got from His Lordship [of Sutherland], and arrived since I came here. And above this is a lake of eighteen miles long, whose name is 'Cromarty', spelt 'Sinn', but in this country goes in the same name as the river. At present the river is impassable everywhere; and they tell me, will probably be so these three weeks, as the lake is quite full. However Your Lordship sees I am pretty secure, as I am master of all the boats.[39]

Loudoun's extended retreat had removed him by 28 miles and three saltwater inlets from 'Old' Fort George at Inverness, which was now stranded beyond any possible hope of relief in the midst of Prince Charles's force of 3,000 men. The tower of the original tower house was still standing inside the newer bastioned outer rampart, which gave the fort two somewhat cramped lines of defence. The governor, Major George Grant, had at his disposal two Independent Companies, those of the Laird of Grant and the Master of Ross, and eighty or so regulars of Guise's 6th who were reckoned 'some of Loudoun's best men'.[40]

On the Jacobite side the Duke of Perth assumed overall command of the siege, rather to the annoyance of O'Sullivan, who believed that he and the Marquis d'Eguilles were managing perfectly well by themselves. On his reconnaissance early on 19 February O'Sullivan saw that the double-layered defences were too formidable for the Highlanders to escalade, and proof against the single cannon then available to the Jacobites, but he spotted the unstable foundations which had caused so much trouble during the construction of the rampart (p. 152) and now made the bastion facing the bridge vulnerable to mining. On the same evening O'Sullivan and Colonel James Grant set men to work to open the mine. They built an emplacement on the Bara Hill overnight, and their gun opened fire on the morning of the 20th.

The defenders were powerless to stop the progress of the mine gallery, for their hand grenades had little effect and they could not depress the barrels of their cannon sufficiently to bring them to bear. Major George Grant feared, with good reason, that the rampart would soon be blown up beneath him, and he surrendered the fort on 21 February. When the news reached Edinburgh the Lord Justice Clerk complained that Grant could have held the Jacobites at bay for a few days more, 'for they had an outer wall five foot thick to go through, and then about thirty or thirty-five foot of earth to get through before they came to the Castle wall',[41] and predictably the Duke of Cumberland exclaimed that he was 'no way able to explain how, or by what it is so, but a silly affair it is'.[42]

The Highlanders plundered the ample provisions they found inside the fort, and Prince Charles ordered the curtain walls to be razed and the bastions blown up, a process which cost the life of a French sergeant who was inspecting a demolition charge that hung fire. His dog fared 'better than his master, for although he was also blown up at the same time, a great height, and was thrown near the side of the river, yet lived, but was sadly lamed'.[43]

CHAPTER 17

Confrontation and Counterstrike

BY THE END OF FEBRUARY 1746 the main forces of the Jacobites had fallen back to Inverness and the country to the east, the Duke of Cumberland and his army had reached Aberdeen, and Lord Loudoun had recoiled behind the Dornoch Firth. The happenings from then until the opening of the brief and decisive campaign of Culloden are certainly the least-known episodes of the rising, but they are among the most varied and intensive. On first principles this time should have been a period of stagnation, for the campaigning season had been pushed far beyond the conventional European limits, and the cruel winter still had weeks to run. Already by 20 February the Duke of Cumberland was convinced that everything had been wound up, and it was left to Sir Andrew Fletcher, the perceptive Lord Justice Clerk, to sound notes of warning:

> As the rebels are possessed of Inverness, the capital in some sort of their country, it is to be feared that their numbers may increase beyond whatever they had in Scotland, at least of Highlanders ... now ... the war is brought home to their very doors, they fight in a manner for the defence of their

---

A peasant soldier with a long lochaber axe

country; the chiefs have told them they are to be extirpated (if they succumb), and made them desperate; their chiefs can tell them that they need only be two or three days from home, and when that is the case, every man that can bear arms will join them and leave their cattle and houses to the care of the women.[1]

Cumberland could not bring himself to take the admonitions seriously, for he assumed that the Jacobites would either strand themselves uselessly in the mountains, or stay at Inverness and be beaten.[2]

The salient features of these complicated episodes are as follows:

❖ In the Western Highlands the Jacobites captured Fort Augustus, but their siege of Fort William was prolonged and unsuccessful. The Royal Navy dominated the seas, supported the defence of Fort William and ravaged the Jacobite coastlands

❖ In the far north-east the Jacobites made an assault crossing of the Dornoch Firth, and scattered the forces of Lord Loudoun. However, a number of the troops and loyalist clansmen rallied in the country of Lord Reay, and captured a vital consignment of French gold which had been destined for the army of Prince Charles at Inverness. The effort to recover the cash and maintain the Jacobite predominance in the Orkney Islands weakened the forces available to the Prince at the time of Culloden

❖ On the main theatre of operations Lord George Murray launched a highly successful raid on the posts of the Argyll Militia in Atholl but was unable to recover Blair Castle. Detachments from Cumberland's army devastated rebellious Strathmore, and raided an arms depot at Corgarff Castle; there were a number of clashes with the forward elements of the army of Prince Charles, which generally turned to the advantage of the Jacobites.

It will be seen that on most occasions the Jacobites had taken the initiative. However, most of the enterprises were shaped by local interests rather than overall strategy, and the Jacobites were unable to regroup in full strength by the time of the last campaign. Some (the Camerons and Clan Donald) were already in an exhausted state when they joined the Prince; some (the MacPhersons), perhaps 'hastening slowly', were just too late; others (Cromartie's men) were beyond reach in the far north-east.

The West

The Siege of Fort Augustus, 3–5 March 1746

The forts Augustus and William had been thorns in the sides of the western clans, and when their chiefs saw how easily Fort George had been taken they clamoured for the siege of those two offending objects. Prince Charles accordingly released the Irish picquets, Royal Ecossais and more than 1,500 of the clansmen of Lochiel, Lochgarry and Keppoch, who descended on Fort Augustus at the end of February:

> God knows what pains we had to send them the artillery, ammunition, meal and even forage, for there was not a scrap to be had in that part of the country; the roads were frozen, the horses reduced to nothing, and not a carter who knew how to drive or guide them. Our small pieces of cannon could be of no great use, only to fire on the barracks. All that we had to depend upon were two pieces of eight that were found in the Castle of Inverness [Fort George], and three or four small mortars that were taken at the battle of Falkirk … there were but sea carriages for our piece of eight pounds. The French ambassador [d'Eguilles] undertook to get carriages made, and so he did, but only one of these pieces arrived, the other carriage broke, and the cannon was left on the road.[3]

It was fortunate for the Jacobites that Fort Augustus had been designed 'more … for ornament than strength',[4] as a demonstration of Hanoverian presence in the Highlands. It was badly sited, the curtain walls were feeble, and vital installations were installed in full view in conical towers on top of the four bastions. The garrison was more powerful than that of Fort George, being made up of three companies of Guise's 6th, but the governor, Major Hu Wentworth, placed one of them in an isolated position in the old barracks of Kiliwhimen on the higher ground to the south.

Lieutenant Colonel Walter Stapleton, as commander of the 'French' troops, evicted the redcoats from the barracks by a straightforward assault, and Colonel James Grant was able to open his first trenches against the fort proper on 3 March. The Jacobite cannon were of little use against even these unimpressive ramparts but on 5 March a bomb from one of the coehorn mortars broke through the roof of the magazine. The resulting explosion breached the bastion beneath, which laid the fort wide open to an assault. The governor surrendered without more ado, which was only sensible, though he was later court-martialled and dismissed from the service.

The Siege of Fort William, 20 March – 3 April 1746

The attention of all parties now shifted to Fort William, as the last surviving strongpoint on the chain of the Great Glen. Cumberland looked on it as 'the only fort in the Highlands that is of any consequence', and claimed that he was 'taking all possible measures for the security of it'.[5] The elderly governor, Alexander Campbell, was described as 'a careful good man',[6] but doubts rose as to his competence during the blockade, and on 15 March he was superseded by Captain Caroline Frederick Scott of Guise's 6th. Scott was the son of a landed family of Bristo, just south of Edinburgh, and few other other lines in Britain were associated so intimately with the reigning house. His diplomat father was already a friend of Elector George of Hanover before he claimed the throne in 1714, and Caroline himself owed his curious name (and possibly, in compensation, his ferocious ways) to his godmother Princess Caroline of Ansbach, who became the queen of George II.

The garrison, as finally reinforced, was made up of two companies of Guise's 6th, two other companies of regulars and a company of the Argyll Militia, about 400 men in all. The fort was more solidly built than Augustus, and its roughly triangular form was calculated to take advantage of the cover afforded by the head of Loch Linnhe, having a north-eastern side giving on to the salt marsh at the mouth of the River Nevis, a western side facing the loch, and three irregular bastions and a ravelin which looked inland to the east. The armament comprised six 12-pounder cannon, eight 6-pounders, seven smaller pieces, two 13-inch mortars and eight coehorns.[7] There was plenty of ammunition, but there was no permanent supply of water within the fort.

On 25 February the garrison began to demolish the service town of Maryburgh so as to clear a field of fire, though nothing could be done to deny the besiegers the use of the outlying heights. Conversely, the location of the fort by the lochside not only gave the place immediate tactical strength, but made it accessible to craft that braved the Jacobite guns at the Corran Narrows. The defenders were supported by the sloop *Baltimore* and on 15 February she was joined by the bomb vessel *Serpent*.

Fort William had long been subject to intermittent blockade by bands of Camerons and Clan Donald,[8] but the chiefs now called for a full-scale siege to take the place by force, and there were some valid reasons for doing so. In friendly hands it would remove an affront to Lochaber, deny the enemy their access to the south-western end of the Great Glen, and, as an offensive base for the Jacobites, enable them to 'make an inroad into Argyllshire

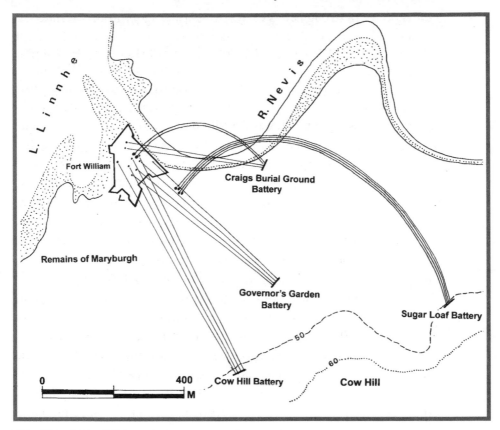

The siege of Fort William

and lay all before them waste'[9] – a prospect which induced Major General John Campbell of Mamore to fortify Inverary.

It is difficult to discover the thinking of the Duke of Cumberland. He expressed great concern for the safety of the fort, as we have seen, but at the same time he was glad that the depredations of the garrison had provoked the Jacobites into besieging the place, for that would 'discourage the men [of the Jacobites] and add to their present distractions'.[10] This interesting statement lends indirect support to the arguments of Prince Charles, who was 'altogether against it ... but the clans looked upon it to be so essential a thing to them, and for the good of the cause, that the Prince consented, though it was exposing himself and them, and even the cause to have the army so scattered'.[11]

The operation was entrusted to the same team which had taken Fort Augustus – Lieutenant Colonel Stapleton, the 'French' regulars and Lochiel's and Keppoch's clansmen. The logistic difficulties were more acute still, and the shortage of strong horses to draw the heavier guns from Inverness was aggravated by that bird of ill-omen, Mirabelle de Gordon, who, Stapleton was amazed to find, had reduced the number of beasts available from twenty-six to fifteen.[12]

One of the precious 8-pounders was overturned on Wade's road beside Loch Ness, and heavy rains in the middle of March swept away two sections of the further road alongside Loch Lochy at Letterfinlay. With uncharacteristic insouciance Colonel James Grant reported that only thirty-four 8-pounder shot were available out of the sixty which were supposed to have been brought from Perth, 'but that will be quite enough, for a single 8-pounder will do the work – that's all we need for a good start, and the Prince's good luck will supply the rest'.[13] Stapleton complained that he meanwhile had to wait uselessly outside Fort William with his 'arms crossed'.[14]

The landward blockade was loose enough to tempt the officers of the garrison to go on recreational walks beyond the ramparts. That was not a good idea, because the local people had suffered much from the garrison, and on 15 February a farmer of the village of Inverlochy shot down Lieutenant George MacFarlane as he was returning by the stepping stones over the River Nevis. In retaliation the governor sent an expedition that burnt down Inverlochy, as being 'the common receptacle of the rebels'.[15]

The Jacobites focused their seaward blockade down Loch Linnhe at the Corran Narrows, where they succeeded in capturing one of the *Baltimore*'s boats. Alexander Campbell determined to 'destroy that nest of rebels'. Early in the morning of 4 March he embarked seventy-one of his men on six boats at Fort William, and over the course of five hours they made their way down the loch, surprised the sentries at the Narrows, and burnt the two ferry houses along with a small settlement a few hundred yards away on the western side. The Jacobites were reported to have had two men killed, 'and many wounded as appeared by the quantities of blood left upon the roads'.[16]

By chance the tender of the bomb vessel *Terror* had been waiting on the seaward side of the Narrows, having been detained on the way to Fort William by adverse wind and tide. The boat was carrying supplies, eighteen Argyll militiamen, and the young engineer Mr John Russell, who had been dispatched to give his expert opinion on the fort. Not knowing what was afoot, the craft weighed anchor at 5 a.m. and fortuitously arrived at the narrows towards the end of the action. 'After ... everything was over, the master and I was standing upon the stern of the boat looking round us as some rascals from behind a boat fired most furiously upon us. We returned their fire with two swivels and a few muskets, but made off very fast for we could not see our enemy: we expected to be seized every hour. Everybody is in high spirits. French artillery will only inspire us with courage, and white cockades will make us desirous after glory.'[17] Russell disembarked at Fort William on the same morning of 4 March, and discovered that the fortifications were 'not in so good repair as I could have wished, the parapet being too low, and some of the wall very old, but the men of war defending one side entirely, I purpose to bring all the guns to the side which is liable to be attacked'.[18]

After having been detained at Castle Stalker by contrary winds, Captain Caroline Scott and the bomb vessel *Serpent* were safely at Fort William on 15 March, and he drew up his rules for the conduct of the defence. Amongst other things, Scott laid down that the garrison must keep up a frequent harassing fire at night with light cannon, and

> send out parties to listen. But take care not to fire while those parties were out. Also keep little patrols going all night on the outside of the walls for securing engineers or another sort of reconnoiterers … When their batteries are raised against us, to ply them well with all the guns we can bring to bear upon their battery from every part of our line, both great and small, and that by degrees, not all at once, but gradually to torment and hinder them from firing or loading their guns with a good direction.[19]

There was no consistency of direction among the Jacobites. The sharp eye of Colonel James Grant had noted that the work was dominated from the south-east by a hill

> whence one may discover everything that passes in the fort. Mr Grant proposed to begin by erecting a battery on this hill to annoy the garrison; and he had observed that one of the bastions projected so far as not to be defended by the fire of the rest, so he proposed to arrive at it by a trench and blow it up. But as he was reconnoitring, he received a violent contusion by a cannon ball, and Brigadier Stapleton having no other engineer, was obliged to send to Inverness for Monsieur Mirabelle, who began on a quite different plan, and succeeded no better at Fort William than he had done at Stirling.[20]

The scheme of attack as actually carried out by Mirabelle de Gordon put the whole weight on the artillery, employing both cannon and 6-inch mortars. The Jacobites opened fire on 20 March and (although there is some uncertainty as to the actual sequence of the initial batteries) it is clear that the earlier sites – on the slopes of Sugar Loaf Hill and the slopes of Cow Hill

– were too distant from the target. On the 23rd, however, a further battery was opened on the Cow Hill but closer to the target. The 6-inch bombs caused Captain Scott some concern for the overhead cover in the fort, but his gunners were hammering back effectively, especially against Cow Hill, and 'we gather up all the splinters of the rebels' shells thrown at us, and broke them small to serve as grape shot'.[21]

It was impossible for the besiegers to creep near the ramparts unobserved, for the nights were clear and moonlit and the only chance the Highlanders had to get to grips with the enemy was when watering parties left the fort. Whilst Scott succeeded in imposing his authority on this garrison, a spirit of division spread among the frustrated Jacobites. There were feuds between the Camerons and the Keppochs, between the 'French' troops and the Highlanders as a whole, and between the Prince's Secretary, Murray of Broughton, and almost everybody else. 'Lochiel and Keppoch are loud in their complaints against him, and the latter has threaten to beat him with a stick … these gentlemen accuse him of having sold off a great quantity of flour to the local people.'[22]

On 27 March the emphasis of the attack shifted from the mortars to the cannon, when the Jacobites unmasked a battery of four 6-pounder pieces on the ground above the Governor's garden. On the night of the 28th the garrison saw a large fire disconcertingly close (at 300 yards) on the hillock of the Craigs Burial Ground, east of the fort, and the next morning the Jacobites opened an artillery attack from this side with red-hot shot, 'which at first burnt some of the fellows' fingers who went to lift the shot till they became more wary'.[23] The aim was to make the cramped interior of the fort untenable, and further missiles included cold roundshot, grapeshot, old nails and (a Jacobite speciality) red-hot lengths of notched iron that were intended to lodge in timbers.

This time Scott was unable to hit back properly with his artillery, for the muzzles of the guns on the Craigs were difficult to see. Instead, upon detecting signs of commotion among the besiegers, he dispatched Captain George Foster with 150 men to assault the battery on the evening of 31 March. There was a muddled relief of the guard between the Camerons and the Keppoch which happened to leave the battery unprotected at the crucial time, and the sortie was able to spike two 6-inch mortars and a 6-pounder cannon, and bring back two more 6-inch mortars and three French 4-pounder cannon. The party then turned against the battery above the Governor's garden, but this time without the advantage of surprise, and Scott had to send two successive reinforcements to get the troops out of trouble. They

Fort William, from the Jacobite battery at the Craigs Burial Ground

returned safely with the captured pieces, and the casualties in the whole affair were even, at eleven or twelve a side.

The siege had dragged on much longer than had been expected, and still to no purpose, and Prince Charles called on Lochiel and Keppoch to bring their men back to Inverness. The fire of the besiegers slackened on 1 and 2 April, and on the 3rd Scott found that the enemy had disappeared, leaving behind their equipment and all but their most easily transportable artillery. 'I shall mount our prize guns (both those we took and the legacy the rebels left me when they marched off), on one corner of our walls that if any general officer comes here, they may be seen at one view.'[24]

The *Baltimore* and the *Terror*, which had done so much to help the defence of Fort William, were units of a flotilla of sloops and surprisingly agile mortar vessels operating under the command of Captain Thomas Noel, from his 20-gun *Greyhound*. As well as supporting the garrisons, Noel had the wider remit of intercepting French sailings, and preventing or deterring the movement of Jacobite clansmen from the western capes and islands to the army of Prince Charles.

The first exercise in retaliatory power (much worse was to follow in the pacification) was entrusted to the naval captain Robert Duff of Logie, who was another of those Lowland Scots who were much embittered against the Jacobites. He took his bomb vessel *Terror* and the small supporting craft *Anne* to Mingary Castle to embark a force of Argyll Militia, and at 4 a.m. on 10 March he landed the troops and fifty-six of his armed sailors on the

Morvern shore of the Sound of Mull. By 6 p.m. the expedition had devastated 14 miles of coast from Drimmin to Loch Aline. The people had been able to escape with some of their effects, but nearly 400 of the houses of the Camerons and MacLeans were destroyed, along with barns, stores of grain, and cattle and horses. Curiously enough these folk were tenants of the Duke of Argyll, whose assets were thereby diminished. On 27 March a further expedition ascended Loch Sunart, and meted out the same treatment along the northern shore of the Morvern peninsula.

Enterprises in the Far North

The Final Defeat of Loudoun

By the last week in February Lord Loudoun with the loyalist clansmen and the men of the 64th were ensconced in Sutherland behind the barrier of the Dornoch Firth and the river and loch of Shin (p. 446), and Lord George Murray was unable to find a means of getting at him there. An astute Jacobite commentator emphasized that it was 'of the utmost importance to disperse Lord Loudoun's little army; it cut off all communication with Caithness, whence the Prince expected both men and provisions, and Lord Loudoun seemed disposed to return to Inverness upon the Prince's leaving it; this discouraged his friends from joining, and would discourage such as had joined from marching south, when there would be occasion. Though Lord Loudoun behaved all along as a gentleman, and was incapable of doing anything inconsistent with that character, people did not care to leave their families and effects exposed to the insults of the enemy'.[25]

By 10 March the demoralized 64th Highlanders and Independent Companies which Loudoun had brought from Inverness had been reinforced by northern clansmen in the shape of 310 of the followers of the Earl of Sutherland, who were shortly to be brought up to a four-company strength of 400, together with 100 of Lord Reay's MacKays. However, the newcomers inspired no great trust, and, far from receiving help from Cumberland, Loudoun was faced with a call from the duke to bring 1,800 of his men by sea to Banff to join the main army. Loudoun pointed out that his four seagoing vessels could transport 300 men at the most, and that the rest of the craft were little ferries and flat-bottomed horse boats which could not venture out of inland waters. In any case the Sutherlands were 'mostly men who have farms', and Loudoun was afraid that 'they will march very thin at this season of the year whenever they discover they are to cross the Firth'. He had still less confidence in the MacKays, who could not be told where they were going until they were actually on board ship.[26]

The first man to hit on a realistic scheme to evict Lord Loudoun was one of Prince Charles's aides de camp, the Irish colonel Richard Warren, who proposed to sweep up all the available fishing boats along the Moray Firth in order to mount an amphibious expedition. 'By friendly approaches and military execution' Warren himself rounded up thirty-eight of the craft and collected them in a main concentration in Findhorn harbour.[27] The boats ought to have been intercepted by the *Vulture* and her sister sloops, but a happy succession of mists and easterly winds had kept the Royal Navy out to sea.

Lieutenant Colonel James Moir of Stoneywood now took charge of the proceedings, and with the aid of a particularly dense fog the fishermen rowed undetected around Tarbat Ness and beached their boats on the sands at Tain at 10 a.m. on 19 March. As overall commander the Duke of Perth marched the landing force thither from a rendezvous at Dingwall, but in the murk the men did not see that the boats had already arrived, and the retreating tide left the craft stranded half a mile from the water. 'We got all to arms in order to launch them, but they were heavy boats; it took us a long time before we could get them afloat.'[28] There were not enough boats to carry the entire force of up to 1,800 men in a single lift, and so an initial 700 or so were embarked as a first wave and approached the Sutherland shore 2 miles west of Dornoch towards 8 a.m. on 20 March. The passage was only about 3 miles across, and the only hazard to navigation was the risk of running aground on the gently shelving sands on the far side.

At this time Loudoun's forces were dispersed behind their water barrier from Dornoch by way of Bonar to Lairg. Loudoun himself had gone up-country on reconnaissance, and the only men within reach of the landing site were forty luckless MacKays and, a little further off, 120 troops of Loudoun's 64th Highlanders under the command of Major William MacKenzie. At the sight of the MacKays the Duke of Perth 'ranged his boats in line so as to be able to disembark his men in order of battle. As soon the water shelved to three or four feet the duke was the first to leap into the water, and all the rest followed his example. They marched in fine order through the sea until the water reached only half-way up their legs, and then delivered their first volley at the enemy'.[29]

The MacKays fled, and by the time Major MacKay hastened up through the coastal dunes with the men of the 64th he could see eighteen boats, of which eight or ten were completing the landing of the first wave, while the others were already making back to pick up the rest. He estimated that 300 of the Jacobites were in full march against him, and another 500 were forming a secure bridgehead for the second wave. It was a highly professional performance by any standard, and the importance of landing in order of battle was something that the British had to relearn a number of times in the course of the eighteenth century.

This part of Sutherland now threatened to become a death-trap for MacKenzie's command, for it consisted of a peninsula enclosed between the Dornoch Firth to the south and by the little Loch Fleet in the rear, which could be crossed only by the passage across the narrows to the Little Ferry. Pursued by the Jacobites, MacKenzie and his troops made first for their base at Dornoch, where they threw some ammunition into a ditch, and then tried to reach the narrows. They gave up the attempt in despair, and the only people to get away were a number of officers who had broken the parole they had given to the Jacobites after Prestonpans and now feared that their surrender would not be accepted. MacKenzie and all the rest laid down their arms. At the Little Ferry the Jacobites also found four ships which had been brought there for safekeeping, and were laden with the stock and valuables of Whiggish merchants and townspeople of Inverness, together with 1,450 muskets and a large consignment of ammunition that had been destined for Lord Loudoun, who learned the full detail of these appalling developments at Invershin.

The line of the Dornoch Firth and the Shin was now completely outflanked on the seaward side, and Loudoun concluded that he must divide his forces. He himself took off to the west with the MacDonalds of Sleat and the MacLeods, and crossed to Skye on 28 March, while he sent the MacKays and the Sutherlands north to Lord Reay's country 'with orders to defend themselves as they can against the rebels, and take particular care in all events that their arms do not fall into the enemy's hands'.[30]

Far Northern Terminations: Cromartie's Campaign and the Loss of Le Prince Charles

After the Jacobites' highly successful expedition across the Dornoch Firth, the Duke of Perth returned to Inverness, leaving 1,500 men who remained in the far north-east under the command of Lord Cromartie. He was accompanied by his eldest son, the 18-year-old Lord John MacLeod, Robert MacGregor of Glencarnock and the old and semi-criminal Coll Ban

MacDonald of Barisdale. Cromartie's MacKenzies were clansmen in the traditional style, but Glencarnock's MacGregors and Barisdale's MacDonalds were not always easy to distinguish from robber bands.

George MacKenzie, 3rd Earl of Cromartie, had been among the last of the traditional leaders to declare for Prince Charles, and according to one source he finally came out 'in the heat of liquor'.[31] Cromartie had then been observed at Perth 'in Highland dress and pistol, white cockade in bonnet, and a large belt before him with the letters *J.R.* cyphered upon the same purse, which … stood for *James Rex*'.[32]

Cromartie and his associates now saw their purposes as being to disarm the fragmented loyalist forces,[33] exact money and settle old scores. The original force divided in three:

❖ Cromartie remained with about 500 men in Sutherland

❖ Cromartie's son Lord MacLeod was operating in Caithness

❖ Barisdale had taken off with his gang to seek revenge on 400 men who had been acting under the authority of the MacKay chief Lord Reay, and 'give a good account of them for the injury they had done to the Prince's efforts'.[34]

The injury was no less than an ultimately fatal blow to the Jacobite cause. Loudoun's last communication to the loyalist northern clansmen had been less than inspiring, as we have just seen, but fate now delivered into their hands a prize of incalculable worth. Put quite simply, Prince Charles was running out of money to pay the forces, who were living in increasingly straitened circumstances in the neighbourhood of Inverness. More than anything else he stood in need of the £15,100-worth of guineas and gold being conveyed from France to Scotland on board *Le Prince Charles*, late His Majesty's snow *Hazard*, which had been captured by the Jacobites at Montrose in November and had been tearing up and down the North Sea between Scotland and French-held ports. The craft was now commanded by the experienced and very tough Franco-Irish frigate captain Richard Talbot. He had with him Colonel Ignatius Brown of the regiment of Lally, six officers and sixty men of the regiment of Berwick, and a number of volunteers from Royal Ecossais, the French Guards and the Spanish service.

On 24 February Talbot was making for the little harbour of Portsoy near Banff when he saw ahead of him the squadron of Commodore Smith (the 40-gun *Eltham*, the 24-gun *Sheerness*, and the sloops *Hound* and *Hawk*). Talbot turned north, and by dint of rowing with the sweeps he was able to

Le Prince Charles, ex-*Hazard*

work around the flotilla overnight and gain the Pentland Firth, the wide strait between the mainland and the Orkney Islands. On the 25th, just when Talbot thought he was clear, he spotted a frigate (*Sheerness*) on his tail, and directed *Le Prince Charles* through the rocky entrance of the nearest inlet, the Kyle of Tongue. The loch was shallow, and just when Talbot was clewing up the sails preparatory to anchoring, the stern of the vessel grounded on a spread of white sand not far up the western side of the entrance. Nevertheless he was able to moor in such a way as to be able to present his little broadside of six 9-pounders down the Kyle.

   Sheerness entered the Kyle at 2.30 p.m. and anchored at a range of half a cannon shot, or about 400 yards. Talbot ran up the white French flag and raised a cry of 'Vive le Roi!'. The British responded with a huzza and a cannon shot, whereupon Talbot fired his broadside and opened combat. The battering went on without intermission until 6.30 p.m., by which time all Talbot's gunners were killed or wounded, and the surviving crew had fled below and were calling on him to surrender. Talbot went below, forced the men up again with his sword, and stationed two Irish soldiers at every gun to keep them at their work.

At seven I sounded the well, and found five and a half feet of water in the hold. I had lost all my masts, yards and steering gear, and seeing how badly the efforts of my crew were flagging, I decided to run the vessel onto the rocks. I accordingly cut the cable at the bitts, and the tide floated us off and threw us on the rocks. As soon as we made contact all my crew, except the officers and six of the sailors, fled to safety ashore, in spite of all I could do.[35]

Talbot and his officers were left to manoeuvre the chests of money down a ramp to the shore with the help of a spare yardarm, and he assigned ten officers and thirty soldiers to guard the gold. He would have liked to have set fire to the abandoned craft, but he had to give up the idea with untransportable wounded still on board. At 10.30 p.m. Talbot and Brown finally went ashore, by which time there was 6 feet of water in the hold, and the 18-pounders of *Sheerness* had shattered the two topmasts, carried away the long bowsprit 11 feet from the end, and scored multiple hits above and below the waterline.

After a debate on the sands Talbot and his officers and troops staggered off at 11.30 in the night in what they thought was the direction of Inverness, and ignorant of whether they were in enemy or friendly country. An hour later they reached the house of William MacKay of Melness, who was one of the Jacobites of his divided clan. He told them that the area was indeed hostile, but he sold them two horses to carry the gold, and provided his two sons as guides on the way to Inverness. By ill fortune the clan chief, Lord Reay, was acting as host to ninety or so officers and men of the 64th Highlanders at Tongue House, on the opposite or eastern side of the Kyle, and soon the troops and increasing numbers of clansmen were on the trail of Talbot's party.

Towards 7 a.m. on 26 February the Jacobites dispersed the first body of forty men who had assembled on a hill opposite them. They broke through five more gatherings on the way south, but they were finally surrounded by a force which Talbot estimated at 320 men. The Jacobites threw what they could of the coins into a nearby loch and among the heather, but then had no other course but to surrender. They were escorted to Tongue House, 'the residence of a Scottish gentleman called Lord Reay, who received us with great kindness and courtesy'.[36]

The Hanoverians believed that they had recovered all the money 'excepting £1,000 which was run away with by a fellow of this country who has not been heard of since'.[37] The fellow was finally discovered to be one John MacKay, 'John who took the gold', and Lord Reay made him return the money as belonging to the public. Deprived of the gold from France, Prince

Charles was reduced to paying his demoralized troops with meal from the dwindling magazines at Inverness, which he believed he must defend even at the cost of a battle.

Visitors to the Orkney Islands

Lord Reay and his people, alarmed at the magnitude of what they had done, embarked on the *Sheerness* rather than face retribution. The first port of call was Stromness on Mainland in the Orkney Islands, where the ship arrived on 1 April.

By chance Orkney then became central to events, with people arriving not only from the mainland but from different continents. The Jacobite lairds had gained the upper hand in this remote part of the world (p. 552), and their position had been strengthened in January when a brig laden with arms, one of four dispatched by the Spanish government, reached Orkney and was piloted into Weddel Sound off Hoy. At about the same time a further ship, the merchantman *Providence* of Boston, Massachusetts, had reached Stromness from Newcastle with a cargo of coal, mixed goods and 150 muskets, and up to a dozen barrels of gunpowder, in addition to an unusually large complement of fourteen carriage guns. Little is known about her master, one Robert Sinclair, though his name suggests that he was a local man, and still less is known about his mission. He claimed that he was putting in for repairs, but that does not explain why he stayed so long.

Rival forces now arrived in rapid succession. Cromartie's son, the Jacobite Lord John MacLeod, had 300 men in Caithness, of which a company's worth took ship from Thurso on 1 April under the command of Alexander MacKenzie of Ardloch, and occupied Kirkwall. The Whiggish Sheriff Depute and the Provost fled to Shetland.

By an extraordinary chance *Sheerness* had just arrived at Stromness towards the western end of the island on the same 1 April. The *Providence* was lying there, with the armaments still aboard. The mate and crew deserted ashore, leaving the ship to Robert Sinclair, and 'upon the *Sheerness*'s coming into the harbour of Stromness he and the Highland gang that was with him got off in a boat; but he [the captain of the *Sheerness*] has brought off the ship, with what arms and ammunition were aboard'.[38]

Lord Reay and his men still shrank from an encounter with the Jacobites, and rather than face Ardloch they remained on board the *Sheerness* when she made for Aberdeen with the *Providence* and the other prizes she had taken. Barisdale's punitive expedition never caught up with them. Ardloch was left in peace to secure the public monies at Kirkwall and

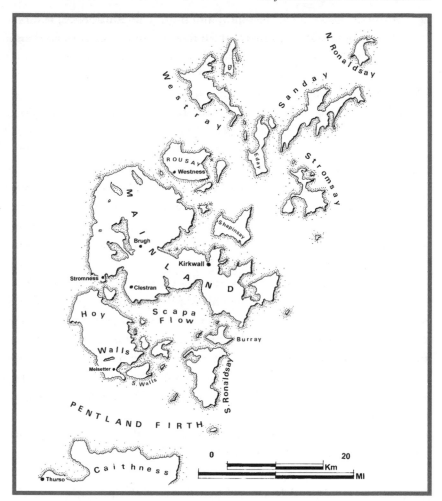

The Orkney Islands

consolidate the Jacobite hold on the islands, then returned to the Scottish mainland on 6 April. Among the local lairds Patrick Fea had made genuine attempts to raise recruits, but the Orkney Islanders were not made for the land service, and the influential Sir James Stewart was chiefly interested in gratifying old grudges. It was going to be a long time before the lairds learned of the overthrow of the wider cause at Culloden.

The End at Dunrobin, 15 April 1746

Cromartie's main force had not strayed from its stamping ground in Sutherland, and had been more interested in exacting contributions than hunting for the lost gold of *Le Prince Charles,* or taking effective measures against the loyalist militia. The militiamen grew in confidence, and on 15 April the commanders learned that there was a good chance of catching Cromartie's 400 troops off guard when they were marching along the coast from Dunrobin to the Little Ferry. The column was strung out, and Cromartie and his officers lagged behind at Dunrobin to pay their respects to their political enemy, the Countess of Sutherland.

Three companies of militia concealed themselves in the broken country which overlooked the fields of the narrow coastal plain, then struck the column in the right flank. The Jacobites made for Loch Fleet, but there was no possible escape around the marshes and rocks at the head of the inlet, and the fugitives crowded at the Little Ferry, where about fifty of them were killed or drowned, and 165 taken prisoner. Those that got away had chopped away the fingers of the men who had clung to the gunwales of the boats in their desperation.

At a signal from a well-wisher in Dunrobin Castle, Ensign John MacKay and a separate force of six militiamen had dashed to the Golspie Burn and got between the column and its officers. Cromartie and his friends fell back to the castle, shut the door behind them, and signalled their plight by ringing bells and waving a flag from the tower. Their men had troubles of their own, as we have seen, and Ensign MacKay took the party prisoner after he bluffed the guard at the door into believing that the officers had already surrendered.

The great loss to the Prince was not the elimination of Cromartie and his people but their absence from the field of Culloden.

Lord George's Atholl Raid and his Siege of Blair Castle, 16–31 March 1746

In the first half of March a kind of strategic vacuum settled over the southern Highlands. This was because the principal Jacobite forces had recoiled towards Inverness, and Cumberland had concentrated his army on the eastern coast. Lord George Murray had been the chief architect of the retreat, but he now began to wonder how the Jacobites might again move forward. Early in the month a number of officers proposed establishing supply depots in Badenoch and elsewhere in the southern Highlands, so that the Jacobites could take advantage of the difficult country even if the Duke of Cumberland marched past them or was successful in open battle. The proposal was rejected as smacking of defeatism.[39]

Towards the middle of the month Lord George was planning an

altogether more concentrated and specific operation, whereby the MacPhersons and the Atholl men would burst through a 10-mile sector of the outposts of the hated Campbell militia between Loch Rannoch and Blair, and irrupt into his home country of Atholl. He disclosed his intentions to Alexander Robertson of Struan on the 15th:

> I heartily sympathise with you and your countrymen for the oppressions they suffer from Argyllshire neighbours and others. You may easily believe me when I saw that it was no fault of mine that a remedy was not applied to that evil sooner; with [Archibald Menzies of] Shian, [David Stewart of] Kynachan and many more brave people we design to attempt breaking up some of their quarters before we sleep tomorrow night. Our design is at one time to pay them a visit at the foot of your loch, at Kynachan, Blairfettie, Bridge of Tilt, Lude and Peter McGlashan's house in Blair. Some cannon will be up the day after to try my brother's Castle ... Would to God I had your advice and personal assistance on this occasion, but I hope your health will continue to last and that you may soon have the pleasure of seeing your Prince and country happily established in peace.[40] [McGlashen's house in Blair was the village inn.]

By this time the enemy forces occupied an outwardly impressive spread of posts across the width of Scotland. We have Cumberland's main concentration about Aberdeen, with a detachment of 500 of his troops based on the castle of Blair Atholl, and another hundred operating from Castle Menzies, guarding the respective axes of Wade's two roads from the north. Cumberland positioned the Hessian mercenaries in support, namely two of their regiments at Perth, and another two regiments and St George's 8th Dragoons at Stirling. Lord Crawfurd was the senior British officer accompanying the Hessians, and he was told that 'if they [the Jacobites] should aim at any such desperate enterprise as a march to break into the Lowlands within reach of the Hessian forces, then His Royal Highness would by all means have Prince Frederick assemble them immediately and march directly to attack them'.[41]

On 9 February Major General John Campbell of Mamore had joined the Duke of Cumberland with four companies of the Argyll Militia. Further detachments of Campbells manned a tripwire of outposts as an eastward extension of the historic clan strongpoints. The principal garrisons in question were located at Bun Rannoch, Kynachan, Blairfettie and Lude. Elaborate arrangements were made so that the garrison of Castle Menzies would support the post of Bun Rannoch in one direction, and Coshieville

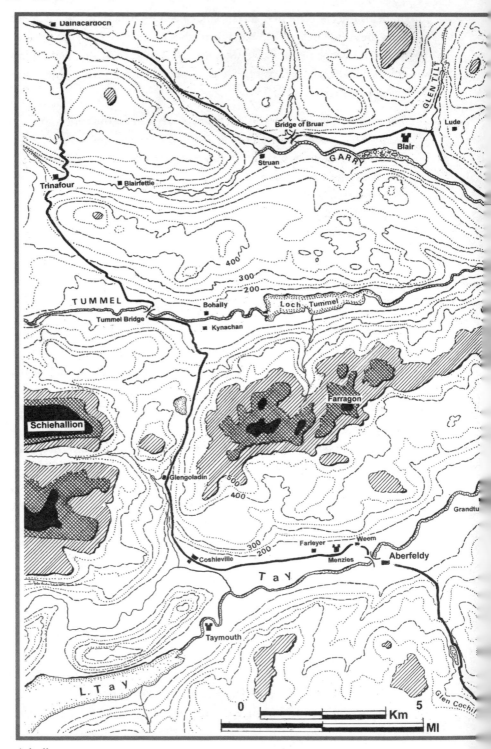

Atholl

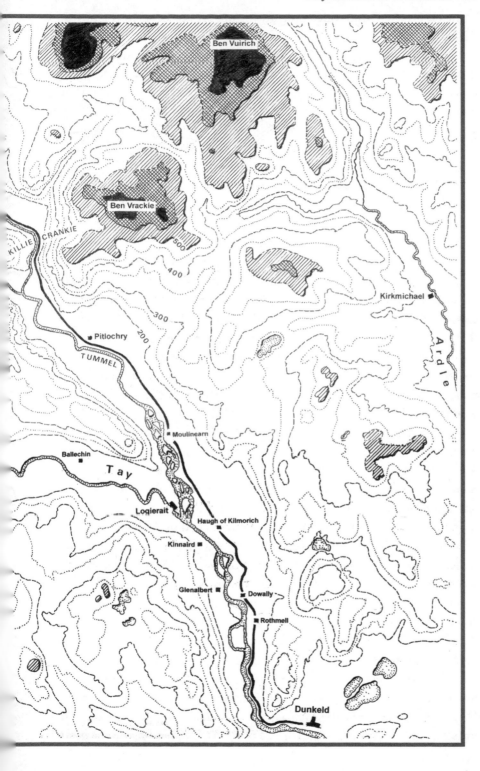

in the other; the Coshieville company in turn was to back up the post at Glengoladin.

However, the majority of the posts were no more than strongly built farmhouses or inns which had no particular provision for defence, and whose weak points were familiar to the evicted Jacobite owners. Nor did the arrangements take any account of the state of mind of the isolated commanders in their hostile environment. Captain Duncan Campbell at Balquhidder observed that 'I and my officers are strangers in this country'.[42] The same applied with greater force to the Hessians, who were overcome with depression at the sight of the mist-shrouded mountains to the north. Their chief, Prince Friedrich, was answerable to his father the Landgrave for the welfare of his troops, and he was not going to risk these valuable and negotiable assets in a cause which inspired him with no enthusiasm.

The Duke of Cumberland was set in his belief that there was no possibility of the friendly forces being surprised,[43] and warnings made no impression on him, even when they were as detailed as that carried by a man who had just escaped from Jacobite captivity, who reported that 'they were whispering that they were to attack those [posts] of the Campbells covering Blair and Castle Menzies, being those parties posted at the foot of Rannoch, Kynachan and Blairfettie, which is the reason for Shian's return back to Badenoch, as he finds the Menzies, the Rannoch men and the men of the Braes of Perthshire won't rise unless those parties are first beat from their posts'.[44]

It would have been difficult to improve on Lord George Murray's planning and execution. He first collected his Atholl Brigade, together with two 4-pounder cannon, and marched from the neighbourhood of Inverness to Strathspey, where on 14 March he gained the surrender of Castle Grant. He left it garrisoned by 100 men, which secured his flank towards Lower Strathspey. In the neighbourhood of Ruthven he was joined by Archibald Menzies of Struan and Cluny MacPherson with 300 local MacPhersons, and a swift march brought the combined force of about 700 men to Dalnacardoch, where the final arrangements were made. The troops were divided into thirty companies or detachments, each assigned to a particular target, and each consisting of both MacPhersons and the Atholl men. They strode across 30 miles of hills to come within reach of their objectives, and 'before they entered upon their black work they secured the Pass of Killiecrankie'.[45]

Much to his later embarrassment, Lieutenant Colin Campbell of Glenure was absent from the 64th's post at Bun Rannoch when it came under assault. 'This news met me at Castle Menzies. It's true that I was away, I wish from my soul that I was not, but my excuse, if one can be, is that I had come down for meal for the party ... which I could not obtain by letters I frequently wrote.'[46] That had been on the 16th. He stayed overnight at Lord Glenorchy's castle at Taymouth, and his return was delayed further when he met with an accident on the road.

Glenorchy wrote to Cumberland in the wretched man's defence that 'he told me, if he were attacked in the night 'twould be impossible to defend it, for the men were scattered in different houses or rather huts, and I was so convinced of its being an improper station that I intended to apply for removing it to a safer and more useful place. As Your Royal Highness will with great reason be angry at this gentleman for being absent from his command, I humbly beg to assure Your Royal Highness that he is a brave and diligent officer but of little experience, having never been in the army before the regiment was raised'.[47] The luckless Glenure finally figured as the victim in the celebrated Appin Murder on 14 May 1752.

The militiamen at Bun Rannoch were drinking themselves into a stupor when they were surrounded by the Jacobites at 11 p.m. on the 16th. 'The sentry upon the officers' quarters fired his musket, but the muzzle of it being beat down the shot did no execution, whereupon he was seized as were three officers and a short time after the whole men.' The next post to the east was Kynachan House, which guarded the important bridge over the Tummel. The place was 'surrounded in the same manner, the sentry who gave an alarm shot was killed, but the men stood some time firing out of slits till an opening being made upon them from the roof, they found they could make nothing of it and were obliged to yield, as were the officers, one of whom stood till he was mortally wounded, and 'tis said he is since dead'.[48] The Jacobite laird of Kynachan, David Stewart, had been assigned to hold Castle Grant, but the entry was effected by Charles Stewart of Bohally, a former gentleman-soldier of the Black Watch who had been paying court to David's daughter and knew the house well.

Altogether at these two posts the garrisons lost two killed and eight or ten wounded, all the rest being taken prisoner. The attacking party at Blairfettie was led by the laird himself, James Robertson, and he was let in by his lady, who had been forced to wait on the Campbells at table.

All the schemes for reinforcing the outposts came to nothing. The party at Glengoladin mutinied without ever having come under attack. The garrison at Coshieville 'declared openly that whatever might come on them they would desert every one of them, that they would do their best for their own safety if we should be attacked in the night, on which and their refusing to march to Glengoladin all the officers of us, after the maturest consideration, were of opinion that it was best to retire here [to Castle Menzies] and bring in the men rather than let them desert'.[49]

All of the objectives were taken, including those of the regulars closest to Blair, and by noon on 17 March Lord George was able to write to O'Sullivan about his initial success:

> I'm so hurried that I can scarce take the time to write you a few lines. I'm afraid I shall be blamed for undertaking too much at one time with my very unequal force, and even success, which often makes atonement for faults, does not hinder me from owing it was too daring ... I need not after this tell you our officers and men behaved well. Cluny [MacPherson] has been indefatigable, and his officers and men bore an equal share in all the parties. What shall be done with all the [captured] Campbells? ... Our men (I own it having been my fault all my life) are too tender-hearted.[50]

Blair Castle was a different proposition, for the grim old pile was held by the cranky and savage Lieutenant Colonel Sir Andrew Agnew, who still had 300 troops with him after making detachments. The garrison had been there for more than a month, every now and then emerging to raid the houses of notorious Jacobites for 5 or 6 miles around. The officers fell into the habit of drinking at David McGlashen's tavern in the village, where one of the attractions was the landlord's daughter Molly, and on the way back they would slash with their swords at the larch saplings that lined the castle drive. Otherwise the garrison was penned up in the castle, which became increasingly foul and verminous: 'The first week of our stay here we had a hard frost, with much snow; then came on a great thaw and wind; immediately after that came a frost again; these sudden changes, and cold windy weather (and by reason of keeping our men so closely confined in Blair Castle) ... breathing in the most nasty scents, which arise from one and the other lying upon straw, almost brought a pestilence among them'.[51]

Early on the morning of 17 March the Jacobites seized a number of small corporals' posts in the neighbourhood – at Bridge of Bruar, the House of Lude, and Bridge of Tilt; all of this, complained Andrew, 'was done before I had information that the rebels were come to attack me, which is a plain demonstration what a villainous country this is'.[52]

Lord George arrived outside his ancestral castle at 9 a.m., 'pipes playing and colours flying. All night and till the moment I marched we had but about thirty-five men, but we gathered fast on our march, and we marched very fast ... There was something very droll about that, but it should not be mentioned'.[53] What had happened was that a villager of Blair had warned

Lord George that Agnew was sallying from the castle to find out who was attacking his outposts:

> It was daylight, but the sun was not yet up. Lord George looking earnestly about him, observed a field dyke (that is a wall of sod or turf) which had been begun as a fence for cattle, and left unfinished; it was of considerable length, and cut in two by a field that was next the bridge ... He ordered his men to follow him, and drew them up behind the dyke, at such a distance from one another that they might make a good show, having the colours of both regiments flying in their front. He then gave orders to the pipers (for he had with him all the pipers, both of the Atholl men and the MacPhersons) to keep their eyes fixed on the road from Blair, and the moment they saw the soldiers appear, to strike up with all their bagpipes at once. It happened that the regiment came into sight just as the sun rose, and at that instant the pipers began to play one of their noisy pibrochs. Lord George Murray and his Highlanders, both officers and men, drew their swords and brandished them above their heads. Sir Andrew, after gazing a while at this spectacle, ordered his men to the right about, and marched them back to the Castle of Blair.[54]

The show was reinforced by bringing in men, women and children from all the neighbourhood, and distributing them among troops on hillocks 'to make an appearance of great numbers'.[55] However, nobody could be found among the Jacobites who dared to deliver a summons to the castle in person, and so it was conveyed by Molly of the Blair Inn. She gave it to a young officer of her acquaintance, who handed it to Sir Andrew in a state of terror. Agnew rejected it out of hand.

The numbers of the Jacobites built up to some 600, and on 18 March they opened fire with all the artillery they had, which amounted to one 4-pounder and one 6-pounder posted on rising ground near the church. In other words, the attack was developing from the north-north-east, from the village now called Old Blair. The first shot was fired by Lady Lude, whose house nearby had been plundered and vandalized by the garrison. However, the guns were puny things to set against the 7-foot-thick castle walls, and 'one of them could not be kept in due position, which obliged them to call on the smith of Blair several times to work at it'.[56] When the cold shot failed, the Jacobites heated altogether 180 shot to red heat in a furnace they set up in the churchyard and fired them at the roof over the course of two days, 'a course,' writes Lord George, 'which I was by no means fond of'.[57] On the 19th the roof took fire, but the flames were extinguished by the exertions of two carpenters who happened to be with the garrison, and of Sir Andrew himself, who found a ladle in the kitchen, and had the shot dropped into tubs of urine: 'Is the loon daft,' he exclaimed, 'knocking down his ain brother's house?'[58]

It was reported on the evening of the 18th that the Jacobites were thinking of opening a trench attack from behind the terrace and ha-ha (sunken wall) near the curling pond.[59] Nothing more is heard of that initiative, and when the cannon were moved there on about the 25th they had no more effect than earlier. The only other means of direct attack would have been through mining, and Lord George thought in fact of digging under the castle wall from behind the cover of the old stables, but could not find the skilled workmen to carry out his project. There was alarm among the defenders when an ominous thudding reverberated from below, but it proved to emanate from a soldier who was chopping up wood in a cellar.

All the time the besiegers peppered the windows with a long-range fire of musketry, which did little harm, and Agnew records that he was 'so ill-provided with ammunition that I took care that our men should not fire till they came near us'.[60] He noticed that a particular window was attracting the Jacobites' attention, and discovered that the fire was aimed at a straw dummy, clad in one of his uniform coats and sporting a spy glass. He made the joker take it down at the risk of his life. Altogether the relationship of Sir Andrew to his charges seems to have been that of a particularly cantankerous schoolmaster with his class.

Although direct attacks proved unavailing, there was good reason that the sheer numbers of the defenders would prove their undoing. For their food before the siege they had depended on fresh consignments of bread from Perth every four days, and now that they looked to their stores of biscuit they found that more than a quarter was mouldy. The only alleviation from the foul stench in the castle was to open the windows, which admitted the freezing air, and the redcoats were so short of firewood that they had to pull down most of the wainscotting of the chambers.

As the siege dragged on, Lord George rode every day towards Dunkeld, through which the combined forces of the Hessians might reasonably be expected to hasten to the relief at Blair. Instead, on hearing of the fall of the outposts in Atholl, Prince Friedrich pulled back his forces at Perth to join those at Stirling. The Duke of Cumberland was furious when he heard of the retreat, and he ordered Friedrich to march on Blair. By 27 March the Jacobites had evacuated their outpost at Dunkeld in the face of the tardy advance of the Hessians and the British St George's Dragoons, and

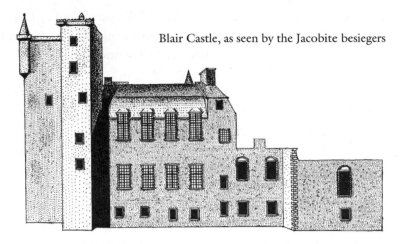

Blair Castle, as seen by the Jacobite besiegers

the following days passed in skirmishing between Dunkeld and the new Jacobite outpost at Pitlochry.

On 30 March a Hessian thrust up the Haugh of Dalskean inaugurated an advance by Hesssian hussars and the British dragoons on Pitlochry, which the Jacobites then abandoned, but they fell back no further than the Pass of Killiecrankie, already identified as 'a most advantageous position at the cntrance to the mountains, where six hundred men can occupy the two sides and deny the passage to an entire army'.[61]

By now Lord George had received repeated demands from Prince Charles to return to the neighbourhood of Inverness, which would shortly receive the attentions of the main Hanoverian army. Lord George raised the siege on 31 March, and brought the Atholl men (swelled by recruits) back north, leaving the MacPhersons on Badenoch to guard the approaches to Inverness from the south. Cumberland sent his congratulations to Sir Andrew Agnew, and authorized him to 'send out sufficient parties, though none further than six miles, to destroy and burn the habitations and effects of all those who may be found in arms contrary to law, or who are out in the present rebellion'.[62]

It is a moot point whether the Atholl Raid, after its brilliant opening, should have been terminated before it became a drain on the resources (as the sieges in the Great Glen proved to be), or whether it should have been continued more energetically than it actually was. Lord George in his history states that on learning of the approach of the Hessians he asked the Prince to send him 1,200 men, which would have been a sure way of defeating the Germans and the British dragoons, and forcing Cumberland to retreat south from Aberdeen.[63] The *Mémoire d'un Ecossais* (1747), attributed to Donald Cameron of Lochiel, puts the requested reinforcement at 1,000 men, and explains that Lord George had been inspired by the news that the Hessians were scattered in three locations, and was confident that he could defeat them, sever communications between the Duke of Cumberland and Edinburgh and Stirling, and so gain ample time to gather his Highlanders and draw on the Lowlands for supplies.

It is difficult to know what to make of this. The punitive expedition to Strathmore (p. 481) shows how sensitive Cumberland was to threats to his landward flank and rear. However, his army was drawing its supplies by sea, not overland, as Gibson points out.[64] Moreover the prolonged siege of Blair (which led only to Perth)[65] was incompatible with the wider scheme as outlined by Lochiel, and the Jacobite forces at the time were dispersed over a triangle whose points were in Atholl, Lochaber and Caithness, leaving the Spey ultimately indefensible against a serious thrust from Aberdeen. Prince Charles genuinely did not have the men to spare. In any case the new scheme represented a radical departure from Lord George's original purpose, which was to liberate Atholl and open it up once more to recruiting. As late as 17 April he offered to return to the army with the recruits he had already raised, 'so if His Royal Highness inclines he may fight them either near Inverness or in Badenoch'.[66]

CHAPTER 18

The Duke of Cumberland in Aberdeen, and the First Pacifications

THE DUKE OF CUMBERLAND AND HIS ARMY arrived in Aberdeen on 27 February 1746, the main force remaining in and about the place until the duke opened his last campaign in April. 'The weather being all this time extremely sharp, with frost and snow and easterly winds, the imflammatory diseases continued. But whilst the men suffered by cold, beds, guards and out-duties, or by their own mismanagement, the officers escaped, who had warm quarters, and were less exposed to cold; only in the beginning of March when the weather was very piercing, some of them were seized with gout.'[1]

At Aberdeen the duke was separated by the great mass of the Grampians from the events in Atholl. He read with concern about the fall of the out-posts, and with anger about the prevaricating Hessians, but otherwise his whole attention was taken up with making ready for the final campaign.[2]

Cumberland and his headquarters needed to chase up Gomes Serra for flour and bread, lay out fresh contracts for forage, and distribute the consignments of blankets and clothing that were being dispatched by the loyalists of Edinburgh and London. Stormy and mostly easterly winds set

A Highlander begging on the streets

in from the beginning of March, which caused heavy snowfalls (worst of all on the 8th), and, to the delight of the Edinburgh Jacobites, left a convoy of biscuit windbound at Leith. A thaw set in on 13 March, which in the short term actually made things worse by swelling the Spey with melt water from the mountains.

The duke's working day began at 4 a.m., and he devoted most of the hours to assembling his forces, training the officers and men, and laying in supplies. He cemented his already excellent relations with his troops, and showed himself 'princely and amiable' to well-affected citizens and gentry,[3] but his conduct and that of his senior officers was not calculated to win them many new friends. At his quarters at Mr Thompson's the duke and his staff helped themselves to the coal, ale, spirits and the milk of the house cow, and they committed atrocities on the table and bed linen. Nearby, in the house of Mrs Gordon of Hallhead, Lieutenant General Hawley took the lady's china 'because it is pretty', and all her clothes except those on her back, 'though for what or for whom he wanted them is a little obscure'.[4]

From Edinburgh the Lord Justice Clerk counselled moderation in the dealings with Aberdeen,[5] but Cumberland was unimpressed, and on coming to the town he 'immediately stopped all the Non-Jurant ministers, and very soon after ordered their meeting houses and the mass houses to be destroyed, which was accordingly executed in both town and country as the army marched along, and indeed none were surprised at this piece of discipline, as these houses were not only illegal, but had in fact proved such nurseries of rebellion'.[6]

Aberdeen at least could be kept under heavy military occupation. The impressive pile of Gordon's Hospital had remained empty ever since it was built in 1732 as a refuge for the children of poor townspeople. It now sprang to life as 'Fort Cumberland', surrounded with palisaded earthworks and garrisoned by 200 men under the ancient Captain John Crosbie, thus securing Aberdeen against the followers of Gordon of Glenbucket, who were even now lurking in the hinterland.

It was a different story in the places that the army had left behind in its passage, and where authority rested with shaky civilian committees of management. When Perth was still garrisoned adequately the loyal citizens made the duke a substantial gift of land in the town,[7] but by the second half of March they were in a state of alarm, fearing alike the Jacobites in their midst, and the prospect of armed bands arriving from the countryside to free the rebel prisoners. George Miller (the Clerk and Sheriff Depute) fled the town, and returned only after receiving stern orders. The government's hold on Montrose was every bit as tenuous, and for the same reasons.[8]

The reports augmented Cumberland's impatience with all things Scottish, and he expressed his regret to the Duke of Newcastle that

> every dispatch of mine must be filled with repeated complaints of the disaffection of this part of His Majesty's dominions, but so it is, that though His Majesty has a considerable and formidable army in the heart of their country, yet they cannot help giving important marks of their ill will, by making efforts to raise men and set prisoners at liberty in the places we have passed through, especially at Forfar, where each of our four divisions lay a night. They had the insolence to conceal three Irish French officers in the town, during the whole time, and after all our troops were passed through, let them beat up for volunteers there; the Magistrates of that town are remarkable for being good politicians, for when they were chosen in the midst of these troubles they made a minute in their Council book that they would not take any oaths, till they should see which side was like to be uppermost.[9]

As a straightforward Germano-English soldier the duke could make little sense of local complexities, and his secretary asked the Lord Justice Clerk to send him some canny Scot who could guide him through 'this wicked scene of confusion and mischief'.[10]

The Corgarff Expedition, 27 February – 5 March 1746

For the time being the duke was in no position to act offensively with his main force. This did not prevent him from launching two expeditions, the first of which he dispatched on 28 February, and by deliberate intent on the day after he arrived at Aberdeen.[11] The overall commander was Lieutenant Colonel William Kerr, Lord Ancrum, with 100 of the 11th Dragoons, and 300 infantry. Their target was the isolated tower of Corgarff, which stood on a hill-top 40 or 50 miles away in a wild landscape at the head of Strathdon, in the country of Gordon of Glenbucket. The expedition would be an act of presence in its own right, and also the means of destroying an important consignment of gunpowder and muskets recently landed by a Spanish privateer at Peterhead, and conveyed to Corgarff by Pitsligo's Horse.

Only six or seven days before the blow arrived, John Knox, the tutor to the sons of the ardent Jacobite, Lady Skellater, had been showing two further young gentlemen around the Corgarff Castle. Forbes of Ballnabodach had been charged by Lord George Murray to defend the place, and he now explained how he proposed to go about it, 'particularly in pulling down a stair and making an opening in the wall whereby they might throw down stones upon anybody that would enter at the gate, that he proposed also to load four hundred guns and call in all the country men that were left about the castle, which ... were about twenty-four'.[12]

Guided by three Presbyterian ministers, Lord Ancrum's expedition set out from Aberdeen on Friday 28 February and traversed the snowy moors and mountains to Tarland. On the way the officers were overheard asking questions about Corgarff and Strathdon. The news was transmitted to Lady Skellater, and 'upon reading of this letter the Lady Skellater immediately thought proper to send an express to Corgarff ... for to put the Governor upon his guard'.[13] By the account of one of the officers of dragoons

> on Saturday morning we marched from Tarland, a most terrible march, to the castle, which stands on the side of the Don, where I dare say never dragoons were before, nor ever will be again, nor foot either, unless Highlanders! Though we marched early in the morning it was past four when we arrived there. We found it abandoned by the garrison, but so lately that the fire was burning, and no living creature except a poor cat sitting by the fire. They had thrown the barrels of powder down the bank into the river in order to destroy them, but had not time – and had conveyed the arms up and down the hills in different directions, and hid the bayonets under a dunghill. However we found all out, and brought away 367 firelocks, 370 bayonets. There were some more arms destroyed, which we could not carry. Ten thousand musket balls we threw into the river and amongst the heather, etc. ... We staved 32 barrels of exceeding fine Spanish powder equal to 69 of our barrels, and threw it all into the river – and afterwards, for want of horses were obliged to burn and destroy so many of the firelocks that we brought but 131 to Aberdeen.[14]

With its mission accomplished, the combined force returned to Aberdeen on the Wednesday, Lord Ancrum having 'behaved with great prudence, and much like an officer'.[15] His troopers had spent two nights slumped in the saddle in the open country, and Ancrum believed that a third night of falling snow would have destroyed them.

Lafansille and the Harrowing of Strathmore

The second expedition was of a different nature, for it was a small campaign which was conducted with some savagery by Major John Lafansille, a man of Huguenot descent who was hostile to anything that smacked of popery. He was now unleashed by Cumberland to pacify the hinterland of Montrose – the Mearns, Strathmore and the nearby glens – which had been the recruiting grounds of the Jacobite regiment of Lord Ogilvy. Many of the troops had deserted to their homes during the hurried retreat, but from the beginning of March reports confirmed that the whole region was in a state of incipient rebellion and that Jacobite bands were roaming the country, the largest being of well over 200 men commanded by Captain David Ferrier, the former Jacobite deputy governor of Brechin. Even the moderate Lord Justice Clerk was calling for measures to curb 'those madmen about Brechin',[16] and King George gave the duke *carte blanche* 'to do whatever is necessary for suppressing this unnatural rebellion, and preventing the further progress and increase of it'.[17]

Major Lafansille was faced with no significant geographical obstacles except the swollen streams on the glens which snaked into the rolling hills to the west. Strathmore itself was a wide alluvial plain, composed of the most part of a fertile light brown earth interspersed with spreads of gravel and sand, like those of the woodlands about Edzell. He reached Montrose on 24 March with a draft of recruits for the Scotch Fusiliers, the 21st, 'really fine fresh young men'.[18] He then put together a force of 300 infantry, and took them on a rough anti-clockwise circuit through the recalcitrant country to burn the Episcopalian meeting houses and plunder the homes of the gentry. The style was set by what he did at the town of Brechin and little Lethnot. He then moved to a temporary base at the ruined sandstone castle of Edzell (where two of his men contrived to fall through holes), and from where he intended to penetrate all the way up Glen Esk to the castle of Invermark, 'the rendezvous of the villains in these parts'.[19] He was prevented by the heavy rains which swelled the Auchmull Burn, the Water of Tarf and the Water of Mark.

The next destination was the castle of the Earl of Airlie at Cortachy, 'a very strong old house, and if they have provisions in that house, one hundred men may defend it for a considerable time against a much larger number'.[20] The conduct of the Airlie family was suspicious in the extreme, for the earl had done nothing to disarm his tenants, and his son, Lord David Ogilvy, was a colonel in the army of Prince Charles and one of the most active of all the Jacobites. Cumberland had sent Captain Hewitt with 100 troops to seize the house and detain the earl, and Lafansille arrived there on the 30th from Montrose, having plundered the house of Alexander Mathers at Mill of Cruke on the way. Cortachy now served as the base for the operations that Lafansille planned for Glen Prosen and Glen Cova. Among the achievements of the redcoats was to capture 'the Grand Rebel' [yet another David Ogilvy], the Laird of Poole, 'very cleverly taken in the embraces of his doxy'.[21]

Lafansille called off his intended expedition up Glen Cova because all of Lord Airlie's tenants were coming in from there to take the oath of loyalty, as well as the men from Glen Prosen, and Ferrier's band had retreated over the Cairngorms. On balance Lafansille decided not to burn Cortachy Castle, for Airlie seemed 'more a fool than a knave', and his lady declared 'she would never go into a meeting house that did not pray for King George'.[22] The expedition returned to Brechin on 2 April. Lafansille completed his work by burning the meeting house there and the one at Careston, and he was back in Montrose by the 4th.

The behaviour of Strathmore weighed heavily with Cumberland when he reflected how best to deal with the Scots. The land had been conquered in the military sense, but a 'petty insolent spirit' had prevented it from being subdued, and the duke was driven to the conclusion that nothing short of 'some stroke of authority and severity' would be capable of eradicating disaffection wherever it might arise.[23]

Sparring over the Spey: Strathbogie (17 March 1746) and Keith (21 March 1746)

On 12 March Cumberland pushed Major General Bland with four battalions from Aberdeen to Inverurie and Oldmeldrum, respectively about 15 and 17 miles to the north-east. Prince Charles concluded that 'it would appear that the enemy is advancing towards us in strength'.[24] However, this was not the opening of an offensive as such, but a means of winning space for the Hanoverian quarters, and perhaps also of inducing the Jacobites to show their hand before they dispersed.[25]

The main Jacobite concentration on this theatre was located on or near Fochabers, where at any one time the Duke of Perth and his brother Lord John Drummond commanded a force of between 1–2,000 men. Their commission was to hold the enemy at arm's length until Lochiel, Keppoch and Lord George returned from their assorted activities in Lochaber and Atholl.

Security rested in the first place on the frontal barrier presented by the Spey. Unlike the coal-black Tay, which progressed majestically through Atholl and Perth on its way to the sea, the Spey never lost its character of a brawling mountain stream, subject to the prevailing weather among its sources in Badenoch. The snowy hills between the Spey and Strathbogie (Huntly) remained a no man's land where on the whole the Jacobites held the advantage, owing to the sympathy of the population and the activities of lively individuals like John Roy Stuart, and the Irishmen Colonel Matthew Baggot and Major Nicholas Glasgow.

On 17 March John Roy Stuart (uncharacteristically off his guard) was lucky not to be caught by the redcoats when Major General Bland launched an expedition against Strathbogie. Bland left the pursuit to a body of Campbells and some of Kingston's Light Horse. They caught up with the Jacobite hussars 2 miles from Keith, and after a flurry of shots chased them through the little town and out to the far side. Every now and then the distance closed to within 200 paces, but the hussars were better mounted, and the race abandoned 2 miles short of the Jacobite concentration at Fochabers on the Spey.[26]

The hussars had dropped pistols and swords in their headlong course, and the Hanoverians were now so confident that they left an outpost in Keith. This was tempting fortune, for the road from Fochabers was good, only 6 or 7 miles long, and the detachment consisted of just seventy Argyll militiamen and thirty of the Kingstons, the whole standing under the orders of Lieutenant Alexander Campbell of Loudoun's 64th. Campbell distributed the Kingstons in billets in the town, and placed the militiamen in the church, with some on guard in the schoolhouse in the yard.

Major Nicholas Glasgow happened to be with Lord John Drummond when they heard that the enemy were keeping a party at Keith, 'so Glasgow said "it was a shame to allow them to come so often," but Lord John said "how could they help it?" so the Colonel Glasgow said "give him 200 men and he would show them they must keep at a great distance"'.[27] Lord John Drummond gave his blessing to the enterprise, and Glasgow put together a force of rather under 200 infantry (mostly of Ogilvy's Regiment), sixteen of the 'French', and twenty-five hussars and mounted gentlemen. Glasgow accompanied the expedition in person, though the operational command lay with Captain Robert Stewart.

The expedition set out from Fochabers overnight on 20/21 March, keeping for the first 5 miles on the road to Keith, then swinging left (east) across country with the help of local guides. The Jacobites marched through Tarmore, crossed the Isla at Milltown of Keith, then regained the main road behind Keith and came at the town from the south, as if they had been reinforcements from Strathbogie. While Lieutenant John Simpson of Auchinhove threw a loose cordon around Keith with the cavalry, Major Glagow made directly for the town with the infantry, arriving at midnight. 'The Campbell's sentry challenged: "Who was there?" It was answered,

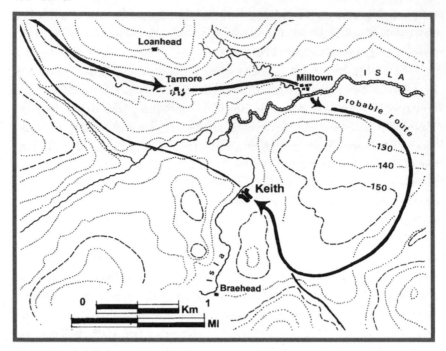

The attack on Keith, 20/21 March 1746

"Friends, the Campbells." He replied, "You are very welcome, we hear the enemies are at hand".[28]

Glasgow seized the man and a second sentry by the scruff of the neck, then went up to a third and shot him. 'After the colonel had shot both his pistols he came up with one of the guards in full arms, did not know what do, but came up briskly and held his empty pistol at his breast, desiring him to surrender, but that he would not do, and pulled out a carbine he had at his side. At which the colonel starts to a side and got out his sword, and cut off his head. Oh, they say he's a brave man and really this story tells he is so.'[29]

Captain Stewart directed the assault on the churchyard, but he suffered a first repulse when the guard turned out of the schoolhouse in force and chased the Jacobites away. However, a second party entered the yard from the far side, and the guards retreated to their main body in the church. Many of Ogilvy's men were wounded in the action, 'as they happened to stand in the south side of the kirk, by the fire from the windows of the kirk'.[30] Stewart himself was shot by a ball which scored both his shoulders, but he made light of his wound, and after half an hour of fighting he finally prevailed on the defenders of the church to surrender. All the same, Alexander Campbell declared that he would yield only to a gentleman, which was stupid as well as pompous. All Jacobites considered themselves to be gentlemen, unless they were ladies, and for this insult he was badly hacked about on the face and wrist. Stewart was now free to help Colonel Glasgow suppress the Kingstons, who had emerged from their billets and were full of fight.

The Jacobites made off with their prisoners before Cumberland's cavalry could arrive in force. The attackers had lost four killed and fifteen wounded, but they believed that they had killed up to twenty-two of the enemy, and they had captured nearly all the rest. However, Captain Alexander Campbell was in such a bad way that he had to be left on the road.

The news of what had happened at Keith was brought to Cumberland by a runaway trooper of the Kingstons, 'a man of no very good conduct, he being subject to drink'.[31] The duke commented that he would have had 'little concern about that accident if it had not been for the loss of Kingston's people'.[32] That was hard on the Campbells, for they had lost some of their best men, and the prisoners were 'removed to Inverness, stripped of their plaids and kilts, led three and three together. The men were much despoiled, one of them my informer told me he saw weep bitterly'.[33] It was convenient to put all the blame on Alexander Campbell, who was supposed to have ignored a positive order not to stay in Keith overnight. He crawled into a roadside house, and was then taken to the home of a Presbyterian minister, who took care of him until he was retrieved on the 27th.

The episode put a great fright into Bland, who now believed that he was about to be attacked by great numbers at Strathbogie, and he recovered his composure only when Brigadier Mordaunt brought up a temporary re-inforcement of four battalions on 22 March. The force at Strathbogie came under the command of William Anne Keppel, 2nd Earl of Albemarle (son of King William's Dutch favourite), who lodged in the house of Governor Hamilton, 'a very pretty situated place'.[34] Bland was content with the arrange-ment, for Albemarle was an easygoing man, but even now the repeated false alarms 'mean that we live like the little men-about-town in Paris or London, turning day into night and night into day'.[35]

In fact the Jacobite horse did little more than exchange pistol and carbine fire across the Isla at Keith, and the Duke of Perth was probably putting up his show of defiance with no more than 300 troops on the eastern side of the Spey. There was a force of 1,000 of so Lowlanders in the neighbour-hood of Fochabers, with posts upstream at Rothes, Elchies, Knockando and Dundurcus. Sir Thomas Sheridan told John Roy Stuart how sorry he was 'that so many of your men have deserted, and that the detachment you sent after them could not overtake them: for, as you say very well, it would be very necessary to make some examples of severity'.[36]

Lord George Murray had not yet returned from his expedition into Atholl, the MacPhersons and Frasers were in their home countries, Cromartie was out of reach in the far north, and Prince Charles still had to retrieve the western Highlanders from the far end of the Great Glen. On 4 April Sheridan wrote in his name to Lochiel and Keppoch that 'His Royal Highness looks upon what has happened at Fort William as but a flea bite, and would not have anybody cast down upon it; what he desires of you is to come away as soon as possible and bring with you all the men you have. We must turn all our fury against the enemy, and that with the utmost expedition ... The Prince would rather have you in three days with five hundred men than with a thousand in three days after ... Those, says the Prince, that love me will follow me, those that will not may stay'.[37]

The appeal was in vain, for even the most biddable of Lochiel's Camerons, the Stewarts of Appin, Keppoch's MacDonnells and the MacDonalds of Clanranald were slow to extricate themselves from Lochaber, and many of their fellow clansmen did not move at all.

Prince Charles and his Army

For all the frustrations that the Duke of Cumberland experienced at Aberdeen, he was still spending his time more productively than Prince Charles. The Jacobite strategy was now being made by Lord George Murray and the clan chiefs, and as a result some of the best forces were dispersed on secondary operations. When he returned from the south Prince Charles had taken up his quarters on 2 March in Inverness, in the house of Anna the Dowager Lady MacKintosh. On the 20th he removed to Elgin, closer to the scene of impending operations.

The Prince paid a number of visits to nearby Gordon Castle, just vacated by the Whiggish Duke of Gordon, and 'the noblest palace in the north ... adorned with pleasant gardens, park, and a final canal, with most agreeable fountains and statues, which the rebels had defaced by shooting at them for their diversion'.[38] However, Charles was confined to his bed for days on end by a fever which sapped his energy, and it is difficult to believe that his malady was purely physical.

The Prince had never faltered in his determination that his army must be organized on a military basis, and that his troops must live on pay as well as motivation. But now the opportunities for exacting cash in enemy territory were limited, and the loss of the French gold on *Le Prince Charles* was going to hit very hard. In a coded message in one of his reports to France, Lord John Drummond wrote that 'we need money for everything, and our great misfortune is that we do not have it … we try to keep the army going on promises, but without money it will surely disperse'.[39] The Prince's secretary, John Murray of Broughton, fell sick at the same time as his master, a man whose basic dishonesty was by no means incompatible with his skills at managing funds and provisions. This essential work now fell into the inexperienced hands of John Hay of Restalrig.

The inexorable weakening of the Jacobite forces did not show itself at once, and the lively riposte at Keith was a flash of the old Jacobite ebullience. According to intelligence received by the Duke of Cumberland, the Jacobites had been encouraged by the long delay at Aberdeen, and as late as 3 April the sloop *Hawk* approached Findhorn basin and discovered the rebels both vigilant and busy at their drilling. However, Rev. James Lumsden was better informed, having been told that

> their affairs on the other side of Spey are in a pitiful situation. Their army extremely much scattered, not one thousand of them in one place. That the clans which were sent off after Loudoun have never returned. That there is the utmost penury of men, the gentlemen obliged to do duty and keep guard every night. That they have made very small levies since their retreat from Stirling. They have but few clans that are the more formidable part of their army … They were frightened of their own shadows. They left my horse in the stable door and went off about a gunshot, imagining two or three of their own men to be Campbell's scouts.[40]

Prince Charles was back in Inverness between 1 and 13 April, and by then it was difficult for the Jacobite officers to conceal their own despair. We find the Master of Lovat and Sir Thomas Sheridan trying to persuade commanders in the field that it was not the first time that armies had been a little short of money, and that it was actually better for the men to have their arrears made up in the fullness of time, instead of being paid day by day.[41]

CHAPTER 19

The Last Campaign,
8 April –15 May 1746

Cumberland's March and the Passage of the Spey,
8–12 April 1746

THE DRY, PERSISTENT SOUTHERLY WIND that had brought transports of provisions to Aberdeen also allowed the turbulent Spey to subside,
and on 8 April most of the forces available to the Duke of Cumberland finally
began to move. Taken as a whole, the routes described a dog-leg that corresponded with the coastline, north to the coast near Banff, then west against
the line of the Spey in the neighbourhood of Fochabers. The actual phas-
ing was fairly complicated, but the movements, as actually executed, may be
summarized as follows

❖ Lord Albemarle's division (second battalion of the Royal Scots, and the
single battalions of Barrell's 4th, Price's 14th, Cholmondeley's 34th and
Munro's 37th, Cobham's 10th Dragoons and Kingston's 10th Light

A British grenadier recalled from the continent to fight at Culloden

Horse), acting as a covering force, remained in its forward position at
Strathbogie until 10 April

❖ Mordaunt's brigade (Pulteney's 13th, Blakeney's 27th and Battereau's
62nd, with four pieces of cannon), functioning as an advance guard,
marched from Oldmeldrum to Turriff on 8 April, and from there to a
potentially exposed position at Banff on the 9th

❖ The concentration at Aberdeen moved in two parts: Cumberland with
the 3rd Division (Howard's 3rd, Bligh's newly arrived 20th, Fleming's
36th, Mark Kerr's 11th Dragoons and six pieces of cannon) took the
direct route north from Aberdeen on 8 April (below); and Lord Sempill's
Division (Wolfe's 8th, Sempill's 25th and Ligonier's 59th) veered out
of the direct line north-west to Inverurie on the 8th, then fell in behind
the rest as a kind of rearguard on the way to Banff.

Commodore Smith's flotilla of warships and transports kept pace offshore,
conveying provisions, and opening fire on whatever Jacobite parties came
within range of its guns.

Inevitably the eyes of posterity fastened on Cumberland, whose division
marched through Whiggish Old Aberdeen, and crossed the Don by the great
single-span bridge of Balgownie. The duke 'endeared himself exceedingly
to the soldiers (if it were possible to increase their affection for him) by walking most of the way with them on foot, generally using one of the soldiers'
tent trees for staff and never going a yard out of the way for a bridge or any
burn they met with, but wading through at the nearest'.[1] The route led
through a number of villages, terminating at the 'poor dirty town of
Oldmeldrum'.[2] On 9 April, in order to reinforce Mordaunt's brigade up
ahead, Cumberland's division executed a forced march to the north-facing
coast at Banff. From Oldmeldrum the column first crossed an undulating
landscape that flattened out towards Turriff, 'this miserable small town' of dark
red sandstone, 'built irregularly on a hillside, which made a much better
prospect at a distance'.[3]

On the far side the landscape opened up to a vast horizon of rolling hills,
and gradually the roadside trees assumed a windswept look, and a dip in the
hills afforded a glimpse of the sea towards the Head of Garness. The march
was a fast-paced one of nearly 20 miles, but the troops were consoled by further evidence of Cumberland's care for them, for the duke had taken a musket
from a soldier to enable him to help his struggling wife who was carrying a
child in her arms.

Towards the end of that day's trek the column began to descend to

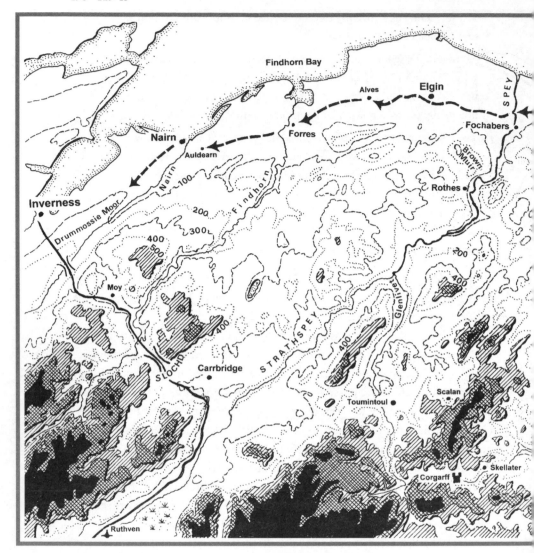

Cumberland's march from Aberdeen to Drummossie Moor

the valley of the Deveron above the port town of Banff. 'His Royal Highness ordered all the army to be drawn up in a great field on this side [of] Banff, and ordered a gill of brandy to every man, to revive him after his long day's march; so that it was eleven o'clock when we entered the town, having been obliged to wade the river, which was very deep.'[4] The division took up quarters in Banff, and the duke stayed in the Old House of the earls of Airlie. Banff made an agreeable impression in the physical sense, but a Jacobite spy, Alexander Kinnaird, had been found tallying the Hanoverian

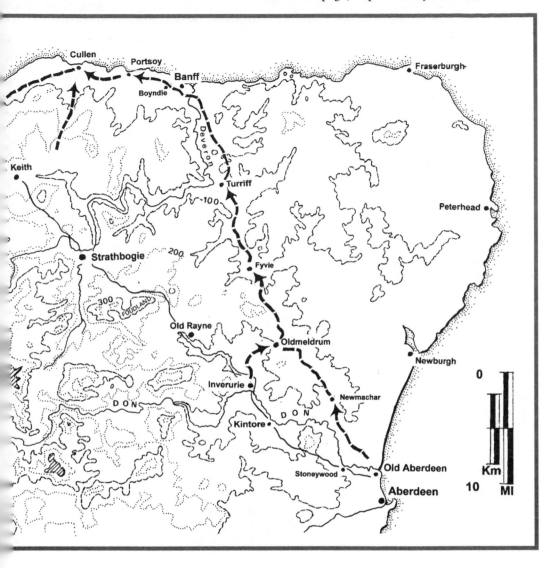

units by making notches on a stick and he was duly hanged from a tree.

After resting at Banff on 10 April the combined forces of Cumberland and Mordaunt set out to the west early on the 11th. The troops were now moving along the coastlands of the Moray Firth, where the spreads of sandy and gravelly soil were easy to cross, although they were intersected by fast-flowing little rivers which were subject to sudden and dramatic floods, of which the spates of the Spey were the most notorious. The landscape west of Banff was typically bare. The redcoats had a further spy with them, but could see nothing suitable to serve as a gallows until they came to Boyndie 2 miles out of town, and hanged him from a projecting gable end: 'his feet touched the ground within five or six inches'. Columns of smoke could be seen from Non-Juring meeting houses in the countryside, 'which our soldiers (very deservedly) took no small pleasure in, as being seminaries for training up Roman Catholics and rebels'.[5] Further along the coast the column reached Portsoy, 'a pretty small village, with the sea coming full up to the town',[6] which had been one of the last ports to remain in Jacobite hands.

Beyond Portsoy the old road climbed towards Redhythe Point, and from there a short march led to the neighbourhood of Cullen, where the infantry were assigned a camping ground for the night in a ploughed field, and the cavalry dispersed to the villages around. Cullen was the first friendly place the troops had seen in a very long time, for the single street of the original town (resited in the 1820s) lay close by Cullen House, the seat of the Whiggish landlord the Earl of Findlater. The house had just undergone a final and comprehensive sacking by the Jacobites, and Lord and Lady Findlater (who had accompanied Cumberland from Aberdeen) assigned the duke to one of the most damaged rooms, by way of showing him what they had suffered for the cause. Cumberland toured the house and saw 'furniture broken and destroyed, trunks, or other lockfast places broken open, and locks broke off all the doors, and several other marks of violence and desolation'.[7]

Lord Albemarle arrived at Cullen on the same day with the troops from Strathbogie, and Cumberland now had all his army together. Fochabers on the Spey had originally been assigned for the rendezvous, and it would have been physically possible for the army to have crossed the river there on 10 April; 'his Royal Highness, on his march to this place, judged it proper to change his disposition two or three times in order to delude the enemy, and by some feint draw them to action. But all hitherto without effect'.[8]

Most of the histories state that the Jacobites ought to have fought the Duke of Cumberland on the Spey. It is hard to agree. If the authority of Frederick the Great, Napoleon and Clausewitz count for anything, then it is very difficult to defend a river line – and they had in mind an obstacle much more formidable than the Spey when the water was low. Stated simply, the defending forces are almost invariably spread out, whereas the attacking forces can concentrate at will. In the present context it is also worth bearing in mind that the redcoats now moved very cautiously whenever they supposed Jacobite forces to be in the offing, and never more so than when crossing a river (p. 144).

The Jacobites would at best have had the chance of inflicting a few minutes' minor tactical damage, even if their forces had been much stronger and
much better found than they were. By this time the Duke of Perth and Lord
John Drummond had at the most 2,500 to defend the line of the Spey.
Colonel O'Sullivan had been sent to inspect the course of the river, now
that the melt waters had subsided, and found it 'fordable in several places
and saw it was needless to pretend to defend the passage of it. We had not
tents to camp, and if we had, we could not pretend to guard all the fords,
beside the country could not make us subsist for four days, and we had but
very slight magazines behind us'.[9] Drawn up behind the Spey, the Jacobites
would have presented static targets to the enemy, and 'when they were driven
from their post, which they must soon be by superior fire, there was no place
they could propose to make a stand till they got to the side of the little River
Findhorn'.[10]

In late March the Duke of Cumberland had dispatched two officers to
prospect the fords of the Spey. Up-to-date information was essential, for a
great volume of water was being forced down a bed which was on average
about 35 yards wide, and where the pebbly channels and beds were constantly shifting. The officers knew the country, and one of them, 'who knew
the Irish language, put on a Highland habit with a white cockade, and rode
up and down … and having sufficiently informed himself, returned undis-
covered'.[11] The spies discovered twelve feasible crossings, having taken into
account the access routes, the nature of the fords themselves, the possible
dangers presented by commanding ground on the far side, and the ways to
further objectives.

Along almost the whole of this stretch of river the 'redcoat' bank
commanded the 'Jacobite' side, which was bordered by level meadows. The
officers recommended in particular the fords at Orton (2 miles above
Fochabers) and Arndilly (1 mile above Rothes). The latter gave access to a
'good road' which led directly to Elgin.[12] This route (corresponding with
the A941) followed the Glen of Rothes behind the screen of Brown Muir, and
a force taking this passage would have cut off any Jacobite forces making a
stand downstream. It is clear that the multiple crossing points rendered the
Spey untenable once the water had fallen below a certain level.

The Jacobites too believed that the redcoats might be tempted by the
ford of Arndilly,[13] but in the event Cumberland chose to make his passage
further downstream, between Fochabers and the sea. He was possibly influenced by the information of John MacCulloch, son of the minister at Bellie
(1 mile below Fochabers), who claimed that the nearby ford was 'not then two

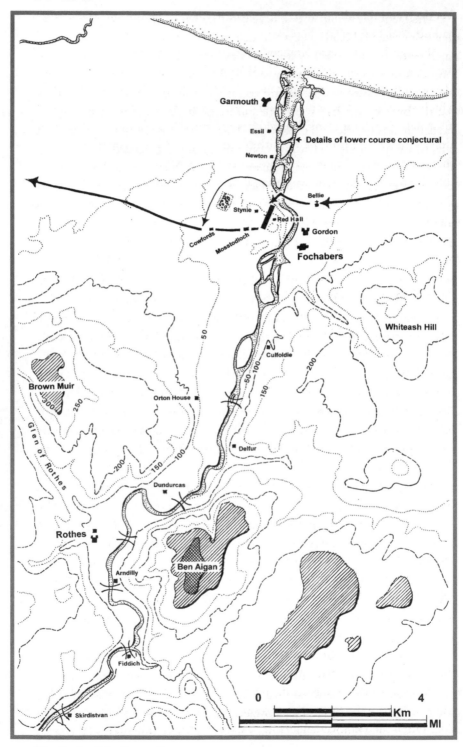

The fords of the Lower Spey

feet deep and that thirty men might cross it without opposition, as the rebels had no guard on sentry there'.[14]

Ensign John Daniel commanded one of the last Jacobite patrols beyond the Spey. He set out at 7 p.m. on 11 April with ten troopers of Balmerino's Horse, and intercepted a message to the Whiggish Duchess of Gordon, which stated that the army would cross the Spey next day. This was vital information, which Daniel should have notified to headquarters immediately.[15] Instead he rode on to within 2 miles of Cullen, where he saw the enemy army drawn up in battle order on the rearward slopes of a hill (probably the Bin of Cullen). The summit itself was unoccupied, which persuaded Daniel and his men to yell defiance from the top and then retreat, 'leaving them to wonder what we meant'.[16] Daniel did not report back until 5 a.m. on 12 April, nor did he convey any great sense of urgency to John Royal Stuart and the lords Perth and Drummond, who were lodging together at Garmouth in the house of the minister Rev. Miln.[17] Considering his duty done, Daniel took himself off to Fochabers to sleep.

A soldier of the Royal Scots records that early on 12 April 'the duke was up … before general beat, giving the necessary orders for the day. He that had seen him reviewing the lines on their long march, would have seen pleasure in his eyes, for we were a fine sight, with clean arms, on as fine a sunshine day as it was'.[18] Soon after leaving Cullen the troops halted on the wider Moor of Arradoul, where Cumberland formed them into three divisions, each separated from the other by an interval of half a mile, with the left-hand of the three assigned to the main road. The march continued through better country, where the ships of their supporting squadron could be seen to the half-right, cannonading enemy hussars on the far side of the Spey.

The Jacobite commanders were still relaxing in the minister's house when a countryman splashed across the river and told them that the land to the east of the Spey was swarming with redcoats. 'But they were so averse to believe it, that when they ran to an eminence and observed them at a great distance, they swore it was only muck heaps; the man said it might be so, but he never saw muck heaps moving before. And they were convinced it was a body of men, still they would only have it to be some of Bland's parties, till their hussars, whom they had sent to reconnoitre, returned and assured them that the whole army under His Royal Highness was coming up.'[19]

Kingston's Horse was acting as Cumberland's advance guard, and halted half a mile from the Spey upon sighting the Jacobite hutted camp on the far side. When the Hanoverian infantry closed up, the enemy set the huts alight and fell back, whereupon the duke ordered the Kingstons to continued down through Fochabers. 'Accordingly we marched through the town … which consists mostly of one very long street, where I [James Ray] observed several good houses, and people of fashion looking at us; but not one person wished us good success.'[20] At about noon John Daniel, literally caught napping, had to escape by a back alley.

The accounts of the crossing places are full of contradictions, though most sources indicate that the main body of the infantry passed at the Ford of Bellie about 1,800 yards downstream from Fochabers, the Duke of Cumberland with Kingston's Horse in the lead, followed by 1,200 Campbells and fifteen companies of grenadiers, then the main body of the infantry, and the artillery and baggage. A stretch of water there still bears the name of the 'Cumberland Pool'.[21]

The most striking feature of this stretch of the river was the hill called the Red Craig, rising to 43 yards on the left bank nearly opposite Fochabers. However, any cannon emplaced there (if the Prince had been willing to bring any up) would have found that the Ford of Bellie was out of reach, at some 1,000 yards, and below the Red Craig the higher ground in any case receded out of musket range of the river bank. Otherwise both the approaches and the exits from the crossings lay across relatively level terrain.

Resistance was minimal. Ray, at least by his own account, was riding at the head of the Kingstons, 'where I very narrowly escaped being shot; for some of the rebels fired at us across the river, kneeling and taking aim as at a blackbird'.[22] A small Jacobite party in Fochabers had fled across the river; 'only one Captain Hunter and a few others waited till the horse were entering the water, when he fired one of his pistols with them without success, and with the other happened to shoot his own horse through the neck; he immediately jumped off his back, got behind his comrade, and galloped off at speed'.[23]

For the rest, the only dangers were presented by the Ford of Bellie, where the men had to follow a zigzag path, 'and to direct them in the true course, four men stood in the river in a line downward, and one or two in another line upward, and all the troops most move directly in those lines'.[24] The infantry and all but one of the cavalry crossed without mishap, but 'the poor women, who among the soldiers are called the heavy train, were also obliged to wade with their clothes packed upon their heads'.[25] The current swept three of the camp followers away, and also a dragoon and his wife who were clinging together – an episode oddly reminiscent of the Jacobite crossing of the Esk on 20 December.

Cumberland could have pressed his advantage by chasing the Jacobites in the remaining hours of daylight, but he did not like the look of a nearby wood, 'and dreaded their lurking, and the loss of men'.[26] He stayed the night in Garmouth in the minister's house, recently vacated by the Jacobite leaders, while his men encamped along the river bank, warmed by a drink from Lord Braco, but lying on prickly barley straw as there was no hay to be found.

To Drummossie Moor, 13–15 April 1746

For three or so weeks now a promising young artist, Robert Strange, had been engaged in Inverness on a particularly interesting commission, namely to design and print a paper currency for the Jacobites. Quantities of the finished notes were ready for distribution at the very time the news arrived that Cumberland had passed the Spey. 'The town was in a general alarm, and even in confusion. Nothing was heard but the noise of bagpipes, the beating of drums and the clash of arms.'[27] In the pandemonium Sir Thomas Sheridan wrote to the Duke of Perth to persuade him that in fact this was most welcome, and that the western clans would shortly arrive with more men than ever. Meanwhile, if the enemy were to continue their advance, Perth was to retire 'safely and deliberately' before them.[28]

The redcoats were indeed on their way. Leaving the banks of the Spey on the morning of the 13th they passed the site of the abandoned Jacobite encampment with its sods, earthen banks, and charred sticks and planks, and marched unresisted along a good road which led across level country towards Elgin. Nearby was the estate of Sir Harry Innes, who had joined Cumberland's army at Aberdeen, leaving his family in Elgin. The Jacobites had confiscated the horses, cattle and grain, though Sir Harry's son James, then aged about 9, found that conditions actually improved when the Innes family came under the protection of Colonel Matthew Baggot and his notorious hussars, who now barricaded the town gates in the face of the advancing Kingston's Horse and then fell back west.

> As soon in the morning as it was thought safe, the gates were opened; some dragoons passed the gate in pursuit; they called to enquire the road to Quarrelwood. I returned and ran to the bank of the Lossie and looking towards the Stone Crop Hill, I saw my father crossing the field the short way to his house at about eight o'clock the Sunday morning. He brought a small sword for me, and by eleven o'clock I was mounted on my old dun pony which the rebels had left, and was presented to the Duke of Cumberland as he led the column to the south of Elgin; the others passed through the town.[29]

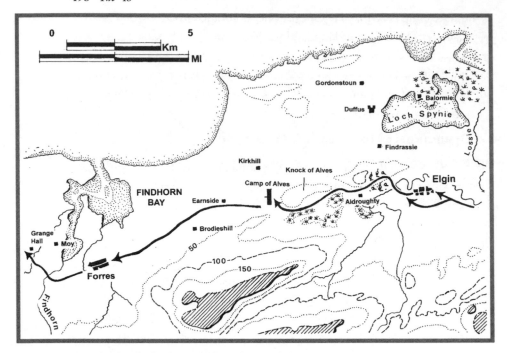

Cumberland's further march – Elgin and Forres

Elgin turned out to be 'a royal borough ... noted for one of the most stately cathedral churches in Scotland ... It was Sunday, and the people were just coming out of church; they crowded about the duke with uncommon alacrity and gladness, pouring out their blessings upon him, and even reckoned themselves happy if they could but kiss his boot; he held out his hands to them in the most condescending and affable manner'.[30]

The Hanoverian army continued its march for 4 miles on the far side of Elgin, and encamped on the gently rising ground at Alves, 'from whence we had a pleasant prospect of the sea, it being fine weather'.[31] They left Alves on the morning of 14 April and continued through Forres.[32] On the far side of town the troops descended to an alluvial plain and waded the River Findhorn, 'which, next to the Spey, is among the largest in the county, and then was excessively deep and rapid'.[33] One of the draught horses collapsed in the middle of the stream, and the cart stuck fast.

> Hawley came up immediately, and fell to lashing the waggoner; the cracks of the whip sounded in the ears of His Royal Highness; he turned about, clapped spurs to his horse, rode into the water, and checked Hawley for his impatience: 'Fie upon it, Hawley, to use any person so, the man is my friend,

and do you not see that he is assisting us?' So, turning to the man, he directed him to loose the harness, and free the horse from his encumbrance; his orders were obeyed, so without further trouble all was set right as before. Hawley became every day more hated, and His Royal Highness increased in favour with the army, who looked upon him as their father, their deliverer, their ornament, their friend.[34]

Colonel O'Sullivan was riding up from the west, and was alarmed at the sight of the troops of the Duke of Perth and Lord John Drummond as they streamed back along the road towards Inverness. That town was less than 25 miles away, and Prince Charles could not afford to yield ground so easily when he was still collecting his forces. O'Sullivan told Perth and his brother that the Prince believed they were falling back too quickly. 'This message put them perhaps too much on their mettle, and might have occasioned their defeat, had the troops under their command behaved with less intrepidity, or the enemy made a desperate attack.'[35]

The first sign of a response came when the Hanoverians were crossing the moors beyond the Findhorn and spotted a body of Jacobites out to left flank, manoeuvring to cut off a party of the staff officers who had set out to prospect the next camp site under the escort of the 1,000 Campbells and fifty of Kingston's Horse. Cumberland ordered Major General Bland to advance all the remaining cavalry, whereupon the Jacobites gave up the attempt. The duke then directed Lord Robert Sutton with the fifty Kingstons and the first fifty Campbells to advance to Nairn, while the rest of the Campbells and the massed cavalry forded the River Nairn above the town.

O'Sullivan responded by advancing three officers and twenty-five men of the Irish regiment of Berwick down to the town bridge, where they set fire to three little carts which were laden with turf, in the hope of imposing some delay. When the vehicles were alight O'Sullivan fell back to the left bank, and arrayed the hussars and the sixty-six men of Captain Shea's squadron of FitzJames' Horse in a line facing the river, with their left flank resting on the town of Nairn. Perth's force was falling back out of reach, but the hussars and the Irish infantry and troopers executed a fighting retreat of 5 miles, turning about repeatedly to face their pursuers, who now amounted to eight squadrons and four battalions. 'The squadron of FitzJames' performed miracles. It was mounted only on crop-tailed horses which we had captured in the two previous battles [Prestonpans and Falkirk], but its disciplined way of manoeuvring had been copied by the rest of the Prince's cavalry, nearly all made up of valiant gentlemen … The enemy horse chased us for four miles as far as a narrow passage, which Lord Drummond lined with part of his rearguard.'[36] The Duke of Cumberland called off the chase, and consolidated his forces – the infantry in a camp at Balblair (just beyond Nairn town), and the cavalry 2 miles further back in quarters at Auldearn on the right bank of the river.

As for Prince Charles, 'His Royal Highness was perfectly well satisfied with what passed, and retired to Culloden House, where he lay that night, that is to say retired, for he never went to bed upon those occasions, and continued the rest of the day in seeing the troops accommodated in the parks and enclosures as well as they could. But they had very little to eat'.[37] Lochiel's Camerons had arrived at Inverness earlier in the day, and the troops from the Spey reached Culloden in the evening. The Duke of Cumberland was informed that the Jacobite forces were gathering on the near side of Inverness, though he could not bring himself to 'believe that they propose to give us battle. All accounts agree that they cannot assemble all their clans, and should they have them all together, I flatter myself the affair would not be long'.[38]

CHAPTER 20

Culloden

FOR THE FIRST TIME SINCE THEY HAD converged in the English Midlands early in December the main forces under the respective personal commands of Prince Charles and the Duke of Cumberland were near enough to close in a decisive encounter. An immediate and bloody resolution was the duke's chief desire. The French ambassador, the Marquis d'Eguilles, knew that the odds were against the Jacobites, for many of their men were beyond recall and those with the Prince were starving and exhausted. The alternative that presented itself to d'Eguilles and his followers was to retire across the upper River Nairn or through Inverness, and put up a protracted resistance on the home ground of the Highlanders in the mountains.

Once the battle was over it was natural to ask what 'can justify the deliberate folly and madness of fighting under such circumstances?'.[1] John Daniel wrongly blamed Lord George Murray, others believed that the Prince; although reluctant, had been unable to 'resist the pleas of the Duke of Perth';[2] another explained that the Prince 'had too high an opinion of the bravery of his men – he thought all irresistible as hitherto they had not been worsted in any encounter, every skirmish had ended to their advantage, and the enemy

---

A caricature of MacDonnell of Keppoch, killed in battle at Culloden

on every occasion had shown the strongest symptoms of fear and diffidence'.[3] Other considerations were less romantic. O'Sullivan himself favoured a retreat into the Highlands, 'but there were difficulties to be met with there too; how could you keep nine or ten thousand men together without meal or money, there was none to be had in the mountains. You could not get them even cows without money, you could not keep them out in the fields in the season we were in, they must be quartered in villages, you could never assemble them in time in case the enemy came upon you, and where were those villages, unless you occupied nine or ten miles … ? There was no reply to this'.[4]

There was no good decision to be made in such circumstances, but just the choice between more or less bad ones. Noon on 15 April found the Jacobite forces drawn up on Culloden Moor, about half a mile south-west of Culloden House. They probably numbered less than 4,500, but 'all the men seemed to be in great spirits, expecting the enemy every moment. The Prince (who was dressed in a tartan jacket and buff vest) rode with his aides de camp from right to left, and addressed each different corps [regiment] with a cheerful smile and salute, which they returned with loud huzzas, especially when any of the scouts came in with an alarm; and the alarm was given several times on purpose to animate them'.[5]

The choice of field had already been a matter of much argument, the details of which are still unclear. On 13 April Lord George Murray sent his aide-de-camp Colonel Henry Ker of Graden[6] and Major Kennedy to the Irish Brigade to prospect a suitable ground. They found something they liked in the neighbourhood of Dalcross Castle, 3 miles to the north-east of where the battle was eventually fought. On the 14th Prince Charles told O'Sullivan to examine the site, in the course of his ride to join the Duke of Perth. The terrain has changed little since the Irishman described it, lying

> near the old Lady MacIntosh's castle that is at the right hand of the road from Inverness to Nairn, over against the five-mile house [Dalcross Castle]. There is a ravine or hollow that is very deep and large and goes in a zigzag, formed by a stream that runs there, just near the castle, so that we were fortified, no enemy could come to us, having this ravine before us. The enemy was to occupy the other side of the ravine where the castle is, which is a rising ground and commands altogether the side we were to occupy. The castle is within musket shot of this ravine, which the enemy was to be in possession of.[7]

O'Sullivan reported unfavourably to the Prince, for he preferred more open ground where the Highlanders could charge in the way that had brought them victory at Prestonpans and Falkirk; they would be lost unfailingly if they were behind an obstacle and exposed to the superior fire of the enemy (p. 118). This way of thinking was not O'Sullivan's alone. When Lord Kilmarnock was asked why the Jacobite had not disputed the passage of the Spey 'he answered that the Highlanders did not like to stand our cannonading; and that the foot in general were against it, as not having cavalry sufficient or good enough to support them'.[8]

Lord George Murray took up the argument again early on the 15th,

Drummossie Moor and surroundings

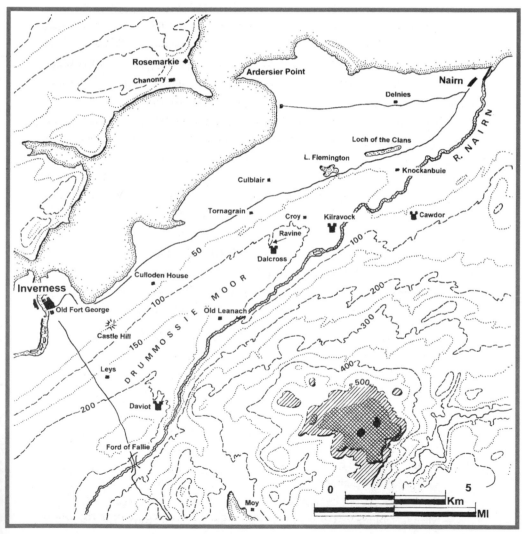

when Colonel Ker, this time accompanied by Brigadier Walter Stapleton, looked at the ground south of the River Nairn towards Daviot Castle, and found it still more rugged and suited to Lord George's preferences than the field by Dalcross. Lord George disliked the terrain near Culloden House as much as before, it being 'a large plain muir, and though in some places it was interspersed with bogs and deep ground, yet for the most part it was a fair field, and good for the [enemy] horse'.' Lord George did not explain how he was going to fight his battle, though he might well have been thinking of a holding action that would win time and enable the army to break free. On the tactical plane Lord George was probably right, for the new Hanoverian army was calculating as well as fast-shooting, and in the battle on the 16th the Jacobites were going to be exposed to superior firepower anyway, which deprived O'Sullivan's reasoning of much of its force. However, the new pro-posal was open to the same objections as before, whether well founded or not, and it was even less acceptable to Prince Charles, for by withdrawing to the southern (right) bank of the Nairn the Jacobites would have left the enemy with a free run to the depots at Inverness.

Later on the 15th the debates were overtaken by the realization that the enemy were not going to appear that day. Cumberland had learned how to pace his army, and he was allowing his troops a complete rest after their exer-tions. They were given spirits and an extra ration of cheese with which to celebrate his 25th birthday, and there was further entertainment at the expense of a 17-year-old lad who had been detected lurking about the camp, and was strung up as a spy. A Presbyterian minister explained to Cumber-land that the boy was a simpleton, and the duke ordered him to be saved. 'The young fellow hung about ten minutes when the reprieve came, but the executioner in cutting him down, cruelly let him fall to the ground, the gal-lows being very high; but as he was young and strong, he was let blood and came to life, though much disordered in his senses when the army went away.'[10]

The Night March on Nairn, 15/16 April 1746

'Four o'clock, nine miles of road to cover, sunrise about 7.23, and light by 7.10 even if the day was dark and tempestuous – in these circumstances Washington reasoned that the advantage of surprise would certainly be lost ... Should the expedition then, be abandoned? ... Washington asked himself the question, but he did not hesitate over the answer ... Day began to dawn when the column of Greene was still two miles from Trenton.' (The march on the Hessian camp at Trenton, 25/26 December 1776, Douglas Southall Freeman, *Washington*, IV, 1951, 311–12.)

'The fighting of Englishmen in the dark is, in general, a very wrong step'

('Remarks on the conduct of Sir J.C. – By an Officer of the Army',
The Gentleman's Magazine, XV, November 1745)

The Prince could not keep his starving and unpaid army together beyond a very few days, and now it seemed that he was being denied his battle. The enemy had even withdrawn their out-parties, which lent credence to a false report that they were entrenching themselves at Nairn. At this juncture Lord George came up with the truly inspired proposal that the Jacobites should attack the enemy overnight in their camp, where the troops were probably doing inebriated justice to the duke's birthday. 'This plan was worthy even of any of the greatest heroes of antiquity, and met with general approbation, particularly among the clans.'[11] It was the way of Prestonpans and Falkirk. It appealed to Prince Charles as a way out of his dilemma, and it also struck the imagination of O'Sullivan, for the redcoat infantry and horse had encamped separately, and would be unable to support each other. When O'Sullivan was asked to draw up the necessary instructions, however, and referred to the author of the scheme, Lord George answered that 'there was no need for orders, that everybody knew what to do'.[12]

The arrangements, such as they were, provided for the troops to march in a single column, Lord George in the lead with 1,200 men, or about one-third of the army, including the Atholl men and the Camerons; the Duke of Perth and Lord John Drummond brought up the rest. Thirty-two of the MacKintoshes, as the local clan, sounded the way ahead, and further parties of them were distributed along the length of the column to keep it together. Prince Charles stationed himself with the 'French' troops at the rear.

Lord George's division was to cross to the right (south) bank of the Nairn about 2 miles short of Nairn town, continue along the right-hand side of the river, and come at the camp of Balblair from the south-east, at the same time as Perth with the rearward division attacked the lines frontally from the west. For the sake of security the march would be directed along the rugged Moor Road, which ran to the south of the Inverness–Nairn highway, and Lord George would delay departure until after dark, for the Royal Navy's flotilla had most inconveniently dropped anchor offshore at 6 p.m. The effect was to cut still further the already short margin of time. By John Daniel's account 'we began our march about seven o'clock, leaving great fires burning in our camp; by some strange infatuation or misfortune the

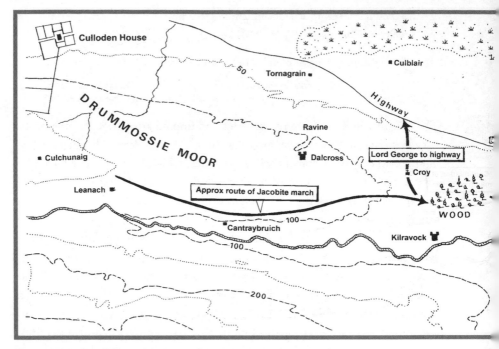

The intended march on the camp of Nairn

road was not rightly taken, either through the ignorance or treachery of Lord George Murray's guide. This still remains doubtful, but this I can say, that with the little knowledge of the country I had, I could have conducted them much better and sooner'.[13]

The initial route for both divisions in any case led through the walled Kilravock (Culraik) Wood, after which Lord George needed to peel off to the right to reach his first crossing of the Nairn, probably at or near the ford from Milton of Kilravock to the Bog of Cawdor. The second division was supposed to continue on its course to the south of Loch Flemington, the Loch of the Clans (much larger then than it is now) and the extraordinary series of scraggy, heather-clad ridges which reached towards Meikle Kildrummie.

It is hard enough today to keep a platoon together in the dark in difficult country; in the driving rain on the night of 15/16 April the Jacobite column must soon have been straggling well beyond its original 1-mile length. Early in the morning Lochiel came to Lord George with the news that many of the clansmen were getting lost in Kilravock Wood; the second division was having difficulty in getting through the breach in the wall into the wood, and the Irish troops in the rear were falling behind the nimble Scots.

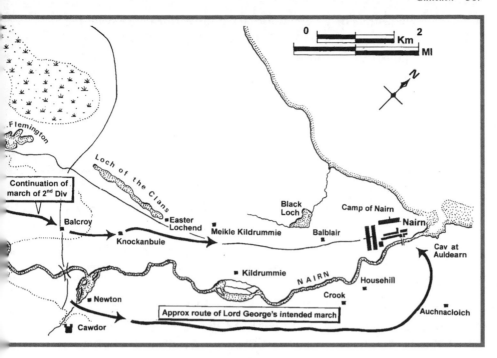

At about 1.45 a.m. Lord George called a halt, and there ensued arguments and some complicated comings and goings, which involved Lochiel, Perth and O'Sullivan making their way to Prince Charles and back again. O'Sullivan told Lord George in the name of the Prince that

> all his confidence is in you, that the loss or gain of the cause is in your hands and depends entirely on you, that you may march to the enemy, that it is morally sure you'll destroy them, having all manner of advantages over them. That you know the situation the Prince is in, neither money or vivres. If you retire you discourage your men, who suffer enough already, you lose all your advantages, and give all over to your enemy; if they come upon you in battle, superior as they are in horse and foot, and their artillery, can you resist them?[14]

Such words, delivered by such a person, probably hardened Lord George in his decision to abandon his own scheme and turn back. The gentlemen volunteers with him were still for pressing on, and John Hay of Restalrig now arrived to claim that the rearward elements had closed up, which cannot have been true. 'He was told the resolution was taken to return, he began to argue upon the point, but nobody minded him. This was the gentleman blamed for the distress they were in for lack of provisions, he having the superintendency of all these things from the time of Mr Murray's [Murray of Broughton's] illness, who had always been extremely active in whatever regarded for providing for the army.'[15]

The halt had lasted no more than a quarter of an hour and Lord George ordered his men to retreat at about 2 a.m. He directed his division past the church of Croy, and then (since there was no further call for secrecy) north to the highway, and back to Culloden Moor. It would be interesting, to say the least, to know how far he had come before he turned back. The accounts are contradictory, but the best evidence places it in the neighbourhood of Balcroy or Knockanbuie farms, which lay about 4 miles from the enemy camp at Balblair,[16] other sources narrowing the distance to 3 miles (Maxwell of Kirkconnell), 2 (Rev. George Innes) or even 1 (O'Sullivan), though it is probable that there is some confusion here with regard to the progress of the second division.

Unaware that Lord George's division had turned off to the north, the second division, led by the MacDonalds of Clanranald, reached the neighbourhood of the Kildrummie farms before morning and near enough to hear the enemy sentries talking in their camp, which lay in the level ground just beyond a gentle rise. Only now did Perth learn that Lord George was on his way back to Culloden. He ordered his troops also to turn about and retreat:

> They had not gone above one hundred yards back when they met the Prince, who called out himself, 'Where the devil are the men a-going?' It was answered, 'We are ordered by the Duke of Perth to return to Culloden House.' 'Where is the Duke of Perth?' says the Prince, 'Call him here.' Instantly the Duke came up, and the Prince, in an angry tone, asked what he meant by ordering the men back. The Duke answered that Lord George with the first line had gone back three-quarters of an hour ago. 'Good God!' said the Prince, 'What can be the matter? What does he mean? We are equal in number, and would have blown them to the devil, pray Perth, can't you call them back yet? Perhaps he is not gone far yet.' Upon which the Duke begged to speak with His Royal Highness. They went aside a very short space. The Prince returned and called out, 'there is no help for it, my lads, march back to Culloden House'.[17]

The disconsolate troops streamed back west, and dispersed among the parks, woods and settlements along the way to Inverness. A number of the Horse Guards progressed only a few miles along the highway before they could go no further. 'We were shown into an open barn, where we threw ourselves down upon some straw, tying our horses to our ankles, and the people assuring us, in case of danger, they should awaken us. They were indeed as good as their promise, for we had slumbered here but a short time before a woman gave us the alarm that the Duke's horse were in sight.'[18]

Prince Charles rode on to Inverness to bring up some of the scanty supplies of biscuit, then rejoined his senior officers, who had collapsed in Culloden House.

> The first man he meets is Lord George. He taxes him without the least anger of his behaviour that night, Lord George throws all the blame on Lochiel. The Prince sends for Lochiel and tells him what Lord George accuses him of. Lochiel will have Lord George confront him in the Prince's presence, and tell him to his face, that he himself was first man who spoke of it, and made them all believe that it would be open day, that the enemy would be prepared, and that not one soul of us would escape, and both and he and his officers talking openly before the men. The Prince would have no other explication, fearing the ill-consequences of it.[19]

The outcome of the abortive night march was to accentuate to an alarming degree the existing contrast between the two armies – the Hanoverians rested, well fed, and well cheered by alcohol, and the exhausted Jacobites who subsisted on water and a few scraps of biscuit. In all probability Lord George would not have had enough time to take the first division over the Nairn and work his way around to be in a position to attack the enemy camp at Auldearn. It might have been different had he abandoned the original plan, continued along the left bank to Kildrummie, waited there for the division of Lord Perth, and then attacked with their combined forces. The way in which the second division made up its time, and its actual arrival at Kildrummie, suggests that this would have been perfectly feasible. The Hanoverian troops were at a disadvantage in half-light (as had been shown at Prestonpans and Clifton) and the duke would not have been available to put them in order, for he was spending the night in lodgings in Nairn town.

'The Streamlet and the Deep Sullen River', 16 April 1746

The choices that presented themselves to the Jacobites when day came on 16 April were in every respect bleak. There was still a case to be made for withdrawing the army out of immediate reach of the enemy to the high ground on the right (south) bank of the Nairn, where it could have occupied the position reconnoitred by Ker and Stapleton on the day before. Lord George was of this opinion, and so, according to his account, were most of the clan chiefs. That, however, would be merely postponing the battle, which would then have to be given either by awaiting the enemy on this ground, or (Elcho's preference) by recrossing the water to attack them on the following night. It is questionable whether the troops had it in them to undertake a further night march, and in any case the margins of time and space were narrowing fast. 'The Prince held a council of war to discuss whether to retreat to Inverness, or await the enemy. He had no money. He had bread for three days only, that after that his forces would have to disperse. This imminent and cruel fate was beginning to dishearten the men, and so the debate was brief. Despite the superiority of the enemy forces the Prince decided he must await them in the position we occupied, which seemed to him better than any of the others thereabouts.'[20]

Possibly, as a biographer of Lord George suggests, in the last resort Prince Charles was swayed by his self-esteem, which would not permit him to evade combat with Cumberland and for which he was willing to sacrifice his army.[21] It is more likely that the Prince was aware that this was the last conceivable occasion on which the armed Jacobite cause could present itself as a formed army, and not as a rabble skulking in the hills. Even Elcho realized that a proper resistance in the Highlands was a logistic impossibility.[22]

In terms of numbers the Jacobites were at a clear disadvantage, at well below the 6,400-odd men who would have been available to them if all their units had been up to strength. They faced some 7,000 Hanoverians. The Prince's army had already overcome adverse odds, but never before had it gone into battle in a worse physical and psychological state than the enemy. The Jacobite artillery consisted of a potentially serviceable train of eleven 3-pounders and one 4-pounder, and indirect evidence suggests that the commander, Captain John Finlayson, knew his business. However, the outstanding Colonel James Grant had been disabled at the siege of Fort William and, apart from a handful of French, there were no professionals available to load and point the pieces. Likewise the Lowlanders and the rearward ranks of the first line were equipped with good French muskets, but the leading troops 'had no targes, for they would not be at pains to carry them'.[23]

Lochiel's Camerons and Keppoch's MacDonnells, or what was left of them, had just arrived from Lochaber, but there were crucial weaknesses in the Clan Donald as a whole, which was the shock force of the army. Barisdale's men were up in the far north of Scotland, and those of Glengarry were at loggerheads with the Clanranalds after Glengarry's son had been shot by accident after the battle of Falkirk. The MacDonalds and the MacDonnells had fought on the right of the first line at both Prestonpans and Falkirk, and Clan Donald came to regard this honoured position as theirs by right. The clan therefore took great offence when, on 15 April, Lord George suddenly invoked a rule (until then ignored) that the regiments of the army must occupy that place in turn. He therefore installed his Atholl Brigade there instead, the first time that this less than fire-eating formation had been placed in the first line. Now on the 16th Lord George desired the Brigade to return to the rest of the Lowlanders in the second line. O'Sullivan refused, probably rightly, for it would have been a recipe for 'order, counter-order, disorder', and in any case by Lord George's logic the post of honour would have fallen by rotation to the Camerons, and not the Clan Donald. Lord Kilmarnock later told his captors that 'on the day before the engagement the rebels were drinking together very cheerfully, but the next morning they almost mutinied about their rank and seniority of posts; for this clan claimed one place, and the other opposed it; so that it was difficult to settle them all with good temper'.[24]

The Hanoverian troops were aroused at 4 a.m. The assembly was beaten and sounded half an hour later, the army was formed at 5 o'clock, and the troops were on the move at 5.15. The redcoats were motivated not just by the desire to get to grips with the enemy after all this time, but by the circulation of a doctored order from Lord George which supposedly instructed the Jacobites to show no quarter.

As regards minor tactics, Cumberland knew that he could rely on the firepower of his foot soldiers, and his recent programme of training had given them confidence in the use of the bayonet. Full credit must also be given to Cumberland and his staff for the highly original and efficient device they employed on the 16th for their march to the field of battle, which permitted the army both to march in four evenly spaced columns (including the cavalry), and to re-form upon command into three front-facing lines. 'You may observe that in this order, if we were attacked in flank, we had on facing to the enemy three lines of five battalions ready formed, with the cavalry at liberty to post itself on either or both flanks; and if we were to be attacked in front, we could form each column wheeling up into each line, and one into the reserve, the dragoons forming two lines and the horse on the right and off the reserve.'[25] The arrangement was equally well suited to doing battle to an enemy drawn upon on Drummossie Moor, or (as Lord George desired) on the far bank of the Nairn (p. 509).

After leaving its encampments the redcoat army inclined to the right, away from the Inverness road, crossed Kildrummie Moss and took up a route which corresponded roughly, and in reverse, to that of the Jacobites on the night before. The wind was cold and gusting from the north-east and threw showers of sleet and rain into the backs of the troops, which was uncomfortable enough, but much better than having to face into the storm as had happened before Falkirk. On being told that the Jacobites were approaching, Cumberland formed the columns into lines, in the elaborate way just described. Lord Cathcart gives the location specifically as between the Loch of the Clans on the right, and Kilravock Wood just to the left; the duke, suspicious as ever of nearby woodlands, caused two of his squadrons of dragoons to face in that direction.[26] His concern proving groundless, Cumberland reconstituted the columns and continued on his way.

The news that the enemy was on the move was conveyed to the Jacobite commanders by outposts of the cavalry and the MacKintoshes, and by a Cameron who had fallen asleep in Kilravock Wood. 'The Prince ordered the pipes to play immediately, the most part of the men were asleep in the villages about. It was pardonable, a great number of them went to Inverness ... Officers were sent to Inverness and the villages about, to make the men join.'[27] The sounds never penetrated the consciousness of some of those who had collapsed during the overnight march, and 'never wakened till they found the enemy cutting their throats'. At noon the Jacobites formed up in a confused way: 'the men were nodding with sleep in their ranks, and at least 1,500 fewer in number'.[28]

With the approach of the enemy confirmed, the Jacobites had to determine in detail how they were going to fight. Colonel O'Sullivan was making the best of a bad job, for he believed that the one chance of victory had come and gone with the march of the night before. The scene of the action was to be on Drummossie Moor, a long barrel-shaped ridge that extended from the sea to the valley of the Nairn. The stretch in question was a piece of gently undulating moorland and rough pasture. Something could be made of it, as far as a hasty view permitted, for the left or northern flank could be protected by the walls of Culloden Park, and the right flank by the enclosures of Culwhiniac Park, which fell away to the River Nairn. Lord George took O'Sullivan to task:

> 'Sir,' says he ... 'the ground is not reconnoitered.' 'I ask pardon,' says O'Sullivan, 'here is as good a position as you could desire. You see the park before you [Culwhiniac] which continues to the river with a wall of six foot high, and them houses [the Leanach steading, and possibly also Culchunaig] near

it, which you can fill with men, and pierce the walls, that is your right. You
see this park here [Culloden] is to be our left, and both in a direct line. If
there be not ground enough, we'll make use of the parks and I'll warrant
you, My Lord,' says Sullivan, 'the horse won't come to you there.' He went
off grumbling.[29]

These considerations were important, for they might help to offset the
Jacobite inferiority in numbers and secure the flanks against the particularly
great preponderance of the Hanoverian cavalry. The enemy horse would
also be impeded by the boggy terrain, some of it under standing water, which
extended in front of the centre-left of the Jacobite line – a consideration that
weighed heavily with some of the Jacobite commanders.[30] By the same token,
however, if the enemy hung back on the far side, this difficult ground would
sap the impetus of any charge that the Highlanders might try to launch
against it.

While the stout walls of the Culloden Park would probably give a measure
of passive protection, more active measures were needed to make the best
use of the enclosure of the Culwhiniac Park 1,100 yards away on the right. To
this end O'Sullivan wished to employ two of the Lowland units of the second
line – the Stoneywood and Avochie battalions of Lord Lewis Gordon's Regiment. O'Sullivan addressed himself to Lord George, who was concerned
about the threat building up against this flank:

> My advice would be, as all their horse is at their left [as most of it was at
> that time], that we should make a breach in this wall, and set in this park
> Stoneywood and the other regiment [Avochie's battalion] that is in column
> behind you, who will take their horse in flank, without fearing in the least that
> they can come upon them. If the horse is taken in flank, with such a wall as
> this between them, and those that fire on 'em, I'll answer they'll break, if
> they are once broke, the foot will not stand, besides, My Lord, if you march
> to the enemy, as you have no other party to take, for I suppose you don't
> pretend to measure your fire with the English troops; in case you are repulsed,
> those same troops that you'll set in the park, will protect your retreat. I'll
> do more. I'd set fifty men in each of those houses (there were three or four
> houses at this right) get the walls pierced, what we call *crenellé*, and that
> will assure your retreat altogether, in case of misfortune.[31]

Lord George asked him huffily if he was in command; O'Sullivan told him he
was not, but that he was only taking the opportunity to give his opinion.
Having thus been put in his place, O'Sullivan did not put the two battalions

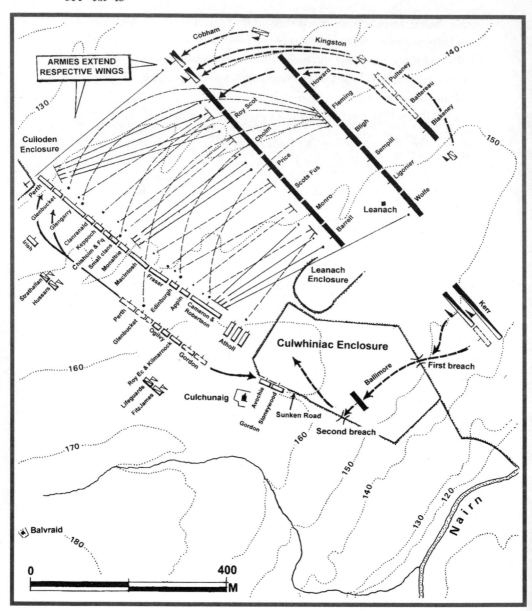

Culloden, 16 April 1746, initial array

inside the enclosure, but posted them in hiding in a sunken lane running outside the western wall of the Culwhiniac enclosure, with a recommendation to place a lookout to keep an eye on the enemy movements. 'Stoneywood, who is a very brave man, assured him that everything would be observed regularly.'[32] The enclosure remained unoccupied.[33]

O'Sullivan began to make his way north along the line to make sure everything was in order. He was puzzled by shouts of '*Close! Close!*' and found that upon Lord George's command the Atholl Brigade and other regiments on the right were re-forming from the standard three-rank line of battle into shallow columns six men deep. This was a good idea in itself, for it halved the frontages and lessened the risk of the units being jammed on the Culwhiniac enclosure and the Leanach farmstead. In fact it was so successful that great gaps opened in the first line, which now had to be filled from the second. John Roy Stuart's Edinburgh Regiment came up to plug the space in the centre-right between the Appin Stewarts and the Frasers. More significantly, Clan Donald drew over to the right to keep contact with the MacLeans, and O'Sullivan had to bring up the regiments of Perth and Glenbucket to fill the gap which opened between the left flank of Clan Donald and the Culloden parks. Two regiments therefore separated the Clan Donald from the protection of the park wall, and in front of them was a patch of particularly boggy and difficult ground.

On his side the Duke of Cumberland concluded that the appearance of new troops on the Jacobite left constituted a threat to his right (northern) flank, which, as his advance progressed, had lost the protection of a tract of marshland that gave out when the redcoats came within 500 yards of the enemy. The duke therefore committed his entire third line to bolster this flank; the first and second lines were now covered by the regiments of Pulteney and Battereau respectively, and the right wing as a whole was prolonged by the two squadrons of Kingston's Horse. In addition he recalled a squadron of sixty of Cobham's Dragoons from patrol, and positioned them on the right of the Kingstons – all of this activity the response to Lord George's reshuffling of the Jacobite first line.

On the far right of the Jacobites the Culwhiniac parks remained empty. This interesting fact was brought to the attention of Major General Bland, the army's arch-tactician, who gained Hawley's authority to pull down a stretch of the long east-facing wall, and feed a significant force through the gap – five squadrons of dragoons (two of Cobham's 10th and three of Kerr's 11th), and a mixed force of loyalist Scots infantry under the command of Captain Colin Campbell of Ballimore (two companies of Loudoun's 64th, and three of the Argyll Militia). Prince Charles was aware of what was afoot, and 'Sullivan is sent to Lord George to pray him to march directly on the enemy, and tells him, "now is the time to have troops in the park that will take the horse in flank when you are marching upon them." Lord George answers him no more, than if he spoke to a stone'.[34]

The Hanoverians therefore had a free run across the interior of the enclosure, and the Scots infantry effected a further breach in the further or western wall, again without opposition, because the two battalions of Lord Lewis Gordon's Regiment were posted too far up the wall to the north to be able to intervene. Lieutenant General Hawley was managing the affair in person, and leaving Ballimore's infantry inside the enclosure, he fed the dragoons through the gap and wheeled them into an attacking position against the right rear of the Jacobite army. Lord George prevented an immediate catastrophe by building a new south-facing flank with the two battalions of Lewis Gordon's Lowlanders, and the only effective mounted troops left to the Jacobites – Elcho's Lifeguards and FitzJames' Horse.

Both sides had been striving for last-moment advantages as at Falkirk, and 'the Prince was all this time going along the lines, encouraging the men, assuring them how much depends on 'em, the obligations he'll owe them, that in serving the King, they serve their country, that they'll be happy after, that the gain of the day depends upon a bold stroke, that they must not amuse themselves in firing, to march directly upon them; in short all that could be imagined to set them in spirits'.[35]

The Jacobites knew that the clash could be only a matter of minutes away, for they could see the enemy advancing in full line of battle, 'but, notwithstanding all our repeated shouts, we could not induce them to return one; on the contrary, they continued proceeding, like a deep sullen river, while the Prince's army might be compared to a streamlet running amongst stones, whose noise sufficiently showed its shallowness'.[36] Prince Charles asked one of the French officers how he thought the battle would go. 'Who answered him, he was sure the day was lost; and the other enquiring his reason, the Frenchman replied that he had observed the Duke's men coming on, but never in his life saw an army move in more cool and regular manner; for they would break and form again with great dexterity of discipline and fine order.'[37]

The battle was probably decided by what happened next, or rather by what did not. In the three previous engagements (Prestonpans, Clifton, Falkirk) the Hanoverian cavalry had plunged (or been plunged) into the fray regardless, and the control of the engagement had passed to the Jacobites.

Now the cavalry was being fed around the two flanks, ready to intervene when the favourable opportunity offered, and for the first time the action on the side of the Hanoverians was left to the artillery.

Towards 1 p.m. Cumberland gave Lord Bury the unenviable task of riding forward in person to reconnoitre what seemed to be a battery of guns in front of the Jacobite army. He came within 100 yards of the objects, which turned out to be some old walls, and drew the first gunfire of the battle. The most relevant maps (those of Cumberland's staff officer and the Hanoverian artillery lieutenant Jasper Leigh Jones) show that the Jacobite artillery was very well sited, with one battery (three guns according to Cathcart; two according to Jones) placed conventionally enough in the centre, but a concentration of guns on either wing – one (four; five pieces) on the right, and one (four; four) on the left – from where they could fire obliquely into the redcoat lines. In addition Cathcart and Jones agree that a further cannon, probably the lone 4-pounder under the French captain du Saussay, was firing throughout the action from the angle of the Culloden Park walls.

The Jacobite artillery ought to have performed much better than it did, which was just to loose off a ragged succession of shots. There were not enough skilled gunners to serve the individual pieces and, although the sun now burst through, the wind continued from the east and blew the powder smoke towards the Jacobites, which was a tactical disadvantage. 'A battery of their cannon bore directly upon the place where he [Cumberland] stood; it did little execution, for a particular Providence guards him, and he trusts to it; several shots narrowly missed him, and one shot took off two men exactly before him.'[38]

The Hanoverians answered with their ten 3-pounders and six coehorn mortars. The range was on the long side, and the Hanoverians had no advantage in the number or the uniformity of their pieces, but the detachments were provided by the Royal Regiment of Artillery, and no longer by a scratch collection of incompetents as at Prestonpans and Falkirk.

Disturbances could be seen among the Jacobites after only a couple of rounds: 'they suffered the cannonade very impatiently, a great many of them threw themselves on the ground, some of them, but very few, gave way and ran off'.[39] The purgatory probably lasted only a few minutes, but it seemed much longer because Lord George was slow to respond to the orders that were being sent by Prince Charles to open the attack. He was disinclined to obey commands that were conveyed by O'Sullivan, and in any case at least one of the messengers was struck down by the artillery. It would also have been natural for Lord George to wait for the redcoats to show their hand in the old blundering style.

At last the Jacobites broke across the tussocky ground in irregular groups. The left wing hardly closed with the enemy at all, probably because the regiments of Perth and Glenbucket on the far left and the small clans towards the centre were looking to Clan Donald for a lead. The Clan had inaugurated the assault at Falkirk in a stylish way, but now they were depleted, remote from their accustomed post of honour, and faced with the task of crossing a stretch of boggy moorland, some of which lay under standing water. The tract of ground to be crossed was not only difficult, but longer (by about 150 yards) than the space in front of the Jacobite right, for the line of battle was not drawn up parallel with the north–south axis of that of the enemy, but slanted towards the north west. The clansmen several times advanced to within a hundred paces of the enemy line, firing their pistols and waving their broadswords, but after each demonstration they fell back, in spite of all the efforts of the Duke of Perth.

These lunges would still have worked very well if they had induced the enemy to act according to type, which was come on piecemeal and in confusion. But this time the redcoats were not going to move before Cumberland saw fit.

> A monstrous hardened wretch, pretending to be a deserter, came running along our lines and begged for quarter, which being a common thing was granted. But soon after, observing my Lord Bury ride by, he took up a firelock that lay upon the ground and discharged it at him, though without effect. This raised a strange bustle and consternation. One of our soldiers, Newman by name, went up instantly and shot him. Lord Bury being an aide de camp to His Royal Highness, the villain certainly took him for the Duke, his regimentals and the fashion of his wig being the very same.[40]

As he looked towards the enemy, another of Cumberland's aides-de-camp, Lieutenant Colonel Joseph Yorke, saw the Jacobites finally coming on by what he described as three wedges. One of them was formed by the lunges of Clan Donald and its neighbours, as just outlined. The other two were generated by the regiments of the centre and right, probably headed respectively by the Farquharsons and the MacKintoshes, and the Appin Stewarts and the Camerons.

The climax of the battle has been described innumerable times, and in the minutest detail, but in essence it was the converging of the central and right-hand wedges into a mass of 1,500-odd men that threatened to overwhelm the regiments of the Hanoverian left wing. Nobody knows for certain why the Farquharsons, MacKintoshes and the other clan units of the centre now

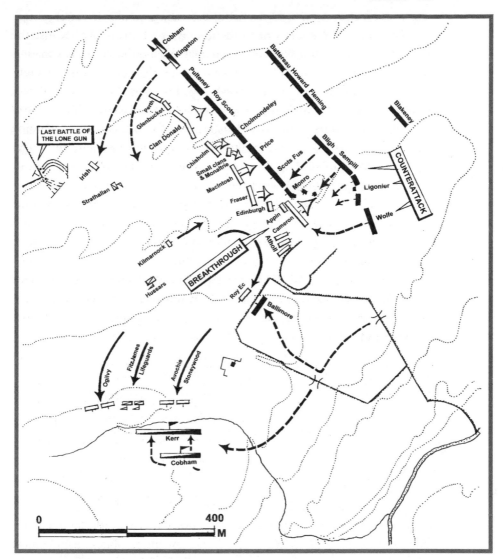

Culloden, the crisis of the battle

veered so markedly towards their right. Perhaps they were steering well clear of the difficult ground in front of the Clan Donald; perhaps also they were shying away from some particularly effective fire of the Hanoverian artillery, which was firing canister instead of roundshot now that the range was closing, and the hail of balls 'made open lanes quite through them, the men dropping down by wholesale'.[41]

The right-hand wedge was advancing more or less directly to its front, and any temptation to incline to the right would have been discouraged by the need to keep clear of the Culwhiniac and Leanac enclosures. It is perhaps worth noting that the scene of the action of the Jacobite right wing as a whole was blanked off from that on the left by an east–west ridge which is too low to register on the standard contour maps, but was a barrier to view for people located on the lower ground on either side.

Barrell's 4th was standing at the extremity of line of redcoat infantry, with its left flank uncovered, and so the Jacobites, having braved volleys of musketry, were able to break into it and kill or disable more than one-third of its rank and file (126 out of 325), in spite of a most determined resistance: 'It was dreadful to see the enemies' swords circling in the air, as they were raised from the strokes! And no less to see the officers of the army, some cutting with their swords, others pushing with their spontoons, the sergeants running their halberds into the throats of the enemy, while the soldiers mutually defended each other, and pierced the heart of his opponent, ramming their fixed bayonets up to the socket'.[42] The MacKintoshes and Frasers from the centre helped to exploit the breach first made by the Appin Stewarts and the Camerons, and the redcoat unit next in line, Munro's 37th, was soon in trouble as well.

A number of moves on the part of Major General Huske, as commander of the second line, prevented the break-in from becoming a full breakthrough. Drawing on his regiments, he brought Wolfe's 8th and Ligonier's 59th around to the south of the Jacobite wedge to an enfilading position which enabled them to pour volley after volley into the densely packed mass. Something also had to be done to halt the forward momentum of the Jacobite wedge. With Barrell's and Munro's still under severe pressure, Huske advanced Bligh's 20th and Sempill's 25th to lend support of the most immediate kind, which was emphasized by a report to the French War Ministry, perhaps from Lord John Drummond himself. The Jacobite charge lacked nothing in impetuosity and violence,

> but it did not have the effect we hoped, for the second line forced the first at bayonet point to hold firm and confront us; the second line carried out this commission with all the more enthusiasm and severity because it was the best means of sheltering itself from the fury of the Highlanders. In addition the ranks were packed so tightly that even the men whom the Highlanders had cut to pieces did not fall down, and the living, the wounded and the dead formed such a solid mass that the Highlanders had to give up any hope of breaking through.[43]

The Jacobite column came to a halt, hemmed in on three sides by the enemy, in a situation strangely reminiscent (with the roles reversed) of the state of

Cumberland's redcoats at Fontenoy. The Highland charge was an all-or-nothing tactic that depended on impetus and the instilling of terror, and now that the advance was checked the Jacobites were at a literally fatal disadvantage. Captain Clifton, commanding the grenadiers of Munro's, found himself face to face with what he calls 'the officer commanding the Camerons', who 'called out to me to take quarter, which I refused, and bid the rebel scoundrel advance, which he did, and fired at me, but providentially missed me, I then fired at him and killed him on the spot; I took from him two pistols and a dirk which are very neat'.[44] Up to 700 Jacobites fell in a matter of minutes, which was a wholly unsustainable rate of loss; the survivors disengaged, threw stones in their frustration, and then fell back in some disorder.

The fighting at Culloden was compartmentalized, in spite of the small dimensions of the field. Close to this heroic blood-letting, but in almost total isolation, a miniature battle was being fought between Hanoverian dragoons and Highlanders on the one side, and units of the Jacobite far right and the scanty reserve of the 'French' regulars.

We left the Hanoverians as the dragoons made their unchallenged passage through the Culwhiniac enclosure, Captain Campbell of Ballimore's company of the 64th staying inside it, lining the north-facing wall, from where they proceeded to shoot up the troops of Royal Ecossais who were standing in the open ground beyond. Encouraged by this success Ballimore's people swarmed over the wall with broadswords in their hands, only to be met in their turn by destructive fire. Ballimore was killed when making his way through a gap and his men ducked back behind the shelter of the wall.

This was small stuff compared with the forces that Major General Bland, having crossed the enclosure from east to west, was arraying on the far side in the shape of his two regiments of dragoons, now subdivided into ten troops. He was now placed to sweep north across the deep rear of the Jacobite army and accomplish its complete destruction. He was foiled by Lord George Murray, who blocked him with his new flank (p. 516), facing south between the little enclosures of the Culchunaig and Balvraid farmsteads, with Elcho's Lifeguards and FitzJames' Horse facing the much superior numbers of the enemy dragoons, but bolstered by Lowlanders on either flank – the two battalions of Lord Lewis Gordon's Regiment on their left, and now also Lord Ogilvy's finely disciplined regiment which Lord George now brought up on the right. This improvised but coherent array now held off the enemy until the rest of the army collapsed.

A disproportionate loss among senior officers usually indicates some kind of falling-away among their rank and file, and it was a very bad sign when a number of Jacobite leaders now had to put themselves in the path of enemy bullets along the main line of battle. 'Cameron of Lochiel, advancing at the head of his regiment, was so near Barrell's that he fired his pistol, and was drawing his sword when he fell, wounded with grape-shot in both ankles. The two brothers, between whom he was advancing, raised him up, and carried him off in their arms.'[45]

Over to the left the Duke of Perth ran to the flinching regiment of the Clanranalds, and declared that he would change his name to 'MacDonald' if they attacked and won the day.[46] There was no question of the Clan Donald striking home when the rest of the left wing was giving way, and three of their chiefs were now felled in rapid succession. The Chevalier de Johnstone was advancing at the side of his friend, MacDonald of Scotus.

> We were on the left of the army, and at a distance of about twenty paces from the enemy, when the rout became general, before we had even given or fired on the left. Almost at the same instant I saw Scotus fall ... I perceived all the Highlanders around turning their backs to fly. I remained for a time motionless, and lost in astonishment; I then, in a rage, discharged my blunderbuss at the enemy, and immediately endeavoured to save myself like the rest; but having charged on foot and in my boots, I was so overcome by the marshy ground, the water of which reached to the middle of my legs, that instead of running I could scarcely walk.[47]

Clanranald himself was disabled by a shot in the head, and Keppoch, scandalized by the flight of his clansmen, 'advanced with his drawn sword in one hand, and his pistol in the other; he had got but a little way from his regiment when he was wounded by a musket shot, and fell. A friend who had followed, conjured him not to throw his life away, said the wound was not mortal, that he might easily join his regiment and retreat with them. Keppoch desired him to take care himself, and going on received another shot, and fell to rise no more'.[48]

Cumberland galloped to Cobham's Dragoons and Kingston's Horse on his far right wing, and launched them in an attack which threatened to cut behind the leaderless Clan Donald. O'Sullivan saw the threat, and he now had a clinching argument to present to Prince Charles, who had been trying to rally the runaways. His original horse had been shot in the shoulder, and was bucking and capering; he had scarcely mounted a fresh animal before his groom was beheaded by a cannon shot, and he refused to leave the field until O'Sullivan at last convinced him that there was no time to lose. Lochiel's cousin Major

Kennedy seized the bridle of his horse, and physically led the Prince away.

Only the few well-disciplined units were able to keep formation. Elcho's Lifeguards and FitzJames' Horse for a number of vital minutes deterred Hawley's dragoons from exploiting the exposed position of the Jacobite far right wing, an action that probably saved the lives of hundreds of fugitives, and helped Avochie's battalion and Ogilvy's Regiment to retreat in good order to the south bank of the Nairn, out of reach of the enemy. Nothing could be done to assist the Royal Ecossais, which was deployed nearer the main battle. Fifty of these blue-bonneted regulars were killed or wounded by the dragoons, and most of the rest were taken prisoner. Lord George Murray too had put himself in the way of danger, but survived all covered with blood and dirt and with his sword hacked about.

Brigadier Walter Stapleton's Irish picquets, the infantry counterpart of FitzJames' Horse, provided cover for Clan Donald by acting like a mobile breakwater against the tide of the Cobhams and Kingstons on the northern flank of the field. Their first ground was a little knoll to the left rear of the original Jacobite line of battle. From there they retreated to the wall of the Black Park (one of the Culloden enclosures), where they made a new stand with the aid of the cannon which was still firing from behind the angle of the Culloden Park wall. The approach of the Hanoverian infantry finally compelled the Irishmen to fall back towards Inverness, carrying the mortally wounded Stapleton with them. They had lost about half their effectives by the time they surrendered in or near the town, on the advice of the French envoy d'Eguilles. The single gun was meanwhile silenced by the fire of four cannon and three coehorns, firing from the closest possible range.

Otherwise the Hanoverian dragoons and light horse had the free run of the field, and there was 'much knapping of noddles',[49] in the sinisterly jocular phrase of James Ray, when they rampaged among the fleeing Jacobites. 'The road to Inverness was covered with dead bodies. And many of the inhabitants not doubting of success, who came out of curiosity to see the action, or perhaps to get plunder, never went home again to tell the story; for they being mixed with their own people, we could not know one from the other.'[50] The surviving MacDonalds, MacDonnells, MacKintoshes and the 120 men of the smaller clans would have been wiped out completely if they had not reached the shelter of the enclosures of Castle Hill towards Inverness, where no cavalry could follow them.

The process of destruction was completed by the murder squads which Cumberland sent out to the fields, parks and scattered buildings in search of the Jacobite wounded. In one incident among many, nineteen of the helpless men were discovered in a barn on the day after the battle. 'They were accordingly taken out, and were set up at a park wall as so many marks to be besported with, and were shot dead upon the spot.'[51] Work of this kind helped to bring the total of the Jacobite dead to the order of 1,500, while the number of prisoners amounted to no more than 154 of the 'rebel' Scots, but 222 of Royal Ecossais, FitzJames' Horse and the Irish picquets, all of whom Cumberland accepted as prisoners of war. A French regular was therefore about four times more likely to be taken alive than one of the rebels.

Hanoverian losses fell overwhelmingly among the battalions of the left wing that had received the main Jacobite impact. Those wounded by the sword, according to Dr Pringle, were 270, who were assembled in two barns (p. 119). No more than fifty were entered on the regimental returns as having been killed. This is suspiciously low, especially as a survey by Glasgow University has identified the mass grave in the 'Field of the English' as a rectangular pit measuring between 50 and 60 yards long and 8 or 10 wide.

After the Battle, 16 April – 15 May 1746

Prince Charles left the field of Culloden under the escort of a detachment of FitzJames' Horse. He crossed the steep-banked Nairn at the Ford of Fallie, dismissed most of his party on the far or southern side, and rode with a few companions up Strathnairn. They then descended to Stratherrick, in one of the most secluded parts of the territories of the Frasers. To the left stretched a line of bogs and the shallow Loch Mhor, and up on the hills to the right stood Gorthleck, the modest house of Lord Lovat's factor Thomas Fraser. Simon, Lord Lovat was there in person, and for the first and last time Prince Charles met the evasive old criminal. The Prince paused to change his clothes and take some glasses of wine, and allow his aide de camp Alexander MacLeod to write to Cluny MacPherson (who had not been at Culloden) that the clan regiments from Culloden were to rally the next day at Fort Augustus, and that the MacPhersons must join them there as soon as possible.[52]

Prince Charles and his party set out at 10 p.m. to address themselves to the difficult climb to the Carn na Dreamaig, from where they took Wade's road down past Loch Tarff to Fort Augustus. They arrived there in the darkness of the early morning of the 17th. It is not known if any rendezvous had been fixed before the battle in the case of a defeat. The fact remains that the greater part of the army was reassembling not at Fort Augustus, but 25 miles away as the crow flies on the far side of the Monadhliath range at Ruthven. There was nobody to meet Charles at Fort Augustus, and the Prince waited there only a matter of hours before he rode down a narrow and woody stretch of the Great Glen to Invergarry Castle, where another disappointment awaited him, for Glengarry was absent and the place bare. After resting in these comfortless surroundings the Prince and his party made their way down the length of Loch Lochy, and turned west for Lochiel's house of Achnacarry, on the shoulder of Beinn Bhan. This was in the heart of the Cameron country, but Lochiel and his armed clansmen were beyond reach, and the servants had not even heard of the battle which had been fought and lost at Culloden. The Prince's flight therefore began later on the 17th, when he took the path along Loch Arkaig towards the western coast (p. 535).

In the course of the same day 2–3,000 men of the beaten army were coming together on the marshy plain of Ruthven. They were secure for the moment, as the route from Inverness via Slochd was 'very narrow, full of tremendous high precipices, where there are several passes where a hundred men could defend against ten thousand, merely by rolling down rocks from the summits of the mountains'.[53] There is some uncertainty about how many messages arrived there from Prince Charles, and what their exact content might have been, though he seems to have thanked his followers for their devotion, and told them to disperse and see to their safety. In reply to a first letter Lord George Murray replied on the 19th to submit his resignation, and chastise the Prince for having ignored his Scots in favour of his incompetent Irish cronies. He and many other leaders had assumed that the fight would be continued among the mountains, and now that Prince Charles had given up the struggle the army broke up. 'We bade one another an eternal adieu. None could tell whether the scaffold would not be his fate. The Highlanders gave vent to their grief in wild howlings and lamentations; the tears flowing down their cheeks when they thought that their country was now at the discretion of the Duke of Cumberland, and on the point of being plundered, whilst they and their children would be reduced to slavery, and plunged, without resource, into a state of endless distress.'[54]

Many of the chiefs still refused to believe that the enterprise had ended there. On 2 May two French ships anchored in Loch nan Uamh, beat off a flotilla of British craft (p. 365), landed large quantities of gunpowder and six casks of gold to the value of £38,000, and embarked with a number of notable fugitives. The kegs of gold caused dissension among the Jacobites from the moment they came ashore, but the landing encouraged Glenbucket, Clanranald, John Roy Stuart and other diehards to meet on the 8th at Muirlaggan at the head of Loch Arkaig, and plan a new coming-together of the clans in the heart of Lochaber. A message reached Prince Charles in his hiding place at Glenboisdale, and he had second thoughts about escaping to France, but the only people to present themselves at the rendezvous at Achnacarry on 15 May were 300 or so of Lochiel's Camerons, and another 300 of the Clan Donald. The Prince was not to be seen. The force, such as it was, scattered rather than be taken in a pincer movement which seemed to be developing on the part of Lord Loudoun, who was advancing from Skye with his heroes, and the Duke of Cumberland, whose advance guard was wrongly reported to have pushed to Fort Augustus.

Had it ever been possible to retrieve anything from the wreck of Culloden? Certainly not with the remains of the army as it assembled at Ruthven, or from the Lowlanders who were making for their own country, or from the Irish or Royal Ecossais, who had been lost at Culloden. No supplies had been collected at Ruthven, and two hard winters in succession had depleted the crops and herds in the Highlands. It would have been necessary at the least to dismiss the Lowlanders, who would have been unable to subsist in that harsh and alien environment.[55] There was more of a case to be made for putting up a guerrilla resistance over the long term, and the Lord President Duncan Forbes feared on 12 June that such a movement might be encouraged by the indiscriminate repression that was now in force. However, the raid on Corgarff Castle had already shown that the redcoats were capable of acting in extreme conditions,[56] and the Highlanders did not have unlimited space at their disposal, for they would have been penned in between Cumberland's army, the Campbells, and the Presbyterian clans of the north. Lochaber itself was insecure because of the enemy garrison in Fort William.

The Duke of Cumberland was now determined to 'teach them an important truth for them to know, by showing them that they can retire to no mountain so barren or remote where he cannot in person lead and subsist a sufficient force from His Majesty's army'.[57] The operations from the camp at Fort Augustus were going to prove that 'the King can, whenever he thinks proper, march his troops into the remotest parts of the mountains and punish 'em as he sees fit'.[58]

Without the presence of a princely leader the resistance was without focus, and Charles had by now effectively forsaken his followers. It was no more or less reprehensible than the actions of Napoleon Bonaparte (another charismatic leader) who was to abandon his armies in Egypt in 1799 and Russia in 1812, and it has had as little effect on their respective devotees ever since. It was entirely in keeping with the Prince's former resolution to confront his enemies with at least the semblance of a regular army; anything short of that held no interest for him.

CHAPTER 21

Repression and Transfiguration

The Pacifications

THE DUKE OF CUMBERLAND WAS, on his own terms, a man of principle. For the whole period of his command he had denied the armed Jacobites and their supporters any consideration under the rules of war. His resolve was if anything strengthened by his recent experiences. Areas of Scotland which he had thought to be under control had returned to rebellion. Now, and entirely predictably, counsels of moderation were heard from the likes of the Lord President Duncan Forbes of Culloden, the Chief Justice Clerk Sir Andrew Fletcher and Lord Crawfurd. A test case was that of the eighty-one Grants of Glen Moriston and Glen Urquhart who had surrendered themselves voluntarily, on assurances from the abominable Ludovick Grant. Sir Alexander MacDonald of Sleat urged that if these men were treated well, it would 'resolve the whole Highlands as to what they are to expect, and what they are to do'.[1]

In the event the Grants were transported into slavery. Cumberland

---

A straggler from the Highland army, the very picture of defeat

feared that compromises and deals by the Scottish Whigs would allow their Jacobite neighbours to resume their way of life until they were next inclined to rebel. There had certainly been executions and forfeitures after the '15, but many of the leading rebels had, in a manner of speaking, been allowed like children to pack up their toys and go home when the game was lost. A final consideration which weighed with the duke was that the greater part of the British Army must be brought back as soon as possible to Flanders, where the French were making important gains, and this in turn pointed to decisive measures. Cumberland realized that the longer he spent in Scotland the less and less he understood of the Scottish mentality, but he grasped that rebellion had deep social roots and that nothing less than a drastic eradication would serve his purpose.

Cumberland's tough measures were promoted by those such as of the earls of Albemarle and Ancrum, Lord Sackville (the hero of Minden), Captain George Munro of Culcairn (the hero of Inverurie), Captain 'Inquisitor' Dunlop of Blakeney's 27th, the naval captains Robert Duff and Caroline Frederick Scott (p. 129), and two men who owed their lives to the clemency of the Jacobites – Lieutenant Colonel Charles Whitefoord of the Marines, and Major W. Alexander Lockhart of Chomondeley's 34th.

Were such proceedings unduly harsh by international standards? They were consonant with British practice as carried through by Lieutenant Governor Lawrence when he devastated Acadia (Nova Scotia) and deported its French inhabitants in 1755. Their descendants in Louisiana are still aggrieved, and 'no amount of genteel whitewashing of Cumberland or the hard men among his followers and imitators should be allowed to cloak the grim realities of the developing Georgian war machine at mid-century'.[2] By way of contrast the French general D'Asfeld adopted a successful policy of conciliation when he pacified the island of Minorca in 1716.

As now practised by the Hanoverian forces in Scotland, the repressions were at first concentrated in the areas where their forces found themselves in the spring of 1746 – by Captain Scott from Fort William, by Lord Loudoun from Skye, and by the Duke of Cumberland from Inverness. The main force of the army then moved to a new base at Fort Augustus, which permitted the Western Highlands to be purged in a more systematic way. Naval flotillas devastated the western islands, and finally brought Orkney under control, and the last stages of the pacification were represented by the business of setting up chains of posts, consigning prisoners to execution or deportation, and enacting a series of repressive laws.

Inverness and the East

The Duke of Cumberland reached Inverness at the head of his dragoons on the afternoon of 16 April 1746, 'all bespattered with dirt, covered with dust and with sweat, and with his sword in his hand'.[3] On the 17th Cumberland detached Lieutenant Colonel Cockayne with 500 men to descend on 'Colonel' Anne MacKintosh at her house of Moy, and bring her to the army. It was not a social call, but Cockayne managed the affair with a sensibility that was rare to find at this time. 'As to my lady, she was mounted upon a gallant steed, and a man in livery after, with a cart that held her baggage and apparel; and so brought to camp; but she alighted just at the entrance, and Colonel Cockayne handed her through the camp to avoid suspicion of being a prisoner, and brought her before the Duke, who committed her.'[4] On the 18th, Brigadier Mordaunt took a force to the Airds, the richest of the Fraser lands, where he confiscated cattle and provisions and burnt Lord Lovat's castle of Beaufort.

Thirty-six recaptured deserters were hanged in the camp, and by way of further diversion the soldiers went to the bank of the Ness to admire the servant girls as they hoisted up their petticoats to wash the household linen, and 'particularly their motion in treading'.[5] Between 23 and 30 April Cumberland was reinforced at Inverness by four battalions which completed a much-delayed voyage from the Thames, but he was disinclined to move for the time being, for he hoped that the rank-and-file Jacobites would respond to terms he had published in February, whereby they could present themselves to a magistrate, deliver their arms, and obtain a temporary protection of six weeks.

The MacPhersons gave themselves up as a clan, and the personal prestige of old Major General Campbell of Mamore gained the surrender of the MacDonalds of Glencoe and some of the Stewarts of Appin. However, the fate of the Jacobite Grants did not inspire much confidence, and the amnesty amounted to little in any case, for after the elapse of the stipulated six weeks the lives and property of the surrendered men were once more at the mercy of the authorities. Not all those who came to hand in their weapons survived that long. On 2 June three Highlanders arrived at Fort William to surrender, and Captain Scott had them drowned by hanging them in a salmon net in a mill flume at Lochoy.

Meanwhile Inverness served as a base for the subjugation of the Jacobite north-east, a task that was entrusted to the Earl of Ancrum. He was too late to track down the men of Ogilvy's Regiment, who arrived in a body at Clova on 21 April and dispersed in their native Strathmore. He therefore dropped off detachments of Cobham's and Kerr's Dragoons in places designated by the duke, and took his troops on an extended *razzia* from Aberdeen.[6]

Aberdeen itself was in the grip of a standing garrison, which was at liberty to treat the place as a captured town in the precedent set at Carlisle. Following Ancrum's lead the officers of Fleming's 36th insulted the towns-people and encouraged their troops to riot on 1 August, when they smashed the windows of more than two hundred homes that had failed to display candles in honour of the birthday of King George. On principle Ancrum set himself against the Lord Justice Clerk's policy of conciliation, 'for the bad consequences of this practice after the last rebellion has appeared of late so plain that, till I have orders, I will go on a very different way'.[7]

The coastlands immediately north of the Tay, along with Perth and Atholl, were fortunate enough to fall within the responsibility of the Hessian contingent, and Prince Friedrich the commander was by now probably a secret Catholic convert, during his time in Britain mixing almost exclusively with known Jacobite sympathizers. The damage in Atholl was inflicted not by the Hessians but by returning Campbell militiamen, who amongst other misdeeds burnt the house of Blairfettie. Thinking it might prove useful as a barracks, they left nearby Kynachan intact; the laird, David of Kynachan, having been among the wounded who had been killed after Culloden.

Nobody ventured to interfere with the MacGregors when they strode across Atholl, and they now made their way home with flying colours, pass-ing by Finlarig Castle where the Campbell militia 'durst not move more than pussies',[8] and defying in broad daylight the posts which Lord Glenorchy had established in the passes. They flaunted their weapons and white cockades in Balquhidder, and the men of Rannoch reverted to their old cattle-steal-ing ways, being tamed only over the course of time by the Commissioners of Annexed Estates from 1755.

The Western Highlands

The Duke of Cumberland was dissatisfied with the progress of pacification and the surrenders, and at last, on 22 and 23 May, he moved Kingston's Horse and eleven out of his sixteen battalions to a great new encampment at Fort Augustus. For many of the troops this was their first experience of the Highlands proper, and Cumberland, as the solicitous leader, offered prizes for horse races. 'Here was also many foot races performed by both sexes, which made many droll scenes. It was necessary to entertain life in

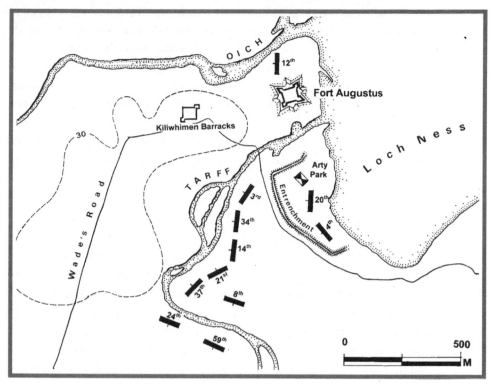

Fort Augustus, with Cumberland's camp

this manner; otherwise, by the constant view of mountains surrounding us, we should have been affected by a hypochondriacal melancholy.'[9]

The army was now able to reinforce the pacification of the Western Highlands, which previously had been penetrated only from the direction of Skye and Fort William. When Cumberland's troops arrived in strength at Fort Augustus the Highlands felt the full weight of repression. Lord George Sackville with a detachment of 500 men set out west for Knoydart and Glenelg, and another 500 troops under the command of Colonel Edward Cornwallis, 'a brave officer of great humanity and honour', descended on the country of the Camerons. On 28 May they destroyed Lochiel's residence at Achnacarry. 'The order was to set fire to his mansion house, but the best of his movables were carried off before the soldiers came; however his fine chairs, tables and all his cabinet goods were set afire and burnt with his house. His fine fruit garden, above a mile long, was pulled to pieces and laid waste.'[10]

Major Lockhart's mission was to purge the lands north of Loch Ness, in Glen Moriston, Strathglass and Glenstrathfarrar. When he was shot down by a sniper, one of the Campbell officers took over the work instead.[11]

On 18 July the Duke of Cumberland set out for England, and relinquished the command to William Keppel, 2nd Earl of Albemarle. Although Albemarle was not by nature as ferocious as the duke, one of his officers wrote from Fort Augustus that 'this country begins to feel a little the consequences of entering into an unprovoked rebellion ... I am inclined to think that our work here will be pretty soon finished, though it must be confessed that these rascals die hard'.[12]

Albemarle approached his work systematically. He divided Scotland into four military divisions: in the north, from the Great Glen to Strathspey; from Strathspey to the eastern coast; south central, from Perth to the Great Glen; and in the far south, the shires south of Stirling. On 9 September he assigned 400 men to guard a first grand cordon, which extended for 62 miles from Strontian in Sunart, across Loch Linnhe to Glencoe and Loch Tay and down to Lennox, thereby covering the Campbell lands and Dunbartonshire. Later cordons covered the eastern shires.

Meanwhile the offending far Western Highlands were receiving the attentions of the Royal Navy and Campbell Militia from the seaward flank. The process was begun by Captain John Fergussone and the shore parties of his converted bomb vessel *Furnace*. He first cruised in the Sea of the Hebrides and the Minch and worked his way north, taking prisoners on Canna and Barra in late April, then patrolling off Lewis in the outer Hebrides. He then turned his attention east, burnt everything of value on Raasay (leaving it in the carbonized condition discovered by Prince Charles during his escape), and on 9 May sailed up the mainland loch of Nevis and burnt the new house of MacDonald of Barisdale. The Jacobites were showing signs of fight, now that two French ships had landed gunpowder as well as gold in Loch nan Uamh on 2 May, and when Fergussone searched the caves on Loch Ailort he came under fire from 500 men under the command of Young Clanranald – who was almost the last representative of the armed Jacobite cause, just as he had been among the first.

The punitive expedition acquired new force on 16 May, when *Furnace* joined another bomb vessel, *Terror*, and Fergussone came under the command of the senior captain, Robert Duff. They launched their first joint expedition on the next day against Morar. The sailors landed on the sandy beach at the western end, and burnt the house of Alan MacDonald. The vessels then turned south, rounded the peninsula and arrived off Arisaig. MacDonald of Borrodale's men opened fire on the approaching boats, and exploded three mines (of French gunpowder) when the sailors reached the stony and rocky shore. Duff and Fergussone retaliated by burning all the houses along the loch.

There were fears of further armed gatherings of Jacobites on the peninsulas to the south, and on 27 May at Tobermory *Furnace* and *Terror* embarked eighty regular troops from Fort William, and 120 of the Argyll militia, which further extended the capabilities of the expedition. On the 28th the combined force made its destructive way to Strontian at the far end of the long dog-leg of Loch Sunart, described by old Major General Campbell of Mamore as 'centrical to all the rebel countries'.[13] He was usually described as a moderating influence, but with reference to the southern shore he wrote of his scheme 'for banishing all the rebellious inhabitants of Morvern, so as to have a new set of people here'.[14] Duff and Fergussone turned back north, left the coastal settlements of Moidart in flames, and on 30 May anchored off the isle of Eigg. Captain John MacLeod and forty men of Clanranald's Regiment were lured by false promises into surrendering, thirty-eight of whom were then confined on board ship (some of them to die on the voyage to the Thames, and the rest destined for slavery in the West Indies). Fergussone then posted detachments around the inland loch of Morar, and on the night of 4/5 June one of his parties captured the invalid Lord Lovat, who was a major prize.

On 19 June Major General Campbell and a force of his militia landed on remote St Kilda, responding to a false report that important Jacobites were hiding there, but he found nothing but innocent islanders. On his return by way of the Outer Hebrides, however, he nearly fell in with the fugitive Prince Charles.

The Far North

The MacKenzies were one of the divided clans, but the Whiggish Lord Fortrose (son of the Earl of Seaforth) raised the loyalists among them to guard the northern passes, even if few Jacobites seemed to have come that way. The Jacobite party among the Orkney Islands had reasserted itself after HMS *Sheerness* and Lord Reay's Munros (alarmed by their success at the expense of *Le Prince Charles* and its cargo of gold) had departed in haste at the beginning of April. The 24-gun frigates *Glasgow* and *Scarborough* showed themselves among the islands on 26 April, heralding the build-up of a small flotilla, but the Royal Navy accomplished little beyond burning the house of Sound on Shapinsay, the home of James Fea of Clestran. All the ships had departed by 15 May, which left Orkney as the only discrete part of the British Isles which could still be counted as under the control of Jacobites.

The pacification of the islands began in a systematic way on 24 May, when

Captain Benjamin Moodie of Melsetter and a party of marines were landed under the protection of the sloop *Shark*. Moodie had a score to settle with the leading Jacobite, Sir James Steuart, who had been responsible for the murder of his uncle on 1 November 1725. He had the satisfaction of taking Steuart prisoner on the same day, and proceeded to burn the houses of prominent Jacobites on Westray, North Ronaldsay and Sanday. The raids continued into September, but Moodie never succeeded in tracking down the surviving lairds William Balfour of Trenaby, Archibald Stewart of Brugh, and the two John Traills (of Westness and Elsness), as they not only had the advantage of local knowledge (and especially of two caves on Westray), but also the local language, which was largely incomprehensible to even quite local outsiders.

Escape, Transportation and Execution

The search for lurking Jacobite notables fell gradually away. Old Lord Pitsligo died in peace in Glenshee, not far from the patrolling redcoats, while Cluny MacPherson skulked in his 'Cage', his rocky hideout on Ben Alder, until he took ship to France in 1755. Stewart of Ardsheal and a few companions concealed themselves behind a waterfall on Beinn a' Bheithir, overlooking Glen Duror. Others got clean away before the end of 1746: Lord George Murray to Holland, the lords Ogilvy and Glenbucket to Norway, and the Chevalier de Johnstone taking the bold and successful course of making straight for London overland. He was nearly denounced on the way, but nothing irked him more than his passage through Forfar. The place had been defiantly Jacobite when Cumberland passed through it, but something must have set de Johnstone against 'this infernal town' imbued with 'Presbyterian fanaticism … that execrable town … its worthless inhabitants … this abominable place … a vile rabble'.[15]

Enterprising French skippers had eluded the enemy warships patrolling off the Western Highlands and islands, and brought away two batches of particularly important people from the shores of Loch nan Uamh: Lord Elcho, Sir Thomas Sheridan, John Hay of Restalrig and the mortally ill Duke of Perth on 3 May; and Lochiel and Prince Charles himself on 20 September.

No other passage of the '45 has been retold so many times as the wanderings and ultimate escape of Prince Charles after Culloden, to the extent that the essentials are in danger of being overlooked in the mass of local detail, topographical word-painting, and digressions concerning picturesque local characters, fly-fishing, deer-stalking, whisky distilling, Highland heroines and the like.

Charles owed his survival as much as anything else to the extreme precautions he took to conceal his whereabouts and intentions, for many Jacobite Highlanders, willingly or not, told the authorities all that they knew
about his travels and contacts,[16] and, without betrayals, the Prince would
not have had as many close shaves as he did. However, the numbers of those
who kept his secret must finally have extended into the hundreds. By general
repute they were the kind of people who would not have hesitated to steal the
shirt off your back, and their loyalty to Prince Charles in the present case
honours the whole episode of the '45.

To attempt to retrace just short stretches of the Prince's path, with all
the advantages of modern maps and equipment, is to realize very soon that we
are dealing not with the effete dandy of hostile legend, but with a very tough
individual. His routes day by day were determined by considerations such as
the kind of ground underfoot, the rumours of the arrival of French shipping,
or the immediate need to avoid cordons, sweeps and outposts. Consequently
he held to ground that even now is peculiarly difficult and remote. There
were times when Charles was reduced to soaked, midge-bitten despair, or
would start awake after a troubled sleep, and 'stare about him … as if disordered in his senses'.[17] More often we find him cheering up his dispirited companions by making light of his troubles or singing them a song in Gaelic.

The wanderings of the Prince may be reduced to a few essential stages.
The first (17–25 April 1746) was a continuation of his flight from Culloden, and carried him rapidly westwards to the shore of Loch nan Uamh.
Between 26 April and 28 June Charles sailed, rowed and walked up and
down the Outer Hebrides. He was drawn north to Lewis, in the vain hope of
taking ship to Norway. He then found refuge in the southern islands, but
the hunt for him grew more and more intense, and his friends had to spirit
him away with the help of a local girl, Flory (Flora) MacDonald. It is curious
to reflect that their voyage 'over the sea to Skye' was not westwards to a
wider world, but on the way back to the mainland. With the passage of time
Flory's role has eclipsed entirely that of another of the MacDonalds, Neil
MacEachain, who was a scholarly and resourceful schoolmaster of South
Uist, and in fact the main instrument of the Prince's salvation.

The Prince reached Skye on 29 June, and the mainland on 5 July. The
western peninsulas were not only beset by the ships of the Royal Navy but
were being sealed off on the landward side by the Argyll Militia. After some
very narrow scrapes, and by dint of some stupendous walking, Charles slipped
through the cordon and on 5 September reached Cluny MacPherson in his
elaborate hideout on distant Ben Alder. The Prince was further than ever

from the sea, but all the more secure for that reason, and the comings and goings of various clansmen gave him a good chance of hearing of any French rescue missions.

Having received a report that the French had arrived off Arisaig, Charles and a few companions set out on 13 September. Early on the 20th the Prince, twenty-three chiefs and gentlemen and 170 Highlanders set sail from Loch nan Uamh, and nine days later he was ashore in Brittany.

Jacobites numbering 3,472 – less enterprising, less well connected, too trusting, or simply unlucky – fell into the hands of the authorities. After formal process 120 of them were executed. This was but a fraction of the numbers who had been given no chance to surrender, who died in prison or in transit, or who were executed under martial law, such as the recaptured redcoat deserters.

Most of the men taken in England were confined in the gaols of the English north country. The officers and sergeants of the Manchester Regiment who were captured at Carlisle were confined at Lancaster, then carted to London for trial. On 19 February 1745 the intimidated Jacobite lad John Collen was taken to point out the more notorious prisoners. At the New Prison in Southwark this juvenile Judas indicated Thomas Syddall, having seen him 'at several places, particularly at Derby, always at the head of the Pretender's advance guard', and at Newgate he identified two further officers, but was then whisked away for his own safety, 'for the prisoners were whispering among themselves and seemed in a mood to attack'.[18]

Many of the Scots were held in Lincoln, and still more in York, the county gaol of Yorkshire, where 227 were being detained in February 1746 in terrible conditions. 'The sickness and close confinement of these wretches may breed contagion ... when the wind sets fair I can almost fancy I smell them ... the steam and stench is intolerable and scarce credible ... walls covered with lice.'[19]

A Mr Masterman was commissioned to carry out the interrogations. At Lincoln he had to call a halt after he had processed fifty-six of the wretches, for 'the rest are either dead, or so distempered that they could not be removed, or brought out of their rooms, without manifest hazard of their lives. Indeed, all those who have been examined were so very nauseous, that I could scarcely bear the room during their examinations. The greatest part of them are so sulky, and so much upon the reserve, that it is scarce to be conceived how difficult it is to get anything out of them, and some of those, who have discovered the least, have taken up more time than those who have been more frank and open'.[20]

Masterman's further examinations in York extended for twelve days, because so many of the names had not been entered on the previous lists, and 'almost half of the prisoners in the gaol are a people who talk a language peculiar to themselves, a language they call "Ersh", which I take to be (in its composition) a mixture of Scotch and Irish, but it seems it is universally spoken in much of the Highlands'.[21]

It was considered too risky to put the prisoners on public trial in Scotland. On 30 May 1746 a first sailing of seven vessels set out from Inverness to carry 570 captives to the Thames. It took an average of three weeks for the ships to arrive, during which time the prisoners were confined below decks, some of them lying on the hard, slimy anchor cables; a number were hauled out and dangled in the sea at the ends of ropes. At the end of the voyage 300 of the prisoners were put ashore, but the rest stayed on board ship. On 20 August 1746 Surgeon Minshaw was sent to report on the state of the men cooped up in the transport *Pamela* at Woolwich. The stench was so bad that it was scarcely possible even to peer into the hold, and the prisoners were instead summoned up one by one, and asked for their details. 'The number of those who came on deck was fifty-four, many of whom were very ill, as appeared by their countenance and their snail-creep pace in ascending the ladder, being only just able to crawl up. Eighteen left below were said to be utterly incapable of coming on deck, unless by sling, which was not thought necessary, as two of the most hardy of the guard went down into the hold and took an account of their names.'[22] By 17 March the next year the prisoners held downstream at Tilbury had been on board ship for eight and a half months; out of the original 157 only 49 survived, and these were transported to slavery in Barbados. The men confined in Tilbury Fort were helped to survive by the kindness of local people and visitors.

Almost exactly one-third of the convicted prisoners were sentenced to be transported to the North American colonies or to the West Indies, where those who survived the voyage laboured under slave-like conditions as indentured servants. The only happy episode concerned the 134 men and fifteen women on board the *Veteran*, which sailed from Liverpool for the West Indies on 8 May 1747. This particular hell ship was intercepted off Antigua on 28 June by Paul Marsal's privateer *Diana*, and taken to his home port of Martinique. The Duke of Newcastle asked for the liberated captives to be returned, but the governor the marquis de Caylus refused, describing how 'these poor wretches cast themselves at my feet … asking for my protection'.[23]

The executions were normally staged in England, for reasons of public order, and the most deplorable or eminent of the malefactors were killed in London. The details remind us that the men who died were not characters in a romantic novel, or players in a costume pageant. Dudley Bradstreet saw five deserters from the Guards shot near the wall of Hyde Park. They were dressed in white, and marched to the spot to the accompaniment of 'drums dismally beating'. The coffins and open graves were ready. The men were told to kneel, caps were placed over their heads, and, with a strange touch of consideration, the orders to the firing party were given silently with a halberd. However, it was impossible to conceal the noise of the final approach from the condemned men, and 'their faces and breasts were all tore to pieces by the balls, and all dead before they fell'.[24]

The captured peers were sent to London to be judged by their fellow lords in Westminster Hall. Two battalions of foot and a detachment of Horse Guards lined the 300-yard route from the Tower to the Green when lords Kilmarnock and Balmerino went to their deaths on 18 August 1746. Kilmarnock had been one of the more tardy and reluctant recruits to the cause. He was now dressed in black mourning clothes, and looked about him in seeming despair before he knelt at the block. The executioner 'raised the axe as high as he could and gave him a deadly stroke; but it did not sever the head from the body, which sprang very high, with a cloud of blood, upon receiving the blow; but with another chop entirely severed it'.

When Balmerino mounted the scaffold the crowds noted with approval his bold and defiant air, and his uniform of blue and red (that of the Jacobite Lifeguards). He was glad to see that the dates on his coffin were accurate, and with aristocratic aplomb asked to feel the edge of the new axe which the executioner produced from its deal case. He pronounced himself satisfied, gave the man three guineas, knelt to place his head on the block and gave the signal without further ado. 'The executioner did not perform this as well as Lord Kilmarnock's, for he mangled him terribly, making three strokes.'[25]

Lord Lovat's life of crime and evasion came to an end on Tower Green on 9 April 1747. The event, almost predictably, was attended with something of the bizarre, for a wooden stand collapsed and killed eighteen of the ghoulish spectators.

For commoners and the ordinary gentlemen, the law laid down the prolonged torture of being hanged until semi-conscious, then let down, laid out and butchered by the executioner. Some of the witnesses were appalled by the scenes, and for one of them the worst vision of all was that of the feeble efforts of a man who was trying to beat the executioner aside as he came at him with the knife.

Colonel Francis Townley of the Manchester Regiment and eight of his companions went to their deaths outside London on Kennington Green on 30 July 1746. They were dignified and defiant, they were hanged together, and the executioner spared them the very worst of the ordeals. Townley was the first to be cut down, after five minutes, and 'laid ... on the stage which was put up there for that purpose. The body being stripped, and laid at his length, but having some signs of life in him, the executioner struck him several violent blows on his breast, and then cut off his head, took out his bowels, and flung them into the fire that was burning near the gallows ... Dawson was the last that was cut down; and when the executioner had thrown his bowels and heart into the fire, the spectators gave three loud huzzas, at the same time crying out 'God bless King George, and all the Royal Family!'.[26]

The severed portions of the various bodies were sent to the places in the kingdom which had witnessed their malefactions, and in such a way a large bag of legal documents, sent by express from London to Carlisle, 'alarmed the country and put the post boys who rode into the night into frights and fears, it being universally believed to be Townley's head'.[27]

Transfiguration

Before long the armed Jacobite cause had suffered the first in a series of ultimately fatal blows. In October 1748 France made peace with Britain. The terms were reasonably advantageous to France, but, as a price for good relations, the British insisted that Louis XV must expel Prince Charles from France, a measure which was implemented in December. Prince Charles now looked to the leaders of the English Jacobites, and in the most bizarre passage of his career he visited London incognito in October 1750, and out of political expediency converted to Anglicanism.

For foreign help, Prince Charles turned to Frederick the Great of Prussia, but the relations between the Prince, the Prussian representative and the English Jacobites were convoluted and strained, and the episode ended in the betrayal of the so-called 'Elibank Plot' in March 1753. The principal intermediary in England had been a brother of Lochiel, Dr Archibald Cameron, who was executed on 7 June – the last of the Jacobites to die for his Prince. Hostilities between Britain and France broke out again in 1755. Prince Charles again came to mind as an instrument against the Hanoverians, but there was no attempt to prepare the ground in Britain, and a great French invasion scheme was literally shipwrecked in the course of the battle in Quiberon Bay on 20 November 1759.

By their own actions the Stuarts were busy ruling themselves out as serious contenders for the crown. In 1747 Prince Charles's brother Henry Benedict accepted a cardinal's hat, a measure that offended the Episcopalian Jacobites, and ruled out all possibility of an alternative succession to Prince Charles, whose private life was in increasing disarray. In fact the French authorities were appalled by his drunkenness even as they were preparing for their expedition in 1759. The Prince was never reconciled with Lord George Murray (who died in Holland in 1760), and he fell out over the course of time with devoted men like his private secretary Andrew Lumisden and John William O'Sullivan. He was deserted in turn by his mistress Clementina Walkinshaw in 1760, and twenty years later by his young wife Louisa von Stolberg, whom he had married in a political match which had been encouraged by the French.

It was some consolation for Prince Charles to be joined by Charlotte, his daughter by Clementina, and they moved together to the Palazzo Muti in Rome. The Prince died there on 30 January 1788, in the same room in which he had been born sixty-seven years before, and forty-two regretted years after his escape from Scotland.

* * *

With the death of the Cardinal Duke of York Henry Benedict on 13 July 1807 the direct Stuart line was extinct, and only the most eccentric legitimists now looked to the remote descent from James II's youngest daughter Anne Marie, from which it proceeded through the Houses of Savoy and Modena to that of the Wittelsbachs of Bavaria in 1919.[28]

Some important props of Jacobite support in Britain had meanwhile fallen away. Prince Charles lost the confidence of activists in England after the failure of the Elibank Plot, while Non-Juring Anglicanism, which had been the ideological and religious foundation of British Jacobitism, died away after a century of distinguished existence. The last known Non-Juring service in England was held, significantly, in Manchester in 1804. The Scottish Episcopalians are said to have ceased to pray for the Stuarts after Prince Charles died in 1788, but the last of the Scottish Non-Juring clergymen, Donald MacKintosh, was still ministering to the diehard Jacobites in his vast parish in eastern Scotland until 1807, the year before he died.

Even some of the Jacobite chiefs and magnates themselves had been active agricultural 'improvers', and wide and probably painful transformations in Highland life were already in prospect before the Hanoverian authorities hastened the process in an altogether brutal way after Culloden.[29]

In such a spirit the new Disarming Act of 12 August 1746 banned the wearing of the Highland dress, as well as the possession of weapons. Just as significantly the chiefs now lost their independent judicial powers over the clansmen, which severed the ties of mutual obligation that bound society together. The Commissioners of the Annexed Estates took over the running of the confiscated Jacobite domains in June 1755, and considered it part of their duty to promote the English language and civilized styles of life.

Surveyors from the Lowlands now began to cast their hard eyes over the crowded straths and glens, and regarded the tacksmen and the ordinary clansmen not as fighting supporters of the chief, but as obstacles to the good management of that chief's estate. The labour-intensive arable plots occupied valuable low ground which could be turned over to winter grazing; the many smallholdings could be consolidated into large units that might be let out at high rents. The tacksmen were the immediate losers thereby, as the middle managers of the clan system. They began to emigrate to North America in large numbers from the mid 1760s, and the loss of these well-set-up men and their families probably did more to destroy Highland society than did the notorious Clearances in the nineteenth century.

What, in spite of everything, prevented the Jacobite spirit expiring with the memory of the victims? What in fact led to its being absorbed, not extinguished, in the British national consciousness? The process certainly had a lot to do with the desire of the later Georges to reconcile the Hanoverian dynasty with strands of British tradition. The middle generation of the family had to die out first.

Signs of degeneration were already evident in the Duke of Cumberland when he travelled back to England in July 1746. He stayed en route with Lord Glenorchy at Taymouth. Glenorchy wrote that in his party 'there were above 140 persons and as many horses. They were all lodged and their bellies filled with meat and drink. The Duke walked a little in the morning and seemed to like the place. I was sorry to see him so fat; he is a good deal more so than when I saw him at Perth going to the North'.[30]

Once the darling of his troops, Cumberland lost their affection by lending support to a harsh disciplinary code, and his military reputation was destroyed in the new war with France, when he was beaten at Hastenbeck on 26 July (N.S.) 1757, and forced to capitulate at Kloster Zeven on 10 September following. He died on 31 October 1765, and his world was already changing.

Cumberland's nephew had come to the throne in 1760, as George III.

The new king was removed by two generations from the arrival of the Hanoverians in 1714. It was not long before he patched up a reconciliation with the English Tories, who had been excluded from public office during the last two reigns. He respected the integrity of the ultra-Jacobite Oliphants of Gask, who refused to recognize him as anything more than the 'Elector of Hanover', and he acted in the style of a true king rather than a usurper when he helped out Jacobites who were in unfortunate straits, like Andrew Lumisden or the Cardinal Duke of York. The cardinal reciprocated by leaving the Stuart family jewels to the Hanoverian Prince George of Wales in his will. That young gentleman had already worn tartan at a ball in 1789, and he became a prime mover in what has been termed very aptly the 'Hanoverian neo-Jacobitism'.

It might have turned out otherwise, for there were strains in Jacobitism which gave it the potential to be a truly revolutionary force, and not just in favour of a deposed dynasty. When revolution came to America, a Jacobite clergyman, John Witherspoon, signed his name to the Declaration of Independence, and Hugh Mercer, who had been a surgeon's mate in the Jacobite army, became one of Washington's brigadier generals, and died of bayonet wounds sustained in the action at Princeton in 1777 (one of his descendants was the General Patton of the Second World War). There were even reports of invitations being extended to Prince Charles by the leading rebels of Boston and Virginia.

In England Jacobitism was the creed of artisans and skilled craftsmen as well as landed gentlemen, and in 1768, at a time of violent radical unrest, the Manchester Jacobite John Holker (now a highly successful entrepreneur in France) had got word to Prince Charles of the opportunities that might now be at his disposal. The Prince followed the events in North America in the 1770s with close interest, but he had been too disillusioned with things British to bring himself to reply to Holker. The scheme was by no means as far-fetched as might be imagined, for Holker was aware of the radical streak in Jacobitism, which objected not only to a usurping dynasty, but to one that had allowed powerful classes to frame laws and shape developments in their exclusive interests. The small people made up the greater part of the Prince's recruits in his brief foray into England, and in that way Jacobitism became the first movement to draw on a pool that was tapped by the Methodists and the Radicals. As late as 1817, when the Manchester Blanketeers went on the march, they chose to follow the route of Prince Charles to Derby. In Ireland there was a direct line of descent from Jacobitism to the Whiteboys of the 1760s, the Defenderism of the 1780s and to elements in the United Irishmen, suggesting parallels with the 'Jacobitism of the Left' of Robert Burns.[31] A Prince Charles, less sunk in decadence than he was in the 1760s, might have emerged as the leader, not of a rising, let alone a 'rebellion', but something of a revolution.

In the absence of a lead from Prince Charles, most of the Jacobites and their descendants became direct or indirect allies of the ruling dynasty in defence of established authority. Flory MacDonald probably had no great interest in politics, Jacobite or otherwise, and she chose to marry a British officer (her neighbour MacDonald of Kingsburgh) with whom she emigrated to North Carolina in 1775. Like the great majority of her fellow Highland immigrants, she identified with King George in the peculiarly savage civil war which developed in those parts, suffering great tribulations in that cause, and she finally returned with Kingsburgh to spend the rest of her days in Skye. The respective sons of Lord Lovat and the Earl of Cromartie, namely Simon Fraser and John MacKenzie, both raised regiments in Scotland for the king, and their examples undoubtedly influenced George III and the government when they returned the confiscated Jacobite estates to their former owners in 1784. The remaining leaders of Catholic Ireland were not disposed to support the American rebels, and when monarchical authority was challenged in a still more direct way in the France of the Revolution, the officers of the red-coated Irish Brigade chose to return to Britain.

By that time, cultural developments had made it possible to identify oneself with the Jacobite cause in ways which did not involve risk or exile, for the outrage against usurpation and injustice was becoming softened, sentimentalized. One of the manifestations owed little originally to Jacobitism as such, and still less to the Edinburgh of the Scottish Enlightenment. The Welsh naturalist and landed gentleman Thomas Pennant was the first author of note to represent to the polite world that there were things worth seeing in the Highlands, and that something of value was being lost there in the interest of 'improvement' (*A Tour in Scotland, and Voyage to the Hebrides, 1772*, 2 vols., Chester, 1774–6). Thus 'the mighty chieftains, the brave and disinterested heroes of old times, [are] by a most violent and surprising transformation, at once sunk into the rapacious landlords; determined to compensate the loss of power, with the increase of revenue'.[32]

The words were shortly to be echoed by Dr Samuel Johnson, in his now much better-known *A Journey to the Western Islands of Scotland* (London 1775). Pennant had a Whiggish reputation, while Johnson's attachment to Jacobitism did not go beyond the sentimental and philosophical. A great deal more was needed to bring together the perceptions of the

Highland landscapes, its suffering inhabitants and the lost Jacobite cause in a way that held a positive appeal. Johnson was at root a sturdy English north midlander, and could not share the excitement being stirred among men and women of sensibility by the bardic poems assembled or invented by James MacPherson in his *Fragments of Ancient Poetry* (1760) and *Fingal* (1761). Johnson had been alert to the injustices being done to good men like M'Queen, a veteran of Culloden, but it was the doctor's young travelling companion James Boswell who found tears springing to his eyes at M'Queen's narrative:

> There is a certain association of ideas in my mind upon that subject, by which I am strongly affected. The very Highland names, or the sound of a bagpipe, will stir my blood, and fill me with a mixture of melancholy and respect for courage; with pity for an unfortunate and superstitious regard for antiquity, and thoughtless inclination for war; in short, with a crowd of sensations with which sober rationality has nothing to do.[33]

Wealthy men of taste of the new generation were banishing the organized formal gardens of the Baroque in favour of the 'natural' (in fact highly artificial) landscapes of dells, hillocks, and carefully positioned copses and sheets of water. The Highlands, which no longer represented a threat to public order, now presented themselves as deliciously wilful extensions of the parklands of a gentleman's seat; the clansmen now stood forth as exemplars of the sentimental cult of primitive virtue, and none more so than the beggar-poor heroes who (or so it was imagined) never considered betraying Prince Charles in order to collect the stupendous reward that was on offer from the authorities.

In such an environment it was possible for Robert Burns, who was (or liked to think he was) a descendant of a persecuted Jacobite of 1715, to link himself as a fellow victim with Lady Nairne, a daughter of the Oliphants of Gask, whose 'Jacobite' ballads (*The Hundred Pipers, Will ye no' come back again?* etc.) were shrilled and tinkled through the drawing rooms of late Georgian Britain.

The year 1805 was crucial in the construction of the Jacobite myth as it has been transmitted to our days, the appeal of which is to sensibility rather than reason. In that year a friend of the Gasks, the Borders lawyer Walter Scott, published an extraordinarily well-received poem, *The Lay of the Last Minstrel*, which represented an ancient, wrinkled harper banished from royal and noble halls, for

A stranger filled the Stuarts' throne;
The bigots of the iron time
Had call'd his harmless art a crime.
A wandering Harper, scorn'd and poor,
He begg'd his bread from door to door.
And tuned, to please a peasant's ear,
The harp, a king had loved to hear.

In 1805 also, Scott penned the first draft of the first historical novel on a Jacobite theme, indeed probably the first historical novel on any subject, the romance *Waverley* (published 1814). The term 'historical novel' is used advisedly, for Scott was aware that he was writing about events only sixty years before he set pen to paper, but separated by fundamental changes from the present. The main characters are depicted sympathetically by Scott, but linked by their involvement with what he regards as the flawed Stuart cause.

Waverley, unlike *The Lay*, is therefore Whiggish in tone, but Scott succeeded in persuading his readers that the place and time in question were capable of stirring the imagination. 'It naturally occurred to me that the ancient traditions and high spirit of a people, who, living in a civilized age and country, retained so strong a tincture of manners belonging to an early period of time, must afford a subject favourable for romance.'[34]

The phase 'old warriors of 1745' is peculiarly significant, for Scott was anticipating by a few years the way in which a large number of thinking people rediscovered the fascinations of the eighteenth century, after all the turmoil of the Revolutionary and Napoleonic periods. In Prussia it can be identified precisely with the labours of the provincial schoolmaster J. D. E. Preuss, author of the nine-volume history *Friedrich der Grosse* (1832–4). In the United States the house of Benjamin Franklin had been demolished as recently as 1812, and the nearby Independence Hall fell into disrepair, but Lafayette's visit in 1824 wrought a transformation. The American Revolution took on a romantic aspect, and after the death in 1832 of Charles Carroll, the last signatory of the Declaration of Independence, Congress itself took measures to trace and reward the remaining veterans.

All the foregoing political and cultural trends found expression in George IV's celebrated visit to Edinburgh in 1822, which Walter Scott stage-managed to brilliant effect. The identity of monarchy in general with a romantically reconstituted Jacobitism was complete. Two years later the remains of James II were reburied with great ceremony at Saint-Germain, and after 1830 the newly exiled Bourbons linked their cause symbolically with that of the extinct

Stuarts, with the loyal peasantry of the Vendée standing in for the devoted Highlanders of Prince Charles.

The remaining eyewitnesses of the '45 were now being sought out and treasured. In Edinburgh in 1822 George IV was introduced to 'Your Majesty's oldest enemy', namely Peter Grant, sergeant major in the Regiment of the MacPhersons, and to Lady Rosemary Clerk (née Dacre), who wore the white cockade which had been given to her by the Highland captain to wear at her christening in 1745. Rosemary was too young to remember the event, but people a little older than herself held on to their recollections of the passage of the Highland army through the straths, glens, alleys and lanes, and their grandchildren were still relating the stories at the end of the nineteenth century.

Conclusions

Uprisings have to make their way by the sword as well as by persuasion, and it is right to give some consideration to the detailed business of manoeuvre and combat. Here the Hanoverian leaders were victims of their own propaganda, which for too long prevented them from recognizing how much they had to learn. Ultimately, however, the Duke of Cambridge triumphed in every military dimension.

There are certainly startling differences in scale between the clashes in the '45 and the great battles that were being fought in the Netherlands in the same period. The rival forces amounted to about 123,000 men at Fontenoy (11 May N.S. 1745), 200,000 at Rocoux (11 October N.S. 1746) and no less than 210,000 at Laffeld (2 July N.S. 1747), along with huge parks of artillery. These combats, gigantic though they were, nevertheless just represented episodes in an entirely familiar process that everyone knew would lead at most to the gain or loss of bargaining points at an eventual congress of peace. On this reckoning the confrontations in the '45 were puny, for 16,300 troops at the very most were deployed in the largest of the encounters (Falkirk, 16 January 1746), and artillery made scarcely any appearance until Culloden. However, the issues were momentous, and in one respect greater still than in the campaigns in North America, which otherwise offer the best parallels. Why was that?

Both Prince Charles and the Duke of Cumberland knew that sovereignty itself was at stake, and each held to his principle with shocking consistency. In his later years the Prince could be overcome with distracted grief whenever he was reminded of what men had suffered on his behalf, but in the rising he regarded his supporters primarily as instruments whereby he could reclaim the crown of Great Britain for his house. To have carried on the fight after Culloden made little sense to him, for it could contribute nothing to that end, and so he abandoned his followers to their fate just as he had the garrison he left behind in Carlisle. The Duke on his side denied his enemies all belligerent rights, as they were understood in regular warfare, and was not content until he had consolidated his military victory by eradicating the social roots of resistance. It was pacification, not peace, and the two were very different things.

The turning points of the '45 were not the combats in themselves, but rather the successive closing down of options that were open to the Jacobites. The council at Derby on 5 December was significant in more than the obvious respect, for up to then the forces of Prince Charles had been held together by offensive action. Back in Scotland, even when reinforced by the troops that had been gathered there by Lord John Drummond, the leaders would once again address themselves to their particular interests. The ridiculous little raid on Ruthven on 29 August had already shown how easy it was to be distracted from the larger purpose, and thus by April 1746 we find the Jacobite forces scattered from the Spey to Lochaber and Caithness, indicating how impossible it would have been to construct a coherent strategy based on a 'Fortress Scotland'.

The Jacobite leaders reached their conclusion at Derby when they were not in immediate contact with the enemy, and the same held true in the later turning points. At Lancaster on 14 December they renounced the chance of doing battle when the Duke of Cumberland had a decided numerical superiority, and the opportunity did not present itself again. The council at Crieff on 2 February was more momentous in its way than the meeting at Derby or even the battle at Culloden, for it was followed by the abandonment of the eastern coastlands of Scotland – and only the way in which the '45 has been generally described and commemorated has prevented us from recognizing how vital that part of the world was to the Jacobite cause. The chance of a last-moment tactical victory came and went with the night march on the camp of Nairn on 16/17 April, and the next day's battle was fought under the most disadvantageous circumstances. The final option of prolonging the resistance in the Highlands did not commend itself to Prince Charles, even if that course had been logistically feasible, for he viewed himself only as a crown prince in command of an army, and not as the leader of a guerrilla band.

Nobody can pretend to offer the last word on the '45. History is constantly reinventing itself, and there are probably three reasons why people will always be tempted to rework the story of the Rising:

❖ Nobody is so divorced from origins and instincts as to be able to avoid 'taking sides', once exposed to this subject matter

❖ There will always appear to be a parallel between the events of the '45, and the wild landscapes in which some of them were played out. It is as if Prince Charles turned back when the good scenery gave out

❖ The period exercises its own fascination, and not least because it was the time when a society based on tradition was about to yield to one directed by industrialization and rationality. Dr Johnson was already busy about his *Dictionary* in 1746, and when it was published nine years later it seemed to stand in a natural succession to some remarkable works which had begun to reduce the world to order: David Hume's *Philosophical Essays Concerning Human Understanding* (1748), the first volume of Denis Diderot's *Encyclopédie* (1751), and the *Species Plantarum* (1752) of Carl Linnaeus. Prince Charles encountered coal-pits and a railway on the field of Prestonpans; his lodgings at Derby stood just down the Derwent from Lombe's great silk mill; he crossed the Carron on the way to Falkirk Muir about 1 mile from the site of the celebrated ironworks that were shortly to bring the Industrial Revolution to the Lowlands.

When we are faced with the divide between the old and the new, it is too easy for us to consign the episode of the '45 to a romantically doomed past, identified completely with the Highland culture – a culture which was in fact shared with the Highlanders who fought for the government, and, at one remove, with the Gaels of Ireland. Jacobitism was also a force beyond the Highlands, and not just in pockets of conservatism, but along the outward-looking Episcopal eastern coastlands of Scotland, in the coal-pits and workshops of the English East Midlands, and in Manchester, which already had the makings of the archetypal city of the Industrial Revolution. Jacobitism has at least the claim to be examined critically in the light of a credible ideological, social and military threat to the regime then obtaining in Britain.

In its striving for legitimacy and equity it was perhaps even the first presage of a future in which its aims, modified by time and circumstance, were to be achieved by other agencies. But amid all the suffering it would be wrong to assume that the men and women of that time regretted what they had done. At Lincoln an officer of the government's law learned that 'on some of the country people going into this gaol and enquiring of the rebels what sort of a man the Pretender was, one of the rebels briskly replied, "I don't know, I never was at St James's"'.[35]

APPENDICES

The Clans, North to South*

THE ORKNEY ISLANDS: THESE ARE A SPRAWL of sixty-seven or so islands situated off the far north-eastern tip of Scotland, from which they are separated by Pentland Firth. They stand on the same latitude as Estonia or Norway, and indeed they belonged to the Kingdom of Norway until 1468. The culture was Norse, not Gaelic, and the Norn language was spoken there until the nineteenth century.

Orkney was not as bleak and forlorn as its situation might suggest, however, for there was good pasture and fishing, the islands actually exported grain to Scotland, while smuggling and shipwrecks could provide a welcome supplement to income. Kirkwall, the capital, stood on the northern side of the wasp waist of the principal island ('The Mainland'), and boasted an ancient cathedral as well as a useful harbour.

The Orkney Islands represented a classic sandwich of competing interests, the top slice comprising the earls of Morton, who exacted feudal dues from the lairds, and who were by tradition Whigs, though at the time of the '45 James Douglas, the 14th Earl, was living in France and trying to negotiate a peace. The twenty-three lairds were Episcopalians and mostly Jacobite, and although they quarrelled amongst themselves, their traditions revived when they found that the factors of the Earl of Morton were altering the traditional measures – the bismars and pundlars – and claiming more in the way of dues than was their right.

There was no effective opposition when, in 1745, the Jacobite lairds awakened to what was happening in Scotland, and took possession of the islands. The most active among them, James Fea of Clestran, offered to raise a regiment in the Jacobite cause, as long as he was made colonel, but Prince Charles was unable to accede for fear of alienating the noisiest of the Jacobites, Sir James Steuart of Burray, who had a long record of resistance to the Mortons. For months on end, therefore, there was no effort to mobilize the resources of Orkney, and the identification of Jacobitism with the turbulent Steuart of Burray was to rebound on the cause when, finally, the islands came to figure in wider events.[1]

The Far North: The northern Highlands form a highly irregular oblong which extends from the north-facing Atlantic coast all the way south to the fault of the Great Glen. The **Sinclairs** had been the historic masters of Caithness, in the generally low-lying north-eastern corner of that region.[2] However, the earls of Sinclair had lost their local dominance along with their wider lands, and although there was potential for

---

*For the purposes of standardization, the style of Scottish surnames given here has been taken from *No Quarter Given. The Muster Roll of Prince Charles Edward Stuart, 1745–46* (Glasgow, 2001).

Jacobite support, their country was hemmed in by natural barriers and the hostile MacKays and Sutherlands. In Caithness the only major representative of the family to 'come out' was George Sinclair of Geese. The local pro-Hanoverian gentry were equally passive. In April 1746 the Lord Justice Clerk in Edinburgh had to tell Commodore T. Smith of the Royal Navy that he did not know any who could be depended upon, other than the retired Captain William Innes of Sandside.

To the west of the Sinclairs a deep zone of bogs and oozing watercourses led to fertile Strathnaver and the adjacent territories of the Presbyterian **MacKays** under their aged and courtly chief, George MacKay, 3rd Lord Reay, who had his seat at Tongue House, by the sandy inlet of the Kyle of Tongue. It was due to Reay's influence that the greater part of his divided clan came out on the side of King George. Cumberland's biographer Andrew Henderson describes the MacKays as in general a noble race, and his views may be taken as representing those of the duke himself. The clan played a tardy but decisive part in the wider context of the rebellion when *Le Prince Charles* was chased ashore in the Kyle of Tongue on 25 March 1746 and her

The Scotland of the Clans

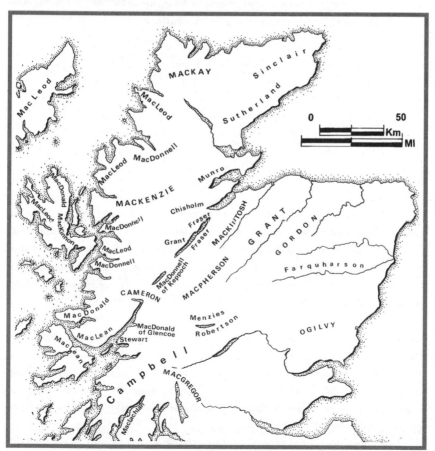

cargo of French gold, which Prince Charles was relying upon to pay his army, was lost to Lord Reay's men, so precipitating the financial crisis which led directly to the battle at Culloden.

South-west of Caithness the extensive territory of the **Sutherlands** owed allegiance to William, Earl of Gordon-Sutherland, who was another supporter of the government. This was 'Hanoverian' territory until the Earl of Cromartie came north with his Jacobites in the spring of 1746 to disperse the hostile clansmen and exact contributions. He wrote to the Countess of Sutherland on 31 March to tell her that he was 'ashamed to be so often troublesome to Your Ladyship on a subject that must be disagreeable to you, as I do assure Your Ladyship it is to me, but the great regard I have for Your Ladyship, and the family of Sutherland, obliges me earnestly to insist with you to endeavour to prevent an evil that must inevitably befall the country and people if they do not give obedience to His Royal Highness's Prince Charles's orders by laying down their arms'.[3] He was still up in the north in April, hoping to retrieve the gold landed from *Le Prince Charles*, but his party was split up and he was captured along with his officers in the Countess's Castle of Dunrobin on the 15th.

Before then the clan had scarcely featured in the events of the '45, and Henderson describes its militia, especially from the coastal regions, as

> among the very refuse of the Highland counties; they are as subject to their lairds … as negroes to their masters. It is notorious what numbers of slaves were sent off to the plantations by MacKay of Scouray & Company in the years 1728 and 1729. In short, these people are as poor, barbarous, inhuman, cruel and revengeful as the worst of the rebels, but less active, more stupid, and not at all given to that outward civility which the latter, but an air peculiar to themselves, affect to show to strangers who come among them. The Earls of Sutherland are certainly as ancient as any in Scotland, but few of them have made a figure in cabinet or field.[4]

The **MacKenzies** counted as one of the major clans, and not least because the government had long used them as one of the instruments of its indirect rule, and at the time of the '45 they predominated along wide stretches of the northern Scottish peninsula from the Minch in the west to the North Sea in the east. The politics of the region were complicated even by the standards of the time. Of the two principal noble families, the Earls of Seaforth had reconverted from Protestantism to Rome, and the last earl of that faith, William 5th, was an enthusiastic Jacobite who had come out in 1715 and again in 1719. He went into exile and lost his estates, but was induced to return and regain his inheritance in 1726 after his clansmen had arranged a pardon with General Wade. He died in 1740, and was succeeded by his eldest son, Kenneth, Lord Fortrose, who declared for the government in 1745. A Presbyterian minister observed after Culloden that 'the gentlemen are mostly Episcopal, and they and their predecessors were at Sheriffmuir and Glenshiel with the last Seaforth, but by the good disposition of the present Seaforth to our happy establishment, they did not think fit to join the late Rebellion, except a few younger brothers who had nothing to lose, who are now prisoners in London'.[5] It had not been as straightforward as that, for his Jacobite wife, Lady Fortrose, remained loyal to the traditions of the clan, and succeeded in detaching many of the men of the MacKenzies from the governmental cause.

The leader of the other great family, George, Earl of **Cromartie**, declared for the Prince in November 1745 and set about raising men from his estates. Easter Ross proved recalcitrant, for the gentry of Tarbat and Tain were independent-minded and unmilitary, and they supported the government so far as they supported anything. They were sheltered to the west by the firmly Presbyterian little clan of **Munro** under its chief, Sir Harry Munro, who held the land towards Dingwall along the northern side of the upper Cromarty Firth. Nobody had a good word to say for these people. Henderson observed that the Munros were no better than the degenerate Sutherlands,[6] while a leading Jacobite described them as 'vultures' who 'devoured the bowels of their country by making war on their other neighbours ... and by plundering houses and farms defended only by women and children'. The noble MacKenzies would have made breakfast of them in open combat.[7] Cromartie had better luck in Wester Ross, where his son John MacKenzie, Lord MacLeod, had been recruiting vigorously in the family estates in that part of the world, and ultimately the Jacobites could count on the support of the greater part of the long stretch of west-facing coastline which extended from Assynt, Coigach, Loch Broom and Loch Carron down to Loch Alsh.

After the Jacobite army retreated from Stirling and regrouped around Inverness in February 1746, it was joined by Cromartie's MacKenzies, the Chisholms and the whole available force of the Frasers. It therefore makes sense to include these people in the survey of the balance of influence in northern Scotland. The **Chisholms** and their more considerable neighbours the **Frasers** by no means constituted a unit, but they had a shared geography and fate. In both their territories the lead was given by the ordinary Jacobite clansmen, for the chief of Chisholm did not come out at all, while the notoriously devious Simon Fraser, Lord Lovat, did not commit himself to Prince Charles until after the battle of Prestonpans. The holdings of the two clans interleaved in the remoter valleys well to the west of the Great Glen: Glen Strathfarrar below Loch Monar was Fraser territory, just as the Chisholms held Glen Cannich and Glen Affric, together with a stretch of the flat-floored Strathglass along with the chief's castle at Erchless. There were many Catholics in Strathglass, but they were surprisingly law-abiding, and they suffered much from the depredations of the Glen Moriston men.

The most advanced part of the Fraser lands was the triangle of the Aird, which stretched just west of Inverness between the Beauly Firth and the river and loch of Ness. It was a rich and fertile land, and sheltered from the winds that roared down the Great Glen. Not far away but very different in character was Stratherrick, a wooded corridor running between the foot of the Monadhliath Mountains and the eastern shore of Loch Ness. Stratherrick provided the Frasers with a handy retreat in time of trouble, and was used by Prince Charles as his avenue of escape immediately after Culloden.

The Frasers would have been in trouble if their immediate eastern neighbours, the **MacKintoshes**, had come out in favour of the government and joined forces with the main body of the Clan Grant. The MacKintosh lands, although somewhat trimmed at the southern end by the MacDonnells of Keppoch after the clan battle of Mulroy in August 1688, still took in Strathnairn, Moy, Badenoch and the valley of the Findhorn. Fortunately for the Frasers, the MacKintosh clansmen obeyed their Episcopal instincts and were turned against their own chief by his wife, the celebrated 'Colonel' Anne. The Grants were nominally committed to the government, but, as we have seen, the chief and his son Ludovick kept people guessing until almost the end of the rising.

The Great Glen and Lochaber: Two green valleys led into the Western Highlands from Loch Ness. These were Glen Urquhart and Glen Moriston, which were the home of a branch of the Protestant **Grants**, who held nominal allegiance to the chief of their clan but who had fallen into the ways of their Gaelic neighbours. They came out in support of Prince Charles, and after the rising they were tricked by the notorious Ludovick into giving themselves up.

Loch Ness terminated at Fort Augustus, but the fault line of the Great Glen continued south-west through a narrow wooded valley and a chain of lochs to Fort William in Lochaber, from where it was prolonged into the salt water as Loch Linnhe. This region may be counted as the heartland of Highland Jacobitism, which was why the government had planted its two forts there in the first place. Glen Garry was another of the westward-leading sub-valleys in the style of Urquhart and Glen Moriston, and was the residence of the **MacDonnells of Glengarry**, 'of a good size, but very poor, and addicted to theft and robbery; if any religion be among them, it is Popery'.[8] They were 'reckoned the most daring and expert thieves in the country, in so much that they overawe all their neighbours. This is much owing to their chief who is an indolent creature, and entirely given up to drink. He did not appear in the late Rebellion, his following being commanded by his second son till some days after the Battle of Falkirk, when he was shot by accident, and after that headed by his cousin Lochgarry'.[9] The Young Glengarry who was shot after Falkirk was Aeneas, and his accidental killer was a MacDonald of Clanranald; this unfortunate man was executed, but the Glengarry MacDonnells were not to be appeased, and many of them deserted.

A further branch of this moody clan, the **MacDonnells of Keppoch**, held Glen Spean and the Braes of Lochaber, which gave them control of a crucial stretch of one of the principal avenues into the Western Highlands. They had consolidated their position there at the expense of the MacPhersons in some of the last of the clan wars, and their current chief, Alexander MacDonnell, hoped that the Stuarts would give him something which he needed, which was proper legal title to his lands.

Meanwhile, he lacked full authority over his clansmen, who were in any case divided between Catholics and Protestants, and the Keppoch MacDonnells became known as the least controllable unit in the Jacobite army. They hung back at Culloden, and Alexander was killed in a gallant one-man charge.

Without the support of Donald Cameron of Lochiel, Prince Charles and his little party would have been forced to return to France before the summer of 1745 was out, and his expedition would scarcely have deserved a footnote in the history books. The largely Episcopalian **Camerons** were in fact the most considerable of the Jacobite clans, and they had been supporters of the Stuarts ever since Donald's famous grandfather Ewen had declared himself in 1646. Even so, Donald weighed up his position very carefully indeed before he committed himself to Prince Charles ninety-nine years later.

The Cameron lands extended over great tracts of mountain and forest on both sides of the Great Glen fault. They blocked the northward expansion of the Campbells, but were themselves almost surrounded by those of the MacDonalds and MacDonnells, with whom the Camerons maintained an uneasy peace. Donald Cameron was a man of affairs and an agricultural improver, and he kept at least the unauthorized cattle-thieving of his men in check. He was at the same time a charismatic clan chief in the old style, who commanded the loyalty not only of the Cameron cadet branches, but clan septs and dependants like the **MacFies** of Glen Dessary, the brigand-like **MacMillans** of Loch Arkaig, and the **MacMartins** of Letterfinlay on Loch Lochy, as well as a still wider following in other people's lands as far distant as Rannoch and Morvern.

The Lochaber chiefs as a whole had a common cause in their opposition to the branch of Marshal Wade's road which reached to Fort William: 'it lessened their influence greatly, for, by admitting strangers among them, their clans were taught that the lairds were not the first of men. But they had another reason much more solid: Lochaber had been a den of thieves, and as long as they had their waters, their torrents and their bogs in a state of nature, they made their excursions, could plunder and retreat in full security'.[10]

The Far West: The peninsulas of the Western Highlands witnessed the earliest scene of the Jacobite '45, and the very last, and the Catholic clansmen who lived there were reckoned to be exceptionally resistant to the influence of the government and the Kirk. The principal clan was that of **MacDonald of Clanranald**, and its branches. The related Clanranalds of Moidart owned Barra and South Uist in the Outer Hebrides, the islands of Rum, Eigg and Canna, and Moidart on the mainland, where the Presbyterians had attempted to found a couple of parishes, 'but by the influence of the gentry, the diligence and insolence of the priests, and the bigotry of the people, the ministers had little success till now'.[11] However, by 1745 the old chief Ranald Clanranald was drunken and decayed, and much under the influence of his brother Boisdale, and Prince Charles was disappointed in his hopes of receiving help from the MacDonalds of the Outer Hebrides.

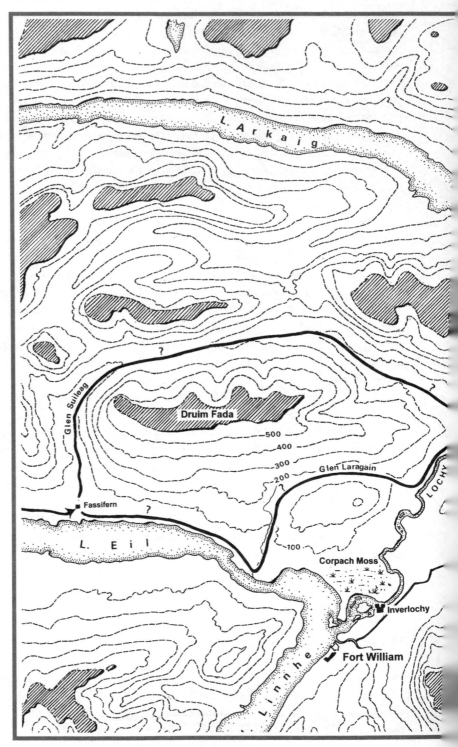

Lochaber, with the route of Prince Charles in August 1745

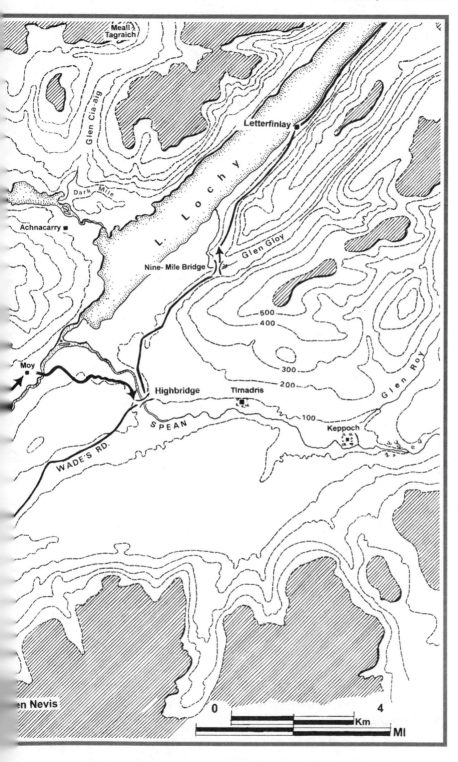

Meall
Tagraich

Glen Cia-aig

Letterfinlay

L. Lochy

Dark Mile

Achnacarry

Glen Gloy

Nine- Mile Bridge

500
400

300

Glen Roy

200

Moy

Highbridge   Tirnadris

100

SPEAN

Keppoch

WADE'S RD.

en Nevis

0   4

Km

MI

It was a different story in the MacDonald territories on the mainland, where Ranald MacDonald of Clanranald of Borrodale ('Young Clanranald') was among the first of the chiefs to declare for the Prince, and began the long process of bringing over the waverers. 'Evidence' Murray of Broughton characterizes him as 'an indolent headstrong boy, guided by his priests, [who] permits his people to act without control'.[12]

If we discount the joint Isle of Lewis and Harris in the Outer Hebrides, Skye was by far the largest of the western islands, and it was a major setback for Prince Charles at the outset of his enterprise when the two major Skye chieftains, Sir Alexander **MacDonald of Sleat** and Norman **MacLeod of MacLeod of Dunvegan**, refused to come out in his favour. Both men were Protestants, along with their people, but the deciding factor in their conduct was that a leading governmental officer, the Lord President, Duncan Forbes of Culloden, had detected them in an attempt to kidnap numbers of their own clansmen and transport them across the Atlantic to slavery. He had kept them under threat of blackmail ever since. Between them the heroic pair held most of the island. The domains of Sir Alexander MacDonald extended along the sheltered eastern coast and the green south-western peninsula of Sleat, while MacLeod of Dunvegan held a great tract of largely useless land in the north-west.

The one countervailing influence on Skye was that of John **MacKinnon of MacKinnon**, whose lands formed the curving southern shore of the great lagoon of the Inner Sound. He was active on behalf of Prince Charles throughout the rising and thereafter, and he helped to detach a number of the minor MacLeod chieftains, including those of Brea, Muiravonside, and in particular Donald MacLeod of Berneray and his cousin Malcolm MacLeod the 10th Chief of **Raasay**. That gentleman was seen in December 1745 leading a large party of MacDonalds, Camerons, MacKenzies and MacKintoshes from Perth to join Prince Charles, and 'he seemed a very active man in the rebel service, and made a very handsome appearance as to himself and his men, who were well clothed and well armed'.[13] Boswell saw Malcolm MacLeod in 1773, when the chief impressed him as the 'perfect representation of a Highland gentleman'. All the same, in 1745 Malcolm had hedged his bets in a typical Highland fashion by making over his estates to his eldest son. If that device failed, he had a second line of defence in an ancient arrangement with the MacDonalds of Sleat. Sir Alexander MacDonald of Sleat was then his political opponent, but '"Don't be afraid," says he: "I'll use all my interest to keep you safe; and if your estate should be taken, I'll buy it for the family." – And he would have done'.[14]

The **Outer Hebrides** could be counted as being beyond the reach of Prince Charles, apart from the help he received there during his escape. Barray, Eriskay, South Uist and southern Benbecula were inhabited by Catholics, but they were sealed off from the mainland both by cruising British warships, and by the unwillingness of MacDonald of Boisdale to come out in support. All the rest of the islands were Protestant, and held by hostile chiefs – North Uist by Sir Alexander MacDonald of Sleat, and Lewis and Harris by the MacLeods and Seaforths.

The Campbells: In 1745 the **Campbells** gave the government its firmest prop of support in the Highlands. The origins of this great clan lay in the region of lochs Awe and Long and the Lennox Hills. From there the principal branch moved its base of power to Inverary near the head of Loch Fyne, a sea loch which gave access to the Firth of Clyde and thence to wider waters. In season the loch teemed with herring, and every night from September to Christmas hundreds of craft exploited the finest fishery on the western coast of Scotland.

On balance, however, the rise of the Campbells derived not so much from geography as from some unique characteristics. No other group equalled them in their capacity to maintain cohesion (despite inevitable rivalries) between the main branch and the cadet lines, to maintain their influence in both the Gaelic and the Lowland worlds, to think strategically through successive generations, or to profit so successfully by major political and social movements in Scotland.

Over the centuries the clan expanded its holdings across a belt of some 112 miles of islands and mainland, from the Inner Hebrides in the west to the borders of Atholl in the east.

The westward drive: The Campbells rose in the shadow of the mighty Clan Donald (MacDonalds and MacDonnells), whose Lordship of the Isles extended over one-third of Scotland in the later Middle Ages, and was acquiring the characteristics of a sovereign state. In 1493, however, the Scottish crown declared the Lordship of the Isles forfeit, and proceeded to entrust the Campbells with the task of 'daunting' the Clan Donald. Here the Campbells benefited indirectly from the military and political campaigns of the English crown against the Gaelic lords of Ireland, which culminated in Elizabeth's Irish War of 1594–1603 and the flight of the Irish magnates ('the Earls') in 1607. The Clan Donald thereby lost its independent Irish base, and its Scottish holdings became more vulnerable than ever when James Stuart united the crowns of England and Scotland in 1603, and devolved wide powers to select client clans – the Gordons in the north-east, the MacKays in the north, and, most significantly, to the Campbells in the south-west. The senior (Argyll) branch of the Campbells completed its expansion at the expense of the MacDonalds when the crown rewarded it with the peninsulas of Kintyre (1607) and Ardnamurchan (1625).

The possessions of the MacLeans were next on the Campbells' menu, and the chance came a couple of generations later when the Earl of Argyll bought up the debts of the bankrupt clan chief, MacLean of Duart, and gained the sizeable island of Mull. The MacLean clansmen resisted the take-over, and they had to be beaten down in a virtual military campaign between 1674 and 1679.

The Argyll Campbells were now in a most advantageous strategic position. They had total control of the Sound of Mull, together with the stronghold of Mingary Castle at the northern side of the seaward entrance, and the harbour of Tobermory, which was tucked away on the Mull shore almost opposite. To the east, where the Sound of Mull merged with the Firth of Lorn, the waters could be controlled by craft operating from the harbour by the castle of Dunstaffnage, an ancient

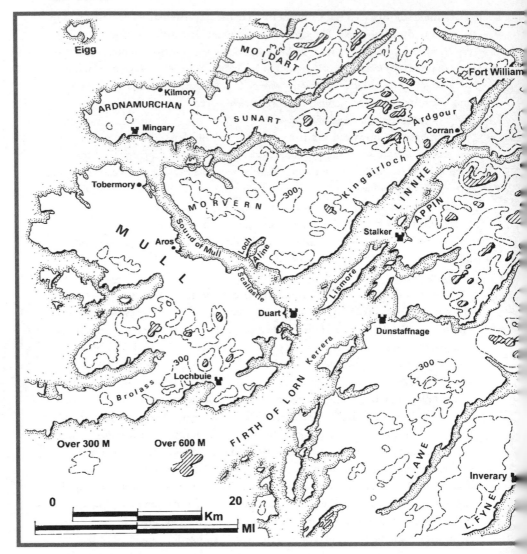

The Campbell lands

stronghold of the MacDougalls which had been in the possession of the Campbells since 1470. Up to the coast to the north, the isolated keep of Castle Stalker had been built in the middle of the sixteenth century by the Stewarts of Appin, and although it was still nominally in their possession, it too was garrisoned by the Campbells in 1745 and 1746. To the south the peninsula of Kintyre approached to within 13 miles of the Antrim coast of Ulster, now heavily colonized by Protestant settlers. The little harbour of Campbeltown prospered from the resulting trade.

The eastward drive: The expansion to the east was mainly the work of the principal cadet branch, the Campbell earls of **Breadalbane**. Their base was Kilchurn

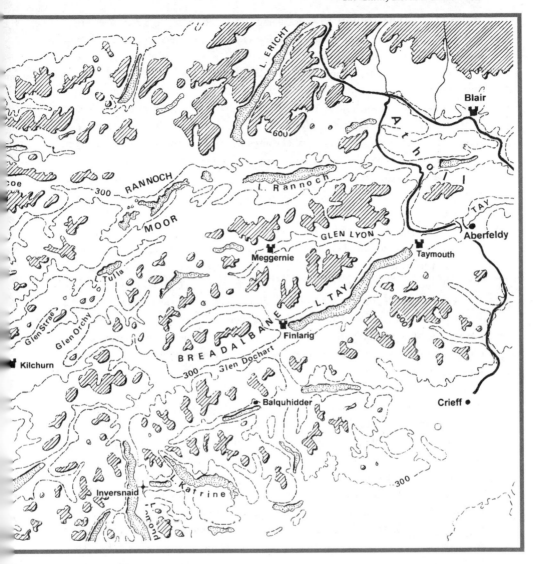

Castle, situated at the far northern end of the inland Loch Awe. The castle was built by Sir Colin Campbell ('Black Colin'), the first Laird of Glenorchy, who died in 1475. Kilchurn as we see it today was refashioned by Sir John Campbell, the eleventh chief and (from 1677) the 1st Earl of Breadalbane. Between 1690 and 1698 he provided the place with a large L-shaped barrack block capable of accommodating 120 soldiers, which made it the first purpose-built barracks in Britain. It is by no means certain in whose interest the work was done, for Sir John had been an ardent Royalist and had contributed to the Restoration in 1660. He seems to have rallied other clan chiefs in support of William III, but he showed his true colours by 'coming out' in 1715, and he was lucky to escape being ruined. His successors drew the appropriate lesson, and the earl of 1745 and his son (Lord Glenorchy) both threw in their lot with the Hanoverians.

From Kilchurn the Campbells of Breadalbane had driven north-west up Glen Strae and Glen Orchy to the shallow Loch Tulla at the foot of the ascent (today's A82) to Rannoch Moor. The methods they employed were force, threats, marriage alliances or, as in this case, a pact with the deluded MacGregors. The next penetrations were to the west by two roughly parallel routes which both led to Loch Tay, namely by way of the gentle Glen Dochart to the western end of the lake, and by the tortuous Glen Lyon to the eastern end. The connection with the MacGregors broke down, and (through another happy intervention of the crown) that turbulent clan was outlawed in 1603.

The outcome was a corridor which projected along the Loch Tay Fault well to the east of the traditional Campbell lands, and which extended athwart, or close to, some of the principal routes from the Lowlands to the Highlands. The gains were secured by castles at the two ends of Loch Tay – Finlarig in the west and Taymouth in the east. Loch Tay itself bore the aspect of a majestic river, and in the course of time the Earls of Glenorchy developed the **MacDiarmid** lands on the rising northern shore into a landscape of farms and parkland. The left flank of the salient was guarded by the crude and violent **Campbells of Glen Lyon** (a much more important route than it is now), who had their seat at Meggernie Castle.

The Campbells in the Eighteenth Century: In a remarkably prescient shift of policy the Argyll Campbells first broke with the house of Stuart in 1638, and fifty years later the 10th Earl was ranked among the foremost supporters of the Glorious Revolution, to the extent of administering the coronation oath to William and Mary. In 1703 he was elevated to duke. By that time the head of the Argyll drew revenues from an area of 500 square miles, and exercised feudal regalities over an area six times that size. The Campbell clan chiefs had the capacity to raise well over 5,000 armed men, namely 3,000 from the duke's lands, more than 1,000 from those of the Earl of Breadalbane, and at least another 1,000 from those of the lesser cadet branches. They had connected stretches of drove road into continuous passages which led to the Lowlands, and they had cultivated social and marriage links with the society of that part of the world – a labour which extended through the generations. All of this confirmed that the Campbells were 'the richest and most numerous clan in Scotland, their countries and boundaries most extensive, their superiorities, jurisdictions and other dependencies by far the greatest in the Kingdom, which makes them the family of the greatest significancy and power in North Britain'.[15]

In 1745 the Campbells were able to deny their core lands to the Jacobites, and by putting their harbours and roadsteads at the disposal of the Hanoverians they permitted the Royal Navy to dominate the western sea lanes, to ravage Jacobite coastlands, to succour Fort William in the weeks before Culloden, and to support the campaign of pacification after the battle. However, there were signs that the clan had over-reached itself. Old John Campbell, 2nd Earl of Breadalbane, had handed over the management of his affairs to his son, Lord Glenorchy, who found that his own Breadalbane men 'showed a great unwillingness to be employed against their nearest relations and neighbours', and could not be trusted to garrison posts in the territories of the Menzies.[16]

The reigning head of the Argyll branch, Archibald, the 3rd Duke, had succeeded in 1743, and was preoccupied with the need to repair various kinds of damage which had been wrought by his ancestors. Most urgently he had to bear in mind that his father, John, 2nd Duke from 1703, had built an outwardly impressive 'argethian' system of political power in Scotland, but had still proved vulnerable to his Whig enemies of the Squadrone faction, as was shown in 1715, when he assumed command of the anti-Jacobite forces in Scotland without the precaution of gaining the necessary authority from London. The Squadrone party, which had its power base in the Lowlands and Borders, and which favoured closer integration with England, was now represented in the capital by Lord Tweeddale as Secretary of State for Scotland. In the autumn of 1745, therefore, when there was a need for drastic measures on the spot in Scotland, Duke Archibald travelled to London to secure his position there.

Archibald had only had two years in which to redress the harm which had been done to the very institution of the clan. From the 1660s the earls of Argyll and Breadalbane had begun to commercialize their lands by reducing the tacksmen's leases from ninety-nine years to nineteen or even less. John, the 2nd Duke, had carried the business further from 1737 by letting out leases in Mull, Morvern and Tiree to the highest bidders, the tacksmen being replaced by factors (estate managers) who had no hereditary claim on the loyalty of the Highlanders. It was typical of the Argylls to anticipate fundamental developments in Scottish affairs, but the result in the short term was to demoralize loyal clansmen, and even give displaced Jacobites the chance to regain their old holdings on new terms. In 1740 cattle raiders penetrated as far as Inverary, which could scarcely have happened if the clan had held together. In 1745 and 1746 the 3rd Duke found it impossible to raise men on Tiree and in other places. Morvern and Ardnamurchan were in open revolt, and became the object of punitive expeditions by his militia and the Royal Navy.

The Neighbours of the Campbells: The Campbells were environed ('surrounded' is too active a word) by predominantly Episcopal clans and families which had suffered under their impact over the generations. We start with the territories which lay to the west of Loch Linnhe and the Firth of Lorn. The attachment of the **MacLeans** to their hereditary chiefs long outlasted the legal loss of some of their prime lands to the Campbells in the 1670s, and in the '15 Sir John MacLean was able to raise 400 of the former MacLean tenants from the islands of Mull, Tiree and Coll, and lead 350 of them to Sheriffmuir. The Jacobites were at something of a disadvantage in 1745, for the new chief, Sir Hector MacLean of Duart, had been arrested while he was on a recruiting expedition for the regiment of Royal Ecossais, and a number of gentlemen proved to be indifferent or hostile to the rising – MacLean of Kingairloch in Morvern, and the MacLean lairds of the isle of Coll, and of Lochbuie and Brolass in the south of Mull. All the same about 180 MacLean fighting men joined from the historic clan lands of Morvern and Ardgour, and made common cause with the local Camerons who were being rallied by Lochiel's uncle, Ludovick Cameron of Trecastle. Only thirty-eight MacLeans are said to have returned home after the rising.

On the 'inland' side of the Campbell territories we encounter a semi-circle of clans which by 1745 had all emerged as enemies of the dukes of Argyll. To the north the **MacDonalds of Glencoe** were the smallest and most isolated group of the 'Great Clan', living in small settlements along Loch Leven and the spectacular valley which bore their name, and existing 'at a distance from politeness, and like many other rebels, drowned in ignorance'.[17] They were reckoned 'false and traitorous, so that they are seldom trusted by their neighbours'.[18] They could show about a hundred armed men, and their chief, Alexander MacDonald, brought them out for the Prince in 1745.

The southern neighbours of the Glencoe MacDonalds were the **Stewarts of Appin**, another small clan of Episcopalians, who held a tract of forest and mountain which reached down to the north-eastern shore of Loch Linnhe. There the resemblance ceased, for the Appin Stewarts were famously law-abiding. Their nominal head was the last of the direct male line, Dugald Stewart the eighth chief, who had been created a Jacobite peer in 1743, but was content to live at home during the '45. The clan was instead raised for Prince Charles by his kinsman Charles Stewart of Ardsheal, who by tradition is acclaimed in most books as 'a brilliant swordsman' (just as Lord George Murray is the 'military genius'), but who was prodded into action by his Jacobite wife Isabel Haldane.[19] Ardsheal's action was more significant than the small numbers of the Stewarts might suggest, for they had long-standing ties with the **MacLarens** (the original clan of the Balquhidder area), the **Carmichaels**, the **Livingstones** (including the great-grandfather of the explorer), the **MacColls**, the **MacCormacks** and the **MacIntyres**.

It was still more risky for Lachlan **MacLachlan**, the 17th chief of his clan, to rally nearly 300 men to the Prince, for his country lay half-way down Loch Fyne, within sight of Inverary, and was surrounded by the Campbells. In the Jacobite army the MacLachlans were brigaded with the **MacLeans**, who were in a similar case, and Lachlan himself became a commissary and was killed at Culloden. A hostile commentator detected the influence of 'the chaplain general of the clans', Rev. John MacLachlan of Kilchoan, 'a most violent Episcopal minister [who] poisoned his chief and the gentlemen of his name to a strange degree, and indeed did more mischief among the clans than any three priests I knew'.[20]

The **MacGregors** had the reputation of being the wildest and most unbiddable of the clans, 'a people very remarkable for wicked achievements',[21] 'seldom to be depended upon, bring frequently delirious ... a very false people, in so much that it is generally said that a MacGregor is never betrayed but by one of his own name',[22] though perhaps their worst crime was to stand in the way of the Campbells.

In 1603 the clan was outlawed and the very term 'MacGregor' forbidden. The clan name was restored under Charles II, but by then the clan lands had already been lost to the Campbells, and the ban on the name was re-enacted in 1693. The original MacGregor lands lay in the volcanic landscape between lochs Lomond and Katrine, which had been very suitable for their purposes. By the time of the '45 many of the MacGregors had adopted the names of Graham, Murray, Drummond or (confusingly) Campbell, and they were scattered from the wastes of Rannoch Moor to the neighbourhood of Balquhidder. There was not even a generally recognized chief, for claims of varying authority could be lodged by the respective MacGregors of Balhaldy, Glencarnaig and Glengyle. However, the MacGregors succeeded in putting together a good clan regiment for the '45; one of the companies did great execution at Prestonpans under the leadership of James Drummond, a son of Rob Roy, and the clansmen proved to be among the last of the Jacobite forces to disperse after Culloden. Their internal cohesion was if anything strengthened by these experiences.

The Highland Margins: The Highlands abated somewhat in their rudeness as they gave way to the lower country to the east and south and became more open to the influence of the farming and maritime communities of the North Sea coast, and that of Perth, Crieff and the smaller market towns.

The lands of the Episcopal **MacPhersons** lay in Badenoch along the upper reaches of the Spey, which were relatively accessible in Highland terms, and the commitment of this clan to Prince Charles had nothing of the desperation which can be detected in the case of folk like the MacLeans. In fact the Macphersons had been generally reckoned to be loyal to the established government, though in dispute with the equally well-affected MacKintoshes concerning the leadership of the **Clan Chattan** (the Clan of the Cat), a loose but ancient confederation which embraced their two clans, along with those of the Clarks, Davidons, Farquharsons, Gows, MacBeans, MacGillivrays, MacPhails, MacQueens and others. Old MacPherson of Cluny declined to 'come out', and his son, Ewan MacPherson the Younger of Cluny, brought over the clan to the Prince only after he had been captured, or allowed himself to be captured, by the Jacobites. The circumstances of the case are still unclear, though Ewan might have been swayed by his close connections with Cameron of Lochiel (his first cousin) and Simon Fraser of Lovat (his father-in-law). His people were probably influenced by the fate of their fellow-clansmen who had enlisted in the Black Watch, and who had suffered for their part in the celebrated regimental mutiny in 1743.

Lower Strathspey was the country of the main branch of the **Grants**. They were Presbyterians, and they had raised a regiment for William during the Glorious Revolution, 'but they suffered so much by the depredations of the Camerons and

MacDonalds that they became rather too cautious at the time of the ... Rebellion; the truth was that they were 'twixt two fires, Lord Lewis Gordon to the east, and MacKintoshes, Camerons and MacDonalds to the west, so that their country must have been severely plundered if they had been more than neuters'.[23]

That was written by a Presbyterian minister who was putting a very favourable gloss on what had happened. The Grants held back when General Cope was retreating to Inverness in late August 1745, and the old chief departed for London after leaving appropriate instructions with his son Ludovick. The conduct of the clan remained suspect even after the Duke of Cumberland brought his army into the neighbourhood in March 1746, for the Jacobites continued to exact contributions of money, meal, straw and transport from lower Strathspey, all in agreement with the gentlemen of four of the parishes. Mrs Penuel Grant asked one of them 'to capitulate for me as you do for yourself, and I shall cause my tenants to observe the articles and terms of your capitulation regularly ... Colonel John Roy Stuart was my husband's friend and comrade before they were engaged in different sides, and am hopeful though they differ about kingcraft he will use his good offices to me on this melancholy occasion'.[24]

Ludovick Grant therefore carried little conviction when he assured the Duke of Cumberland that he could bring out 600 reasonably armed men in his support. Cumberland wrote to the Duke of Newcastle to complain that

> the general villainy and infidelity of the Highlands opens itself every day more, for whilst Lord Seaforth and Mr MacKenzie are with Lord Loudoun their wives are in open rebellion, and, to complete this scene, I yesterday was informed by Mylord Findlater [father-in-law of Ludovick] ... that the clan of Grants had accepted and signed a treaty of neutrality with the rebels, and had given hostages for the observance of it. I am almost certain that the reason of Mr [Ludovick] Grant's leaving the country and coming to me with those few men he brought, was to be out of the way when it was done.[25]

On instructions from London the duke told Lord Findlater to pass on to Ludovick the message that 'he and the forces under his command would use all those gentlemen who treat with the rebels, and refuse to obey you in serving their King and country, as rebels'.[26] Cumberland intended this missive to serve as a threat to Ludovick himself.

Ludovick soon gave further proof of his greatness of mind. On the day of Culloden, although he was absent from the field, he submitted an itemized statement of the expenses he had incurred on behalf of His Majesty in the course of the rebellion.[27] After the battle he persuaded the rebel Grants of Loch Ness to surrender on assurances of good treatment. He then stood aside when, owing to a 'misunderstanding', they were taken into custody and shipped to England under hideous conditions.

With the **Farquharsons** we reach the last clanned family of Aberdeenshire. These people were dedicated Episcopalians, and lived along the green valley of the Dee between Braemar and Cromar, but like the Gordons they were 'esteemed bad mimics of the real clans'.[28] The chief, John Farquharson of Invercauld, had come out for the Jacobites in 1715, but he was too old to respond to the call in 1745, which was instead answered on behalf of the clan by his nephew Francis Farquharson of Monaltrie. Another contribution of the Farquharsons was to have provided the Lady Anne who seduced the MacKintoshes from their loyalty to her husband, their chief.

In Perthshire the Highlands gave on to the Central Lowlands in a region of two great ducal estates, those of Perth and Atholl. The whole constituted a sweep of Highlands and Lowlands that extended in the one direction from Perth and Glenshee to the Trossachs, and in the other from the Ochils to Drumochter. The greater part could be counted as being in the Jacobite interest, though the swampy valley of the upper Forth proved resistant, which was probably due to the influence of the Graham Gentry and the Duke of Montrose, who decided to stay out of the quarrel.[29]

James Drummond, 3rd Duke of **Perth**, was the head of a Catholic and historically Jacobite family. He was deeply committed to the cause, and in addition to raising a regiment of mixed Highlanders and Lowlanders he became the Prince's spymaster and chief of intelligence. His mother, the fierce dowager duchess, meanwhile kept a close watch on the happenings in the neighbourhood of their home in Drummond Castle for the people of Crieff (although rehoused) remembered how the Jacobites had burnt their town as part of Lord Mar's 'scorched earth' policy when he was retreating in the face of the Duke of Argyll's forces in 1716.

The **Atholl** lands proper had a Highland character, but in 1670 the Earl of Atholl inherited the earldom and estates of Tullibardine, which by 1703 had become the Dukedom of Atholl. Together the Atholl estates extended along the Garry, the Tummel, the Tay, and down Strathardle, Glenalmond and Strathearn into the Lowlands, where the Ochils and the estate of Blairingone in Clackmannan formed ducal outposts. Nowadays the land of the dukes of Atholl is associated most immediately with the beautiful and continuous valley which is formed by the lower Garry and the middle Tay, and stretches from Blair Atholl (where the old castle was being remodelled in 1745) to the site of the new mansion at Dunkeld. The vale already wore a park-like aspect:

> The mountains, though very high, have an easy slope a good way up, and are cultivated in many places, and inhabited by tenants who, like those below, have a different air from other Highlanders in the goodness of the dress and the cheerfulness of their countenances.
>
> The strath, or vale, is wide, and beautifully adorned with plantations of various sorts of trees: the ways are smooth, and in one part, you ride in pleasant glades, in another you have an agreeable vista ... the satisfaction [writes Edmund Burt] seemed beyond comparison, by comparing it in our minds with the rugged ways and horrid prospect of the more northern mountains.[30]

These impressive landscapes did not prevent the Atholl holdings from having something of the cobbled-together and artificial about them. The Highlanders set great store by tradition, and they were aware that the local Stewart line of the old earls of Atholl had died out, and that the title had been taken up in 1629 by John Murray of Tullibardine, whose family was of Lowland origin. More significantly, the three elder surviving sons of the 1st Duke of Atholl (d. 1724) had fallen out among themselves, with the middle son, James, now being installed by the London government as the 2nd Duke, and his two brothers continuing to support the Jacobites. William, the eldest son, was recognized by Prince Charles as the lawful duke, while the youngest of the trio, the celebrated Lord George Murray, set himself up to be the military commander of the Jacobites in the '45.

On the evidence, the 'Hanoverian' Duke James was a nonentity in the style of the Duke of Gordon. On the approach of the Prince in 1745 he vacated Blair Castle, and left the management of his affairs in the hands of his factor, Thomas Bissett. In February the next year the Jacobites recoiled towards Inverness, and the Duke of Cumberland instructed his aide-de-camp Lieutenant Colonel Joseph Yorke to direct the reoccupation of Atholl. The language used on this occasion was revealing:

> The melancholy part of this story [so writes Yorke] is that there is no trusting to any people in this whole country to give intelligence; for they all abuse each other to indifferent people, but hold together in the national part of being Jacobites, or at least lukewarm, which I look upon in the same light exactly. The Presbyterian ministers are the only people we can trust, and to give you an idea of one small part of the country, I mean the county of Atholl, the minister, one Ferguson of Logierait, told me that if you were to hang throughout all that country indiscriminately, you would not hang three people wrongfully. I am grieved to say it is mostly so throughout the whole country of the hills, and if it is not rooted out now, you'll have another insurrection in two years' time.[31]

The redcoats arrived to occupy the Atholl lands, which were plainly regarded as reconquered hostile territory, to the extent that the men were instructed to present themselves at Dunkeld and at Kirkmichael in Strathardle 'to await His Grace's further orders'. Sir Andrew Agnew, as commander of the new garrison in Blair Castle, was told that Duke James was coming to take possession of his estate, and would supply him with the names of the local Jacobites. These were to be taken into custody, 'and you are to burn and entirely demolish their houses and habitations'.[32] The duke promised to raise 'five hundred good men who had not bowed their knee to Baal'.[33] He failed completely in this undertaking, just as 'all the men that he raised for Lord Loudoun's Regiment deserted with their officers to the rebels at the first breaking out of the rebellion'. Cumberland concluded that he carried no weight whatsoever in his own country.[34] The recruiting broke down altogether when Lord George Murray arrived on the scene in the course of his 'Atholl Raid', forced his brother to scamper to safety beyond the Pass of Killiecrankie, and besieged Agnew in Blair Castle.

With the Murrays feuding among themselves, we have to look unusually closely at the relations among the lairds and other traditional leaders of the local clans, in this case those of the **Menzies**, **Robertsons** (Clan Donnachaidh) and **Stewarts**. The Murrays had no blood relations among them, and both the Stewarts and the Robertsons were descended from the ancient Gaelic earls of Atholl, which gave them a certain moral advantage over the parvenu Murray dukes.

From the strategic point of view probably the most important estates were held by Sir Robert Menzies, who held lands extending south from his castle at Weem in fertile Strathtay, and along the northern shore of Loch Rannoch to the Moor itself, the bleak home of dispossessed MacGregors, MacDonalds and Camerons. Sir Robert was a large, bookish, placid and club-footed man who held to the government, and the initiative was snatched from him by a devoted Jacobite, his own factor, Archibald Menzies of Shian, who had an estate of his own up on Glen Quaich, but kept his eyes on affairs in Strathspey from his house of Farleyer. Shian's authority brought out the Clan Menzies for the Jacobites.

James Robertson of Blairfettie also declared for the Prince, and ancient allegiances of the Clan Donnachaid as far distant as Perth were raised in the same cause by the ancient and eccentric Alexander Robertson of Struan, whom many of the Robertsons still regarded as their blood chief. He led the Robertsons to Prestonpans and he returned in triumph to Atholl, wearing Cope's wolfskin coat and being dragged along in the general's coach by his clansmen. The Stewart lairds were by tradition Jacobite, and among the dozen who came out in the '45 the leading representatives were probably those of Kynachan, Grandtully and Ballachallan. The latter, David Stewart of Ballachallan, was a gentleman trooper in Strathallan's Perthshire Horse, and is described as being 'about five foot ten inches high, a black [swarthy] man, well set, not very fat, but well looked'.[35] However, force was much in evidence when it came to raising fighting men for the Prince, for this was a borderland society, and many otherwise sympathetic clansmen were under the influence of Lowland ways and the rule of law.

The Jacobite Army in Review

THE FORCES WHICH PRINCE CHARLES led into England late in 1745 were about nine-tenths Highland in character. Lord John Drummond had meanwhile been recruiting in Scotland, and incorporating reinforcements of regulars from France. Prince Charles and his men returned to Scotland on 20 December, and by the time of the battle of Falkirk (17 January 1746) the army had attained almost its full range of diversity, with a distinct 'layering' in the battle array:

❖ First Line: Highlanders, with the chiefs and the gentlemen in the first of the three ranks

❖ Second Line: Lowlanders

❖ Third Line: Franco-Irish and Franco-Scottish regulars, with small parties of horse.

CLAN OR PREDOMINANTLY HIGHLAND UNITS

Camerons of Lochiel
Commanded by Colonel Donald Cameron, Younger, of Lochiel, the effective chief. Joined Prince Charles at Glenfinnan on 19 August 1745. The largest and most important of the clan regiments, and prominent in all major actions – Prestonpans (up to 600), Falkirk (900, having been reinforced by 450 further Camerons brought up by Ludovick Cameron of Torcastle), Culloden (400).

Chisholms of Strathglass
A very small unit raised in and about Strathglass after the battle of Falkirk. About 30 of an estimated total of 80 were killed at Culloden.

Earl of Cromartie's
Raised by George, 3rd Earl of Cromartie, from his own estates, and from the Black Isle, Tain and Dingwall. Fought at Falkirk (200), but otherwise engaged in the north of Scotland, where it was ultimately wiped out at Dunrobin on 15 April 1746.

Frasers of Lovat
Commanded by Lieutenant Colonel Charles Fraser of Inverallachie, the Master of Lovat. Raised in the Fraser lands of Aberdeenshire in late October 1745. At Falkirk (500, with the Chisholms) and Culloden (400).

Gordon of Glenbucket's

Raised by old John Gordon of Glenbucket in Strathavon, Glenbucket, Strathbogie and the Cabrach in September 1745 (*c.* 400). On the invasion of England, and lost one company as part of the garrison left behind in Carlisle. In the trenches before Stirling at the time of Falkirk; in unknown strength in the second line at Culloden.

MacDonalds of Barrisdale

Formed by the unscrupulous Lieutenant Colonel Coll Ban MacDonald of Barrisadale, who was on detachment from the regiment of the MacDonnells of Glengarry. Took part in Cromartie's expedition to the far north, and unable to return in time for Culloden. A small unit of no great worth.

MacDonalds of Clanranald

Commanded by Colonel Ranald MacDonald, Younger, of Clanranald. The first body to rally to Prince Charles, and prominent in all episodes of the rising. At Prestonpans (200), Falkirk (350), Culloden (200). Predominantly Catholic.

MacDonnells of Glengarry

The clan chief, John MacDonnell, failed to come out, and the regiment was commanded initially by his second son, Angus MacDonnell, Younger. At Prestonpans (400). After the invasion of England reinforcements enabled the regiment to field two battalions at Falkirk (900). Angus was killed by accident immediately after the battle. Donald of Lochgarry assumed command, but the regiment had suffered a severe blow to morale. Barrisdale's battalion (above) was detached to the far north, leaving a single battalion (420) to fight on the left wing at Culloden, where it was hit very hard. Incorporated elements as diverse as the MacLeods of Bernera and Raasay, the Grants of Glen Moriston and Glen Urquhart, and the MacDonalds of Scotus. Second in size only to the Camerons, but not particularly well disciplined.

MacDonnells of Keppoch

Command by the clan chief, Colonel Alexander MacDonnell of Keppoch. Especially important in the early days of the rising. Alexander rallied to Prince Charles on 19 August 1745, and Major Donald MacDonnell of Tirnadris had opened hostilities in the action at Highbridge on the 16th. Reinforced by the MacKinnons of Skye under John Dubh MacKinnon of MacKinnon (up to 120), the MacDonalds of Glencoe and the Glengyle MacGregors. At Prestonpans (250), Falkirk (400), and at Culloden (200), where Keppoch was killed in heroic circumstances. He had no documentary title to his lands, which made for a certain instability in his regiment, as did the mixture of Catholics and Protestants. The most disorderly of all the clan units.

MacGregors

Raised in September 1745 by John MacGregor of Glengyle, Ewan MacGregor of

Glencarnock, and two sons of Rob Roy – James Mòr and Ronald. About 40 MacGregors fought alongside 160 men raised by the Duke of Perth (below). Sixty men remained under Glengyle at Doune, while the main force joined in the invasion of England. After the return to Scotland the MacGregors reunited at Stirling. Attached to Lochiel's Regiment at Falkirk. Some of the MacGregors were then committed against Loudoun in the far north, while the rest fought at Culloden. The survivors made their way home in large, defiant bodies.

'Colonel' Anne's MacKintoshes and Clan Chattan

Raised from late 1745 from the MacKintoshes and many smaller elements by Lady Anne Farquharson of Invercauld, in defiance of her husband and clan chief Aeneas MacIntosh. Commanded by Alexander MacGillivray of Dunmaglass. Joined the army in January 1746. At Falkirk (300) and Culloden (350).

MacLachlans

Commanded by the 17th chief, Colonel Lachlan MacLachlan of MacLachlan. Incorporated the nearby MacLeans. A small but brave regiment which fought at Prestonpans (100), Falkirk, and at Culloden, where Lachlan was killed.

MacPhersons of Cluny

Raised in Badenoch by Ewan MacPherson of Cluny, who had commanded a company of Loudoun's 64th Highlanders, but went over to the Jacobites after having been captured by them in August 1745. Prominent in the invasion of England. Fought at Clifton, and at Falkirk (400), but were guarding the communications at Inverness at the time of Culloden.

Stewarts of Appin

Commanded by Charles Stewart of Ardsheal, by reputation a vigorous and dedicated Jacobite, though described by a Hanoverian spy as 'a big fat man, troubled with lethargy'.[1] Incorporated many members of allied family groups, and fought at Prestonpans (200, possibly including the company of MacGregors), Falkirk (300), and at Culloden (250), where the clan banner (blue silk field with yellow saltire) was rescued by Donald Livingstone, and was therefore spared the general combustion of the Jacobite flags by the public hangman. The regiment's performance was impressive, considering the diminutive size of the core clan.

MIXED OR LOWLAND UNITS

Atholl Brigade

Raised from the Atholl tenants, and from the southern Highland lands of Menzies of Weems, Menzies of Shian, Robertson of Struan and the Stewart gentlemen. The three battalions were commanded respectively by Lord George Murray, Lord Nairne and Duncan Robertson of Struan. Fought at Prestonpans (250), Falkirk (900) and Culloden (500), and had the leading part in the Atholl Raid. Large and important.

Bannerman of Elsick's

An independent company raised in the Mearns by Sir Alexander Bannerman, 3rd Baronet of Elsick. Fought at Inverurie in a strength of about 100. In the second line at Culloden, and escaped mostly intact to the north of Scotland where the survivors settled around Dingwall and in Sutherland.

Lord Lewis Gordon's

A large force, always termed a 'regiment', though its structure qualified it as a brigade. It comprised:

❖ Crichton of Auchengoul's Company, raised in Aberdeenshire, the Highland battalion of Lieutenant Colonel Francis Farquharson of Monaltrie. Fought at Inverurie (*c.* 200), and in the first line at Falkirk (150) and Culloden (150).

❖ The Lowland battalion of Lieutenant Colonel John Gordon of Avochie (400) raised in the Strathbogie. In the second line at Falkirk and Culloden.

The recruiting methods of Lord Lewis were particularly brutal, and the regiment included an unusually large number of men who had been enlisted by force.

The Duke of Perth's

Commanded by James Drummond, Duke of Perth. The original core was raised by the MacGregors (above), and the battalion was distinguished at Prestonpans (300, including about 40 MacGregors). Many prisoners were incorporated after the battle, but most of them soon deserted. John Hamilton raised a Lowland battalion in Aberdeenshire in time for the invasion of England, which brought the total to about 750. On the retreat Hamilton and half his battalion were left behind in Carlisle and were lost. Not engaged at Falkirk, and the two battalions fought as an amalgamated unit at Culloden.

Lord Ogilvy's Regiment

First raised in Forfarshire through the local prestige of young David, Lord Ogilvy, the heir to the house of Airlie. The original unit (200) took part in the invasion of England, while Lieutenant Colonel Sir James Kinloch raised a second battalion (300) which fought at Inverurie, and helped to secure the eastern coast for landings from France. The reunited regiment was engaged at Falkirk (900) and Culloden (*c.* 500). The regiment was probably the best drilled and disciplined unit which the Jacobites ever raised in Scotland, and it retired intact from the field of Culloden.

John Roy Stuart's Edinburgh Regiment
Raised after Prestonpans by Colonel John Roy Stuart, one of the few Jacobite officers with experience of regular service. The elements were very disparate – Edinburgh townsmen, English deserters and fifty Strathbraan men drafted from the Atholl Brigade. The little regiment took part in the invasion of England and the siege of Stirling Castle, and fought at Culloden (200).

ENGLISH VOLUNTEERS

The Manchester Regiment (up to 250, reducing to 118)
Raised in Lancashire and Manchester by Colonel Francis Townley. Marched to Derby, but depleted by desertion, and lost almost in its entirety with the rest of the garrison of Carlisle. Most of the rank and file suffered deportation, and Townley and nearly all his officers and NCO were executed in grisly circumstances. Among those who paid with his life was Thomas Chadwick. 'When the rebels first came to Manchester the defendant put on a plaid waistcoat, laced hat, and white cockade, and enlisted in the Manchester Regiment as a lieutenant, and was busy there enlisting men. The defendant marched to Derby and back to Carlisle, armed with a brace of pistols and a small sword and gun ... In the churches at Derby and Lancaster the defendant played several tunes upon the organ – amongst others that called *The 29th of May*, or *The King Shall Enjoy His Own Again*, which made him much esteemed by all the officers of the rebels.'[2]

CAVALRY

Lord Strathallan's Perthshire Horse
The original unit of Jacobite cavalry, raised in Perthshire in early September 1745 by William Drummond, 4th Viscount Strathallan. At Prestonpans (where the Jacobites had no other cavalry) it was posted at Tranent to guard the prisoners. Incorporated with Kilmarnock's Horse Guards for the invasion of England. The two units separated again after the retreat to Scotland. In the reserve at Falkirk. Numbered 82 in February 1746, though many of the men were dismounted. At Culloden joined Baggot's Hussars in a combined strength of only 75; Strathallan was killed in hand-to-hand combat.

Lifeguards
Raised after Prestonpans. Both troops were uniformed splendidly in blue coats turned up with red and brass buttons, scarlet waistcoats with gold lace, tricorn hats with gold lace, and shoulder belts mounted with tartan. The Lifeguards provided the ceremonial escort for Prince Charles, but also carried out important reconnaissance and diversionary functions.

❖ First (Lord Elcho's Troop): The first and always the stronger of the two troops, raised by David, Lord Elcho, as colonel. He was 'young, smooth-faced, inclined to fat, and passionate and wore a fox-skin cap with the ears pricked up, which made him, on horseback, at the head of his men, look very formidable'.[3] The troop reached a strength of 125 (the equivalent of a good squadron), but by the time of Culloden it had been reduced to 30 or 40 mounted men, and was brigaded with FitzJames' Horse. Some of the dismounted men probably served with Kilmarnock's Foot Guards

❖ Second (Lord Balmerino's Troop): The second troop was to have been commanded by Lord Kenmure, who deserted before he could take charge. He was replaced by the Hon. Arthur Elphinstone, who became 6th Lord Balmerino upon the death of his elder brother in January 1746. The troop numbered 40 before the invasion of England, but sank to 16 at Culloden, where it provided Prince Charles's mounted escort. Lord Balmerino was captured, and he made a defiant show at his execution on Tower Hill.

Lord Kilmarnock's Horse Guards (30–50)

Raised after Prestonpans by the near-bankrupt William Boyd, 4th Earl of Kilmarnock. Temporarily incorporated Strathallan's Horse for the invasion of England. In February Kilmarnock turned over the horses to FitzJames' Horse, and his little unit was trans-mogrified into the Foot Guards. Recruiting had always suffered from the competition offered by the glamorous Lifeguards, who succeeded in raising troopers even in the neighbourhood of Kilmarnock's home town of Falkirk.

Lord Pitsligo's Horse (132)

Raised in Aberdeenshire by the old Alexander Forbes, 4th Earl of Pitsligo. On 9 October 1745 it entered Edinburgh to a notable welcome, and was described as a squadron consisting of '132 knights, freeholders and landed gentlemen, besides their servants, all extremely well mounted and accoutred. They are all gentlemen of experience, and are mostly above forty years of age'.[4] Pitsligo's Horse was active in the invasion of England, but took little part at Falkirk, and in February its horses were ruined by the retreat from Aberdeen through the snow. The surviving mounts were turned over to FitzJames' Horse, and most of the men absorbed into Kilmarnock's Foot Guards.

The Hussars (80)

Raised under the nominal command of John Murray of Broughton, Prince Charles's secretary of state. The Hussars ran away at Clifton on 18 December 1745, but became more effective, if less socially exclusive, when they were taken in hand by the

Franco-Irish major Matthew Baggot, described variously as a 'very rough sort of man, and so exceedingly well fitted to command the banditti of which that corps was composed'[5] and 'a wise, courageous and virtuous man, [who] behaved himself in his station to the admiration of all, regulating his corps with such order as to make our enemies and the country, even fifty miles distant from us, have more fear of them than almost the whole army'.[6] Heavily engaged at Culloden alongside Strathallan's Horse; Baggot was wounded and captured. The Hussars had a very distinctive dress of short coats, long and close-fitting tartan waistcoats, and a Tartar-style cap with a fur rim, and a long red tail or plume.

UNITS FROM THE REGULAR FRENCH SERVICE

Royal Ecossais (400)

Raised in France in 1744 by Lord George Drummond, brother of the Duke of Perth. Landed at Montrose on 24 and 25 November 1745 as part of a larger embarkation which was intercepted by the Royal Navy. Wore white breeches and gaiters, but also short blue coats and blue bonnets in the Highland style. Its picquets and grenadier company were largely responsible for the little victory at Inverurie, and formed a composite battalion with the Irish infantry at Falkirk. The regiment was present as a unit at Culloden, by when its complement had fallen to 300 or less.

The Irish Picquets of the Regiments of Dillon, Lally and Roth

In this context the term 'picquets' derives from the eighteenth-century practice of drawing small elements from all available units when it was a question of making up a force for detached and potentially hazardous service. This precaution prevented any one unit being wiped out in the event of a catastrophe – a wise precaution in this case, for the expedition to Scotland was made up of a reinforced picquet company from each of the six regiments of foot of the Irish Brigade, and half of them were captured on board *Le Louis XV* on 28 November 1745. However, three picquets, to the total of 150 officers and men, had been landed a couple of days earlier at Montrose, Stonehaven and Peterhead, and the complement was brought up to 300 by local recruiting, especially from Hanoverian prisoners and deserters. Colonel Walter Stapleton acted as brigadier, and commanded the Irish with great distinction. They helped to keep matters in hand during the disorganized later stages of the battle of Falkirk, and Prince Charles testified that afterwards 'the Irish officers were of vast use in going through the different posts of the army, and assisting in the various dispositions that were made'.[7] The continuing siege of Stirling cost the Irish dearly, 'since all the labour fell upon them, the Highlanders not wishing on any account to get involved'.[8]

A Scottish officer commented that on the abortive night march on Nairn on 15 April 1746 the Highlanders made good progress, but the Irish picquets in the rear were 'not so clever in marching, and the muir they went through was more splashy than they expected, and they were obliged to make some turns to shun houses and there were two or three dykes that took up a good deal of time to pass'.[9] On the next day at Culloden the Irish infantry helped to save the Clan Donald from complete destruction. Stapleton was mortally wounded, there were casualties among his men, and the survivors were taken prisoner. The Irish infantry wore coats of red, but cut in the same voluminous style as those of the French regulars.

FitzJames' Horse (130)

Part of a much larger intended contingent of Irish horse, this squadron of heavy cavalry reached Aberdeen safely on 22 February 1745. Its horses together with the other three squadrons were intercepted by the Royal Navy three days later, and Kilmarnock's Horse Guards had to yield up its animals in order to mount the Irish. Hard service reduced the effectives to about seventy by the time of Culloden, where the Irish were positioned alongside Elcho's Lifeguards on the right wing of the second line.

Apart from their iron breastplates, painted black, the Irish troopers were uniformed almost identically with their enemy dragoons, with red coats turned up with royal blue, tin buttons, and buckskin breeches. Indeed, the troops of the Irish Brigade as a whole wore coats of the same red that had been inherited from the army of James II in the 1690s.

Orders of Battle

Within each line the sequence of formations and units is from right to left

Prestonpans, 21 Sep 1745

JACOBITES (SINGLE LINE AND RES)

Duke of Perth's Division: Clan Donald regiments of Clanranald, Glengarry and Keppoch

Lord George Murray's Division: regiments of Perth, Appin Stewarts and Camerons

Reserve: Atholl Brigade, cavalry of Lord Strathallan and Sir John MacDonald

HANOVERIANS (LT GEN COPE)

Infantry Line (Col Lascelles) Lee's 55th, Murray's 57th, Lascelles' 58th, Murray's 43rd, Loudoun's 64th

Dragoons: Gardiner's 13th, Hamilton's 14th

Artillery (Major Griffith and Lt Col Whiteford) 6 1½-pdrs, 4 coehorns

Falkirk, 17 Jan 1746

JACOBITES

First Line Lord George Murray's Division: Clan Donald regiments of Keppoch, Clanranald and Glengarry; regiments of Appin Stewarts, Camerons, Farquharsons, Cromartie (precise order uncertain)

Second Line Atholl Brigade (3 bns); regiments of Ogilvy and Gordon

Reserve Irish picquets and Royal Ecossais

Cavalry Regiments of Elcho, Balmerino, Pitsligo, Kilmarnock and Hussars

HANOVERIANS (Lt Gen Hawley)

First Line Ligonier's 59th, Price's 14th, Royal Scots (1st of Foot), Pulteney's 13th, Cholmondeley's 34th, Wolfe's 8th

Second Line Battereau's 62nd, Barrell's 4th, Fleming's 36th, Munro's 37th, Blakeney's 27th, Howard's 3rd

Locally raised Forces

Right Rear: Lt Col Campbell of Mamore's coys of 43rd (Black Watch, one), Loudon's 64th (three), Campbell Militia (twelve)

Left Rear: Glasgow Regiment and Paisley Volunteers, With Artillery Train:Yorkshire Blues

Cavalry Dragoon regiments of Cobham's 10th, Ligonier's (late Gardiner's) 13th, Hamilton's 14th

Artillery (Capt Cunningham) About seven cannon

Culloden, 17 April 1746

JACOBITES

First Line Lord George Murray's Division: Atholl Brigade (3 bns), regiments of Camerons and Robertsons, Appin Stewarts

Lord John Drummond's Division: regiments or compound units of Frasers, Mackintoshes, Monaltrie's bn of Aberdeen, MacLeans and MacLachlans, Chishoms

Duke of Perth's Division: Clan Donald regiments of Keppoch, Clanranald and Glengarry

2nd Line or Reserve (John Roy Stuart) Regiments of Gordon (2 bns), Royal Ecossais, Ogilvy, Edinburgh (John Roy Stuart), Kilmarnock's Footguards, Glenbucket, Perth, Irish picquets

Cavalry Lifeguards, FitzJames' Horse, Hussars, Strathallan

Artillery (Capt Finlayson) 11 3-pdr cannon 1 4-pdr cannon

HANOVERIANS

Mixed Advance Guard (Maj Gen Bland) Ballimore's Highland Bn Cobham's 10th Dragoons, Kerr's 11th Dragoons

First Line (Lt Gen Albemarle) Regiments of Royal Scots (1st of Foot), Cholmondeley's 34th, Price's 14th, Royal Scots Fusiliers (21st), Munro's 27th, Barrell's 4th

Second Line (Maj Gen Huske) Howard's 3rd, Fleming's 36th, Bligh's 20th, Sempill's 25th, Ligonier's 59th, Wolfe's 8th

Reserve (Brig Mordaunt) Pulteney's 13th, Battereau's 62nd, Blakeney's 27th Kingston's 10th Light Horse (divided between the two wings)

Artillery (Maj Belford) 10 3-pdrs, six coehorns

The Skies: Scotland's Weather, 8 July 1745 – 16 April 1746

THE SECTION 'THE SKIES' (pp. 380–91) INCORPORATES a whole range of available meteorological data, including the diary entries of scientifically minded professional men and gentry, and comments made by participants in the '45. Material is presented in a more systematic way in the logs maintained by the officers of His Majesty's Ships which operated around the British Isles in this period. Both operational effectiveness and physical survival depended on a correct reading of the weather, and the officers entered their observations twice every twenty-four hours. The terms used in the logs are limited but consistent, and lend themselves to a simplified version of the standard meteorological symbols, and in turn to the kind of map which appears in newspapers and on television. There are six renditions of wind velocity, namely 'calm', 'light', 'moderate', 'fresh', 'strong' and (very rare) 'hard', which became the basis of the later Beaufort Scale, but do not translate directly into that scheme.

Thanks to the configuration of the British Isles, many of the ships spent their time not only at sea, but also 'inland' at locations like Greenock on the Clyde, Leith on the Firth of Forth, and Woolwich on the Thames not far below London. The most representative logs have been found to have been those of His Majesty's Ships *Baltimore, Eltham, Gloucester, Granado, Greyhound, Hawk, Lion, Milford, Pearl, Scarborough, Serpent, Syren* and *Terror.*

The data has been incorporated in the narrative and maps which appear in Chapter 14, but in the present Appendix applied more particularly to the weather in Scotland. The percentages given are those of the readings. It will be seen that the winter arrived unseasonably late, but hit eastern Scotland very hard in early spring.

WESTERN SCOTLAND

July
General: A sunny month, with sun at 46.8% and rain only 10.4%. Mainly moderate winds, with westerly predominating by 69.4%

August
General: Weather not so favourable, with rain at 43.6% and sun just 30.0%. Winds again on the moderate side, but fresh at 27.8%. Westerly predominating by only 0.96%

September
General: A balmy autumn month, with sun at 57.6% and rain at 7.6%. Moderate winds at 45.0%, with east and west registering equally

October
General: Almost equal balance of sun and cloud (without rain) at 32.1% each, and rain at 30.3%. A windy month, with fresh accounting for 28.8% and strong for 30.7%. W winds predominated by 19.3%, with SW accounting for 27.4% of the total

November
General: A foretaste of winter. Sun 30.3%, cloud (without rain) 42.8%, rain only 10.6%, but first appearance of snow at 8.9%. E winds predominated by 22.0%

December
General: Sun 32.0%, cloud (without rain) 22.6%, rain 26.4%, snow only 3.7%. It is evident that true wintry weather had still to arrive. Winds mainly light to fresh, with easterly predominating by 19.2%, and especially from the SE

January
General: Sun 25.7%, cloud (without rain) 24.2%, rain 31.8%, snow still low at only 6.0%. A generally windy month, with strong registering 36.0%, and hard 19.6%. W winds predominated by 28.5%

February
General: Sun 32.6%, cloud (without rain) 26.5%, rain 28.5%, snow still unseasonably low at just 2.0%. Winds mainly moderate and fresh, with E predominating by 12.1%

March
General: Sun 43.9%, cloud (without rain) 27.2%, rain 10.6%, snow 6.0% – almost as much as in January. Characteristic winds moderate to fresh, with E predominating by 48.0%

April 1–16
General: Fine spring weather, with sun at 60.4%, cloud (without rain) and rain at 16.6% each, and no snow. Mainly light to moderate winds, with E predominating by 37.1%

EASTERN SCOTLAND

8 July to 24 October
Insufficient data from logs

25–31 October
General: Calm late autumn weather. Virtually rainless, with sun obscured by haze at 60% rather than cloud at 40%. E winds predominated by 45.3%

November

General: Sun 34.5%, cloud (without rain) 13.5%, rain 16.0%, haze a considerable 27.1%, snow only 4.9% but heavy on the days it fell. Winds light, with W predominating by 24.3%

December

General: Sun 22.2%, cloud (without rain) 36.1%, rain 20.0%, haze 24.4%, no snow recorded in the logs. A windy month, with fresh at 44.2%. E predominated by 33.3%

January

General: Sun 43.3%, cloud (without rain) 36.1%, rain 9.6%, snow a low 4.8%. Mainly moderate and fresh winds. W winds predominated by 17.7%

February

General: Sun 21.6%, cloud (without rain) 23.4%, rain 15.3%. The snow at 20.7% indicated that the winter had at last begun to bite. Winds mainly light and fresh. W winds predominated by 5.5%

March

General: Sun 13.3%, cloud (without rain) and rain 23.4 each, snow a heavy 17.0%. E winds predominated by 71.0%. The winter finally arrived in full force early in the month, but a pronounced (and militarily significant) thaw set in from the 12th

April 1–16

General: Sun 48.6%, cloud (without rain) 19.7%, rain 14.4%, no recorded snow. Generally light winds (50.0%), E predominating by 56.8%. A period of tame weather, with one local but highly important exception

Patterns: Light winds interspersed with calms, with fair weather, occasional haze and cloud prevailed from the 1st to the 6th, with rain off Peterhead on the 4th, and cloud off Banff on the 5th. On the 7th there was cloud and haze in the Moray Firth, and rain followed by sun at Edinburgh. Easterly winds set in on the 8th, with haze and fog on that day, haze and cloud on the 9th, cloud, haze and rain on the 10th and (with sunny spells) on the 11th and 12th. The winds on the 13th were light and calm NE to SE, with sun on the southern shore of the Moray Firth, but cloud further north. E and NE winds on the Moray Firth 14th, with cloud, haze and showers, but a light SE wind at Aberdeen with sun. A strong ENE wind with haze and squalls of rain blew along the southern shore of the Moray Firth on the 15th (when the Jacobites undertook the night march on the camp of Nairn), and again on the 16th (the day of Culloden).

Percentages of Log Readings

WESTERN SCOTLAND

	8–31 July	Aug	Sep	Oct	Nov	Dec	Jan	Feb	Mar	April
Sky										
Sun	46.8	30.9	57.6	32.1	30.3	32.0	25.7	32.6	43.9	60.4
Cloud (without rain)	29.7	25.4	21.1	32.1	42.8	22.6	24.2	26.5	27.2	16.6
Rain	10.6	43.6	13.4	30.3	10.6	26.4	31.8	28.5	10.6	16.6
Haze	12.1	–	7.6	5.3	3.5	15.0	12.1	6.1	12.1	6.2
Fog	–	–	–	–	3.5	–	–	4.0	–	–
Snow	–	–	–	–	8.9	3.7	6.0	2.0	6.0	–
Wind Velocity										
Calm	2.2	6.5	9.8	–	3.6	6.8	3.2	2.1	–	–
Light	20.0	16.3	17.6	17.3	43.6	24.1	6.5	17.0	20.6	36.3
Moderate	57.7	39.3	45.0	23.0	27.2	25.8	34.4	31.9	41.3	47.7
Fresh	20.0	27.8	17.6	28.8	12.7	29.3	36.0	31.9	35.3	15.9
Strong	–	9.8	9.8	30.7	12.7	13.7	19.6	17.0	2.5	–
Hard	–	–	–	–	–	–	–	–	–	–
Wind Direction										
N	12.7	–	–	3.2	–	–	3.0	2.0	–	4.1
NNE	6.3	1.5	–	–	1.8	–	–	4.0	2.3	2.0
NE	2.1	7.8	3.9	3.2	15.0	3.4	6.1	–	14.2	25.0
ENE	2.1	7.8	–	–	3.7	1.7	–	8.1	11.1	18.7
E	–	6.2	3.9	6.4	11.3	5.1	1.5	6.1	4.7	4.1
ESE	–	–	5.8	–	5.6	3.4	4.6	2.0	8.7	–
SE	2.1	14.0	17.6	16.1	15.0	20.6	6.1	14.2	7.9	4.1
SSE	–	6.2	9.8	11.2	5.6	13.7	10.6	12.2	15.8	4.1
S	4.2	1.5	9.8	4.8	1.8	12.0	7.6	4.0	7.1	4.1
SSW	–	6.2	3.9	8.0	3.7	6.8	9.2	6.1	3.9	2.0
SW	8.5	23.4	27.4	27.4	9.4	13.7	15.3	4.0	5.5	14.5
WSW	19.1	1.5	3.9	–	–	8.6	7.6	2.0	1.5	2.0
W	12.7	6.2	1.9	9.6	5.6	–	6.1	6.1	0.7	2.0
WNW	4.2	–	–	1.6	1.8	1.7	1.5	2.0	2.3	2.0
NW	8.5	6.2	3.9	8.0	7.5	1.7	12.3	10.2	3.9	4.1
NNW	17.0	1.5	–	–	7.5	–	–	6.1	4.7	–
Variable/ calm	–	9.3	8.0	–	3.7	6.8	7.6	10.2	4.7	6.2

EASTERN SCOTLAND

	25–31 Oct	Nov	Dec	Jan	Feb	Mar	April
Sky							
Sun	–	34.5	22.2	43.3	21.6	13.3	48.6
Cloud (without rain)	40.0	13.5	33.3	36.1	23.4	23.4	19.7
Rain	–	16.0	20.0	9.6	15.3	23.4	14.4
Haze	60.0	27.1	24.4	6.0	15.3	20.2	11.8
Fog	–	3.7	–	–	3.6	2.12	5.2
Snow	–	4.9	–	4.8	20.7	17.0	–
Wind Velocity							
Calm	77.7	3.9	1.9	1.5	3.1	2.5	9.3
Light	22.2	39.4	13.4	6.2	31.2	13.9	50.0
Moderate	–	27.6	28.8	35.9	23.9	40.5	25.0
Fresh	–	18.4	44.2	42.1	32.3	39.2	15.6
Strong	–	10.7	9.6	14.0	9.3	2.5	–
Hard	–	–	1.9	–	1.0	1.2	–
Wind Direction							
N	–	1.3	1.6	1.1	5.5	3.4	1.6
NNE	5.3	4.9	2.3	5.5	1.1	3.2	
NE	10.0	2.6	11.4	2.3	6.4	7.9	19.6
ENE	–	6.6	3.2	–	3.6	6.8	13.1
E	30.0	5.3	3.2	1.1	8.2	9.0	8.1
ESE	10.0	1.3	4.9	–	1.8	5.6	9.8
SE	10.0	8.0	24.5	2.3	8.2	26.1	9.8
SSE	20.0	3.0	9.8	4.7	5.5	17.0	1.6
S	–	1.3	3.2	2.3	3.6	3.4	1.6
SSW	–	3.0	4.9	3.5	0.9	1.1	3.2
SW	10.0	5.3	18.0	22.6	3.6	2.2	–
WSW	–	5.3	1.6	28.5	0.9	2.2	6.5
W	10.0	14.6	3.2	8.3	9.1	1.1	–
WNW	–	12.0	–	7.1	1.8	–	1.6
NW	–	10.6	3.2	9.5	13.7	2.2	3.2
NNW	–	2.6	–	–	13.7	3.4	3.2
Variable/calm	–	9.3	1.6	3.5	7.3	6.8	13.1

Scottish, Northern English and Period Vocabulary and Usages

PLACE NAMES IN GAELIC (here rendered in italics) are usually very specific, and an acquaintance with some of the more common terms will often give a clue to the local geography.

aber: river mouth

achadh: field

aig: bay

allt: stream

annat: church

aonach: hill

àrd: high

argethian: an adjectival form of 'Argyll,' applied to the management of the Scottish political system by the 2nd Duke of Argyll in the first half of the eighteenth century

auchter, ochter: upper part of

bàgh: bay

ballach, bealach, belloch: mountain saddle, pass

barmkin: outer enclosure wall of stronghold, usually for retaining cattle

beag, beg: small

ben, beinn: mountain

bie, by: settlement

blair, blàr: battlefield, plain

boll: unit of weight, corresponding to a heavy hundredweight

bost: farmstead

brae: steep slope, hillside

buie: yellow, as in Drambuie, the liqueur

bun: foot, or bottom of; river mouth

caddy: porter, messenger

Callum: Malcolm

caol: narrows

carr, carse: low-lying ground along a water course, often swampy

clachan: settlement around a church

close: narrow passageway between buildings, usually covered

cleugh, clough: narrow valley, ravine

coile, coll: wood

coire: corrie, glaciated hollow towards a mountain top

condescension: (period) consideration shown by a superior

corps: (period) regiment

craig, creag: rock

dal, dale: valley

doocot: dove cot

dyke: wall, esp. of loose stones; not, as usual in England, ditch, the retaining embankment of a watercourse

eilean: island

enthusiastic: (period) fanatical

factor: estate manager, usually a more considerable figure than his English counterpart

fermtoun: farm, small settlement

gale: (period) could be applied in the eighteenth century to any wind, regardless of velocity. Thus 'Cool gales shall fan the glade' did not imply that the beloved was to be swept away by an icy blast

gate: street. Very common usage in places of Danish influence, where 'gate', in the sense of entrance, is often rendered as 'port'

gleann, glen: narrow valley, as opposed to *strath* (below)

haugh, heugh: open field, meadow – often damp

inch, innis: meadow, island

inner, inver: river mouth

kil: church

knock: knoll

kyle: narrow strait

laggan: small hollow

law: rounded hill

letter: steep slope

liath: bluish grey, wolf-coloured

loan: grassy lane

loch: body of water; not necessarily identical with the English 'lake', because sometimes connected with the sea

lochan: small loch

luib: bend

machair: sandy fields behind coast

mains: home farm of larger estate

manse: clergyman's house

Master of: term applied to eldest son of baronet

meal, meall, meol: rounded hill

meal: oatmeal

mercat cross: market cross; the symbolic gathering place of a town, esp. for proclamations

merse: flat land along coast or estuary

monadh: hill, mountain ridge

moor, muir: upland waste

mór: big

nan: of the

nervous: (period) strong

ness, *nish*: cape, headland

odhar: pron. almost as 'oo-ar', tawny yellow, as of bracken in winter

outrageous: (period) as applied to stream or river, liable to overflow banks

passenger: (period) any traveller, including travellers proceeding on foot or on horseback

pathetic: (period) moving

pend: covered passage

philibeg: kilt, as opposed to the voluminous wrap-around plaid

Piskie. Episcopalian

policy: plantation

port: gate of town

rannoch: bracken

roy, ruadh: red

rig, rigg: ridge, raised strip of ploughland between furrows

Sandy: Alexander

security: (period) over-confidence

sgorr, sgurr: steep hill or mountain

shambles: butcher's stall

shieling: summer pasture

slach, sloch, slochd: hollow between hills

strath: wide valley, nearly always coupled with name of relevant stream or river

tarf, tarff: bull

thwait: clearing

tolbooth: originally the literal meaning, but by the eighteenth century had evolved into town hall, often with court of justice, prison and other appurtenances

toun, tun: farm

tron: public weigh beam

tullie, tulloch, tully: little hill

uamh, weem: cave

vennel: alley

wath: ford

wind, wynd: lane, pronounced as in 'winding'

Some Pronunciations

'ea' in Gaelic names: 'ay' as in 'slay', thus 'Rea' sounds as 'Ray'

Badenoch: 'Baydenoch', with stress on the first syllable

Bernera: 'Bernaira', with stress on the second syllable

Cholmondeley: 'Chumley'

Corrieyairack: 'Corry-Yarrick'

Culloden: in Scotland the 'o' is pronounced as in 'lodge'

Fiennes: 'Fines'

Gaelic: 'Gallic'

Glamis: 'Glarms'

Grosvenor: 'Grovenor'

Kingussie: 'Kingoosie'

Menzies: 'Mingies'

Morar: 'Mow-Ar'

Muthill: the 'th' sounded as in 'other'

Powrie: 'Poo-Ree'

Ruthven: 'Riven'

Stanhope: 'Stannup'

Wemyss: 'Weems'

The 'y' in the 'ay' suffix in the northern islands should not be pronounced; thus Islay is pronounced as 'Isler,' not 'Islay' as spelt

Some Duplications and Near-Duplications

Callendar House (near Falkirk); Callander town

Cheadle (Cheshire); Cheadle (Staffordshire)

Meggernie Castle (Glen Lyon); Mingary Castle (Ardnamurchan)

Moy Hall (south of Inverness); Moy House (near Fort William); Moy House (by Findhorn Bay)

Nairn (river and little town); Nairne (Lord and Lady)

Newcastle under Lyme (Staffordshire); Newcastle upon Tyne (Northumberland)

Richmond (Surrey); Richmond (Yorkshire)

Notes

Abbreviations

CP   Cumberland Papers, Royal Archives, Windsor
         Castle
DoC   Duke of Cumberland
DoN   Duke of Newcastle
Fawk   Sir Everard Fawkener
NP   Newcastle Papers, British Library, Add. Ms.
         32,705, 32,706
SHAT   Service Historique de l'Armée de Terre, Vincennes
SP   State Papers Domestic, Public Record Office, Kew
TS   Papers of the Treasury Solicitor, Public Record
         Office, Kew

PREFACE

East Lothian, 19–21 September 1745

1. Whitefoord, 1898, 93

2. SP 36/38, Deposition of Richard Jack,
21 September 1745

3. Carlyle, 1860, I, 180

4. Elcho, 1907, 266

5. *The Caledonian Mercury*, 23 September 1745,
letter from the headquarters of Prince Charles, 21
September 1745

6. Chambers, 1869, 114

7. Norie, 1901, II, 77–8

8. TS 20/88, testimony of Alan Stewart, Whitehall, 7
August 1746

9. Johnstone, 1822, 32

10. O'Sullivan, 1938, 77

11. *A Report of the Proceedings of Lieutenant General
Cope*, 1749, 86–7

12. The church at Tranent was much enlarged in
1799–1800, and in Victorian times the churchyard was extended about 20 yards to the east

13. Carlyle, 1860, I, 140

14. Henderson, 1748, 29

15. Lascelles, in *A Report of the Proceedings of
Lieutenant General Cope*, 1749, 65

16. Carlyle, 1860, I, 140–41

17. Crichton (*Woodhouselee MS*), 1907, 38

18. CP 9/152, 'A Narrative of the Behaviour and
Conduct of Colonel Peregrine Lascelles at the
Battle of Preston'

19. 'Journal and Memoirs of P…C… Expedition',

Lockhart Papers, 1817, II, 490

20. CP 6/111, Lieutenant Colonel Whitney to
Colonel Lascelles, Berwick, 11 October 1745

21. CP 9.152, 'A Narrative of the Behaviour and
Conduct of Colonel Peregrine Lascelles at the
Battle of Preston'

22. Marchant, 1746, 105

23. *The Westminster Journal*, 22 March 1746; Norie,
1901, II, 100

24. Crichton (*Woodhouselee MS*), 1907, 38–9

25. Carlyle, 1860, I, 143

26. Crichton (*Woodhouselee MS*), 1907, 38

27. Rev. John Waugh to Dr Bettesworth, Carlisle, 21
September 1745, Moundsey, 1856, 24

28. Rev. John Waugh to Dr Bettesworth, Carlisle, 2
October 1745, Ibid., 27

29. *The General Advertiser*, 1 November 1745, Letter
from a Lady in Edinburgh to her Daughter in
London; *The Caledonian Mercury*, 8 November
1745

30. Henderson, 1748, 32

31. 'Journal and Memoirs of P…C…Expedition',
Lockhart Papers, 1817, II, 449–50

32. Henderson, 1748, 31

33. SP 36/79, 'Extract from a Letter from an English
Officer, now Prisoner at Perth', undated

34. CP 6/111, Lieutenant Colonel Whitney to
Colonel Lascelles, Berwick, 11 October 1745

Introduction

1. Defoe [1724–6], 1927, II, 727

2. Johnson [1775], 1996, 33. For a similar response
see CP 9/55, Alexander Robertson to Fawk,
Perth, 10 January 1746

3. Burt [1754], 1818, II, 245, 285

PART ONE

CHAPTER 1

The Historical Setting

1. Burt [1754], 1818, II, 225

2. Defoe [1724–6], 1927, II, 541

3. Quoted in Lenman and Gibson, 1990, 94

4. Vernon to Lord Vere Beauclerk, *Royal George* in the Downs, 27 September 1745, 'Vernon Papers', 1757, 470–71

5. Lenman, 1984, 77

6. John Clerk of Penicuik, 1912, 91

7. For this argument see Sankey and Szechi, 2001, No. 3, passim

8. Wade to George I, in Burt [1754], 1818, II, 281, 276

9. Lieutenants' logs of the *Lion*, National Maritime Museum, Greenwich, Adm/L/129

10. *More Culloden Papers*, 1923–30, IV, 10

11. Ibid., IV, 12

CHAPTER 2

The Divided Lands:
England, Wales and Ireland

1. *The Penny London Post*, 28 September – 1 October 1745

2. Rev. Donald MacQueen of Kilmuir, 'A Dissertation on the Government of the People in the Western Highlands', 17 November 1774, in Pennant [1774–6], 1998, 658

3. Eardley-Simpson, 1933, 18

4. Information from the late John Caruana, Royal Artillery Museum, Woolwich

5. Tomasson, 1958, 20

6. Santa Cruz [1724–30], 1735–40, IV, 224

7. Yorke, 1913, I, 479

8. SP 36/81, Deposition of Dr Robert Hopwood, London, 15 February 1746

9. SP 36/73, Mr A. Baron to the DoN, 15 November 1745

10. Hughes, 1746, 48

11. Norie, 1901, II, 189, 163

12. Maxwell of Kirkconnell, 1841, 77

13. Stuart Papers, Windsor Castle, Laurence Wolfe to Colonel Daniel O'Brien, 24 January (NS?) 1746

14. SP 36/74, the Duke of Devonshire to DoN, Chatsworth, 25 November 1745

15. Ritchie, 1956, 106

16. Maxwell of Kirkconnell, 1841, 77

17. SHAT A1 3512, Duc de Richelieu, Boulogne, 16 January (NS), 1746

18. SP 36/76, Anonymous report, Dudley, 10 September 1745

19. SP 36/71, Lord Tyrawley to the DoN, Mount Edgcumbe, 11 October 1745

20. Quoted in Atkinson, 1957, 123

21. Marchant, 1746, v

22. Lord Hardwicke to Archbishop Herring of York, 12 September 1745, Yorke, 1913, I, 450

23. SP 36/73, C. Stanley to the DoN, Cross Hall near Ormskirk, 10 November 1745

24. SP 36/70, the Duke of Norfolk to the DoN, Worksop, 8 October 1745

25. *The Universal Spectator and Weekly Journal*, 5 October 1745

26. SP 36/83, Deposition of Charles Hewit, undated

27. SP 36/69, the Bishop of London to the DoN, Whitehall, 28 September 1745

28. SP 36/79, Anonymous and undated intelligence

29. Butler's 'Reports as to Prospects of Invasion and Place of Landings', Eardley-Simpson, 1933, 259–60

30. *The Northampton Mercury*, 26 December 1745

31. *The General Evening Post*, 12 December 1745

32. The Earl of Shaftesbury to the DoN, 5 October 1745. See also *The General Advertiser*, 11 October 1745

33. SP 36/76, Thomas Blake (Collector of Customs at Minehead) to William Wood of HM Customs London, Minehead, 8 December 1745

34. SP 36/74, Lord Edgcumbe to the DoN, Mount Edgcumbe, 19 November 1745

35. SP 36/37, the DoN to the Duke of St Albans, 28 September 1745

36. *The London Evening Post*, 23 November 1745

37. SP 36/73, Walter Wyatt to the DoN, Stamp office, Oxford, 2 October 1745

38. SHAT A1 3521, 'Rapport du Mr Wolfe envoié de Paris à Londres à la fin du 9bre dernier, et parti de Londres le 2 janvier'

39. Stuart Papers, Windsor Castle, 272/92, Laurence Wolfe to Colonel Daniel O'Brien, 24 January 1746; SP 36/70, Mr Waugh to the DoN, Carlisle, 5 October 1745

40. *A Genuine Account of the Behaviour ... of Francis Townley*, etc, 1746, 17

41. *The London Evening Post*, 1 October 1745

42. SO 36/73, the DoN to the Lord Cholmondeley, 16 November 1745; SP 36/75, 'Mrs H.' to Lord Chief Baron Parker, 26 November 1745

43. SHAT A1 3153, 'Rapport du Mr Wolfe'

44. SP 36/70, Haldanby Moor to the DoN, London, 5 October 1745

45. SP 36/78, Anon. To the DoN, Manchester, 10 January 1746

46. *A Genuine Account of the Behaviour ... of Francis Townley*, etc., 1746, 8

47. Ibid., 10

48. The Earl of Derby to the DoN, Knowsley, 22 October 1746

49. O'Sullivan, 1938, 99

50. *The Northampton Mercury*, 7 October 1745

51. NP 32, 705

52. *A Genuine Account of the Behaviour ... of Francis Townley*, etc, 1746, 16

53. SP 36/83, 'A Calendar of the Prisoners being confined in the Castle of York upon Suspicion of High Treason', 9 March 1746

54. *Gentleman's Magazine*, XVI, January 1746, 42

55. SP 36/70, ' A True Copy of the Information of John Purvis against George Turnbull', 8 October 1745

56. SP 36/85, information of James Wilson, 2 May 1746

57. Pennant [1774–6], 1998, 646

58. SP 36/83, Information of James Usher, 4 April 1746; the DoN to Sir Edward Blacket, 15 April 1746; Sir Edward Blacket to the DoN, 15 April 1746; minutes of the special meeting of 17 April 1746

59. SP 36/83, depositions of William Wright and Andrew Daniel

60. Yorke, 1913, I, 459

61. Ó Ciardha, 2002, 270

62. SP 36/78, Dudley Bradstreet to Sir Edward Stone, 24 December 1745

63. NP, Lord Chesterfield to the DoN, 2 September 1745

64. NP, Lord Chesterfield to the DoN, 24 October 1745

65. Ó Ciardha, 2002, 310

66. CP 12/244, S. Poyntz to the DoN, London, 6 March 1746

CHAPTER 3

The Divided Lands: Scotland

1. Lenman and Gibson, 1990, 16

2. Burt [1754], 1818, I, 213–14

3. CP 11/153, the Lord Justice Clerk to Fawk, Edinburgh, 28 February 1746. See also Rev. Goldie to Mr Waugh, Dumfries, 6 May 1746, in Moundsey, 1856, 220

4. CP 12/91, Rev. Alexander Gordon to Fawk, Kintore, 13 March 1746

5. Letter of 3 April 1746, in *The Westminster Journal*, 17 May 1746

6. CP 12/275 Major General Bland to Fawk, Strathbogie (Huntly), 22 March 1746

7. Ray, 1754, 289

8. Seton and Arnot, 1928–9, III, 131

9. Ray 1754, 284

10. CP 10/124, Lords Kinnoul and Dupplin to Fawk, London, 8 February 1746

11. Johnson [1775], 1996, 142

12. Lady Jane Nimmo to Lord Marchmont, 'Marchmont Correspondence', 1933, 331–2

13. 'Memorial anent the True State of the Highlands', Allardyce, 1895–6, I, 167

14. Pennant [1774–6], 1998, 498

15. CP 12/28, the DoC to the DoN, Aberdeen, 9 March 1746

16. 'Memoirs of the Rebellion in 1745 and 1746, so far as it concerned the Counties of Aberdeen and Banff', Blaikie, 1916, 120

17. Ibid., 119–20

18. Ibid., 121

19. TS 20/87, Examination of James Barclay, 19 November 1746

20. Chambers, 1869, 260–61

21. Mr George Carre to Lord Marchmont, Nisbet, 10 September 1745, 'Marchmont Correspondence', 316

22. Webster's analysis [1755] passim, in Kyd, 1952; CP 9/27, Mr Stack to M. Delpeck, Stirling, 24 January 1746

23. CP 9/27, Mr Stack to M. Delpeck, Stirling, 24 January 1746

24. Pennant [1771], 2000, 127

25. Pennant [1774–6], 1998, 365–6

26. Burt [1754], 1818, II, 65–6

27. Smout, in Wateley, 2000, 87

28. Willis, 1973, 97

29. Burt [1754], 1818, II, 34–5

30. Ibid., II, 87

31. Ibid., II, 86

32. SP 36/82, Mr Masterson to the DoN, York, 9 April 1746

33. Johnson [1775], 1996, 30

34. Ibid., 81

35. Pennant [1774–6], 1998, 345–6

36. Ibid., Appendix XI, Rev. Donald MacQueen of Kilmuir, 'A Dissertation on the Government of the People in the Western Highlands', 750

37. Lieutenant Colonel Watson, 'Proposals offered to Major General Blakeney', 1747; 'Memorial anent the Thieving and Depredations in the Highlands of Scotland', 1747 (?); 'Description of the Hills,

Glens and Passes in the Counties of Aberdeen, etc,', 9 July 1747, Allardyce 1896, II, 493–508

38. MacQueen's 'Dissertation', Pennant [1774–6], 1998, 750

39. Watson, 'Proposals', Allardyce, 1896, II, 493

40. Marchant, 1746, 19

41. Burt [1754], 1818, II, 22

42. MacQueen's 'Dissertation', Pennant [1774–6], 1998, 751–2. See also Burt [1754], 1818, II, 21–2

CHAPTER 4

The White Cockade

1. De Vattel, 1835, II, 76–7

2. Maxwell of Kirkconnell, 1841, 82–3

3. Johnstone, 1822, 165

4. O'Sullivan, 1938, 83

5. Maxwell of Kirkconnell, 1841, 156–7

6. Ibid., 61

7. From *The True Patriot*, in *The Gentleman's Magazine*, November 1745, XV, 645

8. O'Sullivan, 1938, 69

9. Lord George Murray, 'Marches of the Highland Army', in Chambers, 1834, 126

10. 'Les Principes Généraux de la Guerre' [1748], Frederick II, *Oeuvres*, 1856, I, 89

11. Horace Walpole to Horace Mann, London, 27 September 1745, Walpole, 1903–5, II, 138

12. Forbes, 1896, I, 263

13. SP 36/77, 'The examination of John McAnzey, Captain of Glengarry's Regiment', 15 December 1745; Gillies, 1991, 42

14. CP 7/201, Deputy Lieutenant of the County of Forfar, and Lieutenant Colonel Sir James Kinloch (second bn of Ogilvy's Regiment) to Lady Powrie, Miltown, 16 November 1745

15. 'An Inquiry into the Causes which facilitated the Rise and Progress of Rebellions and Insurrections in the Highlands of Scotland', 1747, in Burt [1754], 1818, II, 361–2. See also Defoe [1724–6], 1927, II, 838–9

16. Mr George Carre to Lord Marchmont, Nisbet, 10 September 1745, 'Marchmont Correspondence', 1933, 316–7

17. 'An Inquiry' in Burt [1754], 1818, II, 361

18. Maxwell of Kirkconnell, 1841, 27, 184

19. Elcho, 1907, 310

20. Crichton (*Woodhouselee MS*), 1907, 17

21. Letter from Lancaster, 27 November 1745, *The Penny London Post*, 30 November – 3 December 1745

22. CP 6/205, Prince Charles, Holyroodhouse, 9 October 1745

23. CP 7/444, 'Order of the Young Pretender', Manchester, 30 November 1745; CP 12/402, Orders, 17 March 1746. See also CP 7/240, Marshall Rider to the DoC, Congleton, 1 December 1745

24. TS 20/87, Examination of Donald Ferguson, 11 November 1746

25. Seton and Arnot, 1928–9, III, 267

26. 'Letter of an Egyptian', in Tayler, A. and H., 1928, 89

27. Elcho, 1907, 377

28. Yorke, 1913, I, 468

29. CP 7/274, the Duke of Devonshire to the commanding officer of the Duke of Montagu's Carabineers, Derby, 3 December 1745

30. Anon., *A Journey through Part of England and Scotland*, 1746, 11

31. SP 36/73, Thomas Richardson to the Postmaster General, Post Office, Penrith, 11 November 1745

32. Lord George Murray, 'Marches of the Highland Army', Chambers, 1834, 30–31

33. Elcho, 1907, 291

34. Evidence of Austin Coleman, Allardyce, 1896, II, 444. Blyde was a practical fellow, being steward of the Duke of Norfolk's estates in Yorkshire

35. SP 36/73, Thomas Richardson to the Postmaster General, Post Office, Penrith, 11 November 1745

36. Chambers, 1869, 257

37. Bradstreet [1750], 1929, 113

38. SP 36/80, Admiral Martin to Mr Norris at Deal Castle, *Yarmouth* in the Downs, 7 January 1746

39. SHAT A1 3152, 'Rapport du Mr Wolfe', Lord Dillon's 'Repartition actuelle des Troupes réglées de la Grande Bretagne', 3 January 1746

40. *The General Advertiser*, 12 September 1745, letter to Edinburgh, 5 September 1745

41. TS 20/83, 'List of Gentlemen concerned in the late wicked unnatural Rebellion not contained in the First Bill of Attainder'

42. SP 36/79, Information of John Lee, undated; SP 36/83, Examination of James Kerby, 28 November 1745; John Vere in Allardyce, 1896, II, 348

43. Riksarkivet, Stockholm, Fond Anglica 328, Ringwicht to the Kanslipresident, 3 November 1745

44. SP 36/78, Mr J. Sutherland to the DoN, 27 November 1745

45. CP 12/346, Archibald Campbell to Lieutenant General Hawley, Strathbogie (Huntly), 26 March 1746

46. Maxwell of Kirkconnell, 1841, 53; SP 36/70, Provost John Goldie of Dumfries to the Postmaster at Lancaster, 27 September 1745

47. *The Gentleman's Magazine*, January 1746, XVI, 31

48. SHAT A1 3152, 'Mémoire pour Monsieur le Duc de Richelieu, par le Chevalier Stuart', undated

49. Burt [1754], 1818, II, 76

50. SP 36/76, Sir Henry Bracken to Fawk, Warrington, 4 December 1745

51. Johnson [1775], 1996, 100

52. George Lockhart of Carnwarth, *The Lockhart Papers*, 1817, II, 453–4

53. SP 36/74, Mr Alexander Spencer to the DoN, Kendal, 19 November 1745

54. SP 36/76, Thomas Drake, Derby, 7 December 1745

55. Lady Jane Nimmo to Lord Marchmont, Redbraes, 30 September 1745, 'Marchmont Correspondence', 1933, 325–6

56. CP 10/Map no. 482, 'A Plan of the Battle at Prestonpans'

57. Johnstone, 1822, 119–20

58. SP 36/80, 'The further Examination of David Morgan, Esq.', 5 January 1746

59. Reid, 1994, 58

60. O'Sullivan, 1938, 151

61. Johnstone, 1822, 114

62. Pringle, 1753, 51

63. NP, Duke of Richmond to the DoN, Goodwood, 6 February 1746

64. TS 20/88, Information of Allan Stewart, 1 July 1746

65. SP 36/74, Alexander Spencer to the DoN, Kendal, 19 November 1745

66. SP 36/76, Henry Bracken to Fawk, 4 December 1745

67. Johnstone, 1822, 111

68. Tomasson, 1958, 177

69. TS 20/87, Examination of William Clarke, 20 November 1746; see also TS 20/87, Examination of Jean Baptiste Froment, 5 November 1746

70. SP 36/77, 'Memorial from John Finlayson, Mathematicall Instrument Maker of Edinburgh', 24 September 1745

71. Johnstone, 1822, 113

72. Maxwell of Kirkconnell, 1841, 133–4

CHAPTER 5

Government and Military Forces in Hanoverian Britain

1. Rev. Thomas Birch to the Hon Philip Yorke, London, 28 September 1745, Yorke, 1913, I, 460

2. Riksarkivet, Stockholm, Fond Anglica 328, Ringwicht to the King of Sweden, London, 7 January 1746

3. Lieutenant Colonel Joseph Yorke to his father, Chancellor Hardwicke, Stafford, 4 December 1745, Yorke, 1913, I, 475

4. CP 14/385, Enoch Bradshaw to his brother in Cirencester, Stonehaven, 11 May 1746

5. SP 36/78, the DoN to Field Marshal Wade, 25 December 1745

6. SP 36/78, the DoN to the DoC, 28 December 1745

7. SP 36/78, the DoC to the DoN, Blackhall, 30 December 1745

8. Lord George Murray, 'Marches of the Highland Army', in Chambers, 1834, 109

9. CP 15/153, Lord George Murray to Prince Friedrich of Hesse–Cassel, 30 March 1746

10. CP 13/67, Prince Friedrich of Hesse–Cassel to the DoC, 31 March 1746

11. Stuart Papers 272/92, Laurence Wolfe to Colonel Daniel O'Brien, 24 January 1746

12. Lady Jane Nimmo to Lord Marchmont, Edinburgh, 7 March 1746, 'Marchmont Correspondence', 1933, 343

13. *The London Evening Post*, 26 October 1745

14. *The Old England Journal*, 3 August 1745

15. Letter from Berwick, 25 September 1745, in Moundsey, 1856, 30

16. CP 9/152, Major John Severin to Colonel Peregrine Lascelles, Edinburgh, 24 January 1746

17. Johnstone, 1822, 167

18. CP 8/166, Lieutenant General Hawley to the DoN, Edinburgh, 31 December 1745

19. NP, the Duke of Richmond to the DoN, Lichfield, 25 November 1745

20. 'Essay on regular and irregular forces', *The Gentleman's Magazine*, January 1746, XVI

21. Burt [1754], 1818, II, 23

22. *The London Evening Post*, 5 October 1745

23. *The Northampton Mercury*, 4 November 1745, letter from Newcastle, 26 October 1745

24. SHAT A1 3152, 'Rapport du Mr Wolfe'

25. SP 36/75, the Duke of Richmond to the

DoN, Lichfield, 30 November 1745

26. Ray, 1754, 202

27. Sir Thomas Sheridan to Colonel Daniel O'Brien, early March 1746, Tayler, A. and H., 1939, 144

28. Major General Bland, *A Treatise of Military Discipline*, 1743, 114

29. CP 9/43, Lieutenant General Hawley to the DoN, Edinburgh, 7 January 1746

30. Knight, 1935, I, 163–4

31. Rev. John Waugh to Bettesworth, Carlisle, 2 October 1745, Moundsey, 1856, 27

32. Carlyle, 1860, 146, 147

33. SP 36/78, Henry Bracken to Fawk, Warrington, 4 December 1745; Information of Thomas Drake, Derby, 7 December 1745. See also Horace Walpole to Horace Mann, 27 September 1745, Walpole, 1903–5, II, 137

34. 'Agricola', in *The Old England Journal*, 9 November 1745

35. 'Les Principes Généraux de la Guerre' [1748], Frederick II, *Oeuvres*, 1856, I, 93

36. SP 36/70, 'Information relating to the rebels in Scotland', 3 October 1745

37. CP 7/199, the Lord Justice Clerk to the DoN, Edinburgh, 22 November 1745. See also CP 7/154, Mr John Hyde to Fawk, 28 November 1745

38. CP 7/324, the DoC to the DoN, Packington, 6 December 1745. The waistcoats were the gift of Quaker merchants, 'to double over the breast and belly, long enough to be worn under the waistbands' (*The Westminster Journal*, 23 November 1745)

39. CP 10/160, the DoC to the DoN, Perth, 10 February 1746

40. CP 14/385, Enoch Bradshaw to his brother in Cirencester, Stonehaven, 11 May 1746

41. SP 36/85, Lord Lion to Ludovick Grant, 28 August 1745

42. 'Letter from Berwick', 25 September 1745, Moundsey, 1856, 29

43. Hawley's directive of 12 January 1745, Elcho, 1907, 460

44. CP 14/385, Enoch Bradshaw to his brother in Cirencester, Stonehaven, 11 May 1746

45. NP, the Duke of Richmond to the DoN, Coventry, 7 December 1745

46. CP 13/44, Major General Bland to Colonel Napier, Strathbogie (Huntly), 29 March 1746

47. 'Memorial Addressed to His Majesty George I concerning the State of the Highlands', Burt, [1754] 1818, II, 262

48. Burt [1754], 1818, II, 23, 24–5

49. Doran, 1877, II, 93

50. Forbes, 1896, 36

51. TS 20/3, No.3, Anonymous Jacobite Journal

52. *More Culloden Papers*, 1923–30, IV, 102

53. 'Journal or Memoirs of P...C... Expedition into Scotland etc. 1745–6. By a Highland Officer in his Army', *Lockhart Papers*, 1817, II, 505

54. CP 10/168, the DoC to the DoN, Perth, 10 February 1746

55. CP 12/198, the DoC to the DoN, Aberdeen, 19 March 1746

56. CP 12/275, Major General Bland to Fawk, Strathbogie (Huntly), 22 March 1745

57. Mitchison, in Wately, 2000, 28

58. CP 11/108, the Lord Justice Clerk to Fawk, Edinburgh, 26 February 1746

59. CP 11/164, 'Memorial Stating the facts relative to the Conduct of the Town of Glasgow during the present Rebellion. With the proper Vouchers', undated, 1746

60. Burt [1754], 1818, I, 252

61. Ibid., I, 252–3

62. Report of 10 December 1724, Ibid., II, 282

63. Ibid., I, 41–2

64. Speck, 1981, 31–2

65. Johnson [1775], 1996, 26

66. Burt [1754], 1818, II, 13

67. Pennant [1771], 2000, 129

68. Ibid., 133–4

69. Ibid., 133

70. Burt [1754], 1818, II, 215

71. Ibid., II, 216–17

PART TWO

CHAPTER 6

From the Western Isles to the Corrieyairack, 22 July – 29 August 1745

1. Johnstone, 1822, 4

2. Chambers, 1869, 28

3. 'Journal and Memoirs of P...C... Expedition', *Lockhart Papers*, 1817, Ii, 480–81

4. At least according to Norie, 1901, I, 154, who takes issue with the earlier historians who had Prince Charles reaching Loch Moidart by sea

5. Murray of Broughton, 1898, 152, 162

6. One of them was the *Princess Mary*, laden with oatmeal for her home port of Renfrew on the

Clyde (*The Westminster Journal*, 31 August 1745)

7. O'Sullivan, 1938, 59

8. Murray of Broughton, 1898, 162

9. Hughes, 1746, 6

10. Norie, 1901, I, 166–8

11. Anon., 'An Account of Proceedings from Prince Charles' Landing to Prestonpans', 1958, 209

12. 'Narrative of the Prince's imbarkation and arrival etc., taken from the mouth of Aeneas MacDonald', Forbes, 1896, I, 293

13. Major Wentworth to Lieutenant General Cope, Fort Augutus, 13 August 1745, *A Report into the Proceedings ... of Lieutenant-General Sir John Cope*, 1749, Appendix, 62

14. Anon., 'A History of the Rebellion in the Years 1745 and 1746', Tayler, H., 1944, 35

15. Lieutenant Colonel Joseph Yorke to the Hon. Philip Yorke, Vilvorde, 1 September 1745, Yorke, 1913, I, 439

16. Stockholm, Riksarkivet, Fond Anglica 326, Ringwicht to the King of Sweden, 6 August 1746

17. Norman MacLeod to Duncan Forbes of Culloden, 2 August 1745, *More Culloden Papers*, 1923–30, IV, 14

18. *The Caledonian Mercury*, 15 November 1745, Letter from Chapel-en-le-Frith, 1 November 1745

19. Stockholm, Riksarkivet, Fond Anglica 326, Ringwicht to the King of Sweden, 16 August 1745

20. Lord Glenorchy to the Hon. Philip Yorke, 7 September 1745, Yorke, 1913, I, 446–7

21. Lieutenant Colonel Whitefoord in defence of Cope, Whitefoord, 1898, 84

22. Ibid., 84

23. Ibid., 85

24. Letter of an officer to his friend, 27 September 1745, Marchant, 1746, 83–4. See also Lieutenant Colonel Whitefoord, Whitefoord, 1898, 85–6

25. Murray of Broughton, 1898, 62

26. MacCulloch, 1995, 12–13

27. 'An Account of Proceedings', 1958, 211

28. Norie, 1901, I, 213–15

CHAPTER 7

Edinburgh and Cope's Last Challenge, 30 August – 30 October 1745

1. Anon., *A Journey along with the Army*, 1747, 62. Work on Blair Castle was resumed almost immediately after the rising, and transformed the place into a stripped-down country mansion in a particularly austere mid-Georgian style, albeit with sumptuous rococo interiors. The castle was reworked in the middle of the nineteenth century, and emerged as a pile in the Scottish baronial mode, which, however, bore little resemblance to its genuinely baronial origins. Callendar House near Falkirk underwent a double transmogrification of the same confusing kind

2. 'Journal of the Prince's imbarkation and arrival, etc., the greatest part of which was taken from Duncan Campbell', Forbes, 1896, I, 208

3. Harley, Lord, 'Journeys in England' [1725], H.M.C. *Portland MSS*, 1901, VI, 117

4. *The York Courant*, 17 September 1745, Letter from a gentleman in Dundee to his friend in Newcastle, 13 September 1745; Ibid., 24 September 1745

5. NP 32,705, enclosed in Chesterfield's of 23 September 1745

6. O'Sullivan, 1938, 68

7. Quoted in Tullibardine, 1908, I, 320

8. Maxwell of Kirkconnell, 1841, 33

9. 'Journal and Memoirs of P...C... Expedition', *Lockhart Papers*, 1817, II, 487

10. Chambers, 1869, 82

11. The road, now a farm track, runs parallel with the busy A811, which had been driven across the mosses to the north

12. O'Sullivan, 1938, 69

13. NP 32,705, enclosed in Chesterfield's of 23 September 1745

14. SP 36/58, Dr David Goldie to Rev. John Waugh, Dumfries, 13 September 1745

15. NP 32,705, the DoN to Lord Chesterfield, 6 September 1745

16. *The London Evening Post*, 10 October 1745, Letter from Stirling, 30 September 1745

17. Chambers, 1869, 84

18. SP 36/70, information forwarded by the Postmaster of Lancaster, 30 September 1745

19. SP 36/68, Deposition of Richard Jack, 21 September 1745

20. Carlyle, 1860, I, 112

21. Crichton (*Woodhouselee MS*), 1907, 15

22. Ibid., 14

23. Carlyle, 1860, I, 117

24. Ibid., I, 118

25. SP 36/68, Deposition of Richard Jack, 21 September 1745

26. Carlyle, 1860, I, 123

27. Crichton (*Woodhouselee MS*), 1907, 21

28. Carlyle, 1860, I, 123

29. SP 36/68, Deposition of Richard Jack, 21 September 1746

30. Chambers, 1869, 98–9

31. Elcho, 1907, 258–9

32. George Carre to Lord Marchmont, Berwick, 18 September 1745, 'Marchmont Correspondence', 1933, 320

33. Tayler, H., 1948, 39

34. SP 36/38, ? to Major General Blakeney, Inverness, 30 August 1745

35. Whitefoord, 1898, 87

36. Burt [1754], 1818, I, 17

37. Ray, 1754, 271

38. Crichton (*Woodhouselee MS*), 1907, 55; *The London Evening Post*, 10 October 1745, Letter from Newcastle, 6 October 1745

39. Crichton (*Woodhouselee MS*), 1907, 58–9

40. Ray, 1754, 271

41. O'Sullivan, 1938, 89

42. *The Caledonian Mercury*, 4 October 1745

43. Ibid, 23 September 1745. The relevant copy is in the Newspaper Library, Colindale

44. *Orderly Book of Lord Ogilvy's Regiment*, 1927, 6

45. Magdalen Pringle to her sister Tib, 13 October 1745, Tayler, H., 1948, 40–41

46. SP 36/72, Major General Huske to the DoN, Newcastle, 23 October 1745

47. Lady Nimmo to Lord Marchmont, Redbraes, 13 October 1745, 'Marchmont Correspondence', 1922, 326

48. Magdalen Pringle to Tib, 13 October 1745, Tayler, H., 1948, 41

49. 'Memoirs of the Rebellion in 1745 and 1746, so far as it concerned the Counties of Aberdeen and Banff', Blaikie, 1916, 117

50. Norie, 1901, II, 137

CHAPTER 8

Invasion: The Bid for a Kingdom, 31 October – 22 November 1745

1. Lord George Murray, 'Marches of the Highland Army', Chambers, 1834, 46

2. TS 20/87, Examination of James Patterson, undated

3. Ray, 1754, 56

4. Johnstone, 1822, 63

5. NP, the DoN to the DoC, 4 September 1745

6. Stockholm, Riksarkivet, Fond Anglica, 326, Ringwicht to the King of Sweden, 17 September 1745

7. Hon. Charles Yorke to Lieutenant Colonel Joseph Yorke, 30 November 1745, Yorke, 1913, I, 462

8. 'Extract of a Letter from Berwick', Moundsey, 1856, 30

9. NP, the DoN to the DoC, 25 September 1745

10. *Orderly Book of Lord Ogilvy's Regiment*, 1927, 13

11. MacLean, 1996, 23

12. Marchant, 1746, 265

13. Pennant [1771], 2000, 168

14. SP 36/77, Account of John Douglas and William Carver, Selkirk, 7 November 1745

15. SP 36/73, Intelligence to Lord Lonsdale, 7 November 1745

16. *The Penny London Post*, 16–19 November 1745, Report from Newcastle, 13 November 1745. See also SP 36/73, James Patinson to Lord Lonsdale, 9 November 1745

17. CP 7/396, Angus MacDonnell to his uncle, the Laird of Struan, Perth, 13 November 1745

18. Defoe [1724–6], 1927, II, 756

19. Quoted in Tomasson, 1958, 72

20. *The Penny London Post*, 9–12 November 1745, Letter from Berwick, 6 November 1745

21. Beattie, 1928, 39

22. CP 6/191, Lord George Murray to Major David Stewart of Kynachan, Jedburgh, 7 November 1745

23. Murray of Broughton, 1898, 238

24. *The London Evening Post*, 16 November 1745, News from Kendal, 13 November 1745

25. Fiennes, 1947, 204

26. Ibid., 202

27. Archbishop Herring of York, probably to the Hon. Philip Yorke, Bishopsthorne, 9 November 1745, Yorke, 1913, I, 465

28. SP 35/69, Sir James Lowther to the DoN, Whitehaven, 25 September 1745

29. Johnstone, 1822, 56. Johnstone misdates the event to the 9th

30. Ibid., 57

31. Beattie, 1928, 67

32. Quoted in Wheatley, 1903, 22–3

33. *The Daily Post*, 21 November 1745, News from Newcastle, 16 November 1745

34. Macdonald of Castleton, 1995, 18

35. Ray, 1754, 96

36. TS 20/83, Examination of John Allen of Fowles in Perthshire, York, 5 April 1746

37. SP 36/73, 'Intelligence from Penrith', 14 November 1745

38. SP 36/76, Rev. John Waugh to the DoN, Barnard Castle, 1 December 1745

39. SP 36/83, Information of Leonard Deane of Kirkwall, Cumberland, 10 March 1746

40. CP 7/62, Rev. John Waugh to the DoN, c.21 November 1745

41. SP 36/81, Examination of John Pearson, Town Clerk of Carlisle, 21 February 1746

42. SP 36/76, Alexander Blair of Elcho's Life-guards to Miss Blair at her house in Brown's Close in Edinburgh, Derby, 5 December 1745

43. SP 36/78, the DoC to the DoN, Blackhall, 30 December 1745

44. SP 36/70, Lieutenant General Cope to the Marquis of Tweeddale, Berwick, 1 October 1745

45. SP 36/70, James Greive to the Postmaster General, Berwick, 11 October 1745

46. SP 36/72, John Renton, enclosed in Handasyde's of 25 October 1745

47. SP 37/73, Lieutenant General Handasyde to the DoN, Berwick, 3 November 1745

48. SP 36/73, the DoN to Field Marshal Wade, 2 November 1745

49. Sir John Clerk of Penicuik, 1892, 187. See also *The London Evening Post*, 26 September 1745, News from Newcastle, 22 September 1745

50. SP 36/70, Major General Huske to the DoN, 4 October 1745

51. *The York Courant*, 15 October 1745, News from Newcastle, 12 October 1745

52. *The Caledonian Mercury*, 14 October 1745, Letter from a gentleman of Northumberland

53. Ray, 1754, 140

54. *The Caledonian Mercury*, 7 October 1745, Letter from Hull, 25 September 1745

55. *The London Evening Post*, 24 October 1745, News from Hull, 19 October 1745

56. *The General Evening Post*, 14 December 1745

57. CP 6/289, Alexander MacKenzie of Arldloch to John Ross, writer in Edinburgh, 28 October 1745

58. NP, Mr Brereton to Lord Chancellor Hardwicke, 27 October 1745

59. SP 36/73, enclosed in Rev. John Waugh to the DoN, Carlisle, 2 November 1745

60. Vienna, HHStA, Berichte England, Karton 88, Wasner to Vienna, 8 November 1745; Stockholm, Riksarkivet, Fond Anglica, 326, Ringwicht to the King of Sweden, 8 November 1745

61. SP 36/73, the DoN to the Earl of Cholmonde-ley, 13 November 1745

62. SP 36/73, Lord Lonsdale to the DoN, Byrom, 14 November 1745

63. NP 32,705, the DoN to the Duke of Richmond, 22 November 1745

64. SP 326/72, Field Marshal Wade to the DoN, 31 October 1745

65. SP 36/73, Field Marshal Wade to the DoN, 5 November 1745. See also *The York Courant*, 12 November 1745, Letter from York, 7 November 1745

66. SP 36/73, enclosed in Field Marshal Wade's to the DoN, Newcastle, 7 November 1745

67. SP 36/73, Lieutenant General Handasyde to the DoN, Berwick, 11 November 1745

68. CP 7/199, the Lord Justice Clerk to DoN, Edinburgh, 22 November 1745

69. Lord Harley, 'Journeys into England', H.M.C. *Portland MSS*, 1901, VI, 130

70. Lieutenant S. Robinson to Lieutenant Colonel Joseph Yorke, 23 November 1745, Yorke, 1913, I, 467

71. SP 36/74, Field Marshal Wade to the DoN, Hexham, 19 November 1745

72. Lieutenant S. Robinson to Lieutenant Colonel Joseph Yorke, Newcastle, 24 November 1745, Yorke, 1913, I, 467–8

CHAPTER 9

Invasion: The Bid for a Kingdom, 18–30 November 1745

1. SP 37/74, Alexander Spencer to the DoN, Kendal, 19 November 1745

2. SP 36/78, Examination of Peter Pattinson, 24 December 1745

3. Defoe [1724–6], 1927, II, 678

4. McLynn, 1988, 184

5. Fiennes, 1947, 198

6. Pennant [1771], 2000, 170

7. MacLean, 1996, 25

8. SP 36/74, Intelligence from Penrith, 21 November 1745

9. CP 7/107, Intelligence from Mr Gilson, Penrith, 22 November 1745

10. CP 7/416, Prince Charles to the High Constable of Penrith, Penrith, 21 November 1745

11. CP 7/199, the Lord Justice Clerk to the DoC, Edinburgh, 22 November 1745; CP 7/446, William Moir to Lord Lewis Gordon, Aberdeen, 30 November 1745

12. SP 36/74, Intelligence of John Cowper, Penrith, 23 November 1745

13. CP 7/149, Intelligence from Kendal, forwarded 28 November 1745

14. Fiennes, 1947, 191

15. The house still stands, just before the traffic lights where the A7 breaks the originally continuous line of Stricklandgate, and strikes off to the right along Sandies Avenue and over the modern bridge

16. *The Daily Post*, 12 December 1745, Letter from Kendal, 25 November 1745

17. Defoe [1724–6], 1927, II, 678

18. Ibid., II, 678

19. Fiennes, 1947, 189. The graphite of Borrowdale remained Europe's only source of pencil lead until a substitute was discovered in the Napoleonic Wars

20. MacLean, 1996, 25

21. CP 7/430, Lord George Murray to O'Sullivan, Lancaster, 25 November 1745

22. SP 36/76, Dr Henry Bracken to Fawk, Warrington, 4 December 1745

23. SP 36/84, Information of James Jackson and his wife Elizabeth, 14 June 1746

24. MacLean, 1996, 26

25. SP 36/77, Information of Thomas Clark, Lancaster, 3 January 1746

26. SP 36/76, Dr Henry Bracken to Fawk, Warrington, 4 December 1745

27. SP 36/75, Information of Mr Furnivall, Congleton, 27 November 1745

28. SP 36/76, the DoN to the DoC, 30 November 1745

29. SP 36/76, Dr Henry Bracken to Fawk, Warrington, 4 December 1745

30. MacLean, 1996, 26

31. *The London Evening Post*, 7 December 1745, Letter from Hull, 4 December 1745

32. 'John Daniel's Progress', in Blaikie, 1916, 168

33. Maxwell of Kirkconnell, 1841, 60. See also SP 36/75, John Knock, Postmaster of Preston, to the DoN, Knutsford, 26 November 1745

34. *The General Advertiser*, 7 December 1745, Letter of a clergyman of West Yorkshire

35. SP 36/74, 'a rebel', to Mrs Mary Hamilton, Preston, 27 November 1745

36. Defoe [1724–6], 1927, II, 678

37. TS 20/88, Information of Edward Chew of Preston, 5 July 1746

38. TS 20/83, Examination of John Allen of Fowles in Perthshire, York, 5 April 1746

39. CP 7/199, the Lord Justice Clerk to the DoN, Edinburgh, 22 November 1745

40. Ray, 1754, 98

41. Jessup and Ward, 1952, 108

42. Ibid., 108

43. NP, Lord Derby to the DoN, Manchester, 15 November 1745

44. NP, Lord Derby to the DoN, Knowsley, 24 November 1745

45. SP 36/76, Major General Bland to Fawk, 1 December 1745

46. Ray, 1754, 113

47. Ibid., 110

48. *The Penny London Post*, 3–5 December 1745, Letter from Liverpool, 30 November 1745. A slightly different version is to be found in Jarvis, 1971–2, I, 244–5

49. SP 36/70, John Waugh to the DoN, Carlisle, 5 October 1745

50. CP 7/13, Lord Cholmondeley to Fawk, Chester, 8 November 1745

51. CP 7/38, Brigadier Douglas to the DoC, Chester, 15 November 1745

52. SP 36/74, Mr Lord to Lord Cholmondeley, Chester, 23 November 1745

53. CP 7/100, Lord Cholmondeley to Fawk, Chester, 23 November 1745

54. Lieutenant Colonel Joseph Yorke to the Hon. Philip Yorke, Lichfield, 1 December 1745, Yorke, 1913, I, 473

55. 'Journal and Memoirs', *The Lockhart Papers*, 1817, II, 458

56. Defoe [1724–6], 1927, 669. The dark, peaty earth of the mosses is still evident on either side of the M62 motorway on the eastern approaches to Liverpool

57. Ibid., II, 668

58. Ibid., II, 664

59. Vienna, HHStA, Berichte England, Karton 88, Wasner to Vienna, 30 November 1745

60. SP 36/175, Lord Cholmondeley to the DoN, undated, mid November 1745

61. CP 7/124, Lord Cholmondeley to the Duke of Richmond, 25 November 1745

62. NP, Lord Cholmondeley to the DoN, Chester, 24 November 1745

63. CP 7/137, the Duke of Richmond to Lord Cholmondeley, Lichfield, 26 November 1745

64. CP 7/192, Brigadier Douglas to the DoN, 30 November 1745

65. Ray, 1754, 132–3

66. Holroyd, in *The Palatine Note-Book*, 1885, I, 66

67. Defoe [1724–6], 1927, II, 675

68. The Chevalier de Johnstone's story of a riot is a fiction, unsupported by reliable accounts such as those of Beppy Byrom, Mr Alexander Spencer, and the constables Fowden and Walley

69. SP 36/81, Deposition of Samuel Lighthorn, undated

70. By a series of near-miracles the house of the Byroms stands as the most complete half-timbered structure in the city, having survived two bombings which devastated central Manchester – by the Germans in 1940, and by the Irish Republican Army in 1996

71. Byrom, Beppy, 1954, 17, 23

72. 'Brief for the defendant in the suit of King vs. William Fowden', H.M.C. *Kenyon MSS*, 1894, Appx Part IV, 481

73. SP 36/81, Deposition of John Chatham, 14 February 1746

74. CP 7/213, Lord Cholmondeley to Fawk, Chester Castle, 30 November 1745

75. 'Brief for the defendant in the suit of King vs. William Fowden', H.M.C. *Kenyon MSS*, 1894, Appx. Part IV, 481

76. SP 36/83, Information of Samuel Maddock, 11 March 1746

77. *The Manchester Magazine*, 24 December 1745

78. SP 36/81, Deposition of Robert Jobb of Manchester, 14 February 1746

79. SP 36/81, Deposition of John Taylor of Hopwood, 14 February 1746

80. SP 36/83, Information of John Dunkerley, 5 March 1746

81. SP 36/81, Deposition of John Wood, 17 February 1746

82. SP 36/81, Deposition of George Smith, 17 February 1746

83. SP 36/81, Deposition of Joshua Wardle, 19 February 1746

84. Jessup, in Jessup and Ward, 1952, 111

85. Quoted in Smith, P. J., 1993, 24

86. Byrom, Beppy, 1954, 41

87. John Daniel's 'Progress', Blaikie, 1916, 187. See also CP 7/269, Letter of Mr Alexander Spencer, 29 November 1745, and Monod, 1989, 341–40

88. Anon., the interrogation of David Morgan, 'The Forty-Five in Staffordshire', *The North Staffordshire Field Club Transactions*, XLVIII, Stafford, 1924, 91

89. CP 7/213, Lord Cholmondeley to Fawk, Chester Castle, 30 November 1745

90. CP 7/226, Thomas Moore to Lieutenant General Ligonier, Holmes Chapel, 30 November 1745

91. CP 7/240, Intelligence forwarded by Marshall Rider to the DoC, Congleton, 1 December 1745

CHAPTER 10

Invasion: The Bid for a Kingdom, 1–30 December 1745

1. Jessup, in Jessup and Ward, 1952, 113

2. By tradition the troops descended to the river by Tiviot (i.e. 'Teviot') Dale, though the present Tiviot Way probably swings too far to the east, for it would have involved the Jacobites in crossing both the Tame and the Portwood Lake (the flood plain of the Goyt). The whole scene has been transformed by the covering over of the junction of the two streams by the Merseyway (1940), and the superimposition of the Merseyway shopping precinct

3. Chambers, 1869, 188

4. Prestbury has a large number of buildings which saw the passage of the Jacobites in 1745, and has been spared the fate of the nearby part of Cheshire, which has been ruined by its incorporation in Greater Manchester

5. SP 36/76, Mr Wright to 'Good Sir', Knutsford, 2 December 1745

6. It is difficult to reconstruct the story of the lower crossings in any convincing detail. However, the reason for assigning them to the Lifeguards and the Manchester Regiment is that both units left Manchester by Deansgate – the Lifeguards very early in the morning, and the Manchester Regiment after it had received the blessing of Dr Deacon outside St Ann's Church. The identity of the various units of cavalry becomes much more difficult to pin down once they have crossed the river. The documents and the secondary sources often fail to distinguish between the patrols on 30 November and those of the day of the crossing. The orders for 1 December assigned Kilmarnock's Horse to cross by the Didsbury (i.e. Gatley) Ford and follow the road at least as far as Altrincham, leaving the manner of rejoining the army at the commander's discretion. The wording is clear, but leaves us uncertain as to whether any particular action was the work of Elcho's troopers or Kilmarnock's

7. Ray, 1754, 143

8. TS 20/93, Deposition of Samuel Cooper, 25 August 1746

9. Davies, 1961, 108

10. SP 36/76, Information of Charles Vernon, Talke o' the Hill, 1 December 1745

11. John Stafford, quoted in Smith, 1993, 32

12. Ibid., 33

13. SP 36/75, Field Marshal Wade to the DoN, camp near Piercebridge, 28 November 1745

14. *The London Evening Post*, 5 December 1745, Letter from Richmond, Yorkshire, 29 November 1745

15. SP 36/75, Field Marshal Wade to the DoN, camp near Piercebridge, 28 November 1745

16. *The London Evening Post*, 5 December 1745, letter from Richmond, Yorkshire, 29 November 1745

17. SP 36/76, Field Marshal Wade to the DoN, Wetherby, 5 December 1745

18. NP, the Duke of Richmond to the DoN, Lichfield, 23 November 1745

19. NP, the Duke of Richmond to the DoN, Coventry, 21 November 1745

20. Anon., *A Journey through Part of England and Scotland*, 1746, 5

21. NP 32,705, the Duke of Richmond to the DoN, Lichfield, 25 November 1745

22. CP 7/147, Brigadier Bligh to the Duke of Richmond, Stafford, 27 November 1745

23. SP 36/75, the DoC to the DoN, Lichfield, 28 November 1745

24. NP, the Duke of Richmond to the DoN, Lichfield, 29 November 1745

25. SP 36/75, the DoC to the DoN, Lichfield, 28 November 1745

26. Lieutenant General Ligonier to an unknown addressee, Lichfield, 28 November 1745, H.M.C., *Eglinton MSS*, 1885, 187

27. CP 7/170, Major Chiverston Hartopp to the Duke of Richmond, Cheadle (Cheshire), 29 November 1745

28. Atkinson, 1943–4, 110

29. CP 7/255, Fawk to Field Marshal Wade, Lichfield, 1 December 1745

30. CP 7/249, the Duke of Kingston to Fawk (?), Congleton Heath, 1 December 1745

31. SP 36/76, Intelligence from William Cotton, Congleton, 1 December 1745

32. SP 36/76, Cornet Smith to the Duke of Kingston, Northwich, 1 December 1745

33. SO 36/76, Major General Bland to Lord Sempill and Fawk, Newcastle under Lyme, 1 December 1745

34. SP 36/80, Examination of Alexander Kelloch of Nether Knutsford, 28 December 1745

35. Ibid.

36. SP 36/80, Examination of John Long the Younger of Nether Knutsford, 27 December 1745

37. SP 36/80, Examination of Martha Brown of Nether Knutsford, 27 December 1745

38. SP 36/80, Examination of Abraham Merrick of Nether Knutsford, 28 December 1745

39. SP 36/82, Examination of Hugh Leech of Nether Knutsford, 18 March 1746

40. SP 36/76, Examination of Mr Furnivall, 2 December 1745

41. SP 36/75, Orders for the Post at Congleton, 29 November 1745

42. TS 20/23, George Lowe to the Treasury Solicitor (John Sharpe), Chester, 20 September 1746

43. SP 36/76, the Duke of Richmond to the DoC, Newcastle under Lyme, 2 December 1745

44. Anon., *A Journey through Part of England and Scotland*, 1746, 6–7

45. SP 36/70, Fawk to the DoN, 2 December 1745

46. Anon., *A Journey through Part of England and Scotland*, 1746, 7

47. MacLean, 1996, 26–7

48. *Orderly Book of Lord Ogilvy's Regiment*, 1927, 21

49. Elcho, 1907, 336

50. *The General Evening Post*, 7 December 1745, Letter from Ford Green, 4 December 1745; Ibid., Letter from Mansfield, 5 December 1745

51. *Orderly Book of Lord Ogilvy's Regiment*, 1927, 22

52. MacLean, 1996, 27. This indicates that the Atholl Brigade, at least, followed the course of the present A52 between Ashbourne and Derby. Eardley-Simpson (1933, 122), however, suggests that the army took the route (later turnpiked) further east by way of Bradley, Hulland Ward, Mugginstonelane End, Weston Underwood and Keldeston, which certainly matches O'Sullivan's account (1938, 100) of marching by difficult by-roads

53. TS 20/91, Examination against Sparks, undated

54. The house as it stood in 1745 dated from about 1700 and was a smallish affair of brick, standing amid gardens enclosed by high walls. The present pile is by Robert Adam, designed to reproduce the grave majesty of the Pantheon in Rome, and was completed in 1765

55. 'A plain, general and authentic account of the Conduct and Proceedings of the Rebels, during their stay at Derby, from Wednesday the 4th, till Friday Morning the 6th December 1745', Allardyce, 1895–6, I, 287–8

56. John Daniel's 'Progress', Blaikie, 1916, 176

57. Accounts of Rev. Henry Cantrell and Hugh Bateman in Eardley-Simpson, 1933, 146–7

58. TS 20/89, Examination of Thomas Drake, Constable of Derby, 7 July 1746

59. TS 20/89, Information of Joseph Sykes, 7 July 1746

60. 'A plain, general and authentic account', Allardyce, 1895–6, I, 288

61. *The Daily Post*, 26 December 1745, Relation of a gentleman of Derby

62. Stuart Papers 272/92, Laurence Wolfe to Colonel Daniel O'Brien, 24 January 1746

63. CP 7/287, the DoC to the DoN, Stafford, 4 December 1745

64. NP, the Duke of Richmond to the DoN, Lichfield, 4 December 1745

65. SP 36/76, the Duke of Richmond to Fawk, Lichfield, 8 a.m., 5 December 1745

66. NP, the Duke of Richmond to the DoN, Stafford, 9 a.m., 5 December 1745

67. SP 36/76, Major General Bland to Fawk, Newcastle under Lyme, 1 December 1745

68. SP 36/76, Mr J. Thornhaugh to the DoN, Hilton, 2 December 1745

69. SP 36/76, enclosed in the Duke of Devonshire to the DoN, Mansfield, 4 December 1745

70. SP 36/76, R. Sutton to the DoN, Newark, 2 December 1745

71. SP 36/76, enclosed in the Duke of Devonshire to the DoN, Mansfield, 4 December 1745

72. The Hon. Charles Yorke to Lieutenant Colonel Joseph Yorke, undated, Yorke, 1913, I, 479

73. CP 2/274, the Duke of Devonshire to Lieutenant Colonel John Creed, Derby, 3 December 1745

74. 'Nathan Ben Sheddai, a Priest of the Jews', Eardley-Simpson, 1933, 271

75. CP 7/287, the DoC to the DoN, Stafford, 4 December 1745

76. CP 7/321, J. Clay to Lieutenant Colonel John Creed, Nottingham Castle, 6 December 1745

77. 'Nathan Ben Sheddai', Eardley-Simpson, 1933, 271

78. Johnstone, 1822, 67

79. 'A plain, general and authentic account', Allardyce, 1895–6, I, 289

80. CP 7/312, Samuel Kirkman to Fawk, Coventry, 6 December 1745

81. SP 36/76, Alexander Blair of the Lifeguards to Miss Blair, Derby, 5 December 1745; Peter Auchterlony to 'Dear Jennie', Derby, 5 December 1745. In the same vein see the letters of 'J.T.' and Bartholomew Sandland, Derby, 5 December 1745

CHAPTER 11

The Council at Derby and the Retreat to Scotland, 5–30 December 1745

1. SP 36/73, Edward Smalley to the DoN, Standish, 11 December 1745

2. O'Sullivan, 1938, 103

3. *A Journey through Part of England and Scotland*, 1746, 5–6

4. Stuart Papers 272/92, Laurence Wolfe to Colonel Daniel O'Brien, 24 January 1746

5. Atkinson, 1943–4, passim; Mellor, 1948, passim

6. Maurice, 1934, I, 142–3

7. CP 7/235, 'Report from Lieutenant General St Clair, in obedience to the order given by His Majesty concerning the ground for encamping the troops between Highgate and Whetstone. And likewise a report of the different roads leading towards London, which the rebels might take either to their right or left, in order to avoid the ground, where His Majesty's Troops are intended to be posted, with an account of the several roads by which His Majesty's troops may march to frustrate any such attempts of the rebels and interrupt their march towards London', undated. The same units (excluding Harrisons's) are listed in the orders issued by the War Office to the relevant regimental agents, instructing them to issue camp equipment and baggage horses (W.O. 4/41, Out Letters of William Yonge to the agents, 5 and 6 December 1745).

8. *The Northampton Mercury*, 16 December 1745, report from London, 10 December 1745

9. Stuart Papers 272/92, Laurence Wolfe to Colonel Daniel O'Brien, 24 January 1746

10. SP 36/76, the DoN to the DoC, 6 December 1745

11. CP 7/235, 'Report from Lieutenant General St Clair'

12. The Duke of Montagu to the DoN, 3 December 1745, Maurice, 1934, I, 141–2

13. Stuart Papers 272/92, Laurence Wolfe to Colonel Daniel O'Brien, 24 January 1746

14. *The General Advertiser*, 9 December 1745

15. Stuart Papers 272/92, Laurence Wolfe to Colonel Daniel O'Brien, 24 January 1746

16. Mitchell, 1965, 726

17. Johnstone, 1822, 77–8

18. Vienna, HHStA Berichte England, Karton 88, Wasner, 15 November 1745

19. Wasner, 19 November 1745

20. Wasner, 6 December 1745

21. Stockholm, Riksarkivet, Fond Anglica, 327, Ringwicht to the Kanslipresident, 5 December 1745

22. SP 36/76, the DoN to the Lord Mayor of London, Whitehall, 6 December 1745

23. W.O. 4/41, William Yonge to Lieutenant General Folliot, War Office, 7 December 1745

24. Vienna, HHStA Berichte England, Karton 88, Wasner, 10 December 1745

25. Stockholm, Riksarkivet, Fond Anglica 328, Ringwicht to the King of Sweden, 3 January 1746

26. Stuart Papers 272/92, Laurence Wolfe to Colonel Daniel O'Brien, 24 January 1746

27. The Hon. Philip Yorke to Lieutenant Colonel Joseph Yorke, London, 10 December 1745, Yorke, 1913, I, 478

28. Stuart Papers 272/92, Laurence Wolfe to Colonel Daniel O'Brien, 24 January 1746

29. 'Journal and Memoirs', *Lockhart Papers*, 1817, II, 495

30. CP 7/306, Dunk Halifax to Fawk, Birmingham, 6 December 1745

31. McLynn, 1988, 127

32. Maxwell of Kirkconnell, 1841, 81–2

33. TS 20/91, Examination against Sparks, undated

34. Johnstone, 1822, 73

35. CP 36/77, 'The examination of John McAnsey, Captain of Glengarry's Regiment', 15 December 1745. Dudley Bradstreet was riding in just such a condition, and it is likely that 'McAnsey' mistook him for Lord George

36. 'A plain, general and authentic account', Allardyce, 1895–6, I, 291

37. Ibid., I, 292

38. CP 7/316, Theophilus Leven to Fawk, Lichfield, 6 December 1745

39. Banner, 1906, 86

40. John Stafford, in Smith, 1993, 38

41. 'Marches of the Highland Army', Chambers, 1834, 58

42. *The Northampton Mercury*, 16 December 1745, Letter from Newcastle under Lyme, 6 a.m., 9 December 1745

43. SP 36/76, Lord Herbert to the DoN, Shrewsbury, 11 December 1745

44. John Daniel's 'Progress', Blaikie,1916, 179; Elcho, 1907, 343

45. Anon., *A Journey through Part of England and Scotland*, 1746, 8

46. *The Northampton Mercury*, 16 December 1745, Report from London, 14 December 1745

47. Ray, 1754, 188

48. Quoted in Smith, 1993, 39

49. SP 36/80, Deposition of Abraham Howarth, 8 January 1746

50. SP 36/80, Deposition of James Tomlinson

51. Kay, 1896, 103

52. Bradstreet [1750], 1929, 135

53. *The General Evening Post*, 17 December 1745, Letter from a lady in Preston to her friend in town, 14 December 1745. This piece shows every sign of having been circulated to the press by the government

54. TS 20/3, No. 3, Anonymous Jacobite Journal

55. SP 36/77, William Monkhowe to 'Dear Sir', Penrith, 16 December 1745

56. SP 36/77, William Monkhowe to 'Dear Sir', Penrith, 16 December 1745. The black horses must have been trophies of Prestonpans

57. *The Gentleman's Magazine*, January 1746, XVI

58. Maxwell of Kirkconnell, 1841, 81

59. CP 7/325, the DoC to Field Marshal Wade, Packington, 6 December 1745

60. NP, the Duke of Richmond to the DoN, Coventry, 7 December 1745

61. Ray, 1754, 187

62. CP 7/369, the DoC to the DoN, Lichfield, 9 December 1745

63. Stockholm, Riksarkivet, Fond Anglica 328, Ringwicht to the Kanslipresident, 10 December 1745

64. Lieutenant Colonel Joseph Yorke to Lord Chancellor Hardwicke (his father), Macclesfield, 11 December 1745, Yorke, 1913, I, 478

65. *The General Evening Post*, 17 December 1745

66. Anon., *A Journey through Part of England and Scotland*, 1745, 7–8

67. Ibid., 11

68. SP 36/76, Field Marshal Wade to the DoC, Wakefield, 11 December 1745

69. Fiennes, 1947, 221

70. Johnstone, 1822, 14

71. O'Sullivan, 1938, 104

72. SP 36/76, Major General Oglethorpe to the DoN, Preston, 13 December 1745

73. O'Sullivan, 1938, 105

74. SP 36/77, 'Memorial for His Highness the Duke', enclosed in the DoC's report of 17 December 1745

75. 'Journal and Memoirs', *The Lockhart Papers*, 1817, II, 460

76. TS 20/3, No. 3, Anonymous Jacobite Journal

77. SP 37/77, John Straw (Mayor of Kendal) to the DoN, 16 December 1745

78. Maxwell of Kirkconnell, 1841, 84

79. Lord George Murray, 'Marches of the Highland Army', Chambers, 1834, 62. N.B. Lord George and O'Sullivan were now on particularly bad terms, and their accounts at this stage of the campaign are full of contradictions

80. CP 8/44, the DoC to the DoN, Preston, 15 December 1745. See also NP 32,705, the Duke of Richmond to the DoN, Preston, 15 December 1745

CHAPTER 12

Shap, Clifton and the Defence of Carlisle, 16–30 December 1745

1. Maclean, 1996, 29

2. TS 20/3, No. 3, Anonymous Jacobite Journal

3. O'Sullivan, 1938, 106

4. MacLean, 1996, 29

5. *The General Evening Post*, 31 December 1745, Letter from Shap, 23 December 1745

6. MacLean, 1996, 29

7. Lord George Murray, 'Marches of the Highland Army', Chambers, 1834, 62–3

8. Ibid., 63

9. 'Journal and Memoirs', *The Lockhart Papers*, 1817, II, 464

10. Johnstone, 1822, 86

11. Ibid., 87–8

12. Ibid., 89

13. 'Journal and Memoirs', *The Lockhart Papers*, 1817, II, 464

14. Fawk to Lord Lonsdale, Blackhall, 25 December 1745, Atkinson, 1957, 124. The Jacobite journal in TS 20/3, No. 3, has Captain George Hamilton of Redhouse being captured by Hanoverian dragoons in their sweep through the Lowther enclosures, and not later on in Clifton, as in the conventional account

15. Quoted in Ferguson, 1889, 220

16. TS 20/3, No. 3, Anonymous Jacobite Journal

17. Ray, 1754, 195. 'Ogden' was Thomas Ogden of Manchester, a weaver

18. O'Sullivan, 1938, 108

19. Lieutenant Colonel Joseph Yorke to Lord Hardwicke, Penrith, 19 December 1745, Yorke, 1913, I, 486

20. CP 8/110, the DoC to Field Marshal Wade, Blackhall, 24 December 1745

21. Thomas Savage, Ferguson, 1889, 221

22. Ibid., 221

23. *The Caledonian Magazine*, 3 January 1746, Letter from York, 21 December 1745

24. Captain Bradshaw, Maurice, 1934, I, 171

25. Captain John Macpherson of Strathmashie, Forbes, 1896, II, 88

26. CP 8/80, the DoC to the DoN, Penrith, 20 December 1745

27. Captain John MacPherson of Strathmashie, Forbes, 1896, II, 88–9

28. TS 20/3, No. 3, Anonymous Jacobite Journal

29. MacDonnell of Lochgarry, Blaikie, 1897, 117

30. TS 20/3, No. 3, Anonymous Jacobite Journal

31. CP 8/190, Cluny MacPherson's account

32. Lieutenant Colonel Joseph Yorke to Lord Hardwicke, Penrith, 19 December 1745, Yorke, 1913, I, 468

33. Hughes, 1746, 18–19

34. Lord Egmont, 13 January 1746, H.M.C. *The MSS of the Earl of Egmont*, 1923, III, 312

35. Lord George Murray, 'Marches of the Highland Army', Chambers, 1834, 72

36. Lieutenant Colonel Joseph Yorke to Lord Hardwicke, Penrith, 19 December 1745, Yorke, 1913, I, 486

37. Stuart Papers 271/121, Sir Thomas Sheridan to Colonel Daniel O'Brien, Dumfries, 21 January 1746

38. Captain John MacPherson of Strathmashie, Forbes, 1896, II, 90. The sword belonged to Lieutenant Colonel Honeywood

39. Thomas Savage, Ferguson, 1889, 222

40. Maxwell of Kirkconnell, 1841, 88

41. Stuart Papers 171/121, Sir Thomas Sheridan to Colonel Daniel O'Brien, Dumfries, 21 December 1745. See also TS 20/3, No. 3, Anonymous Jacobite Journal

42. TS 20/3, No. 3, Anonymous Jacobite Journal

43. O'Sullivan, 1938, 111; Johnstone, 1822, 100; John Daniel's 'Progress', Blaikie, 1916, 188

44. Lord George Murray, 'Marches of the Highland Army', Chambers, 1834, 75

45. *The General Evening Post*, 31 December 1745, Letter from Penrith, 23 December 1745

46. Lieutenant Colonel Joseph Yorke to Lord Hardwicke, before Carlisle, 24 December 1745, Yorke, 1913, I, 488

47. CP 8/41, Walter Lutwidge (Sheriff of Whitehaven) and five others to the DoC, Whitehaven, 15 December 1745

48. CP 8/52, the DoC to the DoN, 17 December 1745

49. Ray, 1754, 202

50. *The York Courant*, 31 December 1745, Letter from Blackhall, 5.30 p.m., 27 December 1745

51. Anon., *A Journey through Part of England and Scotland*, 1746, 14

52. Anon., *A genuine Account of the Behaviour, Confessions and Dying Words of Francis Townley*, etc., 1746, 10–11

53. CP 8/89, the DoC to the DoN, Blackhall, 22 December 1745

54. *The York Courant*, 31 December 1745, Letter from Blackhall, 5.30 p.m., 27 December 1745

55. *The York Courant*, 31 December 1745, Letter from Penrith, 28 December 1745

56. Ray, 1754, 203–4

57. NP, the Duke of Richmond to the DoN, Upperby, 30 December 1745

58. CP 8/209, 'Records of the Councils of War at Carlisle', 22–29 December 1745

59. NP, the Duke of Richmond to the DoN, Upperby, 30 December 1745

60. SP 36/80, Major General Howard to the DoN, Carlisle, 6 January 1746

61. Prebendary Wilson to Rev. John Waugh, Carlisle, 9 January 1746, Moundsey, 1867, 186

62. NP, James Hewitt to his son John, joiner in Coventry, Carlisle, 9 January 1746

63. NP, James Hewitt to William Hewitt, linen draper in Coventry, undated

64. SP 36/82, Major Farrer to Lord Lonsdale, 24 February 1746

65. SP 36/77, Dr Sterne to the DoN, York, 14 December 1745

66. SP 36/78, the DoN to Dr Sterne, 30 December 1745

67. CP 8/77, Henry Pelham to Fawk, 20 December 1745

68. SP 36/80, 'The King's friends' to the DoN, Manchester, 10 January 1746

CHAPTER 13

Meanwhile, in Scotland ...

1. Lieutenant Colonel Joseph Yorke to Lord Hardwicke, Stirling, 3 February 1746, Yorke, 1913, I, 496

2. CP 7/199, the Lord Justice Clerk to the DoN, Edinburgh, 22 November 1745

3. CP 7/702, Lieutenant Colonel John Campbell to Lieutenant General Guest, Inverary, 12 November 1745

4. CP 7/28, Lord Loudoun and Duncan Forbes to Field Marshal Wade, Culloden, 13 November 1745

5. CP 6/274, Lord Lewis Gordon to John Murray, Huntly Castle, 28 October 1745

6. CP 7/385, James Moir to Lord Lewis Gordon, Aberdeen, 4 November 1745

7. SHAT Al 3512, Lord John Drummond, Perth, 12 December 1745

8. Ibid.

9. Ray, 1754, 174

10. CP 11/340, Deposition of Robert Skinner, Aberdeen, 7 March 1746

11. CP 7/439, James Moir to Lord Lewis Gordon, Aberdeen, 27 November 1745

12. CP 11/109, 'Names to enquire into character of Jacobites', Montrose, 26 February 1746

13. CP 12/49, Rev. George Aitken to the Managers of Montrose, 11 March 1746; CP 12.113, Testimonial of the Managers of Montrose, 15 March 1746

14. *The General Evening Post*, 12 December 1745, Letter from a gentleman of Angus

15. *The Westminster Journal*, 16 November 1745, Letter from a gentleman at Perth to a friend at Berwick, 1 November 1745

16. CP 12/172, Deposition of Andrew Forsyth, Perth, 18 March 1746

17. CP 7/385, James Moir to Lord Lewis Gordon, Aberdeen, 4 November 1745

18. CP 10/148, 'Proceedings of the Committee appointed by His Royal Highness to compose the Magistracy of Perth 'till the same can be regularly settled', Perth, 9 February 1746

19. Account of Mrs Fraser, sister of Duncan Forbes of Culloden, *More Culloden Papers*, 1923–30, IV, 102–4. See also CP 6/274, Lord Lewis Gordon to John Murray, Huntly Castle, 28 October 1745

20. CP 8/177, Duncan Forbes to Norman MacLeod of Dunvegan, Culloden, 13 December 1745

21. TS 20/3, No. 3, Anonymous Jacobite Journal

22. 'Memoirs of the Rebellion in 1745 and 1746, so far as it concerned the counties of Aberdeen and Banff', Blaikie, 1916, 141

23. Ibid., 143

24. Ibid., 142–3

25. TS 20/3, No. 3, Anonymous Jacobite Journal

26. Anon., 'A History of the Rebellion in the Years 1745 and 1746', Tayler, H., 1944, 133

27. 'Memoirs of the Rebellion in 1745 and 1746, so far as it concerned the counties of Aberdeen and Banff', Blaikie, 1916, 145

28. CP 13/260, Deposition of John Stewart, Supervisor of the Excise in Turriff, Banff, 10 April 1746

29. John Daniel's 'Progress', Blaikie, 1916, 178–9

30. CP 7/420, James Moir to Lord Lewis Gordon, Aberdeen, 22 November 1745

31. SHAT Al 3152, Lord John Drummond, Perth, 12 December 1745

CHAPTER 14

The Elements: The Seas and the Skies

1. National Maritime Museum Adm/L/Baltimore 3

2. Seton and Arnot, 1928–9, II, 25

3. CP 10/160, Rear Admiral Byng to Fawk, *Gloucester*, off Montrose, 10 February 1746

4. TS 20/91, 'The Joynt and Several Information of Thomas Hill, late commander of His Majesty's Sloop Hazard, Michael Burgess lieutenant, William Bendall gunner, W.M. Murphy purser and Benjamin Hill clerk of the said sloop'

5. James Moir to Lord Lewis Gordon, Aberdeen, 22 November 1745

6. TS 20/91, 'The Joynt and Several Information'

7. SHAT Al 3152, Lord John Drummond, Perth, 12 December 1745

8. CP 14/219, Rear Admiral Byng to Archibald Scott, London, 14 April 1746

9. CP 9/66, the DoC to Lieutenant General Hawley, London, 11 January 1746

10. CP 9/89, Rear Admiral Byng to the DoC, *Gloucester*, in Leith Roads, 16 January 1746

11. CP 12/198, the DoC to the DoN, Aberdeen, 19 March 1746

12. SHAT Al 3152, 'Instruction Générale pour les troupes qui doivent embarquer aux ordres du Mr le duc de Richelieu', undated

13. Admiral Vernon to the Secretary of the Admiralty, Portsmouth, 17 August 1745, 'Vernon Papers', 1958, 451

14. Admiral Vernon to the Secretary of the Admiralty, Deal, 27 October 1745, Ibid., 496–7

15. Richmond, 1920, II, 180

16. SHAT Al 3152, Marshal Richelieu to the comte d'Argenson, 5 January (OS) 1746

17. SHAT Al 3152, Marshal Richelieu to the comte d'Argenson, 15 January (OS) 1746

18. Bannatyne, 1923, 126

19. NP 32,706, the Duke of Richmond to the DoN, Goodwood, 29 January 1746. See also Captain Samuel Bagshawe to Dr Thomas Fletcher, Eastbourne, 7 February 1746, in Guy, 1990, 49

20. Admiral Vernon to the Secretary of the Admiralty, Deal, 13 December 1745, 'Vernon Papers', 1958, 520

21. Charles Stuart to Admiral Vernon, Flushing, 22 December 1745, Ibid., 568

22. CP 9/29, Major General Ellison (?), 'Observations and Remarks', 3 January 1746

23. CP 12/43, 'The Report of Lieutenant General St Clair', 11 March 1746

24. Admiral Vernon to the Secretary of the Admiralty, *Norwich*, in the Downs, 20 December 1745

25. CP 12/43, 'The Report of Lieutenant General St Clair'

26. Alexander MacDonald (Alasdair MacMhaighstir Alasdair), quoted in Gillies, 1989, 22

27. Quoted in Whatley, in Devine (ed.), 1990, 6

28. Barker, quoted in Kington, 1988, 60, 18

29. Quoted in Tomasson, 1958, 15

30. NP 32,705, John Pelham to the DoN, Crowhurst, 11 and 16 December 1745; *The York Courant*, 20 August 1745

31. *The London Evening Post*, 14 November 1745

32. Abbé Butler to the Duke of Ormonde, undated, August 1745, Tayler, A. and H., 1939, 139. See also Maxwell of Kirkconnell, 1841, 158

33. Quoted in Gillies, 1989, 25

34. Lady Hardwicke to Lieutenant Colonel Joseph Yorke, London, 17 September 1745, Yorke, 1913, I, 453

35. The Lord Chancellor Hardwicke to the Hon. Philip Yorke, London, 21 September 1745, Ibid., I, 457

36. SP 36/70, report of John Giles, Carlisle, 3 October 1745

37. *The Edinburgh Evening Courant*, 19 November 1745

38. CP 7/199, the Lord Justice Clerk to the DoN, Edinburgh, 22 November 1745

39. CP 7/200, correspondent of the Lord Justice Clerk, Perth, 19 November 1745

40. Anon., *A Journey through Part of England and Scotland*, 1746, 3

41. CP 10/160, Rear Admiral Byng to Fawk, *Gloucester*, off Montrose, 10 February 1746

42. CP 11/154, the Lord Justice Clerk to Fawk, Edinburgh, 1 March 1746

43. CP 12/28, the DoC to the DoN, Aberdeen, 9 March 1746

44. CP 13/38, the Earl of Albemarle to Colonel Napier, Strathbogie (Huntly), 25 March 1746

45. CP 13/88, the DoC to the DoN, 31 March 1746

46. CP 13/149, the Earl of Albemarle to Colonel Napier, 10 a.m,, 4 April 1746

47. Ray, 1754, 312

48. Poem of John Roy Stuart, in Gillies, 1989, XXX, 41

PART THREE

CHAPTER 15

The Campaign of Stirling and Falkirk, 20 December 1745 – 1 February 1746

1. CP 10/220, Anon., 'Anent the March of the Highland Army,' undated

2. CP 8/96, the Lord Justice Clerk to Field Marshal Wade, Edinburgh, 22 December 1745

3. Lord George Murray, 'Marches of the Highland Army', Chambers, 1834, 76

4. MacLean, 1996, 30

5. Johnstone, 1822, 104

6. Pennant [1774–6], 1998, 99; Johnstone, 1822, 104

7. Chambers, 1869, 206, 207

8. Pennant [1774–6], 1998, 105

9. Ibid., 106

10. MacLean, 1996, 30

11. Hamilton Palace was demolished in the twentieth century on account of subsidence caused by coal mining. The famous Mausoleum in the park now stands forlornly just to the west of the M74 motorway

12. John Daniel's 'Progress', Blaikie, 1916, 191

13. Ibid., 191

14. Ray, 1754, 232; Savile, in Devine, 1999, 10; Burt [1754], 1818, I, 22; Carlyle, 1860, I, 75

15. Fergusson, 1951, 57

16. CP 11/164, 'Memorial Stating the facts relative to the Conduct of the Town of Glasgow'; Chambers, 1869, 211; John Daniel's 'Progress,' Blaikie, 1916, 191

17. SP 36/77, Field Marshal Wade to the DoN, Ripon, 15 December 1745

18. CP 8/166, Lieutenant General Hawley to the DoN, Newcastle, 31 December 1745

19. CP 9/43, Lieutenant General Hawley to the DoN, Edinburgh, 7 January 1746

20. Horace Walpole to Horace Mann, 17 January 1746, Walpole, 1903–5, II, 168

21. SP 36/80, Dr Goldie to Rev. John Waugh, Dumfries, 12 January 1746

22. CP 9/43, Lieutenant General Hawley to the DoN, Edinburgh, 7 January 1746

23. CP 9/81, Lieutenant General Hawley to the DoN, Edinburgh, 15 January 1746

24. SP 36/80, Dr Goldie to Rev. John Waugh, Dumfries, 12 January 1746

25. CP 11/164, 'Memorial Stating the facts relative to the Conduct of the Town of Glasgow'

26. Ray, 1754, 258

27. Johnstone, 1822, 113, 136

28. CP 9/82, Major General Huske to Lieutenant General Hawley, 14 January 1746

29. MacLean, 1996, 31

30. Ray, 1754, 263

31. Crichton (*Woodhouselee MS*), 1907, 84

32. CP 9/196, Colonel Grant to O'Sullivan, Alloa, 10 January 1746

33. 'A Narrative of Sundry Services performed, together with an Account of Money Dispensed in the Service of the Government during the Late Rebellion by Walter Grossett', Blaikie, 1916, 356

34. Ibid., 357

35. CP 9/208, Lord George Murray to O'Sullivan, Falkirk, 12 January 1746

36. Walter Grossett's 'Narrative', Blaikie, 1916, 360

37. CP 9/82, Major General Huske to Lieutenant General Hawley, Linlithgow, 14 January 1746

38. CP 9/81, Lieutenant General Hawley to the DoC, Edinburgh, 15 January 1746

39. Ibid.

40. Anon., *A Journey through Part of England and Scotland*, 1746, 54

41. CP 9/82, Major General Huske to Lieutenant General Hawley, Linlithgow, 15 January 1746

42. Johnstone, 1822, 119

43. TS 20/3, No. 3, Anonymous Jacobite Journal

44. O'Sullivan, 1938, 116

45. TS 20/3, No. 3, Anonymous Jacobite Journal

46. CP 9/102, 'The Case of Archibald Cunningham late Captain in the Royal Regiment of Artillery', undated

47. Home, 1822, 128

48. CP 9/102, 'The Case of Archibald Cunningham'

49. John Daniel's 'Progress', Blaikie, 1916, 194

50. Probably the lowest in Reid, 1996, 99, and the highest in Livingstone of Bachuil, Aikman and Hart, 2001, 230–1

51. Poem of Alexander Cameron, Gillies, 1989, 38

52. John Daniel's 'Progress', Blaikie, 1916, 195

53. Johnstone, 1822, 121–2

54. Ibid., 122–3

55. CP 9/115, Lieutenant General Hawley to the DoC, Edinburgh, 19 January 1746

56. Bailey, 1996, 139

57. O'Sullivan, 1938, 118

58. Ibid., 118

59. Chambers, 1869, 237

60. CP 9/110, Captain Fitzgerald, 'Relation of the Battle of Falkirk', dated 18 January 1746, probably composed much later

61. CP 9/115, Lieutenant General Hawley to the DoC, Edinburgh, 19 January 1746

62. O'Sullivan, 1938, 118

63. Elcho, 1907, 377

64. Johnstone, 1822, 127

65. Major General Cholmondeley to Charles Fleetwood Weston Underwood, H.M.C., *Eglinton MSS*, 1885, 441

66. Gillies, 1989, 77

67. CP 9/101, 'The Case of Archibald Cunningham'

68. CP 10/17, Testimony of William King, undated

69. Lord George Murray, 'Marches of the Highland Army', Chambers, 1834, 87-8

70. CP 9/110, Captain Fitzgerald, 'Relation of the Battle of Falkirk'

71. Johnstone, 1822, 127–8

72. Chambers, 1869, 235. The house, later No. 121 High Street, was demolished in about 1900

73. Johnstone, 1822, 128

74. Chambers, 1869, 241

75. Bailey, 1996, 170–1

76. TS 20/3, No. 3 Anonymous Jacobite Journal

77. John Daniel's 'Progress', Blaikie, 1916, 198

78. Chambers, 1869, 257

79. CP 14.381, Deposition of John Crosbie of Westmeath, Perth, 11 May 1746

80. Johnstone, 1822, 133

81. Account of Lord Egmont, H.M.C., *MSS of the Earl of Egmont*, III, 1923, 313

82. CP 10/176, Deposition of Miss Agnes Grahame, 6 February 1746

83. CP 10/172, Major Lockhart's Case, undated

84. Anon., 'A History of the Rebellion in the Years 1745 and 1746,' Tayler, H., 1944, 157

85. Sir John Clerk of Penicuik, 1892, 195

86. James Pringle to Lord Marchmont, Edinburgh, 29 March 1746, 'Marchmont Correspondence, 1933, 350

87. Pennant [1771], 2000, 160

88. CP 9/52, the Duke of Perth to O'Sullivan, Stirling, 21 January 1746

89. Johnstone, 1822, 137-8

90. Ibid., 138

91. CP 9/134, Lieutenant General Hawley to the DoC, Edinburgh, 23 January 1746

92. TS 20/3, No. 3, Anonymous Jacobite Journal

93. SP 36/84, Information of Mary Grant, 20 June 1746

94. *The Westminster Journal*, 15 February 1746, Letter from Edinburgh, 1 February 1746

95. Chambers, 1869, 250

96. For a detailed review of the considerations weighing with the Jacobites at this time, see Bailey, 1996, 174–85

97. Blaikie, 1897, 76–7

98. CP 9/110, Captain George Fitzgerald, 'Relation of the Battle of Falkirk'

99. Chambers, 1869, 244–5

CHAPTER 16

The Retreat to the Highlands

1. Maxwell of Kirkconnell, 1841, 115–16

2. CP 10/220, 'Anent the March of the Highland Army through Kirrimuir, Glamis, Brechin, and Montrose on the 4th, 5th, 6th and 7th of February 1746', by a Presbyterian minister of Angus

3. O'Sullivan, 1938, 127

4. SHAT A1 3154, Lord John Drummond, Gordon Castle, 21 March 1746

5. CP 10/229, 'Anent the March of the Highland Army'

6. O'Sullivan, 1936, 128

7. CP 11/10, Deposition of Henry Fife, Perth, 20 February 1746

8. O'Sullivan, 1938, 128. Katherine Tomasson (*The Jacobite General*, 1958, 177) writes that Lord Lewis Gordon took seventeen small cannon by way of Dunkeld and Blair, that Lord George left thirteen 8-pounders and 12-pounders duly spiked and unserviceable at Perth, and that he took two more of the 8-pounders to Blair. However, Lord Lewis's guns were in any case assigned to the column of Prince Charles, and, on the last point, it is possible that there is some confusion with the pieces which Lord George already found in battery at Montrose

9. CP 10/220, 'Anent the March of the Highland Army'

10. John Daniel's 'Progress', Blaikie, 1916, 202

11. CP 10/160, Rear Admiral Byng to Fawk, *Gloucester*, off Montrose, 10 February 1746

12. CP 10/196, Rear Admiral Byng to Fawk, *Gloucester*, off Montrose, 12 February 1746

13. John Daniel's 'Progress', Blaikie, 1916, 203

14. CP 10/256, Anonymous intelligence, 15–17 February 1746

15. Anon., *A Journey through Part of England and Scotland*, 1746, 56

16. Ray, 1754, 262

17. Anon., *A Journey through Part of England and Scotland*, 1746, 58

18. CP 10/233, the DoC to the DoN, Perth, 14 February 1746

19. CP 10/206, the DoC to Lord Loudoun, Perth, 12 February 1746

20. CP 10/131, the DoC to the DoN, Perth, 8 February 1746

21. CP 10/233, the DoC to the DoN, 14 February 1746. For more detail on the Hessians, please see the author's forthcoming *The Hessians in Scotland*

22. CP 10/130, Fawk to lieutenant colonels Agnew and Leighton, Perth, 8 February 1746

23. Anon., *A Journey through Part of England and Scotland*, 1746, 59-60

24. Ibid., 63–4

25. CP 13/306, Miss Isabel Stuart to Miss Anne Haldane, Inverness, 29 March 1746

26. CP 10/95, Sir Robert Menzies to the Lord Justice Clerk, Castle Menzies, 7 February 1746

27. CP 10/96, Robert Robertson to Duke James of Atholl, Kirkmichael, 7 February 1746

28. CP 36/85, Ludovick Grant to Lord Loudoun, 11 February 1746

29. CP 13/306, Isabel Stuart to Anne Haldane, Inverness, 29 March 1746

30. MacLean, 1996, 33

31. Pennant [1771], 2000, 124

32. CP 12/206, the DoC to Lord Loudoun and Duncan Forbes, Perth, 12 February 1746

33. CP 13/306, Isabel Stuart to Anne Haldane, 29 March 1746

34. Stuart Papers 273/52, Sir Thomas Sheridan to Colonel Daniel O'Brien, 12 March 1746

35. CP 12/71, Lord Loudoun to Lord Stair, Dornoch, 2 March 1746

36. CP 13/306, Isabel Stuart to Anne Haldane, Inverness, 29 March 1746

37. CP 12/71, Lord Loudoun to Lord Stair, Dornoch, 2 March 1746

38. CP 11/58, Lord Glenorchy to the Lord Justice Clerk, 24 February 1746

39. CP 12/71, Lord Loudoun to Lord Stair, Dornoch, 2 March 1746

40. CP 11/153, the Lord Justice Clerk to Fawk, Edinburgh, 28 February 1746

41. Ibid.

42. CP 11/159, the DoC to the DoN, Aberdeen, 28 February 1746

43. Ray, 1754, 365

CHAPTER 17

Confrontation and Counterstrike

1. CP 11/87, the DoC to Fawk, 25 February 1746

2. CP 11/159, the DoC to the DoN, Aberdeen, 28 February 1746

3. O'Sullivan, 1938, 137

4. CP 11/154, the Lord Justice Clerk to Fawk, 28 February 1746

5. CP 12/177, the DoC to Major General John Campbell of Mamore, Aberdeen, 18 March 1746

6. CP 11/267, Major General Campbell of Mamore to Captain Caroline Scott, Inverary, 7 March 1746

7. CP 12/82, Captain Scott to Colonel Napier, Castle Stalker, 12 March 1746

8. Maxwell of Kirkconnell, 1841, 120

9. CP 12/82, Captain Scott to Colonel Napier, Castle Stalker, 10 March 1746

10. CP 13/152, the DoC to the DoN, Aberdeen, 4 March 1746

11. O'Sullivan, 1938, 136–7

12. CP 11/324, Lieutenant Colonel Stapleton to O'Sullivan, Fort Augustus, 5 March 1746

13. CP 11/326, Colonel Grant to O'Sullivan, Fort Augustus, 5 March 1746

14. CP 12/361, Lieutenant Colonel Stapleton to O'Sullivan, Fort Augustus, 9 March 1746

15. CP 10/266, Alexander Campbell to Fawk, Fort William, 17 February 1746

16. CP 11/257, Alexander Campbell to Major General Campbell of Mamore, Fort William, 4 March 1746

17. CP 11/256, John Russell to D. Campbell, Fort William, 4 March 1746

18. CP 11/256, John Russell to Major General Campbell of Mamore, Fort William, 2 March 1746

19. CP 12/119, Captain Scott, 'Prospect for the Defence of His Majesty's Castle of Fort William in case of a siege,' Fort William, 15 March 1746

20. Maxwell of Kirkconnell, 1841, 120–1

21. CP 13/383, Captain Scott, 'Journal of a Siege,' enclosed in Scott to Colonel Napier, Fort William, 31 March 1746

22. CP 12/382, Colonel Kennedy to O'Sullivan, before Fort William, 14 March 1746

23. CP 13/83, Captain Scott's 'Journal'

24. CP 11/235, Captain Scott to Colonel Napier, Fort William, misdated '5 March', probably 5 April 1746

25. Maxwell of Kirkconnell, 1841, 91, 129

26. CP 12/31, Lord Loudoun to the DoC, Dornoch, 10 March 1746

27. SHAT A1 3154, 'Victoire remportée par les troupes du prince Edouard sur Milord Loudon et sur l'avantgarde du duc de Cumberland'

28. MacDonnell of Lochgarry's narrative, in Blaikie, 1897, 120

29. SHAT A1 3154, 'Victoire remportée'

30. CP 12/351, Lord Loudoun's orders, Invershin, 20 March 1746

31. Henderson, 1746, 211

32. TS 20/87, Examination of Henry Fyffe, merchant of Perth, Whitehall, 17 July 1746

33. CP 13/366, Lady Sutherland to Lord Cromartie, Dunrobin, 2 April 1746

34. CP 13/313, Patrick Feat to James Fea, Thurso, 30 March 1746

35. Talbot, 'The Loss of the *Prince Charles*', Taylor, H., 1948, 178-9

36. Ibid., 179

37. CP 13/313, Patrick Fea to James Fea, Thurso, 30 March 1746

38. CP 13/179, the DoC to the DoN, 6 or 7 April 1746. See also CP 13/315, Patrick Fea to John Stewart of Burray, Thurso, 30 March 1746; CP 13/365, Archibald Stewart, William Balfour and John Traill to Lord MacLeod, Kirkwall, 8 April 1746

39. 'Copy of a Letter, said to have been written by Lord George Murray, or one of his friends,' Forbes, 1896, I, 266. The attribution to Lord George is unconvincing

40. CP 12/384, Lord George Murray to Robertson of Struan, 15 March 1746

41. CP 12/132, Fawk to Lord Crawfurd, Aberdeen, 18 March 1746

42. CP 12/123, Captain Duncan Campbell to Lord Crawfurd, Balquhidder, 14 March 1746

43. CP 12/28, the DoC to the DoN, Aberdeen 8 March 1746

44. CP 12/36, in George Schaw to Fawk, 10 March (?) 1746

45. CP 12/279, Intelligence of Rev. John Macinnes, 22 March 1746

46. CP 12/141, Lieutenant Colin Campbell to Lord Glenorchy, Castle Menzies, 17 March 1746

47. CP 12/153, Lord Glenorchy to the DoC, Perth, 18 March 1746

48. CP 12/192, Sir Robert Menzies to Lord Glenorchy, Murthly, 19 March 1746

49. CP 12/155, Archibald Campbell to Lord Crawfurd (?), Castle Menzies, 17 March 1746

50. CP 12/404, Lord George Murray to O'Sullivan, Blair Atholl, noon, 17 March 1746. Lord George's communications with O'Sullivan at this time are relaxed and friendly, which suggests a temporary reconciliation

51. Anon., *A Journey through Part of England and Scotland*, 1746, 64

52. CP 13/145, Lieutenant Colonel Agnew to Fawk, Blair Castle, 4 April 1746

53. CP 12/404, Lord George Murray to O'Sullivan, Blair Atholl, 17 March 1746

54. Home, 1822, 148

55. CP 12/194, Intelligence of Rev. Stewart, 19 March 1746

56. Ibid.

57. Lord George Murray, 'Marches of the Highland Army', Chambers, 1834, 108

58. Tullibardine, 1908, I, 329

59. CP 12/194, Intelligence of Rev. Stewart, 19 March 1746

60. CP 13/145, Lieutenant Colonel Agnew to Fawk, Blair Castle, 4 April 1746

61. SHAT A1 3154, Lord George Drummond, Gordon Castle, 21 March 1746

62. CP 12/310, the DoC to Lieutenant Colonel Agnew, Aberdeen, 7 April 1746

63. Lord George Murray, 'Marches of the Highland Army', Chambers 1834, 110

64. Gibson, 1994, 98-9

65. CP 12/35, the Lord Justice Clerk to Fawk, Edinburgh, 10 March 1746

66. CP 12/404, Lord George Murray to O'Sullivan, Blair Atholl, 17 March 1746

CHAPTER 18

The Duke of Cumberland in Aberdeen, and the First Pacifications

1. Pringle, 1753, 44

2. CP 11/236, the DoC to the DoN, Aberdeen, 5 March 1746

3. Henderson, 1746, 236

4. Tayler, A. and H., 1928, 64

5. CP 11/108, the Lord Justice Clerk to Fawk, Edinburgh, 26 February 1746

6. 'Memoirs of the Rebellion in 1745 and 1746, so far as it concerned the Counties of Aberdeen and Banff', Blaikie, 1916, 156

7. CP 11/211, 'The Petition of the Loyal Burgesses and Inhabitants of the Burgh of Perth, for managing the affairs of Perth', Perth, 13 February 1746

8. CP 13/32, George Schaw to Fawk, Perth, 30 March 1746; CP 13/71, the Lord Justice Clerk to Fawk, Edinburgh, 31 March 1746; CP 10/183, George Murison to Fawk, Montrose, 11 February 1746; CP 12/9, George Murison to Fawk, Montrose, 8 March 1746

9. CP 12/28, the DoC to the DoN, Aberdeen, 9 March 1746

10. CP 12/208, Fawk to the Lord Justice Clerk, Perth, 12 February 1746

11. CP 11/326, the DoC to the DoN, 5 March 1746

12. CP 12/38, Evidence against Lady Skellater, 10 March 1746

13. Ibid.

14. Allardyce, 1895–6, II, 311

15. CP 11/236, the DoC to the DoN, Aberdeen, 5 March 1746

16. CP 11/182, George Ogilby and Andrew Molison to James Harrison, Kirrer, 28 February 1746; CP 12/108, the DoC to the DoN, Aberdeen, 14 March 1746; CP 12/169, the Lord Justice Clerk to Fawk, 18 March 1746

17. CP 12/266, the DoN to the DoC, 21 March 1746

18. CP 12/323, Major Lafansille to Colonel Napier, Montrose, 25 March 1746

19. CP 12/206, Captain John Gore to Colonel Napier, Montrose, 24 March 1746

20. CP 12/300, Major John Gore to Colonel Napier, Montrose, 23 March 1746

21. CP 13/104, Major Lafansille to Colonel Napier, Cortachy, 1 April 1746

22. CP 13/104, Major Lafansille to Colonel Napier, Cortachy, 1 April 1746

23. CP 12/209, the DoC to the DoN, Aberdeen, 15 March 1746

24. CP 13/374, Sir Thomas Sheridan to O'Sullivan, quoting Prince Charles, 13 March 1746

25. CP 13/88, the DoC to the DoN, 31 March 1746

26. CP 12/181, Major General Bland to Fawk, Strathbogie (Huntly), 19 March 1746

27. CP 13/306, Isabel Stuart to Anne Haldane, Inverness, 29 March 1746

28. Captain Robert Stewart's account, in Forbes, 1896, II, 216

29. CP 13/306, Isabel Stewart to Anne Haldane, Inverness, 29 March 1746

30. Stewart's account, in Forbes, 1896, II, 217

31. Ray, 1754, 299

32. CP 12/353, the DoC to the DoN, 26 March 1746

33. CP 12/349, Information of Alexander Wilson, 26 March 1746

34. CP12/234, Lord Albemarle to Colonel Napier, Strathbogie, 25 March 1746

35. CP 13/6, Lord Albemarle to Fawk, Strathbogie, 27 March 1746

36. CP 13/352, Sir Thomas Sheridan to Colonel John Roy Stuart, Inverness, 6 March 1746

37. CP 13/51, Sir Thomas Sheridan to Lochiel and Keppoch, Inverness, 4 April 1746

38. Ray, 1754, 320

39. SHAT A1 3154, Lord John Drummond, Gordon Castle, 21 March 1746

40. CP 12/328, Rev. James Lumsden to Rev. James Pollock, Fyvie, 25 March 1746

41. CP 13/327, the Master of Lovat to Colonel Charles Fraser, 1 April 1746; CP 13/360, Sir Thomas Sheridan to the Duke of Perth, Inverness, 7 April 1746

CHAPTER 19

The Last Campaign, 8 April – 15 May 1746

1. 'Memoirs of the Rebellion in 1745 and 1746, so far as it concerned the Counties of Aberdeen and Banff,' Blaikie, 1916, 159

2. Ray, 1754, 312

3. Anon., *A Journey through Part of England and Scotland*, 1746, 78; Ray, 1754, 313

4. Hughes, 1746, 33

5. Anon., *A Journey through Part of England and Scotland*, 1746, 79

6. Ray, 1754, 315

7. Quoted in Tayler, A. and H., 1928, 92

8. Lieutenant Colonel Joseph Yorke to Lord Hardwicke, Speymouth, 12 April 1746, Yorke, 1913, I, 519

9. O'Sullivan, 1938, 148–9

10. Maxwell of Kirkconnell, 1841, 138. Confirmed by Lord Kilmarnock, see Hughes, 1746, 49

11. Anon., 'A History of the Rebellion in the Years 1745 and 1746', Tayler, H., 1944, 196

12. CP 13/108, Shaw and Stuart, 'Observations and remarks on the fords of the Spey beginning with that of Orton two miles above Fochabers', enclosed in Lord Albemarle to Colonel Napier, Strathbogie (Huntly), 1 April 1746

13. CP 13/332, Colonel Roderick Chisholm to Colonel John Roy Stuart, Rothes, 2 April 1746. Roderick was the youngest of the five sons of the chief of the Chisholms, but he led the clan to war. He was killed at Culloden

14. CP 13/150, Intelligence from Strathbogie, 4 April 1746

15. Reid, 1996, 125

16. John Daniel's 'Progress', Blaikie, 1916, 269

17. CP 13/56, the Duke of Gordon to Fawk, Haddo House, 30 March 1746

18. Soldier of the Royal Scots, in Leask and McCance, 1915, 149

19. 'Memoirs of the Rebellion in 1745 and 1746, so far as it concerned the Counties of Aberdeen and Banff,' Blaikie, 1916, 160

20. Ray, 1754, 317

21. For Ray's account to make complete sense, Kingston's Horse must have ridden down the right bank from Fochabers to Bellie. The maps of the time differ considerably in detail, and the frequent changes of channels make it impossible to match the crossings with the topography of the river today

22. Ray, 1754, 317–18.

23. Henderson, 1748, 110. 'Captain Hunter' was Captain David Hunter of Burnside, of the Life-guards, and the incident is also described in TS 20/88, Testimony of Andrew Robinson, 19 July 1746

24. 'A History of the Rebellion in the Years 1745 and 1746', Tayler, H., 1944, 202

25. Hughes, 1746, 35

26. Soldier of the Royal Scots, in Leask and McCance, 1915, 149

27. Strange, 1855, I, 55. A set of the engraved printing plates was discovered on the field of Culloden in the nineteenth century

28. CP 13/399, Sir Thomas Sheridan to the Duke of Perth, Inverness, 10 a.m., 13 April 1746

29. H.M.C., *The Manuscripts of the Duke of Roxburgh etc.*, 1894, Appendix, Part III, 49

30. Ray, 1754, 321; Henderson, 1746, 245

31. Ray, 1754, 322

32. Pennant [1771], 2000, 99

33. Officer of Bligh's 20th, Moundsey, 1856, 222

34. Henderson, 1746, 246

35. Maxwell of Kirkconnell, 1841, 130

36. SHAT A1 3154, 'Relation de la bataille de Colloden'

37. O'Sullivan, 1938, 153

38. CP 13/294, the DoC to the DoN, Nairn, 15 April 1746

CHAPTER 20

Culloden

1. Strange, 1855, I, 61

2. SHAT A1 3154, O'Donovan's relation

3. Maxwell of Kirkconnell, 1841, 144

4. O'Sullivan, 1938, 150

5. 'Narrative of Rev. George Innes', Forbes, 1896, II, 275

6. O'Sullivan, 1938, 148

7. Ibid., 151

8. Hughes, 1746, 49

9. 'Copy of a Letter, said to have been written by Lord George Murray or one of his friends,' Forbes, 1896, I, 257

10. Hughes, 1746, 36

11. Strange, 1855, I, 56

12. O'Sullivan, 1938, 154

13. John Daniel's 'Progress', Blaikie, 1916, 212

14. O'Sullivan, 1938, 157–8

15. 'Copy of a Letter', Forbes, 1896, I, 260

16. Tomasson, 1958, 211; 'A Copy of Colonel Henry Ker of Gradyne, his account', Forbes, 1896, I, 360

17. From the MS. of the Laird of Mackinnon, 'A Genuine and full Account of the Battle of Culloden', Forbes, 1896, I, 6–7

18. Strange, 1855, I, 59

19. O'Sullivan, 1938, 159

20. SHAT A1 3154, 'Relation de la bataille de Colloden'

21. Tomasson, 1958, 222

22. Elcho, 1907, 430

23. Ibid., 433–4

24. Hughes, 1746, 48–9

25. Whitefoord, 1898, 76–7

26. CP 12/4, Lord Cathcart to the DoC, 'Description'

27. O'Sullivan, 1938, 160

28. 'Narrative of the Rev. George Innes', Forbes, 1896, II, 277

29. O'Sullivan, 1938, 161

30. SHAT A1 3154, 'Relation de la bataille de Colloden'

31. O'Sullivan, 1938, 162

32. Ibid., 163

33. Most histories blame O'Sullivan for the failure to occupy the enclosure. Not least of the services of Stuart Reid has been to bring home the prime responsibility to Lord George, see Reid, 1994, 87–8, and 149–50

34. O'Sullivan, 1938, 164. See also Johnstone, 1822, 188–9

35. O'Sullivan, 1938, 163

36. John Daniel's 'Progress', Blaikie, 1916, 213–14

37. Hughes, 1746, 49

38. *The Caledonian Mercury*, 24 April 1746, Letter from an officer to his friend in Edinburgh, 18 April 1746

39. Elcho, 1907, 431

40. Hughes, 1746, 42–3

41. Ibid., 41

42. Quoted in Maurice, 1934, I, 183

43. SHAT A1 3154, 'Relation de la bataille de Colloden'

44. *The York Courant*, 29 April 1746, letter of Captain Clifton, Inverness, 17 April 1746. The man killed by Clifton cannot be Lochiel himself, who survived the battle, but possibly Captain Allan Cameron, or Sergeant Malcolm ('Whiskie') Cameron

45. Home, 1822, 172

46. O'Sullivan, 1938, 164

47. Johnstone, 1822, 214

48. Home, 1822, 173

49. Ray, 1754, 337

50. Hughes, 1746, 44

51. Account of Lady Robertson, Forbes, 1896, I, 218

52. McLaren, 1957, 198

53. Johnstone, 1822, 199

54. Ibid., 203

55. Maxwell of Kirkconnell, 1841, 158

56. Reid, 1996, 128

57. Whitefoord, 1898, 70

58. Lieutenant Colonel Joseph Yorke to the Hon. Philip Yorke, Fort Augustus, 3 August 1746, Yorke, 1913, I, 542

CHAPTER 21

Repression and Transfiguration

1. Sir Alexander MacDonald of Sleat to Duncan Forbes, Urquhart, 4 May 1746, *More Culloden Papers*, 1923–30, V, 79

2. Guy, in Woosnam-Savage (ed.), 1995, 42

3. Henderson, 1746, 259

4. Hughes, 1746, 50

5. *A Journey through Part of England and Scotland*, 1746, 88

6. CP 14/354, Lord Ancrum to Fawk, Aberdeen, 9 May 1746

7. CP 14/384, Lord Ancrum to Colonel Napier, Aberdeen, 15 May 1746

8. Quoted in Tullibardine, 1908, I, 330

9. *A Journey through Part of England and Scotland*, 1746, 95

10. Hughes, 1746, 55, 56–7

11. Simpson, 2000, 108–9

12. Lieutenant Colonel Joseph Yorke to the Hon. Philip Yorke, Fort Augustus, 3 August 1746, Yorke, 1913, I, 543

13. Fergusson, 1951, 197

14. Ibid., 217

15. Johnstone, 1822, 257

16. See the many statements made on board warships in TS 20/94.

17. TS 10/94, Statement of Malcolm MacGregor, Raasay, 21 July 1746.

18. SP 36/81, 'Carrington's Account of the Prisoners in Newgate and New Prison', 19 February 1746

19. Archbishop Herring and Thomas Place, in Oates, 2000, 49

20. SP 36/82, Mr. Masterman to the DoN, undated, March 1746

21. SP 36/83, Mr. Masterman to the DoN, York, 9 April 1746

22. Tayer, A. and H., 1928, 261–2

23. Craig, 2000, 164

24. Bradstreet [1750], 1929, 157

25. Ibid., 164

26. *A Genuine Account of the Behaviour, Confession, and Dying Words of Francis Townley*, etc., London 1746

27. TS 20/30, Philip Carteret Webb to the Treasury Solicitor, 7 August 1746

28. Peter Pinski (*The Stuarts' Last Secret: The Missing Heirs of Bonny Prince Charlie*, Edinburgh 2002), made out a well-documented case for an

illegitimate line of descent to his own by way of the Prince's grand-daughter, Marie-Victoire

29. SP 36/82, 'Some Thoughts of what appears to be necessary for extinguishing, or weakening that spirit of sedition and rebellion, which prevails in Scotland, or rather the northern parts of it', undated

30. Lord Glenorchy to the Hon. Philip Yorke, Taymouth, 24 July 1746, Yorke, 1913, I, 549

31. On this, and much else, see Ó Ciardha, 2002, passim

32. Pennant [1774–6], 1998, 376

33. Boswell [1785], 1996, 257–8

34. Scott, W., *Waverley* [1814], 1994, 6–7

35. TS 20/38, Philip Carteret Webb to the Treasury Solicitor, Lincoln, 23 July 1746

APPENDIX I

The Clans, North to South

1. On all of this see Fereday, 1980, passim

2. Pennant [1771], 2000, 120

3. CP 13/310, the Earl of Cromartie to the Countess of Sutherland, 31 March 1746

4. Henderson, 1748, 45

5. Alexander MacBean, 'Memorial concerning the Highlands', Blaikie, 1916, 76–7

6. Henderson, 1748, 45

7. TS 20/3, No. 3, Anonymous Jacobite Journal

8. Henderson, 1748, 6

9. Murray of Broughton's 'Account of the Highland Clans', The Tower, 22 August 1746, Murray of Broughton, 1898, 441

10. Pennant [1771], 2000, 136

11. Alexander MacBean, 'Memorial concerning the Highlands', Blaikie, 1916, 79

12. Murray of Broughton's 'Account', Murray of Broughton, 1898, 442

13. TS 20/87, Examination of Hugh Ross, 16 December 1746

14. Boswell [1785], 1996, 285

15. 'Memorial anent the True State of the Highlands', Allardyce, 1895–6, I, 167

16. CP 12/202, Lord Glenorchy to the DoC, Perth, 20 March 1746

17. Henderson, 1748, 6

18. Murray of Broughton's 'Account', Murray of Broughton, 1898, 443

19. Craig, 2000, 20

20. Alexander MacBean, 'Memorial concerning the Highlands', Blaikie, 1916, 85

21. 'Memorial anent the True State of the Highlands', Allardyce, 1895–6, I, 170

22. Murray of Broughton's 'Account', Murray of Broughton, 1898, 444

23. Alexander MacBean, 'Memorial concerning the Highlands', Blaikie, 1916, 85

24. CP 12/273, Mrs Penuel Grant to John Grant, Ballindalloch, 12 March 1746

25. CP 12/108, the DoC to the DoN, 14 March 1746

26. CP 12/109, the DoC to the DoN, 14 March (later) 1746

27. CP 14/9, 'Account of Money disbursed by Ludovick Grant of Grant Esq.', 16 April 1746

28. Murray of Broughton's 'Account', Murray of Broughton, 1898, 444

29. Smith, 1995, 18

30. Burt [1754], 1818, I, 332

31. Lieutenant Colonel Joseph Yorke to the Hon. Philip Yorke, Perth, 8 February 1746, Yorke, 1913, I, 500

32. CP 10/230, the DoN to Sir Andrew Agnew, Perth, 13 February 1746

33. CP 11/154, the Lord Justice Clerk to Fawk, Edinburgh, 28 February 1746

34. CP 13/88, the DoC to the DoN, 31 March 1746

35. TS 20/87, Examination of Andrew Johnstone, 19 November 1746

APPENDIX II

The Jacobite Army in Review

1. John Vere, in Allardyce, 1896, II, 362

2. Allardyce, 1896, II, 441. For a detailed analysis of the Manchester Regiment see Monod, 1989, 331-40

3. Bradstreet [1750], 1929, 137–8

4. Annand, 1982, 227

5. Memoirs of the Rebellion in 1745 and 1746 so far as it concerned the counties of Aberdeen and Banff,' Blaikie, 1916, 151

6. John Daniel's 'Progress', in Ibid., 202

7. Browne, 1853, III, 196

8. SHAT A1 3154, Lord John Drummond, Gordon Castle, 21 March 1746

9. 'Copy of a letter, said to have been written by Lord George Murray or one or his friends', Forbes, 1896, I, 264

Bibliography

Manuscript Sources

Cumberland Papers (Windsor Castle). The principal manuscript source. Contains material of political and local as well of military interest, and also the captured Jacobite military correspondence.

Haus-Hof- und Staatsarchiv, Berichte, England, Karton 88 (Vienna; reports of ambassador Wasner)

Hessiches Staatsarchiv, Bestand 4H 2787, *Feldzug in Schottland* (Marburg)

Military Survey of Scotland, 1747–52, Colonel David Watson and William Roy. British Library (London), Maps C9b

National Maritime Museum, series Adm/L, lieutenants' logs (Greenwich)

Newcastle Papers, XX, XXI, Add. MS. 32,705 (British Library, London)

Public Record Office, Kew

— State Papers Domestic 36/44 etc.

— Treasury Solicitor's Papers TS 20/3 etc.

— War Office Papers

Riksarkivet, Fond Anglica, vols. 326 and 328, reports of Caspar Joachim Ringwicht to the King of Sweden and the *Kanslipresident* (Stockholm)

Stuart Papers (Windsor Castle). Holds the scanty correspondence between the headquarters of Prince Charles and France.

Royal Society, London. *A Meteorological Diary kept by the late John Hooker Esq. of Tunbridge, begun the 18th of August 1728 and continued to the 26th of June 1765, being a term of 37 years*

Service Historique de l'Armée de Terre, A1 3152, 3154, *Campagne d'Ecosse*. Esp. for the reports of Lord John Drummond direct to France

Quotations from the Cumberland Papers and the Stuart Papers are by gracious permission of Her Majesty the Queen.

Documentary Collections; Memoirs, Letters and Commentaries of Contemporaries and Near-Contemporaries

'The Albemarle Papers. Being the Correspondence of William Anne, Second Earl of Albemarle, Commander-in-Chief in Scotland 1746–1747', *New Spalding Club*, 2 vols., Aberdeen, 1902

Allardyce, James (ed.), 'Historical Papers relating to the Jacobite Period 1699– 1750', *New Spalding Club*, 2 vols. with continuous pagination, Aberdeen, 1895– 6

Anon., *A Genuine Account of the Behaviour of ... Francis Townley*, etc., London, 1746

Anon. (ed. Tayler, Henrietta), 'A History of the Rebellion in the Years 1745 and 1746', *Roxburgh Club*, Oxford, 1944

Anon., *A Journey through Part of England and Scotland. Along with the Army under the Command of His Royal Highness the Duke of Cumberland*, London, 1746

Anon. (Ranald MacDonald the Younger?), 'An Account of Proceedings from Prince Charles' Landing to Prestonpans', *Miscellany of the Scottish History Society*, IX, Edinburgh, 1958

Anon., 'A Plain, General and Authentick Account, of the Conduct and Proceedings of the Rebels, during their Stay in Derby, from Wednesday the Fourth, till Friday morning the Sixth of December 1745', *Proceedings of the Society of Antiquaries of London*, 2nd series, III, London, 1864–7

D'Argenson, marquis, *Journal et Mémoires* (ed. Rathery, E.J.B.), 9 vols., Paris, 1859–67

Atkinson, C.T., 'Some Letters about the "Forty-Five"', *Journal of the Society of Army Historial Research*, XXVII, London, 1959

The Weather Journals of a Rutland Squire. Thomas Barker of Lyndon Hall, (ed. Kingston, John), Oakham, 1988

Blaikie, Walter Biggar, 'Origins of the 'Forty-Five and other Papers Relating to that Rising', *Scottish History Society*, 2nd series, II, Edinburgh, 1916. Includes John Daniel's *Progress*. Blaikie was the figurative granddaddy of modern scholarship relating to the '45, as well as being the uncle of Alastair and Henrietta Tayler, who carried the tradition into the next generation.

Bland, Humphrey, *A Treatise of Military Discipline*, 5th ed. Dublin, 1743

Boswell, James, *The Journal of a Tour to the Hebrides with Samuel Johnson* [journey made in 1773, 3rd ed., 1785], new ed. by McGowan, Ian, with Johnson's *A Journey to the Western Islands of Scotland*, Edinburgh, 1996

The Life and Adventures of Captain Dudley Bradstreet [1750] (ed. Taylor, G.S.), London, 1929

'Burdett's Map of Derbyshire 1791', ed. Harley, J.B.; Fowkes, D.V.; Harvey, J.C., *Derbyshire Record Society*, Derby, 1975

Burt, Captain Edward, *Letters from a Gentleman in the North of Scotland to his Friend in London*, 2 vols., London 1818. The classic account of a surveyor engaged in the building of Wade's roads. This edition includes Wade's memoranda of the 1720s. A useful single-volume edition, ed. Simmons, A., was published in Edinburgh in 1998 as *Burt's Letters from the North of Scotland* but without the additional material

Beppy Byrom's Diary. An Eye-Witness Account of Bonnie Prince Charlie in Manchester, (ed. Thompson, W.H.), Manchester, 1954

Autobiography of the Rev. Dr. Alexander Carlyle Minister of Inveresk, 2 vols., Edinburgh and London, 1860. For the fall of Edinburgh to the Jacobites, and the battle of Prestonpans

Chambers, Robert (ed.), *Jacobite Memoirs of the Rebellion of 1745*, Edinburgh, 1834. Includes Lord George Murray's 'Marches of the Highland Army'

'The Diary of James Clegg of Chapel-en-le-Frith 1708–1755', *Derbyshire Record Society*, III, Part 2, Derby, 1979

'Memoirs of the Life of Sir John Clerk of Penicuik', *Scottish History Society*, XIII, Edinburgh, 1892

A Report into the Proceedings and Opinion of the Board of General Officers, on their Examiinto the Conduct, Behavior, and Proceedings of Lieutenant-General Sir John Cope, Knight of the Bath, Colonel Peregrine Lascelles and Brigadier-General Thomas Fowke, Dublin, 1749

'Letters of Spencer Cowper, Dean of Durham 1746', *Surtees Society*, CLXXV, Durham and London, 1956

Crichton, Patrick, *The Woodhouselee MS. A Narrative of Events in Edinburgh and District during the Jacobite Occupation*, London, 1907. By a dyed-in-the-wool Edinburgh Whig. His use of the local idiom increases with his indignation.

Anon., *Culloden Papers*, London, 1815

More Culloden Papers (ed. Warrand, Duncan), 5 vols., Inverness, 1923–30. Esp. for the papers of Duncan Forbes of Culloden; the material is related only indirectly to the battle

Defoe, Daniel, *A Tour through the Whole Island of Great Britain* [1724–6], 2 vols., London, 1927

De Vattel, Emerich, *The Law of Nations*, 2 vols., London, 1835

Elcho, David Lord, *A Short Account of the Affairs of Scotland in the Years 1744, 1745, 1746 by David Lord Elcho* (ed. Charteris, E.), Edinburgh, 1907 (facsimile reprint), Edinburgh, 1973

Ferguson, the Worshipful Chancellor, 'The Retreat of the Highlanders through Westmorland in 1745', *Transactions of the Cumberland and Westmorland Antiquarian and Archaeological Society*, X, Kendal, 1889

The Journeys of Celia Fiennes (ed. Morris, Christopher), London, 1947

Forbes, Robert, 'The Lyon in Mourning or a Collection of Speeches Letters Journals etc. Relative to the Affairs of Prince Charles Edward Stuart', *Scottish History Society*, 3 vols., Edinburgh, 1896. A famous collection by a Non-Juring bishop

Frederick II ('The Great'), King of Prussia, *Oeuvres Militaires de Frédéderic le Grand*, 3 vols., Berlin, 1856

Henderson, Andrew, *The Life of William Augustus Duke of Cumberland*, London, 1746

— *The History of the Rebellion, 1745 and 1746*, London, 1748

Home, John, *The History of the Rebellion in Scotland*, Edinburgh, 1822. By a Whig volunteer. He was captured at Falkirk, and escaped from Doune Castle

Hughes, Michael, *A Plain Narrative or Journal of the Late Rebellion begun in 1745*, London, 1746. Another Whiggish volunteer

Jessup, Arthur; Ward, Ralph, 'Two Yorkshire Diaries. The Diary of Arthur Jessup and Ralph Ward's Journal' (ed. Whiting, C.E.), *The Yorkshire Archaeological Society Record Series*, CXVII, no place of publication, 1952. Jessup was an apothecary of Lydgate, near Holmfirth in the West Riding

Johnson, Samuel, *A Journey to the Western Islands of Scotland* [1775], new ed. by McGowan, Ian, with Boswell's *Journal of a Tour to the Hebrides*, Edinburgh, 1996

Johnstone, James Chevalier de, *Memoirs of the Rebellion in 1745 and 1746*, London, 1822

'The Diary of Richard Kay, 1716–51, of Baldingstone, near Bury. A Lancashire Doctor', (ed. Brockbank, W.; Kenworthy, F.), *Chetham Society*, XVI, Manchester, 1968

Ligne, Charles Prince de, *Mémoires Militaires*,

Littéraires et Sentimentaires, 34 vols., Dresden, 1795–1811

Lockhart of Carnwath, George, etc., *The Lockhart Papers* (ed. Aufrere, A.), 2 vols., London, 1817

McDonnell, Hector, 'Some Documents Relating to the Involvement of the Irish Brigade in the Rebellion of 1745', *The Irish Sword*, XVI, No. 62, Dublin, 1984

MacLean, John, *Witness to Rebellion. John MacLean's Journal of the 'Forty-Five and the Penicuik Drawings* (ed. Brown, Iain; Cheape, Hugh), East Linton, 1996

Marchant, John, *The History of the Present Rebellion*, London, 1746

'Marchmont Correspondence Relating to the '45', (ed. Hepburne Scott, G.F.C.), *Scottish History Society*, third series, XII, Miscellany, Edinburgh, 1933

Maxwell of Kirkconnell, James, 'Narrative of Charles Prince of Wales' Expedition into Scotland in the Year 1745', *Maitland Club*, No. 53, Edinburgh, 1841. The most judicious of the Jacobite memoirs

Murray of Broughton, J.M., *Memorials of John Murray of Broughton sometime Secretary to Prince Charles Edward 1740–1747* (ed. Bell, R.F.), Edinburgh, 1898

'Orderly Book of Lord Ogilvy's Regiment', *Journal of the Society for Army Historical Research*, II, London, 1927

O'Sullivan, John William (ed. Tayler, Alastair; Tayler, Henrietta), *1745 and After*, London, 1938. The account of the Jacobite chief of staff, still not fully integrated into the historiography of the 'Forty-Five

Pennant, Thomas, *A Tour in Scotland and Voyage to the Hebrides 1772* [1774–6], (ed. Simmons, Andrew), Edinburgh, 1998

— *A Tour in Scotland 1769* [1771], (ed. Osborne, Brian), Edinburgh, 2000

Pringle, John, *Observations on the Diseases of the Army, in Camp and Garrison*, 2nd ed., London, 1753

Ray, James, *A Compleat History of the Rebellion. From its first Rise, in 1745, to its total Suppression in the glorious Battle of Culloden, in April 1746*, no place of publication, 1754

Santa Cruz y Marcenado, A.N. [1724–30], *Réflexions Militaires et Politiques*, 12 vols., The Hague, 1735–40

'Secret Commentary. The Diaries of Gertrude Savile 1721–1757', *Thoroton Society of Nottinghamshire*, XLI, Nottingham, 1997

Memoirs of Sir Robert Strange ... and of his Brother-in-Law Andrew Lumisden (ed. Dennistoun, James), 2 vols., London 1855

'The Royal Stuart Papers at Windsor' (ed. Gain, Marion F.), Royal Stuart Society, *Royal Stuart Papers*, XVII, Huntingdon, 1981

Tayler, Henrietta (ed.), *A Jacobite Miscellany. Eight Original Papers on the Rising of 1745–1746*, Roxburgh Club, Oxford, 1944

'The Vernon Papers' (ed. Ranft, Brian), *Navy Records Society*, XCIX, London, 1958

'Manchester and the Rebellion of 1745 (The Diary of One of the Constables of Manchester in 1745)' [i.e. Thomas Walley], *Transactions of the Lancashire and Cheshire Antiquarian Society*, new series, VII, Manchester, 1889

The Letters of Horace Walpole Fourth Earl of Oxford (ed. Toynbee, P.), 16 vols., Oxford, 1903–5

The Whitefoord Papers being the Correspondence and other Manuscrips of Colonel Charles Whitefoord and Caleb Whitefoord from 1745 to 1810 (ed. Hewins, W.A.S.), Oxford, 1898

Yorke, P., *The Life and Correspondence of Philip Yorke, Earl of Hardwicke, Lord Chancellor of Great Britain* (ed. Yorke, P.C.), 3 vols., Cambridge, 1913

Publications of the Historical Manuscripts Commission

Report on the Manuscripts of the Earl of Eglinton, etc., for *The Manuscripts of Charles Fleetwood Weston Underwood Esq. of Somerby Hall, Lincolnshire*, London, 1885

Manuscripts of the Earl of Egmont, vol. III, London, 1923

The Manuscripts of Lord Kenyon, Appendix Part IV of the 14th Report, London, 1894

Report on the Manuscripts of the Duke of Portland, K.G., vol. VI, London 1901

The Manuscripts of the Duke of Roxburgh, etc., Appendix Part III of the 14th Report, London, 1894

Report on the Manuscripts of Alexander Stuart, Esq., of Eaglescarnie, London, 1881

Newspapers

The Caledonian Mercury, Edinburgh

Manchester Vindicated. Being a compleat Collection of Papers lately published in Defence of that Town, in the Chester Courant, Chester, 1749

The Daily Post, London

The Edinburgh Evening Courant, Edinburgh

The General Advertiser, London

The General Evening Post, London

The Gentleman's Magazine, London

The London Evening Post, London

The Manchester Magazine, Manchester

The Northampton Mercury, Northampton

The Old England Journal, London

The Penny London Post

The Universal Spectator and Weekly Journal, London

The Westminster Journal, London

The York Courant, York

Secondary Literature

Adam, Frank (revised, Innes of Learney, Sir Thomas), *The Clans, Septs and Regiments of the Scottish Highlanders*, new ed., Edinburgh and London, 1970

Annand, A.McK., 'The Hussars of the '45', *Journal of the Society for Army Historical Research*, XXXIX, London, 1961

— 'Lord Pitsligo's Horse in the Army of Prince Charles Edward Stuart, 1745–6', *Journal of the Society for Army Historical Research*, LX, London, 1982

Anon., 'The Forty-Five in Staffordshire', *The North Staffordshire Field Club Transactions*, XLVIII, Stafford, 1924. For the examination of David Morgan

Astle, William, *'Stockport Advertiser' Centenary History of Stockport*, Stockport, 1922

Atholl, 7th Duke of, *Chronicles of the Families of Atholl and Tullibardine*, 5 vols., London, 1908

Atkinson, C.T., 'Jenkins' Ear, the Austrian Succession and the Forty-Five', *Journal of the Society for Army Historical Research*, XXII, London, 1943–4

— 'Culloden', *Journal of the Society for Army Historical Research*, XXXV, London, 1957

Ayton, J., 'Dr. Samuel Johnson: Was he a Jacobite?', *The Jacobite. Journal of the 1745 Association*, CII, Inverness, 2000

Bailey, Geoff B., *Falkirk or Paradise! The Battle of Falkirk Muir 17 January 1746*, Edinburgh, 1996. Important

Baker, Thomas, 'The 1745 Rebels and Manchester', *Palatine Note-Book*, 1881–5

Bancroft, S.F., 'Scotland's Last Non-Jurant Priest', *The Jacobite*, CVIII, Aberdeen, 2002

Bannatyne, R., *History of the 30th Regiment*, Liverpool, 1923

Banner, Francis, 'The "Going-Out" of Prince Charles in 1745', *Transactions of the Historical Society of Lancashire and Cheshire*, LVII, Liverpool, 1906

Barnes, June, 'Carlisle in 1745', The 1745 Association, *A Jacobite Anthology*, Aberdeen, 1995

Barty, Alexander, *The History of Dunblane* [1944], Stirling, 1994

Beattie, David, *Prince Charles and the Borderland* [1928], reprinted Carlisle, 1995

Bil, Andrew, 'The Formation of New Settlements in the Perthshire Highlands 1660–1780', *Northern Scotland*, XII, Aberdeen, 1992

Black, Jeremy, *British Foreign Policy in the Age of Walpole*, Edinburgh, 1985

— 'Jacobitism and British Foreign Policy under the First Two Georges 1714–1760', *Royal Stuart Papers*, XXXI, Huntingdon, 1988

— 'The Forty-Five Re-examined', Royal Stuart Society, *Royal Stuart Papers*, XXXIV, Huntingdon, 1990

— *Culloden and the 'Forty-Five*, London, 1990

Blaikie, Walter Biggar, 'Itinerary of Prince Charles Edward Stuart', *Scottish History Society*, XXIII, Edinburgh, 1897. The foundation of modern historical research into the 'Forty-Five

— 'Perthshire in the 'Forty-Five', in Tullibardine, 1908

— 'Edinburgh at the Time of the Occupation of Prince Charles', *The Book of the Edinburgh Club*, II, Edinburgh, 1909

Blench, Brian, 'Symbols and Sentiment: Jacobite Glass', in Woosnam-Savage (ed.), 1995

Brewer, John, *The Sinews of Power. Money, War and the English State, 1688–1783*, London, 1989

Broadbent, A.; Dyer, B., *An Introduction to Clifton in Cumberland. Site of the Last Battle Fought on English Soil*, Clifton, undated

Browne, James, *A History of the Highlands and Highland Clans*, new ed., London, Edinburgh and Dublin, 4 vols., 1855–9

Broxap, H., *A Biography of Thomas Deacon. The Manchester Non-Juror*, Manchester, 1911

Bryce, W.M., 'The Flodden Wall of Edinburgh', *The Book of the Edinburgh Club*, II, Edinburgh, 1909

Bull, Stephen, 'Battles of the '45', in Woosnam-Savage (ed.), 1995

Cameron, Marion, 'Tirnadris – Pattern of Chivalry', The 1745 Association, *A Jacobite Anthology*, Aberdeen, 1995

Carswell, Allan L., '"The Most Despicable Enemy that Are" – the Jacobite Army of the '45', in Woosnam-Savage (ed.), 1995

Chadwick, F., *Jacobites. A Volley, Bayonet and Glory Supplement*, 2 vols., Calumet (Pennsylvania), 1999. Wargame scenarios, accompanied by an excellent commentary

Chambers, Robert, *History of the Rebellion of 1745–6*, 7th ed., Edinburgh and London, 1869

Charnock, John, *Biographia Navalis*, 6 vols., London, 1794–8

Cheape, Hugh, 'Highland and Jacobite Culture', in Mackenzie *et al.*, 1996

Collyer, Cedric, 'Yorkshire and the 'Forty-Five', *Yorkshire Archaeological Journal*, XXXVIII, Wakefield, 1955

Conway, Stephen, 'War and Nationality in the Mid-Eighteenth-Century British Isles', *The English Historical Review*, CXVI, No. 468, London, 2001

Craig, Maggie, *Damn' Rebel Bitches. The Women of the '45*, Edinburgh and London, 2000

Crawford, Patrick, 'Did the First of Foot Once Play a Small Role in What Could Have Changed the Course of British Domestic History?', *Journal of the Society for Army Historical Research*, LXXV, London, 1997

Cregeen, Eric, 'The Changing Role of Argyll in the Scottish Highlands', in Phillipson and Mitchison (eds.), 1996

Crofton, H.J., 'Scots and Manchester after the '45', *Transactions of the Lancashire and Cheshire Antiquarian Society*, N.S. XXVI, Manchester, 1908

Croston, James, *Historic Sites of Lancashire and Cheshire*, Manchester, 1883

Cruikshanks, Eveline, *Political Untouchables. The Tories and the '45*, London, 1979

— 'The Oglethorpes: A Jacobite Family 1689–1760', Royal Stuart Society, *Royal Stuart Papers*, XLV, London, 1995

Curley, Thomas M., 'Johnson's Tour of Scotland and the Idea of Great Britain', *British Journal for Eighteenth-Century Studies*, XII, No. 2, Oxford, 1985

Dalton, J.P., 'Durham in the 'Forty-Five', *Transactions of the Cumberland and Westmorland Antiquarian Society*, N.S. XLVI, Kendal, 1947

Davies, C.S., *A History of Macclesfield*, Manchester, 1961

Dawson, June E., 'The Origins of the "Road to the Isles". Trade, Communications and Campbell Power in Early Modern Scotland', in Mason and MacDougall (eds.), 1992

De Courcy Ireland, J., 'The Seamen of the Forty-Five', *The Irish Sword*, II, No. 8, Dublin, 1956

Dent, J.S., 'Recent Excavations on the Site of Stockport Castle', *Transactions of the Lancashire and Cheshire Antiquarian Society*, N.S. LXXIX, Manchester, 1977

Devine, Thomas M. (ed.), *Conflict and Stability in Scottish Society 1700–1850*, Edinburgh, 1990

— *The Scottish Nation*, London, 1999

— 'A Conservative People? Scottish Gaeldom in the Age of Improvement', in Devine and Young (eds.), 1999

Devine, Thomas M.; Young, John R. (eds.), *Eighteenth Century Scotland: New Perspectives*, East Linton, 1999

Dickson, W.K., *The Jacobite Attempt of 1719*, Edinburgh, 1895

Dodghson, Robert A., *From Chiefs to Landlords. Social and Economic Change in the Western Highlands and Islands, c. 1493–1820*, Edinburgh, 1998

Doran, John, *London in Jacobite Times*, 2 vols., London, 1877

Douglas, Hugh, *Jacobite Spy Wars. Moles, Rogues and Treachery*, Stroud, 1999

Douglas, Hugh; Stead, Michael, *The Flight of Bonnie Prince Charlie*, Stroud, 2000

Douglas-Hamilton, Hugh, 'The Titular Charles III and the Stewart Crown of Scotland', in Scott-Moncrieff (ed.), 1988

Duncan, J.G., 'Trade and Traders: Some Links between Sweden and the Ports of Montrose and Arbroath 1742–1830', *Northern Scotland*, VII, Aberdeen, 1986–7

Eardley-Simpson, L., *Derby and the Forty-Five*, London, 1933

Edwards, Owen D., 'The Long Shadows. A View of Ireland and the '45', in Scott-Moncrieff (ed.), 1988

Everitt, Alan, *Landscape and Community in England*, London, 1985

Fairweather, Barbara, 'Jacobite Standards', The 1745 Association, *A Jacobite Anthology*, Aberdeen, 1995

Fereday, R.P., *Orkney Feuds and the '45*, Kirkwall, 1980

Fergusson of Kilkerran, Sir James, *Argyll in the Forty-Five*, London, 1951

Forbes, A., *The Black Watch. The Record of an Historic Regiment*, London, 1896

Fraser, Donald C., 'Some Highland Causes of the '45', in Scott-Moncrieff (ed.), 1988

Gibson, John S., *Ships of the '45. The Rescue of the Young Pretender*, London, 1967

— '"The Summer's Hunting": Historiography of Charles Edward's Escape', in Scott-Moncrieff (ed.), 1988

— *Lochiel of the '45. The Jacobite Chief and the Prince*, Edinburgh, 1994

— *Edinburgh in the '45. Bonnie Prince Charlie at Holyroodhouse*, Edinburgh, 1995

Gillies, William, 'The Prince and the Gaels', in Scott-Moncrieff (ed.), 1988

— 'Gaelic Songs of the Forty-Five', *Scottish Studies*, XXX, Edinburgh, 1989

Gooch, Leo, *The Desperate Faction. The Jacobites of North-East England 1688–1745*, Hull, 1995

Grimble, Ian, 'Houses Divided', in Scott-Moncrieff (ed.), 1988

Guy, Alan J. (ed.), 'Colonel Samuel Bagshawe and the Army of George II 1731–1762', *Army Records Society*, London, 1990

— 'King George's Army, 1714–1750', in Woosnam-Savage (ed.), 1995

Halford-Macleod, 'The Battle for the Ford at Fochabers', *The British Army Review*, No. 113, Upavon, 1996

Hancox, Joy, *The Queen's Chameleon. The Life of John Byrom. A Study of Conflicting Loyalties*, London, 1994

Harrison, William, 'The Development of the Turnpike System in Manchester and Cheshire', *Transactions of the Lancashire and Cheshire Antiquarian Society*, N.S. IV, Manchester, 1886

— 'Pre-Turnpike Highways of Lancashire and Cheshire', *Transactions of the Lancashire and Cheshire Antiquarian Society*, N.S. IX, Manchester, 1891

— 'The Ancient Fords, Ferries and Bridges of Cheshire', *Transactions of the Lancashire and Cheshire Antiquarian Society*, N.S. XIV, Manchester, 1896

— 'The History of a Turnpike Trust (Manchester and Wilmslow)', *Transactions of the Lancashire and Cheshire Antiquarian Society*, N.S. XXIV, Manchester, 1916

Hay, D.; Linebaugh, P., *et al.*, *Albion's Fatal Tree. Crime and Society in Eighteenth-Century England*, London, 1975

Haydon, Colin, '"The Mouth of Hell": Religious Discord at Brailes, Warwickshire, *c.* 1660 – *c.* 1800', *The Historian*, LXVIII, London, 2000

Holroyd, Abraham, 'Long Preston Peggy: A Ballad of 1745', *Palatine Note-Book*, 1881–5

Holtby, R.T., 'Thomas Herring as Archbishop of York, 1743–1747', *Northern History*, XXX, Leeds, 1994

Houlding, J.A., *Fit for Service. The Training of the British Army, 1715–1795*, Oxford, 1981

Jarvis, Rupert C., 'The Jacobite Rising and the Public Monies', *Transactions of the Lancashire and Cheshire Antiquarian Society*, N.S. LIX, Manchester, 1947

— 'The Forty-Five and the Local Records', *Transactions of the Lancashire and Cheshire Antiquarian Society*, N.S. LXV, Manchester, 1955

— 'The Jacobite Occupation of Manchester in 1745: The Impressment of Horses: the James Clayton Chorlton MS', *Transactions of the Lancashire and Cheshire Antiquarian Society*, N.S. LXXV, Manchester, 1965

— *Collected Papers on the Jacobite Risings*, 2 vols., Manchester, 1971–2

Jenkins, M., 'Should the Prince Have Turned Back?' The 1745 Association, *A Jacobite Anthology*, Aberdeen, 1995

Kay, Thomas, 'Remains of the Town Wall of Stockport', *Transactions of the Lancashire and Cheshire Antiquarian Society*, N.S. XIV, Manchester, 1896

Kerr, John, *Wade in Atholl*, Blair Atholl, 1896

Knight, C.R., *Historical Records of the Buffs. East Kent Regiment (3rd Foot)*, I, London, 1935

Kyd, J.G., 'Scottish Population Statistics including Webster's Analysis of Population 1755', *Scottish History Society*, XLIV, Edinburgh, 1952

Lamb, H.H., *Climate, History and the Modern World*, London, 1995

Lamont, Claire, 'Dr. Johnson, the Scottish Highlands, and the Scottish Enlightenment', *British Journal for Eighteenth Century Studies*, XII, No. 1, Oxford, 1998

Leask, J.C.; McCance, H.M., *The Regimental Records of the Royal Scots (The First or the Royal Regiment of Foot)*, Dublin, 1915

Leneman, Leah, *Living in Atholl, 1685–1785*, Edinburgh, 1986

Lenman, Bruce P., *The Jacobite Clans of the Great Glen 1650–1784*, London, 1984

— '1745. Prince Charles Edward Stuart and the Jacobites', in Woosnam-Savage (ed.), 1995

Lenman, Bruce P.; Gibson, John S., *The Jacobite Threat – England, Scotland, Ireland, France: A Source Book*, Edinburgh, 1990

Lindsay, J.M., 'Some Aspects of the Timber Supply in the Highlands, 1700–1850', *Scottish Studies*, XIX, Edinburgh, 1975

Livingstone of Bachuil, Alastair, 'A Morvern Hero', The 1745 Association, *A Jacobite Anthology*, Aberdeen, 1995

Livingstone of Bachuil, Alastair; Aikman, Christian W.; Hart, Betty S. (eds.), *No Quarter Given. The Muster Roll of Prince Charles Edward Stuart's Army, 1745–46*, Glasgow, 2001

Lynch, Michael (ed.), *The Oxford Companion to Scottish History*, Oxford, 2001

Lyon, David, *The Sailing Navy List. All the Ships of the Royal Navy – Built, Purchased and Captured – 1688–1860*, London, 1993

MacCulloch, Donald B., 'The Route of Prince Charles's Army from Fassifern to Moy', The 1745 Association, *A Jacobite Anthology*, Aberdeen, 1995

Macdonald of Castleton, Donald J., 'A Tale of a White Cockade', The 1745 Association, *A Jacobite Anthology*, Aberdeen, 1995

MacDonald, Norman H., 'Alasdair MacMhaighstir Alasdair the Jacobite Bard of Clanranald', The 1745 Association, *A Jacobite Anthology*, Aberdeen, 1995

— 'The Seven Men of Moidart', The 1745 Association, *A Jacobite Anthology*, Aberdeen, 1995

— 'The Skirmish of Highbridge', The 1745 Association, *A Jacobite Anthology*, Aberdeen, 1995

Macinnes, Allan I., 'The Aftermath of the '45', in Woosnam-Savage (ed.), 1995

— 'Scottish Jacobitism: In Search of a Movement', in Devine and Young (eds.), 1999

Mackenzie, Ross, *et al.*, National Trust for Scotland, *The Swords and the Sorrows*, catalogue to 'An Exhibition to Commemorate the Jacobite Rising of 1745 and the Battle of Culloden 1746', Edinburgh, 1996

Mackillop, Andrew, 'Highland Estate Change and Tenant Emigration', in Devine and Young (eds.), 1999

Mackintosh, Alexander, *The Forfarshire or Lord Ogilvy's Regiment*, Inverness, 1914

MacLaren, Moray, *Lord Lovat of the '45. An End of an Old Song*, London, 1957

MacLean, Alasdair, 'Jacobites at Heart. An Account of the Independent Companies', in Scott-Moncrieff (ed.), 1988

McLynn, Frank J., 'Ireland and the Jacobite Rising of 1745', *The Irish Sword*, XIII, No. 53, Dublin, 1979

— 'Seapower and the Jacobite Rising of 1745', *Mariner's Mirror*, LXVII, London, 1981

— *France and the Jacobite Rising of 1745*, Edinburgh, 1981

— *Charles Edward Stuart. A Tragedy in Many Acts*, London, 1988. Unlikely to be replaced as the standard biography

— 'Unpopular Front. Jews, Radicals and Americans in the Jacobite World-View', Royal Stuart Society, *Royal Stuart Papers*, XXXI, Huntingdon, 1988

McMillan, James F., 'Mission Accomplished? The Catholic Underground', in Devine and Young (eds.), 1999

Macpherson, A.G., *A Day's March to Ruin. A Documentary Narrative of the Badenoch Men in the 'Forty-Five and a Biography of Col. Ewan Macpherson of Cluny, 1706–1764*, Newtonmore, 1996

Mansel, Philip, 'The Influence of the Later Stuarts and their Supporters on French Royalism, 1789–1840', Royal Stuart Society, *Royal Stuart Papers*, XXI, London, 1983

Marshall, Rosalind K., 'Prince Charles Edward Stuart', in Woosnam-Savage (ed.), 1995

Mason, Roger; MacDougall, Norman (eds.), *People and Power in Scotland. Essays in Honour of T.C. Smout*, Edinburgh, 1992

Maurice, Sir Frederick, *The History of the Scots Guards*, I, London, 1934

Maxwell, Gordon S., *The Romans in Scotland*, Edinburgh, 1989

Mellor, G.R., 'Hogarth's "March to Finchley"', *Journal of the Society for Army Historical Research*, XXVI, London, 1948

Mitchell, A.A., 'London and the Forty-Five', *History Today*, XV, No. 10, London 1965

Mitchison, Rosalind, 'The Government and the Highlands, 1707–1745', in Phillipson and Mitchison (eds.), 1996

Monod, Paul K., *Jacobitism and the English People*, Cambridge, 1989

Moss, Fletcher, *Didsburye in the '45*, Manchester, 1891

— *A History of the Old Parish of Cheadle, in Cheshire*, Manchester, 1894

Moundsey, G.G., *Authentic Account of the Occupation of Carlisle in October 1745, by Prince Charles Edward Stuart*, London, 1856

Muir, Augustus, *Scotland's Road of Romance. Travels in the Footsteps of Prince Charlie*, 2nd ed., London, 1937

Murdoch, Alexander, 'Emigration from the Scottish Highlands to America in the Eighteenth Century', *British Society for Eighteenth-Century Studies*, XXI, No. 2, Oxford, 1998

— 'Scotland and the Idea of Britain in the Eighteenth Century', in Devine and Young (eds.), 1999

Newton, the Lady, *The House of Lyme. From its Foundation to the End of the Eighteenth Century*, London, 1917

Nichols, Kenneth, 'Celtic Contrasts. Ireland and Scotland', *History Ireland*, VII, No. 3, Dublin, 1999

Nicholson, Robin, 'The Tartan Portraits of Prince Charles Edward Stuart: Identity and Iconography', *British Society for Eighteenth-Century Studies*, XXI, No. 2, Oxford, 1998

Norie, William Drummond, *The Life and Adventures of Prince Charles Edward Stuart*, 4 vols., London, 1901. An ultra-romantic biography. However, there is much useful detail among the purple passages, and the topographical descriptions and photographs are of particular interest

Oates, J., 'York and the Rebel Prisoners, 1745–52', *York Historian*, XVII, York, 2000

Ó Ciardha, Éamonn, *Ireland and the Jacobite Cause. A Fatal Attachment*, Dublin, 2002. Important

The Palatine Note-Book, ed. Eglinton-Bailey, J.S., 5 vols., Manchester, 1881–5

Parsons, Robert F., 'The Role of Jacobitism in the Modern World', Royal Stuart Society, *Royal Stuart Papers*, XXVIII, Huntingdon, 1986

Petrie, Sir Charles, *The Jacobite Movement. The Last Phase 1716–1807*, London, 1950

— 'Irishmen in the Forty-Five', *The Irish Sword*, II, No. 8, Dublin, 1956

Phillipson, N.T.; Mitchison, Rosalind (eds.), *Scotland in the Age of Improvement*, new ed., Edinburgh, 1996

Pittock, Murray G., 'The Rights of Nature: The Ideal Images of Jacobite Ruralism', *British Journal for Eighteenth-Century Studies*, XIII, No. 2, Oxford, 1990

— 'Jacobite Culture,' in Woosnam-Savage (ed.), 1995

— *The Myth of the Jacobite Clans*, Edinburgh, 1996

— 'The Social Composition of the Jacobite Army in Scotland in the Forty-Five', Royal Stuart Society, *Royal Stuart Papers*, XLVIII, London, c. 1996

— *Jacobitism*, Basingstoke, 1998

Pittock, Murry G.; Pollard, T.; Oliver, N., *Two Men in a Trench*, London, 2002. Battlefield excavations by Glasgow University, including Culloden

Prebble, John, *Culloden*, London, 1961, and multiple reprints

— *John Prebble's Scotland*, London, 2000

Procter, Richard W., *Memorials of Manchester Streets*, Manchester, 1874

Reed, Michael, *The Landscape of Britain from the Beginnings to 1914*, London, 1990

Reed, Peter (ed.), *Glasgow. The Forming of the City*, Edinburgh, 1999

Reid, Stuart, *Like Hungry Wolves. Culloden Moor 16 April 1746*, London, 1994

— *1745. A Military History of the Last Jacobite Rising*, Staplehurst, 1996. A ground-breaking account, and the first to be informed by a consistent sense of military realism

Reid, Stuart; Embleton, Gerry, *Culloden*, London, 2002

Richmond, Sir Herbert, *The Navy in the War of 1739–1748*, 3 vols., Cambridge, 1920

Ritchie, Carson I., 'The Durham Assocation Regiment', *Journal of the Society for Army Historical Research*, XXXIV, London, 1956

Roberts, Alasdair, 'Aspects of Highland and Lowland Catholicism on Deeside', *Northern Scotland*, X, Aberdeen, 1990–91

Robertson, James I., *Atholl in the Rebellion of 1745*, Aberfeldy, 1994

— *The Lady of Kynachan*, London, 1995. A highly readable novel, informed by detailed local knowledge

Ross, David R., *On the Trail of Bonnie Prince Charlie*, Edinburgh, 2000

Sankey, M.; Szechi, D., 'Elite Culture and the Decline of Scots Jacobitism 1716–1745', *Past and Present*, No. 173, Oxford, 2001

Saville, Richard, 'Scottish Modernisation prior to the Industrial Revolution, 1688–1763', in Devine and Young (eds.), 1999

Scott, John, 'The Jacobites in Kirkintilloch', The 1745 Association, *A Jacobite Anthology*, Aberdeen, 1995

Scott, Walter, *Waverley* [1814], Edinburgh, 1994

Scott-Moncrieff, Lesley (ed.), *The 45. To Gather an Image Whole*, Edinburgh, 1988

Selkirk, Malcom G., 'Crieff in the '45', The 1745 Association, *A Jacobite Anthology*, Aberdeen, 1995

— 'Hugh Mercer and Lord Pitsligo's Horse', The 1745 Association, *A Jacobite Anthology*, Abedeen, 1995

Seton, Sir Bruce; Arnot, Jean, 'The Prisoners of the '45. Edited from the State Papers', *The Scottish History Society*, 3 vols., Edinburgh, 1928–9

Simpson, John, 'The Causes of the 45', in Scott-Moncrieff (ed.), 1988

Simpson, Peter A., *The Independent Highland Companies 1603–1760*, Edinburgh, 1996

— *Culloden and the Four Unjust Men*, no place of publication, 2000

Smith, Annette M., 'Annexed Estates in Eighteenth-Century Scotland', *Northern Scotland*, III, No. 1, Aberdeen, 1977–8

— 'Dundee and the '45', in Scott-Moncrieff (ed.), 1988

Smith, Archibald K., *The Noblest Jacobite of All* [i.e. James Drummond, Duke of Perth], *Jacobite Perthshire, Jacobite Trossachs*, Callander, 1995

Smith, John, 'Two Generals. Cumberland and Cornwallis', *History Ireland*, VII, No. 3, Dublin, 1999

Smout, T.C., 'The Landowner and the Planned Village in Scotland', in Phillipson and Mitchison (eds.), 1996

— 'Improvers and the Scottish Environment: Soils, Bogs and Woods', in Devine and Young (eds.), 1999

Speck, W.A., *The Butcher. The Duke of Cumberland and the Suppression of the '45*, Oxford, 1981

Stell, Geoffrey, *Dunstaffnage and Castles of Argyll*, Edinburgh, 1994

Suffolk, Philip, *Catholic Brailes. Some Note on its History*, no place or date of publication

Szechi, Daniel, *The Jacobites, Britain and Europe 1688–1788*, Manchester, 1994

Tabraham, Chris; Grove, Doreen, *Fortress Scotland and the Jacobites*, London, 1995

Tayler, Alastair; Tayler, Henrietta, *The Jacobites of Aberdeenshire and Banffshire in the Forty-Five*, Aberdeen, 1928

— *The Stuart Papers at Windsor*, London, 1939. The siblings Tayler were nephew and niece of Walter Biggar Blaikie

Taylor, William, *The Military Roads in Scotland*, Newton Abbot, 1976

Tomasson, Katherine, *The Jacobite General*, Edinburgh and London, 1958

Tomasson, Katherine; Buist, Francis, *Battles of the '45*, London, 1962

Tullibardine, The Marchioness of (ed.), *A Military History of Perthshire 1660–1902*, Perth, Glasgow and Edinburgh, 1908

Turner, Roger, 'Manchester in 1745', Royal Stuart Society, *Royal Stuart Papers*, XLIV, London, c. 1997

Turnock, David, *The Historical Geography of Scotland since 1707: Geographical Aspects of Modernisation*, Cambridge, 1982

Tyson, Robert E., 'Demographic Change', in Devine and Young (eds.), 1999

Ure, John, *Bird on the Wing. Bonnie Prince Charlie's Flight from Culloden Retraced*, London, 1992

Walton, K., 'Population Changes in North East Scotland, 1691–1951', *Scottish Studies*, V, Edinburgh, 1961

Waugh, M., *Smuggling in Kent and Sussex 1700–1840*, Newbury, 1998

Welsh, Frank, *The Companion Guide to the Lake District*, Woodbridge, 1997

Wemyss, Alice, 'Lord Elcho and the '45', in Scott-Moncrieff (ed.), 1988

Wateley, Christopher A., 'How tame were the Scottish Lowlands during the Eighteenth Century?', in Devine (ed.), 1990

Wheatley, J.S., *Bonnie Prince Charlie in Cumberland*, Carlisle, 1903

Whitworth, Rex, *Field Marshal Lord Ligonier*, Oxford, 1958

— *William Augustus, Duke of Cumberland*, Oxford, 1992

Whyte, Ian D., *Scotland before the Industrial Revolution*, London, 1995

— 'Urbanization in Eighteenth-Century Scotland', in Devine and Young (eds.), 1999

Whyte, Ian D.; Whyte, Kathleen, *On the Trail of the Jacobites*, London, 1990

Willis, Virginia (ed.), *Reports on the Annexed Estates*, Edinburgh, 1973

Winslow, Cal, 'Sussex Smugglers', in Hay, Linebaugh, et al., 1975

Winter, H.A. (ed.), *Battling the Elements*, Baltimore, 1998

Woosnam-Savage, Robert C. (ed.), *Prince Charles Edward Stuart and the Jacobites*, Edinburgh, 1995

Young, John R., 'The Parliamentary Incorporating Union 1707: Political Management, Anti-Unionism and Foreign Policy', in Devine and Young (eds.), 1999

Youngson, A.J., *After the Forty-Five. The Economic Impact on the Scottish Highlands*, Edinburgh, 1973

Index